A Companion to Latin American History

BLACKWELL COMPANIONS TO WORLD HISTORY

Published
A Companion to the History of the Middle East
Edited by Youssef M. Choueiri

A Companion to Japanese History
Edited by William M. Tsutsui

A Companion to Latin American History
Edited by Thomas Holloway

In preparation
A Companion to Russian History
Edited by Abbott Gleason

BLACKWELL COMPANIONS TO HISTORY

Published
A Companion to Gender History
Edited by Teresa A. Meade and Merry E. Wiesner-Hanks

A Companion to International History 1900–2001
Edited by Gordon Martel

A Companion to Western Historical Thought
Edited by Lloyd Kramer and Sarah Maza

A COMPANION TO LATIN AMERICAN HISTORY

Edited by

Thomas H. Holloway

BLACKWELL PUBLISHING
350 Main Street, Malden, MA 02148-5020, USA
9600 Garsington Road, Oxford OX4 2DQ, UK
550 Swanston Street, Carlton, Victoria 3053, Australia

First published 2008 by Blackwell Publishing Ltd

1   2008

Library of Congress Cataloging-in-Publication Data

A companion to Latin American history / edited by Thomas H. Holloway.
    p.   cm. – (Blackwell companions to American history)
    Includes bibliographical references and index.
    ISBN 978-1-4051-3161-2 (hardcover : alk. paper)   1. Latin America–History.   I. Holloway,
Thomas H., 1944–

    F1410.C727 2008
    980–dc22

                                        2007031624

A catalogue record for this title is available from the British Library.

Set in 10 on 12 pt Galliard
by SNP Best-set Typesetter Ltd., Hong Kong
Printed and bound in Singapore
by Utopia Press Pte Ltd

The publisher's policy is to use permanent paper from mills that operate a sustainable forestry policy,
and which has been manufactured from pulp processed using acid-free and elementary chlorine-free
practices. Furthermore, the publisher ensures that the text paper and cover board used have met
acceptable environmental accreditation standards.

For further information on
Blackwell Publishing, visit our website:
www.blackwellpublishing.com

Contents

Figures, Tables, and Maps

Notes on Contributors

Adrian A. Bantjes is Associate Professor of History at the University of Wyoming and author of *As if Jesus Walked on Earth: Cardenismo, Sonora, and the Mexican Revolution* (1998) and articles on the political, cultural, and religious history of revolutionary Mexico. He is currently completing a book on revolutionary anti-religious campaigns.

Judy Bieber is Associate Professor of History at the University of New Mexico. Her areas of research specialization include slavery and race relations in the Americas and Brazilian history. She is the author of *Power, Patronage and Political Violence: State Building on a Brazilian Frontier, 1822–1889* (1999).

Sarah C. Chambers, University of Minnesota, has written widely on gender, ethnicity, law, and politics during the transition from colonialism to independence. She has published *From Subjects to Citizens: Honor, Gender, and Politics in Arequipa, Peru, 1780–1854* (1999) and co-edited *Honor, Status and Law in Modern Latin America* (2005). Her current research focuses on family and politics in Chile.

Julie A. Charlip is Associate Professor of history at Whitman College in Walla Walla, WA. She is the author of *Cultivating Coffee: The Farmers of Carazo, Nicaragua, 1880–1930* (2003), and co-author of *Latin America: An Interpretive History*, 8th edition (2007), with the late E. Bradford Burns.

Tom D. Dillehay is Chair and Distinguished Professor of Anthropology at Vanderbilt University. He has carried out extensive archeological and anthropological research in Peru, Chile, the United States, and other countries. He also has numerous publications on topics ranging from the peopling of the Americas and the rise of early Andean civilization to the spread of the Inca state.

John Fisher is Professor of Latin American History in the School of Languages, Cultures, and Area Studies at the University of Liverpool. He has published extensively on Spanish imperial policy during the Bourbon period, commercial relations in the Hispanic world, and the processes that led to Peruvian independence from Spain.

Duncan Green is Head of Research at Oxfam, Great Britain. He is the author of several books on Latin America including *Silent Revolution: The Rise and Crisis of Market Economics in Latin America* (2003), *Faces of Latin America*, 3rd edition (2006), and *Hidden Lives: Voices of Children in Latin America* (1998).

Aline Helg is Professor of History at the University of Geneva, Switzerland. She has published the award-winning *Our Rightful Share: The Afro-Cuban Struggle for Equality, 1886–1912* (1995) and *Liberty and Equality in Caribbean Colombia, 1770–1835* (2004), as well as several articles on race relations in the Americas.

Thomas H. Holloway is Professor of History at the University of California at Davis. His works include *The Coffee Valorization of 1906* (1975), *Immigrants on the Land* (1980), and *Policing Rio de Janeiro* (1993). He has served as President of LASA (2000–1), and Executive Secretary of CLAH (2002–7).

Robert McKee Irwin, Associate Professor of Spanish at University of California at Davis, is author of *Mexican Masculinities* (2003) and *Bandits, Captives, Heroines and Saints: Cultural Icons of Mexico's Northwest Frontier* (forthcoming 2007); and co-editor of *Hispanisms and Homosexualities* (1998), *The Famous 41* (2003), and the forthcoming *Diccionario de estudios culturales latinoamericanos*.

Franklin W. Knight is Leonard and Helen R. Stulman Professor of History at Johns Hopkins University. Among his publications are *Slave Society in Cuba during the Nineteenth Century* (1970), *The Caribbean: The Genesis of a Fragmented Nationalism* (1978), and *The Slave Societies of the Caribbean* (1997). He is currently writing a general history of Cuba.

Hal Langfur teaches the history of Latin America and the Atlantic world at SUNY Buffalo. He is the author of *The Forbidden Lands: Colonial Identity, Frontier Violence, and the Persistence of Brazil's Eastern Indians, 1750–1830* (2006) and editor of the forthcoming *Native Brazil: Beyond the Cannibal and the Convert, 1500–1889*.

Aldo A. Lauria-Santiago is Associate Professor of Latino/Hispanic Caribbean Studies and History at Rutgers University. He is the author of *An Agrarian Republic: Commercial Agriculture and the Politics of Peasant Communities in El Salvador, 1823–1914* (1999) and (with J. Gould) *To Rise in Darkness: Revolution, Repression and Memory in El Salvador, 1929–1932* (2007).

Colin M. Lewis is Reader in Latin American Economic History at the London School of Economics and Political Science, and Associate Fellow of the Institute for the Study of the Americas, University of London. He is currently working on a study of British enterprises in the Argentine. His publications include *Argentina: A Short History* (2003) and (with Christopher Abel) *Exclusion and Engagement: Social Policy in Latin America* (2002).

David R. Mares is Professor of Political Science at the University of California, San Diego, and was previously Professor at El Colegio de Mexico. He has written and consulted widely on interstate conflict, civil–military relations, drug politics, and energy policy. His latest book is *Drug Wars and Coffeehouses* (2006).

Luis Martínez-Fernández is Professor of History at the University of Central Florida. His books include *Protestantism and Political Conflict in the Nineteenth-Century Hispanic Caribbean* (2002) and *Fighting Slavery in the Caribbean* (1998). He is Senior Editor of the *Encyclopedia of Cuba: People, History, Culture* (2003) and is currently writing a concise history of the Cuban Revolution.

Nara Milanich is Assistant Professor of History at Barnard College. Her lastest book, *The Children of Fate: Families, Social Hierarchies and the State, Chile, 1850–1937*, is forthcoming. Her work has appeared in the *American Historical Review*, the *Journal of Social History*, and *Estudios Interdisciplinarios de América Latina*.

John Monaghan is Professor and Department Head at the University of Illinois at Chicago and Adjunct Curator at the Field Museum. He has carried out ethnographic and archival research on Highland Maya communities of Guatemala and Mixtec-speaking groups in Southern Mexico, and is editor of the *Handbook of Middle American Indians, Ethnology Supplement* (2000).

Rachel Sarah O'Toole is Assistant Professor of the Early Modern Atlantic World at the University of California, Irvine with research interests in Andean colonial indigenous communities and the African Atlantic. She has published articles in the *Journal of Colonialism and Colonial History* (Spring 2006) and *The Americas* (July 2006).

Carla Rahn Phillips, Union Pacific Professor in Comparative Early Modern History at the University of Minnesota, currently works on

Spanish seafaring. Pertinent publications include *Six Galleons for the King of Spain* (1986) and *The Treasure of the San José: Death at Sea in the War of the Spanish Succession* (2007).

William D. Phillips, Jr., Professor of History and Director of the Center for Early Modern History at the University of Minnesota, has co-authored two prize-winning books with Carla Rahn Phillips, *The Worlds of Christopher Columbus* (1992) and *Spain's Golden Fleece* (1997), and has edited *Testimonies from the Columbus Lawsuits* (2000).

Jeffrey Quilter is Deputy Director for Curatorial Affairs, Peabody Museum, Harvard, and Curator for Intermediate Area Archaeology. His recent research has focused on ceremonial centers in Costa Rica, Moche art and archeology, and excavation of a colonial period town in Peru. His books include *Cobble Circles and Standing Stones: Archaeology at the Rivas Site, Costa Rica* (2004) and *Treasures of the Andes* (2005).

Susan Elizabeth Ramírez teaches Latin American History at Texas Christian University. She is the author of *To Feed and Be Fed: The Cosmological Bases of Authority and Identity in the Andes* (2005), *The World Upside Down: Cross-Cultural Contact and Conflict in Sixteenth-Century Peru* (1996 and 1998), and *Provincial Patriarchs: Land Tenure and the Economics of Power in Colonial Peru* (1986).

Mary A. Renda teaches history and chairs the Department of Gender Studies at Mount Holyoke College in South Hadley, MA. Her work tracks the imprint of gender and racism in US imperialism. She is the award-winning author of *Taking Haiti: Military Occupation and the Culture of US Imperialism, 1915–1940* (2001).

Jaime E. Rodríguez O. is Professor of History at the University of California, Irvine. His publications include *The Independence of Spanish America* (1998) and *La revolución política en la época de la independencia: El Reino de Quito, 1808–1822* (2006); and, as editor, *The Divine Charter: Constitutionalism and Liberalism in Nineteenth-Century Mexico* (2005) and *Revolución, independencia y la nuevas naciones de América* (2005).

Lise Sedrez is Assistant Professor of History at California State University, Long Beach. Her research interests include urban environmental history, history of science, and modern Brazil. She is working on a book on the Guanabara Bay in Rio de Janeiro, and edits the Online Bibliography on Latin American Environmental History <http://www.csulb.edu/laeh>.

Patricia Seed, Professor of History at the University of California, Irvine, wrote "The Conquest of the Americas" for the *Cambridge Illustrated History of Warfare*, and two prize-winning books, *To Love, Honor, and Obey in Colonial Mexico* (1988) and *American Pentimento* (2001), as well as *Ceremonies of Possession in Europe's Conquest of the New World* (1995).

Kevin Terraciano is Professor of History and Chair of Latin American Studies at UCLA. He specializes in colonial Latin American history, especially the indigenous cultures and languages of central and southern Mexico. His many writings on colonial Mexico include *The Mixtecs of Colonial Oaxaca: Ñudzahui History, Sixteenth through Eighteenth Centuries* (2001).

Peter Wade is Professor of Social Anthropology at the University of Manchester. His publications include *Blackness and Race Mixture* (1993), *Race and Ethnicity in Latin America* (1997), *Music, Race and Nation: Música Tropical in Colombia* (2000), and *Race, Nature and Culture: An Anthropological Perspective* (2002).

Joel Wolfe teaches Latin American History at the University of Massachusetts at Amherst. He is the author of *Working Women, Working Men: São Paulo and the Rise of Brazil's Industrial Working Class, 1900–1955* (1993) and the forthcoming *Autos and Progress: The Brazilian Search for Modernity*.

Andrew R. Wyatt is a PhD candidate at the University of Illinois at Chicago. He is currently conducting research on agriculture terracing at the Chan site, an ancient Maya farming village in western Belize, investigating agricultural intensification and the role of farmers in the political economy.

Introduction

Thomas H. Holloway

This is a compendium of descriptive and interpretive material on the history of Latin America, organized around coherent themes and periods commonly of interest to Latin Americanist scholars and their students, as well as the interested public. The essays are supported by the latest research, assessed and synthesized by trained and experienced specialists, and presented in a sequence organized thematically and chronologically. The standard meta-narrative for the region as a whole is represented here, with considerable illustrative material and case studies ranging widely in time, space, and theme; they are accompanied by more than 1400 bibliographical references and suggestions for further reading, grouped at the end of each thematic essay.

The chronologically organized units in that overarching timeline include the indigenous and Iberian backgrounds, conquest and colonization, the process of independence, the establishment of new nations in the nineteenth century, the varied processes by which the region modernized and developed through the twentieth century. It is also common in surveys of Latin American history to focus specifically on several case studies of major transformation, such as the Revolutions in Mexico and Cuba; to consider the emergence of the United States as a dominant presence in the economic and political affairs of the region; and to focus on other issues better treated thematically than as divisions along the lines of geography and chronology that still dominate historical scholarship and pedagogy.

In keeping with the comparative approach common to historical surveys of such a diverse region of the world, there is no effort here to provide the national narrative of each colonial region or independent nation. Inevitably, the specific experience of some countries looms larger than others. Devoting separate essays to Brazil in the colonial era and again in the nineteenth century is justified on the intellectual grounds that Brazil's colonial trajectory as well as its functioning constitutional monarchy from independence in 1822 to 1889 merits separate consideration from Spanish America. It is also meant to provide readers whose entry into Latin American history is mainly via the Spanish-language regions with material that deals with the distinctive Brazilian experience on its own terms.

Coverage

It is not the intent of this volume to provide complete coverage of the history of Latin America. However completeness might be defined, or the degree to which it is attained, it is always the result of a consensus among specialist scholars as well as what the reader might be seeking or expecting. Historians recognize that "completeness" is a chimera, and any assertion that it has been achieved is an illusion. The list of chronological and thematic chapters in this volume is unavoidably idiosyncratic, and in a sense personal. In developing it, I started with the lists of topics around which I have organized my own yearlong undergraduate survey courses on Latin America as those course syllabi have evolved over the past three and a half decades. The list of chapters also reflects some of the directions the study of Latin American history has gone in the recent past. An introductory survey course of thirty years ago would have dealt with the Mexican and Cuban Revolutions, but there would have been no unit on "Central America in Upheaval." The relevance of that theme for a volume such as this one emerged only in the late 1970s, with the Sandinista Revolution in Nicaragua and civil wars in Guatemala and El Salvador, and faded again in the early 1990s. Central America had been there before, of course, but it came into the meta-narrative more as a stage for US expansion in the early twentieth century, with its Banana Empires and occupations by US Marines and the building of the Panama Canal. At this writing, with Central America once again largely absent from the daily concerns of the English-speaking academic world and its students, it becomes imperative to recall the trajectory of that part of the world in the recent past. In a similar vein, the National Security State dictatorships in several larger South American nations date from the 1960s and 1970s, but what were topics of current events then can now be treated with some historical perspective. We now have enough experience with the neoliberal era, following the many changes of the late 1980s and early 1990s, to include it here. A future edition will no doubt be able to deal with the shift to what might be called the neo-Left, a political phenomenon that began to be felt in the early 2000s and continues as I write this in early 2007.

Other topics represented here reflect emerging concerns of scholars, as well as the societies to which they belong and from which their students are drawn. Three decades ago there would not have been much to say in a chapter on the history of women, gender, and the family in Latin America, because there was little academic production that dealt with those themes. The same could be said for environmental history. In a similar way, there is more here on the indigenous and Afro-Latin American experience than would probably have appeared in a similar collection compiled three decades ago.

The reader will also find a variety of ways of approaching the themes treated in these essays. Some tend to be more historiographical, some more narrative and descriptive, and some more interpretive. While I have made no deliberate effort to encourage such methodological diversity, neither have I attempted to push chapter authors into a formulaic mold. The results present the users of the book with a range of ways of dealing with the topics treated, thus enriching the practical value of this collection. There are also occasional instances of apparent chronological and thematic overlap. For example, the background to the Cuban Revolution or the Central

American conflicts of the 1980s must deal with the expansion of US influence in the Caribbean, and a discussion of the Mexican Revolution must consider Mexico's relationship with its neighbor to the north. But US policies and influences in the first half of the twentieth century also deserve treatment on their own terms.

A word about illustrations and maps: it is time for those working mainly with print sources to accommodate to and recognize the existence of considerable amounts of easily available visual material in digitized form, especially on the World Wide Web. At this writing, one very useful "mother site" or "link farm" that constitutes a portal to many other sites focusing on Latin America and its history is <http://lanic.utexas. edu/>. Other entry points into this material include the list of "Useful Links" on the website of the Conference on Latin American History <http://www.h-net.org/ ~clah/index.html>, and the site of H-Latam, the online Latin American History discussion forum <http://www.h-net.org/~latam/>. Through such websites and internet search engines (Google.com and Yahoo.com are two in widespread use at the time of this writing), it is possible to find many more maps and illustrative materials than it would be possible to include in this volume. One of the issues users of the internet face is the need to sort wheat from chaff, but the wheat is there, a few mouse clicks away. An immense array of maps, portraits, data, depictions of historical events, and – for the period since the mid-nineteenth century – photographs, is now available for consultation online. Text searches also provide access to many historical documents, many of them in translation, as well as interpretive scholarship.

Regarding the bibliographies attached to each essay: these lists combine both the titles specifically referenced in the text, together with suggestions for further reading on the themes discussed and interpretative statements made in each chapter. Just as coverage in the text cannot claim to be complete, the bibliographies do not claim to be exhaustive. But they will provide the reader with an authoritative and up-to-date entry into the voluminous intellectual resources currently available on many aspects of the history of Latin America.

What's in a Name?

What constitutes "Latin America" and its "history"? All three of these words merit some consideration, to trace parameters for both the place (Latin America) and the topic (history). It is not the result of some teleological process by which what is today commonly termed Latin America came to be, for which we can identify a starting point and visualize a neat and discrete evolutionary trajectory. And history itself needs to be distinguished from other fields of scholarly inquiry. To begin such a discussion, it is as useful as it is obvious to recall that these and similar descriptive labels are the products of human mental activity, and did not emerge from natural phenomena or processes. The region of the world now commonly referred to as Latin America existed long before the term emerged as the mental construct that it is. And in the recent past the validity of the label has come under fundamental question (Mignolo 2005), despite the fact that it continues in academic and public discourse – and in the title of this volume – as a shorthand label of convenience. In a companion to Latin American history, it is thus appropriate to sketch both the origin and evolution of the label, and what constitutes the history of the region of the world so designated.

Map 1 The Countries of Latin America
Source: Cathryn L. Lombardi, John V. Lombardi, and K. Lynn Stoner, *Latin American History: A Teaching Atlas* (Madison, WI: University of Wisconsin Press, 1983). © 1983. Reprinted by permission of The University of Wisconsin Press.

We can assume that the indigenous peoples who lived in what is now called Latin America in ancient times, whatever cosmological and descriptive notions they developed to locate themselves in time and space, probably did not have a conception of territory and peoples stretching from what we now call Mexico to the southern tip of South America. They located themselves in relation to other culture groups they were aware of and the landforms and bodies of water they were familiar with, as well as in relation to how they explained how they came to be – their "origin myths," in the condescending terms of Western anthropology. Indeed, the same could be said for other peoples of the ancient world, including those who lived in what is now called Europe, right through to the Age of Discovery roughly in the century from 1420 to 1520, the external manifestation of the European Renaissance. In the imagination of Europe, people and places in the rest of the world only began to exist when they entered the European consciousness. That consciousness then proceeded to categorize and compartmentalize regions, "races," and cultures in ways convenient for the purposes of European hegemony (Wolf 1982).

One of those compartments has become Latin America, which we need to define more explicitly. Following the informal consensus among most historians, and most of the historiography they have produced, there are several parts of the Western Hemisphere that are *not* normally included in the rubric Latin America. Most obviously, these are Canada and the United States, despite the fact that a considerable proportion of the population of the former speaks French, a neo-Latin language; and despite the relevance of the latter in discussions of Latin America's international relations, particularly in the twentieth century. Through the colonial era and up through the taking of about one-third of Mexico by the USA as of 1848, what is now Texas, New Mexico, Arizona, Nevada, and California, plus some territory beyond, figured on maps as part of what we now call Latin America. The European-descended populations in those regions spoke primarily Spanish. In the more recent past immigration and cultural assertion by people who trace their origins to former Spanish- or Mexican-held territories makes the US–Mexican border less relevant in distinguishing Anglo America from Latin America (Acuña 1972).

Also not treated here are the three Guianas (French Guiana, technically decolonized by being designated an overseas department of continental France in 1946; Suriname, formerly known as Dutch Guiana; and Guyana, known in the colonial era as British Guiana and before that as Demerara), as well as Belize (formerly British Honduras). Their historical trajectories have more in common with the non-Spanish Caribbean islands than with Latin America, and historically they were never effectively occupied by either Spain or Portugal. Haiti comes into the historical narrative of Latin America especially because of its importance as a sugar-producing colony of Saint-Domingue in the eighteenth century, as well as the resounding message sent to other slave societies by its independence process, following an uprising of the slave majority and Haiti's establishment of the second independent nation in the Western Hemisphere, after the United States of North America (Trouillot 1995; Fischer 2004). Similarly, Jamaica and all of the Lesser Antilles, from the Virgin Islands just east of Puerto Rico to Trinidad just off the coast of Venezuela, as places eventually colonized by European powers other than Spain and Portugal, do not figure in the conventional definition of Latin America as such. These omissions hint at the usual informal definition of what constitutes Latin America historically: Those areas of the

Western Hemisphere originally claimed (even if not completely or effectively occupied) by Spain and Portugal, and where the dominant national language today is either Spanish or Portuguese.

Geographers, it should be noted, giving priority to contiguous landmasses and bodies of water rather than to historical processes or cultural commonalities, traditionally divide the Americas into two continents and two regions. The continents are North America (from northern Canada to the isthmus of Panama) and South America (from the Panama–Colombia border to the southern tip of Tierra del Fuego, an island south of the Strait of Magellan). The subregions are Central America (from Guatemala to Panama) and the Caribbean (the islands from the Bahamas and Cuba in the northwest to Trinidad and Tobago in the southeast). These different approaches to regional divisions and groupings have led to confusion as frequent as it is superficial. For example, Mexico might be placed in North America by geographers (and in the names of such economic and political arrangements as the North American Free Trade Agreement, NAFTA), but it is definitely part of Latin America for historians. And Puerto Rico, an island of the Caribbean, is politically attached to the United States, but is historically and culturally part of Latin America.

These considerations lead to a question central to the label itself: What is "Latin" about Latin America? There are several historical and cultural issues that, in fact, make the term quite problematic. The language of the Iberian groups engaged in conquest and colonization was not Latin, despite the roots of the Spanish and Portuguese languages in the Roman occupation of Iberia in ancient times. While Latin remained the language of the Roman Catholic Church so central to the Iberian colonization project, there is no apparent connection between church Latin and the label "Latin America." Christopher Columbus himself, mistakenly insisting until his death in 1506 that he had reached the eastern edge of Asia, used the term *Indias Occidentales*, or the Indias to the West. That term lingers today, after being perpetuated especially – and perhaps ironically – by British colonials, in the West Indies, the conventional English term for the islands of the Caribbean Sea eventually colonized by Great Britain, France, the Netherlands, and Denmark.

It is commonly known that the more general term "America" derives from the name of Amerigo Vespucci (1451?–1512), another navigator of Italian origin who made several voyages to the Caribbean region and along the coast of northern Brazil from 1497 to 1502. Unlike Columbus, Vespucci concluded that Europeans did not previously know about the lands he visited in the west, and he thus referred to them as the New World. In a 1507 map by German cartographer Martin Waldseemuller, America appears for the first time with that name. While the protocol of European exploration usually gives primacy to the first "discoverer," there would seem to be some justification for naming the newly known landmass after the navigator who recognized it as separate from Asia (Amerigo Vespucci) rather than for the first European to report its existence, but who subsequently insisted that he had confirmed a new way to reach Asia (Christopher Columbus) (Arciniegas 1990).

In subsequent centuries, Europeans and their colonial descendants applied the term America to the entire Western Hemisphere (which half of the globe is called "Western" and which is called "Eastern" is itself a convention of European origin). That usage continues today in Latin America, where it is commonly taught that there is one continent in the Western Hemisphere: America. The Liberator Simón Bolívar famously convened a conference in Panama in 1826 to work toward a union of the American republics. He included all nations of the hemisphere in the invitation, and it would not have occurred to him to add "Latin" to the descriptors, because the term had not yet been invented. When in 1890 the United States and its commercial and financial allies around Latin America established the Commercial Bureau of the American Republics, which became the Panamerican Union in 1910 and the Organization of American States in 1948, no terminological distinctions were made by culture or language. In the modern era "America" has of course become the common shorthand name of the nation that developed from the 13 English colonies on the eastern seaboard of North America. This apparent appropriation by one nation of a label that traditionally refers to the entire Western Hemisphere has been a recurring source of puzzlement and occasional resentment among Latin Americans (Arciniegas 1966).

Historically, the first use of the term "Latin America" has been traced only as far back as the 1850s. It did not originate within the region, but again from outside, as part of a movement called "pan-Latinism" that emerged in French intellectual circles, and more particularly in the writings of Michel Chevalier (1806–79). A contemporary of Alexis de Tocqueville who traveled in Mexico and the United States during the late 1830s, Chevalier contrasted the "Latin" peoples of the Americas with the "Anglo-Saxon" peoples (Phelan 1968; Ardao 1980, 1993). From those beginnings, by the time of Napoleon III's rise to power in 1852 pan-Latinism had developed as a cultural project extending to those nations whose culture supposedly derived from neo-Latin language communities (commonly called Romance languages in English). Starting as a term for historically derived "Latin" culture groups, *L'Amerique Latine* then became a place on the map. Napoleon III was particularly interested in using the concept to help justify his intrusion into Mexican politics that led to the imposition of Archduke Maximilian as Emperor of Mexico, 1864–7. While France had largely lost out in the global imperial rivalries of the previous two centuries, it still retained considerable prestige in the world of culture, language, and ideas (McGuinness 2003). Being included in the pan-Latin cultural sphere was attractive to some intellectuals of Spanish America, and use of the label "Latin America" began to spread haltingly around the region, where it competed as a term with "Spanish America" (where Spanish is the dominant language), "Ibero-America" (including Brazil but presumably not French-speaking areas), and other subregional terms such as "Andean America" (which stretches geographically from Venezuela to Chile, but which more usually is thought of as including Colombia, Ecuador, Peru, and Bolivia), or the "Southern Cone" (Chile, Argentina, Paraguay, and Uruguay) (Rojas Mix 1991).

Not until the middle of the twentieth century did the label Latin America achieve widespread and largely unquestioned currency in public as well as academic and intellectual discourse, both in the region (Marras 1992) and outside of it. With the establishment of the Economic Commission for Latin America (ECLA, later adding Caribbean to become ECLAC) under United Nations auspices in 1948, the term became consolidated in policy circles, with political overtones challenging US hegemony but largely devoid of the rivalries of culture, language, and "race" of earlier times (Reid 1978). The 1960s saw the continent-wide Latin American literary "boom" and the near-universal adoption of "Latin American Studies" by

English-language universities in the USA, Great Britain, and Canada. This trend began with the establishment of the Conference on Latin American History in 1927 and was consolidated with the organization of the interdisciplinary Latin American Studies Association in 1967. Despite the widespread and largely unproblematic use of the term in the main languages of the Western Hemisphere since that era, regional variations remain: In Brazil *América Latina* is commonly assumed to refer to what in the United States is called Spanish America, i.e., "Latin America" minus Brazil.

While discussing the spontaneous creation of such collective labels, we need to recognize that the terms "Latino" or "Latina/o" now widespread in the United States have no basis in any specific nation or subregion in Latin America. Like the latter term, from which it is derived linguistically, Latina/o is an invented term of convenience – a neologism built on a neologism (Oboler 1995; Gracia 1999; Dzidzienyo & Oboler 2005; Oboler & González 2005). Whatever their origins, Latino or Latina/o have largely replaced the older "Hispanic" or Hispanic American" within the United States, although that English-derived term, problematic on several counts, lingers in library subject classifications.

But there are other questions that need to be posed, in the age of identity politics and the assertion of alternative ethnicities and nationalisms. By its historical and intellectual origins and the claims of pan-Latinism, the term Latin America privileges those groups who descend from "Latin" peoples: Spain and Portugal (but not, ironically enough, the French-speaking populations of Canada or the Caribbean). By another set of criteria, what is now commonly called Latin America might be subdivided into those regions where the indigenous heritage is strong and native identity has reemerged to claim political space, especially in Mesoamerica and the Andean region; Afro-Latin America, especially the circum-Caribbean region and much of Brazil; and Euro-Latin America, in which relatively massive immigration from 1870 to the Great Depression of the 1930s transformed the demographic and cultural makeup of southern Brazil, Uruguay, and Argentina (Rojas Mix 1991). In other words, Latin America as a term ignores or claims dominance over other cultures in the region, which have recently come to reassert their distinctive traditions, including a plethora of languages spoken by tens of millions of indigenous people – none of which have any relationship to Spanish or Portuguese (or Latin) beyond a scattering of loan words. The current condition of peoples of indigenous and African heritage has a historical relationship to conquest, colonialism, subjugation, forced assimilation, exploitation, marginalization, and exclusion. Those are not processes to celebrate and use as the basis for national or regional identity challenging the hegemony of the Anglo-Saxon "race," as was the thrust of pan-Latinism of yore. But they are the basis for claiming cultural and political space – as well as territory and access to resources – within Latin America, today and into the future (Monaghan and Wyatt; Terraciano; Knight; Helg; and Wade, this volume).

BIBLIOGRAPHY

Acuña, R. (1972) *Occupied America: The Chicano's Struggle Toward Liberation*. Canfield Press, San Francisco.

Arciniegas, G. (1966) *Latin America: A Cultural History*. Knopf, New York.

Arciniegas, G. (1990) *Amerigo y el Nuevo Mundo*. Alianza, Madrid.

Ardao, A.(1980) *Génesis de la idea y el nombre de América Latina*. Centro de Estudios Latino-americarnos Rómulo Gallegos, Caracas.

Ardao, A. (1986) *Nuestra América Latina*. Ediciones Banda Oriental, Montevideo.

Ardao, A. (1993) *América Latina y la latinidad*. Universidad Nacional Autónoma de México, Mexico City.

Barker, N. N. (1979) "The Factor of 'Race' in the French Experience in Mexico, 1821–1861," *Hispanic American Historical Review*, 59:1, pp. 64–80.

Dzidzienyo, A. & Oboler, S. (eds.) (2005) *Neither Enemies nor Friends: Latinos, Blacks, Afro-Latinos*. Palgrave Macmillan, New York.

Elliot, J. H. (1972) *The Old World and the New, 1492–1650*. Cambridge University Press, Cambridge.

Espinosa, A. M. (1919) *América Española, o Hispano América: El término "América Latina" es erróneo*. Comisaria Regia del Turismo y Cultura Artística, Madrid.

Fischer, S. (2004) *Modernity Disavowed: Haiti and the Cultures of Slavery in the Age of Revolution*. Duke University Press, Durham.

Gracia, J. J. E. (1999) *Hispanic/Latino Identity: A Philosophical Perspective*. Blackwell Publishing, Malden, MA.

Hale, J. R. (1968) *Renaissance Exploration*. British Broadcasting Corporation, London.

Marras, S. (1992) *América Latina, marca registrada*. Grupo Zeta, Mexico City.

McGuinness, A. (2003) "Searching for 'Latin America': Race and Sovereignty in the Americas in the 1850s." In N. Appelbaum, A. S. Macpherson, & A. Rossemblat, (eds.), *Race and Nation in Modern Latin America*. University of North Carolina Press, Chapel Hill.

Mignolo, W. (2005) *The Idea of Latin America*. Blackwell Publishing, Malden, MA.

Oboler, S. (1995) *Ethnic Labels, Latino Lives: Identity and the Politics of (re) Presentation in the United States*. University of Minnesota Press, Minneapolis.

Oboler, S. & González, D. J. (eds.) (2005) *The Oxford Encyclopedia of Latinos and Latinas in the United States*. Oxford University Press, New York.

O'Gorman, E. (1961) *The Invention of America: An Inquiry into the Historical Nature of the New World and the Meaning of Its History*. Indiana University Press, Bloomington.

Parry, J. H. (1961) *The Establishment of European Hegemony, 1415–1715: Trade and Exploration in the Age of the Renaissance*. Harper & Row, New York.

Phelan, J. L. (1968) "Pan-latinisms, French Intervention in Mexico (1861–1867) and the Genesis of the Idea of Latin America." In *Conciencia y autenticidad históricas: Escrito en homenaje a Edmundo O'Gorman*. Universidad Nacional Autonónoma de México, Mexico City.

Reid, J. T. (1978) "The Rise and Decline of the Ariel–Caliban Antithesis in Spanish America," *The Americas*, 34:3, pp. 345–55.

Rojas Mix, M. (1991) *Los cien nombres de América: Eso que descubrió Colón*. Lumen, Barcelona.

Scammell, G. V. (1981) *The World Encompassed: The First European Maritime Empires c. 800–1650*. University of California Press, Berkeley.

Schurz, W. L. (1954) *This New World: The Civilization of Latin America*. Dutton, New York.

Trouillot, M.-R. (1995) *Silencing the Past: Power and the Production of History*. Beacon Press, Boston, Mass.

Wolf, E. (1982) *Europe and the People without History*. University of California Press, Berkeley.

Chapter One

Early Population Flows in the Western Hemisphere

Tom D. Dillehay

Setting the Stage

The early history of human exploration and achievement in the Americas is a register of ideas inferred from the combination of archeological, paleoecological, biological, and linguistic data. Scholars have recognized many patterns in the data and proposed several interpretative scenarios, at local and continental scales, and their recurrence in time and space. These scenarios have emphasized the variable biological, social, and cultural capacities of the first humans to spread throughout the New World and their adaptations to changing environmental circumstances and their symbolic and material expressions. These adaptations across the Americas involved many cultural continuities and changes through the selective invention and exchange of cultural elements (Dillehay 2000; Adovasio & Page 2002; Meltzer 2003b).

The focus here is the first few millennia or so of human settlement in the New World, spanning the late Pleistocene and early Holocene period, from approximately 15,000 to 9,000 years ago, with implications for later periods. This coverage does not terminate the late Pleistocene at the usual arbitrary cut-off point of 10,000 years ago when deglaciation ended in most regions. That date prevents the late Pleistocene period from being considered as part of the social and cultural contributions made to later prehistory. In the pages that follow, the scholarly ideas and scientific evidence about this period are summarized, illustrating how our knowledge of the first Americans continues to develop. Although I primarily emphasize the technologies and economies of the first Americans, I also attempt to address social and other issues in hopes of imbricating the deep past with more recent indigenous cultural transformations.

Much rethinking about the peopling of the Americas has occurred in recent years as a result of new discoveries in archaeology and paleoanthropology. Several archeological sites in both North and South America have much potential to document earlier traces of human occupation (Dixon 1999; Dillehay 2000; Meltzer 2003b). The eastern woodlands of the United States in particular have yielded more convincing evidence of sites ancestral to the widely documented 11,300-year-old Clovis culture, which is best known for its fluted bifacial projectile point and big game hunting tradition. Meadowcroft Shelter in Pennsylvania, Cactus Hill in Virginia,

Topper Site in South Carolina, and others suggest that groups of generalized hunters and gatherers may have lived in those areas as far back as 16,000 to 13,000 years ago (Figure 1.1) These possibilities are supportive of the 12,500-year occupation at Monte Verde and slightly later sites in South America, because if people first came into the New World across the Bering land bridge, we would expect earlier dates in North America. It also is likely that multiple early migrations took place and people moved along the edge of the ice sheets from Siberia to Chile (Fladmark 1979; Dixon 1999; Dillehay 2000) and possibly from northern Europe into eastern North America (Stanford and Bradley 2002). Recently, there is renewed discussion of possible influences from Australia and Oceania and even Africa. Some paleoanthropologists, led by the Brazilian Walter Neves (Neves et al. 2003), suggest that the oldest skeletal material from eastern Brazil more strongly affiliates with ancient Africans and Australians than with modern Asians and Native Americans. This suggests the presence of non-Mongoloid as well as Mongoloid populations in the Americas (cf. Steele & Powell 2002). Neves does not believe that these migrants came directly from Africa or Australia, but that they splintered off from an earlier group that moved through Asia and eventually arrived in Australia and America.

Linguists and geneticists also postulate earlier and multiple migrations. Johanna Nichols (2002) believes that a high diversity of languages among Native Americans could only have developed from an earlier human presence in the New World, perhaps as old as 30,000 to 20,000 years ago. Several geneticists present a similar argument derived from genetic diversity (e.g., Schurr 2004). Based on comparisons between certain genetic signatures shared by modern Native Americans and modern Siberians, it has been estimated that people from Siberia entered the New World at least 20,000 to 14,000 years ago. These first immigrants are believed to have followed a Pacific coastal route into the Americas, where they spread into all interior regions. Later interior migrations possibly moved into North and Central America where they mixed with earlier populations.

These new discoveries and ideas are not without their critics. Advent Clovis proponents who defend the Clovis-first theory still hold to the notion that the first Americans were mainly big game hunters who entered the Americas from Siberia no earlier than 12,000 to 11,500 years ago and spread rapidly throughout the Americas. These proponents believe that notions of a pre-Clovis presence at earlier sites are based on questionable radiocarbon dates, site stratigraphies, and interpretations of the evidence. Although these criticisms are often constructive and warranted for some earlier and often outlandish claims and encourage a more rigorous approach to the study of the first Americans, they are usually based on anecdotal tales, emotive vindication, and little scientific evidence.

The Pre-Clovis and Clovis Dilemma

In the 1950s, the discovery of fluted projectile points at Blackwater Draw, near Clovis, New Mexico, the type site of the Clovis culture, set the standard by which all other point types and early cultures would be measured for the next 50 years. Based on the later discoveries of more Clovis points at sites throughout North America, the Clovis culture came to be known as the first "migratory culture" in the

Figure 1.1 Location of major archeological sites of the late Pleistocene period in the New World

Americas. In essence, the Clovis point was equated with the first Americans and with early human migration from Siberia to Tierra del Fuego. The argument for the Clovis-first model has been based primarily on the stylistic association of a few similar traits such as fluting on lanceolate projectile points. Every time these and other traits have been found in the Americas, they have been uncritically interpreted as evidence of a Clovis culture and a Clovis migration. As a result, the Clovis culture has continually widened to include technologically distinct point types, such as the Fishtail, Restrepo, Paijan, and Ayampitin points in South America. None of these distinct types fit culturally, stylistically, and technologically with the Clovis point and with the Clovis-first scheme. It also remains unclear as to what Clovis culture is and the criteria employed to define it (cf. Haynes 1969; Dillehay 2000). Although there is a good understanding of Clovis stone tool technology, little still is known about the subsistence, social, domestic, and mobility patterns of regional Clovis cultures and even less about their possible relation to the early cultures and peoples of the Southern Hemisphere.

Despite the continuing debates over the first peopling of the Americas and the ambiguity and paucity of evidence, four issues are becoming clearer. Although Clovis culture is the most widely distributed early record in North America and accounts for a major portion of the first chapter of human history in the north, it fails to explain early cultural and biological diversity in all of the Western Hemisphere, especially in South America. Second, Northern Hemisphere agendas about the peopling of the New World, which were developed in the historically better investigated regions of North America, have created unrealistic expectations or preconceptions about the significance of cultural developments in South America. Despite the likely migration of early people from the north to the south, the archeological records of each continent must be viewed in their own terms and not be judged by preconceived notions usually based on meager evidence or overextended interpretative models (Dillehay 1999, 2000; Meltzer 2003). Third, many anthropologists now no longer consider the Clovis people to be purely big game hunters, but also small game hunters and gatherers of plants. And fourth, regardless of the quality of evidence, early American populations seem to present a cultural and biological melting pot for a long time and probably had their physical, genetic, and cultural roots in different areas. A lingering question is whether Clovis people developed from an earlier population in the Americas, or whether they were only some of the first Americans in some areas.

It is my belief that there were pre-Clovis populations in the New World sometime between 20,000 and 15,000 years ago. I also believe that the first migrants into the Americas adapted to many different environments quickly, creating a mosaic of contemporary different types of hunters and gatherers (i.e., big game hunters, generalized interior foragers, coastal foragers) immediately after they entered new environments. Further, in my opinion, a key issue is not rapid migration but rapid social change, cultural exchange, and a steep "learning curve" across newly encountered environments – adaptation of technological, socioeconomic, and cognitive processes over several generations (cf. Dillehay 1997, 2000; Meltzer 2003). As the early archeological records of South America and parts of the eastern United States suggest, this was not a single unitary process, but many. While different types of hunter and gatherer groups were settling into one new environment, others were probably just moving into neighboring areas for the first time. Others probably stayed for longer periods in more productive environments. All of these processes must have begun sometime before 12,000 years ago in order to produce the types of technological and economic diversity reflected in the archeological record by 11,000 years ago in most regions of the Americas (Bryan 1973; Dillehay 1999, 2000). The record left behind by these processes is characterized by variable site sizes, locations, functions, occupations, artifact assemblages, and internal structures that reflect different adaptations to different environments and various degrees of social interaction between different populations.

Interdisciplinary Evidence and Words of Caution

It may be argued that one of the most direct evidences of humans in the Americas are the languages spoken by peoples of the hemisphere and the genetic linkages between them and others. However, there is no consensus among specialists as to the validity of historical linguistics and genetics in constructing models of American origins as far back as 10,000 years ago and more. Both historical linguistics and genetics can suggest likely places of origin of a language and genetic group, and the geography of its spread from such a point of origin, but on their own they cannot convincingly achieve a chronology for the spread of a language group or genetic population or the dating of a particular language stage and genetic mutation.

In regard to chronology, language and genetics do not change at a constant rate and we do know that language replacement can occur rapidly. What is required is a material indicator of the language spoken and of the genetic mixture to provide a correlation of language and date. As expected, such correlations are very difficult to find. These difficulties aside, it is important to consider the linguistic and genetic information for the Americas in relation to the archeological and biological evidence. The information gained from these disciplines enables the highlighting of the differences that exist between the current communities of the area, and warns of the complex associations between these communities in the present and the past. However, it must be kept in mind that it is difficult to associate historical linguistics directly with material evidence. And the genetic evidence must be derived from human skeletons. Further, both the linguistic and genetic chronologies must depend on radiocarbon and other dating techniques in archeology.

In this essay, I primarily consider archeology (including the scant skeletal material available for the late Pleistocene) to be the only reliable direct indicator of a human presence in the Americas, and the paleoenvironmental evidence, which may be used to provide a proxy (i.e., not direct) record of human presence. The environmental evidence, like the genetic and linguistic evidence, has problems related to its utility and interpretation. The archeological record also is problematic. It generally is not well preserved and often is disturbed by numerous natural processes that may destroy and mix evidence. Furthermore, early archeological sites are generally characterized by a narrow range of cultural materials and few internal site traits (e.g., hearths, activity areas). In fact, most early sites contain stone artifacts and, when preservation permits, the bone remains of animals. This forces archeologists to over-rely on technologically distinct and temporally sensitive stone projectile points, for example, in order to maximize information about the first Americans, which also is problematic.

To elaborate briefly, traditional approaches to the peopling of the Americas have relied too heavily on subjective aesthetic definitions of point styles (e.g., Clovis, Folsom, Fishtail, Paijan) from a wide variety of archeological sites in North and South America. Not yet fully integrated into these approaches are systematically contextualized archeological traits such as internal site patterning of non-projectile point stone tools, other artifacts and features (e.g., hearths, storage pits), and inter-site quantitative and qualitative comparisons between these and other variables. Point styles may be valid chronological and functional markers but not valid indicators of late Pleistocene social organizations, economic strategies, and patterns of early human entry and dispersion throughout the New World. Arguments for long-distance migration in the Americas must be founded on something more scientifically rigorous than a simple reference to the appearance of a single, possible foreign trait – that is, the flute on a Clovis point – and its possible association with a single similar trait elsewhere. A narrow focus on a single trait or small group of traits may conceal many other cultural possibilities. The lack of explicit study of a wide range of artifact sites and inter-site comparisons across the Americas impedes communication by restricting our understanding of what is meant by different artifact styles and their associated traits within and across different types of sites in different environments.

The New World during the Last Glacial Maximum

During the period 25,000 to 10,000 years ago shifting dry and hot or cold conditions prevailed over much of the hemisphere. This climatic regime peaked 21,000 to 15,000 years ago, during a period called the Last Maximum Glaciation, or LGM. Extensive areas of the northern half of North America and limited high-altitude and high-latitude areas of South America were glaciated during the LGM. During this period the sea level stood approximately 130 m below present level, so that the continents were larger than they are now. Much of the continental shelf that is now ocean floor was comprised of low-lying plains. Some would have been a continuation of dunefields and other geological formations, but others were resource-rich coastal lakes and lagoons, forests, and rugged hills, plateaus, canyons, and river valleys. Cooling of the ocean resulting from reduced glaciation decreased evaporation, and consequently throughout many regions precipitation was less.

Extensive dune whorls in the North American southwest and mid-Atlantic seaboard and in parts of northern South America dated to this period suggest a strong semi-permanent high-pressure system over many regions. The lack of warm sea in high-latitude areas and increasing land surfaces due to glacial retreat reduced the onshore movement of tropical rain depressions. Inland aridity was intense enough that lakes as far south as Chile and Argentina dried up, forests retreated, and some animals became extinct. Over the high-latitude regions severe cold, drought, and strong winds discouraged vegetation growth in some regions.

After the LGM world temperatures increased, the Northern and Southern Hemisphere icecaps began to shrink and as a response the level of the sea rose. A surge came at 15,000 years ago, when the North American ice sheets melted, but ice sheets in Antarctica began their retreat at 12,000 years ago. The land area shrank, and the present coastline began to form about 6,000 years ago. From 14,500 years ago, tree lines climbed about 800 m in many areas, while glaciers and surrounding alpine and subalpine environments in the Rocky Mountains of North America and the Andean Mountains of South America retreated. This shift in the location of higher-altitude forests often restructured the diversity and type of resources available to people, especially in hilly and mountainous areas. In many areas, temperature increased by 5–6 °C. In the interior of both North and South America, especially in the temperate woodlands of eastern North America and in the tropics of the Amazon Basin, there was sufficient humidity and cooler temperatures to sustain vegetation, and dune building decreased. Progressively, dunefields across the continent stabilized and forests replaced former shrubby grassland and savanna. From 11,500 years ago many plant species in mountainous environments migrated inland and to higher altitudes, replacing grasslands and savannas.

When people first arrived in the Americas and dispersed across the continents, they faced a continual series of environmental challenges that persisted throughout the late Pleistocene and early Holocene. The adaptability and endurance in colonizing the Americas produced early cultural diversity across these environments, including specialized big game hunters in open terrain such as the Great Plains in North America and the Pampa and Patagonian grasslands in Argentina and Chile, specialized maritime foragers along both the Pacific and Atlantic shorelines, and various kinds of generalized foragers in various parkland, savanna, and forest habitats.

Extinction of Megafauna

Most mammal species inhabiting the Americas in the late Pleistocene survived into modern times. Those that did not survive include most of the largest species. These extinctions occurred as mosaics of individual events in different parts of the Americas over many thousands of years. Late Pleistocene extinctions included mastodont, wooly mammoth, American horse, giant armadillo, ground sloth, ancient bison, and others. During the late Pleistocene nearly all animals had a larger body mass than their modern descendents. Many researchers believe that some of the large species did not become extinct at all, but simply became smaller because of a strong selective force for smaller body size as modern climatic conditions approached. Such a trend is particularly notable among the grazing animals.

There are different explanations for why so many animal species, especially the larger ones, became extinct within the last several millennia. The main arguments concern environmental changes of natural origin, and over-hunting. However, no single cause is sufficient to explain the disappearance of a large and diverse range of animals adapted to such a wide range of habitats. Least evident is the part humans may have played in the process. An extreme view of the human intervention explanation is the "*blitzkrieg* hypothesis," formulated by Paul Martin (1984) to explain animal extinctions in North America. This argument is that the larger animal species were eliminated by "overkill" shortly after people first arrived in the continent. Other less extreme positions are that small-scale but continuous hunting of megafauna, or large-scale burning which changed the landscape, had cumulative long-term effects that threw megafauna into an irreversible decline. There also are multi-causal explanations that combine human intervention with climatic change, offering a scenario of sustained hunting of species that were ecologically stressed by the onset of the LGM and already on the path to extinction.

Despite the discovery of many archeological sites with megafauna bones, there is not an overwhelming number of megafauna-kill sites in North America and only a small handful in South America (Meltzer 1993; Dillehay 2000). Kill sites are rare anywhere in the world, so it is not surprising that few have been identified in South America. Generally, archeologists believe that this is a limitation of the archeological record rather than a true indication of late Pleistocene subsistence. Even if more kill sites exist, as we believe they must, there is the problem of how to identify them. Projectile points have been found with the bone remains of megafauna in many sites throughout the New World, but they also could represent fortuitous mixing of natural and cultural debris or even human scavenging of natural death localities. Further, stone artifacts and megafauna remains have been found stratified together in many caves and in beds of springs. In the absence of direct evidence, this evidence may only mean that humans and megafauna frequented the same places at different times. More often the bones are intrusive in the critical levels and their association is spurious. The marks of butchering tools are difficult to demonstrate and other marks on megafauna bone are from teeth of predators, scavengers, and tree roots. Even evidence of burnt bones found with stone tools is not always sufficient evidence alone to assume a human association. I point this out because there has been a tendency in archeology, especially in North America, to overinterpret the archeological evidence toward big game hunting, which is understandable in many cases because only stones and bones are preserved in sites and many scholars view the depletion and pursuit of big game as the primary factor motivating people to migrate rapidly to new environments in search of food.

Motivating Migration

What motivated people to explore and colonize distant lands? It is unlikely that we will ever really know what motivated people to travel along interior rivers and other routes and along coastlines or possibly across the sea to settle America. There may have been "push–pull" effects (Anthony 1990) in migration from northeast Asia across Beringia to Alaska or from western Europe along the ice sheets to the northeast shores of Canada. Factors pushing people to migrate might be perceived as overpopulation of certain resource zones, feuding, expulsion, environmental catastrophe, and/or adventure. Pull factors might be through the maintenance of contacts with related groups that had already settled elsewhere. Other pull factors might be the need to develop new alliances through intermarriage for population purposes and the developing knowledge of easy resource exploitation in pristine environments. Whatever the motivation, and whether exploration and colonization were by interlopers or seafarers or both, the next consideration is where they came from.

Based on current evidence, all that can be established is that if people moved southwardly along the northern Pacific and/or Atlantic coastlines, they must have crossed some distances greater than swimming range and therefore watercraft must have been required. It is not likely they were out to sea and had no land in sight; the coastlines were probably always in view. In this sense, archeologists may be underestimating the early archeological capacity for sea voyaging as suggested by new archeological finds in other parts of the world. For instance, rockshelters in the northern Solomon Islands contain occupation debris dating back to about 28,000 years ago. The nearest land from which people could have traveled to the Solomons was New Ireland, 180 km away off northeast Australia. Earlier views considered that people in unnavigable boats could only have achieved occupation of Alaska or New-foundland by accidental drift voyages. What we do know is that people had crossed the sea to settle Australia and New Guinea at times of lower sea level before 40,000 years ago. At the height of LGM, many more islands and high points in the landscape of the Northern Hemisphere were connected by large areas of lowlands and river channels.

It is presumed among many archeologists that there was less constraint in follow-ing coastlines, because they offered the best chance of survival in a new unknown land. This premise of dependence on the resources of the sea and littoral zone is the basis of the coastal hypothesis proposed by Knut Fladmark (1979), who postulated that the first colonists subsisted primarily on fish, shellfish, and small terrestrial animals, and that they had little interest in moving inland. This scenario would explain the rapid peopling of the New World. He and others argued that human settlement was confined to the coastline for many centuries, and that only later did people expand along the river corridors to exploit the rich aquatic resources of inland water bodies.

As the number of known early sites has increased, their distribution has broadened to include non-coastal habitats, and there is no comfortable fit between Fladmark's model and these inland findings. Further, the coastal economy is a highly specialized economy of the littoral zone, not the more generalized exploitation typical of many indigenous groups living along the American coasts in historical times. The coastal model implies that people were so specialized that that they were unable to adapt to environmental conditions away from the coast. While some coasts were richly endowed with food resources, others were almost bereft of them. Inland there were vast expanses of tropical and temperate forestlands and woodlands, and grasslands inhab-ited by grazing animals. An alternative scenario is progressive colonization of various environmental zones – the better-watered regions first and the arid areas last. Wood-lands were prime country because they supported a greater diversity of plant and animal species, which would have permitted a broad-spectrum diet of large and small game, aquatic resources, and plants.

The first human inhabitants of the Americas probably stepped ashore somewhere along the coasts, probably in Alaska and possibly in northeast Canada. Archeology cannot provide a precise answer about the timing of first settlements because much of these regions remains to be explored and excavated, and also there is a margin of error or uncertainty in chronometric age determinations. During the foundation era of first colonization, the human population was probably very small and may not have left sufficient traces to be archeologically visible. It is possible, therefore, that people arrived more than a few thousand years earlier than the dates determined for the oldest traces of human occupation of sites.

Thus, at the moment there is no clear resolution as to whether one or the other of these possible migration scenarios accounts for the patterns observed in the early American Pleistocene record. I am convinced that there were multiple migrations, with varying degrees of longevity and interior penetration from different places throughout the late Pleistocene. There are many sites that have not yet been investigated, particularly along the coast and in the interior regions of Alaska, Canada, and Central and South America. It would come as no surprise if there were new data suggesting occasional contacts with western Europe.

One of the earliest migrations must have been from Eurasia to western to eastern Beringia. Several sites in what is now Alaska and Yukon Territory suggest the presence of people in late Pleistocene times (see Fig. 1.1). Possible bone tools and later stone tools at Bluefish Caves date between 20,000 and 12,000 years ago. Sites associated with bifacially flaked points and other tools date between 11,800 and 11,000 years ago in the Nenana Valley of Alaska. Later Nenana sites produced wedge-shaped cores and microblades reminiscent of tool industries in northeastern Asia. Although the early archeological evidence from the far northwest is scarce, it is becoming clearer that people with similar economies and technologies were moving back and forth across Siberia and Beringia by at least 11,500 years ago. The question is when and where these same people moved farther south and east, which would have been difficult at the time. Beringia was surrounded by massive ice sheets that provided few openings into new lands unless people followed the Pacific coastline. Much debate is centered on the movement of people through habitable openings in the ice sheets and initially along the edges of ice and farther south along an exposed coastal plain, where recently excavated sites such as On Your Knee Cave and Daisy Cave in North America and Quebrada Jaguay and Quebrada Tacahuay in Peru are beginning to shed new light on early maritime adaptations.

The archeological record below the ice sheets is different. The fluted point sites of the Clovis and later Folsom and Dalton cultures, dating between 11,300 and 10,500 years ago and 10,500 and 9,500 years ago, respectively, are the first established indicators of widespread late Pleistocene occupation in North America. Some of the best-documented sites are Kimmswick, Vail, Bull Brook, Shawnee-Minisink and Shoop, Flint Run, Debert, Clovis, Murray Springs, Gault, Aubrey, and others. Although many of these localities appear to represent specialized big-game kill sites, especially in the southwest and Great Plains, those in the eastern woodlands suggest generalized foragers (e.g., Meltzer 2003a), exploiting a wide range of animal and plant species. One site in particular, Meadowcroft Shelter in Pennsylvania, which dates in pre-Clovis times to at least 16,000 years ago, yielded a wide range of artifactual and ecofactual materials indicative of a broad-spectrum economy focused on large and small game and vegetal species.

Unfortunately, little is known of Mexico and the remainder of Central America. A few sites have produced Clovis, Fishtail, and other point types. In Mexico several early sites have been dated between 30,000 and 10,000 years ago, but archeologists question the contexts and, to date, little validity has been given to them. The only certainty is the promise that more research in this region will yield important information to allow us to not only recognize many new patterns in the Central America register but also to relate this region as a lengthy transformative bridge between the different histories of human migration in the Northern and Southern Hemispheres.

As I and others have stated before, South America is different from North America because no single culture dominated the continent the way the Clovis culture, with its representative fluted points, may have done for a relatively short period of time in North America. The Southern Hemisphere differs for several reasons. First, there are no extensive ice sheets possibly blocking human movement, except those in the high altitudes of the central Andes and the high latitudes of southern Chile and Argentina. Second, there is no clear stratigraphic sequence of continental and regional projectile point styles, such as Clovis and Folsom and Clovis and Dalton. In South America, the earliest technologies consisted of different kinds of stone tools, including a wide variety of spear points, unifacial tools made of flakes, and sling stones, which is different from North America. A wide variety of point styles are known in South America. They include long bipointed forms like the El Jobo points from Venezuela and the Monte Verde points from southern Chile; the stemmed Paijan and Fishtail style from various areas; and the triangular and subtriangular point types from the central Andean highlands. We know that these and other point styles began to pro-liferate around 11,000 to 10,500 years ago. Some stone tool industries of South America, especially those from late Pleistocene sites in eastern Brazil (Lagoa Santa, Lapa Vermelha IV), also were based on unifacial industries that coexisted with and had different characteristics from bifacial ones. Based on current evidence, the only possible link between North and South America has been the so-called fluting on the Fishtail and Clovis points, and this association is controversial and unconvincing. Although Fishtail points have been dated by radiocarbon means between 11,100 and 10,200 years ago in southern Patagonia, the southernmost tip of South America, they are no older than 10,500 years ago in other areas of South America and in Central America, leading Alan Bryan, William Mayer-Oakes, and other archeologists to suggest that they were invented in the far south and diffused to the north. Too, the South American stemmed Paijan point is earlier than its North American coun-terpart. Earlier "fluted" and stemmed points in South America have prompted some archeologists to ask why more models of early south-to-north migration are not considered. But, here again, this suggestion is based on aesthetic point associations and not on systematically analyzed inter-site and intercontinental trait comparisons. Third, the earliest evidence from a wide variety of South American sites indicates dietary breadth and cultural diversity at the outset of human entry and dispersion, with many areas witnessing the development of broad forager diets long before 11,000 years ago (Bryan 1973; Dillehay 2000; Salemme & Miotti 2003). Big game hunting was simply one of many different economic practices, and apparently never achieved the importance it allegedly did in North America.

It is not known when people first moved into South America, although it can be reasonably assumed that they came from North America by way of the Pacific and/or Atlantic coastlines and by various interior routes through the Panamanian isthmus. Although people had already reached the far southern tip of the continent in Tierra del Fuego by at least 11,000 years ago, the terminal Pleistocene between at least 11,300 and 10,500 years ago saw the establishment of human settlements in Amazonia (Monte Alegre, Lapa do Boquete), the high Andes (Tibito, Tequendama, Lauricocha), and the grasslands of Uruguay and Argentina. By about 11,000 to 10,000 years ago, people were moving into caves and rockshelters immediately after deglaciation in the high Andes of Peru (e.g., Cueva Pachamachay, Cueva Telarmachay, Cueva Uchumachay) and northern Chile (San Lorenzo), and in Andean foothills of southern Patagonia (Los Toldos, Piedra Museo, Cueva Fell,

Tres Arroyos). How much earlier were they there? Fifteen to twenty thousand years ago is certainly a possibility, but until more archeological evidence is available, it is uncertain.

As a final point here, in recent years, several sites have raised issues that are timely and important for the study of early plant and human interaction. Although vegetal matter usually is not preserved in the archeological record, where it *is* preserved, there is considerable evidence that the subsistence basis of the late Pleistocene and early Holocene was varied, though with widespread, recurrent elements in it. The absence of plant remains in most sites may result from sampling error, poor preservation, and/or non-use. However, where it is preserved, such as the 12,500-year-old site of Monte Verde in south-central Chile, various cave and rockshelter sites in eastern Brazil (e.g., Lapa do Boquete, Santana do Riacho), and open-air sites such as Pena Roja in the tropical lowlands of Colombia, it indicates that people gave equal or more emphasis to plant gathering and possibly manipulation than the exploitation of game animals. Most significant, terminal Pleistocene cultigens such as squash (*Lagenaria* sp.), gourds (*Cucurbita* sp.), and quinoa (*Chenopodium quinoa*) (Piperno & Pearsall 1998) also exist in the Central Andes, which suggests very early plant manipulation and dependency.

Just as the effects of expanding global systems have generated new interest in relationships between societies formerly conceived as occupying different rungs of a developmental social ladder, there should be more study of the applicability of different plant uses by specialized terrestrial hunters and maritime fishermen and gatherers (exploiting seaweed and other aquatic plants) and by generalized hunters and gatherers and of the relationships between these different, at times, coexisting economic groups from 12,000 to 9,000 years ago. The paradox in these differing economies is the creation and maintenance of diversity, likely involving new and continued reliance on wild plant and animal resources at a time when people were exploring and filling new niches and establishing more permanent exchange relations with neighbors and long-distance groups.

Unfortunately, little is known of the social organization associated with these different economic types in the late Pleistocene and early Holocene periods. Based on the current evidence, we can only presume that semi-mobile to mobile band societies in both North and South America cooperated and shared resources. At the outset of human exploration and movement, highly mobile foragers entering unpopulated lands had unlimited access to a wide variety of resources and must have relocated themselves regularly, especially in vast open areas like the high-latitude tundra of northern North America. The internal structure of domestic spaces at some sites, such as the open-air localities of Monte Verde in Chile, were well preserved, showing the remains of hut structures, hearths, and activity areas. The post-hole remains of possible shelters and other features at the Thunderbird site in the eastern woodlands of the United States reveal significant developments in the separation of public and private spaces and suggest seasonal, if not, yearly aggregation of people. Other sites like Aubrey and Gault in north Texas, Tres Arroyos in southern Patagonia, Paijan sites on the north coast of Peru, and many others throughout the Americas, also suggest that domestic spaces and especially hearths were important centers of social and economic activities. Once domestic areas were divided and designated for special purposes, some degree of communal, if not social, differentiation might have occurred.

Later in the early Pleistocene period, Paijan sites in northern Peru and other localities such as Acha 2 on the north coast of Chile exhibit multiple permanent household structures made of stone, which suggest long-term occupation, social aggregation, planning, and more intensified exploitation of local resources. Enough evidence now exists to indicate that broad-spectrum diets in the eastern woodlands of North America and in many different environments of South America were intensified from the late Pleistocene to the early Holocene period, which set the stage for increased regional experimentation and restructuring of subsistence economies between 11,000 and 8,000 years ago. Many human populations began to focus on seasonally abundant and storable resources, which led to increased sedentism, social interaction, and probably institutionalized management of human energy and time. Perhaps most important was the level and degree of social interaction between geographically proximal groups practicing different types of subsistence economies, and how this interaction was organized.

In regard to the social and ritual life of the earliest Americans, nothing is known of their mortuary practices and religious beliefs because only a small handful of human skeletal remains dating to the late Pleistocene period have been found in the New World. This may suggest different burial patterns from what is known for hunters and gatherers in other parts of the world. However, beginning around 9,500 years ago, several early skeletal remains have been recovered from both North and South America, including Kennewick Man, Spirit Cave woman, and others in the United States, several skeletons from cave and rockshelter sites in Colombia, eastern Brazil, and southern Chile and Argentina, among others. The craniometric evidence from these later remains suggests possible biological differences that may have their roots in earlier immigrants (<11,000 years ago) and later Paleoindians (11,000 to 10,000 years ago). That is, the early Holocene data reveal a wide range of craniofacial variation compared to later middle Holocene skeletons (c.7,000 to 5,000 years ago), with little to no shared physical traits between them. Such differences suggest that the early and late populations were derived from temporally and possibly geographically different migrations, although genetic drift and regional adaptation may account for some of this variation (Steele & Powell 2002; Neves et al. 2003). This evidence generally agrees with the cultural and economic diversity suggested in the archeological record of the Americas. Despite the paucity of early biological data, most of the current and later genetic and skeletal data suggest close biological linkages between early populations from Eurasia/East Asia and early Holocene Native American groups.

Continuities and Complexities

In many areas of the New World, early Holocene foragers continued many of the economic and technological patterns and fundamental restructuring of the society and the way different populations interacted, which characterized the late Pleistocene period, although there are important local variations, such as the appearance of cave art in Brazil in terminal Pleistocene times and the development of cultigens, elaborate mortuary practices, and social changes in several regions in early Holocene times. In Mexico, the Central Andes, and the eastern woodlands of the United States, some terminal Pleistocene groups discovered horticulture and new, more complex lifestyles such as semi-sedentism and population aggregation that set the stage for the subsequent construction of public places (e.g., ritual plazas and mounds) and social differentiation between 7,000 and 6,000 years ago in parts of the Americas (e.g., Watson Brake site in Louisiana, Nanchoc sites in Peru). Although the late Pleistocene and early Holocene environments of the landscape determined the resource structure and influenced the human response to the exploitation of resources, people produced the social conditions and structures in which they lived and, in turn, were shaped by the institutions and beliefs that either they controlled directly or that were beyond their control. As discussed above, many of the first Americans were generalized foragers, specialized hunters, maritime gatherers and hunters, or invariably different combinations of these economic strategies in a wide variety of environmental contexts. These diverse economies must have entailed different degrees of technological innovation, planning, risk management, resource sharing, mobility and territoriality, and social interaction. Not well understood by archeologists are the patterns of interaction operating among these different societies, especially in spatially proximal places like the Andean mountains and Pacific coast and ecotones like the Great Plains and the eastern woodlands of the United States, and how this interaction created new and different institutions and sociocultural complexities. However, it is becoming more apparent that different pathways were taken by different groups in the North American southwest and eastern woodlands and in the arid and tropical lands of Mexico and South America to incipient complexity and to different scales of interaction between these and other different types of societies. It also is important to recognize that these regional developments did not fully emerge in some areas like Mexico and the Central Andes until plant and animal domestication occurred in terminal Pleistocene and early Holocene times.

Most archeologists treat each early specialized hunting, gathering, and fishing economy differently. Yet, each bears a relationship to others as components of a hemisphere-long framework of the first Americans. None of these component economies is more or less important; they must have interacted with each other, as suggested by the shared stone tool technologies of the Clovis, Fishtail, Paijan and other point styles, and together comprised the conceptual framework through which participant regional groups interpreted and generated increased stylistic designs and ever increasingly different lifestyles. This interpretative and participatory framework must have shifted with respect to the relations between different people as they adapted to different social and physical environments. Perhaps most adaptable was a generalized economic organization, which would have allowed for flexibility in responding to various instances of what may be essentially the same basic participation at different locations and times in places. Specialized economies, on the other hand, allowed localization and more intimate linkages with specific types of environments, such as big game hunting in open terrain, fishing, and shellfish collecting along coastlines. Other societies seasonally combined different hunting, collecting, and possibly incipient horticultural strategies by practicing long-distance transhumance between different environments and/or by establishing exchange relations with other groups to access a wider variety of resources.

It is generally assumed that the advantages of early mixed hunting, gathering, and incipient horticultural economies were self-evident in terms of the security of food supply, ease of storage, and stability of settlement, and that these advantages were offset only perhaps by the greater labor input required, especially by fixed-plot cultivation. This kind of activity would explain the emergent complexity of riverine societies in the eastern United States and of coastal societies in Ecuador and Peru. But the advantages of different forms of subsistence could only have been self-evident in a social context where more food, more permanent settlement, and more cooperation and sharing were desired (cf. Woodburn 1982; Kelly 1995). Interaction and cooperation between different groups could have been more advantageous than individualism in order to improve food gathering or to defend against others. It is perhaps more that small cohesive groups, such as those documented in several early Holocene sites on the north coast of Peru (Dillehay et al. 2003), were the best setting for the emergence of cooperation; in these groups, the practices and identities of the other members are known, there are multiple opportunities for reliable interaction, and there likely was egalitarianism.

Likewise it is often assumed that settlement expansion and population growth are natural consequences of the adoption of agriculture, virtually without reference to the nature of the communities that adopted it in its various forms. Unfortunately, the scarcity of internal site structure and domestic architecture in early sites prohibits archeologists from inferring the social structure and internal activities of early communities. Emergent complexity also likely developed due to internal parameters such as population growth and intensification of land use in resource-rich areas and to social aggregation and greater care of the dead. As mentioned earlier, it is not until the 9,500 period that human skeletal material begins to appear more consistently in the archeological record of the Americas. It also must have taken shape and changed as a direct outcome of the social interactions of different populations in constant flux, especially where the crafting of incipient complexity involved material resources, but also invisible resources, such as the manipulation and invention of forms of meaning and abstract units of social organization.

In summary, the late Pleistocene period laid some of the social and economic foundations for the significant cultural changes that were to follow in the early and middle Holocene period (10,000–6,000 years ago). Early cultural developments show cultural diversity at the outset of human entry into many regions of the New World, especially South America, and the later establishment of ever increasingly distinct regional economic combinations. Although the evidence is still too scanty to discern the specifics of these developments, two general transitions can be discerned. The first was a change in adaptive strategies and organizational abilities during and at the end of the Pleistocene period. This transition signifies the rapidly increasing ability of people to recognize the environmental potentials that existed in some areas, to communicate these potentials to others and to take advantage of them, and to develop the social organization required to exploit resources in a wider variety of environments. Second, early people probably learned many hunting techniques, and on occasion employed them to bring down quite large animals. But with the exception of big game in largely open habits like the Great Plains and other grasslands, there is no hard evidence to show that hunting was the mainstay of the earliest known coastal and woodland economies. The social and psychological requirements of hunting probably played an important part in molding group organizational skills. But the same can be said of collecting plants and maritime resources. But I see these issues as secondary to the real prime mover of greater social complexity, and that is the practice of sharing food and ideas within organized, aggregated social groups practicing different complementary lifestyles.

Epilogue

The emergence of humans in the Americas is probably far more complex than the current models depict. At the moment, the evidence points towards the presence of humans in the New World sometime between 18,000 and 13,000 years ago and their arrival from east Asia, with possibilities of immigrants from other places at other times. At the moment, none of the archeological, genetic, skeletal, and linguistic data are reconciled to produce a coherent model to explain human dispersion and cultural variation. The reconstruction of early American society necessarily depends upon the imaginative reconstruction of archeologists and other scholars, and the fact that the evidence is so sparse does not mean that we refrain from making some informed speculations, often grounded in the observed behavior of ethnographic foraging societies.

Part of my concern here also is that traditional approaches to the study of the peopling of the Americas have relied too heavily on subjective aesthetic definitions of projectile point styles from a wide variety of archeological sites in North and South America. Not yet fully integrated into these approaches are systematically contextualized archeological traits such as internal site patterning of non-projectile point stone tools, other artifacts and features, and inter-site quantitative and qualitative comparisons between these and other variables. Until we carry out inter-site and intercontinental studies of organizational strategies and mobility patterns, we will not more fully understand the peopling of the Americas.

Several new directions need to be taken in the future of first American studies. First, we need to use the ecological conditions of resource exploitation and the resource structures of population distributions to explore the shifting organization and relationships through time of different scales of specialists, generalists, mixed strategies, and interactionalists. The result is a picture of widespread and systematic relationships between what is usually viewed as "separate" desert, woodland, coastal, highland, and tropical peoples with separate maritime, hunting, and gathering economies. In this regard models like Clovis big game hunting encourage us to look for development and control by a single economic mode when in fact elusive and less conspicuous forms of exchange, economic synchronization, and social interaction also must have existed to link various peoples settling into and flowing through different landscapes. The shifting connections among these peoples surely have been a long-term feature in the regional dialogue through which territorial identities were eventually fashioned and transformed into the corporate styles of later ethnicities, polities, and state societies. Certain research questions can guide us in the ways these different early societies operated in terms of their practical deployment of different material conditions; the way that practice reworked the structured social and economic principles of organization; the way practice and social agency mutually worked to meet historical contingencies; and the way they accessed different sets of material conditions and the mechanism of interaction operating between them. Another research direction should involve domestic archaeology – the living sites of past people – which has been a topic of increased research among archeologists in later periods, but has received minimal attention as a social unit among early people specialists. This is unfortunate, because it would help to counter the kill-site bias that plagues late Pleistocene archeology. Future work also needs to define better regional chronologies and to excavate larger areas in sites to identify and study activity areas and the internal spatial structure that make up local and regional systems.

BIBLIOGRAPHY

Adovasio, J. & Page, J. (2002) *The First Americans*. Random House, New York.

Anthony, D. W. (1990) "Migration in Archaeology: The Baby and the Bathwater," *American Anthropologist*, 92, pp. 895–914.

Bryan, A. L. (1973) "Paleoenvironments and Cultural Diversity in Late Pleistocene South America," *Quaternary Research*, 3, pp. 237–56.

Clapperton, C. M. (1993) *Quaternary Geology and Geomorphology of South America*. Elsevier, Amsterdam.

Dillehay, T. D. (1997) "Monte Verde: A Late Pleistocene Site in Chile." In *The Archaeological Context*, Vol. II. Smithsonian Press, Washington, DC.

Dillehay, T. D. (1999) "The Late Pleistocene Cultures of South America," *Evolutionary Anthropology*, 24, pp. 13–32.

Dillehay, T. D. (2000) *The Settlement of the Americas: A New Prehistory*. Basic Books, New York.

Dillehay, T. D., Rossen, J., Maggard, G. K., Stackelback, K., & Netherly, P. (2003) "Localization and Possible Social Aggregation in the Late Pleistocene and Early Holocene on the North Coast of Peru," *Quaternary International*, 109–10, pp. 3–11.

Dixon, J. (1999) *Bones, Boats and Bison*. University of New Mexico Press, Albuquerque.

Fladmark, K. (1979) "Routes: Alternate Migration Corridors for Early Man in America," *American Antiquity*, 44, pp. 55–69.

Haynes, C. V. (1969) "The Earliest Americans," *Science*, 166, pp. 709–15.

Kelly, R. (1995) *The Foraging Spectrum: Diversity in Hunter-Gather Lifeways*. Smithsonian Institution Press, Washington, DC.

Martin, P. S. (1984) "Prehistoric Extinctions: The Global Model." In P. S. Martin & R.G. Klein (eds.), *Quaternary Extinctions: A Prehistoric Revolution*. University of Arizona Press, Tucson, pp. 354–403.

Meltzer, D. (1993) *Search for the First Americans*. Smithsonian Books Press, Washington, DC.

Meltzer, D. (2003a) "Lessons in Landscape Learning." In M. Rockman & J. Steele (eds.), *Colonization of Unfamiliar Landscapes: The Archaeology of Adaptation*. Routledge, London, pp. 224–41.

Meltzer, D. (2003b) "Peopling of North America," *Developments in Quaternary Science*, 1, pp. 539–63.

Neves, W., Prous, A., Gonzalez-Jose, R., Kipnis, R., & Powell, J. (2003) "Human Skeletal Remains from Santana do Riacho, Brazil: Implications for the Settlement of the New World," *Journal of Human Evolution*, 45, pp. 759–82.

Nichols, J. (2002) "The First American Languages." In N. Jablonski (ed.), "The First Americans, the Pleistocene Colonization of the New World," *Memoirs of the California Academy of Science*, 27, pp. 273–93.

Piperno, D. & Pearsall, D. (1998) *The Origins of Agriculture in the Lowland Neotropics*. Academic Press, New York.

Salemme, M. & Miotti, L. (eds.) (2003) "South America: Long and Winding Roads for the First Americans at the Pleistocene/Holocene Transition," *Quaternary International*, 109–10, pp. 1–179.

Schurr, T. (2004) "Molecular Genetic Diversity in Siberians and Native Americans Suggests an Early Colonization of the New World." In D. Madsen (ed.), *Entering America: Northeast Asia and Beringia before the Last Glacial Maximum*. University of Utah Press, Salt Lake City.

Stanford, D. & Bradley, B. (2002) "Ocean Trails and Prairie Paths: Thoughts on the Origins of Clovis." In N. Jablonski (ed.), "The First Americans, the Pleistocene Colonization of the New World," *Memoirs of the California Academy of Sciences*, 27, pp. 255–74.

Steele, G. & Powell, J. (2002) "Facing the Past: a View of the North American Human Fossil Record." In N. Jablonski (ed.), "The First Americans, the Pleistocene Colonization of the New World," *Memoirs of the California Academy of Sciences*, 27, pp. 93–122.

Woodburn, J. (1982) "Egalitarian Societies," *Man*, 17, pp. 431–51.

Chapter Two

MESOAMERICA

John Monaghan and Andrew R. Wyatt

Introduction

The term "Mesoamerica" refers to the civilization that originated some 4,000 years ago in the present-day countries of Mexico, Guatemala, Belize, Honduras, and El Salvador. Mesoamerican people independently invented agriculture and writing, made sophisticated temporal and celestial measurements, built great cities, and created beautiful artistic traditions. After the European conquest of the sixteenth century, Mesoamerican people maintained their communities under the colonial governments that institutionalized the subordination of conquered peoples and attempted to replace native religions with Christianity. Although colonialism ended in the nineteenth century, Mesoamerican people continued to be subject to changes imposed by outsiders, from the privatization of their lands, to the introduction of short-lived economic development schemes, to the elimination of indigenous languages – all, usually, in the name of progress. Despite all this there are today millions of Mesoamerican people living in North America. Many maintain distinctive traditions and continue to speak indigenous languages, and in recent decades have begun to form broad-based ethnic coalitions to demand not only full rights as citizens in their home countries, but that their special status be constitutionally recognized by national governments.

The term Mesoamerica was originally proposed by anthropologist Paul Kirchoff (1943); he defined it by a series of what scholars of the day called culture area traits. For Kirchoff these included writing, the use of calendars, stepped pyramids, the ball game, particular religious practices and beliefs (some of which involved human sacrifice), complex social stratification, and distinctive technologies and economic practices. Although anthropologists today no longer define Mesoamerica as a simple collection of traits, instead focusing on the socioeconomic processes, evolutionary patterns, and historical developments that led to the intense interaction and exchange among specific societies in the region, we know now that many more items could be added to Kirchoff's list which either originated in Mesoamerica and/or make it distinct from adjacent regions. As is true of any conceptual definition of a civilization, there are obvious weaknesses, since boundaries are never permanent, no pedigree is ever pure, and there is the danger that we overly reify and fetishize a scholarly construct. Nonetheless people throughout the region today speak languages that are historically descended from languages spoken in the area thousands of years ago, despite the presence of Spanish loan words; men and women dance before the gods as a form of prayer, even though the gods may be Saint James and Saint Cecilia; and people consider corn and beans as essential elements of good nutrition just as in ancient times, even if the particular species of bean they consume was domesticated in China, not Mesoamerica. Perhaps most significantly, Mesoamerican people continue to draw boundaries between themselves and non-Mesoamerican people on the basis of language, society, and culture.

As an organizing basis for scholarship the concept Mesoamerica values and institutionalizes certain kinds of specific knowledge that are highly relevant, such as the learning of languages, the immersion in history, and the appreciation of expressive culture. While it is true that the roots of areal classifications lie in national projects, it is also true that the concept of Mesoamerica points to a shared heritage that transcends national boundaries. Kirchoff, like many early Mesoamericanists, was an anthropologist, but Mesoamericanist scholars come from many disciplines, including Art History, History, Human Biology, Literature, Linguistics, Philology, and Religious Studies, and the areal focus allows for a fruitful, though often contentious, exchange of disciplinary views.

Archeology of Mesoamerica

Archeologists divide the Mesoamerican past into a number of distinct periods: Paleoindian, Archaic, Formative, Classic, and Postclassic. Each of these combines broad evolutionary changes with chronology, and each has been subdivided for more precision. Although periodization of this sort no longer plays the analytical role it once did in archeology, these temporal/evolutionary classifications continue to be widely used as heuristic tools.

The Paleoindian period begins as the first foragers move into what is now Mexico and Central America. The earliest known archeological sites in Mexico date from about 14,000 years ago, but, given the accumulating evidence for earlier human habitation in other areas of the Americas, it is probable that there were hunting groups in the region much earlier. A great deal of archeological work has been carried out in this region, but the vast majority of archeologists focus on later periods when the complex societies emerged and flourished; therefore knowledge of the Paleoindian period is relatively undeveloped, especially when compared to the work done in the United States. As is true throughout North America, the Paleoindian period comes to an end with climate changes at the end of the Pleistocene and the extinction of the large mammals that forced them to adapt to the environment in new ways. The idea that Paleoindians relied primarily on large mammals such as the mammoth is falling out of favor. It is likely that early Americans had a varied diet that relied primarily on small animals and gathered plant material.

In the Archaic Period, from roughly 10,000 to 4,000 years ago, Mesoamerican people created new storage and food-processing technologies, including the *mano* (pestle) and *metate* (grinding stone), and began to cultivate a suite of plants that became the basic elements of the Mesoamerican diet: corn, beans, squash, tomatoes, chilies, avocado, mamey, guava, vanilla, tuna cactus, and cacao; as well as cotton and indigo. As is true of foragers in general, these early peoples' movements tracked environmental fluctuations. In the Tehuacán Valley of Puebla, for example, foragers congregated in the dry season along rivers and permanent water holes and moved up the valley sides during the rainy season, as berries and other foods became available (MacNeish 1975). As this suggests, Archaic people diversified their subsistence base by exploiting a larger variety of seasonally available resources than was true in the Paleoindian period. Eventually, people in the Archaic period throughout Mesoamerica adopted a more settled, although in many cases not completely sedentary, lifestyle as they slowly changed to almost full-time agriculturalists (Flannery 1986). Many of the earliest sedentary people were located in lacustrine and estuarine environments such as the Pacific Coast in Chiapas and around Lake Texcoco. The diversity of resources in these areas allowed for very early permanent settlements.

Because agriculture has such far-reaching consequences for human life, and because Mesoamerica is one of the very early centers of its development, a great deal of attention has been paid to the origins and processes by which Mesoamerican people first domesticated wild plants. It appears that the first food plants cultivated were squashes, which people grew for their seeds and probably for their use as storage containers. According to the evidence available, early peoples began to broadcast the seeds of wild varieties of squash, so that when they returned to the area later they would be more abundant. This intervention in the reproduction process was the beginning of a steady process of selection that caused these wild plants eventually to undergo dramatic genetic change. What was true for squash was also true for the other early cultigens. At the beginning of the Archaic period, many of these plants looked nothing at all like their modern manifestations. Maize, for example, was a kind of grass growing in the highlands of Mexico when people began to cultivate it 5,000–6,000 years ago.

The Formative period, from about 4,000 years ago to AD 250, was marked by massive technological changes as Mesoamerican people adopted increasingly intensive forms of agriculture, the first permanent villages and towns on the Pacific and Gulf coasts appeared, and the socially stratified societies, often called chiefdoms, emerged. The evidence suggests that early chiefdoms were led by a family group ranked above other members of society, and that religion played a major role in this ranking. It was also during this period that a distinctive pan-Mesoamerican iconography and civic-ceremonial complex appeared, made up of a plaza surrounded by temples, palaces, ball courts, and other specialized buildings. A key center of these developments was the Gulf Coast of the present-day Mexican states of Tabasco and Veracruz, where the Olmecs built the major sites of La Venta and San Lorenzo. Originally founded as farming villages, archeologists have been able to trace their transformation, from 1,500 BCE to 100 BCE, into major polities whose influence spread over a large area. The centers contained massive public buildings; in San Lorenzo it involved reshaping a natural hill with large quantities of fill to level it into a plateau. The spring at El Manati near San Lorenzo preserved carved wooden offerings with the baby-faced motif in the surrounding mud, as well as dozens of rubber balls, suggesting the Olmecs were playing some variant of the ball game, which Kirchoff signaled as one of the traits of Mesoamerican civilization. While the Olmec have long been seen as the Mesoamerican Ur culture (Coe & Koontz 2002), the idea of such a foundational culture has been questioned by those working with Formative materials from other areas. Sharer & Grove (1989) argue that Mesoamerican culture emerged out of the interactions of many Formative groups, and things like the baby-faced motif were designs shared throughout the region, with perhaps variant local meanings, so it is not possible to say they originated with the Olmecs.

The Classic period, from AD 250 to 900, is marked by the presence of state-level societies throughout the region. Unlike chiefdoms, in state-level societies there are complex bureaucracies, large urban centers, and a complex stratification, and polities rule over larger territories (Blanton et al. 1993). Significant examples of such developments include the Central Mexican center of Teotihuacán, the hilltop site of Monte Albán in the Valley of Oaxaca, the Maya sites of Tikal in Guatemala, and Copán in Honduras. Although most of these sites originate in the Formative, they reached the peak of their expansion in the middle Classic. All of these cities are architectural jewels and, today, well-known tourist sites. Teotihuacán, for example, extended over 20 square miles, and its very carefully planned urban core was made up of large public buildings and grid blocks organized around a wide causeway about a mile and a half long. To one side of the causeway is the Pyramid of the Sun, one of the largest pyramids in the world. Scattered throughout the city were large multi-family compounds that included workshops as well as living areas. It is even said that at its height Teotihuacán was the largest city in the world, with a population of over 100,000 in AD 600.

Early scholars believed the Classic period to be the highest expression of Mesoamerican civilization, with the subsequent Postclassic, AD 900–1521, a period of decline. Classic period polities, so the story went, were ruled by philosopher kings, who were more interested in the movement of the stars and the passage of time than in expanding their realms. However, it turns out that Classic period polities, far from being peaceful states, carried out extensive wars of conquest and took pride in the tribute they forced others to give and the captives they took from defeated enemies. This appears to be the main theme, for example, of the celebrated eighth-century murals of Bonampak, which depict the celebration at the Maya court of the site when it received payments from tributaries and prepared captives for sacrifice. Nonetheless, between AD 700 and 900 there was a major disruption in the area since many of the important centers of the Classic period were abandoned within a relatively short time, and what were major states appear to have dissolved. Thus, sometime around 650 the center of Teotihuacán was burned, and Monte Albán was largely empty of people by AD 800. The most dramatic case is what has become known as the "Maya collapse" in the lowland tropical forest region covering parts of southern Mexico, Guatemala, and Honduras.

The Maya collapse has been a topic of research for several generations of archeologists. One school of thought believes that the demands of feeding a large and growing population led to massive deforestation and erosion. The subsequent agricultural failure from this environmental degradation contributed to the exodus of the population from the lowlands. Another school suggests that increasing warfare among Maya polities led to populations fleeing the city centers to escape the escalating violence. A third hypothesis proposes that social unrest and an uprising against the demands of the ruling elite led to the collapse of Maya cities. However, most researchers believe it to be the complex interaction of environmental, demographic, social, and political factors that made it no longer possible to sustain the complex political and social structures that characterized the Classic period in this region (for a review, see Webster 2002). Current research is also questioning the extent of the Maya collapse, as some cities were not completely depopulated, and continued to exist as functioning centers up to the arrival of the Spanish. However, it is clear that something happened in the Maya world between AD 900 and 1000 that not only resulted in the abandonment of most of the large Maya cities, but also made it impossible for Maya polities to reestablish themselves in much of the lowland area.

The complete depopulation of a region at the end of the Classic was the exception, so that while cities such as Monte Albán in Oaxaca and Teotihuacán in Central Mexico were abandoned, many others sprang up nearby, and there is evidence that some of these were founded by former inhabitants of the great Classic cities. Populations then increased throughout most of the Postclassic period, and the landscape was covered by numerous city-states or "community-kingdoms" with distinct identities, customs, and traditions. At the heart each kingdom was a ruling dynasty, which often kept deep genealogies as a way of justifying their claims to rule. Rulership was passed down in family lines although we now know the long, unbroken family trees which rulers had depicted in books were the exception, rather than the rule, since conquest, dynastic intrigue, and the vagaries of life often meant that children did not succeed parents (Gillespie 1989). City-states might have been allied to one another; they might have been bound in larger kingdoms through tribute relationships; or they might have been in open conflict with one another, leading some observers to refer to this as the "balkanization" of Mesoamerica (Flannery & Marcus 1983). Even the largest polities, such as the Mexica or Aztec empire, were made up of a number of kingdoms bound to one another by alliances and tribute relations. The Mexica were originally vassals of the Tepanec king of Azcapotzalco, who used them as mercenaries. In 1428 they banded with other groups (the Acolhua of Texcoco and the Tepanec of Tlacopan) to form the Triple Alliance and defeat the Tepanec of Azcapotzalco. The Triple Alliance eventually held sway over some 50 city-states in the Valley of Mexico and about 250 outside the valley, administered as 38 tribute-paying provinces. About 100 of these city-states were clients – that is, they paid tribute and supported military operations of the empire but were independent. There were other states in the Valley of Mexico that remained independent and competed with the Aztecs, notably Tlaxcala, itself the center of a confederacy of city-states, bitter enemies of the Triple Alliance.

Over the last 40 years scholars have vastly improved our understanding of ancient Mesoamerica. Perhaps one of the more significant findings has been that the region was much more integrated than previously thought. Although high transportation costs (there were no pack animals or wheeled vehicles in ancient Mesoamerica) limited the circulation of bulky goods, vast networks of trade and exchange in luxury goods, low-weight commodities, and special foodstuffs such as cacao and salt linked groups not only in the core Mesoamerican region, but well beyond, reaching into the Pueblo societies of the US southwest and the chiefdoms and tribal societies of lower Central America. Early Spanish observers marveled at the size of Mesoamerican markets and the variety of items that could be obtained in them. Long-distance trade was tied up with politics: colonies were established far from polity centers to guarantee the supply of precious items, and empires reorganized markets for imperial aims. Although the most detailed information on trade and exchange comes from later periods, it is clear that the basic elements of trade in prestige goods were in place by the Formative period throughout Mesoamerica (Braswell 2004; Sharer & Traxler 2005).

The movement of things was accompanied by the movement of peoples. Biological archeologists have demonstrated on the basis of diet and skeletal morphology that people born in many different regions were found in the large cities and imperial capitals, suggesting that it was not just the merchants who were traveling long distances. Iconographic analysis carried out by art historians and epigraphers has demonstrated the existence of complicated systems of alliance and intermarriage connecting the elite of different centers to one another, a pattern that continued in select areas long after the conquest. Moreover, in the Postclassic period we know that a marriage tie between polities might involve not only the movement of members of the elite, but also the relocation of large groups of farming families attached to the marriage partners (Byland & Pohl 1994).

Another area where great strides have been made in the understanding of the Mesoamerican past is through research on ancient scripts. Mesoamerican people independently developed a number of complex literary traditions. At the time of the conquest there were four distinct writing systems in use: Maya, Zapotec, Mixtec, and Central Mexican. An early Zapotec monument from San José Mogote, in Oaxaca, indicates that the calendar and related glyphs were in use by 600 BCE. Monuments found in the Isthmus of Tehuantepec provide evidence for a fully developed writing system at 100 BCE, although its relationship to later writing systems is not clear, and there is recent evidence of an Olmec script. Although almost all of our knowledge of early Mesoamerican writing comes from inscribed monuments (and in the Maya area in particular polychrome pottery), we know from the Postclassic period that Mesoamerican people also composed books. Mesoamerican books, or codices, are beautifully illuminated screenfold manuscripts often inscribed on paper or on a stiffened animal hide covered with gesso. These books contain the histories of particular royal lines, genealogies, genesis-like religious accounts, and ritual manuals. Although many of these books were destroyed or lost, a number survived, and Mesoamerican scribes continued to produce documents in the native tradition well into the colonial period (Boone 2000). The decipherment of Mesoamerican scripts has advanced considerably, and scholars of the Maya script are now able to understand much of what the ancient scribes set down (Macri & Ford 1997; Houston et al. 2001).

It appears that Mesoamerican writing developed within a tradition of recitational literacy – in other words, the texts were meant to be read aloud. Specialists have advanced the idea that the screenfold format of Mesoamerican books facilitated the oral reading of the text, and that these readings were part of a larger performance, which included poetic language, drama, and dancing. Indeed, Mesoamerican texts are highly artistic, and the Maya word for scribe in many languages comes from a root that means both painting and writing. What we know of scribes indicates that they were from the upper strata of society. Classic Maya scribes even signed their names to their creations.

Much of the research on Mesoamerican writing has tended to focus on technical questions of decipherment. Because many of the monumental texts are fairly laconic – mentioning little more than a place, a ruler, a date, and some delimited action by the ruler – research has concentrated on the identification of places mentioned in the texts, the construction of Precolumbian dynastic sequences, and a charting of the waxing and waning fortunes of particular sites (a good example is Houston 1993). However, it has become increasingly clear that these texts provide a unique historical resource for the Americas, since they present views of pre-Columbian society unmediated by Spanish colonialism. Some Postclassic codices, for example, recount events that go back as far as AD 900, providing an indigenous view of the Classic/Postclassic transition and other changes that we know of through the archeological record. In some areas enough manuscripts survived that one can be used to fill gaps in the story told by another, and to develop a sense of a regional perspective on events. A good example of this concerns the Mixtec ruler 8 Deer Tiger Claw, who lived from the mid-eleventh century to the mid-twelfth century and who extended his rule through a series of deft alliances and expansionist wars until he was finally murdered in an ambush by his rival, Lord 4 Wind, and his empire divided. The life of 8 Deer Tiger Claw is discussed in three different codices, produced in different political centers. Each of these sources varies somewhat in the story, and one, the Zouche-Nuttal, contains information about Lord 8 Deer's early life that is not found anywhere else. They also individually emphasize certain of his actions or downplay others, which has been seen by scholars as evidence that the story is being recorded from the perspective of particular political points of view (Byland and Pohl 1994). Archeologists have even uncovered graffiti scribbled on the sides of ancient buildings, although its significance is difficult to determine. Others have begun to use Mesoamerican texts as a window onto ancient beliefs, values, symbolism, and world view (see Houston et al. 2006).

Mesoamerica after the Conquest

Mesoamerican history is conventionally divided into a Preconquest or pre-Columbian period and a Postconquest or Colonial period, to highlight the significance of the Spanish conquest in changing the fortunes of Mesoamerican people. Hernán Cortés and his soldiers arrived in Mexico in 1519, and although the last independent Maya kingdoms were not conquered until the end of the seventeenth century, most of Mesoamerica came into some kind of contact, if not outright Spanish control, by the 1540s. Traditionally, the conquest was viewed as a time of utter devastation that marked the end of Mesoamerican civilization. The Spanish imposed a number of foreign institutions on the people of the region; they converted many of them to Christianity; and they instituted polices such as the *congregación*, or the consolidation of indigenous settlements into more easily monitored locations, that reordered native society. It was felt that the conquest, if not exactly putting an end to Mesoamerican civilization, certainly sent it on the road to decline and disappearance. Indeed Mesoamerica is often spoken of as something that is past, and lay people are sometimes surprised to learn that Maya or "Aztec" people exist today.

In recent years subtle historical analysis, employing documents produced by Mesoamerican people as well as Spanish writers, presents a much more complicated picture of what went on in the sixteenth century; it makes Mesoamerican people appear to be somewhat less of the victims that the traditional view supposed and allows us to see that Mesoamerican civilization did not come to an end in 1519. After all, in

Central Mexico, once Tenochtitlán, the capital of the Triple Alliance Mexica, fell, the conquest was essentially over, so that most of the city-states in the region remained untouched. Even areas that were conquered, such as Chiapas and Veracruz, were then largely abandoned by the Spanish who, once they finished looting the major settlements, moved off to new areas and did not return for years. Rather than replacing native institutions, practices, and beliefs with Spanish ones, what has become clear is that the sixteenth-century Spanish needed to make many accommodations to Mesoamerican traditions for the colony to function, and in key areas it was the Spanish who had to adapt to Mesoamerican norms, not the other way around. Cortés himself depended on Mesoamerican allies to carry out his conquest (Hassig 2005, Seed, this volume). When he set off for Honduras in 1524 he had with him some 300 Europeans, but also 3,000 Mexican allies. The Tlaxcalans, who enjoyed a special status in Spanish law due to their early alliance with Cortés and their continued loyalty to the Spanish regime, were key figures in the colony, and Tlaxcalan populations were resettled to troublesome frontiers to provide stability.

Without denying the fact that Mesoamerican people were increasingly incorporated into the colonial and later Atlantic economy, Spanish law invested property rights in indigenous communities and placed many administrative functions in the hands of community members, which tended to reinforce communal identities. Institutions emerged that mediated local interaction with the market, Spanish taxing agencies, and even the court system, so that areas of indigenous life, if not beyond colonial control, were certainly insulated, and spaces remained where Mesoamerican people could act without direct censorship. Many of the Spanish policies were revised during the late eighteenth-century period of the Bourbon Reforms, which sought to obtain a greater share of indigenous wealth in the colony, and indirect rule was to be replaced by close bureaucratic regulation. Although in the Yucatan this amounted to what has been called a "second conquest" (Farriss 1984), in other areas these reforms remained largely on paper, and were never effectively applied.

It has also become clear that the issue of translation during the colonial period is even more complicated than previously thought. The concept of syncretism, while descriptive of the diverse roots of particular cultural forms, is too general to be of much analytical use in understanding the subtleties of Mesoamerican/Spanish interaction and exchange. For example, unlike the Judeo-Christian tradition, where god is a unique and transcendent divinity, in Mesoamerica the universe was not viewed as distinct from divinity. Thus if the Christian god created the universe apart form himself, in Mesoamerica the universe emerges from the deity. The Tzeltal today say that "when the world appeared, so did god," indicating that one did not exist before the other, and many groups view the earth as a divine thing, with the landscape spoken of in terms of corporeal images. Similarly, many Mesoamerican groups hold that the kind of afterlife one experiences is dependent on the manner in which one dies, not one's moral conduct during life. Reconciling such subtle ideas with those of Christianity is not an easy thing to do. Conversion was thus rarely the straightforward theological change from one type of religious belief to another that the Spanish imagined. What tended to occur was a kind of opportunistic selectivity, creativity, and just plain misunderstanding of Spanish beliefs on the part of Mesoamerican people. Indeed there are Mesoamerican people today who express basic theological beliefs that are very close to what their ancestors held, despite hundreds of years of living with Christian doctrine. Today Jesus is equated with the Sun in many areas, one of the principal forces of the Mesoamerican universe (thus Mixtec say Bethlehem is where the sun rises, and Jerusalem is where the sun sets, corresponding to the idea that the sun is born anew each morning and dies and goes into the underworld each evening).

Even though Mesoamerican people in many places practice a kind of popular religion that is obviously rooted in both Christianity and Mesoamerican beliefs, we have also come to understand that the story is not simply one of two discrete traditions meeting and blending or clashing with one anther. Rather, Christianity, and how it was presented to Mesoamerican people, changed over time, so that what was orthodox in one period might not be orthodox in another. This led to the ironic situation that practices originally allowed or even taught by the Church in one period led to conflict with the Church later on. Astrology for example, was considered a legitimate form of knowledge in the sixteenth century, and learned Spanish friars made systematic inquiries into the Mesoamerican calendar and consulted with Mesoamerican divinatory specialists. By the end of the seventeenth century, however, the Inquisition was sanctioning Mesoamerican calendar specialists for practices based on illegitimate knowledge. Similarly, the cult of the saints, so important in colonial Spanish religion, is seen by some priests today as a kind of idolatry. In the 1970s the priests in the Maya town of Aguacatán, Guatemala even eliminated most of the saints from the church and forbade people from worshiping them. To further complicate matters, religion practiced by Mesoamerican people during the colony and afterwards was influenced not only by Spanish priests, but also by popular European beliefs, by Africans brought to the New World as slaves, and by other Mesoamerican people who spread local innovations to other areas. Some observers feel that even today orthodox Protestantism, which has spread to an increasingly large number of Mesoamerican people (it is estimated that about one-fourth of people in Guatemala are now practicing Protestants, and in Mexico about 10 percent of the speakers of indigenous languages now identify as Protestants), is now in the same position vis-à-vis how religion is practiced among Mesoamerican people as is Orthodox Catholicism (Monaghan 2000).

While the Spanish colonial efforts at transforming Mesoamerican civilization are less straightforward than once believed, we have learned that the biological effects of the conquest were profound. The effects of European infectious diseases on New World populations have been recognized for some time. An infected soldier in Cortés's party exposed Mesoamerican populations to smallpox in 1519, with devastating results. It is said that Cortés owes much of his success to the fact that disease often preceded the conquistadors, so that by the time they arrived in a place the population was ill or dying. Over the next 80 years Mesoamerican people suffered through repeated epidemics of typhus, diphtheria, whooping cough, chicken pox, measles, and influenza as well as smallpox. These are all highly infectious diseases that devastated the New World populations that had not been exposed to them, but had a lesser effect on Old World populations that had built up resistance. In fact, the lack of exposure to endemic diseases was often fatal to European-descended people raised in the New World who traveled back to Spain. It is estimated that there were 18 million to 30 million people living in Mexico when Cortés arrived in 1519, and by 1600 there were fewer than two million. Thriving towns disappeared, the Spanish began to import African slaves to replace the native populations, and certain areas were completely abandoned. Some estimate that Latin America as a whole did not regain its preconquest population until well into the twentieth century. It is no co-incidence that a number of Mesoamerican intellectual and artistic practices, such as Mesoamerican writing, disappear at this time.

The biological conquest of Mesoamerica did not end with infectious diseases. The conquest also altered the environment in dramatic ways. The Spanish introduced a number of aggressive plants that took over large areas: some were weeds; others were grasses. The Spanish were also pastoralists as well as farmers, and brought with them cattle, pigs, sheep, goats, chickens, horses, donkeys, and other animals that thrived in the New World and which in turn altered the environment in dramatic ways. It is estimated that cattle herds in Mexico doubled every 15 years during the sixteenth and seventeenth centuries, so that beef became a very inexpensive commodity. Rats, unwelcome stowaways on European ships, also spread throughout the New World. It is important to see the different species – grasses and weeds, cattle, pigs, and chickens, European people, infectious disease – as being of a set, since animals species which lived off the introduced plants were often carriers and vectors of infectious disease, while at the same time being part of a whole European way of life (Crosby 2003).

Although the Mesoamerican population was reduced by as much as 90 percent in the sixteenth century, a demographic recovery began in the seventeenth century and has continued to this day. In 2000, Mesoamerican people made up roughly 10 percent of the Mexican population as a whole, and 40 percent of the Guatemalan population. However, these numbers, which are based on either self-identification, ability to speak an indigenous language, or some sort of easily recognized symbol, fail to take into account what Guillermo Bonfil Batalla (1996) called "México pro-fundo," the idea that Mesoamerican values, beliefs, and practices permeate the lives of people who do not overtly identify as indigenous. The modernist project in Mexico, Bonfil Batalla argues, is to deny this heritage, even though it is part of the daily life of millions of Mexicans, not just those who speak an indigenous language. It will be interesting to see whether, as being indigenous becomes a less stigmatized identity, as appears to be happening in some urban areas of Mexico, the numbers of people self-identifying as a member of an indigenous Mesoamerican group will increase at a rate that approaches or exceeds the rate of natural demographic increase.

Mesoamerican people today are frequently classified as such based on the languages they speak. It is estimated that, at the time of the conquest, there were anywhere between 100 and 190 languages spoken in the region. This wide range is due to the difficulty in determining whether a tongue named by early observers but which became extinct before it could be recorded is a regional variant of another language. It is clear, however, that successive waves of migration, coupled with the difficult topography, which tended to isolate early hunting and farming groups, made Meso-america a place of extreme linguistic diversity. Mesoamerican languages are classified into some 14 distinct families, plus a number of isolates, and they can be as different from one another as Russian is from Italian. The Otomaguean languages, for example, which include Mixtec and Zapotec, are tonal, like Southeast Asian languages. In Mixtec most words are a simple combination of two syllables, each made up of one consonant and one vowel (cvcv). Words are then distinguished from one another by tone, which functions as a phoneme. There are usually three tones. Thus a word written as *cuca* can mean "rich" or "comb" depending on the tone given each syllable. Nahuatl, on the other hand, a member of the Uto-Aztecan family, creates very long words by making extensive use of prefixes and suffixes and compounding. Within languages dialect continua sometimes prevails, so that the people of one town may not understand the people from six towns away, even though intelligible communication takes place between each of the neighboring towns. Some linguists, who distinguish languages based on levels of intelligibility, conclude that some languages, such as Zapotec, are actually many different languages (38 in the case of Zapotec). This diversity of languages led to the use of Nahuatl as a kind of lingua franca in the late Postclassic in Central Mexico, something the colonizers adopted in the sixteenth century as policy for Mesoamerica in general and which no doubt contributed to the use of Spanish for the same purpose later on. However, Mesoamerican people who travel through areas with dialect continuity develop a recognition of the systematic differences that occur between towns, and are able to communicate without having to switch to Spanish or some other lingua franca.

In the twentieth century the governments of Mexico and Central American countries such as El Salvador made the elimination of indigenous languages a policy goal. The assumption was that in order to have a viable national identity the nation should be made up of people who speak a common language. Moreover, since indigenous languages were considered to be lesser forms of communication, by learning Spanish rural people would best be able to compete in the market and participate in civic life. The tool for this was the school system, and teachers would often impose Spanish by a mixture of appeals to progress, the humiliation of individual students, and threats of punishment. Although Mexican intellectuals and indigenous people began to oppose these polices as early as the 1940s, and a bilingual program was established in the national school system, the pressure to assimilate remains high, and bilingual education, largely confined to the primary schools, is treated mainly as a way of teaching Spanish, as opposed to preserving an indigenous language.

Today there are some 70 Mesoamerican languages spoken by an estimated 20 million people. In southern Mexico and Guatemala speakers of these languages make up a significant proportion of the population, and many languages continue to see the numbers of speakers expand. There are over a million speakers of Nahuatl, K'iche', and Yucatec respectively, and Mam, Kaqchikel, Q'eqchi', Zapotec, and Mixtec are each spoken by around half a million people. However, there are Mesoamerican languages such as Ixcatec that are only spoken by handful of older people. Even in the cases where the numbers of speakers continues to grow, this growth is usually below the prevailing rate of demographic expansion. Moreover, the number of monolingual speakers of all languages is shrinking as a percentage of overall speakers, and the number of towns where Mesoamerican languages are spoken is also decreasing, even in the case of those languages where the numbers of speakers has increased (Monaghan 2000).

Of all the periods since the conquest, our understanding of Mesoamerican civilization in the nineteenth century is the least robust (see Carmack et al. 1996). This is partly due to the nature of the archival record. The learned treatises by Spanish friars that have done so much to illuminate the colonial period were no longer being produced. Moreover, as the nineteenth century wore on, increasingly fewer documents were produced in native languages, so that we do not have this important source for an understanding of Mesoamerican cultural categories. There are exceptions, such as the work that has been done on the nineteenth-century Caste War of Yucatán. In 1847–8 the Maya revolted against the Mexican government and overran most of the Yucatán Peninsula (Reed 1964). Even after they were driven out of the major towns they continued to resist from the southern and eastern forests, and did not submit to the central government until the early years of the twentieth century. Maya scribes produced a documentary record, often in Yucatec, which, combined with Mexican records, oral histories, and archeology allows us insight into Maya beliefs and motivations during this important period in Yucatán's history (Alexander 2004).

Another reason why our understanding of Mesoamerica is so sketchy for the nineteenth century has to do with the dominant scholarly focus. While historians of the colonial period have a deep interest in Mesoamerican people and their adaptations to colonial rule, for the nineteenth century historians have largely been consumed with questions of nation building and the accompanying struggles over political ideology, processes in which rural people, and Mesoamerican people in particular, seemed, for a long time, to play only a marginal role. Historians who work on the period thus tend not to refer to Mesoamerican people in terms of the communities they belong to or the languages they speak, preferring terms such as "Indian" or "peasant," the implication being that the most important element in their identities was how they fit into an ethnic hierarchy or the kind of articulation they maintained with the world economy. Yet recent scholarship has made it increasingly clear that in the first half of the nineteenth century, after national elites sought to reconstitute different portions of the Spanish New World empire as independent states, populism was the key to power, and political leaders sought to appeal to a cross-section of groups, including indigenous communities. Indeed Mesoamerican people made up a significant portion of the Mexican armies that fought for independence from Spain. The popular appeal often centered on local rights, privileges, and independence, and elites made considerable concessions to Mesoamerican people, even when the concessions violated central tenets in the dominant political ideologies of the time (Mallon 1995; Guardino 2006). It is also becoming clear that the liberal program to transform rural society in the second half of the nineteenth century by dissolving corporate property and turning rural people into individual landholders did not have uniform results, as some groups, far from losing corporate lands, actually began to use the market to expand landholdings and extend collective control over land (Lauria-Santiago, this volume).

In the late nineteenth and early twentieth century the first ethnological reports on Mesoamerica began to appear. These began as anthropologically informed traveler's accounts, which were followed by anthropological expeditions, and finally by the close study of particular groups over a relatively long period of time. These early ethnologists came to the conclusion that Mesoamerican people should not be viewed in the same terms that the native peoples of North America were viewed, that is, as members of tribes. Instead the most significant social unit was the town or community, often with its distinctive dress, ways of speaking, customs, and high levels of endogamy. Although this first generation of ethnographers were sometimes too quick to assume that everything they observed was some relic of an ancient past, and in their accounts often ignored the contemporary political and economic forces that shaped people's lives, they created the first detailed record of Mesoamerican beliefs and practices since the early colonial period. A number of institutions arose during this period to promote Mesoamericanist scholarship, such as the National Museum of Anthropology in Mexico City.

Mesoamerican people changed in important ways during the twentieth century. Population growth, marginal land bases, and environmental degradation made it increasingly difficult to subsist as small-scale farmers; so many sought other ways of making a living. Like other rural populations throughout Latin America, they participated in the massive rural–urban migration that led to the growth of the primate cities of their countries. Many entered service industries and began to occupy low-level jobs in the public sector, and many others, particularly women and children, entered the urban informal economy. Mesoamerican men and women also began to travel further than ever before to work as seasonal agricultural laborers. Migration of Mesoamerican people has extended into the United States and Canada, although it is still not widely recognized that many of the "Hispanic" migrant workers in agriculture, food processing, and construction are actually people who speak a Native Mesoamerican language. However, rather than simply losing population, some rural communities and households instead acquire an additional component. In the cities, people from the same town tend to live in close proximity to one another and work in the same industries, while constantly moving back and forth between their urban and rural homes. Formally organized migrant associations are also formed by city dwellers, both as social clubs and as ways to channel resources and other aid to the home community, and communities have revised traditional civic arrangements to accommodate migrants' need to be absent for long periods. It remains to be seen whether these patterns will persist beyond the lives of the first generations of migrants.

Rural–urban and transnational migration, expanded educational opportunities, and the possibilities of steady professional employment has meant that an indigenous identity, unlike 100 years ago, is no longer synonymous with being part of a rural farming household. Ethnic-based political movements, usually led by intellectuals who studied in urban areas, have appeared in several regions of Mesoamerica and in the United States. It is quite significant that Mesoamerican people, trained as anthropologists, historians, and linguists, have begun contributing to Mesoamericanist studies by carrying out their own scholarly projects.

BIBLIOGRAPHY

Alexander, R. (2004) *Yaxcaba and the Caste War of Yucatan*. University of New Mexico Press, Albuquerque.
Blanton, R., Kowalewski, S., Feinmen, G., & Laura Finsten, L. (1993) *Ancient Mesoamerica: A Comparison of Change in Three Regions*. Cambridge University Press, Cambridge, UK.
Bonfil Batalla, G. (1996) *México Profundo: Reclaiming a Civilization*. University of Texas Press, Austin.
Boone, E. (2000) *Stories in Red and Black: Pictorial Histories of the Aztecs and Mixtecs*. University of Texas Press, Austin.
Braswell, G. (ed.) (2004) *The Maya and Teotihuacan: Reinterpreting Early Classic Interaction*. University of Texas Press, Austin.

Byland, B. & Pohl, J. (1994) *In the Realm of Eight Deer: the Archaeology of the Mixtec Codices.* University of Oklahoma Press, Norman.

Carmack, R., Gasco, J., & Gossen, G. (1996) *The Legacy of Mesoamerica.* Prentice Hall, New York.

Carrasco, D. (ed.) (2001) *The Oxford Encyclopedia of Mesoamerican Cultures.* Oxford University Press, Oxford.

Coe, M. & Koontz, R. (2002) *Mexico: From the Olmecs to the Aztecs.* Thames and Hudson, New York.

Crosby, A. (2003) *The Columbian Exchange: Biological and Cultural Consequences of 1492,* 2nd ed. Praeger, New York.

Evans, S. (2000) *Archaeology of Ancient Mexico and Central America: An Encyclopedia.* Taylor and Francis, New York.

Farriss, N. (1984) *Maya Society under Colonial Rule.* Princeton University Press, Princeton.

Flannery, K. (1986) *Guila Naquitz: Archaic Foraging and Early Agriculture in Oaxaca, Mexico.* Academic Press, New York.

Flannery, K. & Marcus, J. (eds.) (1983) *The Cloud People.* Academic Press, New York.

Gillespie, S. (1989) *The Aztec Kings: The Construction of Rulership in Mexican History.* University of Arizona Press, Tucson.

Guardino, P. (2006) *The Time of Liberty: Popular Political Culture in Oaxaca, 1750–1850.* Duke University Press, Durham.

Hassig, R. (2006) *Mexico and the Spanish Conquest.* University of Oklahoma Press, Norman.

Houston, S. (1993) *Hieroglyphs and History at Dos Pilas: Dynastic Politics of the Classic Maya.* University of Texas Press, Austin.

Houston, S., Chinchilla Mazariegos, O., & Stuart, D. (eds.) (2001) *The Decipherment of Ancient Maya Writing.* University of Oklahoma Press, Norman.

Houston, S., Stuart, D., & Taube, K. (2006) *The Memory of Bones: Body, Being and Experience among the Classic Maya.* University of Texas Press, Austin.

Kirchoff, P. (1943) "Mesoamerica: Its Geographic Limits, Ethnic Composition and Cultural Characteristics." In J. Graham (ed.), *Ancient Mesoamerica.* Peek Publications, Palo Alto.

MacNeish, R. (ed.) (1975) *Prehistory of the Tehuacan Valley.* University of Texas Press, Austin.

Macri, M. & Ford, A. (eds.) (1997) *The Language of the Maya Hieroglyphs.* Pre-Columbian Art Research Institute, San Francisco.

Mallon, F. (1995) *Peasant and Nation: The Remaking of Post-Colonial Mexico and Peru.* University of California Press, Berkeley.

Monaghan, J. (ed.) (2000) *Supplement to the Handbook of Middle American Indians,* Vol. 6, *Ethnology.* (General editor: Victoria Bricker). University of Texas Press, Austin.

Reed, N. (1964) *The Caste War of Yucatan.* Stanford University Press, Stanford.

Sharer, R. & Grove, D. (eds.) (1989) *Regional Perspectives on the Olmec.* Cambridge University Press, Cambridge, UK.

Sharer, R. & Traxler, L. (2005) *The Ancient Maya,* 6th ed. Stanford University Press, Stanford.

Webster, D. (2002) *The Fall of the Ancient Maya: Solving the Mystery of the Maya Collapse.* Thames and Hudson, New York.

Chapter Three

TRADITION AND CHANGE IN THE CENTRAL ANDES

Jeffrey Quilter

Introduction

No matter how well prepared the traveler might be, no amount of reading, video viewing, or web surfing can come close to the experiences of standing in the ruins of an adobe city that stretches for kilometers or viewing ancient irrigation systems flowing with water and cut-stone terraces still under cultivation in the Central Andes. The ubiquity of the material remains of prehistoric cultures and the pervasiveness and tenacity of old life-ways make a deep impression on both laypeople and scholars alike.

In studying the Andean past, one approach may be termed "civilizational," in which studies are carried out in the emic mode, attempting to understand ancient cultures on their own terms. At the other extreme, some archeologists have engaged with the remains of the past as in a New World "laboratory" to examine large anthropological issues on the origins of plant and animal domestication, the evolution of political economies, and similar issues from an etic perspective. Many scholars fall somewhere between these two extremes. In this essay, I will present information drawn from both kinds of approaches. I will begin by discussing the spatial, temporal, and formal dimensions of the domain of study and then follow with a broad narrative of the culture history of the region as commonly and currently accepted (Richardson 1994; Moseley 2001; Stone-Miller 2002; Quilter 2006).

Space, Time, and Form

The Central Andes is commonly conceived as coterminous with the extent of the Inca Empire. The territory included stretches from the Ecuador–Colombian border to Santiago, Chile, and from the Pacific Ocean to the fringes of the tropical forest in the east, across the Bolivian altiplano, southwards to incorporate northwestern Argentina and northeastern Chile. In practice, however, the region is more narrowly defined. The peripheral areas of the Inca Empire are or are not considered part of the Central Andes depending on the time period in question and the topics under investigation. For example, Ecuador was only under Inca dominion relatively late in prehistory.

In general, the Central Andes is comprised of three major environmental zones: the desert coast, the highlands, and the tropical forest. The altiplano of Bolivia might be considered another zone, as may the *ceja de la selva*, the high tropical forest on the eastern slopes of the Andes. In all but the altiplano, river valleys play important roles. On the coast they served as oases in the harsh desert. In the highlands they were essential routes of communication and offered valuable bottom lands in the vertical world of the Andes. In the tropical forest, again, rivers served as principal communication routes, mostly by canoes.

While the Central Andes might be broadly divided into three major zones, lesser environmental features made critical differences in the lives of ancient inhabitants. Thus, while the coast in one area or another may seem equally barren to the casual visitor, apparently minor variations in geomorphology and ecology can make critical differences. These include the depth of the water table, making "sunken garden" agriculture more or less feasible; the presence of sandy or rocky shorelines offering different mollusks for exploitation; the presence or absence of estuarine resources near the coast; and the location of fog-fed *lomas* vegetation on coastal hills in relation to other resources.

The Humboldt Current runs from south to north, close to the shore. The cold waters up-well nutrients which, in turn, feed a rich and diverse group of fish, pinnipeds, sea birds, and other exploitable resources. Water vapors blown eastwards across the desert are borne upwards by heat radiating off the desert coast to fall as rain in the highland, leaving the coast a parched desert. The water then returns to the Pacific in river valleys roughly parallel to one another.

On the central coast, the foothills of the Andes run into the sea. The hills thus block some of the mists, known locally as *garua*, and support unique forms of xerophytic vegetation in the *lomas*. These verdant fields offered oases in the barren coastal deserts for pre-agricultural populations and, later, pasturage for highland herds of camelids. The central coast also is distinctive in that the lower floodplains of three of its major rivers – the Chillón, the Rimac, and the Lurín – nearly merge into one another. This large agricultural zone was highly productive in late prehistory, supporting one of the densest populations and most powerful polities of pre-Columbian Peru.

On the north coast, from the modern city of Trujillo northwards, there are fewer Andean foothills close to shore and the Humboldt Current gradually turns westwards. *Lomas* are not as common but the local climatic regime is wetter, so that more luxuriant and permanent vegetation increases northwards. In addition, river valleys tend to be parallel to one another rather than merging, as on the central coast, and desert regions between adjacent valleys are distinct. The *Pampa de Paiján* separating the Chicama and Jequetepeque Valleys is the largest stretch of desert north of Lima and south of the Sechura Desert. Although cultural patterns sometimes ignored this boundary, there were notable subregional cultural variations and different languages were spoken on either side of the Paiján desert in late antiquity.

Similar regional variations were present throughout the Andes. The Santa is the only major river on the Pacific watershed in the highlands that flows northwards for a considerable distance before turning towards the ocean. This long valley corridor, known as the *Callejón de Huaylas* in its upper reaches, served as a communication route through the highlands and down to the coast and affected cultural patterns for centuries. The high table land (*puna*) around Lake Junín is another example, among many others, of an environmental zone that supported distinct regional cultural patterns.

Although environmental conditions constrained and influenced cultural patterns throughout the Central Andes, regionally, larger geocultural conformities are in evidence. To the north, separate Peruvian and Ecuadorian co-traditions are in evidence as early as the third millennium BCE (Burger & Raymond 2003: 469–71), yet this frontier region was highly porous so that, in later prehistory, the cultural practices on the north coast of Peru share as much, if not more, with Ecuadorian cultures to the north as they do with southern neighbors. In addition, in the north the relative distances between the coast, *sierra*, and tropical forest are among the shortest in the Central Andes and the height of the passes are among the lowest, perhaps fostering more continuous communication between residents of these zones than in other areas where each zone is larger.

South of Lima the coastline and mountains trend more eastwards and river valleys tend to be less deeply entrenched. Movement between the coast and highlands was fairly easy and there were long-standing patterns of interaction between South Coast peoples and those of the southern highlands of Peru and the Bolivian altiplano.

Chronology building for the Andean past uses both relative and chronometric dating systems. When the Spanish arrived the Incas told them that nothing but barbarism had preceded them. But Inca stories were inconsistent and even to many Spaniards it was clear that past events had been complex. In the last third of the eighteenth century, the archbishop of Trujillo, Martínez de Compañon recorded the vast adobe ruins of Chan Chan, capital of Chimor, the great rival of the Inca. By 1851, the first director of the National Museum, Marfiano Rivero y Ustáriz, and his Swiss colleague, Jakob von Tschudi (1851), published the first book devoted to Andean prehistory, *Antigüedades Peruanas.*

A German, Max Uhle (1902), pioneered archeology in Peru at the end of the nineteenth century. Through excavations at the great and long-used pilgrimage center of Pachacamac, in the Lurín Valley, as well as work in the Moche Valley on the north coast, he established the basic chronological system used today (Uhle 1913). Uhle noted that Inca hegemony had been preceded by an era of regional ceramic styles corresponding to regional polities. This was already known (now called the Late Intermediate Period) but Uhle identified a widespread style in existence immediately before the era of regionalism, adding a new era (now called the Middle Horizon) of considerable time depth to prehistory. He also conducted research at the Huaca de la Luna on Moche burials (Early Intermediate Period) and even earlier remains in Supe and Ancon.

In the 1920s and 1930s, a highland Indian who became an internationally respected figure, Julio C. Tello, further refined the chronology of the Andes. Whereas scholars before him saw the birth of Andean civilization on the coast, Tello sought its origins in the highlands, at the magnificent stone-built temple complex of Chavín de Huantar, located in the upper reaches of the Marañon River, on the eastern side of the continental divide (Tello 1943, 1960). Chavín's dazzling baroque art style was distinct, powerful, and combined imagery of plants and animals from the Pacific Ocean, the highlands, and the tropical forest. In addition, many images, such as the "Staff God" on the Raimondi Stela, appeared to be the first representations of symbols that were repeated, with variations, throughout the rest of Andean prehistory, although their meaning may have varied in later cultures (Isbell & Knobloch 2006). Thus, to Tello, it was the tropical lowlands and highlands that were the sources of Andean civilization and Chavín had been the mother culture that had given it birth.

Thanks to Tello, the Andean past gained greater time depth than ever before. The completion of the chronological framework occurred in several subsequent stages to Tello's work. In 1934–7 a young US archeologist, Junius Bird (1938), supervised excavations at several sites in Patagonia including Fell's Cave, which yielded the remains of extinct Pleistocene animals and spear points similar to finds made slightly earlier near the towns of Folsom and Clovis, New Mexico. This and other discoveries at the tip of South America confirmed that humans had been there in remote antiquity. Lacking any means to precisely date these remains, however, made it difficult to determine how they related to later phases of prehistory.

Bird (1948; Bird & Skinner 1985) again made history in 1946–7 when he and his wife and children spent 11 months at Huaca Prieta, at the mouth of the Chicama River, on the north coast of Peru. The site was a large mound, built up from the accumulated refuse of daily life by people who had made their living by fishing and simple farming in a time before the adoption of pottery. Although the concept of a period of "primitive fisherfolk" had long been entertained by archeologists, Bird's work helped to clarify who these people were and to define the Preceramic Period. The sophistication of their twined textiles, some with elaborate designs, and other aspects of their material culture, made it clear that these people had already adapted themselves well to the local environment at a time period later than the Fell's Cave occupation but well before Chavín.

Work by a number of scholars, aided by the use of radiocarbon dating, which became available in the late 1950s, helped to complete the framework of Andean chronology in the 1960s. In a chronological system developed by John Rowe (1962) and Dorothy Menzel, the vast period of time from the entry of humans into South America to the first use of pottery was named the Preceramic Period (Figure 3.1). The first use of ceramics, some time between 1700 and 1500 BCE was designated as the Initial Period. There followed three periods, known as horizons, in which a distinctive artistic style was widespread, suggesting some kind of religious or political unity: the Early Horizon, the time of Chavín; the Middle Horizon when Tiwanku and Wari styles were widespread; and the Late Horizon, the time of the Incas. Sandwiched between these horizons were two periods, the Early Intermediate Period and the Late Intermediate Period, when numerous regional art styles and sociopolitical systems prevailed.

The Rowe–Menzel chronology is used by most North American and European Andeanists and many Peruvians. In Peru, however, a chronology proposed by Luis Lumbreras (1974), based on an avowedly evolutionary framework, is equally popular. It progresses from the Lithic to the Archaic to the Formative Period, followed by more descriptive terms: Regional Developmental, Wari Empire, Regional States, and the Inca Empire. The major temporal blocks, especially in the later periods, are similar to those in the Rowe–Menzel system. Other schemes are employed in the other Andean countries based on different perspectives on the past and national traditions of research in them.

B.C	3000	2000	1000	500	0	500	1000	1500

Preceramic Period	Initial Period	Early Horizon	E.I.P	Middle Horizon	L.I.P	L.H.

Sechin
Kuntur Wasi
Recuay
Chimu
Aspero Kotosh
Moche
Lambayeque
Wari
Paloma Caral La Galgada
Pacopampa
Lima
Inca
Manchay
Chavin
Tiwanaku
Lupaca
El Paraiso
Paracas
Nasca
Colla

Archaic	Formative	Regional Developmental	Wari Empire	Regional States

B.P.	5000	4000	3000	2500	2000	1500	1000	500

Figure 3.1 Chronogram of Central Andean cultures and sites with Rowe–Menzel (top) and Lumbreras (bottom) chronological systems. Divisions within the Preceramic Period and earlier eras prior to Archaic not shown. Blank box on far right of Lumbreras system is Inca

The formal characteristics of Andean cultures vary through time. There are a number of constants, however. Andean peoples domesticated the potato and a number of tubers, such as oca (*Oxalis tuberosa*) and ullucu (*Ullucus tuberosus*). They also grew a variety of different beans and fruits such as lucuma (*Lucuma obovata*), pacae (*Lutzomyia (migonei) pacae*), and avocados. The llama and alpaca are domesticated versions of wild guanacos and vicuñas. The guinea pig, or *cuy*, also was domesticated for food and was, and remains, an important and reliable source of meat. Camelids were not only used for meat but the llama was used also as a pack animal, driven in herds. Alpaca wool, and to a lesser extent llama wool, also was woven in textiles, as was domesticated cotton.

Western South America is famed for its high mountains but also hosted one of the world's great maritime cultures. Seafaring was carried out by the use of reed boats and rafts on Lake Titicaca as well as the Pacific. Long-distance exchange was carried out by means of these watercraft and a wide variety of fishing techniques were employed in subsistence practices.

Although there were specialized merchants who traveled long distances for exotic goods in late prehistory, market systems were not common in Andean culture. Instead, as John Murra (1972) pointed out, kin groups distributed their members throughout the "vertical archipelago" of different, stacked resource zones up and down the slopes of the Andes. The core unit of those kin groups is the *ayllu*, a term which has received extensive discussion but which can be defined as a clan-like group relying on kinship for membership but not exclusively so (Bastien 1985). Such communities tended to be scattered across the landscape with urban-like complexes the exception, rather than the rule, in prehistory.

A common, widespread Andean world view was based on asymmetrical dualism: two almost equal entities dependent on each other and dynamically related (Burger & Salazar-Burger 1993). At the same time, however, boundaries between the living and the dead or human and natural were fluid (Salomon 1995). Important deceased ayllu elders as well as the Inca sovereign were preserved as mummies and treated as continuing members of the community. So too, mountains, rock formations, ancient ruins, and other places were considered as sacred, living entities with mana-like power. They as well as smaller objects were termed *huacas* in Inca Quechua.

A host of specific items of material culture has long been in use in Andean culture. These include the foot plow (Quechua: *chaki taklla*), metallurgical techniques such as depletion gilding, engineering feats (canals and terraces, rope bridges), a rich tradition of weaving both technically complex and symbolically rich (Boone 1996), and the valuation of the *Spondylus* shells of warm equatorial waters. Patterns of feasting including the drinking of *chicha* (fermented beverage) were long-lived in the Andes, as well as chewing coca. When and how these things and behaviors were invented or adopted in the Andes are questions that remain to be investigated, in many cases.

A Summary of Andean Culture History

First peoples

Homo sapiens sapiens evolved in the Old World and entered the Western hemisphere some time later. When, exactly, the first entry was made is the subject of considerable debate. The model held from the 1950s to the 1980s was that people migrated from Beringia, the large land mass connecting Asia and Alaska, when the large continental ice sheets in the late Pleistocene lowered sea levels worldwide. It was thought that during a warm period an ice-free corridor opened, allowing human entry. Humans then rapidly filled the continent in perhaps only a thousand years or so, reaching the tip of Patagonia by 10,000 BCE.

Several investigations during and since the 1980s have challenged this view (Dillehay et al. 2004). Evidence now suggests that some kind of simple seafaring capabilities existed as early as possibly 40,000 to 30,000 years ago when Australia, already isolated from mainland Asia, was first populated by humans (Brown 1997). Few serious scholars suggest that the New World was inhabited this early, but the dates open the possibility of very early human entry along the coast – "island hopping" in remote antiquity, perhaps much earlier than the *c*.10,000 BCE date commonly considered. Research at Monte Verde, in southern Chile, suggested site occupation at about 12,500 years ago, a millennium earlier than secure dates for New World occupancy (Dillehay 1997 and this volume).

The earliest humans are commonly conceived of as "Big Game Hunters" who may even have helped in the extermination of the large megafauna, such as mammoths and mastodons, at the end of the Ice Age. Also known as Paleoindians, these mobile hunters are best known for the large spear-points they chipped from flint and similar materials (Lynch 1983; MacNeish et al. 1983). By 10,000 BCE different tool traditions were already in existence with "fluted" (Clovis and Folsom) points common in North America into northwestern South America and "fishtail" in western South America. Differences in the forms of these points are presumed to be related to function, but archeologists have assumed that they may also represent some kind of ethnic identity. In Peru, the earliest known distinctive point is Paiján, associated with an early hunting–gathering–fishing culture on the North Coast (Chauchat and Pelegrin 2004).

There is a general pattern of research consistently pushing dates for "firsts" further back in time. Recently, isotopic analyses have produced evidence suggesting that the bottle gourd (*Laganeria sicereria*) entered the New World already domesticated, *c*.10,000 BP and were widely used by 8,000 BP (Erickson et al. 2005). Similarly, research on the south coast of Peru, at Quebrada Jaguay (Sandweiss et al. 1998) and the Ring Site (Sandweiss et al. 1989) indicates a very early maritime adaptation, beginning *c*.13,000 BP. Thus, an older picture of relatively late entry of humans and a specialization of hunting large Pleistocene mammals is gradually yielding to a more complex view than previously thought of an earlier entry, possibly via a number of different means and routes, and an earlier diversification in resource exploitation. Plant and animal management began early as well. In the highlands, some groups began to specialize in hunting wild camelids while others diversified their subsistence strategies. A number of cave sites such as Guiterrero Cave (Lynch 1983), Pikimachay (Rick 1980), and others have been excavated exploring these patterns. Seasonal transhumance between highlands and coast was practiced by some groups (Lynch 1967). Elsewhere, seasonal movement was restricted to environmental zones within larger settings, such as movement between *lomas* fields, river valleys, and the shore (Richardson 1992). Semi- or full sedentism occurred in locations where various resource zones could be exploited over the course of a year from a single locale, such as the Paloma site in the Chilca Valley (Benfer 1984; Quilter 1989).

The construction of large-scale architecture occurred much earlier in Peru than in Mesoamerica with huge complexes being built by 2000 BCE. Recent work by Ruth Shady (2001, 2004, 2006; Shady & Leyva 2003) and her colleagues at sites in the Supe Valley have made claims for the "earliest city" and the "earliest civilization," at the site of Caral. While these dates are quite early, they are a reasonable extension into the past of a tradition of large-scale constructions already known (Quilter 1991).

The monumental constructions of the Late Preceramic and early Initial Periods were impressive, requiring great amounts of labor. The Sechín Alto Complex in the Casma Valley, for example, consists of 10 square kilometers of sites with overlapping occupations from the Late Preceramic (*c*.1850 BCE calibrated) into the Initial Period (*c*.1300 BCE calibrated) (Pozorski & Pozorski 2002). The latest site complex, Sechín Alto, consisted of a main mound 250 by 350 meters in plan and 30 meters in height fronted by a plaza more than a kilometer long and almost a half-kilometer wide. These sites grew by the layering of new construction over old but nevertheless required great amounts of labor.

What is fascinating about continuing research on the Late Preceramic and early Initial Period is the growing evidence that between 2000 and 1500 BCE there were several different regional styles of monument construction. One of the best known of these is the Manchay Culture, consisting of large U-shaped complexes on the central coast of Peru and including the type site of Manchay Bajo in the Lurín Valley and others in Central Coast Valleys between it and Chancay (Burger & Salazar-Burger 1990, 1991).

Farther north, the Supe Valley sites reflect a contemporary North Coast architectural and ceremonial tradition of sunken circular courts in front of stepped pyramids. Other patterns can be seen in the north highlands, with terraced platforms such as at Pacopampa (Morales, in press). A "Little Tradition" of small kiva-like subrectangular to circular rooms with benches and central fire pits is known as the Kotosh Religious Tradition, named after the highland type site on a river system draining to the Amazon (Burger & Salazar-Burger 1986). This likely very early ceremonial tradition appears to have been incorporated and reworked at some of the larger complexes, such as at La Galgada (Grieder et al. 1988), located between the coast and highlands.

Great temple complexes were built for 500 years or more during the Preceramic Period and continued into the Initial Period when ceramics, metallurgy, and loom weaving were added into the inventory of material culture. Ceramics were first used much earlier in Ecuador and Colombia and the reasons for the late appearance of pottery in Peru remain to be explained. The adoption of ceramics may have had more to do with the elaboration of a prestige economy and feasting (see DeBoer 2001) as a means of achieving or maintaining social rank, since irrigation, agriculture, and many of the other "hallmarks" of civilization were already practiced in the Preceramic.

The origins of civilization

The great cult emanating from the highland site of Chavín de Huantar was dubbed by Julio C. Tello (1943, 1960) as the "Mother Culture" of Peruvian civilization (Burger 1988, 1992; Lumbreras 1989, 1993; Rodríguez Kembel & Rick 2004). With its powerful art style, it still is seen as the first great unifier of much of Peru as its art and, inferentially, its religious cult, were adopted over much of the Central Andes. Richard Burger (1981) demonstrated that Chavín was actually a relatively late phenomenon, spreading its influence around 400 BCE. It was the synthesizer of the cults and art of the great temple complexes of the Initial Period, combining tropical forest, coastal, and highland iconography and concepts in a unique way, as has been pointed out by various scholars, particularly Donald Lathrap (1971, 1985).

The Chavín phenomenon may have been an institutionalized revitalization cult, taking old ideas and reinterpreting and repackaging them in a pan-Andean movement. Influences were particularly strong on the South Coast. A series of massive El Niño events may have shaken the foundations of Initial Period of society, providing the opportunity for a synthetic cult to arise (Burger 1988; Sandweiss & Quilter, in press). More El Niños, with massive rains and floods on the coast and droughts in the highlands, may have contributed to the subsequent fall of Chavín. The archeological record is murky between 200 BCE and AD 200, which appears to have been a kind of "Dark Ages." Near the Chavín heartland, the Recuay culture (Lau 2002–4) eventually emerged with a distinctively simplistic, apparently "rustic" stone sculpture style which seems to have been a rejection of the elaborately produced, baroque "high art" style of Chavín (see Quilter 2001). On the South Coast, Chavín influences fade and local styles emerge. This change marks the end of the Early Horizon, in which Chavín rose and fell, and the beginning of the Early Intermediate Period.

The Early Intermediate Period

Regional cultures such as Recuay, Nasca, Lima, and Moche emerged in the Early Intermediate Period. "Regional" is a relative term since some of the art styles of these archeological cultures spread over broad areas and through long periods of time. The Moche style, for example, stretched 500 miles from the hills behind the Sechura desert through the north coast to the Nepeña Valley and lasted from circa AD 100 to 700 (Larco Hoyle 2001; Quilter 2002).

Recently, scholars have begun to reexamine earlier assumptions of a one-to-one correlation of Moche art (mostly ceramic) style and polity. While some still adhere to the idea of a conquest state based in the Moche Valley, near Trujillo, others are exploring the idea of a more complicated past which included valley-centered polities. Given that the art style, temples, and other material culture which denote "Moche" were extant for seven centuries, it is likely that political history in the region was complex and probably included phases of political unification of two or more valleys as well as times of more locally based power.

On the South Coast, the Nasca style was shared by communities, probably organized in small political units, which were engaged in raiding-style warfare in which trophy head taking was practiced (Silverman & Proulx 2002). The famous geoglyphs known as the "Nasca Lines" may have been a place of pilgrimage, as may have been the large architectural complex of Cahuachi (Silverman 1993). The Recuay culture of the central highlands also may have been divided into small polities, while on the central coast large sites, such as Maranga, may have had direct control of irrigation systems, perhaps with strong managerial and political control.

The arts and crafts of the Early Intermediate Period are famous for their technical virtuosity and diversity of styles. The Moche are famed for their modeled and painted bichrome ceramics of white and red-brown depicting animals, people, and mythological creatures and scenes. The Nasca are known for the rich color palette used to decorate finely made ceramics. The Nasca also are famed for their rich textile tradition, first begun in the Early Horizon by the Paracas culture in which mummies were wrapped with multiple layers of magnificently embroidered fabrics. Recuay is among the first art styles to emphasize the affairs of ordinary humans, depicting high-ranking lords with their llamas or groups of men and women in council or ritual. Recuay was in contact with the Moche who also depicted people in their art. The Nasca of the South Coast shared similar styles and ideas with the peoples of the southern highlands and the area around Lake Titicaca, Bolivia (Plourde & Stanish 2006). It is from these highland realms that the next great wave of consolidation came in the Middle Horizon.

The Middle Horizon

There has been a tremendous amount of new research on the great powers of the Middle Horizon, Wari (Cook 2004) and Tiwanaku (Kolata 1993, 1996a,b, 2003; Young-Sánchez 2004; Stanish 2005). Thirty years ago it was difficult to distinguish between the two traditions outside of their heartlands as their art styles have superficial similarities. It was clear, however, that there was a frontier between the two cultures, with Tiwanaku extending its influence from present-day Bolivia southwards into northern Chile and Wari influencing central Peru. Research in the last three decades has advanced our abilities to distinguish between Tiwanaku and Wari remains but their political, social, and economic relations are still unclear. For example, we now know that the Moquegua Valley in southern Peru was occupied by both Wari and Tiwanaku populations, who retained their identifies (Williams & Nash 2002; Goldstein 2005). Like the Moche, we are probably looking at very complex political processes, perhaps similar to the kinds of relations between France and Germany in the late nineteenth and early twentieth centuries – two polities with different languages (Quechua and Aymara?), quite similar material cultures, and complex cultural–political relations that included borrowing, emulation, and antagonism, at times.

Both Tiwanaku and Wari were based in large urban-like complexes. The site of Huari has not received extensive study as it is located in what was the heartland of the Shining Path (*Sendero Luminoso*) guerrilla movement in the 1980s and 1990s. From earlier work, the sprawling site is known for the use of huge stone blocks in the creation of large, multi-story building complexes that included the tombs of high-ranking individuals. Tiwanaku, however, has been studied extensively and has revealed a more formal plan with orientations to nearby mountains and large plazas and pyramids for state rituals (Isbell & Vranich 2004).

The exact nature of the political organizations associated with Wari and Tiwanaku are not known with certainty. The size and nature of the urban-like complexes suggest state-like organizations although these sites could have been centers for pilgrims rather than imperial capitals. Inca origin myths traced ancestry to the Tiwanaku realm while scholars have argued that Wari first employed many aspects of Inca state administration, such as roads, administrative centers, and perhaps even *khipus* (knotted string records used by the Incas).

Wari dominated the great pilgrimage center of Pachacamac, in the Lurín Valley, and the Central Coast, in general, and it may have been from there that it extended its power along the coast, northwards, to the Moche realm. The degree to which Wari and Tiwanaku spread their influences through the use of religious proselytization, economic machinations, or, for Wari, through militarism, is uncertain. Eventually, however, their power waned. As in the case of earlier eras, archeologists have tended to rely on environmental factors as explanations for these collapses. Although the issues are still vague, it is possible that demographic pressure on carrying capacity and, possibly, a series of severe droughts in the highlands, may have contributed to political instability.

The Late Intermediate Period

As in earlier times, the vacuum created by the collapse of highland powers led to the emergence of regional art styles and associated polities. On the North Coast, the Moche style ended, possibly aided by a series of devastating El Niño events (Moseley 1983) followed by some kind of intrusion by Wari. After a period of instability, two kingdoms emerged: Lambayeque, in the north, and Chimu, farther south (Moseley & Cordy-Collins 1990). The Chimu apparently conquered their northern neighbors and expanded southwards along the coast to create an imperial domain that eventually rivaled and was defeated by the Incas.

On the Central Coast, a local polity called Ichma (Rostworowski de Diez Canseco 1977), was in control of Pachacamac and the old Lima Culture territory. Around Lake Titicaca and the southern highlands the kingdoms of the Lupacas and the Chancas arose (Arkush, in press). On the South Coast, near the mouth of the Chincha Valley, a large settlement of specialized long-distance seafaring merchants was established.

There is a distinct international flavor in Late Intermediate Period archeology, including long-distance *spondylus* trade by the Chimu and, possibly, the Chincha of the South Coast. The growth of international styles suggests the movement of peoples and goods across great ranges of space, including pilgrimage centers, and widely shared artistic conventions such as geometric designs, which seem less highly charged with distinctive symbolism than earlier imagery. It was in this interconnected world that the Inca arose.

The Late Horizon

The study of the Incas (D'Altroy 2002) and their times is not dominated by archeology; even archeologists have to know the extensive colonial documents in order to excavate Inca sites knowledgeably. Interpreting colonial period documents is a field unto itself. Recent studies of documents have tended to avoid accepting chronicles at face value but understanding them as the products of writers with specific backgrounds and agendas. The availability of many documents also allows for the investigation of issues that would be extremely difficult to pursue without them, such as the nature and role of knotted string records, *khipu*, used by Inca administrators (Quilter & Urton 2002; Urton 2003).

The Inca conquest of western South America was rapid, with estimates of the initial expansion shortly before 1450 and ending with the arrival of the Spanish in 1532. Rebellions against Inca hegemony were common despite the ruthlessness with which they were suppressed. The Incas manipulated ancient ideas of unequal reciprocity in order to create patron–client relations between themselves and subject peoples. If a group willingly entered the empire, the local political system was left in place with only an Inca governor, an Inca sun temple, and taxation in labor and produce demanded. Nevertheless, the arrival of the Spanish was seen by some as an opportunity to throw off the yoke of Inca dominion to aid the Europeans in the conquest of the Incas (Seed, this volume).

Pizarro and his band of men landed in Peru late in 1532. Following strategies and tactics developed by Cortés in Mexico, the capture of the Inca Emperor, Atahualpa, engaged at the time in a civil war, was a key to Spanish victory; it was aided by a plague ravaging the populace. In many ways, however, the Spanish Conquest was not secure until the 1570s when the last Inca resistance was ended by Viceroy Toledo, who imposed order on a chaotic situation which had included not only Inca revolts but also civil wars between the conquistadors.

There has been little archeology of the conquest and early colonial period of the last two-thirds of the sixteenth century. Most of our understanding of these events has been developed through reading early Spanish chronicles and the work of later mestizos, who used writing to justify their statuses or to make claims within the Spanish judicial system. One such chronicler was Felipe Guaman Poma de Ayala

(1980 [1615–16]), who wrote a thousand-page letter to the King of Spain, including illustrations of Inca Emperors and ways of life as well as the injustices of the Spanish against native peoples.

The Incas commonly claimed that before them no civilized societies had existed in Peru and that only through their conquest and consolidation of the empire were people raised from the most primitive of states. It is perhaps common for great empires to make such claims. However, the extensive archeological record of millennia of prehistory is testament that western South America was the locale of a unique and rich set of cultural traditions with deep roots in the past, and of creative people who created unique and vibrant forms of civilization many times over since remote antiquity.

ACKNOWLEDGMENTS

Many thanks to Richard Burger and Gary Urton for reading a draft of this chapter and offering very helpful comments on it.

BIBLIOGRAPHY

Arkush, E. (In press) "Warfare, Space, and Identity in the South-Central Andes: Constraints and Choices." In A. E. Nielsen & W. H. Walker (eds.), *Warfare in Cultural Context: Practice, Agency, and the Archeology of Conflict.* Amerind Foundation Advanced Seminar Series, Dragoon, AZ.

Bastien, J. W. (1985) *Mountain of the Condor: Metaphor and Ritual in an Andean Ayllu.* Waveland Press, Prospect Heights, IL.

Benfer, R. A. (1984) "The Challenges and Rewards of Sedentism: the Preceramic Village of Paloma, Peru." In M. N. Cohen (ed.), *Paleopathology at the Origins of Agriculture.* Academic Press, Orlando, FL, pp. 531–58.

Bird, J. B. (1938) "Antiquity and Migrations of the Early Inhabitants of Patagonia," *Geographical Review*, 28:20, pp. 250–75.

Bird, J. B. (1948) "Preceramic Cultures in Chicama and Virú." In W. C. Bennet (ed.), *A Reappraisal of Peruvian Archaeology*, Memoirs of the Society for American Archeology, 4, pp. 21–8.

Bird, J. B. & Skinner, M. (1985) "The Preceramic Excavations at the Huaca Prieta Chicama Valley, Peru." In J. Hyslop (ed.), *Anthropological Papers of the American Museum of Natural History*, Vol. 62, Part 1. New York.

Boone, E. H. (1996) *Andean Art at Dumbarton Oaks*, 2 vols. Dumbarton Oaks Research Library and Collection, Washington, DC.

Brown, P. (1997) "Australian Palaeoanthropology." In F. Spencer (ed.), *History of Physical Anthropology: An Encyclopedia* (2 vols.). Garland Publishing, New York, pp. 138–45.

Burger, R. L. (1981) "The Radiocarbon Evidence for the Temporal Priority of Chavin de Huantar," *American Antiquity*, 46:3, pp. 592–602.

Burger, R. L. (1988) "Unity and Heterogeneity within the Chavín Horizon." In R. W. Keatinge (ed.), *Peruvian Prehistory.* Cambridge University Press, Cambridge and New York, pp. 99–144.

Burger, R. L. (1992) *Chavin and the Origins of Andean Civilization.* Thames and Hudson, London and New York.

Burger, R. L. & Raymond, J. S. (eds.) (2003) *Archaeology of Formative Ecuador.* Dumbarton Oaks Research Library, Washington, DC.

Burger, R. L. & Salazar-Burger, L. (1986) "Early Organizational Diversity in the Peruvian Highlands: Huaricoto and Kotosh." In R. Matos, S. A. Turpin, & H. H. Eling Jr. (eds.), *Andean Archeology: Papers in Memory of Clifford Evans.* Monograph 27, Institute of Archeology, University of California, Los Angeles, pp. 44–64.

Burger, R. L. & Salazar-Burger, L. (1990) "The Chronology and Function of Cardal's Public Architecture." Paper presented at the 18th Annual Midwest Conference on Andean and Amazonian Archeology and Ethnohistory. University of Chicago, Chicago.

Burger, R. L. & Salazar-Burger, L. (1991) "The Second Season of Investigations at the Initial Period Center of Cardal, Peru," *Journal of Field Archeology,* 18:3, pp. 275–96.

Burger, R. L. & Salazar-Burger, L. (1993) "Dual Organization in Early Andean Ceremonialism: A Comparative Review." In L. Millones & Y. Onuki (eds.), *El mundo ceremonial Andino,* Senri Ethnological Series, No. 37, Tokyo, pp. 97–116.

Chauchat, C. & Pelegrin, J. (2004) *Projectile Point Technology and Economy: A Case Study from Paiján, North Coastal Peru.* Texas A & M University Press Consortium, College Station, TX.

Cook, A. G. (2004) "Wari Art and Society." H. In Silverman (ed.), *Andean Archeology.* Blackwell, Malden, MA and Oxford, pp. 146–66.

D'Altroy, T. N. (2002) *The Incas.* Blackwell, Malden, MA and Oxford.

DeBoer, W. (2001) "The Big Drink: Feast and Forum in the Upper Amazon." In M. Dietler & B. Hayden (eds.), *Feasting in the Archeological Record.* Smithsonian Institution Press, Washington, DC, pp. 215–40.

Dillehay, T. D. (1997) "Monte Verde: A Late Pleistocene Settlement in Chile," *Smithsonian Series in Archeological Inquiry,* Vol. 2. Smithsonian Institution, Washington, DC.

Dillehay, T. D., Bonavia, D., & Kaulicke, P. (2004). "The First Settlers." In H. Silverman (ed.), *Andean Archeology.* Blackwell, Malden, MA and Oxford, pp. 16–34.

Erickson, D. L., Smith, B. D., et al. (2005) "An Asian Origin for a 10,000-Year-Old Domesticated Plant in the Americas," *PNAS,* 102:51, pp. 18315–20.

Goldstein, P. S. (2005) *Andean Diaspora: The Tiwanaku Colonies and the Origins of Empire.* University of Florida Press, Gainesville.

Grieder, T., Bueno Mendoza, A., et al. (1988) *La Galgada, Peru.* University of Texas Press, Austin.

Guaman Poma de Ayala, F. (1980 [1615–16]). *Primer nueva corónica y buen gobierno,* ed. J. Murra & R. Adorno, trans. J. L. Urioste. Siglo Veintiuno, Mexico City.

Haas, J. & Creamer, W. (2006) "Crucible of Andean Civilization," *Current Anthropology,* 47:5, pp. 745–75.

Isbell, W. H. & Knobloch, P. J. (2006) "Missing Links, Imaginary Links: Staff God Imagery in the South Andean Past." In W. Isbell & H. Silverman (eds.), *Andean Archeology III: North and South.* Springer, New York, pp. 307–51.

Isbell, W. H. & Vranich, A. (2004). "Experiencing the Cities of Wari and Tiwanaku." In H. Silverman (ed.), *Andean Archeology.* Blackwell, Malden, MA and Oxford, pp. 167–82.

Kolata, A. L. (1993) *The Tiwanaku: Portrait of an Andean Civilization.* Basil Blackwell, Oxford, England and Cambridge, MA.

Kolata, A. L. (1996a) *Valley of the Spirits.* John Wiley & Sons, New York.

Kolata, A. L. (1996b) *Tiwanaku and Its Hinterland: Archeology and Paleoecology of an Andean Civilization. Volume 1: Agroecology.* Smithsonian Institution Press, Washington, DC.

Kolata, A. L. (2003) *Tiwanaku and Its Hinterland: Archeology and Paleoecology of an Andean Civilization. Volume 2: Urban and Rural Archeology.* Smithsonian Institution Press, Washington, DC.

Larco Hoyle, R. (2001 [1938/1939]) *Los Mochicas, Tomos 1 & 2.* Museo Arqueológico Rafael Larco Hoyle. Lima, Peru.

Lathrap, D. (1971) "The Tropical Forest and the Cultural Context of Chavin." In E. Benson (ed.), *Dumbarton Oaks Conference on Chavin (1968)*. Dumbarton Oaks Research Library and Collection, Washington, DC, pp. 73–100.

Lathrap, D. (1985) "Jaws: The Control of Power in the Early Nuclear American Ceremonial Center." In C. B. Donnan (ed.), *Early Ceremonial Architecture in the Andes*. Dumbarton Oaks Research Library and Collection, Washington, DC, pp. 241–67.

Lau, G. F. (2002–4) "The Recuay Culture of Peru's North-Central Highlands: A Reevaluation of Chronology and Its Implications," *Journal of Field Archeology*, 29, pp. 177–202.

Lumbreras, L. G. (1974) *The Peoples and Cultures of Ancient Peru*, trans. B. Meggers. Smithsonian Institution Press, Washington, DC.

Lumbreras, L. G. (1989) *Chavín de Huantar en el Nacimiento de la Civilización Andina*. Instituto Andino de Estudios Arqueológicos, Lima.

Lumbreras, L. G. (1993) *Chavín de Huantar. Excavaciones en la Galería de las Ofrendas*. Materialien zur Allgemeinen und Vergleichenden Archäeologie, vol. 51. Comisión für Allgemeine und Vergleichende Archäologie. Philipp von Zabern, Mainz am Rhein.

Lynch, T. F. (1967) *The Nature of the Central Andean Preceramic*. Occasional Papers of the Idaho State University Museum 21, Pocatello.

Lynch, T. F. (1980) *Guitarrero Cave: Early Man in the Andes*. Academic Press, New York.

Lynch, T. F. (1983) "The Paleo-Indians." In J. D. Jennings (ed.), *Ancient South Americans*. W. H. Freeman and Company, San Francisco, pp. 87–137.

MacNeish, R. S., Vierra, R. K., et al. (1983) *Prehistory of the Ayacucho Basin, Peru Volume IV, The Preceramic Way of Life*. University of Michigan Press, Ann Arbor.

Morales, D. (In press) "Pacopampa: Architecture and Iconography." In W. J. Conklin & J. Quilter (eds.), *Chavin: Art, Architecture and Culture*. Cotsen Institute of Archeology, University of California, Los Angeles.

Moseley, M. E. (1983) "The Good Old Days Were Better: Agrarian Collapse and Tectonics," *American Anthropologist*, 85:4, pp. 773–99.

Moseley, M. E. (2001) *The Incas and Their Ancestors: The Archeology of Peru* (rev. ed.). Thames and Hudson, London and New York.

Moseley, M. E. & Cordy-Collins, A. (eds.) (1990) *The Northern Dynasties: Kingship and Statecraft in Chimor*. Dumbarton Oaks Research Library and Collection, Washington, DC.

Murra, J. (1972) "El control vertical de un máximo de pisos ecológicos en la economía de las sociedeades Andinas." In J. Murra (ed.), *Formaciones Económicas y Políticas del Mundo Andino*. Instituto de Estudios Peruanos, Lima.

Plourde, A. M. & Stanish, C. (2006) "The Emergence of Complex Society in the Titicaca Basin: The View from the North." In W. Isbell & H. Silverman (eds.), *Andean Archeology III: North and South*. Springer, New York, pp. 237–57.

Pozorski, S. & Pozorski, T. (2002) "The Sechín Alto Complex and Its Place Within Casma Valley Initial Period Development." In W. Isbell & H. Silverman (eds.), *Andean Archeology: Variations in Sociopolitical Organization*. Plenum, New York, pp. 15–20.

Quilter, J. (1989) *Life and Death at Paloma: Society and Mortuary Practices in a Preceramic Peruvian Village*. University of Iowa Press, Iowa City.

Quilter, J. (1991) "Late Preceramic Peru," *Journal of World Prehistory*, 5:4, pp. 387–438.

Quilter, J. (2001) "Moche Mimesis: Continuity and Change in Public Art in Early Peru." In J. Pillsbury (ed.), *Moche: Art and Archeology in Ancient Peru*. Studies in the History of Art 63, Center for Advanced Study in the Visual Arts Symposium Papers XL. National Gallery of Art, Washington, DC, pp. 21–44.

Quilter, J. (2002) "Moche Politics, Religion, and Warfare," *Journal of World Prehistory*, 16:2, pp.145–95.

Quilter, J. (2006) *Treasures of the Andes: The Glories of Inca and Pre-Columbian South America*. Duncan Baird, London.

Quilter, J. & Urton, G. (2002) *Narrative Threads: Accounting and Recounting in Andean Khipu*. University of Texas Press, Austin.

Richardson III, J. B. (1992) "Early Hunters, Fishers, Farmers and Herders: Diverse Economic Adaptations in Peru to 4500 B.P." *Revista de Arqueología Americana* 6: (July–December). Instituto Panamericano de Geografía e Historia, México City, pp. 71–90.

Richardson III, J. B. (1994) *People of the Andes*. Smithsonian Books. St. Remy Press, Montreal.

Rick, J. W. (1980) *Prehistoric Hunters of the High Andes*. Academic Press, New York.

Rick, J. W. (1988) "The Character and Context of Highland Preceramic Society." In R. W. Keatinge (ed.), *Peruvian Prehistory*. Cambridge University Press, New York, pp. 3–40.

Rivero y Ustáriz, M. E. de & Von Tschudi, J. (1851) *Antigüedades Peruanas*. Imprenta Imperial de la Corte y del Estado, Vienna.

Rodríguez Kembel, S. & Rick, J. W. (2004) "Building Authority at Chavín de Huantar: Models of Social Organization and Development in the Initial Period and Early Horizon." In H. Silverman (ed.), *Andean Archeology*. Blackwell, Malden, MA and Oxford, pp. 51–76.

Rostworowski de Diez Canseco, M. (1977) *Señoríos indígenas de Lima y Canta*. Instituto de Estudios Peruanos, Lima.

Rowe, J. H. (1962) "Stages and Periods in Archeological Interpretation," *Southwestern Journal of Anthropology*, 18:1, pp. 40–54.

Salomon, F. (1995) "The Beautiful Grandparents." In T. Dillehay (ed.), *Tombs for the Living: Andean Mortuary Practices*. In Dumbarton Oaks Research Library and Collection, Washington, DC, pp. 247–81.

Sandweiss, D. H., Heather McInnis, H., et al. (1998) "Quebrada Jaguay: Early South American Maritime Adaptations," *Science*, 18 vol. 281, no. 5384, pp. 1830–2.

Sandweiss, D. H., Richardson III, J. B., et al. (1989) "Early Maritime Adaptations in the Andes: Preliminary Studies at the Ring Site, Peru." In D. Rice, C. Stanish, & P. R. Scarr (eds.), *Ecology, Settlement and History in the Osmore Drainage, Peru*. British Archeological Reports, International Series, pp. 35–84.

Sandweiss, D. H. & Quilter, J. (eds.) (In press.) *El Niño, Catastrophism, and Culture Change in Ancient America*. Dumbarton Oaks Research Library and Collections, Washington, DC.

Shady, R. (2001) *La ciudad sagrada de Caral-Supe y los orígenes de la civilización Andina*. Museo de Arqueología y Antropología de la Universidad Nacional Mayor de San Marcos.

Shady, R. (2004) *Caral: La ciudad del Fuego Sagrado*. Centura, Lima.

Shady, R. (2006) "America's First City? The Case of Late Archaic Caral." In W. Isbell & H. Silverman (eds.), *Andean Archeology III: North and South*. Springer, New York, pp. 28–66.

Shady, R. & Levya, C. (eds.) (2003) *La ciudad sagrada de Caral-Supe: Los origines de la civilización Andina y la formación del estado pristíno en el Antiguo Perú*. Instituto Nacional de Cultura, Lima.

Silverman, H. (1993) *Cahuachi in the Ancient Nasca World*. University of Iowa Press, Iowa City.

Silverman, H. & Proulx, D. A. (2002). *The Nasca*. Blackwell, Oxford.

Stanish, C. (2005) *Ancient Titicaca: The Evolution of Complex Society in Southern Peru and Northern Bolivia*. University of California Press. Berkeley and Los Angeles.

Stone-Miller, R. (2002). *The Art of the Andes: From Chavin to Inca*, 2nd ed. Thames and Hudson, London and New York.

Tello, J. C. (1943) "Discovery of the Chavin Culture in Peru," *American Antiquity*, 9, pp. 135–60.

Tello, J. C. (1960) *Chavin: Cultura matriz de la civilización Andina, Primera Parte*. Universidad Nacional Mayor de San Marcos. Lima, Peru.

Uhle, M. (1902) "Types of Culture in Peru," *American Anthropologist*, 4, pp. 753–9.

Uhle, M. (1913) "Zur Chronologie der alten Culturen von Ica," *Journal de la Société des Américanistes de Paris*, New Series, 10, pp. 341–67.

Urton, G. (2003) *Signs of the Inka Khipu: Binary Coding in the Andean Knotted-String Records*. University of Texas Press, Austin.

Williams, P. R. & Nash, D. J. (2002) "Imperial Interaction in the Andes: Huari and Tiwanaku at Cerro Baúl." In W. Isbell & H. Silverman (eds.), *Andean Archeology: Variations in Sociopolitical Organization*. Plenum, New York, pp. 243–66.

Young-Sánchez, M. (2004) *Tiwanaku: Ancestors of the Inca*. Denver Art Museum/University of Nebraska Press, Lincoln and London.

Chapter Four

Portuguese and Spaniards in the Age of European Expansion

William D. Phillips, Jr. and
Carla Rahn Phillips

The history of humankind in the Western Hemisphere had already passed through many millennia before voyagers from the Eastern Hemisphere first made contact with them, and the character of that contact was shaped to a great extent by the prior experience of the peoples involved. Previous chapters have traced the various strands of human history in the Americas during those millennia. It is therefore appropriate for this chapter to begin with a brief synopsis of the history and interaction of the three component parts of the Old World of the Eastern Hemisphere: Europe, Africa, and Asia.

By the fifteenth century, educated Europeans knew that they were part of that broader world, though some of their ideas bore little resemblance to the geographical reality defined in later centuries. The traditional view of the earth in medieval Europe was depicted in a variety of flat circular maps. Regardless of their individual characteristics, these maps all reflected the idea that only a portion of the earth, well above the equator, was habitable. Below the equator lay what was usually called the Torrid Zone, too hot for human habitation. Christianity assumed that God the Father created the earth and that human history centered around the life and death of his son Jesus. Accordingly, Christian mapmakers depicted Jerusalem – the holy city of Judaism, Christianity, and Islam – at the center of the inhabited world. The known continents were arrayed around Jerusalem, with Europe and Africa together about the size of Asia by itself.

Such depictions of the world are generally called T-O maps, a shorthand description of their layout and presentation. The Mediterranean Sea formed the base of a "T" with Jerusalem at its head; the arms of the T were the Don River and the Nile River. Reinforcing the blending of religion and geography, many of these maps located the Garden of Eden, described in the Bible as the terrestrial paradise, in the eastern part of Asia. An all-encompassing and uncharted ocean, the "O" of the map, surrounded the landmass of Eurasia (Kimble 1938; Westrem 1991; Harvey 1996; Larner 1999). The T-O maps have frequently been used as evidence of medieval ignorance of the true shape of the earth. A compelling counterargument is that the T-O maps depicted spiritual rather than physical truths; they were drawn schematically in the full knowledge that the scheme did not represent the physical world. In much the same way that maps of modern subway systems bear little resemblance to the exact shape of the tracks beneath the urban landscape, they were symbolic representations of an intellectual reality (Phillips 1988: 188–9).

North Africa and the Middle East provided Europeans with access to the products of Africa and Eurasia, and European geographical knowledge tended to follow from the trade goods they imported. For example, once Europe began to import Asian products regularly in the twelfth century, Europeans became fairly well informed about Asia. They were much less well informed about Africa for several reasons: the limited trade in products from sub-Saharan Africa; European assumptions about the inhospitable nature of the Torrid Zone; and Muslim zeal to keep Christians out of direct trade to Africa. The existence of two continents in the western ocean between Europe and Asia lay completely outside the knowledge of even the best-educated Europeans in the fifteenth century.

Europeans gained their knowledge of Asia through contacts that began in ancient times. While the Roman Empire held sway in Europe and the Middle East, its trading networks radiated from Rome westward to the British Isles and eastward to the Indian subcontinent. Once the overarching authority of Roman rule disintegrated, those networks unraveled. Asia receded from European reality, while persisting in the European imagination as the source of luxury and wealth and the site of the Christian terrestrial paradise. From the end of the Roman Empire until the First Crusade – or, from the fifth to the late eleventh century – western Europe was poor, backward, and underdeveloped, both by the standards of the old Roman Empire and by comparison to its successor empires in Byzantium and the Islamic world. In the early Middle Ages, westerners had to defend themselves from a series of outside attacks. Beginning in the early eighth century, the Muslims conquered most of the Iberian Peninsula and raided the kingdom of the Franks north of the Pyrenees, following their explosive conquests in the Middle East and North Africa. In the ninth century, Viking raiders harried western Europe and established their own kingdoms in France, England, and Italy. In the ninth and tenth centuries, the Magyars attacked Central Europe from the east. The Catholic Church was one of the few consistent forces acting for Christian unity during that tumultuous period.

By the tenth century, the tide of invasion had ebbed, as the invaders were incorporated (in the case of the Vikings), defeated (in the case of the Magyars), or held at bay (in the case of the Muslims). Thereafter, in the absence of major external threats and with monarchs working with the Church to limit internal warfare, Europe began to prosper. A rising population, stimulated by innovations in agriculture and stockbreeding, led to an expansion of land under cultivation. The increased food supply supported not only a continuing rise in the population but also an expansion of towns, cities, and commercial activity.

In Spain, Christian leaders in the north directed a series of campaigns against the Muslim lands of the south. By the mid-1080s, they had reached the center of the peninsula, conquering Toledo in 1085 and Valencia (though only temporarily) a few years later. During the same time, and inspired by the Spanish reconquest, legal scholars at the papal court in Rome developed the idea of the "just war." According to their formulations war could be justified – despite the oft-professed pacifism of Christianity – on any of several grounds. The most important for the struggle against Islam was that war was justified to regain lands that once had been in Christian hands.

This doctrine applied clearly in the Spanish case and it could easily be applied to Syria and Palestine, which had been ruled by Christian emperors from the legalization of Christianity in the Roman Empire in 393 until the seventh century, when the Muslims conquered the area (Russell 1975; Muldoon 1979; Johnson 1997; Mastnak 2001).

The traditions that Iberians developed in their reconquest of territory from the Muslims helped to shape their attitudes and actions as they moved overseas, first in the Canaries and later in the Americas. Castilians in particular had long experience, stretching over centuries, of acquiring land by conquest and then controlling it by settlement. In the initial conquests, many commoners gained economic advantage and moved higher in the social ranks through military daring and success. Those who joined successful expeditions led by kings or by noble captains could expect to share in the rewards. They would receive a portion of the movable booty and, more important in the long run, citizenship in the new municipalities created subsequently. The elite among them received more substantial rewards and grants of land along with royal offices, most notably that of *adelantado* or governor of a newly incorporated area (O'Callaghan 2003).

The defeated Muslims faced a variety of fates in Iberia. Conquered warriors were held captive until ransomed, and if ransoms were not forthcoming, they often ended up as slaves. The populations of the conquered towns usually had the choice of leaving or remaining to live under Christian rule. They could retain their religion and customs but faced pressures to convert to Christianity and assimilate to Christian norms. Later, in the Canaries and the Americas, conquered people had little choice but to convert and assimilate.

Spaniards in the Americas were the heirs of the traditions of the reconquest. They knew how their forebears had gained land from the Muslims and established control over that land and its inhabitants. The history of gallant feats and the rewards of the reconquest found reinforcement in the ballads and tales that were still current in the sixteenth century and that helped shape the mental world of the conquistadors in the Americas (Leonard 1949).

In the early 1090s the Byzantine emperor Alexius Comnenus requested the help of Pope Urban II in enlisting a contingent of western knights to help protect Constantinople from the Muslim Seljuk Turks in Asia Minor. The pope agreed to help and preached a sermon in the southern French city of Clermont in 1095 that went far beyond the emperor's request, calling for western knights to march to Jerusalem and free Christianity's most holy city from Muslim control. He described Palestine as a land of milk and honey and promised that those who died while fighting the Saracens (another European name for the Muslims) would enter into heaven. The rapid response must have exceeded his fondest dreams. In a few months, Urban witnessed the formation of four major armies of experienced knights, along with several mobs of inexperienced commoners. They set off for the Middle East to reclaim the birthplace of Christianity, and within five years Jerusalem was in their hands. This nearly spontaneous eruption of Christian militancy has come to be known as the First Crusade, which would be followed by three other major crusades and several minor ones in the course of two centuries.

For the knights who joined the crusades, and for the nobles who led them, the compensations for hardship and danger were more than adequate. They could gain spiritual rewards for participation; they benefited from a papal moratorium on their debts while they campaigned; and they could hope to gain lands for themselves in the conquered territories. This last incentive was especially important as Europe coped with an impressive rise in population, which made land for seigniorial holdings increasingly difficult to find.

The crusader states lasted for nearly two centuries before the Muslims regained control over the territory. Although their existence became precarious by the late thirteenth century, the crusader states continued to produce sugar for their own use and for export. When the Muslims drove the last westerners from the Middle Eastern mainland in 1291, Christian refugees took the knowledge of sugar production with them. In the islands of the Mediterranean and the eastern Atlantic, and on the mainland of states in the western Mediterranean, they introduced large sugar plantations producing for export. The commerce in sugar between Muslim and Christian lands also continued, with ports in Syria and Egypt continuing to provide western merchants with sugar, as well as spices and other goods. Sugar would be introduced to the Atlantic islands by Spanish and Portuguese settlers, and to the Americas by Columbus, who took sugar-cane plantings to Española on his second voyage. In other words, Columbus would provide the link between sugar production in the Old World and the New, as he would provide other crucial links in the development of global trade.

Even though the Crusades failed to establish lasting control of the Christian holy places, they gave western Europeans first-hand knowledge of the Middle East and a hint of the vastness of Asia that lay beyond. The end of the Crusades by no means ended Europe's connection to the Middle East, and through it, to the farthest reaches of Asia. Many of the luxurious and exotic products prized by the European elite continued to arrive from Asia via the Middle East, but political and economic conditions over that vast land mass determined whether trade was profitable or even possible. For many years in the eleventh and twelfth centuries, competing empires in Asia habitually disrupted trade. During the thirteenth and fourteenth centuries, however, the long overland routes from the Black Sea to China opened again, in the aftermath – ironically – of a terrifying series of conquests by the Mongols of Central Asia, disciplined masters of mounted warfare.

Under the leadership of Genghis Khan, "ruler of the universe," and his grandson Kublai, the Mongols conquered much of Asia, relying on terror, rapine, and pillage to defeat their largely sedentary enemies and hold them in submission. Genghis and then Kublai conquered most of Asia to the eastern fringes of Europe during the thirteenth century. Stiff resistance in Egypt and their lack of expertise in jungle warfare and naval engagements finally brought the Mongol conquests to a halt, and the empire broke up in the fourteenth century (Morgan 1986). For a period in the thirteenth and fourteenth centuries, however, the Mongols guaranteed the safety of travelers along the overland routes spanning their vast empire, in what is often called the "Pax Mongolica," an echo of the "Pax Romana" throughout much of Europe and the Middle East in ancient times. The Pax Mongolica allowed contacts between Europe and Asia that were impossible beforehand, including a series of visits to Asia by Christian missionaries and merchants from Europe, who returned to tell their stories to Europeans fascinated by tales of faraway lands and untold riches.

Long-distance trade with Asia suffered a stunning blow after 1347, when bubonic plague arrived by way of the Asian caravan routes at the shores of the Black Sea. From there it spread like wildfire throughout Europe, where it was known as the Black Death, killing between one-quarter and one-third of the population in a few years (Cohn 2002; Benedictow 2004). The Black Death also devastated the population of the Middle East and paralyzed long-distance commerce for a generation or more (Dols 1977). Adding to the chaos, a dissident Mongol tributary named Timur the Lame (aka Tamerlane) carried out a series of brutal conquests from Persia to India during the late fourteenth century. At the same time the Ottoman Turks carved out an empire in Anatolia and the eastern Mediterranean. The combination of plague and political disruption starting in the mid-fourteenth century ended the golden age of trade and contact between Europe and Asia that had been protected by the Mongols.

While it lasted, the Pax Mongolica had brought more Asian goods, and Asia itself, within the reach of Europeans. Mediterranean merchants explored the possibilities for direct trade with the markets of Asia. Missionaries explored the possibilities of converting the huge Asian populations to Christianity. Popes and princes became aware that, beyond the Islamic world, lived other peoples who might be willing to form alliances against the Muslims of the Middle East. The more Europeans learned about the world east of Jerusalem, the more they searched for ways to travel there. Their fascination with reaching Asia would inspire Columbus and others of his generation to explore outward from Europe to find a seaborne route to the riches and potential converts of the Far East, avoiding the strongholds of Islam.

Europeans were quite familiar with parts of the Islamic world, particularly North Africa and the Kingdom of Granada in southern Spain. Despite centuries of reconquest and crusades, and despite frequent attacks from Muslim pirates at sea, Christians of the western Mediterranean regularly traded in the ports of North Africa. The gold of West Africa enriched Muslim rulers in the black African empires, as well as trading cities south of the Sahara. In the ports of the southern Mediterranean, European merchants obtained African gold brought across the Sahara Desert by Muslim caravans. But in Africa as in the Middle East and Asia, the politico-religious barrier between Christianity and Islam prevented European merchants from reaping the full benefits of long-distance trade.

To overcome this disadvantage, Europeans established trade routes that did not depend upon the goodwill of Muslim states. The reasons for their success were embedded in the history of Europe in general, and of Iberia in particular. Even during the depression that followed the Black Death, some cities had remained vital centers of manufacturing, trade, government, religion, and culture. Those cities were poised for further growth once the depression lifted. Moreover, despite recurring plagues and other setbacks, the population of Europe was growing again by the late fifteenth century, and the wealthiest citizens sought out exotic goods that displayed their distinction from more ordinary folk.

International trade played an important role in supplying the luxuries demanded by the European elite, both during the depression and thereafter (Lopez 1971; Poston 1973). In the Mediterranean, trade in general gave rise to sophisticated bookkeeping and credit instruments, as well as maritime insurance and international commercial law. Itinerant merchants carried their commercial techniques with them, helping to disseminate advanced methods all over Europe. These developments provided the structure for financing voyages and organizing and regulating trade that were later used for overseas exploration. Foreign merchant colonies played an important role in the commercial life of many important European cities in the late fifteenth century. Lisbon, for example, already harbored a community of Italians, many of them merchants, when Columbus arrived in Portugal in the 1470s. Some families had been there for a century or more. Italian communities were also well established in Seville, Cádiz, Córdoba, Cartagena, and elsewhere in Castile. Foreign merchant enclaves are sometimes viewed as outposts of their home countries, yet merchants of all nations tended to have a good deal in common. The role that local and foreign merchant communities in Iberia played in backing voyages of exploration has long been acknowledged. New research into business contracts and related documents is allowing us to deepen and broaden our understanding of those roles, and the importance of expanding commerce in promoting European expansion (Dollinger 1970; Hunt & Murray 1999).

European society in the fifteenth century organized itself in a hierarchical pyramid. A very small privileged elite, probably comprising no more than 10 percent of the total population, stood at the top, controlling much of the landed and movable wealth, as well as local and national governments. Some members of the elite sprang from families that had earned their position through military service to a patron or lord. Others had grown wealthy through trade and then had abandoned trade for the more prestigious status of landowner, earning their income by renting land to tenant farmers. Still others were members of the elite by virtue of holding important positions in the religious hierarchy of the Roman Catholic Church, the only Christian church in western Europe in the fifteenth century. In one way or another, the elite had power over the vast majority of the population, which included everyone from the poorest beggars to wealthy merchants outside the social elite.

It is difficult to define levels of economic well-being precisely in fifteenth-century Europe, but general impressions provide grim reminders of the vast disparity between rich and poor. The truly destitute probably accounted for about 10 percent of the total population. In years of bad harvests, the proportion of people falling into destitution might rise to 20 percent. The poorest of the poor would rise and fall in number depending upon the fortunes of the working poor – those who managed to survive most of the time through farming or other labor, but who occasionally fell into destitution through illness, injury, bad harvests, or some other catastrophe. The working poor probably included at least 50 percent of the population. Farmers with some land of their own (and perhaps a few animals), artisans, and shopkeepers represented those with a slightly better lot in life, and perhaps some small savings to tide them over in hard times. This group probably included no more than 15–20 percent of the population. Except for the elite, those who had sufficient food and other necessities all or most of the time would have been a small proportion of the total population. Members of the clergy came from virtually every part of the social hierarchy, and ran the gamut of wealth and status from the highest church official to the lowest parish priest. By virtue of their membership in the clergy, however, they rarely faced starvation.

The social hierarchy was supposed to be unchanging, with everyone expected to remain at the same level into which he or she was born. Reality was rather different.

Within the Church, for example, bright and talented individuals might rise to the top ranks of the hierarchy, despite humble birth. A similar upward mobility was possible through a military career. European wars in the fourteenth and fifteenth centuries provided the opportunity for many men to acquire noble status, or at least to acquire wealth as the spoils of war. As in medieval times, service to the monarchy remained a popular avenue to wealth and status. Christopher Columbus himself, the son of a weaver and small merchant of Genoa, could aspire to noble status as a result of his service to the king and queen of Spain. His career was by no means unique. Conversely, a family high in status – designated as noble because of illustrious deeds in the past – might lose its wealth and be forced to live quite humbly, while retaining the legal status of nobility. In short, there was much more social mobility in Europe than we might expect based on definitions of legal status alone, but the relative percentages of rich and poor persisted. As the population grew and the economy quickened its pace, the opportunities for social mobility, both upward and downward, tended to increase, and traditional definitions of wealth and status began to erode (Braudel 1981).

Europe contained a wide variety of governments in the late fifteenth century, from free cities and city-states to duchies, counties, principalities, and large territorial monarchies. Although European political units differed from one another in many ways, they shared certain characteristics. For instance, they were each governed by a body of law, both written and customary, that placed limits on the actions of individuals and their leaders and regulated their behavior for the general good of society. In southern Europe the traditions of written law were especially strong, stemming from the ancient law codes of the Romans, and revised over the centuries since then. The law codes in effect in the late fifteenth century dealt with virtually every aspect of human existence: marriage and inheritance; civil and criminal wrongs; the definition and legal implications of social hierarchy; morals and manners; religion; relations among states and peoples; trade and commerce; war; and a host of other topics. Judges and lawyers occupied an important position all over Europe, applying the law as a living reflection of their changing societies.

National monarchies far outstripped smaller units such as city-states in resources. In the late fifteenth century, their kings and queens enjoyed power and territories far beyond the dreams of their medieval predecessors. They had a permanent and substantial tax base for the support of governmental administration and foreign policy. Moreover, they could use their authority to encourage activities such as exploration that benefited both the state and its subjects. It is no accident that Columbus and his brother sought support from all four of the wealthiest national monarchies of their time: Spain, France, Portugal, and England. Although Columbus himself was Genoese, the city-states of northern Italy did not command the resources of the new monarchies, nor, because of their identification with the Mediterranean, were they as likely to be officially interested in Atlantic exploration. Genoese merchants who wished to enter the transoceanic Asian trade realized they would have to work through intermediaries or attach themselves to national monarchies in Western Europe (Hay 1966; Aston 1968; Cardini 1989).

We should be careful not to assume too much about the power of the national monarchies, however. Their kings and queens had established centralized authority at the expense of powerful subjects within their realms, often through open warfare.

In the fifteenth century, the matter of who should rule was by no means settled. For centuries thereafter, many European monarchs faced serious challenges to their authority from within, as well as having to deal with foreign rivals. Moreover, the amount of money available to the rulers of national monarchies was seldom sufficient to cover the costs of their ambitious foreign policies. Instead, rulers were often forced to rely for support on the same powerful subjects that they were trying to control. The trick was to inspire their loyalty to the throne and at the same time to make it worth their while to demonstrate that loyalty. In this endeavor, the presence of a foreign enemy could prove useful, and enemies lay close at hand in the Islamic world.

The eastern Mediterranean lay firmly in the hands of the Muslims, beyond the control of Christian leaders in Europe. Although Christians and Muslims clashed periodically in the long centuries between the rise of Islam and the late fifteenth century, their warfare was hardly continuous. Between periods of open fighting, a great deal of trade occurred, brokered by merchants from Italian cities such as Venice and Genoa, which had reached a practical accommodation with the Islamic world. In Iberia north of the frontier between Christian and Muslim forces, Christian rulers also reached fairly amicable agreements with their Muslim counterparts, despite intermittent warfare. The situation began to change in the fifteenth century, because of the expansion of a militant new force within Islam – the Ottoman Turks – who challenged the traditional Muslim rulers in the eastern Mediterranean and began a concerted campaign to extend the lands under Muslim control (Creasy 1961; Inalcik 1973; Goodwin 1999).

The Ottomans directed their main thrust in the fifteenth century against the Christian Byzantine Empire, which ruled extensive lands in southeastern Europe from its capital at Constantinople. After gradually encircling the city with conquests in the Balkans, the Ottomans took Constantinople in 1453, a bitter defeat for Christian Europe. For the Genoese and the Venetians, the expansion of the Ottomans meant the loss of their colonial outposts in the Black Sea and the Aegean. For Christian Europe as a whole, the loss of Constantinople meant that the Ottomans held a dagger at the heart of Christian civilization.

By the late fifteenth century, the essential hostility between Islam and Christianity was an acknowledged fact, although Italians still traded in Muslim port cities, and Christian pilgrimages to Jerusalem continued. The dream of the warriors and crusaders of earlier times to recapture the holy places of Christianity from Muslim control continued as well, with renewed fervor. This dream served as a powerful inspiration for many of the explorers and mariners of southern Europe, whatever national differences might have divided them.

Muslims, particularly the Ottoman Turks, posed a major threat for Christian rulers in the late fifteenth century. The possibility that explorers could provide information about Muslim power induced several reigning monarchs to support exploration (Phillips 1988: 60–73). The Portuguese dreamed of carrying a Christian holy war to the heart of Islam. The Castilians shared that dream, but first they had to complete their own reconquest of Muslim Granada.

A curious legend about a Christian emperor named Prester John, supposedly descended from one of the Three Magi, encouraged their hopes that a holy war against the Muslims could succeed (Slessarev 1959; Gumilev 1987; Beckingham &

Hamilton 1996). The legend found its way into medieval chronicles, gathering embellishments and shifting in geographical focus in the process. Portuguese voyages down the Atlantic coast of Africa in the early fifteenth century were ordered to collect news or even rumors about Prester John's kingdom, and later in the century King João II sent an overland expedition to seek him in the Middle East. The Portuguese eventually found a kingdom in East Africa whose people had been Christian since the fourth century, converted by the Copts of Egypt. Unfortunately, their leader – though called an emperor – hardly measured up to the legendary Prester John in power or resources. Despite this disappointment, there is little doubt that the politico-religious goal of seeking allies beyond the centers of Ottoman power helped to inspire European exploration and incursions into Africa.

The ultimate destination, however, remained Asia. Europeans had sought to travel overland to the Far East since the twelfth century. As far as we know, the first European attempt to sail to Asia around Africa was launched in 1291 – exactly two centuries before Columbus – and its leaders, like Columbus, were Genoese. Italian and Iberian sailors probed the Atlantic sporadically thereafter, discovering nearby islands and charting the mainland shores. Through trade and settlement, they also found ways to profit from their discoveries (Pérez Embid 1948: 51–8; Phillips 1988: 156–8).

The Canary Islands, known to classical antiquity as the Fortunate Isles, began to interest Europeans in the course of the fourteenth century. With patents from the rulers of Castile or Portugal, various adventurers visited the islands and attempted to conquer their inhabitants, the Guanches, establishing competing claims to overlordship and the right to establish colonies. Several successive popes granted the islands to other petitioners, and the rulers of England and France watched the process closely, concerned that whoever gained the Canaries might tip the balance of power in what was later called the Hundred Years' War. Though the monarchs of Portugal and Castile did not directly challenge the pope's authority to grant sovereignty over the Canaries, Portugal claimed the first modern discovery. Castile trumped that by asserting that the Visigoths of Spain had seized the islands from infidels centuries before, and that they belonged to the Castilian monarchy as the heir of the Visigoths.

The arrival of the Black Death in 1348 suspended plans for any large-scale attempts at conquest, but the major contenders continued to send small expeditions to the area, and the king of Aragon sent out several expeditions of his own from Majorca that included both missionaries and settlers. Attempts to convert the Canary Islanders to Christianity had evidently been going on for some time and continued through the rest of the fourteenth century. By the 1390s, sailors from Andalusia also visited the islands fairly regularly, but only in 1402 was the expedition launched that began the definitive conquest of the Canaries by Castile (Pérez Embid 1948; Rumeu de Armas 1956; Ladero Quesada 1979; Fernández-Armesto 1987).

In the mode of its conquest, colonization, and economic organization, the experience of the Canaries set many precedents that would later be repeated in the Americas. Successive kings of Castile in the early fifteenth century granted private individuals permission to pursue the conquest in the name of the Crown. The Catholic monarchs Ferdinand of Aragon and Isabel of Castile tightened royal control over the process late in the century, partly as a general move to strengthen their authority, and partly in recognition of the strategic importance of the Canaries in the struggle with Portugal. The definitive conquest of the last Guanche strongholds did not occur until 1496, under royal authority and with backing from Genoese merchants resident in Andalusia. The conqueror, Alonso Fernández de Lugo, used modern army tactics and followed the standard practice of securing allies among the Christianized islanders to use against the pagans. Nonetheless, the final conquest took nearly three years. At one point the local inhabitants ambushed and defeated his troops, forcing the survivors to abandon the islands temporarily.

The Guanches did not know how to work metal and were primarily herders, though some bands practiced agriculture on the island of Gran Canaria. The Castilians made treaties with some of the bands on various islands and conquered others. In the initial phases of conquest, the conquerors needed quick profits to repay creditors who had financed the expeditions. The capture and sale of slaves offered an obvious and easy way to repay those loans. Many enslaved Guanches were taken to be sold in Spain or in the Madeira Islands settled by the Portuguese; other slaves remained in the Canaries to work for European settlers, most frequently in household service. According to medieval law, it was legal to enslave the members of bands that resisted the Spanish incursion – those who, in other words, were captured during a "just war." It was not legal to enslave members of bands that submitted voluntarily. However, bands allied with the Europeans who later rebelled or refused to carry out the terms of their treaties could be enslaved as "captives of a second war" (*de segunda guerra*). Conquerors and colonists often circumvented the laws, however, eager for the profits to be made from the slave trade and from sugar plantations worked by slave labor (Marrero Rodríguez 1966; Lobo Cabrera 1982; 1996: 103–17).

European settlers introduced sugar cane quite early in the Canary Islands, although production would not reach its peak until early in the sixteenth century, when 29 mills functioned. The Canaries served as a way station for Spanish sugar production between Europe and the Americas. Cuttings for the propagation of sugar cane, and sugar-processing techniques, would be taken from the Canaries to the newly discovered Caribbean islands early in the colonizing process (Camacho y Pérez-Galdós 1961; Crosby 1986).

The relations between European and native peoples in the Canaries also foreshadowed experiences in the Americas (Ladero Quesada 1979; Mercer 1980; Férnandez-Armesto 1982; Aznar Vallejo 1983). In the Canaries slaves were used both as laborers and as commodities for sale elsewhere, but the Guanche population was relatively small to begin with, and its numbers fell drastically through epidemic disease and warfare after the European incursion. Moreover, members of many bands could not be enslaved legally, and those enslaved frequently attained manumission. Consequently, the natives of the Canaries did not account for a substantial or long-lasting addition to the international slave trade. The Canarian slave trade to Europe ceased altogether in the early sixteenth century, as the islanders increasingly assimilated into European culture and intermarried with the colonists.

In short, local people never filled the need for labor in the colonial economy of the Canaries, and settlers anxious to develop the islands' economy solved the labor shortage in various ways. A number of free Castilian and Portuguese settlers emigrated to the Canaries, and some wealthy settlers brought their own slaves with them from the Iberian Peninsula. In addition, Portuguese slave traders brought in black

Africans from the west coast of the continent, and Castilians raided the mainland coasts for North Africans, Berbers, and others, to enslave. Many of the Africans, especially the North Africans, were soon freed, and there was even a voluntary emigration of Muslims and converted Muslims (Moriscos) from Spain and North Africa to the Canaries. Following the first Spanish contact with the Americas, a few Caribbean natives were sold in the Canaries, but the Spanish Crown quickly outlawed the slave trade in Indians. The initial search for quick profits through the slave trade, followed by the establishment of more lasting bases for the colonial economy, shaped the relationship between Europeans and local inhabitants in both the Canaries and the Americas.

Like the Canaries, the Madeira Islands were the focus of rivalry among several groups of European explorers between their discovery in the thirteenth or early fourteenth century and their definitive settlement by the Portuguese in the early fifteenth century. Given the wind patterns in the eastern Atlantic, it was only a matter of time before some group of European seafarers discovered the Madeiras, and Iberian mariners were ideally situated to be the first.

In the late fourteenth and early fifteenth centuries, Portuguese and Castilian ships visited the Madeira Islands for easily obtainable items such as wood and the dyestuff called "dragon's blood," the resin of the so-called dragon tree (*Dracaena draco*). Pirates used the islands as occasional bases as well. The Portuguese Crown was not very interested in the Madeiras until 1417, when their Castilian rivals visited the islands with a large force. Faced with potentially serious Castilian competition, João I of Portugal sent an expedition of about one hundred people, mostly from southern Portugal, to the principal islands of the Madeiras – Madeira and Porto Santo – to establish permanent settlements. Christopher Columbus later married the daughter of one of the expedition's leaders, Bartolomeo Perestrelo, an Italian naturalized in Portugal. In 1433 Portugal's new king Duarte made his brother Prince Henrique (known to history as Henry the Navigator) lord of the Madeiras for life (Duncan 1972; Diffie & Winius 1977; Vieira 1992). Prince Henrique later created administrative divisions called captaincies in the islands, which he bestowed on the early expedition leaders as hereditary rights (Russell 2000).

The Madeiras were uninhabited and fertile, but the land required careful and extensive preparation before sugar or other crops could be successfully grown there. The Portuguese burned forests and built irrigation canals and terraces to balance the effects of irregular and insufficient rainfall. By about 1450 the Madeiras began to generate profits based on grain production, and the Portuguese built a water-powered flour mill on Madeira in 1452. Thereafter, sugar production and other agricultural pursuits expanded to support a much larger population (Vieira 1991, 2004). The Venetian Cadamosto reported some 800 people living on the island of Madeira in 1455, and the Portuguese Azurara, writing in the same decade, gave a similar estimate. By the early sixteenth century the population stood at 15,000 to 18,000, including some 2,000 slaves.

From the mid-fifteenth century on, the Portuguese took slaves to work in the Madeiras: Moroccans and Berbers, black Africans, and native islanders from the Canaries. There was a limit to the number of slaves who could be profitably employed, however, because the Madeiran sugar plantations were relatively small in comparison to the later Caribbean and Brazilian plantations. Besides, the growth of population in Portugal in the sixteenth century induced many free Portuguese laborers to migrate to Madeira, depressing the market for slaves. The use of slave labor soon began to decline, and there were even proposals to expel the Canary Islanders to reduce the labor supply. In short, during the fifteenth century, the development of Madeira, like the Canaries, proceeded along lines that later characterized American colonial development, with a reliance on slave labor for commercial plantations. In the sixteenth century, however, Madeira came to rely much more heavily on free labor, phasing out a system of slave labor that did not suit the situation there.

São Tomé, which later became a crucial entrepot for the transatlantic slave trade, also experienced a sugar boom in the sixteenth century, and in many ways the island served as a prototype for sugar production in the islands of the Caribbean. The Portuguese established sugar production on other Atlantic islands as well, but none rivaled the early profits of the Madeiras. Sugar enjoyed little success in the Azores because of the unsuitable climate; grain and dyestuffs were always more important there. Portuguese development of the Cape Verde Islands concentrated on cereals and fruits, as well as cattle-raising.

Overall, in the fifteenth century, Iberians and their Italian associates developed two modes of exploitation in newly colonized areas. In one mode, the Portuguese set up factories or trading posts along the African coast, sometimes fortified, sometimes not, that enabled them to tap into existing networks of trade. In Africa, Europeans had to contend with major obstacles to any grandiose plans for Christian proselytizing or control of local resources. Many African kingdoms and other states were willing to trade, but they would not allow Europeans to dominate them and had the strength to resist attempts at conquest in the fifteenth century. The Portuguese soon abandoned any thoughts of territorial conquest they might have entertained and instead negotiated with each local ruler for trading privileges. Endemic diseases in Africa also prevented European colonial incursions into the African mainland. Tropical Africa hosted a variety of diseases unknown in Europe. Local populations had developed tolerance or even immunity to these diseases, but Europeans had never been exposed to them and succumbed in great numbers. Together, the insalubrious environment and the strength of African states prevented Europeans from establishing a territorial base in West Africa. The Portuguese found ample compensation in trade, however, and were content to act as merchants in their coastal enclaves.

The other mode of European exploitation, developed in the Atlantic islands, differed greatly, even though the island groups were discovered and settled by Iberians at the same time that they explored West Africa. The Azores, the Madeiras, and the Cape Verdes were uninhabited, and all but the Cape Verdes were mild enough in climate and similar enough to Europe to allow Europeans to settle there with ease and without conflict. The Canary Islanders maintained a long resistance to European domination but ultimately failed, limited by their stone technology and their lack of immunity to common European diseases. In all the Atlantic islands, a new mode of colonial control and exploitation developed, initiated by a forceful European incursion, then followed by the development of profit-making ventures in agriculture and mining, with the use of coerced non-European labor. This mode of operation would not work in regions such as mainland Africa and India, but it would be repeated profitably and with devastating effects across the Atlantic.

Exploitation of the Atlantic islands by Portuguese and Castilian settlers was a logical extension of the search for commercial profits that had engaged southern Europeans for centuries. That search formed one of the two major sets of motivations that drove Europeans to try new ventures and explore new lands. The other major motivation was religion, the militant Christianity that had propelled both the reconquest of Iberia from the Muslims and the Crusades that took the battle to the heartland of Islam. Together, religious and economic motivations had shaped European experience for centuries, particularly in the south. They came together in the late fifteenth century to inspire Columbus's great leap of imagination. But as compelling as these motivations were, they would have had no practical consequences without the appropriate means to act upon them. If motivations were to be turned into realities, Europeans needed a wide range of technology and technical skills, including capable ships and the knowledge of how and where to sail them.

Columbus was not the only European to think about reaching Asia by sailing west, or even the first. Moreover, if he had not obtained support for his voyage, some other mariner would probably have done so within the same generation. The logic of hundreds of years of European sailing experience pointed in that direction. In the late fifteenth century Basque whalers ventured farther and farther into the Atlantic as they hunted their prey. The king of Portugal sponsored at least one voyage westward before 1492, and, in the same decade that Columbus reached the Caribbean, the king of England sponsored several voyages westward at more northerly latitudes, following earlier probes westward by English merchants.

Both Columbus and his contemporaries saw his first voyage as part of a long process extending European trade over increasingly large areas. In that sense, Columbus's voyage differed only in direction from earlier voyages in the eastern Atlantic and along the western coast of Africa. Many Christians, including Columbus himself, also saw his voyage as an extension of the militant Christianity that had launched the Crusades against Islam in the Middle East and the Iberian Peninsula.

Columbus thought the greatest accomplishment of his first voyage was to have reached the outlying fringes of Asia, where he expected to find populations receptive to the Christian message as well as fabulous wealth. Until his death, he publicly asserted that he had arrived in Asia, even though his private letters on the fourth voyage suggest that he knew it was not the part of Asia known to European travel books. It took decades for Europeans to realize the full implications of Columbus's epochal voyage. Instead of the long-sought passage to Asia, he had brought the knowledge of vast lands in the Western Hemisphere into the consciousness of Europe and, ultimately, the rest of the Old World. The long traditions of conquest and colonization by land in the Iberian reconquista, and conquest and colonization by sea in the Canaries, helped shape the attitudes of Iberians as they confronted the Americas. Long before Europeans knew the full extent of that New World, they had carried their crusading zeal, their technology, their administrative, legal, and social structures, and their unfamiliar and devastating diseases to its peoples.

BIBLIOGRAPHY

Aston, M. (1968) *The Fifteenth Century: The Prospect of Europe*. Harcourt, Brace, and World, New York.

Aznar Vallejo, E. (1983) *La integración de las Islas Canarias en la Corona de Castilla (1478–1526): Aspectos administrativos, sociales, y económicos.* Universidad de Sevilla and Universidad de La Laguna, Seville and La Laguna.

Beckingham, C. F. & Hamilton, B. (1996) *Prester John, the Mongols, and the Ten Lost Tribes.* Variorum, Aldershot.

Benedictow, O. J. (2004) *The Black Death, 1346–1353: The Complete History.* Boydell, Woodbridge.

Braudel, F. (1981) *The Structures of Everyday Life: The Limits of the Possible.* Harper & Row, New York.

Camacho y Pérez-Galdos, G. (1961) "El cultivo de la caña de azúcar y la industria azucarera en Gran Canaria (1510–1535)," *Anuario de Estudios Atlánticos,* 7, pp. 1–60.

Cardini, F. (1989) *Europe 1492: Portrait of a Continent Five Hundred Years Ago.* Facts on File, New York.

Cohn, S. K. (2002) *The Black Death Transformed: Disease and Culture in Early Renaissance Europe.* Oxford University Press, New York.

Creasy, E. S. (1961 [1854–6]) *History of the Ottoman Turks,* 2 vols. Khayat, Beirut.

Crosby, A. W. (1986) *Ecological Imperialism: The Biological Expansion of Europe, 900–1900.* Cambridge University Press, Cambridge, UK.

Diffie B. W. & Winius, G. D. (1977) *Foundations of the Portuguese Empire, 1415–1580.* University of Minnesota Press, Minneapolis.

Dollinger, P. (1970) *The German Hansa.* Stanford University Press, Stanford.

Dols, M. W. (1977) *The Black Death in the Middle East.* Princeton University Press, Princeton.

Duncan, T. B. (1972) *Atlantic Islands: Madeira, the Azores, and the Cape Verdes in Seventeenth-Century Commerce and Navigation.* University of Chicago Press, Chicago.

Fernández-Armesto, F. (1982) *The Canary Islands after the Conquest: The Making of a Colonial Society in the Early Sixteenth Century.* Clarendon Press, Oxford.

Fernández-Armesto, F. (1987) *Before Columbus: Exploration and Colonization from the Mediterranean to the Atlantic, 1229–1492.* University of Pennsylvania Press, Philadelphia.

Goodwin, J. (1999) *Lords of the Horizon: A History of the Ottoman Empire.* Henry Holt, New York.

Gumilev, L. N. (1987) *Searches for an Imaginary Kingdom: the Legend of the Kingdom of Prester John.* Cambridge University Press, Cambridge, UK.

Harvey, P. D. A. (1996) *Mappa Mundi: The Hereford World Map.* University of Toronto Press, Toronto.

Hay, D. (1966) *Europe in the Fourteenth and Fifteenth Centuries.* Holt, Rinehart, and Winston, New York.

Hunt, E. S. & Murray, J. M. (1999) *A History of Business in Medieval Europe, 1200–1550.* Cambridge University Press, Cambridge, UK.

Inalcik, H. (1973) *The Ottoman Empire: The Classical Age, 1300–1600.* Praeger, New York.

Johnson, J. T. (1997) *The Holy War Idea in Western and Islamic Traditions.* Pennsylvania State University Press, University Park.

Kimble, G. H .T. (1938) *Geography in the Middle Ages.* Methuen, London.

Ladero Quesada, M. A. (1979) *Los primeros europeos en Canarias (Siglos XIV y XV).* Colección Guagua, Las Palmas de Gran Canaria.

Larner, J. (1999) *Marco Polo and the Discovery of the World.* Yale University Press, New Haven.

Leonard, I. A. (1949) *Books of the Brave, Being an Account of Books and of Men in the Spanish Conquest and Settlement of the Sixteenth-Century New World.* Harvard University Press, Cambridge, MA.

Lobo Cabrera, M. (1982) *La esclavitud en las Canarias orientales en el siglo XVI: Negros, Moros, y Moriscos.* Cabildo Insular de Gran Canaria, Gran Canaria.

Lobo Cabrera, M. (1996) "Esclavitud y azúcar en Canarias." In Alberto Vieira (ed.), *Escravos com e sem açúcar – actas do seminário internacional, Funchal, 17 a 21 de junío de 1996.* Centro de Estudos de História do Atlántico; Secretaria Regional do Turismo e Cultura, Funchal, pp. 103–17.

Lopez, R. S. (1971) *The Commercial Revolution of the Middle Ages, 950–1350.* Prentice-Hall, Englewood Cliffs.

Marrero Rodríguez, M. (1966) *La esclavitud en Tenerife a raiz de la conquista.* Instituto de Estudios Canarios, La Laguna de Tenerife.

Mastnak, T. (2001) *Crusading Peace: Christendom, the Muslim World, and Western Political Order.* University of California Press, Berkeley.

Mercer, J. (1980) *The Canary Islanders: Their Prehistory, Conquest and Survival.* Collings, London.

Morgan, D. (1986) *The Mongols.* Blackwell, Oxford.

Muldoon, J. (1979) *Popes, Lawyers, and Infidels: The Church and the Non-Christian World, 1250–1550.* University of Pennsylvania Press, Philadelphia.

O'Callaghan, J. F. (2003) *Reconquest and Crusade in Medieval Spain.* University of Pennsylvania Press, Philadelphia.

Pérez Embid, F. (1948) *Los descubrimientos en el Atlántico y la rivalidad castellano–portuguesa hasta el Tratado de Tordesillas.* Escuela de Estudios Hispano-Americanos, Seville.

Phillips, J. R. S. (1988) *The Medieval Expansion of Europe.* Oxford University Press, Oxford.

Phillips, W. D. & Phillips, C. R. (1992) *The Worlds of Christopher Columbus.* Cambridge University Press, Cambridge, UK.

Poston, M. M. (1973) *Medieval Trade and Finance.* Cambridge University Press, Cambridge, UK.

Rumeu de Armas, A. (1956) *España en el Africa atlántica.* C.S.I.C., Madrid.

Russell, F. H. (1975) *The Just War in the Middle Ages.* Cambridge University Press, Cambridge, UK.

Russell, P. E. (2000) *Prince Henry "The Navigator": A Life.* Yale University Press, New Haven.

Slessarev, V. (1959) *Prester John, the Letter and the Legend.* University of Minnesota Press, Minneapolis.

Vieira, A. (1991) *Os escravos no arquipélago da Madeira, Séculos XV a XVII.* Centro de Estudos de História do Atlántico, Funchal.

Vieira, A. (1992) *Portugal y las islas del Atlántico.* MAPFRE, Madrid.

Vieira, A. (2004) "The Sugar Economy of Madeira and the Canaries, 1450–1650." In S. B. Schwartz (ed.), *Tropical Babylons: Sugar and the Making of the Atlantic World, 1450–1680.* University of North Carolina Press, Chapel Hill, pp. 42–84.

Westrem, S. (1991) *Discovering New Worlds: Essays on Medieval Exploration and Imagination.* Garland, New York.

Chapter Five

EXPLORATION AND CONQUEST

Patricia Seed

Spaniards and Portuguese initially occupied the New World in order to secure commercial networks and ensure a steady flow of goods back across the Atlantic. In both kingdoms the first official organizations to oversee the new colonies were boards of trade (Andrews 1978: 55). Such trade dominated Spanish expansion until 1518 (Sauer 1966: 205–7), and Portuguese expansion until 1550. After that period, both nations embarked on policies of agricultural settlement that would continue until the end of the colonial era. How each of these two nations pursued such settlement differed, given the divergent native communities and commercial opportunities they encountered in the Americas.

Contrary to later English political propaganda – that Spanish and Portuguese subjects arrived in the New World to pursue military objectives – both first arrived in the New World prepared both to explore and to trade. Surveying newly navigable coasts and searching for tradable goods went hand in hand, since the coasts were the paths for trade.

As the first Spanish emissary, Christopher Columbus and his crew, coasted past Antillean Islands and along Caribbean shores, they searched for signs of habitation and indications that the residents were friendly and might have valuable goods to trade (Sauer 1966: 95; Andrews 1978: 9). His Portuguese counterparts, the brothers Miguel and Gaspar Corte Real, also first sailed past the shorelines of Brazil with the same initial objectives: charting coastlines and searching for communities producing tradable commodities.

That much of the early exploration of the New World shared similar aims and policies did not emerge accidentally. Both policies originated in an earlier Portuguese pattern of trading along the West African coast (Bensaúde 1940: 133–86). When Columbus landed in the New World, he had long been married into a Portuguese noble family on the Madeira Islands and had been active in their business dealings. Furthermore, he already had personally journeyed on at least one African trading voyage, sailing between 1480 and 1482 to the Portuguese trading center in El Mina (in modern-day Ghana). On the West African coast he witnessed Portuguese techniques of negotiating with people who spoke an entirely different language. He also saw how they traded with people who observed customs and rituals of exchange very different from those operating during European commercial transactions. While

Columbus may have fantasized about encountering Asian nobility in the New World, he had practical experience in trading with people unfamiliar with Asian or European customs of exchange.

Portuguese expeditions to Africa had to meet a second requirement as well. The ships' pilots were expected to carefully follow the coastline of previously uncharted terrain, and to bring back information that could be used on future voyages. Eventually Portuguese leaders came to call this process of reconnoitering "discovery." When drafting many of the early official authorizations for travel to the New World, Spanish officials borrowed the language and the goals from those already established by their Lusitanian neighbors. Ships sent to the New World from both countries were instructed to study systematically these previously undeciphered coastlines (Sauer 1966: 40–8, 105, 111; Weddle 1998: 107–31). In dealings with previously unknown people and territories over the next 300 years, Spanish and Portuguese explorers were to focus on delimiting uncharted coasts and trading in unfamiliar, preferably lucrative, goods. As later settlements began to move away from the coasts, both Spanish and Portuguese officials insisted on mapping land-based trade routes (Kelsey 1998: 56–90).

The search for trade goods and the routes to them depended upon private capital in both Spanish and Portuguese empires. This pattern also originated with Portuguese West African voyages. First, most Portuguese voyages had to raise all the costs of their expeditions from private sources. Some had the personal wealth to pay for building and outfitting a ship, hiring a crew, and supplying them with the supplies necessary to survive. Those lacking such funds would enter into agreements with wealthy investors to underwrite the costs of their journeys. These wealthy individuals placed their funds at the disposal of expeditionary leaders in the expectation of a profit. In the Spanish New World, Columbus's initial voyages aside, each subsequent voyage required large amounts of private capital (Sauer 1966: 105).

Columbus's discovery of the Caribbean occurred by accident, after Portuguese officials had rejected it as based on erroneous information. Unlike the Spanish king and queen, King John II of Portugal possessed an accurate idea of the distance between Iberia and the eastern coast of Asia. Hence in 1485 he rejected Columbus's proposal because he knew that no ship could carry sufficient provisions for a journey of that length. (Even with the tip of South America as a way station and a fairly accurate idea of the distance involved, many of Magellan's men starved to death on the voyage across the Pacific during the first circumnavigation of the earth, 1519–21.)

However, Columbus managed to convince the less geographically knowledgeable monarchs of Spain that the East lay within a reasonable sailing distance. In April 1492, Isabella and Ferdinand, flush from the retaking of Granada the preceding autumn, took the usual step of funding this unusual voyage. In the "Capitulations of Santa Fe" they granted Columbus's outsized demands for his initial voyage, perhaps anticipating that the expedition might very well fail, and hoping to motivate him to carry through with his plans. If successful, Columbus would become Admiral of the Ocean Sea (then the most common name for the Atlantic), Viceroy, and Governor General of the Asian regions, along with a host of other privileges.

When the voyage succeeded contrary to all expectations because Columbus ran into the Caribbean Islands (by accident rather than design), the instigator of this voyage soon proved far less adept a leader than he had imagined himself to be.

Columbus's substantial titles and colossal rights were quickly rescinded over his protests. Future authorizations for travel to the New World granted leaders more reasonable privileges resembling the traditionally more modest goals of Lusitanian expeditions.

Vessels from both Spain and Portugal followed the same pattern during the initial years of contact: raising private funding and searching for tradable goods so that an exploratory expedition would turn a profit. While both powers continued modified versions of these explorations until the end of the colonial era, both eventually had to establish permanent settlements in the New World in order to secure the trade networks they had established. Spaniards became the first to establish significant permanent settlements.

An initial ramshackle encampment of men left behind by Columbus's sinking of his own flagship the *Santa María* failed. The survivors fell to quarreling among themselves, leaving them vulnerable to attacks from the natives. When Columbus returned the following year, no one from this initial group remained alive. Rather than abandoning the program of settlement, Columbus established a small base on the northwest coast of Hispaniola, which his brother moved in 1496 to the location that today serves as the capital of the Dominican Republic – Santo Domingo. These initial settlements lay along the coast, where goods produced in the interior could be loaded onto ships for transport across the Atlantic.

In addition to the impulse to establish port bases in the Caribbean, Spanish arrivals soon encountered a second motive to settle in the New World – a metal with obvious commercial potential, which offered prospects of immediate and vast wealth. Only by remaining on the island to supervise the natives collecting gold could they realize their dreams of riches, rapidly settling on the islands to speed the process of becoming rich.

With the gold rush Spaniards soon took up permanent residence in the Caribbean. Employing the large number of indigenous inhabitants or Tainos on the gold-rich island of Hispaniola, newly settled Spaniards coerced many to perform the tedious labor of panning, for the gold on Hispaniola lay close to the surface of mountains. Rains and rivers over the centuries had washed the gold downhill, where it rested in streams and riverbanks; thus the gold could be recovered by continually sifting through the pebbles and stones for gold. As in any gold rush, new arrivals became preoccupied with searching for the mineral, neglecting to invest time and effort in growing food. Since the natives could not keep up with Spanish demands for both food and gold, and Spaniards quarreled bitterly among themselves over the right to use native labor for panning, a central authority was instituted in 1501 to keep order among the Spanish settlers.

The sudden descent of large numbers of Europeans with all their contagious bacteria and viruses upon this small island community had natives dying off in record numbers (Cook & Borah 1971–9: I, 376–410; Casas 2003). Slaving began in 1499, and the almost industrially paced demands for native labor to sustain the new colony led Queen Isabella to approve taking "hostile" Indians as slaves in 1503 (Sauer 1966: 112). The label of "hostile" remained open to broad interpretation, allowing Spaniards, in effect, to gather native slaves from any region they located. Even with these liberal rules, Spaniards soon exhausted the supplies of labor on nearby islands. Six years later the labor shortage again became so acute that King Fernando ordered the enslavement of Lucayans from the Bahama Islands. The next year some 40,000 Lucayans were forcibly taken to Hispaniola. By the time of Ponce de Leon's voyage the following year (1513), the Bahamas had become deserted. Two years later the inhabitants of St. Croix suffered the same fate, as did those of Barbados (Sauer 1966: 192–4).

"Discovery and Rescue"

As the first official government center in the New World, Santo Domingo soon became the launching point for other voyages around the Caribbean. Because of the centralized nature of Spanish exploration, the instructions for such voyages became formulaic (Ramos Pérez 1981). The shorthand title for these exploratory expeditions was "discovery and rescue." "Discovery" in these instructions signified the same thing that it had when first used for Portuguese voyages down the coast of West Africa – methodically exploring previously unknown regions. However, the term "rescue" in these instructions is a perversion of both its modern meaning and its original significance. During the centuries-long battles between Christians and Muslims on the Iberian Peninsula, hostage taking was widespread on both sides. To prevent their co-religionists from falling permanently into enemy hands a ransom of some kind had to be arranged to "redeem" or "rescue" the hostages. Since poor people were frequently unable to pay any significant sum for their own redemption, the word "rescue" originally implied saving these captives of war from being sold into slavery. Since the unransomed sometimes abandoned their faith for that of their captors, the act of Catholic rescue implied preserving their Christian faith by removing them from Muslim control (Seed 2001: 92–3). While "rescuing" aimed at averting enslavement in Europe, in the Caribbean it became a pretext for enslavement rather than a means of preventing it.

The rationale for slavery as "rescue" had two separate components. First, was the idea – never carefully investigated – that individuals being sold by brokers were somehow already slaves. In purchasing the allegedly enslaved individual, the Spanish explorer merely was paying ransom to "rescue" an individual or group from their indigenous owners. A second, more perverted, version of the word "rescue" allowed Spaniards to contend that by capturing and even enslaving these people themselves they were in fact liberating them from a life of servitude to the devil or pagan superstition. Because one of the conditions of slave holding was seeing to the religious instruction of those he owned, enslavement to a Christian overlord could be rationalized on religious grounds. While sincere believers in the redemptive qualities of enslavement to Christians can, no doubt, be found, the cynical manipulation of this category seems to have prevailed (Seed 2001: 104–6).

Despite the devastation of native inhabitants and loss of labor, Spaniards continued to pour into the Caribbean, drawn by legendary tales of vast stores of gold. Coupled with the headlong reckless speed with which the Spanish residents first exhausted the existing stores of gold, then depleted neighboring islands of labor, and finally spread illness among unsuspecting local inhabitants, the opportunities for commercial profit soon dwindled to nearly nothing. Even the gold itself was soon exhausted. Gold in Hispaniola lasted 25 years and in Puerto Rico and today's Haiti half that time.

With increasingly smaller quantities of gold left for new arrivals to make their fortunes, many began to inquire about exploring other islands – where perhaps equally large stores of gold might well be found. However, some enterprising subjects realized the need to supply the gold-rush islands. Diego de Nicuesa and Alonso de Ojeda successfully petitioned the Crown to give them gold-free Jamaica to grow food and other supplies for the other islands.

Consequently other Spaniards soon sought to explore other islands in search of gold. These expeditions, like the Portuguese trade to West Africa, had to find private investors. In 1508 Juan Ponce de Leon took over Puerto Rico and in 1511 Diego Velázquez de Cuéllar set out in three ships to settle Cuba; three years later he had succeeded. A year after Velázquez left for Cuba, Ponce de Leon left for what was thought to be the large island of Florida. Not all Caribbean islands offered gold or large supplies of labor (Sauer 1966: 178–86, 199, 216, 292).

The word "exploration" today brings to mind traveling down a backcountry road, or setting off to wander around an unfamiliar town or neighborhood. Had departing to find new lands in the Caribbean followed such a model, venturing forth would have been as simple as raising the capital, finding a captain, a crew, a boat, and supplies, and then setting sail. However, Spanish officials in the Caribbean followed an organized centrally controlled model of discovery that their Portuguese counterparts had set in place during the previous century. In order to limit access to the valuable goods being encountered along the African coast, Prince Henry initiated a system requiring central authorization for all voyages, including privately funded ones. Only in this way could he be assured that he would receive his 20 percent tax on the goods being imported. In addition to taxes, Prince Henry would gain systematic rather than slapdash information on the newly encountered coastal outlines of western and southern Africa.

For similar reasons – ensuring the collection of royal taxes and methodically garnering information on the surrounding regions – Spanish officials set a similar centrally controlled structure in place in the Caribbean (Ramos Pérez 1981). While private investors had to put up the capital for explorations, they were not free to set off in any direction they wished. Before setting forth, the organizer of an expedition had to obtain official permission – usually from the local governor or, for larger, more ambitious expeditions, from a more distant royal authority in Spain. While no physical force prevented an individual from setting out on his own, a subtly more effective pressure kept individuals from so doing. Without official permission, any and all wealth obtained during the voyage could be seized by government officials upon his return. Any hope such an individual had of establishing independent political authority on another island or nearby region similarly vanished. While individuals who encountered wealth on new islands tried to keep knowledge of the full amount of their acquisitions from colonial officials, paying a 20 percent tax on some of it was preferable to losing all of it.

Just as the Spanish king and queen had authorized Columbus's initial voyage to the New World, they continued to control the conditions under which their subjects set out to explore new territories and search for new sources of wealth. While minor expeditions could proceed with only the approval of the Caribbean governor, other more adventurous proposals required approval from the Crown itself. When Ponce de Leon sought authorization for a trip to discover the fountain of youth (which might have been located in Eden) he returned to Spain to garner royal approval. Similarly when Pizarro and his financial backers learned of the potentially wealthy areas further to the south, he too went to Spain to obtain broader authorization and privileges than was customary on the shorter-lasting voyages of "discovery and rescue."

Hernán Cortés famously and egregiously violated his limited directive for exploration. Authorized by Cuba's governor to explore only a limited stretch of the coast of what we now know as mainland Central America and to rescue Spaniards possibly being held captive by Native Americans, Cortés soon deviated from his instructions. Upon learning of the vast riches within a short journey up the coast – and clearly beyond his designated area – Cortés resorted to several subterfuges to set aside the rules and establish himself as leader of the new expedition (Cortés 1986).

The discovery of the immensely wealthy, densely populated, and sophisticated Aztec empire in 1519 changed Spanish patterns in the New World forever. The traditional practice of "discovery and rescue" only worked as long as Spaniards encountered relatively small nuclei of settlement. When faced with large-scale populations such practices became absurd. Hence another strategy had to be devised – one which would try to conserve the large empires, but under Spanish imperial dominion.

The conquests of first Mexico and then Peru remain among the most famous campaigns in the history of the hemisphere. Full of drama, tragedy, and triumph, the unfolding events in sixteenth-century Mexico and Peru have been retold for generations – and in nearly every language (Prescott 1843, 1847; Heming 1970; Hassig 2006). Contributing to the widespread appeal of these conflicts lies a tale of an encounter with civilizations reminiscent of the long-disappeared classical civilizations of Greece, Rome, India, China, and Egypt, but with their own novelties: exotic monumental architecture, untold quantities of gold, silver, and precious metals often worked into intriguing alien designs, and an unprecedented number of unfamiliar birds and plants that produced brilliant new colors for painting and clothing. To Europeans accustomed to wars lasting a hundred years or more, Spaniards strode to military victory over both Aztec and Inca empires in a phenomenally short period of time. The capitals of both empires succumbed in less than five years. To Spaniards, the speed of their victories proved their superiority over all other powers of the era. Indeed, sixteenth-century Spanish accounts of these victories dwell on the small numbers of their own troops (less than a thousand for Cortés and perhaps 2,000 for Pizarro) against armies numbered in the tens of thousands (Restall 2003: 3).

For 17 years after Spaniards landed in the Caribbean, they had no conception of the landmass that lay directly west of Cuba, nor the extent of South America. The native navigators whom they employed to guide them traveled along a traditional route that took them north from the Venezuelan coast through the Caribbean and then further northward to Florida and back. Only a storm-driven wreck on the coast of Yucatán accidentally brought Spaniards into contact with the slender length of continent to their west (Díaz del Castillo 1956). For nearly two decades the Caribbean-dwelling Spaniards lacked even the slightest inkling of the existence of an immense empire a little over a hundred nautical miles away.

Cortés, ordered by Diego Velasquez, the governor of Cuba, to retrace the route of shipwrecked vessels, reached the Yucatán uneventfully. There, for the first time, a Spaniard learned of the existence of an immense and wealthy empire a short distance up the coast from the Yucatán. The expedition preceding Cortés reported on a large empire, but apparently to the south, and most likely the Mayan communities. No Spaniard (outside of a few isolated castaways) had previously heard of the Aztec empire of central Mexico. Cortés's orders limited him to exploring the traditional short length of coastline in the region of the marooned vessel. Upon hearing of the immense potential wealth to his north, Cortés proceeded to disobey his instructions for a limited journey, and moved north along the coast to attempt to seize control of the newly discovered empire. At what became Veracruz he organized a municipal government which then elected Cortés Captain General, providing a cover of political legitimacy for his new objectives. He then marched inland toward the Aztec capital, defeating and subsequently making alliances with several native groups along the way, notably the Tlaxcalans, traditional enemies of the Aztecs.

On November 8, 1519 the Spaniards entered Tenochtitlán, the Aztec capital, and were received as guests. Some of Cortés's men returned to Cuba rather than accompany him into the interior, and informed Velazquez of what had transpired. The furious governor of Cuba immediately sent a large fleet toward Mexico authorizing his own (legitimate) attack on the newly found empire. (Had he or any other Spaniard ever had an inkling of such a large empire, they would have pursued it far sooner.) But by the time the governor's lawful expedition arrived on the coast of Mexico, Cortés's men were already residing in the halls of Montezuma, enjoying the hospitality of the ruler of the Aztecs, whom they subsequently took prisoner, following long-established tactics of European conflict with non-Christian peoples. In a rush to prevent the arriving shiploads of Spaniards from taking over the conquest from him, Cortés left the capital without putting anyone in charge of the troops residing with Montezuma. While he was on the coast successfully persuading most of the new arrivals to accept his leadership, the Spaniards remaining in the capital decided to massacre Montezuma's court (Sahagún 1950–82: XII, 53).

Bitter retribution followed when Aztecs learned of their leader's capture – and possible execution at Spanish hands – and prepared an offensive. Forewarned of the coming assault, the Spaniards attempted to slip out of the capital along one of the causeways before the onslaught, in the early hours of July 1, 1520. But with their big, distinctive horses and clanging armor, the Spaniards were soon detected and surrounded by Aztec warriors. Those overburdened with gold were easily knocked off their horses or lost their footing and drowned under the weight of their own greed (Sahagún 1970: 65–7). Cortés, who returned just in time to see the defeat, led his troops back out of the valley of Mexico, and into the land of the Aztec's long-time enemies, frequently defeated by Montezuma's troops on the field of battle. Delighted to have an opportunity to partner with a potentially victorious ally, the Tlaxcalans welcomed Cortés, trained with his troops, and in turn were equipped with stronger bronze-tipped spears and arrows. Ten months after the defeat on what became known by Spaniards as the *Noche Triste* (Sad Night) Cortés, accompanied by tens of thousands of trained and well-equipped Tlaxcalans, once again marched toward Tenochtitlán. After a siege lasting months, the victorious Spaniards again entered the vanquished capital of the Aztec empire on August 13, 1521 (Hassig 1988: 245, 249, 250).

Despite his oratorical and military skills, Cortés was never a very appealing figure. His letters to the King of Spain detailing the events leading up to the capture of the

Aztec capital in 1521 admit no tactical or military mistake, express no remorse for the slaughter of unarmed civilians in the town of Cholula, and offer no apology for barbarically torturing Cuauhtémoc, Montezuma's successor, in an unsuccessful effort to steal even more gold from the vanquished Aztecs (Cortés 1986). His only admission of culpability was self-serving. Having clearly and directly violated the king's New World delegate (Velazquez) by invading the Aztec empire, he ceaselessly excused his disobedience. But without such extensive and repeated justifications, Cortés stood to forfeit all of the gold, silver, precious minerals, and other rare goods that he had acquired during the conquest. His only mistake, he believed, was the failure to garner prior approval. But given the proximity of the Mexican coast to long-established Spanish colonies, Cortés could not risk traveling to Spain for official permission to follow up on his sudden and unanticipated discovery of the Aztec empire; in the interval, the governor of Cuba or other properly authorized royal officials would have appointed their own military commanders and Cortés would have lost out completely on the great riches of Mexico.

A less accomplished orator than Cortés would have found himself stripped of all his immense, newly acquired riches. But in a series of humble and suppliant letters to the Crown (Cortés 1986), along with extravagant and exotic gifts later presented at court, Cortés successfully petitioned for recognition of his conquests. Among these gifts appeared rare parrot feathers, gold jewelry, and an emerald shaped like a pyramid with a base as broad as the palm of the hand. While King Charles I (Charles V of the Holy Roman Empire) made his displeasure at Cortés's disobedience known, he grudgingly granted the successful conquistador the recognition he sought.

While Cortés had no prior knowledge of the Aztec civilization, the leader of the other major Spanish conquest of an indigenous empire did have advance information of the Inca kingdom to the south. Just as the conquest of Mexico had begun from an unprepossessing Caribbean settlement, the events that led to the conquest of Peru began in the initially profitable gold fields in what is now Panama. Called "Golden Castile" (*Castilla del Oro*) for the wealth originally found there, the settlement was headed by Don Pedro Arias de Avila, or Pedrarias, as he was usually named. Given the easier land passage to the north, Pedrarias ordered expeditions to explore Central America, reaching both Costa Rica and Nicaragua (Sauer 1966: 248–50, 268–9).

After Vasco Nuñez de Balboa traversed the narrow isthmus of Panama in 1513, the first sighting by Europeans of the Pacific Ocean, others soon followed in his wake. But undertaking a land voyage to the south proved daunting. Just south of Panama lies the rainiest region in all the Americas, the Darién and what is now the Colombian province of Chocó. Faced with this impenetrable jungle, in 1522 Pedrarias gave his permission for a seaborne expedition tentatively dispatched south of Panama, which returned with news from natives along the coast of a potentially large and wealthy kingdom even further south. Francisco Pizarro, who had few funds himself, sought out an older, somewhat wealthier, partner, Diego de Almagro, and the two turned to a third, the wealthy vicar of Golden Castile, Hernando de Luque, to fund a lengthier coastal exploration in 1524, once again with the approval of governor Pedrarias. Once they eventually had succeeded in sailing past the soggy Chocó, Pizarro and Almagro encountered a number of distinct indigenous communities and found significant quantities of gold – and rumors of still more to the south. They returned determined to launch another seaborne adventure. The second expedition, which once again enjoyed government approval, set forth in 1526, sailing further south than the earlier voyage; it reached what is now the southern coast of Colombia and encountered native villages of 2,000 or more inhabitants. But conditions on board ship and the poor provisions provided the sailors led to complaints against Almagro, head of one of the ships, and displeased the governor of Golden Castile so much that when the vessel returned to Panama, he refused to authorize further voyages southward.

Equally difficult conditions prevailed on Pizarro's vessels. And on Rooster Island (*isla del Gallo*) Pizarro allegedly drew a line in the sand, challenging members of the expedition to continue to follow him to the south. According to legend only 13 men crossed the line, while the rest returned to Panama. The fortunate 13 soon reached the first large Pacific port, Guayaquil in modern-day Ecuador, and crossed over to the large inhabited town of Túmbez on the northern edge of Peru, where they encountered their first Inca *curaca* (leader). Still coasting along the northern coast of Peru, they eventually reached the bank of the Moche River, near which they turned the vessel around and returned to Panama.

Pedrarias's replacement as governor remained unimpressed by Pizarro's returning finds, calling them "heap display of gold and silver toys and a few Indian sheep." Hearing of the tremendous physical hardships endured on the southward voyages, he refused to authorize additional journeys. With the local authority banning future expeditions, the trio had no choice but to send one of their members to Spain to plead for official authorization from the Crown. After some difficulty in raising the necessary funds, Pizarro, in the spring of 1528, sailed from Panama, taking with him several natives, two or three llamas, several indigenous cloth fabrics, and a few gold and silver ornaments. While nothing to compare with the emerald as broad as a man's hand, these exotic items expedited the affair, and on July 26, 1529 Emperor Charles V's consort, Queen Isabella, authorized the expedition. Pizarro was given six months to raise sufficient funds and outfit a ship to undertake the expedition further to the south.

Having trouble meeting the Crown's minimum requirements for men and supplies, Pizarro slipped out of port, leaving a single undermanned ship behind. The crew on that ship deceptively claimed that the supplies had sailed ahead with Pizarro, and the remaining vessel departed. In January 1531, the vessels, with approximately 180 men and 27 horses, assembled for the third and final attempt to locate a wealthy kingdom down the western coast of South America. Losing a dozen men to battle and illness, Pizarro received unexpected reinforcement from a small boat with 30 men captained by Sebastián Benalcázar, and then another 100 men and horses led by Hernando de Soto (who would later die while exploring the Mississippi River). Following their first large seizures of gold and silver, Pizarro melted them down, sent the king's fifth back to Panama, and the rest to repay the men who had financed the expedition, including both the ships and the supplies.

At the time of Pizarro's arrival, the Inca Empire was torn politically in a competition for the imperial throne between half-brothers Huascar and Atahualpa, following the death of their father, the emperor Huayna Capac. After founding a base at the coastal town named San Miguel de Piura, Pizarro set forth into the heart of Inca territory where Atahualpa, the military victor in the succession struggle, was camping. Meeting with hospitality from the natives along the way, with fewer than 200 men he passed through community after community, meeting no resistance. Heading toward the encampment of Atahualpa, Pizarro decided to capture the native leader – emulating Cortés's capture of Montezuma, but also following long-standing tactics in European warfare. On November 16, 1532, Pizarro and his men hid behind the low stone buildings in the small town of Cajamarca waiting for Inca to arrive. Once trapped with his retinue in the small enclosed central square, Pizarro and his troops charged from all four corners, slaughtering over a thousand attendants, and grabbing Atahualpa. By holding the Inca leader captive until he had filled two large rooms with precious metals from floor to ceiling – one with silver, the older with gold – Pizarro and his followers gained a fortune. The 168 men who participated in the assault became rich beyond their wildest dreams (Lockhart 1972).

The dramatic capture of Atahualpa and the ransom made up of tens of millions in gold and silver constitutes one of the most spectacular episodes in the conquest of the Americas. However astonishing the quantity of precious metals obtained, the underlying practice of seizing members of an opposing army for ransom long featured in medieval Iberian warfare between Christians and Muslims. Both sides retained the poorer captives as slaves; both also held the wealthier captives for maximum revenue before releasing them.

But just as the process of "ransom" had earlier become perverted into slavery in the Caribbean, this process of "ransom" on the mainland became extortion. Payment did not result in Atahualpa's release to return to his own people. Rather, Pizarro executed the Inca leader after he had paid the ransom, on August 29, 1533. Nor had Pizarro been the first to extort gold in a phantom ransom demand. Cortés had similarly attempted to extort gold from Montezuma and later from the young Cuauhtémoc, defeated leader of the Aztec forces (Sahagún1950–82: XII, 45). Realizing that no more gold was to be had, Cuauhtémoc too was executed.

Despite the capture of Atahualpa, the Spaniards in Peru continued to be greeted everywhere with hospitality. While waiting for the ransom to arrive in Cajamarca, Pizarro sent his older brother to explore the situation in surrounding towns. Even when destroying the temples of Inca gods, and stealing the precious minerals and jewels that had adorned their altars, they met with no armed resistance. Villages were burnt and temples and palaces were plundered, as Spanish men moved toward the Inca capital of Cuzco. The Inca call to arms failed to materialize. Beginning on the outskirts of Xauxa, however, Pizarro and his men began to encounter increasing military resistance. How and why the signal for resistance went out, we do not know. But soon Spaniards encountered burnt villages, destroyed bridges, and heavy stones moved into the pathways to prevent horses from moving swiftly. As Iberians passed through a narrow mountain pass in Vilcacongo, Incas inflicted the first significant casualties and injuries on the Spanish forces since their arrival in Peru. Their efforts slowed, but failed to halt the Spanish forces.

Unable to stop their advance on the Inca capital, Manco, brother of Huascar and contender for the Inca throne, decided to enlist the Spaniards' support for his rule. Manco emerged from Cuzco to meet Pizarro, who declared his support for Manco's leadership of the Inca Empire. Thus his troops entered Cuzco without opposition. Once inside, however, Pizarro's forces set about plundering Inca palaces and temples for gold and silver, just as they had looted the surrounding countryside on their way to Cuzco. Considerably less gold and silver was seized in Cuzco than was taken at

Cajamarca. Furthermore, the total needed to be divided among nearly 500 men, making the individual shares less than at the earlier attack.

Manco soon realized that, far from gaining Spanish support for his role as head of the Inca Empire, he had merely been duped into becoming their pawn. Imprisoned by Spanish authorities, he plotted to escape. First, he led Francisco's brother Hernando Pizarro to hidden stores of gold, gaining the latter's confidence. Then, using the ruse of a secret cave in the Andes containing even greater treasure, Manco departed Cuzco accompanied by only two soldiers. The next time Spaniards encountered Manco he was leading an army of tens of thousands of Inca warriors occupying an unassailable mountain stronghold to the east of the Inca heartland.

Faced with an immense and rapidly multiplying Inca army, Spanish troops originally sent to retrieve Manco Inca retreated in haste to the walled city of Cuzco. But even there they remained vulnerable. Manco's forces launched flaming balls into the city, destroying all of its wooden and thatch buildings. For the next five months, Inca forces kept the Spaniards under siege. Four hundred fresh troops sent to relieve the besieged Spaniards at Cuzco never arrived, all presumably killed by Inca forces.

In the end the Inca leader was forced to lift the siege, not under military pressure from the Spaniards, but because his army consisted of peasants. In August, the start of the Southern Hemisphere spring, his men had to return to their villages to plant crops or face starvation. Thus Manco Inca gave the order to lift the siege and retreated to an impregnable mountain fortress with a small army of men.

Never again was the Inca leader able to field such a massive army against the Spaniards. The arrival of more Spaniards disrupted Inca networks and weakened the populace. Spaniards began flooding the countryside, appropriating native labor for their own ends, and, with their animals, spreading diseases that would initially weaken and ultimately decimate the native population of Peru (Alchon 1991; Cook 1998). Manco Inca remained in his stronghold, from where he launched successful raids on convoys of goods and supplies traveling from the coast to Cuzco for the next three years.

Just as all the later arrivals in the Caribbean remained convinced that supplies of gold lay just over the horizon, so too did the Spaniards, disappointed at their apparently meager shares of gold and silver from Cuzco. Convinced that even greater treasures lay elsewhere in the Americas, they sought and received authorizations for further explorations. In 1534 Almagro led a force of 300 men to explore the land to the south of Peru. In 1540 Francisco's other brother, Gonzalo, was authorized to explore the lands to the east of Quito. Neither man found anything of immediate economic value, but Gonzalo's expedition suffered the greatest devastation. For to travel east, they first traversed high mountain passes, from which they descended into the tropical climate and headwaters of the Amazon. Realizing that no easily found riches lay further east, Gonzalo returned up the eastern side of the Andes to Quito. One out of every two Indians who accompanied Gonzalo Pizarro perished, as did two out of every three Spaniards. The small group Gonzalo sent downriver on rafts to search for supplies, led by Francisco de Orellana, eventually surfaced months later at the mouth of the Amazon.

Almagro traveled south, following the well-built Inca roads along the Andes until the latter ended in the rugged mountain passes and treeless high plateau of what is now Bolivia, where his men perished from cold and starvation. Reaching the conclusion that nothing of commercial value lay to the south, Almagro, determined not to repeat the experience of the deadly cold, took his men down the Andes to the coast. Unfortunately, the Atacama desert lay along the coast between him and Cuzco. Three fruitless years later Almagro and his men returned. During Almagro's absence, Pizarro's friends became ensconced in power and sought to limit the jurisdiction Almagro had legitimately acquired for his role in the conquest of Peru. Faced with bureaucratic foot dragging, Almagro attacked and defeated Pizarro's followers in the former Inca capital. For the next seven years, armed conflict erupted between the followers of Pizarro and those of Almagro.

Less than a decade after the immense seizure of wealth at Cajamarca, on June 26, 1541, Francisco Pizarro was killed in Lima by allies of his former partner Almagro, the man with whom he had planned and provisioned the expedition leading up to the capture of the Inca Empire. Almagro in turn was killed by Pizarro's brother Gonzalo, and the latter was ultimately hanged by a Spanish official sent to end the conflict. Of the Pizarro brothers only Hernando survived, by virtue of spending 20 years incarcerated in a Spanish prison. Manco Inca, who backed the Almagro faction in the civil wars, was ultimately killed by angry Almagro partisans following a defeat. Manco's troops then slaughtered the Spaniards.

Like Cortés and countless other Spaniards, Pizarro ceaselessly mythologized his victories as those of a handful of Spaniards against tens of thousands of indigenous people. The reality of the Inca conquest – as that of the Aztecs – was that both depended on an initial element of surprise, followed by highly successful exploitation of traditional indigenous rivalries. Initially staggered by the newcomers' novel tactics and strategies, the disoriented native communities in Mexico and Peru delayed taking up arms. But they faced an additional disadvantage (Seed 1995). Once armed, native communities did not operate a united front. Both Cortés and Pizarro successfully persuaded old enemies to betray their opponents' secrets and to arm thousands of their own community to march against old rivals. The opportunity to settle old scores proved irresistible. When the would-be avengers realized they had been deceived, it was too late. Cuauhtémoc perished; Manco Inca survived but only briefly managed to hold the Spaniards at bay until he, too, was murdered by Spaniards in 1544.

The delay in responding created the pause while another, more deadly, army began to make itself felt. That army's members remained invisible to the naked eye, yet within it marched microbes, bacteria, viruses, and parasites – Old World diseases to which the natives of the Americas had no biological immunity (Crosby 1972; Mann 2005). This undetectable enemy would become the true conqueror of the Americas. While debates over the original size of the indigenous population of the Americas prior to the arrival of Europeans have become among the most contentious, the amount of the decline remains remarkably consistent. Over a 100-year period, commencing with the first contact, 90 percent of America's indigenous population died. While the culprits were numerous, the end result was the same: devastation of the native populace in waves of illness and death (Cook and Borah 1971–9; Alchon 1991; Cook 1998; Henige 1998).

The most commonly offered explanation remains the most likely. Tens of thousands of years separated the overwhelming majority of the continent's inhabitants from contact with people from Asia, Africa, or Europe. During that period, immune capacity declined, leaving the inhabitants vulnerable. During Cortés's final assault on Tenochtitlán, both leadership and ranks of the Aztec military were weakened by smallpox (Sahagún 1950–82: XII, 81). Unexpected disease that had traveled overland from the Venezuelan coast to Peru may have killed the Inca emperor Huayna Capac in 1527, along with the expected heir to his throne, setting the stage for a dispute over succession before the arrival of Pizarro and his band. Pizarro was then able to exploit the resulting conflicts among Inca factions to his advantage. Even more deadly than first contacts were the continued waves of European arrivals, each carrying a potentially lethal microbe in his cloak, or a deadly parasite in the intestine of his innocent-looking sheep. Natives would survive one epidemic, only to fall to the next, or the next, or the next. In this fashion the major population centers of the New World, and the empires that governed them, collapsed.

While surviving inhabitants of the large empires fell under Spanish authority, residents of small isolated communities initially managed to survive by being ignored. While their communities, too, fell to rampaging disease, they were equipped with something the earliest fallen were not, namely knowledge of the enemy, his weapons, his tactics, and his strategies.

For 300 years the Mapuche of Chile attacked Spanish convoys, launched guerrilla raids on military forces only to melt back up into the hills with their mission accomplished (Vargas Machuca 1892). Armed with horses escaped or captured from the Spaniards they became intimately acquainted with, the Mapuche could attack at will. Eventually Spanish officials signed truce agreements with the Mapuche to supply the frontier centers founded by Pedro de Valdivia in the sixteenth century.

On the northern frontier, Juan de Oñate led an expedition north across the Rio Grande to establish a base among the indigenous communities of what is now New Mexico. In between this northern outpost and Spanish settlements in central Mexico lay hundreds of miles of open territory, often beset by native attackers equipped, like their counterparts in southern South America, with knowledge of the Spaniards and with horses descended from those brought by the Spaniards.

While the men involved in fighting the wars of New World conquest came from many different walks of life, few were professional soldiers (Lockhart 1972; Restall 2003: 27–37). But it was not the professional credentials of the participants that lent the Spanish enterprise of the Indies its military identity. Rather, warfare became the basis for legitimizing the official Spanish legal acquisition of New World domains; the military strategy of capture and ransoming justified Iberian political, economic, and military tactics in the New World.

Seeking to create lawful grounds for the Spanish settlement of the New World in the second decade of contact, legal advisors to the Crown reinterpreted the classic summons to Islam used during Muslim expansion into new territories, but now in a Christian framework. The carefully composed text, called the Requirement, insisted that the natives acknowledge the superiority of Catholicism, and allow the Christians to enter their country for the purpose of conversion (Palacios Rubios 2007). However, any resistance to this demand would result in the immediate use of force. Although mumbled into beards from behind trees, with little comprehension of the meaning of the words among either Spaniards or Indians, nonetheless the act of reading the text aloud constituted sufficient grounds for the Crown of Spain to claim the New World for itself from 1512 forward (Seed 1994: chap. 3).

Within the Spanish Empire, however, there existed a wide range of convictions on the legitimacy of military rationale for conquest, ranging from the proponents of war without any reservation – conquerors such as Francisco Pizarro, Gonzalo Fernández de Oviedo, and Hernán Cortés – for whom a declaration of war was not only imperative but indisputable, to Bartolomé de Las Casas, whose uncompromising advocacy of peaceful methods of domination situated him securely at the opposite end of the spectrum (Cortés 1986; Casas 2003).

War was more than merely a method of enforcing the legitimate political authority of the Spanish Crown. Justly launched by the reading of the Requirement, war also sanctioned Spanish acquisition of the natives' gold, silver, and other possessions under the well-established classical Greek and Roman principle permitting plunder to victors in military engagements. In addition, these same classical principles under some conditions also entitled Spaniards, as military winners, to enslave the natives as well.

Attacking the legitimacy of warfare as a method of establishing sovereignty also directly or indirectly undermined the entire economic basis of the conquest for both private citizens and the Crown. Hence within Spain, these internal critiques of the military option were highly controversial both within government circles and among those who had benefited financially from the conquest. Those who had acquired great wealth opposed eliminating the military rationale. Although the Crown listened to the critics who claimed that the Requirement bore its Islamic heritage too openly, it was loathe to abandon its long-utilized rationale for settlement. Eventually it renamed the Requirement the "Ordinance of Peace," increasing the number of times that natives had to be summoned to accept Christian preachers in their domains, but with the same result: should such requests be ignored or refused, military action and forcible subjugation would follow.

Although comparatively few in number against the large contingents of indigenous warriors arrayed against them, Spanish military expeditions in the conquest era had several distinct advantages. First, they were backed by sea power, which all Native American empires lacked. Hence they could continually replace fallen combatants and resupply their own forces even across great distances. Unlike the early Norse expeditions to the New World, the new Iberian-designed ships and navigational techniques permitted not merely a handful, but thousands of Europeans to eventually reach American shores. The sheer variety and numbers of people also brought the second invisible army of conquest – disease – to the New World. Secondly, Spaniards had recently concluded a centuries-long struggle against various Muslim-held territories and Berber invaders. Such experiences had prepared them for unorthodox strategies and tactics including hostage taking, "rescues," and ransoms. More recently Spain had been engaged in military conflicts in northern Italy, where it had proved itself the most capable conventional army in western Europe at the time. Third, and finally, like their Portuguese counterparts, Spanish leaders made strategic alliances with native communities, successfully leveraging already simmering antagonisms and rivalries to their own advantage (Seed 1995: 140). Centuries of experience in carefully recruiting allies from within the ranks of quarreling but powerful Muslim enemies provided Iberian leaders with practice in discerning cracks in seemingly united fronts and exploiting existing animosities to their own political advantage. (Subsequent European invaders would lack that experience.)

What began as a search for new trade goods and routes soon began to incorporate long-familiar practices of armed Iberian conflicts – hostage taking, exploiting internal rivalries, justifying their presence in the New World by a military summoning of natives to Christianity – all emerging from an often unacknowledged Islamic precedent. Even their politically successful strategy of incorporating large indigenous settlements borrowed from an Islamic prototype (Seed 2001: 72–90). A newer development – Spaniards' recently acquired expertise at long-distance voyaging – provided them with a crucially important continual stream of men and munitions as well as the inadvertent microbial hitchhikers whose spread would also impact the Spanish settlement of the New World.

BIBLIOGRAPHY

Alchon, S. A. (1991) *Native Society and Disease in Colonial Ecuador.* Cambridge University Press, New York.

Andrews, K. R. (1978) *The Spanish Caribbean: Trade and Plunder, 1530–1630.* Yale University Press, New Haven.

Bensaúde, J. (ed.) (1940) *O manuscrito "Valentim Fernandes."* Editora Atica, Lisbon.

Casas, Bartolomé de las (2003) *An Account, Much Abbreviated, of the Destruction of the Indies, with Related Texts*, trans. Andrew Hurley, Introduction by Franklin Knight. Hackett Publishing, Indianapolis.

Cieza De Leon, P. de (1998) *The Discovery and Conquest of Peru: Chronicles of the New World Encounter*, trans. and ed. Alexandra Parma Cook and Noble David Cook. Duke University Press, Durham.

Cook, N. D. (1998) *Born to Die: Disease and New World Conquest, 1492–1650.* Cambridge University Press, New York.

Cook, N. D. & Lovell, G. (eds.) (1991) *Secret Judgments of God: Old World Disease in Colonial Spanish America.* University of Oklahoma Press, Norman.

Cook, S. F. & Borah, W. (1960) *The Population of Central Mexico in 1548: an Analysis of the Suma de Vistas de Pueblos.* University of California Press, Berkeley.

Cook, S. F. & Borah, W. (1971–9) *Essays in Population History: Mexico and the Caribbean*, 3 vols. University of California Press, Berkeley.

Cortés, H. (1986) *Letters from Mexico/Hernan Cortes*, trans.and ed. Anthony Pagden. Yale University Press, New Haven.

Crosby, A. W. (1972) *The Columbian Exchange: Biological and Cultural Consequences of 1492.* Greenwood Publishing, Westport.

Díaz del Castillo, B. (1956) *The Discovery and Conquest of Mexico, 1517–1521*, trans. A. P. Maudslay. Farrar, Straus, and Giroux, New York.

Guamán Poma de Ayala, F. (1615–16) *El primer nueva corónica y buen gobierno*, ed. Rolena Adorno. Royal Library, Copenhagen <http://www.kb.dk/elib/mss/poma/> (accessed January 12, 2007).

Hassig, R. (1988) *Aztec Warfare: Imperial Expansion and Political Control.* University of Oklahoma Press, Norman.

Hassig, R. (2006) *Mexico and the Spanish Conquest*, 2nd ed. University of Oklahoma Press, Norman.

Heming, J. (1970) *The Conquest of the Incas.* Macmillan, London.

Henige, D. (1998) *Numbers from Nowhere: The American Indian Contact Population Debate.* University of Oklahoma Press, Norman.

Kelsey, H. (1998) "Spanish Entrada Cartography." In D. Reinhartz & and G. Saxon (eds.), *The Mapping of the Entradas into the Greater Southwest.* University of Oklahoma Press, Norman.

Lockhart, J. (1968) *Spanish Peru, 1532–1560: A Colonial Society.* University of Wisconsin Press, Madison.

Lockhart, J. (1972) *The Men of Cajamarca: A Social and Biographical Study of the First Conquerors of Peru.* University of Texas Press, Austin.

Lockhart, J. (ed.) (1993) *We People Here: Nahuatl Accounts of the Conquest of Mexico.* Wipf & Stock, Eugene.

Mann, C. C. (2005) *1491: New Revelations of the Americas before Columbus.* Knopf, New York.

Padgen, A. (1993) *European Encounters with the New World: From Renaissance to Romanticism.* Yale University Press, New Haven.

Palacios Rubios, J. L. (2007 [1512]) An English translation of the full text of the "Requirement" is located at <http://en.wikipedia.org/wiki/Requerimiento> (accessed January 13, 2007).

Prescott, W. H. (1843) *History of the Conquest of Mexico, with a Preliminary View of the Ancient Mexican Civilization, and the Life of the Conqueror, Hernando Cortés.* Harper & Brothers, New York.

Prescott, W. H. (1847) *History of the Conquest of Peru, with a Preliminary View of the Civilization of the Incas.* Harper & Brothers, New York.

Ramos Pérez, D. (1981) *Audacia, negocios y política en los viajes españoles de descubrimiento y rescate.* Casa-Museo de Colón, Valladolid.

Restall, M. (2003) *Seven Myths of the Spanish Conquest.* Oxford University Press, New York.

Sahagún, B. de (1950–82) *General History of the Things of New Spain: Florentine Codex.* School of American Research, Santa Fe.

Sahagún, B. de. (1970) *Florentine Codex: General History of the Things of New Spain,* trans. and ed. Arthur J. O. Anderson & Charles E. Dibble, 2nd. ed., rev. The School of American Research. Santa Fe.

Sauer, C. (1966) *The Early Spanish Main.* University of California Press, Berkeley.

Seed, P. (1994) *Ceremonies of Possession in Europe's Conquest of the New World.* Cambridge University Press, New York.

Seed, P. (1995) "The Conquest of the Americas." In G. Parker (ed.), *Cambridge Illustrated History of Warfare.* Cambridge University Press, New York.

Seed, P. (2001) *American Pentimento: The Invention of Indians and the Pursuit of Riches.* University of Minnesota Press, Minneapolis.

Tedlock, D. (ed.) (1996) *Popol Vuh: the Mayan Book of the Dawn of Life,* rev. ed. Simon & Schuster, New York.

Torre, M. de la (ed.) (1983) *El Lienzo de Tlaxcala.* Text by Josefina García Quintana and Carlos Martínez Marín. Cartón y Papel de México, Mexico City.

Vargas Machuca, B. de (1892) *Milicia y descripción de las Indias: volumen primero y segundo.* V. Suarez, Madrid.

Vega, G. de la (1966) *Comentarios reales de los Incas. English Royal Commentaries of the Incas, and General History of Peru,* trans. Harold V. Livermore, Foreword by Arnold J. Toynbee. University of Texas Press, Austin.

Weddle, R. S. (1998) "Coastal Exploration and Mapping: A Concomitant of the Entradas." In D. Reinhartz & G. Saxon (eds.), *The Mapping of the Entradas into the Greater Southwest.* University of Oklahoma Press, Norman.

Zárate, A. de (1968) *The Discovery and Conquest of Peru: A Translation of Books I to IV of Agustín de Zárate's History of These Events,* trans. J. M. Cohen. Penguin Books, Baltimore.

Chapter Six

COLONIAL BRAZIL (1500–1822)

Hal Langfur

The traditional view that the Portuguese mariner and nobleman Pedro Álvares Cabral (1467/8–1520?) happened on Brazil merely by accident on his way to India no longer convinces most experts. Mounting evidence suggests greater intention behind Portugal's south Atlantic ventures, making the discovery a predictable outcome of the age of European expansion. Following Columbus's Caribbean landfall in 1492, Portuguese diplomatic pressure convinced Pope Alexander VI to revise a bull that gave Spain title to all newly discovered lands beyond a meridian 100 leagues west of the Cape Verde Islands. The original line would have assigned the Americas in their entirety to Spain. The revised 1494 agreement, the Treaty of Tordesillas, pushed the divide another 270 leagues west, establishing the precedent for Portugal's later claim to Brazil's Atlantic bulge as the Portuguese strove to secure and extend their authority in the south Atlantic.

For most of the fifteenth century, Portugal's sailors had been advancing southward along the African coast, gradually raising expectations that an all-water route could be found to the Indies and their lucrative spice trade. Five years before Columbus's discovery, Bartholomeu Dias left Lisbon in command of a fleet that became the first to round the southern tip of Africa. King Manuel I (r. 1495–1521) dispatched Vasco da Gama to follow up that achievement in 1497. Avoiding the doldrums before steering for the Cape of Good Hope, da Gama's fleet of four ships sailed south by southwest far enough into the Atlantic to spot birdlife that suggested land lay to the west. Such a discovery held the promise of providing Portugal with a valuable way station on the route around the Cape. An account of a clandestine voyage the following year by the cosmographer Duarte Pacheco Pereira (?–1533), once considered apocryphal but now widely judged credible, would make him the first known Portuguese navigator to explore Brazil's littoral. Pereira claimed to have sailed along the northern coast to the mouth of the Amazon River, territory that the Treaty of Tordesillas would have placed in Spanish hands, hence the presumed secrecy exercised by King Manuel in ordering the voyage and concealing its findings (Couto 1998: 149–60).

Cabral's reputed discovery of Brazil can thus be deemed accidental only in a technical sense (if at all), especially since Pereira was a prominent member of Cabral's expedition. Upon da Gama's return from India in 1499, the Crown entrusted Cabral with command of a second armada bound for the Orient, the largest the Portuguese had ever assembled, composed of 13 ships and 1,500 men. Carried off course by winds or currents or, as specialists now generally concur, purposefully veering farther west than da Gama (who with Pereira provided sailing directions), Cabral reached the coast of South America on April 22, 1500, at a point near present-day Porto Seguro, well within the Portuguese zone. In the name of the Crown, he took possession of the territory. He called it the Land of the True Cross in a letter drafted by his scribe, Pero Vaz de Caminha. Cabral lingered for eight days before resuming his voyage to India, establishing contact with the region's natives and sending one of his supply ships back to Portugal to report the landfall. Cynically, according to the revisionist interpretation, Manuel deemed the discovery "miraculous" when conveying the news to the Spanish monarchs Ferdinand and Isabella, his relatives and rivals. He then quickly dispatched a subsequent fleet of three caravels under the command of Gonçalo Coelho, with Amerigo Vespucci serving as chronicler. This expedition (1501–2) explored more than 3,000 kilometers of coastline, returning to Lisbon with samples of a red dyewood (brazilwood, *Caesalpina echinata*). This product, known from similar species since ancient times, would give the territory its permanent name and become its most significant initial export commodity.

Caminha described the indigenous inhabitants of the new land as "colored in a reddish manner, of good faces and good noses, [and] well-made . . . They care about neither covering themselves nor showing their shame; and in this they have as much innocence as in showing their faces" (Caminha 1974). Thus began a long history of interaction, misinterpretation, attraction, revulsion, conflict, alliance, cooperation, and cooptation on both sides of an encounter that would unfold throughout the course of the colonial period. Estimates vary widely for Brazil's total indigenous population on the eve of contact, the most reliable figures ranging between two and four million. While causing severe depopulation stemming from disease, relocation, and forced labor, the encounter resulted neither in the effective eradication of Amerindians that largely characterized Caribbean history nor the decisive conquests that occurred in Mesoamerica and the Andes. More appropriate comparisons can be found in the experience of the native inhabitants of North America and of Spanish American peripheries beyond the urban centers of the great sedentary civilizations defeated by Spanish conquistadors. Unlike the Aztec and Inca empires, native polities in Portuguese America were small, fragmented, and thus resistant to capitulation en masse. The mobility of these non-sedentary peoples, along with Portugal's more pressing interests in Asia, further explains the ensuing slow pace of colonization. Without wealth amassed from agricultural surpluses or gold, Brazil's Indians presented few immediate objectives for conquest, and the task of binding their labor to remunerative commercial production required prolonged effort. The plodding pace of territorial conquest, far from complete even at the end of the colonial period, meant that ethnocide never precluded the possibility of ethnogenesis. As some ethnic groups vanished, new ones formed in response to altered circumstances. Violent clashes at some points of contact did not rule out intensive collaboration at others. Migration into the vast interior long remained an option to avoid contact altogether.

Scholars conventionally divide the indigenous population encountered by the first European traders and settlers into two large groups, the Tupi–Guarani and the

Tapuia. The semi-sedentary Tupi–Guarani occupied most of the Atlantic coastal strip. The semi-nomadic Tapuia inhabited the interior and a few isolated stretches of littoral. This classificatory scheme, borrowed from the first colonists who learned it from the Tupi, does not do justice to the diversity of native groups and their varied historical experience. The Tupi–Guarani, as their name suggests, combined two subgroups: the Guarani, who controlled the region south of present-day São Paulo, including the river basins that form Brazil's southern border; and the Tupi, who dominated the remainder of the coast north to the Amazon. The Tupi were further subdivided into numerous village-based groups, which shared linguistic and cultural origins but engaged in constant warfare with one another. These wars yielded territory and captives, some of whom the victors consumed in cannibalistic rituals that imposed cosmological vengeance and elevated successful warriors to headmen. A pejorative term used by the Tupi to describe hostile Indians who spoke other languages, the designation Tapuia obscured great cultural differentiation among dozens of distinct inland clans and tribes, the majority of them speakers of Gê, Carib, and Arawak languages. The heteronym Tapuia served colonists well in their bid to vilify all groups who resisted incorporation.

For several decades, peaceable relations based on the exigencies of survival and trade, if not mutual understanding, characterized contacts between the Portuguese and Brazil's coastal Indians. Following a successful model developed along the African coast, Portugal established several trading posts or *feitorias* where goods manufactured in Europe were bartered for tropical products. Decisively outnumbered, the traders who visited these posts negotiated with native allies for protection and food, especially the ubiquitous manioc root, a native cultivar and dietary staple. In exchange for hoes, axes, knives, cloth, beads, mirrors, and assorted trinkets, they also obtained brazilwood, monkeys, and parrots, all of which were prized in Europe. In the 1530s, as agriculture began to replace barter, advantage shifted to the Portuguese. The Tupi and other groups now became a barrier to colonization, inhibiting efforts to clear and cultivate land. They also represented the most obvious source of agricultural labor. Thus began the drive to conquer, assemble, enslave, and, where this proved impossible, dislodge or destroy the colony's native peoples. Previous generations of historians, however, underestimated the capacity of natives to continue to exert at least some control over their fate, to adapt to the disruptions of colonization, and to influence the course of subsequent events.

Focused on the wealth of Asia, the Portuguese Crown did not turn seriously to the task of colonization until imperial rivalries, particularly with the French, threatened the loss of Brazil. Refusing to recognize the Treaty of Tordesillas, France insisted on the principle of *uti possidetis* or effective occupation as the only legitimate basis for territorial claims in the Americas. Along Brazil's undefended coastline, French corsairs engaged in piracy and bartered for dyewood. They entered into alliances with indigenous groups at odds with those trading with the Portuguese. Indians and Europeans, sometimes unwittingly, became participants in each other's power struggles. Increasing disorder prompted João III (r. 1521–57) to sponsor the expedition of Martim Afonso de Sousa (1500–71), who led 400 settlers to found the royal colony of São Vicente, near present-day Santos, in 1532. The following year the Crown divided Brazil into hereditary captaincies, distributed among 12 loyal donataries. The divisions conformed to borders drawn along latitudes, each separated by a stretch of coastline ranging from 25 (130 km) leagues to more than 60 leagues (310 km). The captaincies extended into the unexplored interior where theoretically they abutted Spanish America at the Line of Tordesillas. The 12 men granted these lands were soldiers of fortune, bureaucrats, merchants, and petty nobles. They received sweeping administrative, judicial, and fiscal powers but not ownership rights, except to a single private tract. The remainder of the land was to be subdivided among favored settlers in royal land grants known as *sesmarias*. Although the French continued their intrusions, establishing short-lived settlements in Guanabara Bay (Rio de Janeiro) in 1555 and, later, along the coast of Maranhão in 1612, the captaincy system effectively answered France's legal challenge concerning possession.

The system did not, however, promote successful colonization. By the middle of the sixteenth century, only two of the donatary captaincies were flourishing. Under the leadership of able lieutenants, Sousa's southern settlement had expanded inland to the fertile Piratininga Plateau, where the village of São Paulo took root by 1554. Benefiting from the energies of donatary Duarte Coelho Pereira, who developed sugar production into a thriving enterprise at the town of Olinda, the northern captaincy of Pernambuco provided the New World's first example of a profitable export other than gold seized from the Aztecs and Incas. The remaining captaincies languished. Experience and capital were scarce, internal dissent pervasive, and Indian attacks unrelenting. Many settlers crossed the Atlantic against their will, exiled to Brazil by the Portuguese courts and the Inquisition, accused of bigamy, witchcraft, and the clandestine practice of Judaism, among other crimes. Over time, the captaincies reverted to the Crown, purchased back from their donatories and administered by the state.

The captaincy system's inadequacy and mounting international pressures convinced João III to dispatch a royal governor general to Brazil for the first time in 1549. He chose the nobleman Tomé de Sousa (r. 1549–53), who had military experience in Africa and India. Sousa led 1,000 settlers – some 300 of them soldiers and another 400 condemned exiles – to build the fortified city of Salvador in Bahia, which would remain the colony's capital until 1763. He strengthened captaincy administration, established municipal councils, and constructed fortifications to defend other coastal settlements, notably Rio de Janeiro. The governor carried royal orders to prevent colonists from provoking Indians to war then enslaving those taken captive, in accordance with the medieval concept of just war. A precursor of future indigenous legislation benevolent in word but repressive in deed, these orders simultaneously directed Sousa to punish those Indians who resisted subjection, "destroying their villages and settlements, and killing and enslaving whatever part of them you consider sufficient" (Bonavides & Amaral 2002: 159).

Traveling with the governor's retinue, a group of six Jesuits, including the charismatic Manuel da Nóbrega (1517–70), arrived to tend to moral matters in the colony and, above all, to catechize the Indians. The Jesuits eschewed life in the Portuguese settlements, residing instead in native villages, founding missions for those converted to Catholicism, and learning their languages. Unwittingly, the missionaries served as conduits for European diseases, which spread more rapidly among natives concentrated in the missions. Some of the earliest missionary successes came among native women and *mameluco* children, the offspring of unions between Portuguese men and their Indian concubines. As cultural intermediaries, the new converts carried the teachings and promises of the missionaries to others whose villages lay far in the interior or *sertão*. In addition to religious conversion, the Jesuits concentrated on turning semi-nomadic Indians into settled agricultural workers. A rift opened between missionaries and colonists who feared losing control over the supply of native labor. The Crown addressed the dispute with its characteristic contradictions, granting the Jesuits final authority over Indians settled in mission villages, while permitting colonists to persist in the practice of enslaving those captured in wars deemed to be just. Accusations of cannibalism and other native offenses abounded as justifications for further inland conquests. Resistance to slavery in colonized areas produced numerous hybrid messianic movements known as *santidades*, led by indigenous prophets. The most important, which occurred in the 1580s at Jaguaripe in southern Bahia, blended Christian symbols with native dances, trances, and tobacco consumption to inspire adherents, including *mamelucos* and some whites, to seek the mythical Tupian "land without evil," free from Portuguese domination (Metcalf 2005: 215–34).

Such cultural resistance and further demographic decline brought by warfare, slavery, and widening epidemics left the growing demand for a pliable labor force unsatisfied. These factors impelled the increasing use of African slaves, whose labor the Portuguese had long ago learned to coerce. The transition varied in time and place, progressing most rapidly in Pernambuco and Bahia, where commercial sugar production proved most profitable. The colonial plantation regime followed models developed first on Madeira, São Tomé, and other islands off the west coast of Africa, where the gainful cultivation of sugar cane depended on the enslavement of blacks (Knight, this volume). The preexisting slave trade in Africa coalesced with the growing demand for compulsory labor. By the early seventeenth century, Brazil's economy came to be dominated by the African slave trade. A unified system arose, linking, on one side of the Atlantic, areas devoted to reproducing, capturing, and shipping slaves and, on the other, enclaves where their labor was consumed for profit. This decisive and enduring connection with Africa has led historians to give ever-greater emphasis to the importance of the wider Atlantic context in understanding colonial Brazil.

As the world's largest producer and exporter of sugar between 1580 and 1680, Brazil became dependent on slavery to such an extent that the system's logic went virtually unchallenged by those who reaped its benefits. The juridical and religious structures of early modern Portuguese society, which enforced social hierarchy, further legitimated the expansion of slavery. By 1810 more than 2.5 million African slaves, most of them young males, had crossed the Atlantic to Brazil, making it by far the largest single slave importer. Over the course of the colonial period, the center of the trade shifted south along the African coast, from Guinea and the Mina Coast in the sixteenth century to the Congo, Mozambique, and especially Angola in the eighteenth century. A similar geographic shift occurred in Brazil, as first Olinda and Recife in the sixteenth century and then Salvador in the seventeenth century relinquished their positions as the colony's preeminent slave ports to Rio de Janeiro in the eighteenth century.

Soaring slave imports reflected planters' balance sheets. During the first half of the seventeenth century, the labor of a plantation slave returned the price of his purchase in less than 16 months. Planters calculated that it was cheaper to replace slaves worked to sickness or death than to sustain them with adequate shelter, nutritious diets, and labor regimes limited to their physical capacity. The resulting high mortality rate required constant replenishment of workers, sustaining the transatlantic trade. As immigrants, slaves outnumbered Portuguese more than two to one. In the fertile Recôncavo, the coastal plain at the center of sugar production in Bahia, slaves comprised as much as 70 percent of the population, most of them born in Africa. Although the wealthiest planters amassed slaves by the hundreds, on average they employed between 60 and 80. Two-thirds were male, a sexual imbalance that reached three-fourths in the fields. Females accounted for almost half of all domestic slaves, working as wet nurses, nannies, cooks, and seamstresses. Many became the objects of their owners' sexual whims, and some were forced into prostitution to earn money for their masters, especially as slavery spread to urban centers. A tenacious myth permeating traditional scholarship, which held that Brazilian slaves suffered less at the hands of their masters than elsewhere in the Americas, has been dispelled by more recent studies.

One explanation for slavery's stability as a labor regime and social matrix was its tendency to create divisions among those of African descent, which derived from a powerful system of incentives and disincentives. Traders in Africa and planters in Brazil intentionally assembled workforces fragmented by ethnicity. Slaves born in Africa, known as *boçales*, were then pressed into the lowest, unskilled positions, especially fieldwork. Skilled positions, as a rule, were reserved for those born in Brazil, called *crioulos*, especially those who demonstrated compliance and who had acquired greater familiarity with Portuguese culture and language. These positions in the countryside included mill workers, muleteers, and even overseers; in urban settings, they included carpenters, masons, bakers, and tailors. A related color-based distinction yielded privileges for lighter-skinned mulattos. Similarly directed toward skilled tasks, they were less likely to suffer corporal punishment and more likely to receive additional rations and rum, as well as opportunities to earn cash, for example, by selling surplus crops they raised on garden plots. They figured disproportionately – particularly females – among those freed on their masters' death or allowed to purchase their freedom after years of loyal service.

The plantation enclaves developed at Pernambuco and Bahia also imposed hierarchies on the free population, creating middle groups whose allegiances tended toward their patrons rather than those of lower status. Manumitted slaves ran the risk of re-enslavement – which could occur arbitrarily or legally – if they ran afoul of their former masters. As day laborers, fishermen, boatmen, artisans, and, especially in the case of women, as food vendors, free persons of color provided essential services, while seeking to distance themselves from their former condition. This sector's population grew dramatically over time, accounting for more than 40 percent of all blacks and mulattos by the end of the colonial period. A significant number became small-scale slaveholders, the surest means of securing the economic and juridical privileges of freedom. Clearing land at the margins of plantation zones, freedmen cultivated foodstuffs to provision the growing rural and urban population. Poor whites engaged in many of the same activities, blurring occupational and economic lines, while creating a basis for racial rivalry. The professional services required to administer the colony were provided by lawyers, bureaucrats, military officers, and clergymen, the great majority of whom were white. A relatively prosperous class of farmers or *lavradores* cultivated much of the cane processed at the sugar mills, known as *engenhos*. The most successful cane farmers owned large tracts of unencumbered land, while others entered into rent or sharecropping agreements (Schwartz 1985).

At the apex of the social hierarchy stood the mill owner or *senhor de engenho*. An Italian Jesuit who arrived in Salvador in the 1680s observed that, "being a plantation owner in Brazil is as esteemed as the titles among nobility are esteemed in Portugal" (Antonil 1997: 75). While planters comprised a colonial aristocracy, they never achieved the status of the hereditary nobility to which they aspired. Their deep involvement in commerce was considered an ignoble activity, although their wealth went a long way toward offsetting this social debility. They invested in cattle ranches, shipping, and urban properties. In addition to their plantation houses, they kept urban residences where they conducted business. They diversified into rum, tobacco, and foodstuffs production to cushion the strain of inconstant sugar prices on the Lisbon, London, and Amsterdam markets. A traditional view of planters as isolated feudal lords, uninterested in and unaffected by mercantile capitalism, can no longer be sustained. Nor can conventional assumptions concerning the extended households, the so-called Big House or *casa-grande*, over which some of them presided. "The social history of the Big House," the influential sociologist Gilberto Freyre wrote, "is the intimate history of practically every Brazilian, the history of his domestic and conjugal life under a slaveholding and polygamous patriarchal regime" (Freyre 1956: 56). That view has changed. Both in plantation zones and to an even greater degree in peripheral areas less geared to large-scale agricultural production, manuscript census data reveal that household patterns were not restricted to large families headed by white male planters who dominated wives and children, mistresses and illegitimate offspring, extended kin and retainers, and the slaves who labored in the house and field. With surprising regularity smaller nuclear families proved the norm. Most were headed by men, but a significant number were formed by single women, often unmarried mothers.

Slavery's stability as an economic and social complex did not mean that its victims lacked all means to oppose the destruction of their lives, families, and cultures. Slaves mitigated work demands by feigning sickness, malingering, breaking tools, and sabotaging mill equipment. They pressured masters for better food, less arduous work hours, and more time and land to plant and market subsistence crops. They fled to neighboring plantations to enlist other planters in complaints against particularly vicious owners and overseers. Persistent attempts to forge and sustain marriages, families, and networks of godparents countered social fragmentation. Slaves did not merely bow to the dominant culture perpetuated by the Roman Catholic Church. They used the church as a means to form protective communal bonds. They sustained African spiritual traditions in the guise of popular Catholicism. They found in music and dance forms of expression not easily silenced.

In its most direct and perilous forms, resistance to slavery brought open rebellion and flight. Even though slave uprisings caused few lasting disruptions during the colonial period, plots and rumors of plots surfaced frequently. This threat left masters constantly uneasy and imposed limits on coercion. Runaway slave communities sprang up throughout the colony, and their prevalence is one explanation for the limited number of rebellions. Known as *mocambos* and *quilombos*, these communities assumed a variety of forms. Some were short-lived, home to just a handful of fugitives. Others endured for generations and sustained substantial populations. Some formed in the distant hinterlands where the colony's vast territory served to conceal them; others in borderland areas where Portuguese jurisdiction remained tenuous; still others on the immediate edge of villages, towns, and major urban centers. Free blacks and even whites were known to collaborate with runaways, exchanging information or trade goods such as salt, alcohol, and cloth for a share of stolen merchandise or agricultural production. There were also documented instances of cooperation between plantation slaves, urban blacks, and runaways, although, as always, sources written by fearful authorities must be treated with caution. Similar runaway communities arose throughout the Americas, yet nowhere with such frequency as in Brazil.

The largest and most durable *quilombo* was known as Palmares, a network of geographically distinct communities that formed in the interior of the northeastern captaincies of Alagoas and Pernambuco early in the seventeenth century. To sustain themselves, fugitives gathered in Palmares farmed and launched raids on local plantations, capturing slaves. Such slaves remained in bondage in the *quilombo*, following African traditions, a practice negating facile assumptions about quilombo inhabitants as freedom fighters. Runaways who reached the community on their own were free. Official estimates placed the population of Palmares at the end of the century at 20,000 or more. An elected ruler or "great lord" named Ganga Zumba presided over this realm. He was succeeded in about 1680 by Zumbi, the quilombo's last leader. Zumbi's power was evident in an official communication dispatched by King Pedro II (r. 1668–1706) in 1685, an attempt to lure him into submission. The king promised forgiveness for "all of the excesses" the African lord had committed, recognizing that Zumbi's "rebellion was justified by the evils practiced by some bad slave-owners in disobedience of my royal orders" (Alves Filho 1999: 87). During the 1680s no fewer than six armed expeditions set out to capture him and destroy Palmares. Not until 1695 did the quilombo finally fall. Despite relentless efforts to stamp out others, they remained a feature of slavery throughout Brazil until abolition in 1888. Zumbi would become an icon of modern Afro-Brazilian solidarity movements.

The profits generated by the sugar trade, despite its internal perturbations, drew the attention of non-Portuguese investors and rival empires. Spanish Hapsburgs occupied the Portuguese throne from 1580, creating the Iberian Union, which endured until 1640. Portuguese autonomy in the union diminished over time, accompanied by increasing resentment. The Dutch, at war with Spain, found their traditional trade with Portugal severed during this period. They occupied Bahia in 1624, only to be expelled the next year by a joint Portuguese and Spanish force. They attacked again in 1630, capturing what was then still the more prosperous captaincy of Pernambuco. The very nature of the export economy, which depended on a few major trans-shipment points, made this occupation possible. The ports of Recife and Olinda could be held with comparative ease. Inland, the Dutch at first faced stubborn military opposition from Portuguese settlers and their Indian and black allies, who exchanged allegiance for promised rewards. Others members of these marginalized groups, however, cast their lot with the Dutch, expecting similar advantages.

The Dutch West Indies Company installed a prince of the House of Orange, John Maurice of Nassau (r. 1636–44), as governor general of the new colony. Considered able and humane, particularly in the sphere of indigenous relations, Maurice extended

Dutch influence south to the São Francisco River, north beyond the Amazon River, and into the Caribbean Basin. He mounted an expedition that seized Angola from the Portuguese, along with a number of West African ports vital to the slave trade. His conciliatory approach to Brazilian planters brought results. Although some abandoned their plantations and took refuge in Bahia and Rio de Janeiro, many others – joined by new Dutch, French, and British immigrants, some of them Jews – eagerly accepted company credit and filled the vacuum left by colonists who fled. Dutch Calvinist ministers less willing to cooperate with Luso–Brazilian Catholics undercut Maurice's enlightened policies. A temporary collapse of sugar prices on the Amsterdam market exacerbated tensions. When the Dutch West Indies Company failed to provide the financial support Maurice required, he resigned in protest. His departure set the stage for a successful rebellion by planters, again joined by blacks and Indians, aided finally by forces sent from Portugal, which had regained its independence from Spain. The Dutch garrison in Recife capitulated in 1654, but not before much of the northeastern sugar economy lay in ruins. Over the long term, the Dutch occupation elevated Bahia as the center of Brazilian sugar production; however, it also contributed to the transfer of technology and know-how to the Antilles, fostering the rise of intense Caribbean competition from Holland, England, and France. The accompanying severe recession in Brazil would not be reversed until gold was discovered in the interior in the late seventeenth century. Even so, over the entire colonial period, sugar production remained the most lucrative economic activity.

The belated discovery of enormous mineral wealth can be traced to the activities of the so-called *bandeirantes*, famed explorers and Indian hunters concentrated in the southern captaincy of São Vicente, later São Paulo. They pushed the limits of Portuguese settlement and geographic knowledge westward, far beyond the line established by the Treaty of Tordesillas. The Paulistas were aided in this endeavor by the advent of the Iberian Union, which eased restrictions on crossing the boundary between the two empires. Missionaries and cattlemen also pushed westward, occupying regions of the Amazon Basin and areas that would later, through the principle of *uti possidetis*, come to form portions of the south, north, and central-west of Brazil. The Paulista expeditions of the sixteenth and especially seventeenth centuries, comprising hundreds and more rarely thousands of colonists and detribalized Indians, covered still greater distances through the wilderness. These *bandeiras* (literally, banners; that is, banner-waving troops) traveled inland from the coast for months, even years, at a time. After initial attempts to locate precious metals met with failure, the economic motive for these ventures turned toward the capture of native slaves, known as *negros da terra* or blacks of the land. The southern coast's less favorable soils and greater distance from European markets left Paulistas at a disadvantage as sugar producers and, consequently, as importers of African slaves. Bonded indigenous labor endured in the region as the linchpin of production far longer than in the northeast. Indians served landowners in viniculture and cotton planting and, most importantly, in wheat cultivation for local consumption and export to the plantation zones. The perpetual and profitable drive to replenish and expand the local labor force – rather than to supply plantation workers to northeastern sugar estates, as historians once thought – galvanized the expeditionary activity.

From the earliest days of settlement in the south, Portuguese men commingled with Tupi women, producing mixed-race or *mameluco* children who sometimes passed for white and, as their lands and wealth increased, rose to prominence in local society. Many became skilled fighters, backwoodsmen, slavers, and cultural intermediaries. Indian males newly incorporated into Paulista society seem to have preferred participating in wilderness expeditions to planting and harvesting, traditionally the work of Tupi women. In settler society, many of the women became domestic servants. Although royal legislation prohibited Indian enslavement, the Paulistas circumvented this limitation through the legal innovation of "administration," which charged landowners with instructing the Indians in Catholicism and western work habits. "Far from enslaving them," as one landowner justified the practice, "we render them an unremunerated service by teaching them to till, plant, harvest, and work for their livelihood" (quoted in Monteiro 1994: 139). Estate inventories demonstrate that such Indians were passed as property from one generation to the next.

One of the most renowned bandeirantes, Antônio Raposo Tavares (1598–1658), a governor's son, left on his first bandeira with some 100 Paulistas and 2,000 Indian auxiliaries in 1628. Raiding Spanish Jesuit missions established in the Guaíra region of present-day Paraná, the expedition seized hundreds of slaves and set in motion a process that forced the missionaries to move their base of operations into increasingly distant areas. Tavares established a great estate along the Tietê River, relying on more than 100 Indian laborers. During the Dutch occupation, he marched forces northward to fight the invaders. His final expedition between 1648 and 1652 traversed more than 10,000 kilometers in three years, following the Paraguay, Mamoré, and Madeira Rivers until reaching the Amazon, which he descended to its mouth before returning to São Paulo with a much reduced troop.

Historians conventionally locate the conclusion of the era of bandeira-led conquest somewhere near the end of the seventeenth century. In fact, military and paramilitary adventures evolved rather than ceased, adapting to altered circumstances. These changes became apparent by the second half of the seventeenth century as the Church responded to Jesuit denunciations by reasserting its formal opposition to Indian slave hunting and as the progressive depletion of native populations made such slaving less efficient. Often called *armações* after the investors or *armadores* who financed them, the later Paulista expeditions became smaller but more numerous. They continued seizing captives, although in reduced numbers. They also turned to new activities, fighting in the northeast, for example, against rebellious Indians in what became known as the War of the Barbarians (1683–1713) and participating in the destruction of the Palmares quilombo. Under crown sponsorship, they also returned to the dream of finding precious metals, which finally yielded spectacular results. Paulista bandeirantes made a series of major gold strikes no later than the 1690s in the southeastern interior, which would come to be called Minas Gerais, that is, the General Mines. Secondary discoveries occurred far to the west in Mato Grosso and Goiás in 1718 and 1725. In all of these regions, adventurers continued to scour lands beyond the primary mining camps for much of the rest of the century, hoping for still greater riches. Mato Grosso became the destination of a particularly impressive form of expeditions – the *monções* or monsoons, massive prospecting and trading parties that traveled from São Paulo along rivers and overland to the distant western gold fields.

In Minas Gerais, the unearthing of the most extensive gold deposits the Americas had ever known produced a rapid economic expansion, a complex inland urban society, and a rich Baroque culture. Two hundred years after the colony's discovery, the first great wave of Portuguese immigrants crossed the Atlantic in pursuit of wealth. During the first six decades of the eighteenth century, more than half a million colonists emigrated from Portugal and its Atlantic islands to Brazil, primarily young peasant men who often borrowed money for their passage. Tens of thousands of them and, in even greater numbers, the African slaves purchased by those who accumulated capital pressed inland from the seaboard. The population of European descent swelled; that of African descent grew even faster, eventually forming the largest regional captive and free colored population in Portuguese America. In the Emboabas War (1708–9), the new European immigrants wrested control of the mining camps from their original Paulista settlers. Vila Rica (later Ouro Preto) blossomed into the gilded capital of the mining district, inhabited by some 20,000 settlers at its demographic peak in the 1740s. To the north, at Tejuco, diamonds were discovered in 1729, adding still greater impetus to the windfall that transformed the colony and the transatlantic commerce linking it to Europe and Africa.

The precious metal and stones that flowed into the South Atlantic economy reoriented the Portuguese overseas empire, temporarily reinvigorated a declining Iberian kingdom, and nourished the burgeoning Industrial Revolution in England, Portugal's exigent ally to the north. In the colony itself economic power shifted toward the mining region and Rio de Janeiro, the port city through which the bulk of the bullion, immigrants, slaves, trade goods, and contraband passed. Before the Portuguese Crown fully acknowledged these changes and transferred the colony's capital from Salvador to Rio de Janeiro in 1763, the inevitable depletion of the mineral washings was already underway. Distrust by crown officials regarding the denizens of the mining district surfaced immediately. Those who departed the coast for the distant gold fields shocked high-ranking observers as "vile people," as "licentious and unchristian," as "criminals, vagabonds, and malefactors," as "unruly and uncontrolled," to cite a few of the slurs marshaled by Brazil's governor general João de Lencastre in 1701 (Rau & Silva 1955–8: 14–17). Through the lens of elite bias, this perspective reflected the marginalized status of the mobile mass of prospectors, adventurers, and common laborers who flocked to the mines. A small minority eventually amassed fortunes from the alluvial deposits that sustained the bonanza. Most, however, lived in the uncertain, often desperate circumstances common to transient gold-rush economies.

As in the plantation districts, African slaves came to perform the bulk of the heavy labor. They comprised nearly half of the estimated 340,000 inhabitants in Minas Gerais in 1776, the year of a captaincy-wide census.[1] Panning for gold, operating sluices, knee deep in icy water searching for diamonds, they encountered work regimes so difficult that their mortality rate appears to have been well above that of slaves in plantation zones during the same period. Quilombos proliferated to an even greater degree than on the coast, spawning a counter force of *capitães do mato* (literally "captains of the forest"), paid runaway slave-hunters, many of whom were free blacks. Among blacks and especially whites, women were far less numerous than men in the mining district, particularly during the early decades of the century, skewing gender relations with peculiar results. Concubinage and prostitution became widespread. Innumerable illegitimate children contributed to the fast growth of a free mixed-race population, as their white fathers sometimes freed them along with their mothers. Emancipation came either upon the father's death or through formal contracts known as *coartações*, which established the terms of self-purchase over a specified number of years. By 1776, free blacks comprised almost a third of the overall population.

A significant number of unmarried women of color navigated the hazards of their vulnerable position and achieved marked upward economic mobility and, less frequently, social acceptance by the white elite. The most famous case was that of Chica da Silva (*c.*1734–96), born into slavery in Tejuco, where by the final quarter of the century free women of color headed more households than any other single group (41 percent), followed by white males (35 percent). Purchased from a Portuguese doctor, Silva gained her freedom and became wealthy as the mistress of one of the colony's most powerful Portuguese officials, the diamond contractor João Fernandes de Oliveira. She had fourteen illegitimate children, all but one of them with the contractor, who returned to Lisbon in 1770 to resolve a legal dispute over his inheritance. She helped ensure the welfare and education of her children and grandchildren through successful business ventures, including the rental to the diamond mines of the many slaves she came to own. Her membership in various lay confraternities associated with the Catholic Church – including separate ones traditionally restricted to blacks, mulattos, and whites – demonstrated both the ambiguities and possibilities of her social position.

The decline of mining, especially gold extraction, during the second half of the eighteenth century further deepened royal suspicions about the conduct of colonists. Loathe to admit to the ephemeral nature of alluvial mining, the Crown became convinced that Brazil's mineral wealth was being secreted away by smugglers without payment of the requisite royal fifth or *quinto*, the largest of the innumerable levies imposed on the mining districts. Historians continue to debate the extent of such contraband. What is certain is that elite jeremiads about the decadence of the postboom era underestimated the degree to which mining's collapse was countered in the colony, especially after about 1780, by economic diversification, the renewed expansion of agricultural exports, the growth of domestic markets tied to population growth, small-scale manufacturing, and the rise of a powerful merchant class in Rio de Janeiro. The same cannot be said of Portugal, which by the middle of the eighteenth century had slipped into a position of deepening dependence vis-à-vis Europe's great powers, especially England. Perhaps more strikingly, the balance of colonial trade came to favor Brazil over the mother country. Profligate spending accompanied by inflation, reliance on British textiles and other manufactured goods, the failure to invest in domestic industrialization, the destruction of Lisbon by an earthquake in 1755, and the lack of an adequate merchant fleet strained the system that tied Portugal to its major colony.

After the less than competent José I ascended to the throne in 1750, his ambitious and autocratic first minister, Sebastião José de Carvalho e Melo (r. 1750–77), the future Marquis of Pombal, set out to reassert mercantilist control of Portuguese America according to the principles of enlightened despotism. The move paralleled the Bourbon Reforms imposed on Spanish America. Pombal established two crown monopolies to rekindle the economy of the northeast and to develop an export trade in forest products, cotton, and rice from the Amazon region. He pursued the twin policies of redirecting to the crown profits being diverted by Brazilian merchants while favoring local elites with administrative positions. Despite the signing of the treaties of Madrid (1750) and later San Ildefonso (1777), which systematized the borders between Portuguese and Spanish America and effectively erased the Tordesillas line, incorporating many of the lands explored by the bandeirantes, Pombal remained concerned about Spanish territorial ambitions. The southern borderlands in particular were a focus of imperial rivalry throughout the colonial period. Tensions reached a violent peak when the expulsion of the Spaniards from territory claimed by Pombal provoked Charles III to launch the largest military expedition Spain had ever ordered to the Americas in 1776.

Pombal was also convinced that Jesuit control of indigenous labor in the Amazon and along Brazil's southern borderlands threatened royal hegemony and commercial profits. He thus stripped the missionaries of the temporal powers they exercised over Indian villages, restricting them to ecclesiastical activities and throwing open the villages to trade with Portuguese merchants and settlers. In 1757, he promulgated a major corpus of indigenous legislation, the *Diretório dos índios* or Indian Directory, drafted by his brother, the governor of the Amazonian captaincies of Grão Pará and Maranhão. While juridically free, Indians living in mission villages were now subject to the rule of lay directors named by the governor himself. The natives were to be Christianized, civilized, and taught the essential skills of trade and agriculture. Assimilation was encouraged through policies favoring marriages between whites and Indians. In these ways, natives would become "useful to themselves, to the colonists, and to the state" (Moreira Neto 1988: 165–203). Pombal then expelled the Jesuits from the colony in 1759.

In Minas Gerais, Pombal redoubled efforts to crack down on smuggling and improve the collection of taxes owed to the royal treasury. He also established a crown monopoly on diamond extraction. Repressive measures were imposed on the free poor, most of them persons of African descent, whose itinerant, subsistence-level existence on the margins of the market economy was seen as fostering a labor shortage that contributed to waning gold production. Pombal permitted some exploration for gold in forested lands lying to the east of the mining region, which the Crown had formerly set off-limits to bar overland access to and egress from the mines. In combination with his radically revised indigenous policies, this opening impelled a drive by the locally powerful to conquer indigenous peoples who had used the coastal forests between Bahia and Rio de Janeiro as a refuge zone since the sixteenth century (Langfur 2006).

Pombal fell from power after José I's death in 1777. The successors to the throne, Queen Maria I and her son João (who took over her duties in 1792 when she was declared mentally incompetent and took the title of regent in 1799), rejected many of Pombal's specific policies but generally continued efforts to centralize and increase the efficiency of colonial administration. The threatened calling in of debts owed the Crown catalyzed a failed nativist intrigue known as the Inconfidência Mineira (1789) in Minas Gerais, the most dramatic consequence of social dislocation and political discontentment in the troubled mining district. Long seen as a heroic first step toward Brazilian independence in 1822, its participants elevated as national icons, the plot later suffered the skeptical reevaluation of scholars less dazzled by the motives of its self-interested wealthy backers, who stood to profit from a tax rebellion (Maxwell 1973). The primary exception, Joaquim José da Silva Xavier (1748–92), a middle-class dragoon officer and dentist known as Tiradentes (the tooth-puller), genuinely advocated the republican cause, heralding Enlightenment principles of liberty and equality, and assumed full responsibility for the conspiracy. He was the sole plotter executed by the Crown. Elsewhere in the colony, the Crown benefited along with colonial elites from an agricultural renaissance produced by circumstances in the wider Atlantic world, including disruptions to the cotton and rice trade caused by the American Revolution and to the Caribbean sugar trade caused by the slave rebellion in Saint-Domingue. Tobacco exports, used in trade for African slaves, also increased.

The sobering mass rebellions that ignited the French and Haitian Revolutions gave pause to dominant white colonists who might have emulated North American patriots in fomenting an independence movement. If the Anglo-American Revolution provided a model, one of its most important lessons concerned the maintenance of slavery in the course of achieving independence. The so-called Tailors' Conspiracy in Bahia (1798) sought to instigate an armed uprising against Portuguese rule and install a republic styled on the French example. The plot, which involved both whites and mulattos, was viciously repressed and manipulated by crown authorities to exploit white fears of a slave revolt. With slave owning so ubiquitous, even among smallholders and the professional class, concerns about social upheaval and loss of privilege outweighed any impulse to precipitate a break from Portugal. Enlightenment ideas and liberalism inspired those who sought more control over colonial affairs, but almost always with an eye toward reform not revolution. Differences between Brazilian-born intellectuals, administrators, planters, and merchants and their Portuguese-born counterparts did not rise to the level of hostility that existed between creoles and peninsulars in late colonial Spanish America. The prosperous condition of the capital Rio de Janeiro, especially the elevation of Brazilian merchants there to positions of substantial wealth and power, further tempered latent antagonisms. Endogenous capital formation, much of it stemming from domestic markets, led commercial interests to be less preoccupied with transatlantic tensions than historians once supposed. Rather than the coalescence of an independent national identity, which only emerged over the course of the nineteenth century, upheaval in Europe following the rise of Napoleon exerted the decisive influence over events leading to independence from Portugal in 1822.

The colonial period assumed its final form after an unprecedented event stemming from that upheaval. In 1807, Napoleon's armies marched across Spain and into Portugal, seeking to seal off Europe from the flow of British goods through Portuguese ports. Escorted by British warships, Prince Regent João escaped to Brazil with his aging mother, the royal family, and more than 10,000 members of the court, becoming the first European monarch to set foot in the Americas. After a brief stop in Salvador, the royal entourage took refuge in March of 1808 in Rio de Janeiro. The capital of the colony would remain the center of the Portuguese Empire for 13 years (Schultz 2001).

Two of the prince regent's earliest actions after the transfer reveal much about the colony during this final period. While still in Salvador, João abolished the 300-year-old system of mercantilist control by opening Brazil's ports to friendly nations, which at the time meant primarily Great Britain. From the monarch's point of view, sanctioning what was already a flourishing contraband trade between the British and the

Brazilians meant that the Crown could at least benefit from taxing this commerce. At the same time, the concession to British pressure presaged future changes as Great Britain pushed to impose free trade and abolition of the transatlantic slave trade. The second action, in contrast, harkened back to the earliest days of Portuguese settlement. Determined to incorporate the vast forested territory that separated the three major nodes of colonial settlement – Bahia, Minas Gerais, and Rio de Janeiro – João declared war on the Botocudo, the zone's semi-nomadic indigenous occupants. Condemning the "invasions" of the "cannibal" Botocudo, he invoked the timeworn principle of just war, pledging a military offensive that would not cease until the Indians, "moved by just terror," submitted to the rule of law, accepting settled life as settled vassals, as others before them had done (Cunha 1992: 57–60). The policy would not be officially abandoned until 1831. These two royal edicts testify to the tug-of-war between continuity and change that characterized the years leading toward independence.

The prince regent was crowned King João VI upon the death of his mother in 1816, a few months after he declared Brazil a co-kingdom, raising it to an equal position with Portugal. That action meant that, in a legal sense, Brazil was no longer a colony. When he finally returned to Lisbon in April 1821, he left his son Pedro behind to rule Brazil. As he seems to have recognized, Brazil would not easily be reduced again to its former subordinate status. The following year, September 7, 1822, Pedro declared independence.

NOTE

1   The estimate is based on specific methodologies applied to the 1776 census data (Bergad 1999: 91).

BIBLIOGRAPHY

Alden, D. (1968) *Royal Government in Colonial Brazil with Special Reference to the Administration of the Marquis of Lavradio, Viceroy, 1769–1779*. University of California Press, Berkeley.

Alden, D. (1996) *The Making of an Enterprise: The Society of Jesus in Portugal, Its Empire, and Beyond, 1540–1750*. Stanford University Press, Stanford.

Alves Filho, I. (1999) *Brasil, 500 anos em documentos*. Mauad, Rio de Janeiro.

Antonil, A. J. (1997 [1711]). *Cultura e opulência do Brasil*. Itatiaia, Belo Horizonte.

Barickman, B. J. (2004) "Revisiting the Casa-grande: Plantation and Cane-Farming Households in Early Nineteenth-Century Bahia," *Hispanic American Historical Review*, 84:4, 619–25.

Bergad, L. W. (1999) *Slavery and the Demographic and Economic History of Minas Gerais, Brazil, 1720–1888*. Cambridge University Press, Cambridge.

Bethell, L. (ed.) (1987) *Colonial Brazil*. Cambridge University Press, Cambridge.

Bonavides, P. & Amaral, R. (2002) *Textos políticos da história do Brasil*, 3rd ed. Senado Federal, Brasília.

Boxer, C. R. (1957) *The Dutch in Brazil, 1624–1654*. Clarendon Press, Oxford.

Boxer, C. R. (1962) *The Golden Age of Brazil, 1695–1750*. University of California Press, Berkeley.

Boxer, C. R. (1969) *The Portuguese Seaborne Empire, 1415–1825*. Alfred Knopf, New York.

Caminha, P. V. de (1974 [1500]) *Carta a el-rei D. Manuel sobre o achamento do Brasil (1 de Maio de 1500)*, ed. M. V. Guerreiro. Imprensa Nacional-Casa da Moeda, Lisbon.

Cohen, T. M. (1998) *The Fire of Tongues: Antonio Vieira and the Missionary Church in Brazil and Portugal.* Stanford University Press, Stanford.

Couto, J. (1998) *A construção do Brasil: Ameríndios, portugueses e africanos, do início do povoamento a finais de quinhentos.* Cosmos, Lisbon.

Cunha, M. C. da (ed.) (1992) *Legislação indigenista no século XIX: Uma compilação (1808–1889).* Universidade de São Paulo, São Paulo.

Davis, D. (1973) "How the Brazilian West Was Won: Freelance and State on the Mato Grosso Frontier, 1737–1752." In D. Alden (ed.), *Colonial Roots of Modern Brazil.* University of California Press, Berkeley.

Diffie, B. W. (1987) *A History of Colonial Brazil, 1500–1792*, ed. E. J. Perkins. Krieger, Melbourne, FL.

Freyre, G. (1956) *The Masters and the Slaves*, 2nd ed., trans. S. Putnam. Knopf, New York.

Furtado, J. F. (2003) *Chica da Silva e o contratador dos diamantes: Outro lado do mito.* Companhia das Letras, São Paulo.

Hemming, J. (1977) *Red Gold: The Conquest of the Brazilian Indians, 1500–1760.* Harvard University Press, Cambridge, MA.

Higgins, K. J. (1999) *"Licentious Liberty" In a Brazilian Gold-Mining Region: Slavery, Gender, and Social Control in Eighteenth-Century Sabará, Minas Gerais.* Pennsylvania State University Press, University Park.

Karasch, M. C. (1987) *Slave Life in Rio de Janeiro, 1808–1850.* Princeton University Press, Princeton.

Langfur, H. (2006) *The Forbidden Lands: Colonial Identity, Frontier Violence, and the Persistence of Brazil's Eastern Indians, 1750–1830.* Stanford University Press, Stanford.

Lewin, L. (2003) *Surprise Heirs: Illegitimacy, Patrimonial Rights, and Legal Nationalism in Luso-Brazilian Inheritance, 1750–1821*, vol. 1. Stanford University Press, Stanford.

Maxwell, K. R. (1973) *Conflicts and Conspiracies: Brazil and Portugal: 1750–1808.* Cambridge University Press, Cambridge.

Metcalf, A. C. (1992) *Family and Frontier in Colonial Brazil: Santana De Parnaíba, 1520–1822.* University of California Press, Berkeley.

Metcalf, A. C. (2005) *Go-betweens and the Colonization of Brazil, 1500–1600.* University of Texas Press, Austin.

Monteiro, J. M. (1994) *Negros da terra: Índios e bandeirantes nas origens de São Paulo.* Companhia das Letras, São Paulo.

Moreira Neto, C. de A. (1988) *Índios da Amazônia: De maioria a minoria (1750–1850).* Vozes, Petrópolis.

Morse, R. M. (ed.) (1965) *The Bandeirantes: The Historical Role of the Brazilian Pathfinders.* Alfred Knopf, New York.

Nowell, C. E. (1936) "The Discovery of Brazil – Accidental or Intentional?" *The Hispanic American Historical Review*, 16:3, pp. 311–38.

Prado Júnior, C. (1967) *The Colonial Background of Modern Brazil*, trans. S. Macedo. University of California Press, Berkeley.

Rau, V. & Silva. M. F. G. da (eds.) (1955–8) *Os manuscritos do Arquivo da Casa de Cadaval respeitantes ao Brasil.* Atlântica, Coimbra.

Russell-Wood, A. J. R. (1982) *The Black Man in Slavery and Freedom in Colonial Brazil.* Macmillan Press, London.

Russell-Wood, A. J. R. (1998) *The Portuguese Empire, 1415–1808: A World on the Move.* Johns Hopkins University Press, Baltimore.

Schwartz, S. B. (1973) *Sovereignty and Society in Colonial Brazil: The High Court of Bahia and Its Judges, 1609–1751.* University of California Press, Berkeley.

Schwartz, S. B. (1985) *Sugar Plantations in the Formation of Brazilian Society: Bahia, 1550–1835.* Cambridge University Press, Cambridge.

Schultz, K. (2001) *Tropical Versailles: Empire, Monarchy, and the Portuguese Royal Court in Rio De Janeiro, 1808–1821.* Routledge, New York.

Souza, L. de M. e (2004) *The Devil and the Land of the Holy Cross: Witchcraft, Slavery, and Popular Religion in Colonial Brazil,* trans. D. Grosklaus Whitty. University of Texas Press, Austin.

Sweet, J. H. (2006) *Recreating Africa: Culture, Kinship, and Religion in the African–Portuguese World, 1441–1770.* University of North Carolina Press, Chapel Hill.

Chapter Seven

INSTITUTIONS OF THE SPANISH AMERICAN EMPIRE IN THE HAPSBURG ERA

Susan Elizabeth Ramírez

Columbus's hope of finding the people who produced nutmeg and cinnamon had not died before the institutional structure of the Western Hemisphere began to take shape. The institutions that exploration, encounter, and colonization elicited appeared gradually with the aim of guaranteeing Spanish hegemony in the "New World." A previous generation of scholars studied the major Spanish institutions that regulated colonial life in America from a legal and structural perspective, while more recent work has penetrated the institutional façade to focus on how individuals made these institutions work. This chapter will describe the institutions of the Spanish colonial empire and then document how their study has changed in the last 60 years or so.

The Spanish Colonial Administrative Structure

Historians such as Charles Gibson and C. H. Haring described colonial institutions designed by the Crown and its agents to order nearly every aspect of existence for peninsular immigrants, their American-born children (the creoles), native peoples, blacks, and the mixed-blooded persons born after contact in 1492. In Spain, the House of Trade (*Casa de Contratación*), established in 1503, supervised commerce, issued licenses to travel to America, controlled shipping and exports and imports and collected the taxes on these, and received consignments of goods and money. Its power as a royal treasury and revenue office increased as the empire expanded. A special judicial department studied and decided civil and criminal cases relating to trade and navigation. Officials of the Casa also trained pilots for the Atlantic crossing; regulated their activities; recorded the progress of geographical discovery; and maintained the master map (Haring 1947; Gibson 1966: 100–1). The second institution of import was an advisory board to the king, called the Council of the Indies, which formally appeared in 1524. It served as a clearinghouse for information coming from the Indies. On the basis of this information, it drafted and issued American decrees and edicts that the king signed, as "*Yo El Rey*." It also served as a supreme court, hearing appeals from Americans on important civil issues.

To administer the affairs of America on site and counter, in part, the rising power of the *encomenderos* – the early conquerors who were rewarded for their service to the Crown with the labor and tribute of groups of native peoples (*encomienda*) with the stipulation that they protect and instruct them in the Catholic religion – the Spanish king appointed alter egos called viceroys (or vice-kings) to represent his person and interests. The power of these high-ranking royal servants extended to all inhabitants subject to the king, be they Spanish, native, black, or some combination of the three (the *castas*). A viceroy ruled at the pleasure of the Crown from Mexico City (formerly the Aztec capital Tenochtitlán) and Lima (or Los Reyes, as it was known in the sixteenth century). A viceroy was a king's man, his deputy in America. Viceroys were almost all Spaniards who came from the established and named nobility, but the office was not hereditary. The usual term of a viceroy was five or six years, a term deemed not long enough to establish an independent basis of power. In some cases viceroys served in Mexico (the kingdom of New Spain) before being sent to serve in Peru (officially, the kingdom of New Castile), which was seen as the culmination of a successful career. In the sixteenth century, viceroys tended to serve as bureaucrats; in the seventeenth, they were more likely to be military men. The first viceroy, Antonio de Mendoza, was appointed in 1535 for New Spain. In 1542 King Charles I (Charles V of the Holy Roman Empire) appointed Blasco Núñez Vela the viceroy of Peru. He set out for the Andes in 1544 and, once there, proved so intransigent in implementing the New Laws of 1542 that would have abolished the *encomienda* at the death of the present holder that a group of incensed *encomenderos* captured and beheaded him. A civil war followed, preventing the establishment of a stable viceregal administration in Peru for some years (Lockhart 1969; Keith 1971; Himmerich y Valencia 1991; Puente Brunke 1992; Grunberg 1994; Avellaneda 1995).

With time, however, the viceroy proved a reasonably effective institution to uphold the Crown's power. As the embodiment of the monarch, surrounded by ritual and a numerous retinue and court, he represented the pinnacle of prestige and authority. He was first and foremost an executive ordered to implement the will of the king. But he could issue edicts and thus had some legislative power. He also was charged with maintaining civil order and, therefore, had some military responsibilities, although these tended to be more illusory than real early in colonial times. He also was vice-patron of the Church with influence in the nomination and appointment of high ecclesiastical officials. The great distance from the metropolis tended to increase the viceroy's authority, but there was a limit to what one man could do in the vast expanse of American viceroyalties.

The jurisdiction of the viceroys was divided into presidencies and captaincies. The viceroys enjoyed political authority over the inhabitants of the presidencies, like Panama, Quito, Chile, and Charcas (Upper Peru). People living in the remotest areas fell under the attention of a captain general who had civil jurisdiction over them. Like the viceroys, the overwhelming majority of captains general were peninsular-born. Although the captain general did not have the rank and prestige of a viceroy, his governance was important because of the remoteness from the capital and continuing problems with unacculturated natives on the frontiers of settlement.

Another important institution was the *audiencia* or supreme tribunal. The main role of the judges (*oidores* – listeners) who sat on the various high courts that were

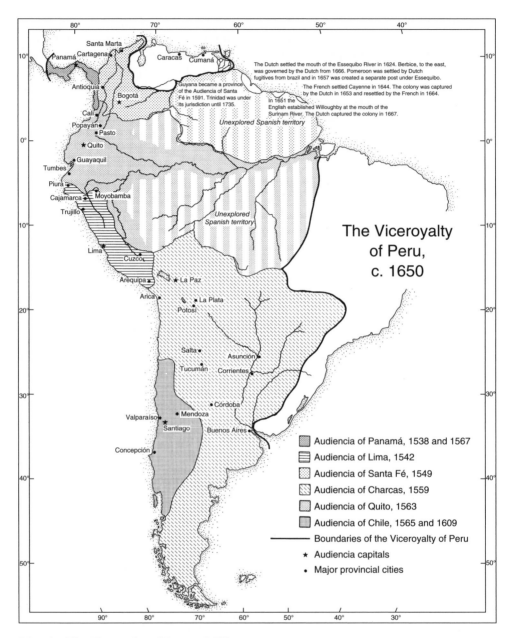

The Dutch settled the mouth of the Essequibo River in 1624. Berbice, to the east, was governed by the Dutch from 1666. Pomeroon was settled by Dutch fugitives from brazil and in 1657 was created a separate post under Essequibo.

Guyana became a province of the Audiencia of Santa Fé in 1591. Trinidad was under its jurisdiction until 1735.

The French settled Cayenne in 1644. The colony was captured by the Dutch in 1653 and resettled by the French in 1664.

In 1651 the English established Willoughby at the mouth of the Surinam River. The Dutch captured the colony in 1667.

Unexplored Spanish territory

Unexplored Spanish territory

The Viceroyalty
of Peru,
c. 1650

▨ Audiencia of Panamá, 1538 and 1567
▤ Audiencia of Lima, 1542
▦ Audiencia of Santa Fé, 1549
▨ Audiencia of Charcas, 1559
▩ Audiencia of Quito, 1563
▥ Audiencia of Chile, 1565 and 1609
── Boundaries of the Viceroyalty of Peru
★ Audiencia capitals
• Major provincial cities

Map 2 The Viceroyalty of Peru, *c.*1650
Source: Cathryn L. Lombardi, John V. Lombardi, and K. Lynn Stoner, *Latin American History: A Teaching Atlas* (Madison, WI: University of Wisconsin Press, 1983). © 1983. Reprinted by permission of The University of Wisconsin Press.

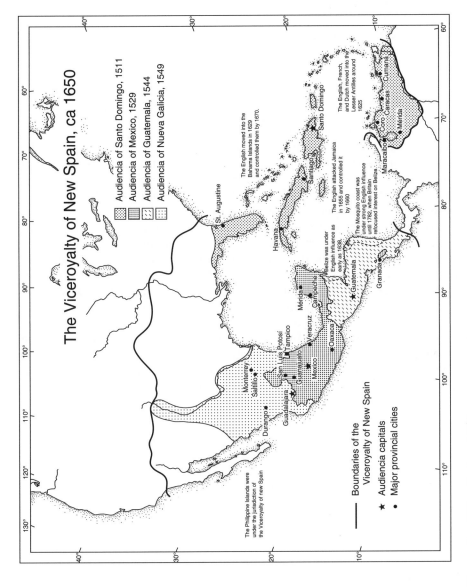

The Viceroyalty of New Spain, ca 1650

Audiencia of Santo Domingo, 1511
Audiencia of Mexico, 1529
Audiencia of Guatemala, 1544
Audiencia of Nueva Galicia, 1549

The English moved into the
Bahama Islands in 1629
and controlled them by 1670.

The English, French,
and Dutch moved into the
Lesser Antilles around
1625

The English attacked Jamaica
in 1655 and controlled it
by 1660

The Mosquito coast was
under strong English influence
until 1782, when Britain
refocused interest on Belize.

Belize was under
English influence as
early as 1638.

The Philippine Islands were
under the jurisdiction of
the Viceroyalty of new Spain

Boundaries of the
Viceroyalty of New Spain
★ Audiencia capitals
• Major provincial cities

St. Augustine
Havana
Santo Domingo
Santiago
Mérida
Coro Caracas Cumaná
Maracaibo
Granada
Guatemala
Campeche
Mérida
Oaxaca
Veracruz
Tampico
San Luis Potosí
Guanajuato
Mexico
Guadalajara
Saltillo
Monterrey
Durango

Map 3 The Viceroyalty of New Spain, *c.*1650
Source: Cathryn L. Lombardi, John V. Lombardi, and K. Lynn Stoner, *Latin American History: A Teaching Atlas* (Madison, WI: University of Wisconsin Press, 1983). © 1983. Reprinted by permission of The University of Wisconsin Press.

gradually established in America (see Table 7.1) was to settle disputes. Most oidores were Spaniards, but toward the end of the Hapsburg rule and into the first years of the Bourbon administration, the number of creoles increased. Like judges of the Supreme Court of the United States, their colonial Spanish American rulings established precedent and had the force of law. In addition to their judicial and legislative roles, the audiencias could under certain circumstances assume an executive role. If both the viceroy and the archbishop (who succeeded him) died in office, the chief judge (president) of the audiencia served as interim viceroy until another vice-king could be sent from Spain (Burkholder 1980: Appendix A).

Supporting these institutions were the officials of the *Real Hacienda* (Treasury) who controlled fiscal and monetary affairs. They received the tax revenues and paid the cost of government. The *Casa de la Moneda*, the mint, struck the coinage, including the world-famous Spanish pieces of eight (*peso de ocho reales*), from the silver and gold bullion from the mines and other sources.

At the local level, the crown representative was akin to a local governor called a *corregidor* or *alcalde mayor*. Theoretically, there were two types. The first was a corregidor of Indians, with jurisdiction over groups of native peoples. He protected the natives, administered justice, and collected tribute. The second was the corregidor of Spaniards, who enjoyed executive power as governor, and judicial and legislative power as judge in the first instance in Spanish towns (*villas, ciudades*). This official was charged with maintaining order and morality and administrating the city. In practice, one man often filled the duties of both the corregidor of Indians and Spaniards. Peninsular regulation established checks on the corregidor's power. The corregidor was not supposed to be a local person, although this sometimes was allowed. Even when a non-local man assumed control, he often became involved with the local elite, through marriage or godparentage ties, both of which made him less effective as a crown agent. The Crown also required him to post bond because he controlled the collection of certain tax and tribute revenues. A substantial bond also assured the government that he would be available for a judicial review (*residencia*, discussed below) after his term expired to answer to any charges of corruption and abuses of power.

Table 7.1 *Audiencias* of mainland Spanish America

Kingdom	Audiencias	Date of creation
New Spain	Santo Domingo	1526
(Mexico)	Mexico	1527
	Los Confines (Guatemala)	1543
	New Galicia (Guadalajara)	1548
New Castile (Peru)	Panama	1535
	Peru (Lima)	1542
	Santa Fé de Bogotá	1549
	Charcas (Upper Peru)	1559
	Quito	1563
	Chile	1609
	Buenos Aires*	1661

*Later suppressed

A second locus of local power rested in the town council or *cabildo*, made up of citizens chosen as aldermen or councilmen (*regidores*) and magistrates (*alcaldes*) with jurisdiction over the urban-dwelling settlers (*vecinos*). Most Spanish municipalities had a dozen or fewer regidores who sat together to elect two of their number as alcaldes each year. Town councils passed laws for the municipality; decided issues like who got what building site (*solar*); and screened applicants for vecino status. Alcaldes also served as judges of minor crimes. Aldermen administered the water supply and public lands around the town, maintained the sanitation system, and guaranteed public order. In addition, they set prices for basic foodstuffs and regulated certain artisanal production. Councilors were appointed at first, but later the positions were sold. Over time, seats on the council became regarded as private possessions that could be renounced and sold or inherited by a male family member.

Church and State

However, the civil bureaucracy and local town councils did not govern alone. In colonial times many of the functions that are today state obligations were charged to the Church. In fact, Gibson, a very well known colonial historian, writes that, "In the complexities of law and precedent it was impossible to say where the church authority ceased and state authority began." The Church was not a monolithic institution. It consisted of two major parts: the regular and the secular clergy. The regular clergy lived by a monastic "rule" in convents and monasteries, and included Franciscans, Dominicans, Augustinians, Carmelites, Jesuits, and other orders. The secular clergy were the parish priests under bishops and archbishops. Together the seculars and regulars, as arms of the state, defined what was proper and "civilized." In so doing, they upheld European morality and championed Spanish culture. Priests also sometimes used the confessional to betray plotters of insurrection and actively neutralized social unrest. They administered charity, running orphanages and feeding the poor. The Church also established the few schools that existed: seminaries and universities for the males and convent classes for the girls. The king charged them with taking censuses and keeping the population registers, including baptismal, marriage, and death records. With no mass media and extremely limited literacy, the clergy became the means to communicate with parishioners, reading edicts and letters from the pulpit during mass. Some orders took a role in health, operating the only hospitals in urban areas. Donations, endowments, fees, and offerings allowed the Church over the years to amass great wealth. In a society without public or private banks until the eighteenth century, these pooled funds were made available as loans at 3–7 percent interest to people with real assets. Thus the Church financed investment and conspicuous consumption of the elite and, in so doing, won additional influence and power (Gibson 1966: chaps. 4 and 5; Schwaller 2000; Silverblatt 2004).

Furthermore, the regulars served as a vanguard in the colonization of the Americas and played a major role in the "spiritual conquest" and the acculturation and protection of the native peoples throughout the colonial era. The Franciscans and Dominicans early became builders of missions, around which congregated the native faithful. The later-arriving, but highly organized and effective Jesuits were given the task of educating the sons of the native nobility (Ricard 1966; Phelan 1970; Langer and Jackson 1995; Burns 1999; Saeger 2000; Alfaro 2001).

Over time, the Crown turned against the regular orders in favor of the secular clergy. The Crown, jealous of its power, controlled the secular church through the institution of the *patronato real*, which gave the king a veto over high ecclesiastical office and the additional power to administer ecclesiastical jurisdictions and revenues and veto papal bulls. Thus, the Crown had final say over who became archbishops and bishops, choosing one who would most likely bend to the royal will from a roster of possible nominees submitted by the Church. Over time then, some missionary regulars, once they had succeeded in baptizing, catechizing, and hispanizing their native charges, were forced to leave the monasteries they had built to start over farther and farther away from the viceregal capitals to minister to ever more remote frontier areas. By this process, the churches and missions of the regulars were transferred to the seculars and, in a sense, the missionaries were penalized for their independence and conversion successes (Gibson 1966: 76).

To further maintain the purity of the faith, Philip II established the Inquisition in Spanish America by decrees of 1569–70, with offices in Mexico City, Lima, and Cartagena. It was made up of a tribunal with judges or inquisitors, a lawyer and a secretary, responsible to its own supreme council in Spain. Its jurisdiction covered clerics and laymen (including blacks, but not Indians). It dealt with all offenses against the faith, such as heresy, blasphemy, sorcery, bigamy, impersonation of the priest-hood, belief in false doctrine, incest, and homosexuality. Specifically outside its jurisdiction were treason, unnatural vice, rebellion, rioting and inciting to riot; forgery of royal letters; rape; arson; housebreaking; highway robbery; robbery of churches; and "other crimes greater than these." It had the power to arrest, excommunicate, incarcerate, embargo goods, fine, humiliate, and burn at the stake. These powers and its secret activities and deliberations inspired horror in the general population. There was no possibility of appeal from its decisions to any secular authority in the Indies. In general, inquisitors lost no opportunity to extend their jurisdiction. One mechanism for doing so was the practice of appointing ecclesiastical judges of the first instance (*comisarios*), in all important centers of population, and a network of *familiares*, honorary lay agents, in all towns to keep their eyes and ears open for infractions of law. Rich and powerful men desired to be familiares because of the prestige associated with the post and because service would give them exemptions (*fueros*) from prosecution in civil courts (Greenleaf 1969).

State Policy

Once these institutions had been described, scholars focused on how these institutions affected whole sectors of the developing economies of Spanish America. Royal officials took a direct role in providing the wherewithal to subsidize activities that proved beneficial to the metropolis. When the sought-after exotic spices proved illusive, the Crown focused on bullion. In theory, one-fifth (the *quinto real*) of the precious metal of native treasures, taken as plunder, delivered as ransom, or obtained through grave robbing, was due the king. Once the sources of these metals were determined and located, crown officials structured local institutions to subsidize mining efforts. For example, in Peru, Viceroy Francisco de Toledo (ruled 1569–81) resurrected an Inca institution, called the *m'ita*, the Quechua term for rotating public labor service, and reformulated it to provide thousands of native workers for the highland mines in the southern Andes (Bakewell 1984; Lohmann Villena 1999).

The mines proved an effective market for the agricultural sector. Alongside native production of corn, potatoes, beans and other grains, and vegetables, Spaniards and creoles began ranching and farming activities soon after arrival. As Spanish towns were founded, citizens received garden plots in suburban areas. After the encomendero protests over the New Laws, additional towns were founded as agricultural centers. The citizens of these new towns received *mercedes*, large grants of land for planting wheat, sugar cane, and other cash crops, often in areas where the native population had declined due to the devastating effects of European diseases. The crown-mandated *reducción* or *congregación* (native resettlement) policy benefited estate owners by forcing natives off good lands and concentrating them in their own towns (*pueblos*). These natives eventually came under the control of the corregidor, who was authorized to establish the *repartimiento* labor distribution system mandating that a certain percentage of able-bodied, adult native males serve on a rotating basis, either as agricultural laborers or shepherds at a fixed wage usually below the market rate (Chevalier 1970; Cushner 1980; Davies 1984; Ramírez 1986: esp. chap. 4; Guevara Gil 1993).

Original mercedes became in time the basis of large estates, of three major types: the *estancias* (ranches); the mixed farms producing cattle and agricultural products called by the generic label *haciendas*; and the specialized farms or plantations (although the latter term was not used in colonial times), variously called *haciendas y trapiches*, *ingenios*, or some variation of the same. Periodically in the sixteenth and seventeenth century, the Crown would send a high-ranking inspector to the provinces to examine land titles (*visitas de la tierra*). These inspections were designed to redress native grievances over land usurpation and to produce revenue for the Crown. Individuals without proper title to all the land that they claimed or used were charged a fee to legalize and regularize their titles. Inspectors sold unused public lands, the *tierras realengas y baldías*, to the highest bidder. Although estate owners paid no property taxes as such in this era, they did send part of the produce as the *primicia* (first fruits) and the *diezmo* (tithe) to support the church (Burga 1976; Ramírez 1986).

Another sector regulated by the royal institutions in Spain and America was commerce, which was important for supplying the overseas kingdoms. The Casa de Contratación, mentioned above, established a state trade monopoly, centered in Seville. For easier control, it limited the ports open to overseas commerce to Santo Domingo, Veracruz, Panama, Cartagena, and Lima-Callao. Trade was restricted between American ports during certain periods. Licenses were required to trade various items, the most famous of which was the *asiento* to trade in slaves. A fleet system was established gradually, beginning in 1526 when a decree prohibited single ships from crossing the Atlantic. In 1537, another established the armada (*flota*) system to protect vessels and enforce the trade monopoly (Artíñano y de Galdácano 1917; Céspedes del Castillo 1945; Haring 1947).

Taxes on this trade were sizable. The *almojarifazgo*, established in the sixteenth century, was an import–export duty. This tax was decreed for Peru in 1573, but because of local resistance not applied until 1591. Then it began as a 5 percent tax on all commercial goods imported into Peru and a 2 percent charge on those exported. In the seventeenth century it fluctuated from 2.5 to 7.5 percent, although some foodstuffs were exempt. Originally, it was directly collected by royal officials, but after 1640 tax farmers or the merchants' guild (*consulado*, discussed below) made collections. Another charge was the *avería*, a convoy duty to support *the Armada del Mar del Sur* (Fleet of the South Sea). It was first instituted in the 1580s by Viceroy Don Martín Enríquez de Almansa (1568–80) after Frances Drake's 1579 raid along the west coast of South America, at the rate of 0.5 percent on all transported merchandise. In 1592 this duty was increased to 1 percent after Thomas Cavendish's raid of 1587. By the 1630s, the duty had been raised to 2 percent (Céspedes del Castillo 1945; Klein 1998).

To provide a voice on issues of trade and taxation, merchants established a guild, the *consulado*. The *hombres de negocio* (literally, businessmen), the mercantile elite of the colonies, tied to transatlantic shipping and mercantile houses in Europe, were centered in Mexico City and Lima. They successfully exerted power on a local level, but could not change the major thrust of royal commercial policy (Moreyra Paz Soldán 1950).

Centralizing Ambiguities

Studies of how some of these governing institutions functioned found that a latent centralization of power was built into the structure. Jurisdictions were designed to be overlapping, so that conflicts between institutions and persons that could not be resolved on a local level were appealed up. The king, as the embodiment of natural and divine law, was the ultimate authority. He had the right, as the best leader, to interpret God's law or master design on earth. Viewed over the long run, the system was a brilliant mechanism for asserting royal power. This system of nebulous and loosely defined jurisdictions built centralization into a system in which the king was the ultimate judge of issues deemed important enough to require his attention.

An example of how the Hapsburg system of vague job descriptions and overlapping authorities resulted in ambiguity and conflict comes from northern Mexico in the 1560s (Parry 1948: 89–90). The Audiencia of New Galicia was a presidency at the time under the authority of Viceroy Luis de Velasco (1550–64). There was no governor, only an Audiencia in Guadalajara. When the viceroy ordered the Audiencia to send someone to protect the scattered Spanish settlements in the north against the intermittent warfare of native Chichimecs, Guachichiles, and Zacatecos, the judges of the Audiencia came into conflict with prominent personages of the region and then with the viceroy himself. The viceroy deemed security essential to provide the conditions to encourage mining, ranching, and other productive activities.

When the first commissioner, Pedro de Ahumada, proved ineffective, the viceroy became convinced that other measures were necessary to maintain order. Therefore, in 1562 Velasco appointed Francisco de Ibarra to be the governor of New Vizcaya, a new jurisdiction farther north. Ibarra was a nephew of one of the first conquerors, Diego de Ibarra, who had powerful connections at court. Diego had used his influence with the viceroy to get Francisco accepted as a page in the viceroy's service in

1550, and in 1554 Francisco got a commission to explore the north. He became the leader of a group that founded the settlements of San Martín, Fresnillo, Sombrerete, and Nieves. It was unsurprising then that in 1562 he was chosen as governor in return for promising to assume the expenses of pacification and settlement.

Conflict erupted because the Audiencia of New Galicia already claimed jurisdiction and had chosen men to head some towns in the area. One was Diego García de Colio, who "was a tough old *conquistador*, who had been at the taking of Mexico [Tenochtitlán] and had served subsequently in Guatemala, and under Francisco Cortés in Chimalhuacán. He was a vecino of Guadalajara, a person of considerable social influence in New Galicia" (Parry 1948: 89–90). When Francisco de Ibarra appeared in the town of San Martín and asserted his authority as governor of New Vizcaya, García de Colio resisted. An angry scene ensued during which García de Colio was injured. Ibarra then expelled him and other municipal officials, refounded the town, and left. After his departure, García de Colio reestablished the jurisdiction of the Audiencia and sent an angry letter of complaint and protest to the king. Meanwhile, Ibarra set up his headquarters in Durango and from there started to extend his jurisdiction toward the Pacific Ocean. The Audiencia of Guadalajara objected. In 1564 Viceroy Velasco died, leaving the viceregal throne empty. The Audiencia of New Galicia appealed to King Philip II, because no favorable decision could be expected from the Audiencia of New Spain in Mexico City. The Audiencia of New Galicia claimed that some towns had been founded before Ibarra arrived and therefore were under its jurisdiction; that it had authority over the population of what was becoming New Vizcaya; and that appeals should be heard by its judges. Ibarra replied that he recognized only the viceregal and audiencia authority in Mexico City. He also said in his defense that the whole dispute resulted from jealousy because the oidores could not do what he was doing. He saw his actions as service to the crown.

The new viceroy, Gastón de Peralta, the Marqués de Falces (1566–7), supported Ibarra, because by granting him jurisdiction he recognized his own authority over the northern settlers. The Audiencia of New Galicia protested again. A 1567 compromise halted the dispute and potential violence temporarily by giving the Audiencia of New Galicia appellate jurisdiction. The judges, however, were still not totally satisfied. They decided to bide their time, hoping that the next viceroy would reverse the order. In 1569 Ibarra asserted his legal victories and marched into the town of Nombre de Dios, where he deposed the officials appointed by the Audiencia. An armed clash was avoided only because the Viceroy Martín Enríquez de Almansa took complete control of the town. In 1576 Philip II ruled (on appeal) that the town was part of New Vizcaya. Thus, the ultimate authority, the Crown, vindicated the viceregal decisions and authority. But this occurred only after the struggle between Ibarra and the Audiencia of New Galicia was redefined by the Viceroy and the Audiencia of Mexico City; situations shifted with changing viceroys, and central authorities compromised to prevent major clashes and violence. Long delays were common. During these, each side bargained, and appealed to the king. Appeals were made to multiple authorities over the years, but the king had the last say.

Usually the viceroy did not intervene in local affairs, but a striking example of viceregal intervention occurred in 1588 over the unlawful marriage of a judge of the Audiencia of New Galicia. The case illustrates the continuing clashes between peninsular and local authority and the calming effect of the clergy (Parry 1948: 170–1). At first glance, this might seem insignificant, even trivial. Viceroys and oidores were forbidden by a decree of 1575 – and later their children too were forbidden – to marry into the local elite and were automatically to be deprived of their office and salary if they did so. In 1588 Nuño Núñez de Villavicencio, a judge of the Audiencia of New Galicia, married the daughter of Juan Bautista de Lomas y Colmenares, a rancher, mine owner, and citizen of Nieves in New Galicia. It was the duty of the president of the Audiencia to deprive Núñez de Villavicencio of his position, but the presidency was vacant. None of the other judges took action against a colleague. The Viceroy Álvaro Manrique de Zúñiga, Marqués de Villamanrique (1585–90), ordered Núñez de Villavicencio to be arrested and held without salary. In response the oidores declared the viceroy without jurisdiction over the population of New Galicia. An outraged viceroy wanted to reduce the tribunal to obedience by force. He ordered an army of 300 men to advance toward Guadalajara. The Audiencia, in reaction, mustered 200 vecinos and their servants, while the local natives fled to the hills and work came to a standstill. Eventually, the bishop interceded, leading a "solemn procession" with the exposed Host in his hands, and with "sermons and showers of tears" he persuaded the commander of the viceroy's army to return to Mexico and avoid civil war.

Reports reached the king, who intervened to prevent civil war by replacing the viceroy with Luís de Velasco, the younger (1590–5). In the end the new viceroy took no action, and Núñez de Villavicencio got to keep his office, his salary, and his wife. Meanwhile, the struggle between viceroy and the Audiencia over a seemingly petty matter became redefined as one of major jurisdictional significance. In principle, the viceroy could intervene in the presidency of New Galicia, but in practice efforts to do so could provoke violent conflict. The king took quick and decisive action when conflict (which was expected) reached a threshold level, above which it was not tolerated. The Church, the traditional bestower of political legitimacy, intervened in a political dispute. Local defiance was tolerated to a degree, but the balance of authority was not to be destroyed.

In the Hapsburg governing system there were also clashes between church and state. For example, a conflict between the Audiencia of New Galicia and the Inquisition over jurisdiction occurred in the 1590s during the viceroyalty of Luis de Velasco, the younger (1590–5, who wanted to organize an expedition to settle what is now the US state of New Mexico (Parry 1948: 177–84). There were two candidates for the job, both from New Galicia: Juan Bautista de Lomas y Colmenares of the town of Nieves, reputed to be the richest man in New Galicia with considerable family influence; and Francisco de Urdiñola, a Basque who had come to the Indies as a "poor gentleman," but who had acquired considerable wealth as a rancher and mine owner. Urdiñola was known as an able soldier and organizer, having settled New León (Coahuila) and founded the city of Saltillo. The incident started in February of 1593 when Urdiñola's wife died. Six months later Domingo de Landaverde, a Spaniard employed by Urdiñola as a mechanic and handyman, disappeared. An official inquiry discovered nothing and the case was closed. After the incident, Urdiñola was summoned to Mexico City to talk with Viceroy Velasco about the expedition (*entrada*) into New Mexico. The Crown had rejected Lomas y Colmenares' proposal because he wanted powers and conditions that were deemed "outrageous." Urdiñola's appointment was almost certain. But, the proceedings were interrupted by an order for his arrest on a charge of murder, issued by the Audiencia of New Galicia.

The Audiencia's case resulted from an anonymous and undated denunciation accusing Urdiñola of poisoning his wife and murdering his employee Landaverde, alleging adultery as the motive. This action was taken after the son-in-law of Lomas y Colmenares, Urdiñola's rival, became a judge of the Audiencia of New Galicia. The Audiencia sent a judge to Nieves to arrest Urdiñola, his steward, and younger brother and sequester his property. But Urdiñola was in Mexico City and the younger brother and steward were absent. Urdiñola appealed to the viceroy who dispatched a letter to the Audiencia, requesting that the trial be removed to Mexico City. The Audiencia refused. Then Urdiñola, as a *familiar*, sought protection of the Inquisition, which took fast action. The next day it sent an order to the Audiencia demanding jurisdiction and that Urdiñola's property be released. The Inquisition also asked civil authorities to keep Urdiñola in Mexico City, safe from arrest by the Audiencia. The Audiencia replied that the Inquisition did not have jurisdiction in cases of murder. The Inquisition replied with a threat to excommunicate and fine the judges and their agents. This impasse forced the parties to negotiate the jurisdiction according to a decree of 1572 that provided that in cases of conflict over criminal jurisdiction, the senior judge of the Audiencia should confer with two Inquisitors. If agreement could not be reached the parties were to send the case to Spain, where the *Suprema* of the Inquisition and Council of the Indies would decide it. Meanwhile, the accused was to be released on bond.

The Audiencia sent an agent, not a judge, so the Inquisitors paid no heed. Finally in May of 1595, a judge arrived in Mexico City. Eventually, the Audiencia and the Inquisition both sent agents to Nieves to hear witnesses. The Inquisition inquiry reported that there was no case against Urdiñola and that he had been framed at the instigation of Lomas y Colmenares to get Urdiñola out of the way so that he would be commissioned to lead the expedition into New Mexico. The case was appealed to Spain where it was decided according to strict law in favor of the Audiencia. Urdiñola was tried in Guadalajara, but the composition of the court had changed. The judgment in the case, given in 1598, found Urdiñola an accessory to the death of Landaverde. Urdiñola appealed to Mexico City and, there, was found innocent. Thus, the Church, specifically in this case the Inquisition, had power and would protect its own (here, a familiar) in disputes over jurisdiction. The conflict expanded and spread upward; a personal dispute became an institutional one. Institutions bargained and negotiated; appeals limited conflict. Yet, as in the cases above, the central power resolved the dispute in the end.

These cases illustrate the general truth that while central power managed to maintain overall authority it was not absolute, nor could it be, considering the size of the Spanish Empire, the vast distances, and the difficulty of communication and control.

Corrupting Contradictions

Contradictions within the system of governance also made practice different than what was expected in principle. For example, the restrictions on local corregidores, who over time became overwhelmingly creoles, were numerous. A man could not be a corregidor in his native region. He was not supposed to hold significant property in the area in which he held office. He was not supposed to be a relative of another office holder. He could not marry a woman under his jurisdiction. The term of office of five years was supposed to prevent him from establishing an entrenched local base of support. Before taking office he had to submit an inventory of his property and personal effects. And he had to secure a bond to guarantee his honesty in handling tribute and taxes and the administration of justice. But because a candidate usually turned to the local elite, be it made up of encomenderos, landowners, miners, merchants, or some combination of these, to put up his bond, he became beholden to them. This made complete impartiality in settling court cases sometimes impossible. When he left town to visit the people under his jurisdiction, for example, he left a lieutenant in his place, occasionally one of his guarantors, who used the delegated power to settle court cases in his own or his kinsmen's or client's interests (Ramírez 1986: 50–1, 80, 87–8, 136, 143, 228).

In the seventeenth century, the corregidor also had to buy his office. Because the state salary was low, the corregidor had to find other ways to recoup the expenditure and otherwise benefit from his office. Thus his interests were financial, as well as administrative. Corregidores of Indians forced natives to buy sometimes non-essential goods, like mules, mirrors, and wine at high and inflated prices. In some areas, too, the corregidor distributed to natives such raw materials as cotton or wool, to spin and weave into cloth, in a rudimentary system reminiscent of the putting-out system of Europe. The corregidor then sold the resulting cloth at a profit (Ramírez 1986: 88–9, 143).

At the end of the corregidor's term, he was required to stand for a review (*residencia*) of his administration, designed to investigate and determine if he had misappropriated funds or abused his power. These proceedings proved moderately effective in the sixteenth century, but over the course of the seventeenth century most became increasingly procedural and ineffective. This was due to the fact that local members of the elite put up the bond to guarantee that the incoming royal official would remain for the official inquiry into his tenure. When the time came, however, these same guarantors had no incentive for denouncing abuses, because they were ultimately responsible for paying any fines incurred for infractions. Secondly, the announcements of the proceedings were made in Spanish by the public crier, thereby leaving natives who did not know the language uninformed of the proceedings. Finally, in these residencias the judge might be – and often was – the incoming royal official, who knew that he too would be subject to the same kind of hearing at the end of his term. This made him sympathetic to his predecessor and may have led to the whitewashing of misdeeds. Only if the abuse was egregious would fines be levied. These contradictions in the system allowed laws to be inconsistently obeyed or implemented, especially at the local level (Ramírez 1986: 51).

These same regulations and the poor pay of most positions, in a social atmosphere that pressured officials to live ostentatiously, motivated most to ease their monetary worries by finding ways to get around them and out of embarrassing predicaments in the spirit of "*hecho la ley, hecho la trampa*" (a law passed begets a trick to bypass it). For instance, the same types of financial pressures experienced by the corregidor also subverted his supervisors and the entire hierarchy of royal officials. Thus, the first viceroy of New Spain, Antonio de Mendoza (1535–50):

in his person and as the monarch's surrogate presented a far more resplendent and impressive symbol of royal, indeed imperial, authority. He belonged to one of the five or six most powerful and prestigious families in Castile. He came of a functioning aristocracy, active in military leadership, civil administration, and the church hierarchy, wealthy in lands and livestock, and responsible in royal service. He was a younger son of Don Iñigo López de Mendoza, Count of Tendilla and Marquis of Mondéjar, the first Christian governor of Granada. In the years of Ferdinand's regency in Castile, when nobles and towns once again tended to autonomy, Tendilla had remained loyal to the principle of centralized authority and by his example and influence kept Andalucia at peace. In New Spain Mendoza maintained a court, a bodyguard of thirty to forty gentlemen, and a staff of sixty Indians, and employed many more. As viceroy he was also president of the audiencia of Mexico, vice-patron of the church, and prime dispenser of patronage. He could and did frame laws, subject to review by the Council of the Indies. He ruled as father to the Indians, governor and mediator among Spaniards, and lesser version of the king. (Liss 1975: 56–7)

Although he himself may have obeyed the rules, they did not prevent other members of his immediate family from breaking them with his help.

From his arrival in New Spain Mendoza had complained of inadequate salary. Apparently, however, he soon found extra official means to sustain himself and his family. His brother Francisco had accompanied him to Mexico and became one of its principal wealthy vecinos, marrying the widow of Juan Jaramillo, whose first wife had been Marina, Hernán Cortés' native translator, confidante, and the mother of his bastard son, Martín. In 1556 Velasco's son Luis, later to be viceroy also, married María de Ircio y Mendoza, the Mexican-born daughter of Mendoza's sister Leonor and Martín de Ircio, and his daughter Ana de Castillo wed the mine-rich conqueror of Nueva Vizcaya, Diego de Ibarra. The second viceroy and his family, too, despite royal orders to the contrary, became actively involved in the economy and society of Mexico. (Liss 1975: 65–6)

Stephanie Blank (1974) and Clara López Beltrán (1998) have documented social networks that operated in a similar fashion in colonial Venezuela and Bolivia, respectively.

Other royal officials were subject to many of the same prohibitions as the corregidor, like not marrying, holding property, or profiting locally. But colonial manuscripts document how such legislation remained often a dead letter. In the 1540s, the oidor Lorenzo de Tejada was denounced for trading with the Indians. He exchanged bad land for twice as much good land and bought property which he improved and built upon for very profitable resale. And, in 1554, some oidores in New Galicia were known to be active in slaving, in mining in Zacatecas, and in related commerce. Luckily, the natives produced enough to satisfy the graft and exigencies of officials all the way up to the vice-king (Liss 1975: 66).

Like royal officials, colonists at all levels developed mechanisms to thwart effective central control. One of these was a studied non-observance of royal decrees. Early in the history of Spanish America, local authorities used the phrase "*obedezco pero no cumplo*" (I obey, but will not comply) to delay or forego the implementation of certain royal proclamations that conflicted with local interests or did not fit local circumstances. In the classical case, an alcalde would read the decree aloud, at a cabildo meeting, for example; hold it over his head; and pronounce the words "*obedezco pero no cumplo*," indicating that he recognized the Crown's authority to issue the decree, but would not enforce it because it did not fit provincial conditions. While he then penned a reply to the Crown explaining his actions, the decree's implementation was held in abeyance. Often, years passed before a reply came from Spain. Meanwhile, the decree was ignored and largely forgotten.

An example of such resistance and effective local autonomy comes from the municipal level where the town council (*cabildo*) represented the power and authority of the local elite. In a climate of serious financial exigencies after the defeat of the Spanish Armada in 1588, the Crown tried to impose a special tax to sponsor and arm an American fleet. Town councils became a lobbying force against the tax. The cabildo of the highland city of Quito invoked the "*obedezco pero no cumplo*" tradition and asked for a suspension, arguing that they were already paying a subsidy to fortify the seaport of Guayaquil. Behind some of the resistance was the thought that the fleet was a mechanism shutting them off from a freer international trade that might have lowered the costs of imported goods. So why, some asked, should citizens living far from the ocean pay for a measure to secure the port of Guayaquil or a fleet to patrol the coast? The cabildo of Quito tried to influence other cabildos, like that of Cuenca, to ally with them on this issue, but they refused, so the Quito council proceeded alone. Eventually, the president of the Audiencia, Dr. Manuel Barros de San Millán, jailed a member of the cabildo. When the vecinos let him out of jail, Barros de San Millán requested military backup from Lima. A few days after Christmas of 1592, fighting broke out. The viceroy of Lima, García Hurtado de Mendoza (1589–96), had dispatched troops and, in response, the vecinos had called up a voluntary militia and begun to talk about independence with the support of England. In the insurrection that followed, a sniper shot a leading citizen and a priest mediated to stop a mob of citizens from attacking the audiencia president. Eventually, in 1593, the Crown sent an independent royal agent to mediate, investigate, and review the situation. He imposed the tax, but dismissed Barros de San Millán because he had not sought a compromise. In the end the Crown won (Pareja Diezcanseco 1958: 269–75). Thereafter, the cabildo as an institution lost power to the corregidor and viceroy. The Crown began to sell cabildo offices to men who had a stake in the system and therefore would not challenge and change it. The signs of decline of the cabildo are seen in the infrequency of meetings and the refusal to serve, especially in smaller towns. In the seventeenth century, municipalities sold off public lands, depriving them of a source of income. They became dependent on the viceroy for money. The scope of their activities declined and they often let crown-appointed corregidores take over some of their functions.

When a legal way could not be invented around a law or regulation, people resorted to corruption. The trade monopoly, heavy taxation, and mercantilistic trade and production restrictions encouraged contraband. To escape paying the royal fifth, Potosí miners sent part of their silver down the river system to the south Atlantic coast to exchange for imports of English manufactured goods and French luxury items. In mid-seventeenth century Peru the sale of fiscal offices to inefficient and dishonest officials "with strong local connections" institutionalized "venality and corruption," negatively affecting royal tax collection efforts. Twenty or twenty-five years later a crown investigator described the Supreme Court judge Bartolomé Salazar as a "dangerous and greedy man, who used his position to build a personal fortune of over 10,000,000 pesos." The same investigator fingered another "major offender," Diego León Pinelo, the crown attorney to the Audiencia and official "protector of the Indians." His large family and numerous debts made him subject to bribes and other forms of graft. However, the most consistent form of corruption concerned the corregidor of Indians. One investigation found that tribute debts from these officials reached nearly 2.5 million pesos in 1664, confirming that the residencia system was in most cases a moot exercise (Andrien 1982: 103–4, 171–2). Another notorious example was the case of Dr. Antonio Morga, who became the president of the Audiencia of Quito. In the second decade of the seventeenth century en route from Mexico to Quito he took with him 40,000 pesos worth of contraband Chinese silks. After the contraband's discovery, it was placed under armed guard, but within days, it had disappeared. Later it was offered for sale at a retail shop in Quito. One of the owners of the store was Dr. Morga's son and namesake. The son's interest in the retail store was "a flagrant violation of royal edicts, several of which prohibited any commercial activity on the part of the unmarried children of magistrates or their servants" (Phelan 1970: 160).

From Institutional to Social History

In sum, social historians have fleshed out the institutional framework earlier studied and described in legal terms, to refocus our attention on how institutions worked on a daily basis and how they affected such social categories, as miners, landowners, or merchants; or, increasingly, specific individuals. The centralized, hierarchical system looked and sounded good and rational in theory. But institutions functioned variably in practice. And, although this discussion suggests that the government institutions affected the life of every social sector, the present state of research shows that they did so on an uneven basis. A viceroy, although theoretically omnipotent, was only one man in figurative control over thousands of people scattered over vast territories which at first had no fixed and recognized boundaries, and across which transportation and communication was difficult and very time consuming. Even corregidores had trouble administering the populations of their much more reduced and specific jurisdictions because of scattered settlement patterns. In addition, the concept of "*obedezco pero no cumplo*"; the compromising ties between peninsular royal officials and the local elites; the fact that more native sons were finding places in the bureaucracy and the Church; overlapping jurisdictions; and inherent contradictions in the institutions designed to impose Hapsburg authority effectively meant that royal mandates were only sporadically and imperfectly enforced. A focus on crown officials and the people they governed shows that the state remained relatively weak during the Hapsburg era. Although such a system was less effective from an official's point of view, it was ultimately efficacious from Madrid's perspective. Legal ambiguities and a tolerance for less than the letter of the law gave the system enduring flexibility that, argues Phelan (1960), allowed Hapsburg Spain to incorporate vast regions and large native populations into a colonial structure and govern Spanish America for more than two centuries.

However, this story is still largely about elites interacting with other elites. Future scholars need to focus on the lives of the common folk as they interacted with these institutions. This points scholarship in the direction taken by Irene Silverblatt (2004) and (to a lesser extent) Surge Gruzinski's (1989) work on the Inquisition and the people in both elite and non-elite sectors that were denounced before this ecclesiastical tribunal. Interactions between church officials and traditional natives push us into the realm of historical anthropology and how the Church, for example, extirpated idolatry. Only by studying these specific and seemingly unimportant individual cases can we learn how the people reacted and in doing so helped shape the institutions of the Hapsburg colonial system (Mills 1997).

BIBLIOGRAPHY

Alfaro, A. (2001) *Los colegios jesuitas en la Nueva España*. Artes de México, México City.

Andrien, K. J. (1982) *Crisis and Decline: The Viceroyalty of Peru in the Seventeenth Century*. University of New Mexico Press, Albuquerque.

Artíñano y de Galdácano, G. (1917) *Historia del comercio con las Indias durante el domonio de los Austrias*. Talleres de Oliva de Vilanova, Barcelona.

Avellaneda, J. I. (1995) *The Conquerors of the New Kingdom of Granada*. University of New Mexico Press, Albuquerque.

Bakewell, P. (1984) *Miners of the Red Mountain*. University of New Mexico Press, Albuquerque.

Blank, S. (1974) "Patrons, Clients, and Kin in Seventeenth Century Caracas: A Methodological Essay in Colonial South American Social History," *Hispanic American Historical Review*, 54:2, pp. 260–83.

Blank, S. (1979) "Patrons, Brokers and Clients in the Families of the Elite in Colonial Caracas, 1595–1627," *The Americas*, 36:1, pp. 90–115.

Burga, M. (1976) *De la encomienda a la hacienda capitalista*. Instituto de Estudios Peruanos, Lima.

Burkholder, M. A. (1980) *Politics of a Colonial Career: José Baquíjano and the Audiencia of Lima*. University of New Mexico Press, Albuquerque.

Burkholder, M. A. & Johnson, L. (2004) *Colonial Latin America*. Oxford University Press, New York.

Burns, K. (1999) *Colonial Habits: Convents and the Spiritual Economy of Cuzco, Peru*. Duke University Press, Durham.

Céspedes del Castillo, G. (1945) *La avería en el comercio de Indias*. Escuela de Estudios Hispano-Americanos, Sevilla.

Céspedes del Castillo, G. (1947) *Lima y Buenos Aires, repercusiones económicas y políticas de la creación del virreinato del Plata*. Escuela de Estudios Hispano-Americanos, Seville.

Chevalier, F. (1970) *Land and Society in Colonial Mexico: The Great Hacienda*. University of California Press, Berkeley.

Cushner, N. P. (1980) *Lords of the Land: Sugar, Wine and Jesuit Estates of Coastal Peru, 1600–1767*. State University of New York Press, Albany.

Davies, K. A. (1984) *Landowners in Colonial Peru*. University of Texas Press, Austin.

Gibson, C. (1966) *Spain in America*. Harper Torchbooks, New York.

Greenleaf, R. (1969) *The Mexican Inquisition of the Sixteenth Century*. University of New Mexico Press, Albuquerque.

Grunberg, B. (1994) "The Origins of the Conquistadores of Mexico City," *Hispanic American Historical Review*, 74:2, pp. 259–83.

Gruzinski, S. (1989) *Man-gods in the Mexican Highlands: Indian Power and Colonial Society, 1520–1800*. Stanford University Press, Stanford.

Guevara Gil, J. A. (1993) *Propiedad agraria y derecho colonial*. Pontificia Universidad Católica del Perú, Lima.

Haring, C. H. (1947) *The Spanish Empire in America*. Harcourt, Brace, and World, Inc., New York.

Haring, C. H. (1918) *Trade and Navigation between Spain and the Indies in the Time of the Hapsburgs*. Harvard University Press, Cambridge, MA.

Himmerich y Valencia, R. (1991) *The Encomenderos of New Spain, 1521–1555*. University of Texas Press, Austin.

Keith, R. G. (1971) "*Encomienda, Hacienda* and *Corregimiento* in Spanish America: A Structural Analysis," *Hispanic American Historical Review*, 51:3, pp. 431–46.

Klein, H. S. (1998) *American Finances of the Spanish Empire: Royal Income and Expenditures in Colonial Mexico, Peru and Bolivia, 1680–1809*. University of New Mexico Press, Albuquerque.

Langer, E. & Jackson, R. H. (eds.) (1995) *The New Latin American Mission History*. University of Nebraska Press, Lincoln.

Liss, P. K. (1975) *Mexico under Spain, 1521–1556: Society and the Origins of Nationality*. University of Chicago Press, Chicago.

Lockhart, J. (1969) "Encomienda and Hacienda: The Evolution of the Great Estate in the Spanish Indies," *Hispanic American Historical Review*, 49:3, August.

Lockhart, J. & Schwartz, S. (1983) *Early Latin America: A History of Colonial Spanish America and Brazil*. Cambridge University Press, Cambridge.

Lohmann Villena, G. (1999) *Las minas de Huancavelica en los siglos XVI y XVII*. Pontificia Universidad Católica del Perú, Lima.

López Beltrán, C. (1998) *Alianzas familiares: Elite, género y negocios en La Paz, siglo 17*. Insituto de Estudios Peruanos Lima.

Mills, K. R. (1997) *Idolatry and Its Enemies*. Princeton University Press, Princeton.

Moreyra Paz Soldán, M. (1950) *El tribunal del consulado de Lima*. Instituto Histórico del Perú, Lima.

Pareja Diezcanseco, A. (1958) *Historia del Ecuador*. Editorial Casa de la Cultura Ecuatoriana, Quito.

Parry, J. H. (1948) *The Audiencia of New Galicia in the Sixteenth Century: A Study in Spanish Colonial Government*. Cambridge University Press, Cambridge.

Phelan, J. L. (1960) "Authority and Flexibility in the Spanish Imperial Bureaucracy," *Administrative Science Quarterly*, V: 1, 47–65.

Phelan, J. L. (1967) *The Kingdom of Quito in the Seventeenth Century*. University of Wisconsin Press, Madison.

Phelan, J. L. (1970) *The Millennial Kingdom of the Franciscans in the New World*. University of California Press, Berkeley.

Puente Brunke, J. (1992) *Encomienda y encomenderos en el Perú: Estudio social y politico de una institución colonial*. Diputacion Provincial de Sevilla, Sevilla.

Ramírez, S. E. (1986) *Provincial Patriarchs: Land Tenure and the Economics of Power in Colonial Peru*. University of New Mexico Press, Albuquerque.

Ricard, R. (1966) *The Spiritual Conquest of Mexico*. University of California Press, Berkeley.

Saeger, J. (2000) *The Chaco Mission Frontier*. University of Arizona Press, Tucson.

Schwaller, J. F. (2000) *The Church in Colonial Latin America*. Scholarly Resources, Wilmington, DE.

Silverblatt, I. (2004) *Modern Inquisitions: Peru and the Colonial Origins of the Civilized World*. Duke University Press, Durham.

Chapter Eight

INDIGENOUS PEOPLES IN COLONIAL SPANISH AMERICAN SOCIETY

Kevin Terraciano

This essay focuses on the fully sedentary, highly organized peoples who came into contact with Spaniards during the colonial period, from the sixteenth through the eighteenth centuries. These groups were located primarily up and down the central Andes (from modern-day Ecuador to Peru and Bolivia) and Middle America (central and southern Mexico and Guatemala). I will not neglect the other regions of Latin America entirely, but I have chosen to focus on these two extended culture areas for three reasons: (1) they were the centers of intensive contact between Europeans, indigenous peoples, and Africans in this period; (2) we know so much more about the native peoples of these areas compared to other areas of Latin America because of the contact; and (3) limitations of length. It is no accident that the Spaniards gravitated to the sedentary peoples and settled among them. The latter shared the most in common with the Europeans, who stood to gain the most from the labor, lands, and resources of these peoples after the military conquests. The countless surviving texts produced by Spanish and indigenous writers from these areas continue to engage us and challenge us to write better histories. This chapter is a summary of relatively recent findings on certain aspects of this complex and important topic.

The sedentary areas of Mexico and Peru became the two great viceroyalties of Nueva España and Nueva Castilla, respectively, and were consolidated by the 1550s. Spaniards went immediately to these promising areas of sedentary native populations, lured at first by gold and then later by silver. After the military conquests thousands of Iberians went especially to the economically flourishing areas of the colonies, where employment and other opportunities were most promising. This process was so rapid that every major Spanish city in the "Indies" had been founded by the end of the sixteenth century.

The conquests of the sedentary peoples were rapid and permanent. The Spaniards enjoyed a tremendous military and technological advantage. Most people had no place to migrate or escape to and chose not to leave their ancestral, sacred lands. In most places, the Spaniards acquired supplies and local allies with each victory, so that each successive conquest in the sedentary areas made the next one easier. But among the more mobile non-sedentary peoples, fighting in many areas went on indefinitely and expeditions could not achieve final results. Forts were built, permanent paid soldiers were stationed on frontiers, and native peoples were brought in from other regions as middlemen to help pacify the war zones. Rebellions or new hostilities continued for centuries. The enslaving of Indians and the establishment of missions – ecclesiastical fortresses where people from a large area were congregated – were typical features of European expansion into the vastly underpopulated regions of Latin America. In places such as northern Mexico, the Río de la Plata region, Venezuela, and the Amazonia, Europeans adopted new strategies to take advantage of local situations.

Contact with Europeans devastated native peoples in many ways. Nothing remained the same. The initial shock of conquest was accompanied or followed soon after by waves of epidemic diseases, a spiritual and cultural crusade against native religions and life-ways, and multiple attempts to reorganize native society. It is difficult to generalize about the experiences of hundreds of culture and language groups under colonial rule. In general, however, it is safe to say that processes of change were more extensive and rapid in areas where many Europeans went, and were delayed in places where Europeans were few. Resistance to change was often complex and subtle, but many changes resulted from cultural contact over the course of generations, so that individuals, groups, or even whole communities could not, over time, resist all aspects of cultural influence from Spaniards and Africans, nor did they always want to. Likewise, Spaniards and Africans were not immune to native cultural influences.

Indigenous peoples of North and South America could not have foreseen or resisted the onslaught of disease that battered them from the very beginning of these dark times. In the first century after contact, the native population declined to approximately 10–20 percent of the preconquest total. In Spanish America, the indigenous population declined steadily until around 1650. Never before or since has mankind witnessed such a staggering loss of life from disease, compounded in some places by warfare, slavery, plague, and malnutrition. In Mesoamerica, the population at the time of contact is estimated at 20 to 25 million; the Andean highlands had at least half as many inhabitants. The total population (Spaniards, Africans, and peoples of mixed racial descent included) did not reach its preconquest level until the twentieth century. The native population never came close to its original numbers again. The epidemics that affected every generation were more extreme than the Black Death of medieval Europe, which killed as many as half the urban residents in some areas. Native Americans had no immunities to the diseases of Eurasia and Africa, such as smallpox, measles, pertussis (whooping cough), and diphtheria, that the Europeans and their domesticated animals introduced in the Americas. It is impossible to imagine the psychological and cultural impact of this death and destruction, which debilitated native peoples' abilities to resist invasion and forms of coercion and domination. Europeans were also vulnerable to diseases such as malaria, especially in the lowland tropical areas; but they were not affected as a group in such a catastrophic way.

Coercive Labor Systems

The economy of the Indies in the early period consisted mainly of the Europeans' use of native and African labor to furnish and produce goods, especially raw materials, for shipment across the Atlantic. In return, merchants supplied European goods to those who needed them in the Indies. In Spanish America, the mining of precious metals made it possible. Mines generated the wealth to attract Spaniards to the Americas, to buy European and Asian goods, and to maintain the Crown's strategic interest in the colonies. The Spaniards were fortunate to find large silver deposits in or near the great sedentary areas of Mexico and Peru, where they could rely on a large supply of cheap or free labor to enrich themselves.

At first, Spaniards relied on the *encomienda* (from *encomendar*, to entrust), a grant by the Crown to a Spaniard, usually for life, to collect a specified amount of labor and tribute from a given indigenous community. A *corregidor* or *alcalde mayor* (local Spanish officials in charge of a given jurisdiction) oversaw this process. The encomienda was given to an important Spaniard (most were *conquistadores*) who resided in the Spanish city, and was based on an existing native sociopolitical unit, which kept its own authorities and its people kept their own land, but through the *cacique* (native leader) they performed labor for and/or paid tribute to the *encomendero*. The encomendero informed the cacique of his demands, and the cacique depended on the already existing labor and tribute mechanisms to produce it. Spanish authorities bullied or replaced resistant caciques if necessary. The functioning of the encomienda depended on the indigenous community's maintenance of its internal government, land resources, and taxpaying mechanisms. If the resources were lost, whether through depopulation or reorganization, then the encomienda would not work well.

This system of labor taxation placed additional burdens on members of indigenous communities, who were required to pay tribute and labor to the encomendero, the native nobility, and the local church, even as the population declined. In central Mexico, Spaniards used tribute lists of the conquered Mexica to determine the types of products that communities produced. In practice, however, Spaniards did not want or need many traditional tribute items such as feathers or maize, but rather preferred items for Spanish consumption, such as wheat. Cotton cloth was one indigenous item that remained in high demand. Eventually, Spaniards demanded tribute in quantities of gold or silver, which communities had to acquire through trade or mining, and thus were forced to enter the money economy.

A generation after the conquest, when most communities had been assigned as encomiendas, when the native population was declining and immigration from Europe was increasing, newly arriving Spaniards began to compete for native labor and tribute and resented the special privileges of encomenderos. This increased competition among the Spanish group led to the decline of the encomienda as a solution for the distribution of native labor. King Charles I abolished the encomienda in the name of justice for the Indians, but he also increased the Crown's own authority by limiting the powers of the Spanish colonial aristocracy. Conquistadors and their descendants resisted this attempt to rein in their powers and fortunes, and in Peru it fueled a civil war, reminiscent of the Comunero Revolts in Spain only two decades earlier. Once the encomienda was abolished, people in the escheated encomienda jurisdiction paid tribute directly to the Crown. Encomiendas that were left vacant were directly assigned to the Crown; in fact, some of the largest and most populous native provinces belonged to the Crown from a very early time because the system would not allow such vast assets to go to any one encomendero.

One solution to the shortage of labor was the *repartimiento* (from *repartir* – to distribute), a system of rotational labor in which colonial authorities assigned small groups of native people to individual Spaniards for specific periods of time, such as three months or a year. Thus more Spaniards could share the wealth of Indian labor while communities continued to rely on traditional mechanisms to provide the labor. In Peru repartimiento labor was called *mita*, using the Quechua term for "turn" or "season." Inca rulers had relied on a similar concept of rotational labor duty, although they did not direct labor drafts almost exclusively to the grueling and often hazardous work of mining, as did the Spaniards. And in preconquest Andean society, each person and each unit was to make a contribution to the general good and receive something in return; when workers did mita duty for the *curacas* (native lords), they received provisions, clothing, or other gifts in return. This was not the case with the repartimiento.

Encomiendas in central Mexico gave way to the repartimiento system by the second and third generations after the conquest. Away from the center, where there was less competition among Spaniards because there were fewer of them, the encomienda tended to last longer. Mining areas relied both on the unskilled labor of repartimiento and the skilled wage labor involved in processing the ore. By the middle of the seventeenth century, the repartimiento in turn gave way in many places to individual wage labor arrangements between Spaniards and Indians or *mestizos*. Again, the timing of this process varied considerably. A form of the repartimiento in areas such as highland Peru and Yucatán persisted until the end of the colonial period and, in fact, continued into the postcolonial period. In general, labor acquisition relied less over time on indigenous communities to channel labor and material resources. In any case, the vast majority of labor arrangements in the sedentary areas relied on the native population in this period.

Political and Economic Reorganization

Recent research has emphasized how central communities were in the organization of indigenous societies, especially among the sedentary peoples. The endurance and strength of these communities, even after massive population loss and numerous colonial and postcolonial challenges, continues to intrigue ethnohistorians. In Mesoamerica, for example, one of many culture and language groups known today as the Nahuas lived in hundreds of small states, with anywhere from a couple of thousand to fifty or even a hundred thousand inhabitants in each. Such a state was called an *altepetl* (Nahuatl "water(s) and mountain(s)," in reference to the people's territory). Everywhere we look in the sedentary areas, there is some close equivalent. What we call the Aztec Empire was a confederation of three altepetl, of which the leading and largest was México-Tenochtitlán (the people of this place were called *Mexica* and/or *Tenochca*), on the site of present-day Mexico City. One would need to go to Istanbul or the Far East to find cities as large as Tenochtitlán just before the Spaniards arrived. Through a series of conquests, the Mexica elites collected tribute of all kinds from many of the other altepetl of the region, and arranged interdynastic marriages with them to their own advantage. In this way they built a broad power base that extended into southern Mexico and unified the regional economy to a large extent. But the people of the whole region did not become Mexica. Some large states, such as the four-part confederation of Tlaxcala, were entirely outside the Mexica network. And even in the area of Mexica dominance, each group still lived within its own separate altepetl, which kept its name, its people, usually most of its territory, and its own dynastic leader. The Tlatelolca, who lived on the island of Tenochtitlán in the lake of Tetzcoco, were closer to the Mexica than any other group, but still considered themselves Tlatelolca. In fact, the Mexica conquered Tlatelolco and forced them into the empire only a few decades before the Spanish invasion. Each altepetl had its own origin legend that recalled some momentous migration or sacred beginning. Each had, in addition to its own rulers, its own market and its own special deity (or deities), who was often a divine ancestor from the origin legend.

The implication of this cultural and political autonomy is that native civilization did not collapse when the larger confederations or empires fell apart. These communities were able to function on their own, even in relative isolation. This isolation benefited the colonizers, who encountered few sustained rebellions that unified communities across entire regions, and thus managed to suppress *tumultos* before they spread. But this isolation has also protected languages and customs from successive attacks by colonizers, modernizers, and nation builders, among others, who have sought to change these people over the last five centuries. Today, the survival of thousands of communities that are based squarely on preconquest settlements is one of the most enduring indigenous legacies of the Americas.

Spaniards made some attempts to reorganize sedentary communities into more nucleated and governable entities, moving communities from their defensive positions on hilltops and slopes to flatter land, and congregating them into more compact settlements. A second *congregación* campaign in the sixteenth century responded to demographic decline that had left the settlements even more dispersed. Spaniards also imposed regional hierarchies by designating some communities as *cabeceras* (head towns) and others as *sujetos* (subject towns), requiring the latter to channel their labor and tribute payments to the cabeceras to facilitate the collection of taxation, among other things. In many cases, the colonial hierarchies and divisions had not existed in preconquest times. Over time many sujetos broke away from cabeceras as soon as possible, creating numerous small independent units that came to be known as undifferentiated Indian *pueblos* (Spanish for "town," as well as "people").

Because it was impossible for even one Spaniard to reside in each of the thousands of communities spread out across the central areas, colonial rule depended on creating Spanish-style town councils, entirely made up of indigenous men. This town council was called the *cabildo*, just as Spanish cities in the Americas had their own cabildos. Spanish officials with wide-ranging administrative and judicial powers, called *alcaldes mayores* and *corregidores*, bought offices, usually for a five-year period, to collect taxation and act as first-instance judges within specified jurisdictions in the largely indigenous countryside. Native officials of the local cabildo were responsible for paying tribute to the Spanish alcalde mayor and reporting major crimes to him. In other words, the Spaniards instituted a form of local government that continued to rely entirely on the same group of local male nobles who had occupied similar political and economic roles before the conquest. They were responsible for serving as intermediaries between their communities and Spanish officials, and played an active role within the new colonial system, seeking to protect and promote their communities within the Spanish legal and administrative system.

In the new cabildo, the old hereditary lord (called *tlatoani* in Nahuatl or *cacique* in Spanish, *curaca* in Peru), usually held the highest office in the cabildo, now called *gobernador*. Thus the most important male of the community was called "cacique and governor." In certain areas, such as the Mixtec region of Oaxaca, there was a female *cacica* for every male cacique who was recognized locally as a dynastic leader. She could not hold the office of governor, but she continued to exercise hereditary leadership. In relatively remote areas such as the Mixteca, the titles of cacicas and caciques continued to be used throughout the colonial period. In most places, however, those rights and privileges associated with the ancient hereditary rulership had disappeared by the eighteenth century, and many of the governors no longer claimed descent from a precolonial dynastic lineage. At the same time, many hereditary rulers lost support within their communities, as distinctions between elites and commoners became less clear, and wealth became more important than claims to hereditary status.

Within indigenous communities, officials continued to handle many conflicts according to local custom, often without a written record, unless it were a violent or serious crime, or if a Spaniard were involved, or if the aggrieved party chose to approach the alcalde mayor with a complaint. In handling such a legal dispute, whether civil or criminal, the alcalde mayor and his staff began a formal investigation with the assistance of cabildo officials by assembling evidence and obtaining preliminary declarations from the parties involved, making arrests, if necessary, and scheduling a hearing with witnesses. In some respects the alcalde mayor, with his legal advisors and staff, personally administered justice at the provincial level. But individuals and groups (men and women, nobles and commoners) could appeal provincial decisions or move the entire proceedings to the *Audiencia* (highest court) in the capital or, in New Spain, to the *Juzgado de Indios*. Both courts exercised overlapping and supercessory jurisdiction over provincial cases involving Indians. They could appeal a case in one court and then, if necessary, approach the other. Even if the case were tried at the provincial level, the alcalde mayor consulted a lawyer from the Audiencia who reviewed the complete dossier on the crime and ratified, overturned, or issued a sentence. In fact, provincial courts in criminal proceedings could not impose sentences of death, mutilation, or slavery upon assailants without consulting Audiencia officials. Sentences passed by trained agents of the court might be influenced by several factors: early Spanish American precedent and law; the concerns of the colony or province; and Castilian codes of law. This complex legal system generated tons of paperwork and allowed a range of checks and appeals, but the system and the letter of the law favored those of high social standing, as it did in Spain.

In the sixteenth century, the encomienda and the Church were the major ties between Spanish and indigenous populations in the central areas. The encomienda's labor and tribute obligations brought large numbers of Indians into temporary contact with Spaniards in cities and mining settlements. Even though most of these people were under the supervision of their own authorities and did not deal directly with Spaniards, they came into contact with Spanish culture. The Spanish city was the headquarters of the vast majority of the Spanish population. Spaniards resided in the cities. This fact created a city/hinterland dichotomy more typical of Spain than of preconquest settlement patterns. The encomienda established a pattern of urban migration from indigenous communities to Spanish cities. Some native individuals and families remained in the cities and mining areas rather than going home, creating a small urban Indian population in a marginalized suburb. In the other direction, workers of the encomendero went out from the city to collect tribute and money from indigenous communities, and to organize Spanish enterprises such as wheat growing and cattle ranching. These people were mainly marginal, poor Spaniards, non-Spanish Europeans, free Africans or slaves, mestizos and *mulatos*. They were few in number at first, and their social and cultural impact on the countryside was not great in the first generations after conquest, but they were the beginning of a movement of people from the Spanish cities into the surrounding indigenous countryside, creating small Spanish-speaking centers outside of the cities that became the basis of provincial cities. Although Spanish law prohibited non-Indians from living in *repúblicas de Indios* without a permit, this law became increasingly outdated by the seventeenth century, when contact could not be avoided in most cases. Likewise, in the early period, Spaniards attempted to prohibit Indians from entering the *traza* or center of Mexico City without work permits, but the law proved too difficult and unrealistic to enforce.

Spaniards also competed with indigenous traders and producers and attempted to take over any profitable enterprise, even when it involved the sale of indigenous goods. For example, many groups across the continent practiced long-distance trade. At first, the new money economy offered all types of traders the prospect of earning pesos for carrying valuable indigenous commodities, such as cloth, dyes, cacao, precious feathers, gems, skins, etc. Some indigenous traders prospered in the early colonial period, but they were displaced by Spaniards and other Spanish-speaking individuals who possessed large pack trains for transport and who could draw on extensive credit lines for the advance purchase of goods. Native people were restricted by law in the number of mules that they could own, discouraged by officials from leaving their communities, and cut off from credit. Cheap cloth produced in Spanish-owned *obrajes* (workshops) competed with locally produced cloth or spun cotton, which was in high demand by local Spanish officials. It did not take long for the Crown to get in on the action. Royal monopolies on *pulque* (fermented alcoholic beverage) and tobacco, among other indigenous products, illustrate the extent of this competition and the disadvantages faced by native producers and traders, who became increasingly confined to the resale of products purchased from Spanish *tratantes* or *mercaderes* and the operation of small stores.

In the early colonial period, large landholdings were not a particularly valuable resource outside of the central areas, because agricultural goods or livestock could not be shipped across the Atlantic and domestic markets far from major cities were too small to demand many of these products. Also, encomienda labor and tribute could satisfy many local demands, and there was no shortage of good land as the indigenous population steadily declined. Agricultural practices requiring intensive labor, such as terracing, were abandoned, and overgrazing by countless flocks and herds who ran amok in the new ecosystem led to severe erosion in some places. Spaniards managed to acquire some of the best available lands closest to Spanish settlements, whether by conquest, royal grant, or purchase, but the real growth of Spanish *haciendas* (rural estates) did not occur until the second half of the colonial period. In the sedentary areas, haciendas grew at the expense of indigenous lands and benefited from the labor of landless peasants. As the total population began to increase in the second half of the seventeenth century, and domestic markets grew apace, Spaniards demanded more land for haciendas. This is when the implications of the privatization of landholding became readily apparent. In this period legislation known as the *composiciones de las tierras* (literally "compositions of lands") restricted the corporate landholdings of *pueblos* and required titles to all remaining lands claimed by communities or individuals. Those who did not possess titles to claimed lands, purchased in Spanish courts, could lose them to confiscation and auction. Native lands were increasingly lost over time, snatched up by people who had much more money and access to credit. Often, community leaders did everything possible to retain their ancestral lands. But many communities were fragmenting into smaller units by this period, spurred on by the incentive to claim pueblo status in order to acquire the maximum allocation of corporate lands, and many lacked the financial and legal resources to resist demands for privatizing land. This was a long and extended process, which continues to the present day, in some places.

The Spiritual Conquest

Friars and priests quickly followed in the footsteps of the conquerors. Like the encomienda, parishes were based on the location of already existing communities in the sedentary areas. Communities redirected a percentage of their labor and tribute toward building the church and maintaining the priest – a provision that often placed friars and encomenderos in direct competition for labor, especially as the indigenous population declined rapidly in the second half of the sixteenth century. Churches were built in the middle of settlements, often from the same stones and on the same sites as the preconquest temples. In the sedentary areas people possessed the technical and organizational skills, combined with new technologies and materials, to build magnificent churches in the colonial period; priests instructed local authorities to oversee church construction and attendance. Each constituency of the community usually built its own church. The Church considered every potential enterprise to sustain their activities, from producing silk and sugar to buying and selling African slaves.

During and after the military phase of the conquest, Christian priests set out to find and destroy temples, images, and native priests. They confiscated and burned indigenous *codices* and created new sacred texts in the form of native-language *doctrinas* or catechisms. They saw the conquest and the effect of European diseases as divine retribution for worshiping false gods and the devil, and sought to learn as much as possible about local beliefs and customs in order to identify and extirpate idolatries. Members of the religious orders developed extensive native-language training programs so that they could communicate with people, preach to large audiences in church patios, and hear confession. They worked with male elites and their sons in schools to develop native-language dictionaries and grammars, teaching them how to write their own languages with the Roman alphabet. There were so few priests that they could not have done it any other way. The orders also introduced edifying plays, established schools, and founded hospitals for the sick.

In the areas of sedentary populations, the Church created parishes based on existing communities and their administrative structures. In peripheral areas of low population density that was not possible, and Iberians adopted the mission as a method of conversion and pacification. The mission differed from the parish church in that it was located in a relatively arbitrarily chosen location, where indigenous people were forced or enticed from a large surrounding area to live in the mission compound. Mission establishments represented an adaptation of the center's rural monasteries to the peripheral zones. In the center, a cloister stood alongside the church, facing onto a large open atrium. The cloister enclosed the entire community: church, convent, storehouses, shops and workshops, and residences for Indians. Its walls defended it against attack. The enclosure in some missions was large enough for grazing livestock. Mission settlements were supervised directly by Spanish priests, usually friars in the regular orders. The Spaniards tried to make the indigenous peoples of the frontiers more like those of the sedentary areas, by creating walled-in settlements and forcing them to plant and harvest crops and perform Spanish-style enterprises. In New Spain, Spaniards relocated indigenous groups (especially the Tlaxcalans) from central Mexico to act as intermediaries in mining towns to the north and as far as New Mexico in the upper valley of the Río Grande. Missions and military forts (*presidios*) were Spanish adaptations to the frontier. The soldiers in these forts, plebeian Spaniards and mestizos, often supplemented their meager salaries by capturing Indians and selling them as slaves.

In northern Mexico there were four areas of mission activity: New Mexico beginning in the late sixteenth century; the Gulf of California in the seventeenth and eighteenth centuries; Texas in the early and mid-eighteenth century; and Alta California in the late eighteenth and into the early nineteenth century. As in central Mexico, the Franciscans were at first the most active order; by 1600 they had 25 establishments in the north. The Jesuits began to develop a northern mission program during the seventeenth century in Sonora, Arizona, and the coastal regions along the Gulf of California, among the Yaqui and Seri and other culture groups. Paraguay was another site of mission activity, where over 100,000 Indians were housed in as many as 30 Jesuit missions by the seventeenth century. Conflict between the Jesuits and Spanish settlers revolved around the right to control Guaraní labor in the region. Although the Jesuits held the high moral ground in this controversy, they nonetheless relied on Indian labor to create profitable economic enterprises and supplied mining areas with the same types of goods that the Paraguayan Spaniards produced. Competition for scarce indigenous labor was fierce in the peripheral regions of Latin America.

Indigenous responses to these attacks on their sacred beliefs and practices spanned the spectrum from outright resistance to apparent acceptance, but many people probably fell somewhere between those two extremes. In the sedentary areas, many native groups had experienced some sort of conquest before and probably expected to receive the deity or deities of the conquerors as a gesture to the victor. However, Christianity demanded the denial and desecration of all other deities. Few native groups were willing to make this drastic break, at least in the first couple of generations after the conquest. More likely, in the presence of Spaniards, people were forced to abandon the most visible forms of traditional worship, while they continued to perform less conspicuous traditional practices, either secretly or embedded within the new religion. As many priests came to realize over the course of the colonial period, numerous non-Christian cultural practices survived, especially within indigenous households and in concealed places. The best evidence for remnants of these practices comes from the modern ethnographic record.

Despite many differences between native religions and Christianity, there were often certain similarities, as well. Christians capitalized on the association between the new church building and the old temple, as they had done during the spread of Christianity in Europe. In Mesoamerica, people knew how to build large, permanent structures by cutting massive stones and moving them to a sacred site. Many communities built large churches in the first few generations after conquest and employed the same name for the new structures as the old temples (for example, Nahuas used the term *teocalli*, "sacred house"). The Mesoamericans had a mainly outdoor religion, since the old platform temples had no interior space; likewise, the monastery church faced onto a great enclosed patio and featured an open chapel, which faced the patio, where mass was said to crowds standing in the open. Multiple images of saints inhabited the new sacred house, headed by a patron saint. The idea of the patron saint as a symbolic protector must have appealed to the corporate nature of communities, serving a similar role as the old local deity. The Christian calendar and its many saints' days resembled Mesoamerican sacred calendars marked by periodic feast days for sacred personages or events.

At the same time, it is easy to overestimate the impact of Christian teachings in this period, as some friars did in their own self-glorifying chronicles. Although conversion was a major objective on the colonial agenda, few Spaniards were actually devoted to this purpose. Most people had very limited contact with priests and friars. Few communities had resident priests in the colonial period. Although indigenous men could work in and around the church as minor officials (*sacristan*, *fiscal*, etc.), they could not become priests. Moreover, despite the shared practices between Christianity and sedentary religions and the many pressures to convert, people who wanted to accept the new system were bound to encounter alien concepts and to interpret many introductions in terms of old beliefs and practices. Many fundamental Christian principles, such as sin, heaven, hell, and the devil, simply had no corresponding equivalents in native cultures. If people did not necessarily reject or embrace Christianity, the fact remains that there were cultural barriers to learning, understanding, and practicing the new faith.

As in other arenas of cultural contact, the extent of the Spanish presence affected the development of local Christianity. Where Spaniards congregated in great numbers, Christianity and indigenous religious traditions tended to converge and coexist. Indeed, Catholicism seems to have had a profound impact on many native communities of Latin America, and continues to have a pervasive influence today. Outside the sedentary areas, however, things were different. Most peoples on the frontiers could not identify with the Spanish introductions and often opposed Christianity or tried to escape it rather than to engage it to some degree. Sometimes, two separate and parallel cults would be maintained in remote areas. A continuation of traditional practices, which Christians viewed as idolatries and witchcraft, shocked friars and priests when they encountered them in these more remote areas. Outright rejections of Christianity, in which native leaders urged people to reject the foreigners and their religion and called on them to return to indigenous practices and beliefs, were more common in those areas than in the centers of colonial settlement. The *Taqui Onqoy* rebellion in the highlands of Peru in the 1560s and the Pueblo revolt of New Mexico in 1680 are two prominent examples of the rejection of Christianity. Ironically, some millenarian movements employed Christian symbols or figures – such as the cross, Jesus, and Mary – against church and colonial authorities and sometimes Spaniards in general. The Cancuc rebellion of 1712 in Chiapas, and the caste wars of Yucatán and Chiapas in the nineteenth century, exemplify these types of resistance.

Writing and Language

In Mesoamerica, the precolonial pictorial writing system on deerskin, fig-bark paper, cloth, stone, ceramics, precious metals, and bones faded away in the course of the colonial period. Alphabetic writing first complemented pictorial writing and finally displaced it by the eighteenth century. Most indigenous groups in Mesoamerica used the Roman alphabet to write in their native languages throughout much of the colonial period. Literacy was confined to elites within these societies. Native-language writers from central and southern Mexico produced countless texts in their own languages, on a wide range of topics, from the histories of the Nahua historian Chimalpahin to the mundane affairs of indigenous municipal councils. These writings are extraordinary sources for the historian. For Mesoamerica, native-language writings are known to exist for Nahuatl, Mixtec, Zapotec, Chocho, Otomí, Purépecha, and the Mayan languages of Yucatec, Chontal, Cakchiquel, and Quiché. Legal and cultural pressures led many communities to adopt Spanish-language writing by the late eighteenth century, at the same time as many indigenous people in these areas were becoming increasingly bilingual. Native-language texts in many of these languages fade out in the early nineteenth century. Alphabetic writing in the Andean area was not as widespread as it was in Mesoamerica, perhaps because the Andeans did not use ink and paper before the conquest (the *quipu*, the primary form of record-keeping, was a memory aid rather than a way of recording language); nonetheless, the Quechua legends of Huarochirí are fabulous examples of this writing.

Bilingualism and native language loss occurred in stages, reflecting the gradual and uneven nature of cultural change. As native-language speakers came into increasing contact with Spanish speakers, the dominant language grew at the expense of local languages. In Mexico independent studies of texts written in Nahuatl, Mixtec, and Yucatec Maya have shown how, a generation or so after contact, people began to borrow words from Spanish to refer to the new objects and ideas that the Europeans brought to the Americas. At first, most of these words were nouns to describe objects. Hundreds of Spanish words streamed into the language throughout the colonial period. For Nahuatl, after 1650 or so, Nahuas also began to borrow Spanish verbs, conjunctions, prepositions, and idioms. Bilingualism became common by the eighteenth century, although the vast majority of Nahuas still spoke Nahuatl. A similar process has been observed for the Mixteca and Yucatán, but the rate of change in these areas corresponds to the extent of contact between native and Spanish speakers, which was much less pronounced there.

Of course, colonial Spanish also adopted thousands of words from native languages (many of which have come into English), but the dominant language of Spanish

America was not as affected as were hundreds of native languages in the Americas. This process continues today. Generally, speech communities that came into greatest contact with Spanish speakers in the colonial period were most likely to adopt Spanish, as the culture and genetic makeup of the population changed over time. This is the main reason why native languages have survived in some areas and not others.

Society and Gender

An upper group of indigenous elites survived the conquest. They owned more property than most indigenous people (and possessed title to it through Spanish courts) and tended to know more Spanish and often dressed like Spaniards. They could benefit from the economic reorientation, at first through their traditional privileges, and then as they figured out how to make money in relation to the Spanish world. In order to preserve their privileges and high status, they were forced to adapt to changing circumstances. Native elites can be distinguished by the Spanish names they adopted. In the sixteenth century, most took prestigious Spanish names and the honorific titles *don* and *doña* at baptism. The highest-status names were those of famous conquerors, viceroys, or well-to-do local Spaniards. One cacique in the Mixteca was bold enough to take the name don Felipe de Austria, after the king Philip II of Spain. In many such cases, the Spaniard probably knew or at least gave the indigenous person his permission and sponsorship. The more distinguished Spanish surnames went only to the highest members of indigenous society. Spanish patronymics ending in -ez were the next level, and were generally adopted by the lesser nobility. Even more common was the use of religious names other than saints, named after the cross or the magi, for example. The most common names consisted of a first name plus a saint's name, such as Alonso de San Pedro. Eventually, the "de San" became superfluous, and the normal lowest-ranking name consisted of two first names: Juan Diego or Juana María. A native person's name usually defined his/her status relative to the Spanish-speaking group, and one's possibility of individual advancement within colonial society. For the vast majority of indigenous people, however, all the names looked alike, and this was no coincidence. Most commoners continued to live and work within their communities. By the middle of the seventeenth century, most people in the sedentary areas had Spanish surnames. Names were one of many indicators of social status and ethnicity, as they were in Spain.

Caciques and members of the nobility, in general, stood at the forefront of cultural contact and change. Most Spaniards recognized native elites as hereditary lords worthy of more respect and privileges than the ordinary commoner, and Spanish officials and religious sought out these elites as indispensable middlemen. In turn, many caciques imitated wealthy Spaniards by dressing like them, being outwardly Christian, obtaining licenses to ride a horse and to carry a sword and dagger, learning how to read and write, and becoming bilingual. They participated actively in Spanish-style local government and learned about the Spanish legal system. Some owned African slaves, mimicking the prestige factor of the dominant society. These were the *indios ladinos* (roughly, Latinized Indians), the acculturated Indians who cooperated with colonial authorities for their own benefit, and who facilitated relations and negotiations between the people whom they represented and colonial authorities. Cooperation with colonial authorities was certainly a more pragmatic and safe option than opposition. Cacicas and other elite women were as adept at this strategy of adaptation and survival as were men, although they were excluded from certain public arenas and practices, whether by local indigenous tradition or by Spanish law (or both); they could not be elected to the local cabildos, nor could they expect to learn to read and write, for example.

Sometimes, caciques who succeeded in conforming to Spanish expectations, or appeared no longer to represent local interests, undermined the support of their own people. Commoners might refuse to provide goods and labor to their palaces and lands. A point of contention between caciques and commoners involved the question of whether a cacique's estate (called a *cacicazgo* in Spanish legal terms) was considered private property or the inalienable possession of the community, vested in the lord but not owned by him. Spanish law dictated that caciques owned private titles to their lands and palaces; some communities came to resent serving lords and working their lands under these circumstances, when they received little in return. At the same time, many caciques were forced to compete with Spaniards for access to labor and tribute, especially as the native population declined over the course of the sixteenth century. Over time, Spanish legislation reduced the amount of labor and tribute to which caciques were entitled, diverting these resources to the tribute rolls and labor services of Spaniards. Depopulation and competition with Spaniards, and changing social relations within communities, led to the decline of lordly establishments, especially where Spaniards were concentrated. In the Valley of Mexico, the decline was already apparent by the end of the sixteenth century, whereas in more remote places to the south of New Spain many elite families retained significant privileges and exercised local authority well into the eighteenth century and beyond.

Commoners were not as likely to come into constant, direct contact with Spaniards, especially if they did not migrate to the city. Most *macehuales* (as commoners were called in New Spain, from the Nahuatl term *macehualli*) lived in their communities, knew no Spanish, performed the traditional work of farming or weaving, and paid tribute. However, they faced an increasing burden of taxation by having to support both the indigenous nobility and Spaniards. Men and women were affected differently, but both needed to earn currency to pay local or royal tribute. Typically, men labored in farms or mines, whereas women spun cotton and wove cloth for external markets. In addition, many women who were unattached to a community ended up working in the households of Indian elites or Spaniards. Domestic servants were prime candidates for extramarital sex with Spanish men, whether consensual or non-consensual. This contact was one factor that gave birth to a largely urban mestizo population, which generally looked more to the dominant Spanish culture for identity. They were more likely to learn Spanish, practice a Spanish craft, and thus be more eligible to move up in the ethnic and occupational hierarchies of colonial society.

The Ethnic Hierarchy

From the earliest period, interethnic sexual contact, usually not based on marriage, led to the creation of new ethnicities and social arrangements. The well-known pattern had been established in Iberia, where late-marrying men typically had informal unions with women often of a lower social and ethnic rank. Normally, the children of these unions were accepted into the family but at the same time subordinated to legitimate heirs; some provision was often made for the mothers, but they could not attain the rank of the women that the men might later marry. These customs were transferred to the Americas, where Iberian men had sexual relations with native and African mistresses and produced mestizo and mulatto children. Such was the case, for example, of the Peruvian-Spanish writer Garcilaso de la Vega, el Inca, whose father was a conquistador and his mother was an Inca noblewoman. In the usual pattern, his father then married a Spanish woman 20 years younger and had a Spanish son who displaced Garcilaso as principal heir when he was 10 years old. Garcilaso's father then arranged a marriage for his mother to a Spanish foot soldier. Garcilaso's father did provide him with an education and certain connections in Spain, where he lived most of his life. In the Indies the vast majority of sexual relationships between Spaniards and Indians were between Spanish men and indigenous women or mestizas. Conversely, indigenous men had little chance of sexual contact with Spanish women.

Over the course of the long colonial period, these extramarital sexual relations and interracial marriages produced an ever-growing mixed population, which no longer necessarily bore the stigma of earlier mestizo generations, except from the point of view of the upper classes. The dominant groups of colonial society were the Iberians, who sought to preserve their status by affirming their own *limpieza de sangre* (purity of blood, or descent) in contrast to the many ethnic mixtures of colonial society that threatened their ideal of purity. From the very beginning, elites devised a hierarchy of types, based on the one in Spain, which ranked people according to their ethnic category.

The three original categories of Spaniard, Black, and Indian gradually evolved into a complex mixture of peoples and cultures, especially in cities. The hierarchy attempted to keep track of a person's *calidad* (quality), a broad term that referred to one's phenotype, education, occupation, cultural behavior, and social status. Those who most resembled the dominant group occupied the upper ranks of the hierarchy. Indians and Africans, especially if commoners and slaves, were at the bottom. By the eighteenth century, especially in cities, there existed dozens of categories to denote the many ethnic/racial mixtures of society. Elaborate classifications were often unrealistic, however, because it was impossible to distinguish one category from many of the others. Most importantly, a great, mixed middle group called the *castas* – free men and women of mixed ancestry – shared many social and cultural characteristics. In this system, status was often negotiable for the middle groups – the castas or mestizos. A mestizo was more likely to identify with his Spanish side in order to avoid prejudices against Indios and to escape paying the royal tribute levied on Indians. A similar process occurred in Spain, where *moriscos* (descended from Muslims) and *conversos* (descended from Jews) called themselves Spaniards and Christians in order to avoid persecution. Mestizas were among the most socially mobile of the castas in that they were sought after as marriage partners by lower-ranking Spaniards, other mestizos, and indigenous nobles alike. If she married a Spaniard, she would probably not be called a mestiza, but rather a Spaniard. In this way, mestizas entered the dominant group. Since Spanish women were not available in the same way, mestizo males could not expect to find marriages with Spaniards. It was much more likely that a child would be classified as mestizo (not Spaniard) if male than if female.

This hierarchy devised by the dominant group must have had its limits. Not everyone or even most people were obsessed with "passing" upward, and it must have meant little to the vast majority of people in these societies who were more interested in subsistence than in social climbing. On the other hand, it is difficult to deny that the terms "indio" and "negro" had (and continue to have) undesirable connotations in many parts of Latin America. And although the obsession with purity of blood was an elite Iberian trait, dominant attitudes about *calidad* and social status trickled down from elites and affected all those who desired to improve their socioeconomic position. Economic success depended to a large extent on one's relationship with local elites and employers, in building and cultivating client–patron relationships with a member of the dominant group. In other words, the ethnic labeling of people reinforced a class order based on phenotype, cultural behavior, and social status. Those who sought to improve their status needed to mind the way that they were perceived by members of the upper group. Enough people internalized the ideology to sustain it. And one might argue that it is sustained today in many places, in both subtle and blatant ways.

Spaniards dominated the most important occupations in the colonies, including the following positions: high officials, large estate owners, professionals (holders of degrees and titles), mine owners and engineers, international merchants, church people (priests, friars, nuns), military officers; and even petty administrative officials. In contrast, with the exception of small groups of indigenous elites who managed to adapt to colonial changes, most native men and women were confined to manual labor and menial tasks, in the fields or in the mines, or as transport workers, petty merchants, street vendors, and domestic servants. Europeans could be found among the lower occupations as well, but they moved up the scale more frequently than any other ethnic group. Internal stratification even within the lower levels was often based on race or appearance. For example, guilds of the European-originated trades discriminated against indigenous, mestizo, and free African artisans. Social mobility was possible, but legal or cultural restrictions and prejudices presented formidable barriers for Indians. Women could be found among all occupations at the bottom levels; a typical occupation of African and native women was selling food and drink on the street or in taverns.

Although today we discuss the relationship between race and class, neither term was used in the colonial era, but loaded terms such as *limpieza* and *calidad* contain many of the same essential ingredients. Simply put, Iberians controlled the means of production and extracted surplus products or labor from those who did not. If race was not as important as wealth in determining one's socioeconomic status by the later colonial period, as some historians have suggested, then the two variables of race and class were still closely related in most places. Most people of European descent owned veritable fortunes compared to Indians and Africans. Those who were called caciques by the end of the colonial period could claim little more than multiple, scattered plots of land and few domestic animals in their last wills and testaments; some owned a horse and many possessed all sorts of domestic and imported goods, but few had much money or many lucrative investments or any property of great value. And yet they were rich compared to most indigenous people.

Spaniards, whether *criollos* born in the Americas or *peninsulares* born in Spain, sought to set themselves apart from the majority, to maintain their prestige, dominance, and wealth. A very small percentage of the population was very wealthy, and the vast majority of this group was European. The monopolization of important positions and resources by Europeans and their descendants, and the unequal distribution of wealth, power, and status between those elites and the vast majority of the population descended primarily from the conquered peoples, is an unmistakable feature of the colonial legacy. Colonialism benefited the colonizers.

After independence, despite the revolutionary rhetoric of social transformation, many continuities stand out. Most indigenous peoples faced new challenges and threats in the nineteenth century. Governments made new and more intensive efforts to change Indians – to force them into the national mainstream, to privatize the corporately held lands of indigenous communities and, at times, to eradicate them with superior military force and weaponry. With good intentions or not, national governments attempted to abolish native languages, cultural practices, and communities. This is one undeniable aspect of the colonial legacy of the Americas. Today, native peoples are among the poorest groups in the hemisphere, nearly always living below the world poverty index. The status and treatment of indigenous communities and individuals within nation-states is in many places as problematic and controversial as ever.

BIBLIOGRAPHY

Adorno, R. (1986) *Guaman Poma: Writing and Resistance in Colonial Peru.* University of Texas Press, Austin.

Anderson, A. J. O., Berdan, F., & Lockhart, J. (eds.) (1976) *Beyond the Codices: The Nahua View of Colonial Mexico.* UCLA Latin American Studies Series, no. 27. University of California Press, Berkeley.

Bakewell, P. (1984) *Miners of the Red Mountain: Indian Labor in Potosí, 1545–1650.* University of New Mexico Press, Albuquerque.

Barrios, L. (1996) *La alcaldía indígena en Guatemala, época colonial, 1500–1821.* Universidad Rafael Landívar, Instituto de Investigaciones Económicas y Sociales, Guatemala.

Boone, E. H. & Cummins, T. (eds.) (1998) *Native Traditions in the Postconquest World.* Dumbarton Oaks Research Library and Collection, Washington, DC.

Borah, W. (1983) *Justice by Insurance: The General Indian Court of Colonial Mexico.* University of California Press, Berkeley.

Borah, W. & Cook, S. F. (1960) *The Population of Central Mexico, 1531–1570.* Ibero-Americana, 43. University of California Press, Berkeley.

Borah, W. & Cook, S. F. (1963) *The Aboriginal Population of Central Mexico on the Eve of the Spanish Conquest.* Ibero-Americana, 45. University of California Press, Berkeley.

Bracamonte y Sosa, P. (2003) *Los Mayas y la tierra: la propiedad indígena en el Yucatán colonial.* Miguel Angel Porrúa: Centro de Investigaciones y Estudios Superiores en Antropología Social, Instituto de Cultura de Yucatán, México.

Brading, D. (1991) *The First America: The Spanish Monarchy, Creole Patriots, and the Liberal State, 1492–1867.* Cambridge University Press, Cambridge.

Bricker, V. (1981) *The Indian Christ, The Indian King: The Historical Substrate of Maya Myth and Ritual.* University of Texas Press, Austin.

Buenahora Durán, G. (2003) *Historia de la ciudad colonial de Almaguer y sus pueblos de indios: siglos XVI–XVIII.* Editorial Universidad del Cauca, Popayán, Colombia.

Burkhart, L. (1989) *The Slippery Earth: Nahua–Christian Moral Dialogue in Sixteenth-Century Mexico*. University of Arizona Press, Tucson.

Carrasco, P. & Broda, J. (eds.) (1976) *Estratificación social en la Mesoamérica prehispánica*. Centro de Investigaciones Superiores, Instituto Nacional de Antropología e Historia, Mexico.

Castillero Manzano, R. M. (2005) *Mezcala: expresión de un pueblo indígena en el período colonial, vicisitudes y fortalezas*. Universidad de Guadalajara, Centro Universitario de Ciencias Sociales y Humanidades, Guadalajara, México.

Chance, J. K. (1978) *Race and Class in Colonial Oaxaca*. Stanford University Press, Stanford.

Chance, J. K. (1989) *Conquest of the Sierra: Spaniards and Indians in Colonial Oaxaca*. University of Oklahoma Press, Norman.

Chocano Mena, M. (2000) *La fortaleza docta: elite letrada y dominación social en México colonial, siglos XVI–XVII*. Bellaterra, Barcelona.

Clendinnen, I. (1987) *Ambivalent Conquests: Maya and Spaniard in Yucatan, 1517–1570*. Cambridge University Press, Cambridge.

Cline, S. L. (1986) *Colonial Culhuacan, 1580–1600: A Social History of an Aztec Town*. University of New Mexico Press, Albuquerque.

Cline, S. L. (ed.) (1993) *The Book of Tributes: Early Sixteenth-Century Nahuatl Censuses from Morelos*. UCLA Latin American Studies Center Publications, Los Angeles.

Cole, J. (1985) *The Potosí Mita, 1573–1700: Compulsory Indian Labor in the Andes*. Stanford University Press, Stanford.

Cook, N. D. (1981) *Demographic Collapse: Indian Peru, 1520–1620*. Cambridge University Press, Cambridge.

Cook, N. D. (1998) *Born to Die: Disease and New World Conquest, 1492–1650*. Cambridge University Press, Cambridge.

Cook, N. D. & Lovell, W. G. (1991) *Secret Judgments of God: Old World Disease in Colonial Spanish America*. University of Oklahoma Press, Norman.

Cook, S. F. & Borah, W. (1960) *The Indian Population of Central Mexico, 1531–1610*. Ibero-Americana, 44. University of California Press, Berkeley.

Cook, S. F. & Borah, W. (1968) *The Population of the Mixteca Alta, 1520–1960*. Ibero-Americana, 50. University of California Press, Berkeley.

Cook, S. F. & Borah, W. (1971) *Essays in Population History: Mexico and the Caribbean*. University of California Press, Berkeley.

Cope, R. D. (1994) *The Limits of Racial Domination: Plebian Society in Mexico City, 1660–1720*. University of Wisconsin Press, Madison.

Corcuera de Mancera, S. (1991) *El fraile, el indio, y el pulque: Evangelización y embriaguez en la Nueva España (1523–1548)*. Fondo de Cultura Económica, Mexico.

Crosby, A. W. (1973) *The Columbian Exchange: Biological and Cultural Consequences of 1492*. Greenwood Press, Westport.

Cutter, C. R. (1986) *The Protector de Indios in Colonial New Mexico, 1659–1821*. University of New Mexico Press, Historical Society of New Mexico, Albuquerque.

Deeds, S. (2003) *Defiance and Deference in Mexico's Colonial North: Indians under Spanish Rule in Nueva Vizcaya*. University of Texas Press, Austin.

Doesburg, S. van (2001) *Códices Cuicatecos: Porfirio Díaz y Fernández Leal. Edición facsimile, contexto histórico e interpretación*, 2 vols. Editorial Porrua, Mexico City.

Escobari de Querejazu, L. (2001) *Caciques, yanaconas y extravagantes: La sociedad colonial en Charcas s. XVI–XVIII*. Embajada de España en Bolivia, Plural Editores, La Paz, Bolivia.

Farriss, N. M. (1984) *Maya Society under Colonial Rule: The Collective Enterprise of Survival*. Princeton University Press, Princeton.

Ferrero Kellerhoff, I. (1991) *Capacho: un pueblo de indios en la jurisdiccion de la Villa de San Cristobal*. Academia Nacional de la Historia, Caracas.

Florescano, E. & García Acosta, V. (eds.) (2004) *Mestizajes tecnológicos y cambios culturales en México*. Centro de Investigaciones y Estudios Superiores en Antropología Social, Mexico.

Gauderman, K. (2003) *Women's Lives in Colonial Quito: Gender, Law, and Economy in Spanish America*. University of Texas Press, Austin.

Gibson, C. (1952) *Tlaxcala in the Sixteenth Century*. Yale University Press, New Haven.

Gibson, C. (1964) *The Aztecs under Spanish Rule: A History of the Indians of the Valley of Mexico, 1519–1810*. Stanford University Press, Stanford.

Gómez Canedo, L. (1982) *La educación de los marginados durante la época colonial: Escuelas y colegios para indios y mestizos en la Nueva España*. Editorial Porrúa, Mexico.

Gonzalez-Hermosillo Adams, F. (ed.) (2001) *Gobierno y economía en los pueblos indios del México colonial*. Instituto Nacional de Antropología e Historia, Mexico.

Gosner, K. (1992) *Soldiers of the Virgin: The Moral Economy of a Colonial Maya Rebellion*. University of Arizona Press, Tucson.

Gruzinski, S. (1988) *El poder sin límites: Cuatro respuestas indígenas a la dominación española*. Instituto Nacional de Antropología e Historia, Mexico City.

Gruzinski, S. (1993) *The Conquest of Mexico: The Incorporation of Indian Societies into the Western World, 16th–18th Centuries*, translated by E. Corrigan. Polity Press, Cambridge, UK.

Guy, D. J. & Sheridan, T. E. (eds.) (1998) *Contested Ground: Comparative Frontiers of the Northern and Southern Edges of the Spanish Empire*. University of Arizona Press, Tucson.

Harvey, H. R. & Prem, H. J. (eds.) (1984) *Explorations in Ethnohistory: Indians of Central Mexico in the Sixteenth Century*. University of New Mexico Press, Albuquerque.

Haskett, R. (1991) *Indigenous Rulers: An Ethnohistory of Town Government in Colonial Cuernavaca*. University of New Mexico Press, Albuquerque.

Haskett, R. (2005) *Visions of Paradise: Primordial Titles and Mesoamerican History in Cuernavaca*. University of Oklahoma Press, Norman.

Hassig, R. (1985) *Trade, Tribute, and Transportation: The Sixteenth-century Political Economy of the Valley of Mexico*. University of Oklahoma Press, Norman.

Herrera, R. A. (2003) *Natives, Europeans, and Africans in Sixteenth-Century Santiago de Guatemala*. University of Texas Press, Austin.

Hill, R. M. (1987) *The Pirir Papers and Other Colonial Period Cakchiquel-Maya Testamentos*. Vanderbilt University Press, Nashville.

Horn, R. (1997) *Postconquest Coyoacan: Nahua–Spanish Relations in Central Mexico, 1519–1650*. Stanford University Press, Stanford.

Hu-De Hart, E. (1981) *Missionaries, Miners, and Indians: Spanish Contact with the Yaqui Nation of Northwestern New Spain, 1533–1820*. University of Arizona Press, Tucson.

Huerta, M. T. & Palacios, P. (1976) *Rebeliones indígenas de la época colonial*. Instituto Nacional de Antropología e Historia, Mexico.

Jackson, R. H. (1994) *Indian Population Decline: The Missions of Northwestern New Spain, 1687–1840*. University of New Mexico Press, Albuquerque.

Jara, Á. (1981) *Guerra y sociedad en Chile: La transformación de le Guerra de Arauco y la esclavitud de los indios*. Editorial Universitaria, Santiago de Chile.

Jimenez, G. M. A. (1986) *La esclavitud indigena en Venezuela, Siglo XVI*. Fuentes para la Historia Colonial de Venezuela, Caracas.

Jones, G. (1989) *Maya Resistance to Colonial Rule: Time and History on a Colonial Frontier*. University of New Mexico Press, Albuquerque.

Kellogg, S. (1995) *Law and Transformation in Aztec Culture, 1500–1700*. University of Oklahoma Press, Norman.

Kellogg, S. & Restall, M. (eds.) (1998) *Dead Giveaways: Indigenous Testaments of Colonial Mesoamerica and the Andes.* University of Utah Press, Salt Lake City.

Kicza, J. E. (2003) *Resilient Cultures: America's Native Peoples Confront European Colonization, 1500–1800.* Prentice-Hall, New Jersey.

Klein, H. S. (1993) *Haciendas and Ayllus: Rural Society in the Bolivian Andes in the Eighteenth and Nineteenth Centuries.* Stanford University Press, Stanford.

Lane, K. (2002) *Quito 1599: City and Colony in Transition.* University of New Mexico Press, Albuquerque.

León-Portilla, M. (1976) *Culturas en peligro.* Alianza Editorial Mexicana, México.

Langer, E. & Jackson, R. H. (eds.) (1995) *The New Latin American Mission History.* University of Nebraska Press, Lincoln.

Lockhart, J. (1991) *Nahuas and Spaniards: Postconquest Central Mexican History and Philology.* Stanford University Press and UCLA Latin American Center Publications, Stanford and Los Angeles.

Lockhart, J. (1992) *The Nahuas after the Conquest: A Social and Cultural History of the Indians of Central Mexico, Sixteenth through Eighteenth Centuries.* Stanford University Press, Stanford.

Lockhart, J. (1993) *We People Here: Nahuatl Accounts of the Conquest of Mexico.* University of California Press, Berkeley and Los Angeles.

Lockhart, J. & Schwartz, S. (1983) *Early Latin America: A History of Colonial Spanish America and Brazil.* Cambridge University Press, Cambridge.

Lockhart, J., Berdan, F., & Anderson, A. J. O. (eds.) (1986) *The Tlaxcalan Actas: a Compendium of the Records of the Cabildo of Tlaxcala, 1545–1627.* University of Utah Press, Salt Lake City.

Lockhart, J., Schroeder, S., & Namala, D. (eds.) (2006) *Annals of His Time: Don Domingo de San Antón Muñón Chimalpahin Quauhtlehuanitzin.* Stanford University Press, Stanford.

MacCormack, S. (1991) *Religion in the Andes: Vision and Imagination in Early Colonial Peru.* Stanford University Press, Stanford.

MacLeod, M. J. & Wasserstrom, R. (eds.) (1983) *Spaniards and Indians in Southeastern Mesoamerica: Essays on the History of Ethnic Relations.* University of Nebraska Press, Lincoln.

Martínez Baracs, A. & Sempat Assadourian, C. (1994) *Suma y epíloga de toda la descripción de Tlaxcala.* Universidad Autónoma de Tlaxcala, Secretaría de Extensión Universitaria y Difusión Cultural; Centro de Investigaciones y Estudios Superiores en Antropología Social, Tlalpan, Mexico.

Mills, K. (1997) *Idolatry and Its Enemies: Colonial Andean Religion and Extirpation, 1640–1750.* Princeton University Press, Princeton.

Mundy, B. E. (1996) *The Mapping of New Spain: Indigenous Cartography and the Maps of the Relaciones Geográficas.* University of Chicago Press, Chicago.

Nesvig, M. (2006) *Local Religion in Colonial Mexico.* University of New Mexico Press, Albuquerque.

Newson, L. A. (1986) *The Cost of Conquest: Indian Decline in Honduras under Spanish Rule.* University of Colorado Press, Boulder.

O'Phelan Godoy, S. (1985) *Rebellions and Revolts in Eighteenth-Century Upper Peru.* Bohlau, Koln.

Oudijk, M. (2000) *The Historiography of the Benizaa: The Postclassic and Early Colonial Periods (1000–1600 A.D.).* Research School of Asian, African, and Amerindian Studies, Leiden, Netherlands.

Pardo, O. (2004) *The Origins of Mexican Catholicism: Nahua Rituals and Christian Sacraments in Sixteenth-Century Mexico.* University of Michigan Press, Ann Arbor.

Pastor, R. (1987) *Campesinos y reformas: La mixteca, 1700–1856.* El Colegio de México, Mexico.

Patch, R. W. (1993) *Maya and Spaniard in Yucatan, 1648–1812.* Stanford University Press, Stanford.

Poole, S. (1995) *Our Lady of Guadalupe: The Origin and Sources of a Mexican National Symbol, 1531–1797.* University of Arizona Press, Tucson.

Powell, P. W. (1952) *Soldiers, Indians, and Silver: The Northward Advance of New Spain, 1550–1600.* University of California Press, Berkeley.

Powers, K. V. (1995) *Andean Journeys: Migration, Ethnogenesis, and the State in Colonial Quito.* University of New Mexico Press, Albuquerque.

Rabasa, J. (2000) *Writing Violence on the Northern Frontier: The Historiography of Sixteenth-century New Mexico and Florida and the Legacy of Conquest.* Duke University Press, Durham.

Radding Murrieta, C. (1997) *Wandering Peoples: Colonialism, Ethnic Spaces, and Ecological Frontiers in Northwestern Mexico, 1700–1850.* Duke University Press, Durham.

Ramírez, S. E. (1996) *The World Upside Down: Cross Cultural Contact and Conflict in Sixteenth-Century Peru.* Stanford University Press, Stanford.

Restall, M. B. (1997) *The Maya World: Yucatec Culture and Society, 1550–1850.* Stanford University Press, Stanford.

Restall, M. B. (1998) *Maya Conquistador.* Beacon Press, Boston.

Restall, M., Sousa, L., & Terraciano, K. (2005) *Mesoamerican Voices: Native-Language Writings from Colonial Mexico, Oaxaca, Yucatan, and Guatemala.* Cambridge University Press, Cambridge.

Retamal Avila, J. (2000) *Testamentos de indios en Chile colonial, 1564–1801.* RiL Editores, Universidad Andrés Bello, Santiago de Chile.

Reyes García, L. (1977) *Cuauhtinchan del siglo XII al XVI: Formación y desarrollo histórico de un señorío prehispánico.* Franz Steiner Verlag, Wiesbaden.

Ricard, R. (1966) *The Spiritual Conquest of Mexico: An Essay on the Apostolate and the Evangelizing Methods of the Mendicant Orders in New Spain: 1523–72,* translated by L. B. Simpson. University of California Press, Berkeley.

Rivera Pagán, L. N. (1995) *Entre el oro y la fe: El dilema de América.* Editorial de la Universidad de Puerto Rico, Río Piedras, Puerto Rico.

Robins, N. A. (ed.) (2005) *Cambio y continuidad en Bolivia: Etnicidad, cultura e identidad.* Plural Editores: Asociación de Estudios Bolivianos, La Paz, Bolivia.

Rodríguez Baquero, L. E. (1995) *Encomienda y vida diaria entre los indios de Muzo, 1550–1620.* Instituto Colombiano de Cultura Hispánica, Bogotá, Colombia.

Romero Frizzi, M. (1990). *Economía y vida de los españoles en la Mixteca Alta: 1519–1720.* Instituto Nacional de Antropología e Historia, Mexico.

Romero Frizzi, M. (1996) *El sol y la cruz: Los pueblos indios de Oaxaca colonial.* Centro de Investigaciones y Estudios Superiores en Antropología Social, Mexico.

Roskamp, H. (1998) *La historiografía indígena de Michoacan: El Lienzo Jucutácato y los títulos de Carapan.* Research School of Asian, African, and Amerindian Studies, Leiden.

Ruiz de Alarcón, H. (1984) *Treatise on the Heathen Superstitions That Today Live Among the Indians Native to This New Spain, 1629,* trans. and ed. J. R. Andrews and R. Hassig. University of Oklahoma Press, Norman.

Ruiz Medrano, E. (1991) *Gobierno y sociedad en Nueva España: Segunda audiencia y Antonio de Mendoza.* El Colegio de Michoacan, Zamora, Michoacan.

Ruz, M. H. (1994) *Un rostro encubierto: Los indios del Tabasco colonial.* Centro de Investigaciones y Estudios Superiores en Antropología Social, Instituto Nacional Indigena, Mexico City.

Sahagún, B. de. (1950–82) *The Florentine Codex: General History of the Things of New Spain*, trans. A. J. O. Anderson and C. E. Dibble, 13 parts. University of Utah Press and School of American Research, Salt Lake City and Santa Fe.

Salas de Coloma, M. (1998) *Estructura colonial del poder español en el Perú: Huamanga (Ayacucho) a través de sus obrajes, siglos XVI–XVIII*. Pontifica Universidad Católica del Perú, Fondo Editorial, Lima.

Salomon, F. (2004) *The Cord Keepers: Khipus and Cultural Life in a Peruvian village*. Duke University Press, Durham.

Salomon, F. & Urioste, G. (eds. and trans.) (1991) *Huarochirí Manuscript: A Testament of Ancient and Colonial Andean Religion*. University of Texas Press, Austin.

Santos Granero, F. (ed.) (1992) *Opresión colonial y resistencia indígena en la alta Amazonia*. CEDIME: FLACSO, Sede Ecuador, Quito, Ecuador.

Schroeder, S. (ed.) (1998) *Native Resistance and the Pax Colonial in New Spain*. University of Nebraska Press, Lincoln.

Schroeder, S., Wood, S., & Haskett R. (eds.) (1997) *Indian Women in Early Mexico*. University of Oklahoma Press, Norman.

Service, E. R. (1954) *Spanish–Guaraní Relations in Early Colonial Paraguay*. University of Michigan Press, Ann Arbor.

Sigal, P. (2000) *From Moon Goddesses to Virgins: The Colonization of Yucatecan Maya Sexual Desire*. University of Texas Press, Austin.

Solís Robleda, G. (2003) *Bajo el signo de la compulsión: El trabajo forzoso indígena en el sistema colonial yucateco, 1540–1730*. CIESAS, Instituto de Cultura de Yucatán, M. A. Porrúa Grupo Editorial, Conaculta, INAH, México.

Spalding, K. (1984) *Huarochirí: An Andean Society under Inca and Spanish Rule*. Stanford University Press, Stanford.

Spicer, E. H. (1962) *Cycles of Conquest: The Impact of Spain, Mexico, and the United States on the Indians of the Southwest, 1533–1960*. University of Arizona Press, Tucson.

Spores, R. (1967) *Mixtec Kings and Their People*. University of Oklahoma Press, Norman.

Spores, R. (1984) *The Mixtecs in Ancient and Colonial Times*. University of Oklahoma Press, Norman.

Stern, S. J. (1982) *Peru's Indian Peoples and the Challenge of the Spanish Conquest: Huamanga to 1640*. University of Wisconsin Press, Madison.

Stern, S. J. (ed.) (1987) *Resistance, Rebellion and Consciousness in the Andean Peasant World, 18th to 20th Centuries*. University of Wisconsin Press, Madison.

Taylor, W. B. (1972) *Landlord and Peasant in Colonial Oaxaca*. Stanford University Press, Stanford.

Taylor, W. B. (1979) *Drinking, Homicide, and Rebellion in Colonial Mexican Villages*. Stanford University Press, Stanford.

Taylor, W. B. (1996) *Magistrates of the Sacred: Priests and Parishioners in Eighteenth-Century Mexico*. Stanford University Press, Stanford.

Taylor, W. B. & Pease, F. (eds.) (1994) *Violence, Resistance, and Survival in the Americas: Native Americans and the Legacy of Conquest*. Smithsonian Institution Press, Washington, DC.

Terraciano, K. (2001) *The Mixtecs of Colonial Oaxaca: Ñudzahui History, Sixteenth through Eighteenth Centuries*. Stanford University Press, Stanford.

Weber, D. (1992) *The Spanish Frontier in North America*. Yale University Press, New Haven.

Wightman, A. M. (1990) *Indigenous Migration and Social Change: The Forasteros of Cuzco*. Duke University Press, Durham.

Wood, S. (2003) *Transcending the Conquest: Nahua Views of Spanish Colonial Mexico*. University of Oklahoma Press, Norman.

Zavala, S. (1978–80) *El servicio personal de los indios en el Peru*. El Colegio de México, Mexico City.

Zavala, S. (1984–95) *El servicio personal de los indios en la Nueva España*. El Colegio de México, Mexico City.

Zavala, S. (1994) *Los esclavos indios en Nueva España*. El Colegio Nacional, Mexico City.

Zeitlin, J. F. (2005) *Cultural Politics in Colonial Tehuantepec: Community and State among the Isthmus Zapotec, 1500–1750*. Stanford University Press, Stanford.

Zulawski, A. (1995) *They Eat from Their Labor: Work and Social Change in Colonial Bolivia*. University of Pittsburgh Press, Pittsburgh.

Chapter Nine

SLAVERY IN THE AMERICAS

Franklin W. Knight

Slavery constitutes the unconditional servitude of an individual usually acquired by purchase and often legally described as chattel or a tangible form of movable property. An ancient form of subordination and labor organization, slavery has been practiced at some time or the other by most social groups around the world. The tradition of slavery is extremely old. Nevertheless, the variants of slavery in the American hemisphere were unusual in many respects. In the Americas slavery became identified with immigrant Africans. It constituted major international commerce involving Europe, Asia, and the Americas. It transformed the economy of the Americas as well as the demography, ecology, and culture of many regions. American slavery was closely identified with property rights, and with social segmentation resulting in mutually reinforcing social cleavages in the more developed slave societies of the hemisphere.

From ancient antiquity slavery constituted an important dimension of social and occupational organization (Finley 1998). The word originated with the sale of Slavs to the Black Sea region sometime during the ninth century and continued to exist in European society until the nineteenth century. Enslavement became the principal source of labor during the process of European colonization (Vieira 2002). Within Europe, however, slavery transformed itself into serfdom, a system of servitude that existed between the eleventh and the nineteenth centuries.

In Africa slavery constituted an integral part of social relations and in many parts of the continent slavery served the purpose of group ascription, enabling groups to supplement the numbers of either males or females as the community saw fit (Meirs & Kopytoff 1977; Lovejoy 1983). One basic difference between slavery in Africa and its later form in the Americas lies in the inalienability of the condition through generations. In Africa children of slave mothers were, more often than not, free and equal members of the community. This automatic social mobility removed the indelible stain that attached itself to slavery in the Americas.

Likewise, forms of slavery existed among the indigenous societies in the Americas before the arrival of Christopher Columbus. Like the African situation, indigenous American slavery did not divide populations into mutually exclusive segments. Slaves and their masters shared ethnicity, language, religion, and culture. Several types of slaves existed in Aztec society. One type was the prisoner of war, a common form of slavery in classical antiquity. The other more common type was the class called *tla-cotin* or *tlacotli*, a group that like their African counterparts appeared to enjoy many attributes not usually identified with slaves in slave societies. Not only were all children fully free and equal members of the community, but slaves could own property, including other slaves, and had considerable geographical mobility. Slaves were automatically considered to be free if they married their masters, or had children with them. In addition, indigent persons could sell themselves temporarily into slavery. Some forms of criminality were punished with enslavement and debtors could also be sold as slaves to their creditors (Gibson 1964: 153–65). Indian forms of slavery, like many other organizational aspects of indigenous society, were rapidly eliminated by Spanish colonial rule.

The reconstruction of the American sphere after 1492, however, created a system of slavery quite unprecedented in human experience. Slavery in the post-Columbus Americas was a patently artificial social and political construct, not a natural condition, and a specific organizational response to a specific labor scarcity brought about by the decimation of the indigenous population of the Antilles. The enslavement of Africans and their descendants in the Americas, then, was a relatively recent development in the course of human history – and quite exceptional in the universal history of slave societies.

Slavery was also unquestionably a form of power relations. Slaves by and large did not have an equal voice in articulating views of their conditions or directly controlling their territorial affairs.[1] But not having an equal voice should not be understood to mean that slaves were powerless. Nor did they arrive in the New World mysteriously bereft of their innate intelligence, social skills, and political abilities. Africans did not undergo "social death" merely by transiting the Atlantic Ocean.[2] Their actions spoke eloquently of their innermost thoughts and represented their reflections on, and reactions to, the world in which they found themselves. Moreover, the successful development of the Americas as well as the prosperity and power of many western European states derived from the unremitting industry of enslaved Africans in the Americas (Solow & Engerman 1987; Solow 1991).

Columbus, desperate to find some commercial commodity in the Antilles, initially thought the people whom he encountered in the Caribbean in 1492 might make good slaves, as he seemed to infer in his log of Friday, October 10, 1492, when he wrote of the locals he saw: "They ought to make good and skilled servants, for they repeat very quickly whatever we say to them. I think that they can easily be made Christians, for they seem to have no religion. If it pleases Our Lord, I will take six of them to Your Highness when I depart, in order that they may learn our language" (Fuson 1987: 77). His monarch, Isabel of Castile, thought otherwise and declared the few indigenous inhabitants he brought back from the first voyage to the newly discovered lands to be her vassals rather than her slaves. Unfortunately for the Indians of the Americas, high ideals succumbed rapidly to the harsh reality of the urgent need for labor in the Americas.

The first Africans who accompanied the early Spanish explorers fell in that ambiguous penumbra between slaves and servants. Some may even have been free (such as Pedro Alonso Niño and Juan Garrido who accompanied Christopher Columbus); and others were servants. Nuflo de Olano, who accompanied Vasco Nuñez de Balboa across the Isthmus of Panama, was, however, a slave. So were Juan Valiente and several others who traveled and fought with Hernán Cortés in Mexico, the Pizarro brothers in Peru, and Pánfilo de Narváez in Florida. Those blacks who sailed with Columbus on his first voyage to the Americas in 1492 were free men. Their descendants presumably were as free as any other Spanish colonist in the Americas. Other blacks who accompanied the early Spanish *conquistadores* might have been servile but were not true slaves as the term was later understood. Estebanico, described as "Andrés Dorantes' black Moorish slave," accompanied Alvar Nuñez Cabeza de Vaca in that amazing journey around the Gulf of Mexico and overland across the southwest to Mexico City in the late 1520s and 1530s. Estebanico learned several local Indian languages with consummate ease and posed, along with his companions, as a holy man gifted with healing powers (Weber 1992: 44). Bernal Díaz del Castillo (1979) describes several "blacks" who accompanied Hernán Cortés to Mexico – one of whom brought wheat; and another, a follower of Pánfilo de Narváez, introduced smallpox with lethal results among the Indians. Of the 168 men who followed Francisco Pizarro to Peru in 1532 and captured the Inca Atahualpa at Cajamarca, at least two were black – and an additional person might have been *morisco* (converted Muslim) (Lockhart 1972: 35–6). Juan García, born in Old Castile, served the expedition as a piper and crier. Miguel Ruiz, born in Seville, was a part of the cavalry and probably received a double portion of the spoils – as did all those who had horses. In the expanding frontier of Spanish America, the important distinction was not between slaves and free but rather between conquistadors and natives, or Christians and non-believers. The frequent use of the word *raza* (race) in early Spanish colonial documents represented not a biological definition but rather a conceptual distinction of cultures.

Given the ambiguity of the nature of slavery in early America before the end of the seventeenth century, it was difficult to ascertain individual status in some areas. Some non-whites arrived from Europe as free or nearly free individuals and other non-whites behaved as though they were always free. A significant proportion of the non-white inhabitants of the American slave societies were not the direct descendants of slaves. That is to say, they were not freedmen, or the descendants of freedmen, but free men and women who could trace their free status through several generations. They comprised a growing segment of the American Creole (native-born) population. These forever-free people formed an important dimension of the history of American slave societies, of the constantly negotiated and ever-changing world of masters and slaves.

The ambiguity of laws pertaining to slavery and the conditions of slaves was reflected in the bewildering variety of circumstances in which slaves found themselves. Slavery in the Americas, therefore, was never a static condition and that makes it difficult to generalize about the institution across the Americas. In the beginning, Spanish slave laws were guided by the famous *Siete Partidas* of Alfonso X, *El Sabio* (1221–84) sometime in the thirteenth century. Colonial American conditions were quite unlike Iberia and so slavery underwent many transformations there.

One of the more ambiguous cases of slavery was the remarkable experience of the slaves and their community of El Cobre in eastern Cuba, described magnificently in two excellent books by Olga Portuondo Zúñiga (1995) and María Elena Díaz (2000). In El Cobre the original copper mining company went bankrupt in 1680 and the slaves as well as the physical property – machinery, lands, and buildings –

reverted to the monarchy of Castile. The slaves of El Cobre became royal slaves with significant traditional privileges, and apparently they knew it better than the officials at the royal court. The slaves successfully exploited Spanish laws and customs to establish a viable self-governing community in which their town council supervised free people. Surely this was a most anomalous situation in the American slave system: enslaved people with more extensive privileges than freeholders. When in 1780 the residents eventually lost their autonomy, the compromise with the copper company for those residents who had not purchased their freedom – or had it purchased for them in the intervening years – was a peculiar category called "wage slaves." The mining company nominally recovered its "slaves" after more than a hundred years of litigation, but it was forced to pay wages to the slaves in the same manner as to the regularly hired free laborers.

As Genaro Rodríguez Morel (2004: 85–114; forthcoming) shows, between 1502 and 1518 Spain shipped out hundreds of black slaves from Iberia to the fledgling American colonies. Some of these slaves, called *ladinos*, were born in Iberia, in the relatively large communities of Africans found between Málaga and Huelva in southern Iberia. As such they were Roman Catholic in religion, and fully Hispanic in culture. Others were recently imported from Portuguese trading posts along the West African coast. In the Americas those slaves worked in the mines of Hispaniola, Mexico, and Peru, dived for pearls off the Venezuelan coast, helped to build the newly founded cities and towns, and supplemented the faltering Indian population everywhere that the Spanish established settlements. From this early population, a growing community of free non-white, non-indigenous people developed throughout the Americas. Those descendants of various mixtures of populations, usually called mulattos and mestizos, were unique to the colonial experience in the Americas.

Most Africans, however, arrived in the Americas as a result of the prolonged trans-atlantic commerce in Africans. The transatlantic slave trade formally began when King Charles I of Spain sanctioned the direct importation of Africans to his colonies in the Americas in 1518, finally acknowledging that the potential supply of indigenous slaves was inadequate to maintain the economic viability of his fledgling overseas colonies.[3] By 1550 thousands of Africans were already being delivered to the Americas, mainly to Hispaniola. By 1550 Peru had more than 3,000 African slaves despite the civil war still raging there (Klein 1999: 22). Shortly thereafter the Portuguese started to import Africans to Brazil to create a plantation society and establish an Atlantic bulwark against other Europeans intruding along the coast. As the demand for labor grew, the number of Africans imported as slaves increased and eventually manual labor throughout the Americas became virtually synonymous with the enslavement of Africans. The transatlantic slave trade became a lucrative international enterprise, and by the time it ended about 1870, more than 10 million Africans were forcibly trans-ported and distributed in slavery throughout the Americas. Many millions more died in Africa or at sea in transit to the Americas (Eltis et al. 1999).

Although the Spanish American colonies participated in the slave trade during its centuries-long trajectory, Spanish merchants actually transported a relatively small number of Africans to the Americas. English, French, and Portuguese merchants dominated the transatlantic dimension of the commerce. These three states accounted for more than 90 percent of Africans transported and sold in the Americas between 1518 and 1870.

The slave trade responded to an interrelated series of factors operating across Africa – at the supply side – and also in the Americas – at the market level (Klein 1999). The trade falls into four phases, strongly influenced by the development of colonialism throughout the hemisphere. In the first phase, lasting to about 1620, the Americas were the exclusive domain of the Spanish and the Portuguese. These Iberian powers introduced about 125,000 slaves to the Americas, with some 75,000 (or 27 percent of African slave exports of the period) to the Spanish sphere, and the about 50,000 (18 percent of the trade) to Brazil. During this period a majority of the slaves traded from the African continent (about 55 percent) went to the tropical African islands of Fernando Po and São Tomé, to Europe proper, or the islands of the Madeiras, Cape Verdes, and the Azores. Indeed, the small island of São Tomé alone received more than 76,000 African slaves during the period, exceeding the entire Spanish American market. There was a relatively small flow averaging about 1,000 slaves per year to the Western Hemisphere colonies, most of whom were supplied from Portuguese forts along the West African coast. By the end of the sixteenth century the sugar-producing estates and vineyards of Lima, Pisco, and the Ica valleys of Peru had more than 20,000 African slaves. By 1640 Lima itself counted more than 20,000 slaves in a variety of urban occupations. But slavery in the towns, farms, and mines of the Americas then employed fewer Africans (about 45 percent of the total Atlantic trade) than did the islands just off the coast of Africa itself.

The second phase of the transatlantic slave trade lasted from 1620 to about 1700. During this time approximately 1,350,000 slaves were distributed throughout the Americas, with an additional 25,000 or so going to markets throughout Europe. During this phase the Americas became the principal destination of enslaved Africans, and the trade was marked by greater geographical distribution, along with the development of a more varied supply pattern on the African side. The first Africans delivered to the mid-Atlantic British North American colonies in 1607 were supplied by the Dutch and probably came from Central Africa. The European component of the trade eventually dwindled to less than 2 percent. Across the Atlantic, Brazil assumed the premier position as a slave destination, receiving nearly 42 percent of all Africans sold on the western side of the Atlantic Ocean during the period. Brazilian preeminence would remain a permanent characteristic of the transatlantic slave trade. Spanish America received about 22 percent, distributed principally in Hispaniola, Puerto Rico, Cuba, Mexico, Central America, and the Andean regions of South America. The English Caribbean colonies received more than 263,000 slaves, or 20 percent of the volume sold in the Americas. The French Caribbean imported about 156,000 slaves, or 12 percent; and the small islands of the Dutch Caribbean bought another 40,000 slaves, or 3 percent of slaves sold throughout the Americas.[4] The growing intensity of the commerce by 1700 reflected the increased specialization in the production of tropical staples by Europeans in the Americas.

This second phase experienced a social and demographic metamorphosis brought about by the sugar revolutions taking place in various parts of the tropical Americas. Slavery evolved from being primarily a supplemental form of labor to being the principal instrument of labor organization in the plantation areas of the Americas – the northeast of Brazil, the fertile intermountain valleys of Peru and Mexico, the Caribbean coastlands, and the readily accessible areas of the southern and mid-

Atlantic North American mainland. By the end of the period the Americas were divided between a number of rival European nations all successfully establishing plantation colonies for the production and export of tropical staple crops such as cotton, tobacco, sugar, indigo, and rice. Slaves became perhaps the most important commercial commodity in transatlantic trade and the desired form of labor on the American plantations. By 1700, although Africans and other non-Europeans could still be listed as either servants or slaves, those of African descent were more consistently and uniformly designated as slaves. Thereafter Europeans in the Americas never listed their fellow Europeans as slaves and the fact of purchase became indicative of slave status.

More importantly, slavery evolved by the end of the seventeenth century into a complex system of labor, commerce, and society which was legally, socially, and ethnically distinct from other forms of servitude, and almost always exclusively applied to the condition of non-free Africans. Two patterns of colonies developed throughout the Western Hemisphere: colonies designed as microcosms of European societies; and colonies designed primarily for the efficient production of export commodities. The first pattern of colonies constituted the settler colonies of the central parts of Brazil, the Caribbean territories of Cuba, Puerto Rico, and Western Hispaniola, the highland zones of Mexico and Peru as well as English and French settlements of North America. In these colonies slaves constituted a minority of the population and did not necessarily represent the dominant labor sector. The second pattern comprised the exploitation plantation colonies, marked by their overwhelming proportion of non-free members, and in which slavery formed the dominant, highly coerced labor system. Most of these colonies began as productive enterprises with a focus more on productive efficiency than on societal recreations. Some settler communities such as the northeast of Brazil, Barbados, the Magdalena River valley of Colombia, and Cuba later were transformed into exploitation societies after they became involved in the sugar revolutions during the eighteenth or nineteenth centuries.

In many regions of the Americas the differences between settler and exploitation slave societies were never sharply or exclusively drawn. Pockets of one type or the other prevailed everywhere. But the changes could be noted in the changing population composition of certain regions. For example, in 1650, of the 100,000 immigrants to British North America only 16,200 were African slaves. At the same time approximately 97 percent of all the inhabitants of the mainland Americas (except Brazil) were classified as white. By 1759, with the recovery of the indigenous population, the mainland proportion of whites fell to about 75 percent. By contrast, the Caribbean population indicated the tremendous demographic impact of the transatlantic slave trade. In 1650 about 75 percent of the Caribbean population was classified as white. A hundred years later that proportion fell below 20 percent.

The third period, between 1701 and 1810, represented the maturation of the slave system in the Americas. During this time slavery became the principal form of labor organization in much of the Americas. This third phase witnessed the apogee of both the transatlantic slave trade and the system of American slavery. During this time entirely new societies were created throughout the tropical Americas. Altogether nearly six million Africans – amounting to nearly 60 percent of the entire transatlantic slave trade – arrived in American ports. Brazil continued to be the dominant recipient country, accounting for nearly two million Africans, or 31 percent, of the trade for the period. The British Caribbean plantations (mainly on Barbados and Jamaica) received almost a million and a half, accounting for 23 percent of the trade. The French Antilles (mainly Saint-Domingue on western Hispaniola, Martinique, and Guadeloupe) imported almost as many, accounting for 22 percent of the trade. The Spanish Caribbean (mainly Cuba) imported more than half a million, or 9.6 percent of the trade. The nearly equal number that went to the Dutch Caribbean accounted for nearly 8 percent of the trade, but most of those Africans were reexported to other areas of the New World. The British North American colonies imported slightly more than 300,000 Africans, or slightly less than 6 percent of the trade; with the small Danish colonies of the Caribbean buying about 25,000 slaves, a rather minuscule proportion of all slaves sold in the Americas.

The eighteenth century formed the watershed in the system of American slavery. Just as it reached its highest proportion of imports and economic development it started to disintegrate. Individuals, and even groups such as the Society of Friends or Quakers, had always opposed slavery and the slave trade from the earliest period. General disapproval of the system, however, only gained momentum from the Enlightenment and its emphasis on rationality, combined with British Evangelical Protestantism during the later eighteenth century. Opposition to slavery became increasingly more coordinated in England and eventually had a profound impact, leading to the abolition of the English slave trade in 1807. Before that, prodded by Granville Sharp and other abolitionists, English Chief Justice Mansfield declared slavery illegal in Great Britain in 1772, giving enormous impetus to the British Anti-slavery Society (West 2005). The British legal ruling immediately freed about 15,000 slaves who found themselves in Britain with their colonial masters, who estimated their immediate property loss at approximately £700,000. In 1774 the Society of Friends abolished slavery among its members.

In 1776 the British philosopher and economist Adam Smith declared in his classic study *The Wealth of Nations* that the system of slavery represented an uneconomical use of land and resources since slaves cost more to maintain than free workers. By the 1780s the British parliament was considering a series of bills dealing with the legality of the slave trade. Before that, several of the recently independent former North American colonies – then part of the United States of America – such as Vermont, Connecticut, and Rhode Island, abolished slavery within their local juris-dictions. New York imposed a conditional abolition of slavery in the state in 1799 and New Jersey followed in 1804. After 1808 – when the British and the Americans legally abolished their component of the transatlantic slave trade – the English initi-ated a campaign to end all slave trading across the Atlantic, and to replace slave trading within Africa with other forms of legal trade. Through a series of outright bribes, diplomatic pressure, and naval blockades, the transatlantic trade gradually came to an end around 1870.

But slavery was not only attacked from above by governments seeking to rational-ize the slave market and international economies. At the same time that European governments contemplated administrative measures against slavery and the slave trade, the implacable opposition of the enslaved themselves in the overseas colonies increased the overall costs of maintaining the system of slavery. Everywhere slave revolts, conspiracies, and rumors of revolts engendered widespread fear among owners and administrators (Craton 1997: 222–70). Small bands of runaway slaves formed stable black communities, legally recognized by their imperial powers in difficult geographical locations such as Esmeraldas in Ecuador, the Colombian coastal areas, Palmares in Brazil, and in the almost impenetrable mountains of eastern and western Jamaica.

The system of slavery has always been as inherently unstable as it was internally contradictory. Within the highly developed and quasi-industrialized plantation slave societies, an overlapping system of castes and classes created frontiers of competition and contentious areas of potential dissatisfaction that from time to time resulted in conspiracies and revolts. The three principal caste-like divisions established by laws and custom were whites, free persons of color, and slaves. Significant distinctions existed within each caste, but those distinctions were not based on common criteria. Whites were subdivided largely by economic indices into principal whites and lesser whites. In the Spanish areas the principal division between the white sectors coincided with locality of birth. Those born in Spain were called *peninsulares* (or in Mexico, *gachupines*) while those born in the Americas were called *criollos*, or Creoles. In the French Antilles the designations were *grands blancs* and *petits blancs*. All whites were assumed to be free and in the Caribbean their superordinate social classification corresponded to their relationship to plantation production or position in local government.

Free persons of color held the intermediate position between the whites and the enslaved and were subdivided mainly by pigmentation. Miscegenated individuals tended to be considered of a higher social class than black individuals. Slightly higher esteem fell on those born in the Americas than those born in Africa, as often indicated in the various Spanish censuses that differentiated this category into *negros libres* and *mulatos*.

While the other two categories entailed varying degrees of freedom, slaves represented a caste apart. Unlike the two categories of legally free whose mobility tended to be socially upward, slave mobility, given the broad spectrum of slave conditions, could be in either direction. Nevertheless, slaves also had their internal class divisions, based on occupation or geographical location. Skilled slaves, domestic workers, or urban slaves generally had a higher prestige than non-skilled field slaves.

No single consistent criterion served as the basis for social differentiation within the slave societies of the Americas and this factor constrained or severely inhibited mobility as well as cohesion. The whites were divided by wealth. The free colors were divided by color. And all slaves were separated by permanent legal disabilities. The result was a series of friction points within American slave systems that were exacerbated by the inescapable ambiguity and contradictions of the societies. Whites constituted organic societies in settler colonies where they formed the majority of the population and therefore were able to establish hegemony of force in most situations. A large critical mass also permitted occupational variety among the group of whites. In most exploitation societies, on the other hand, whites constituted a minority and therefore depended on the military services of their metropolis for the security of their persons and their property. Minority demographic status also forced whites to depend on non-whites for some essential services, thereby prohibiting some forms of occupation exclusion and discrimination found in some settler societies. Nevertheless, those whites continued to agitate for greater colonial independence of action, which they often expressed as a form of inherent liberty. At the same time whites tended to advocate a restriction of the conditions of free persons of color, even in cases where that sector duplicated the wealth and education of the white upper classes. Both elements of the free sector exploited and circumscribed the working and daily living conditions of their slaves, thereby engendering continual resistance from below.

Each segment of the American slave society had grievances that they expressed in different ways. The free people tended to use avenues of political communication with the metropolis either through the town councils in the Spanish colonies, representative chambers in the French colonies, or elected assemblies in the English colonies. The slaves resisted in any way they could, constantly negotiating with their masters the parameters of liberty enjoyable at any given moment. When negotiations broke down individually or collectively the result was often disaster. Not surprisingly, by the middle of the eighteenth century visitors to the slave societies of the Americas could begin to observe the palpable tension between the ranks of residents.

That tension exploded uncontrollably in 1791, when the slaves of Saint-Domingue, taking their cue from the French Revolution, revolted successfully under Toussaint Louverture (1743–1803) and a number of other local leaders. The radical French commissioner in the colony, Léger Félicité Sonthonax (1763–1813) saw the futility of defeating the local revolt and declared the emancipation of all slaves and their immediate admission to full citizenship (1793), a move ratified the following year by the revolutionary government in Paris that extended the emancipation to all French colonies. Napoleon Bonaparte revoked the decree of emancipation in 1802, but failed to make it stick in Saint-Domingue, where the ex-slaves and their free colored allies declared the independence of Haiti – the second free state in the Americas – in 1804.[5] Haiti clearly represented a significant turning point in the history of slavery in the Americas.

The fourth and final phase of the transatlantic trade lasted from about 1810 to 1870 and was overshadowed by the Haitian Revolution. During that phase approximately two million Africans were sold as slaves in a greatly reduced area of the Americas. With its slave trade continuing until 1850 (although illegal after 1830), Brazil imported some 1,145,400 Africans or about 60 percent of all slaves sold in the Americas after 1810 (Conrad 1972: 21–2). The Spanish Antilles – mainly Cuba and Puerto Rico – imported more than 600,000 Africans (32 percent), the great majority of them illegally introduced to Cuba after an Anglo-Spanish treaty to abolish the Spanish slave trade in 1817. The French Antilles imported approximately 96,000 slaves, equivalent to about 5 percent of all slaves sold during that period, mainly for the small, marginally productive sugar plantations of Martinique and Guadeloupe. The Southern United States also imported about 50,000 slaves, or slightly less than 3 percent of all slaves sold, despite formally agreeing to end their international slave trade in 1807.

During the nineteenth century the American system of slavery inevitably collapsed, sometimes with a whimper but occasionally with the clamor of civil war, as in the United States of America or in Cuba. Abolition began with the untidy general emancipation of the slaves in French colonies in 1794. This was a French metropolitan response to the serious revolt that broke out in Saint-Domingue in 1791. As Laurent

Dubois and John Garrigus (2006) carefully explain, both the revolution in France as well as the colonial variants were affected by the unpredictable turn of political events in Paris, which saw the execution of the French monarch in 1793 and the ongoing imperial rivalry that encouraged England and Spain to support colonial revolt before they realized the profound implications for their own empires. The French National Convention not only announced the emancipation of all French slaves; it also made them citizens of the empire, greatly exacerbating the anomaly between freedom and liberty in the slave society.

The Haitian Revolution inculcated a "terrified consciousness" in all whites across the Americas.[6] After that, slavery and the slave system would never be the same. Slave revolts increased across the hemisphere (Gaspar & Geggus 1997; Geggus 2001; Geggus 2003). During the succeeding decades, slave emancipation became a part of the platform for political independence across Spanish America.

Conditions of Slavery

The system of slavery in the Americas was generally restrictive and harsh, but significant variations characterized the daily lives of the enslaved across time and space. The exhaustive demands of the plantation societies in parts of the Caribbean and Brazil, combined with skewed sexual balances among the slaves, resulted in excessively high mortality rates, unusually low fertility rates, and consequently a steady demand for imported Africans to maintain the required labor forces (Curtin 1990: 17). The recovery of the indigenous populations in places such as Mexico and the Andean highlands led to the use of other systems of coerced labor rather than African slaves. Importation of Africans declined where local Indian labor was available after 1700, and that partly explains the declining import figures for Africans throughout Spanish America (except for Cuba) after about 1700. Frontiers of grazing economies such as the *llanos* of Venezuela, the southern parts of Brazil, and the pampas of Argentina and Uruguay required only modest supplies of labor, and so African slaves constituted an insignificant proportion of the local population. The city of Buenos Aires was an exception in 1810 since the black population equaled the white population in 1800 (Andrews 2004: 41). Only in the United States did the slave population reproduce itself dramatically over the years, supplying most of the expanding internal demand for slave labor during the nineteenth century.

In general death rates were highest for slaves engaged in sugar production, especially on newly opened areas of the tropics, and lowest among domestic urban workers, except during periodical outbreaks of epidemic diseases (Higman 1984; Engerman & Higman 1997). But slavery represented an artificial situation entirely hostile to the health and well-being of the enslaved. With the abolition of slavery the demographic profile of people of African descent made a dramatic rebound (Knight 1974: 46–8). George Reid Andrews makes the point dramatically when he points out that:

> During the period of slavery, ten times as many Africans came to the Spanish and Portuguese America (5.7 millions) as to the United States (560,000). By the end of the 1900s, Afro-Latin Americans outnumbered Afro-North Americans by three to one

(110 million and 35 million respectively) and formed, on average, almost twice as large a proportion of their respective populations (22 percent in Latin America, 12 percent in the United States). (Andrews 2004: 3)

The relationship between slave imports and surviving Afro-American populations in the post-abolition period remains extremely complex. Slavery was a clear legal designation but the terminology of Afro-American is socially constructed, imprecise, and eternally variable. The attack on the slave trade paralleled growing attacks on the system of slavery throughout the Americas. The self-directed abolition from below that occurred in Saint-Domingue/Haiti in 1793–1804 was not repeated elsewhere. Instead, a combination of internal and external events eventually determined the course of abolition throughout the region. The issue of slavery became a part of the struggle for political independence for the mainland Spanish American colonies (Helg, this volume).

Resistance to Slavery

Overt and bloody revolt was not the only, much less the major, form of resistance to the institution of slavery. Just as the poor do not accept their poverty, slaves did not benignly accept slavery. Michael Craton (1997: 222) points out that:

> Slave resistance was as inevitable as slavery itself. Slaves "naturally" resisted their enslave-ment because slavery was fundamentally *unnatural*. Slave resistance of one kind or another was a constant feature of slavery. Only the forms varied across time and place, according to circumstances and opportunities, mutating in rhythm to an internal dynamic, if not also in relation to the larger historical context . . . If slave resistance was endemic, it was overt only in special circumstances.

Overt rebellion was, of course, the most dramatic objection to slavery by far (Gaspar & Geggus 1997).

Most rebellions started with small conspiracies and often planters were prone to exact tremendous retribution based on their paranoid fear of the ultimate conse-quences of such revolts. This is exactly what happened in 1843 in Matanzas, Cuba – a place that ironically means in English "the place of the massacres." In Cuba the authorities murdered hundreds of slaves and free people of color, some in cold blood, because they felt that some slaves were about to start a rebellion.

Other forms of resistance were more prevalent, more endemic, than outright revolt. Certainly more pervasive in time and place were the deliberate absences from the work regime and running away from the plantation during slavery. This perennial absconding took two forms. The first was the mass desertion that left deliberately with the intention never to return. The refugees sometimes formed independent communities in the relatively inaccessible hills near plantations and towns, and oper-ated in a symbiotic relationship with established colonial society. Such mass desertion was called *gran marronage*, and gave rise to the various maroon communities all across the Americas. In Spanish these communities were called *palenques*, and in Brazil they were referred to as *quilombos* or *mocambos*. Some maroon communities lasted only briefly. Others lasted for centuries, as was the case of the Jamaica Maroons. Determined communities in Bahia and Palmares in Brazil, in Esmeraldas in Ecuador, in Maracaibo in Venezuela, and in Le Maniel in French Saint-Domingue lasted for many decades.

Concomitant with *gran marronage* was the more individual occurrence, called *petit marronage* – the spontaneous decision of an individual slave to leave his or her master for a short period. *Petit marronage* reflected the strong individual will of the slave to resist forced or unpleasant labor, to procrastinate, or to defy authority. It was never designed to create a viable alternate to the slave society, as was *gran marronage*. At its most serious, *petit marronage* remained a personal conflict between master and slave, as illustrated in the relations between Thomas Thistlewood and his slaves in eighteenth-century Jamaica (Hall 1999; Burnard 2004).

Other forms of slave resistance were equally personal and vindictive. Suicide among slaves was endemic in the American slave society. Domestic slaves poisoned themselves and their masters, and across the Caribbean whites spoke often in fear of the magical powers of slaves who they suspected of having cast spells on them. Slaves also malingered and feigned ignorance, pretended not to understand the common plantation language of their drivers, broke the farm equipment, killed or maimed the cattle, set fires to the cane fields at harvest time, destroyed the cane carts and milling machinery, or even sold the produce of the plantations. By these various forms of industrial action slaves sabotaged the production and productivity of the plantations and increased the overall cost of the system to their owners.

It is extremely difficult to determine what constituted conscious modes of resistance and what actions resulted from the inadvertent consequence of random carelessness on the part of the slaves. But abundant evidence exists to suggest that slaves were largely in command of their world even when they lacked the force to alter it. They were not entirely powerless in shaping the world in which they lived, although their influence over their daily lives should not be overestimated.

Writers such as Gordon K. Lewis and Michael Craton (1997) are wont to evaluate all actions of slaves as part of a conscious pattern of resistance. Lewis (1983: 175) divides resistance into three categories:

1   The category of patterns of accommodation and of habits of learned survival in the daily experience of plantation life: this involved the whole gamut of slave response, short of escape and rebellion, to the general slavery situation, and included everything from feigned ignorance, malingering, sabotage, slowed-down work habits, suicide, and poisoning of masters, on to the endless invention of attitudes that reflected a general war of psychological tensions and stresses between both sides in the master–slave relationship.
2   The category of alternative lifestyle: this category includes the manifold ways whereby the slave populations nourished and developed their own autonomous world of culture – in the areas, variously, of family, religion, language, song and dance, and even economic organization.
3   The category of escape and open revolt.

Writers such as Lewis and Craton obviously view the entire existence of slave life as a form of sociopolitical resistance, a necessary precondition to a life in freedom but also a vital manifestation of their own dignity and humanity. Emilia Viotti da Costa has written:

> Creating a black community in the slave quarters and holding on to traditions repre-
> sented resistance to slavery because slavery implied not only the subordination and
> exploitation of one social group by another, but also the confrontation of two ethnic
> groups. The slave could resist in different ways: as a slave to his master, as a black man
> to a white man, and as an African to the Europeans. In the context cultural resistance
> could be interpreted as a form of social protest. (1977: 301)

Nevertheless, viewing the slave systems as merely an enduring inescapable pattern of coercion and resistance is rather narrow and constricting and eventually leads to an intellectual cul-de-sac. It fails to do full justice to the varied, dynamic, and nuanced world of the American slave systems. Such a narrow view perpetuates an indelible victim mentality and fails to reflect the totality of slavery throughout the Americas, while at the same time minimizing the monumental resilience, the astonishing creativity, and magnificent contribution of Africans and their descendants in the making of the modern world.

Africans, whether free or enslaved, profoundly affected every aspect of American society regardless of the location in which they found themselves. Antonio de las Barras y Prado noted for Havana around the middle of the nineteenth century that, "the people of color serve the whites in every domestic, agricultural and industrial job."[7] According to the monumental statistical compilation done by Jacobo de la Pezuela (1863–6) for Cuba during the nineteenth century, non-whites demonstrated an amazing versatility and industry across a wide variety of occupations. Occupational designations varied from place to place, making direct comparisons difficult. Nevertheless, a general pattern can de discerned. Slaves and non-whites dominated lower-skilled and non-skilled occupations such as bakers, bricklayers, barbers, carpenters, and daily-paid workers, in agriculture and in industry. They also were found disproportionately as hatters, house painters, masons, muleteers, musicians, potters, saddlemakers, sawyers, shoemakers, silversmiths, tailors, water carriers, and watchmen. Female slaves and non-whites were found overwhelmingly in dressmaking, washing, and domestic help. Slaves and free non-whites were excluded from the upper levels of the clergy, the military, and the police, as well as the imperial bureaucracy, or large-scale businesses.

Since the daily life of the enslaved across the Americas varied so much, it is difficult to categorize neatly. Certainly it cannot be done satisfactorily within the restrictive bipolar forms of accommodation or resistance. It should not surprise us that slaves performed many of the tasks in any society, although they tended to dominate the unskilled categories. They lived their lives as best they could and when slavery was abolished adjusted as well as the situation permitted. Slavery was never a static institution. It changed enormously through time, and even in the same locality. The post-emancipation societies also varied, presenting new challenges to populations largely excluded from economic and political power for centuries. Indeed, a great number of people described as Africans or as African slaves in the Americas were not in any way overtly coerced. Their lot was quite removed from that of the quasi-industrialized plantation field slaves, especially in the last century of the American slave system. Together, the enslaved and the non-white free made indelible contributions to every American society.

NOTES

1 A significant exception is that within the Ottoman Empire Janissaries were slaves who had prestige, authority, and political as well as military power.
2 This is the untenable position espoused by Patterson (1982), which unfortunately has been quite influential in the later historiography.
3 According to Rodríguez Morel (forthcoming), licenses might have been granted for slave importation to Seville before 1518 but after issuance was formalized and taxes imposed on the imports. See also Palmer (1997: 9–44).
4 Calculations are based on Curtin (1969). Other authors have recalculated the figures provided by Curtin but their overall variations fall well within his margin of error of plus or minus 20 percent.
5 The bibliography on the Haitian Revolution is extensive. See the selected bibliography in Dubois & Garrigus (2006).
6 The phrase "terrified consciousness" appears in Anthony Maingot (1996), and as the title of a chapter in Ramchand (1970: 23).
7 De las Barras y Prado (1925: 107). The memoir was written between 1850 and 1862 and published posthumously.

BIBLIOGRAPHY

Andrews, G. R. (2004) *Afro-Latin America, 1800–2000*. Oxford University Press, New York.

Bowser, F. P. (1974) *The African Slave in Colonial Peru, 1524–1650*. Stanford University Press, Stanford, Calif.

Burnard, T. (2004) *Master, Tyranny and Desire. Thomas Thistlewood and His Slaves in the Anglo-Jamaican World*. University of North Carolina Press, Chapel Hill, NC.

Conrad, R. E. (1972) *The Destruction of Brazilian Slavery, 1850–1888*. University of California Press, Berkeley.

Conrad, R. E. (1986) *World of Sorrow: The African Slave Trade to Brazil*. Louisiana State University Press, Baton Rouge.

Craton, M. (1997) "Forms of Resistance to Slavery." In F. W. Knight (ed.), *UNESCO General History of the Caribbean, volume III. The Slave Societies of the Caribbean*. UNESCO/Macmillan, London.

Curtin, P. (1969) *The Atlantic Slave Trade: A Census*. University of Wisconsin Press, Madison.

Curtin, P. (1990) *The Rise and Fall of the Plantation Complex. Essays in Atlantic History*. Cambridge University Press, New York.

Da Costa, E. V. (1977) "Slave Images and Realities." In V. Rubin & A. Tuden (eds.), *Comparative Perspectives on Slavery in New World Plantation Societies*. Academy of Sciences, New York.

De la Pezuela, J. (1863–6) *Diccionario geográfico, estadístico, histórico de la isla de Cuba*, 4 vols. Mellado, Madrid.

De las Barras y Prado, A. (1925) *Memorias: La Habana a mediados del siglo XIX*. Ciudad Real, Madrid.

Díaz, M. E. (2000) *The Virgin, The King, and the Royal Slaves of El Cobre. Negotiating Freedom in Colonial Cuba, 1670–1780*. Stanford University Press, Stanford.

Díaz del Castillo, B. (1979 [1800]) *The True History and Conquest of Mexico*, trans. M. Keatinge. Renaissance Press, La Jolla, CA.

Dubois, L. & Garrigus, J. (2006) *Slave Revolution in the Caribbean, 1789–1804. A Brief History with Documents.* Bedford/St. Martin's, New York.

Eltis, D., Behrendt, S., Richardson, D., & Klein, H. (eds.) (1999) *The Trans-Atlantic Slave Trade; A Database on CD-ROM.* Cambridge University Press, Cambridge.

Engerman, S. & Higman, B. W. (1997) "The Demographic Structure of Caribbean Slave Societies in the Eighteenth and Nineteenth Centuries." In F. W. Knight (ed.), *UNESCO General History of the Caribbean, volume III. The Slave Societies of the Caribbean.* UNESCO/Macmillan, London.

Finley, M. (1998) *Ancient Slavery and Modern Ideology.* Markus Wiener Publishers, Princeton.

Fuson, R. (trans.) (1987) *The Log of Christopher Columbus.* International Marine Publishing Company, Camden, ME.

Gaspar, B. & Geggus, D. (eds.) (1997) *A Turbulent Time. The French Revolution and the Greater Caribbean.* Indiana University Press, Bloomington.

Geggus, D. (1997) "Slavery, War, and Revolution in the Greater Caribbean." In B. Gaspar & D. Geggus (eds.), *A Turbulent Time. The French Revolution and the Greater Caribbean.* Indiana University Press, Bloomington.

Geggus, D. (ed.) (2001) *The Impact of the Haitian Revolution in the Atlantic World.* University of South Carolina Press, Columbia.

Geggus, D. (2003) "The Influence of the Haitian Revolution on Blacks in Latin America and the Caribbean." In N. P. Naro (ed.), *Blacks, Coloureds and National Identity in Nineteenth-Century Latin America.* Institute of Latin American Studies, London.

Gibson, C. (1964) *The Aztecs under Spanish Rule. A History of the Indians of the Valley of Mexico.* Stanford University Press, Stanford.

Hall, D. (1999) *In Miserable Slavery. Thomas Thistlewood in Jamaica, 1750–86.* University of the West Indies Press, Mona, Jamaica.

Higman, B. W. (1984) *Slave Populations of the British Caribbean, 1807–1834.* Johns Hopkins University Press, Baltimore.

Klein, H. (1999) *The Atlantic Slave Trade.* Cambridge University Press, New York.

Knight, F. W. (1974) *The African Dimension in Latin American Societies.* Macmillan, New York.

Lewis, G. K. (1983) *Main Currents in Caribbean Thought.* Johns Hopkins University Press, Baltimore.

Lockhart, J. (1972) *The Men of Cajamarca. A Social and Biographical Study of the First Conquerors of Peru.* University of Texas Press, Austin.

Lovejoy, P. (1983) *Transformations in Slavery: A History of Slavery in Africa.* Cambridge University Press, New York.

Maingot, A. (1996) "Haiti and the Terrified Consciousness of the Caribbean." In G. Oostindie (ed.), *Ethnicity in the Caribbean: Essays in Honor of Harry Hoetink.* Macmillan, London.

Meirs, S. & Kopytoff, I. (eds.) (1977) *Slavery in Africa: Historical and Anthropological Perspectives.* University of Wisconsin Press, Madison.

Palmer, C. (1997) "The Slave Trade, African Slavers, and the Demography of the Caribbean to 1750." In F. W. Knight (ed.), *UNESCO General History of the Caribbean, volume III. The Slave Societies of the Caribbean.* UNESCO/Macmillan, London.

Patterson, O. (1982) *Slavery and Social Death: A Comparative Study.* Harvard University Press, Cambridge, MA.

Portuondo Zúñiga, O. (1995) *La Virgen de la Caridad del Cobre: Símbolo de cubanía.* Editorial Oriente, Santiago de Cuba.

Ramchand, K. (1970) *The West Indian Novel and its Background.* Macmillan, London.

Rodríguez Morel, G. (2004) "The Sugar Economy of Española in the Sixteenth Century." In S. Schwartz (ed.), *Tropical Babylons. Sugar and the Making of the Atlantic World, 1450–1680*. University of North Carolina, Chapel Hill.

Rodríguez Morel, G. (forthcoming) "Black Slavery in the Hispanic Caribbean in the Sixteenth and Seventeenth Centuries." In F. W. Knight (ed.), *UNESCO General History of the Caribbean, volume III. The Slave Societies of the Caribbean* (rev. ed.). UNESCO/Macmillan, London.

Solow, B. (ed.) (1991) *Slavery and the Rise of the Atlantic System*. Harvard University Press, Cambridge, MA.

Solow B. & Engerman, S. (eds.) (1987) *British Capitalism and Caribbean Slavery: The Legacy of Eric Williams*. Cambridge University Press, New York.

Vieira, A. (ed.) (2002) *História do Açúcar. Rotas e Mercados*. Centro de Estudos de História do Atlântico, Madeira.

Weber, D. (1992) *The Spanish Frontier in North America*. Yale University Press, New Haven.

West, S. (2005) *Though the Heavens May Fall. The Landmark Trial That Led to the End of Human Slavery*. Da Capo Press, Cambridge, Mass.

Chapter Ten

Religion, Society, and Culture in the Colonial Era

Rachel Sarah O'Toole

This chapter explores indigenous adaptations to Spanish Catholicism in Mesoamerica and the Andes during the height of colonial rule between the mid-sixteenth and the mid-eighteenth centuries, with additional comparisons to Afro-Brazilian society of the eighteenth and nineteenth centuries. Some colonized "Indians" seized on ecclesiastical institutions such as religious sodalities to build new, urban identities while African-descent slaves could employ the Inquisitorial courts to defend themselves against their owners' abuses. At the same time, ecclesiastical judges prosecuted indigenous healers just as clerical leaders excluded free men of color from taking religious vows or entering institutions of higher learning. Yet, subaltern engagements with ecclesiastical beliefs, practices, and corporations as well as clerical responses reveal how diverse colonial communities expressed their social ties through the institutions of the Catholic Church and, in so doing, shaped public performances, religious worship, and definitions of kinship in colonial Latin America.

Colonial Evangelization and Becoming Catholic

Catholic evangelization in the sixteenth century was a double-edged sword. Catholic missionaries worked to eradicate indigenous and African religious practices while Catholicism also provided a justification for the enslavement and colonization of African and indigenous peoples. Initially, Nahua ("Aztec"), Mayan, and Andean societies responded to proselytization by incorporating their cultural practices and previous spiritual interpretations into Catholic rituals and church locales. Enslaved Southwestern Atlantic Africans continued to practice Catholicism while West Africans adapted themselves to Catholic institutions to form evolving transatlantic Afro-Latin American identities. Simultaneously, conversion to Catholicism facilitated the inclusion of indigenous communities and, to a lesser extent, enslaved Atlantic Africans into the Catholic "body" as vassals of a Catholic monarch.

In the sixteenth century, missionaries from the regular orders (including Franciscans, Dominicans, and Augustinians) worked among indigenous communities and populations in Mesoamerica with great dedication. Friars at first assumed that indigenous peoples had not been exposed to Catholicism or certainly not given the chance to embrace its teachings. Based on an interpretation of indigenous people as rational beings ready to receive conversion, the first waves of Iberian missionaries learned indigenous languages in order to correctly communicate Christian doctrine. During what some scholars have interpreted as a hopeful moment of cultural coexistence, Franciscan missionaries cast Nahua actors in religious dramas that included native songs and local costumes. The friars employed indigenous artisans to paint murals on church walls that incorporated autochthonous flora and fauna as well as indigenous imagery and motifs (Burkhart 1989: 20).

Millenarian zeal informed the furious pace of the Franciscans. The friars taught indigenous neophytes "correct external behavior" that, in time, they believed would grow into a deeper, spiritual awakening if not a ready adherence to Catholic practice (Clendinnen 1987: 47–8). By the 1560s, the Franciscans in the Yucatán had discovered that Mayas continued to worship deities that they had sworn to abandon. Acting from a sense of intense betrayal, the Franciscans employed unauthorized Inquisitorial procedures to try, sentence, and punish (sometimes with death) the Mayan "offenders." Regardless, missionaries incorporated indigenous people into the creation of Catholic colonial culture, a fact not erased by the eventual end of the initial utopian religious project.

In the seventeenth century, indigenous communities and individuals continued to combine Catholic imagery and rituals with local celebrations as "Indians" increasingly identified as Christian. Resettled into colonial villages, Nahuas recognized particular Catholic saints as sacred symbols of their communities or representations of influential ancestors. In Sula, Mexico, two elderly leaders dreamt that Santiago (St. James) appeared to announce himself as the people's saint while elsewhere local artisans depicted St. Francis alongside the former Mexica ("Aztec") rulers of Tenochtitlán. Nahuas also included Catholic saints into household altars adorned with candles, flowers, and incense or housed in separate "saint-houses" adjacent to family homes (Lockhart 1992: 236, 238). During *fiestas* that also coincided with seasonal observances (such as rain-making ceremonies), Mayas (as well as other indigenous communities) honored their saints with abundant food and drink as well as demonstrated their gratitude with bullfights, dances, and (eventually) fireworks. Thus, independently, Mesoamericans made Catholic rituals and Catholic objects part of their households and villages as indigenous religiosity and Catholicism itself underwent a colonial transformation.

In the Andes, clerics accompanied Spanish conquerors, but only after intra-Spanish conflicts ceased and Inca armed resistance retreated in the 1550s did secular clergy and local elites establish monasteries, cathedrals, and parish churches. Initial evangelical attempts were quickly revealed as cursory and ineffectual in the 1560s when a rural priest reported that groups of "Indians" danced and trembled into altered states. Those affected by the "dancing sickness," or Taki Onqoy, spoke as Andean *huacas* (deities) who rejected Spanish religion as well as European food and clothing. In response, Catholic authorities met in Lima for the Third Council (1582–3), where they resolved to eradicate Andean practices, destroy sacred sites, and reeducate indigenous communities in a series of anti-idolatry campaigns that continued (sporadically) into the eighteenth century. At the same time, Catholic clergy renewed their intentions to learn indigenous languages as well as composing manuals and sermons in Quechua. Andean evangelization combined punishment and entreaties.

Still, Andean people incorporated Christian religious imagery into their social landscapes. As extirpators desecrated sacred sites or huacas with crosses, Andean people continued their pilgrimages and devotions to these familiar locations. Additionally, indigenous communities created new saints. In the early 1580s, two kin groups on the shores of Lake Titicaca could not choose between the version of the Virgin Mary known as La Candelaria or the image of St. Sebastian as their intermediary with God. Threatened by bad harvests and severe drought, the community sent one member, Francisco Tito Yupanqui, to apprentice himself with a master image-maker in Potosí. There, the indigenous artisan crafted an image of the Virgin Mary known as Our Lady of Copacabana, whose miracles continue to attract pilgrims (Salles-Reese 1997: 20, 27). As indigenous peoples, such as those of Lake Titicaca, incorporated statues and paintings of saints, rosaries, and other holy relics into their personal possessions and public lives, Catholic imagery spread throughout the Andes and beyond.

Exclusion and Inclusion into the Catholic "Body"

Still, individually, some indigenous men and women retained or transformed previous religious practices and, in a way, capitalized on European perceptions of "Indians" as categorically unorthodox. Though discouraged by Catholic authorities, Europeans and their descendants consulted indigenous practitioners for remedies to illness or advice on their relationships. In Guanajuato (Mexico), a *criolla* (i.e., born in the colony, of Spanish descent) consulted an indigenous local healer on how to punish a man who had reneged on his promise to marry (Behar 1989: 192). Clients of María de Arriero, an Andean indigenous practitioner of love magic, included Spanish women who washed in water with flowers and herbs supplied by their "Indian witch" in hopes of binding their lovers to them (Mills 1997: 116–17). As their prosecution by the Inquisition indicates, indigenous ritual specialists were arguably beyond the boundaries of orthodox religious practice but could be central in the daily lives of Spanish colonial inhabitants.

A diverse clientele also sought out Atlantic Africans and their descendants for assistance with divination and healing that included Catholic imagery, practices, and beliefs. Elite Spanish women as well as free and enslaved people of color consulted María Martínez, a *mulata* diviner in urban Peru who "had a fierce reputation for straightening out questions of passion and justice" (Silverblatt 2004: 172–4). According to women clients who testified to Inquisitors, María Martínez derived her powers from a sexual, and heretical, pact with the devil. Likewise, free and enslaved men and women of color provided elite women in colonial Guatemala with ritual objects, spells, and divination services designed to bring wealth, to cure illness, or to promote business (Few 2002: 106–10). The social, economic, or racial distance between a ritual practitioner and a client often contributed to the perception of marginal potency as colonizers imagined non-white women as powerful in their heterodoxy.

As colonizers grew more dependent on the labor of enslaved women and men, slaveholders and colonial authorities associated Africans and their descendants, in particular, with demonic magic and witchcraft. Slaveholders feared that slaves employed amulets, curses, and powders to bewitch and to kill their owners. In turn, enslaved people may have seized on the opportunity afforded by colonizers' associations as a means to avoid physical punishment or other abuses. According to Inquisition documents, a slaveholder in early eighteenth-century Pernambuco (Brazil) was so fearful of his slave's sorcery that he refused to allow him to pray (Souza 2003 [1986]: 126–7). Whether or not the enslaved man used his amulet (a "mandinga pouch") to curse his owner remains unknown, but the slaveholder's fear was evident. Owners also employed Atlantic African diviners to achieve "balance and harmony in the slave community," as in the case of a planter in Bahia who hired a Congo man to locate a murderer on his estate (Sweet 2003: 120–1). When completed, the slaveholder had settled a dispute according to the culture of the enslaved community itself. In this way, both slaveholders and slaves operated according to a spiritual and religious logic that stressed the influence of Atlantic Africans outside of Catholic orthodoxy.

Other Atlantic Africans insisted they were members of the Catholic community regardless of slaveholders' prejudices and fears. In the early modern Atlantic world, as explained by Herman Bennett (2003), the Spanish Crown and the Catholic Church categorized enslaved Africans and their descendants as both royal vassals and, once baptized, as legitimate Christians. Likewise, Portuguese colonizers in Brazil recognized the Christian identities of enslaved Atlantic Africans, especially those sold from Central Africa where inhabitants of the Kingdom of Kongo as well as Portuguese Angola and Benguela came from practicing Catholic communities (Heywood 2002: 91–113; Thornton 2002: 72–90). Furthermore, Iberian slaveholders were bound by ecclesiastical agreements and theological precepts to teach enslaved men, women, and children basic doctrine and to allow slave couples to marry and to be buried according to Catholic standards. Once in the Americas, even Africans from Senegambia and the Bight of Benin (where Catholic missionaries had been less successful) converted voluntarily and benefited from partial protections offered by the Catholic Church.

Thus, enslaved or free, Atlantic Africans and their descendants incorporated Catholic imagery and, in some cases, transformed its meaning. In colonial Brazil, Africans employed pieces of consecrated Catholic altars (*pedra d'ara*) as talismans and, most popularly, in *bolsas de mandinga* or amulets designed to protect owners from harm. Far from rejecting Catholicism, slaves and free people venerated the pieces of stone that had been blessed by a Catholic priest (Sweet 2003: 203–4). In nineteenth-century Brazil, some Africans may have baptized each other in order to wash away sins that included the evils of sorcery and the devil (Karasch 1987: 257). Atlantic Africans, therefore, chose Catholic objects or religious rituals that fit into previous beliefs and current practices. They incorporated Catholicism into their communities and concurrently included themselves into Catholicism.

If indigenous and African people were Catholic, Spanish and Portuguese colonizers and slaveholders imagined that "blacks" and other people of color inhabited a distinctive space in Catholic colonial culture from that of "Indians." Christian Iberians had long associated blackness with sin as well as cultural inferiority in a manner that linked "black blood" with an irredeemable status of servitude (Sweet 1997: 149, 154, 159; Martínez 2004: 4). In the colonial setting, Spanish colonial authorities employed categories such as *negro* and *negra* to transform "Africans" into "slaves" (Bennett 2003: 180). Colonial perceptions regarding the nature of Atlantic Africans and their descendants served to further justify slavery and the subsequent regulations of both enslaved and free people. According to Inquisitors and their notaries, "black" women were naturally rebellious and dangerously sensual while Spanish jurists regulated "black" men as categorically uncivilized. If indigenous people were weak and ignorant in colonial discourses, blacks were described as bellicose and cunning (Lewis 2003: 2, 31, 101, 159). According to colonial law, indigenous people were to be incorporated into a Catholic body (if segregated in social practice). However, dependency on skilled captive labor also caused Iberian colonials to exclude and reject "blacks" from colonial society. Colonial regulations marked people of color as foreign outsiders whose true conversion to Christianity and loyalty to the Crown was continually suspect.

Membership of the secular clergy and religious orders therefore was not open to indigenous or African men and women. Early in the Postconquest period mendicants in Mexico entertained the possibility that indigenous men would be able to take vows in the formal orders, while some missionaries in the Andean regions suggested that with the proper education "Indians" could become priests. Yet, monasteries and the priesthood quickly became the domain of men who could prove legitimate descent from married Christians and those who could publicly claim a Hispanic heritage. While some *mestizos* and men of African descent eventually took religious vows, the clergy was primarily Spanish. Even Cuzco's first convent, founded to include the *mestiza* daughters of local *conquistadores* and Inca noble women, gradually segregated and eliminated indigenous nuns. Nuns of the black veil would be those considered Spanish while indigenous women and their descendants took the lesser, white veil (Burns 1999: 15–40). Although included as practitioners, indigenous and African peoples were excluded from religious leadership.

Still, African and indigenous people were integral to Catholic religious institutions. In colonial convents, indigenous and African-descent women provided the daily labor that allowed professed nuns to devote their lives to prayer. Servants, slaves, and dependents staffed the convent's kitchens, gardens, and laundry rooms as well as selling foodstuffs on the streets of colonial cities to support their owners. In fact, enslaved women and indigenous servants were often liaisons who provided news to cloistered nuns that would be necessary for the management of the convent's communal (and members' individual) properties. Likewise, enslaved men tended the churches and the infirmaries of colonial monasteries even if they were unable to take formal vows.

Colonial religious institutions could not categorically bar pious men and women of color. Indigenous women established *beaterios* for a laity who could not profess but lived in seclusion or served local communities. Thus, lay religious institutions as well as monasteries and convents operated as hospitals or orphanages regardless of members' abilities to take formal vows. Within monasteries and convents, African men and women became *donados* or *donadas*, as enslaved people who "donated" themselves to religious service. In Lima, the slave Ursula de Jesús devoted her life to cleaning Santa Clara's chapel and praying for the souls in purgatory. Martín de Porres, a free man of color, also undertook the treatment of the sick and poor within and beyond the walls of Lima's Dominican monastery. His piety as well as charity, illustrated by his first miracle (to bring the cat, the dog, and the mouse together to eat from one bowl), so impressed the inhabitants of Lima that they nominated him for sainthood following his death in 1639. Despite the exclusionary practices of religious institutions, subaltern individuals in some cases superseded colonial expectations that African and indigenous descendants were incapable of such saintly commitments.

Many African-descent people considered themselves to be devout Catholics and, along with indigenous communities, understood how inclusion in the Catholic body alleviated their outsider status. In the 1560s, when Franciscan missionaries realized that the Yucatán Maya had not completely converted to Catholicism, they still noted that the symbol of crucifixion had penetrated indigenous imaginations (Clendinnen 1987: 186). Mayas may not have employed the image of Jesus on the cross in an orthodox manner, but the crucifixion image had become a part of their religious practices. By the mid-seventeenth century, some Andeans had internalized the damning sermons of the extirpators and expressed shame over sexual or social practices as had been taught in doctrine classes. They confessed real fear of the devil, who could appear as "a dark and sinister man" (Mills 1997: 225, 228). Unlike the capricious and ambiguous spirit of precolonial Andean beliefs, the devil was "black" and categorically dangerous. Likewise, Atlantic Africans saw themselves as Catholic despite colonial claims of their "dangerous" and "devilish" position. Thus, evangelization of indigenous and African colonial peoples was a force of elimination of non-Christian religious practices, but also an entry into colonial society.

Between Orthodox Catholicism and Heterodox Catholics

With their membership, however tenuous, into the Catholic body politic, indigenous and African colonial peoples employed social and cultural institutions of the Church to defend their interests. Indigenous communities claimed to be loyal subjects of a Catholic King in order to defend their land from encroaching private Spanish landholders throughout the seventeenth century. Until the end of slavery in the nineteenth century, enslaved Africans and their descendants demanded that their owners recognize their status as married Catholics and keep their families intact. Secular and ecclesiastical authorities may have dismissed the commitments of indigenous and African-descent peoples. Subaltern groups, nevertheless, seized on the possibilities of Catholic institutions in order to secure economic resources, as well as to shape colonial public culture, household structures, and religious beliefs in Iberian–American societies.

The colonial creation of *doctrinas* or "Indian" parishes allowed some indigenous communities to maintain control over Preconquest landholdings and water rights. In central Mexico, the parishes often had the same borders as the Preconquest institution of the Nahua *altepetl*, a community of people who held dominion over territory such as a city-state or a village (Lockhart 1992: 29). Among the Maya, the Franciscans often respected native boundaries so that colonial parish administration helped to preserve previous hierarchies of subordinate hamlets (or annexes) to "head" parishes. Into the twentieth century, parishioners of Tetiz continued to take their saint on a 10-kilometer procession to the district's Preconquest principal town in the northwest Yucatán (Farriss 1984: 149, 151). Parish divisions, although imposed by colonial overlords, allowed indigenous communities to maintain social and political continuities into and beyond the era of Spanish colonization.

In the Andes, Viceroy Toledo (and some predecessors) resettled dispersed indigenous communities and distinct kinship groups (*ayllus*) into colonial *reducciones* in the 1570s that were also intended to constitute a single parish. In many cases, as in Mesoamerica, colonial officials settled related (if not antagonistic) Preconquest communities (or *parcialidades*) into colonial towns. Yet, Andean reducciones were also intended to reorganize indigenous social structures. Crown officials conceptualized colonial "Indian" villages based on a grid plan, with straight streets radiating out from a plaza on which the parish church and the municipal buildings (including the jail) stood as firm indicators of the dual centralizing authorities. In addition to concentrating Andeans so that a priest could better teach Catholic doctrine and ensure regular attendance at Mass, colonial reducciones were supposed to impose heteronormative and monogamous standards on Andean families. Rather than living with and among groups of kin, colonized Andeans were ordered to form nuclear families and marry in the church (Spalding 1984: 214, 216).

Secular and ecclesiastical officials instructed priests to destroy Andean religious practices, including any attempts to maintain sacred sites associated with ancestor worship. Priests were supplied with printed sermons, confession manuals, and doctrinal guides to instruct Andean communities in a language that reflected an ecclesiastical perception of indigenous people as timid, "fragile," and easily "infected" by idolatry. Through the practice of annual confessions, the clergy instructed indigenous people in the norms of sexual behavior, including detailed descriptions to avoid "deviant" practices such as fornication, adultery, sodomy, bestiality, and other sexual sins (Harrison 1994: 135–50). Thus, the colonial rural parish in the Andes was a site where indigenous communities underwent radical rearrangements of social relations on the most intimate level.

In both the Andes and Mesoamerica, indigenous leaders could employ the official definitions of the colonial parish as well as its offices to enforce a limited governance of their communities. In the urban areas, parishes gave new shape to regional identities, as Cuzco's parochial churches housed Andeans of particular ethnicities such as Cañaris of Santa Ana. In rural areas, Andean men elected their fellows to the positions of sexton, choir leader, and constable as well as a schoolmaster who received a salary from the village community fund (Spalding 1984: 218). Among the Maya, the choirmaster kept track of births, marriages, and deaths, supervised the catechism, and selected local children for further education. In fact, the man in this position investigated whether members were fit to be married, led liturgies, and buried the dead and baptized the young if the priest was unavailable (Farriss 1984: 335–6). In this way, indigenous men transformed their communities into villages based on Catholic family structures and Iberian government hierarchies.

Africans and their descendants also established collective identities within particular churches through their memberships in *cofradías* or *irmandades* (sodalities or religious brotherhoods). Unlike indigenous populations, colonial officials did not assign enslaved or free Africans and their descendants to particular lands or urban neighborhoods. Yet, sodalities often provided religious services in the absence of an officiating cleric or priest. Like indigenous personnel in rural parishes, officers of the sodality led prayers, organized Masses, fed the poor as well as buried and prayed for the dead (Bowser 1974: 247–50). Africans and their descendants joined these religious organizations in order to claim the dignity of a Catholic burial as well as the opportunity to join in public religious processions of annual feast days. In Brazil, such sodalities could grow from building altars for their saints in elite churches, to establishing their own chapels. Members chose officers who would collect funds, obtain candle wax needed for processions and burials, and keep the account books (Karasch 1987: 83–6). Members also developed exclusive societies based on a shared African ethnicity as a *congo* or a *mina* as well as free or enslaved status and even occupation. In this way, sodalities reflected colonial hierarchies as well as proved a public presence for collectivities of Africans and their descendants.

Africans and their descendants also employed sodalities to worship black saints and to perform their own spiritual practices within the bounds of Catholicism. In Brazil, Africans transformed Catholic images into "African-style ancestral spirits" who could be called on for protection. For example, St. George assisted men during fights and St. Peter helped those who wanted to identify thieves. Saints helped ward away illness, assisted in childbirth, and could cure specific diseases (Sweet 2003: 206–8). In some cases, Catholic saints were also associated with spiritual entities or *orixás* at the center of Candomblé and Umbanda religions, as the image of Our Lady of Sorrows may have correlated with the Yoruba deity Iemanjá. Likewise, the image of Judas may have been associated with Exú, a powerful *orixá* who controlled unruly spirits (Karasch 1987: 277–84). African and African-descent people transformed saints' images into humanized beings that lived and breathed as well as drank and snored. As familiar assistants, black saints such as St. Benedict the Moor were simultaneously benevolent and destructive. In 1849, the powerful saint supposedly punished Rio de Janeiro with a yellow fever epidemic after whites refused to process his image on their shoulders. The organized worship of saints provided Africans and their descendants with a powerful means to attract fortune, health, and status as they warded off evil within and outside of orthodox Catholicism.

Indigenous people also employed the economic aspects of Catholic sodalities as they adapted to the significant material changes of Spanish colonization. In the rural areas, indigenous villages employed sodalities as a means to retain and to expand communal property as Andean *cofradías* held lands that they had collectively purchased or had been donated by devoted members (Spalding 1984: 45). *Cofradía* leaders then employed the income to sponsor religious celebrations including bullfights, processions, and feasts. Among the Maya, cofradía officers organized biannual trade expeditions to exchange cacao for scapulars, images, and cash along commercial routes that were active before Spanish colonization. Yucatán Mayan cofradías invested their communal funds in the untraditional yet profitable enterprise of cattle ranching that provided a dependable income and relief from famine. In the rural areas, Maya cofradía officers maintained the association's account books and were often more permanent than the rotating priests. Simultaneously, as demands grew for labor in the mines and the growth of significant urban areas created rural and urban migrations throughout the southern Andes, cofradías provided a means for individuals to integrate themselves in new environs. New indigenous elites in the cities emerged as cofradía officers of migrant communities while market women reinvested their profits and marked their wealthy status through their participation in public processions. Religious sodalities provided an institutional means to survive the disruptions of Spanish colonization and, in some cases, profit the colonial economy (Farriss 1984: 154–5, 267, 270, 326, 338).

In the rural and urban areas, indigenous people also employed the parish churches or chapels that adjoined monasteries and convents for their own religious purposes. In the Yucatán, one indigenous community continued to bury their dead underneath the altars and in the crypts of their parish church in the precolonial flexed position with a jade bead in the mouth. Andeans appropriated the image of St. James and linked the Catholic saint with the mountain thunder god Illapa. In this way, the didactic murals on the walls of rural Andean churches could become message boards for "resistance-in-acquiescence," as Andean-ized saints became intermediaries to God for indigenous communities (Silverblatt 1988: 190–1). Likewise, the immense paintings of the Corpus Christi procession in Cuzco communicated an incorporation of Inca elites as pious patrons and reverent participants of one of the most important celebrations of the Catholic calendar (Dean 1999: 95–6). While the physical location of parish churches may have initially communicated a Spanish dominance of indigenous societies, individuals and communities appropriated these structures and its artwork for their own communiqués.

Likewise, enslaved Africans and their descendants employed the practice of baptism to build necessary social networks. Adults who had been forcibly traded from the Atlantic African coasts were often baptized in a perfunctory way. Yet, African parents in colonial Brazil secured a new kin relationship with a prosperous and powerful individual when they chose the godparents of their children (Karasch 1987: 257, 349). In some cases a godparent was an owner or another slaveholder who may or may not have been willing to help in the manumission of the child. In most cases, however, relatives or friends purchased the freedom of a beloved godchild or members of a sodality offered funds. Baptism as a Catholic institution helped enslaved Africans build social networks that might eventually help secure the freedom of their families (Bowser 1974: 280, 282, 288).

Indigenous people also employed the Catholic institution of *compadrazgoi*, or godparentage, to express non-kin relationships and build new connections with other adults. Migrants among the Maya forged new relationships by asking local people to serve as godparents to their children. These relationships would create "a supplementary or alternate network of mutual obligations" that could help individuals and groups survive recurrent famines, epidemics, and other disasters of colonization (Farris 1984: 220, 250, 259). Indigenous women and men called each other *comadre* or *compadre* in order to express a "sense of connection, obligation, and reciprocity achieved voluntarily rather than by birth" that was strengthened with regular rituals and events (Stern 1995: 105). Use of the Catholic institution of godparentage could also obligate indigenous individuals and communities to their Spanish "kin." In the Andes, Spaniards employed ties of godparentage to organize labor for private enterprises such as mining (Spalding 1984: 288). In Guatemala, European traders employed their compadrazgo ties to secure cacao from native producers at lower prices (Herrera 2003: 51). Still, indigenous people could call on their ties with Spaniards to gain assistance in the colonial courts, to secure a loan, or to find work. Godparentage, while involving sometimes burdensome obligations, could be a useful tool.

While indigenous women and men established long-term relationships and familial bonds within Catholic institutions, they could be reluctant to enter into formal matrimony. Some Maya, and members of other indigenous groups, disagreed with Catholic prohibitions of bigamy, adultery, incest, and divorce that were central to orthodox Catholicism. Maya officials who resisted punishing community members engaging in these practices often faced the dilemma of a colonial intermediary: enforcement meant rewards from colonial authorities, but resistance from the home community could jeopardize local leadership positions. Because colonial tribute was imposed on married male heads of households, couples were pressured into formal Catholic unions at an early age as communities struggled to keep up with colonial demands (Farriss 1984: 170; Spalding 1984: 175). Indigenous communities may have pushed couples into matrimony, in contrast to the usual courtship and trial marriages practiced by native Andeans. Marriage fees for the announcement of the banns and the wedding Mass could also be prohibitive to impoverished indigenous couples and families so that matrimony was more common among indigenous elites. Thus, even as colonial villages and parish structures lent themselves to heteronormative structures, some indigenous people resisted this fundamental expectation of Catholic families.

Indigenous men and women, however, entered into marriage in order to formalize economic partnerships and to secure social networks. In the seventeenth century, Andean indigenous migrant men (*forasteros*) married into local ayllus in order to join an established community and thereby gain access to abandoned lands. Urban indigenous couples in colonial Potosí married and then pooled their resources to set up businesses such as *pulperías* (stores), bakeries, or other commercial enterprises. Indigenous women retained control of their investments and, in contrast to Spanish women, were often the urban operator or the public seller while a husband helped to supply the business (Mangan 2005: 145–6, 156). Colonial Spanish Americans also developed reciprocal understandings of sexual relations within marriage. If a husband pursued additional sexual liaisons outside of the marriage, a wife still could expect continual economic support and freedom from physical abuse or "cultural humiliation." If a wife was going to feed the family (no small task in a colonial household), then she could expect a husband to provide for his dependents including herself and her children (Stern 1995: 86). Domestic and sexual abuse was still part of indigenous relationships, but an ideal marriage was understood as a useful partnership – free from exploitation – that could attract indigenous people.

Depending on their married lives, indigenous and many other colonial women experienced widowhood as a liberation or as a time of great uncertainty. In Santiago de Guatemala, Spanish widows continued to operate the businesses of their husbands and profited from their new independence (Herrera 2003: 34). In colonial Quito, mestiza widows ran pulperías that they inherited from their husbands to achieve a moderate level of prosperity, while Spanish widows lent money at a considerable interest rate (Gauderman 2003: 82, 87). Yet, for lower-status indigenous and urban women, widowhood was an ambiguous period of their lives. Communities in colonial Mexico characterized widows as morally treacherous and sexually dangerous, similar to other lone, deviant women who lived outside the purview of a male head of household. Poor widows, like other subaltern independent women, could be more vulnerable to male violence and, in indigenous communities, "married male tributaries might stigmatize widows and redistribute their 'excess' lands" (Stern 1995: 66, 117, 197–8). Yet, in colonial Potosí, most widows (Spanish or indigenous) engaged in petty trade as much as their married counterparts. While some widows were able to continue or expand their husbands' trades or businesses, others subsisted on very marginal ventures such as selling cooked food or living from the earnings of their slaves (Mangan 2005: 135, 147–9). In either case, widowhood could mean, but did not ensure, a profitable, independent livelihood.

Free men and women of color also developed profitable and useful partnerships even as enslaved Atlantic Africans and their descendants continued to struggle to claim the right to marry. Since the early sixteenth century, the Spanish Crown affirmed the right of enslaved Africans to marry as a means to impose orthodox Catholicism. Slave owners, on the other hand, were reluctant to allow slaves to marry, as canon law prohibited separating couples and their children. Following ecclesiastical rules could result in additional costs rather than benefits for owners. Even if an enslaved man and woman were able to secure permission from their owner and pay the necessary fees, parish priests questioned their abilities to understand Christian doctrine. Still, enslaved men and women in Mexico, Brazil, and Peru married each other and often chose partners from the same region of origin. Africans who claimed their right to marry also rejected being labeled as property and claimed their identities as Christian vassals (Karasch 1987: 287, 290; Bennett 2003: 44–7, 80–1, 102).

On the other hand, enslaved men and women may have also rejected the holy bonds of matrimony as incongruous with their world view. The high numbers of enslaved men in relation to enslaved women in mid-eighteenth-century Rio de Janeiro suggest that monogamy was not an option for many enslaved adults; women may have had more than one partner. Furthermore, the high number of children born to enslaved "single" mothers also suggests that Atlantic Africans created alternative family structures. For example, two "Guiné" slaves appeared for the baptism of their twins, but both parents were listed in the parish records as "single." Parenting did not equal Catholic matrimony. Slaveholders might also require slaves to marry, which could also encourage enslaved adults to seek more consensual and fulfilling relationships outside of such forced unions. Marriage, therefore, was a tool for building relationships and families that some enslaved and free people of color employed, and others rejected, based on realities of gender ratios and accessibility of priests (Sweet 2003: 37, 39, 41, 43).

Even in death, Atlantic Africans and their descendants appropriated Catholic funeral rituals for their own ends. In Lima free people of color organized lavish funerals with processions and masses to honor the dead (Bowser 1974: 320). In spite of slave owners' disrespect for deceased slaves and discouragement of public ceremonies, enslaved men and women buried their relatives according to Central African traditions in Brazil. Slaves asked the deceased if they had sufficient food, tobacco, and other necessities to ensure that the spirits of the dead were appeased. Enslaved Brazilians also participated in large gatherings where they drank, ate, and drummed to ensure the deceased's proper passage to the next world (Sweet 2003: 176–9). In urban environs, large processions led by a master of ceremonies, drummers, kin, and community accompanied the deceased to their burial in the slaves' church or a mass grave, depending on the wealth and status of the individual (Karasch 1987: 252–3). People clapped, sang, and carried the body in fine clothing, with altar boys and priests officiating only after the deceased had been honored outside the church during the lengthy procession. In this way, slaves employed Catholic rituals to honor their kin and community.

Indigenous communities also transformed Catholic rituals into ceremonies for their kin and ancestors during celebrations of All Souls' Day or the Day of the Dead. Rituals associated with the dead were meant, like those conducted by Central Africans and their descendants in Brazil, to ensure that the deceased were fed and cared for so that they would not return to harm the living. These indigenous concepts merged with the day on the Catholic calendar when the faithful were to pray for the restless souls in purgatory. On this occasion, the colonial Maya staged elaborate masses to honor elite ancestors and filled the churches with the smoke of candles and incense intended to nourish the dead. Families provided food as well as drink to feed ancestors as well as themselves in a practice that would migrate in the nineteenth century to new, suburban cemeteries (Farriss 1984: 323). Fitting native beliefs into Catholic practices allowed indigenous people to continue to worship dead kin and, in this way, care for their communities.

Indigenous and African peoples employed orthodox Catholic institutions for heterodox ends. Their participation indicated an intense piety and a wish to fully comply with the requirements of the Catholic rite of passage. In the same instance, subaltern communities could employ their Catholic status to continue rituals and to transform their relations in colonial and slavery societies.

Beyond the Church: Spiritual Lives and Popular Entertainments

Not all subaltern beliefs, practices, and entertainments fit into Catholic institutions and ritual. For instance, viceregal and regional elites jockeyed for honorable positions in public processions, both religious and civic. Their location in the parade as well as their clothing and attendants communicated their prestige and status to other elites as well as commoners, whose role was to serve as spectators (Burkholder 1998: 29). Processions marked public celebrations (most often religious holidays) when plebeians, enslaved and free as well as African and indigenous, joined in the revelry. In the Andes, the town council or other patrons paid for fireworks displays, bullfights (or bull "runs"), and asked local communities to perform particular dances as artisans and venders pooled their resources to construct decorative arches. Some elites who paraded distributed coins to the crowds, as guilds and cofradías used these authorized public events to express their loyalty to the Crown or religious devotion. Yet, paintings of the Corpus Christi procession in the highland town of Cuzco suggest that some plebeians would rather chat, smoke, or laugh even while elites processed the images of saints before them on city streets. In some cases, the crowds that pressed against the paraders, to the dismay of local officials, contained women mixed with men as participants hotly debated their place within the public ceremony rather than focus on the purpose of the event.

Informal parties that took place after the officially sponsored processions were often the big draw for the majority of colonial inhabitants. In Brazil, free and enslaved Africans and their descendants met to dance in the evenings and into the night on Saturdays and before holy days. Laborers and marketers retired to impromptu taverns to drink *chicha* (in the Andes) or *pulque* (in Mexico), where they gambled, flirted, and played guitars sometimes until the morning hours. Others would flock to cockfights or horse races as people moved through city streets listening to musicians, eating holiday foods, and viewing the altars built especially for the occasion (Chambers 1999: 116–17). Intoxication could lead to knife fights, brawls, or ugly exchanges of words as plebeians surged into the streets and packed the plazas, in some cases to express their political sentiments but mostly to enjoy themselves with friends, family, and new acquaintances.

Beyond ecclesiastical control and secular oversight, colonial people engaged in sexual practices that were categorically forbidden by the Catholic Church. According to baptismal records and Inquisitorial confessions, men and women engaged in consensual vaginal intercourse regardless of their marital status or their fears of exposure. Additionally, according to Pete Sigal (2003: 8–9), the evidence of sexual desire on the part of two male partners, the active and the passive, remains inconclusive, yet highly suggestive that the penetrator not only attempted to dominate his partner, but seduce him. Sexual assaults and other acts of violence and domination were also common, yet consensual sexuality that deviated from Catholic norms also formed a deep if mostly hidden aspect of colonial society.

In fact, colonial people attributed sexual prowess and success to the help of the devil. According to Mexican Inquisition records, Spanish, mestizo, and African-descent men claimed that, in exchange for their souls, the devil helped them to seduce women. In one recorded case, a young *pardo* ejaculated and then gave his semen to the devil in order to inseminate his beloved (Cervantes 1994: 87). Colonial women also employed the devil to fulfill their sexual desires. In both Mexico and Peru, women of any status sought out ritual specialists, mostly other women, who would be able to cast spells, provide charms, or supply herbal potions that would allow them to increase the ardor of their lovers, partners, and husbands. Women also sought out practitioners of love magic to punish *compañeros* who had not been faithful or adulterous husbands, as the devil became an assistant and, sometimes, an attentive lover (Behar 1989: 183, 191). The gendered calls to the devil for assistance underlined the unequal locations of most men and women in colonial society, as free men could assert their sexual prowess as a sign of their masculine potency while free women were beholden to some form of patriarchal power. Regardless, enslaved men and women had to submit to their owners' preferences and demands, often undercutting Atlantic African masculinity. Still, enslaved men sought to control their female partners, as judicial authorities tried Felipe Mina, a slave in colonial Trujillo, for assaulting his lover with a knife. Sexual activity was riddled with colonial tensions as well as definitive acts of domination.

Inquisitors, clerics engaged in anti-idolatry campaigns, and ecclesiastical inspectors attempted to monitor and punish subaltern practices they considered deviant. Yet despite Inquisitorial persecution, Atlantic Africans in Rio de Janeiro developed a religion around leaders who could make charms that protected slaves from abusive owners and could cure illnesses by expelling evil from the body (Karasch 1987: 263). Similarly, some indigenous communities continued to support religious specialists who cared for Pre-Columbian sacred spaces and drew on these supernatural powers to combat epidemics and individual sickness (Mills 1997: 107–8). The very demands of slaveholders and colonizers fueled the needs of subaltern communities to develop alternative interpretations of colonial society that could be tools for survival as well as resistance.

Conclusions

Colonized and enslaved Catholics adapted beliefs and rituals to cultural and social institutions of the colonial Church. In doing so, they enmeshed themselves within Catholic hierarchies and sexualities. Nonetheless, the structures of Catholicism provided a location for indigenous people as well as some enslaved Atlantic Africans to stand as part of a collectivity in colonial Latin America. By participating in the various institutions of the Church, indigenous and African people as well as their descendants would be able to claim their rights as loyal subjects to Catholic monarchs despite the condescension of local Spanish and Portuguese colonizers and slaveholders. In this juncture, subaltern peoples participated in the creation of the societies and cultures of the Iberian Americas, both within and at the margins of acceptable practices and orthodox religion.

BIBLIOGRAPHY

Behar, R. (1989) "Sexual Witchcraft, Colonialism, and Women's Powers: Views from the Mexican Inquisition." In A. Lavrin (ed.), *Sexuality and Marriage in Colonial Latin America*. University of Nebraska Press, Lincoln, pp. 178–206.

Bennett, H. L. (2003) *Africans in Colonial Mexico: Absolutism, Christianity, and Afro-Creole Consciousness, 1570–1640*. Indiana University Press, Bloomington.

Bowser, F. P. (1974) *The African Slave in Colonial Peru 1524–1650*. Stanford University Press, Stanford.

Burkhart, L. M. (1989) *The Slippery Earth: Nahua–Christian Moral Dialogue in Sixteenth-Century Mexico*. University of Arizona Press, Tucson.

Burkholder, M. A. (1998) "Honor and Honors in Colonial Spanish America." In L. L. Johnson & S. Lipsett-Rivera (eds.), *The Faces of Honor: Sex, Shame, and Violence in Colonial Latin America*. University of New Mexico Press, Albuquerque, pp. 18–44.

Burns, K. (1999) *Colonial Habits: Convents and the Spiritual Economy of Cuzco, Peru*. Duke University Press, Durham.

Cañizares Esguerra, J. (1999). "New World, New Stars: Patriotic Astrology and the Invention of Indian and Creole Bodies in Colonial Spanish America, 1600–1650," *The American Historical Review*, 104:1, pp. 33–68.

Cervantes, F. (1994) *The Devil in the New World: The Impact of Diabolism in New Spain*. Yale University Press, New Haven.

Chambers, S. C. (1999) *From Subjects to Citizens: Honor, Gender, and Politics in Arequipa, Peru 1780–1854*. Pennsylvania State University Press, University Park.

Clendinnen, I. (1987) *Ambivalent Conquests: Maya and Spaniard in Yucatan, 1517–1570*. Cambridge University Press, Cambridge.

Cope, R. D. (1994) *The Limits of Racial Domination: Plebeian Society in Colonial Mexico City, 1660–1720*. University of Wisconsin Press, Madison.

Dean, C. (1999) *Inka Bodies and the Body of Christ: Corpus Christi in Colonial Cuzco, Peru*. Duke University Press, Durham.

Farriss, N. M. (1984) *Maya Society under Colonial Rule: The Collective Enterprise of Survival*. Princeton University Press, Princeton.

Few, M. (2002) *Women Who Live Evil Lives: Gender, Religion, & the Politics of Power in Colonial Guatemala*. University of Texas Press, Austin.

Gauderman, K. (2003) *Women's Lives in Colonial Quito: Gender, Law, and Economy in Spanish America*. University of Texas Press, Austin.

Gruzinski, S. (2001) "Image Consumers." In S. Gruzinski, *Images at War: Mexico from Columbus to Blade Runner (1492–2019)*. Duke University Press, Durham.

Harrison, R. (1994) "The Theology of Concupiscence: Spanish–Quechua Confessional Manuals in the Andes." In F. J. Cevallos-Candau, J. A. Cole, N. M. Scott, & N. Suárez-Aráuz (eds.), *Coded Encounters: Writing, Gender, and Ethnicity in Colonial Latin America*. University of Massachusetts Press, Amherst, pp. 135–50.

Herrera, R. A. (2003) *Natives, Europeans, and Africans in Sixteenth-Century Santiago de Guatemala*. University of Texas Press, Austin.

Heywood, L. M. (2002) "Portuguese into African: The Eighteenth-Century Central African Background to Atlantic Creole Cultures." In L. Heywood (ed.), *Central Africans and Cultural Transformations in the American Diaspora*. Cambridge University Press, Cambridge, pp. 91–113.

Jaffary, N. (2004) *False Mystics: Deviant Orthodoxy in Colonial Mexico*. University of Nebraska Press, Lincoln.

Karasch, M. C. (1987) *Slave Life in Rio de Janeiro 1808–1850*. Princeton University Press, Princeton.

Lewis, L. A. (2003) *Hall of Mirrors: Power, Witchcraft, and Caste in Colonial Mexico*. Duke University Press, Durham.

Lockhart, J. (1992) *The Nahuas after the Conquest: A Social and Cultural History of the Indians of Central Mexico, Sixteenth through Eighteenth Centuries*. Stanford University Press, Stanford.

MacCormack, S. (1991) *Religion in the Andes: Vision and Imagination in Early Colonial Peru*. Princeton University Press, Princeton.

Mangan, J. E. (2005) *Trading Roles: Gender, Ethnicity, and the Urban Economy in Colonial Potosí*. Duke University Press, Durham.

Martínez, M. E. (2004) "The Black Blood of New Spain: *Limpieza de Sangre*, Racial Violence, and Gendered Power in Early Colonial Mexico," *The William and Mary Quarterly*, 61:3, pp. 479–520.

McKnight, K. (2003) "'En su tierra lo aprendió': An African *Curandero*'s Defense before the Cartagena Inquisition," *Colonial Latin American Review*, 12:1, pp. 63–84.

Metcalf, A. (1999) "Millenarian Slaves? The Santidade de Jaguaripe and Slave Resistance in the Americas," *The American Historical Review*, 104:5, pp. 1531–59.

Mills, K. (1997) *Idolatry and Its Enemies: Colonial Andean Religion and Extirpation, 1640–1750*. Princeton University Press, Princeton.

Ricard, R. (1966) *The Spiritual Conquest of Mexico; An Essay on the Apostolate and the Evangelizing Methods of the Mendicant Orders in New Spain, 1523–1572*. University of California Press, Berkeley.

Salles-Reese, V. (1997) *From Viracocha to the Virgin of Copacabana: Representation of the Sacred at Lake Titicaca*. University of Texas Press, Austin.

Sigal, P. (2003) "(Homo)Sexual Desire and Masculine Power in Colonial Latin America: Notes toward an Integrated Analysis." In P. Sigal (ed.), *Infamous Desire: Male Homosexuality in Colonial Latin America*. University of Chicago Press, Chicago, pp. 1–24.

Silverblatt, I. (1988) "Political Memories and Colonizing Symbols: Santiago and the Mountain Gods of Colonial Peru." In J. D. Hill (ed.), *Rethinking History and Myth: Indigenous South American Perspectives on the Past*. University of Illinois Press, Urbana, pp. 174–94.

Silverblatt, I. (2004) *Modern Inquisitions: Peru and the Colonial Origins of the Civilized World*. Duke University Press, Durham.

Souza, L. de M e. (2003 [1986]) *The Devil and the Land of the Holy Cross: Witchcraft, Slavery, and Popular Religion in Colonial Brazil*. University of Texas Press, Austin.

Spalding, K. (1984) *Huarochirí: An Andean Society under Inca and Spanish Rule*. Stanford University Press, Stanford.

Stern, S. J. (1995) *The Secret History of Gender: Women, Men, and Power in Late Colonial Mexico*. University of North Carolina Press, Chapel Hill.

Sweet, J. H. (1997) "The Iberian Roots of American Racist Thought," *The William and Mary Quarterly*, 54:1, pp. 143–66.

Sweet, J. H. (2003) *Recreating Africa: Culture, Kinship, and Religion in the African–Portuguese World, 1441–1770*. University of North Carolina Press, Chapel Hill.

Thornton, J. K. (2002) "Religious and Ceremonial Life in the Kongo and Mbundu Areas, 1500–1700." In L. Heywood (ed.), *Central Africans and Cultural Transformations in the American Diaspora*. Cambridge University Press, Cambridge, pp. 71–90.

Twinam, A. (1999) *Public Lives, Private Secrets: Gender, Honor, Sexuality, and Illegitimacy in Colonial Spanish America*. Stanford University Press, Stanford.

Van Deusen, N. (2004) *The Souls of Purgatory: The Spiritual Diary of a Seventeenth-Century Afro-Peruvian Mystic, Ursula de Jesús*. University of New Mexico Press, Albuquerque.

Villa-Flores, J. (2002) "'To Lose One's Soul': Blasphemy and Slavery in New Spain, 1596–1669," *Hispanic American Historical Review*, 82:3, pp. 435–68.

Wightman, A. M. (1990) *Indigenous Migration and Social Change: The Forasteros of Cuzco, 1570–1720*. Duke University Press, Durham.

Chapter Eleven

IMPERIAL RIVALRIES AND REFORMS

John Fisher

Introduction: Europe and Ibero-America 1700–1808: an Overview

Six European powers – England, France, the Netherlands, Portugal, Russia, and Spain – competed for both territory and commerce in the American hemisphere in the seventeenth and eighteenth centuries. They were joined after 1783 by the United States of America (USA), which by a combination of diplomacy, trade, and purchasing power began to expand by the early nineteenth century into vast regions in North America formerly claimed by Spain and/or France. By the early eighteenth century the Dutch were largely a spent force, despite retaining a number of Caribbean possessions. Similarly Russia, although in danger at various points in the eighteenth century of coming into open conflict with England and/or Spain as it tried to expand down the Pacific coast of North America from Alaska, was not a major player in the imperial chess games contested in North America. Accordingly, this chapter will concentrate upon the rivalries, aims, and policies of, first, Spain (allied for most of the period with France) and, second, Portugal, which normally sided with England during the international conflicts of the eighteenth and early nineteenth centuries. The chapter begins by providing a summary of war and diplomacy in the Americas from 1700. This is followed by an analysis of the aims/intentions/results of the Bourbon reforms in Spanish America, and a brief summary of Portuguese policy toward Brazil. It concludes with a discussion of attitudes toward the Iberian imperial powers of Spanish Americans and Brazilians respectively on the eve of the Napoleonic invasions of Spain and Portugal in 1807–8.

War and Diplomacy

Following the death in 1700 of Spain's last Hapsburg king, the childless Charles II, the major European powers – on one side England and Austria and, on the other, France and Spain – and their satellites lurched inexorably in 1702 toward the War of the Spanish Succession (Kamen 2001: 1–33). Although this conflict, like the world wars of the twentieth century, had its origins in Europe, it was also fought in the great powers' overseas empires, particularly in the Americas. For Spain and Spanish America an immediate consequence of the alliance of its new Bourbon king, Philip V, with his native France was the opening up of the hitherto exclusive imperial commercial system to the new protecting power: first through the transfer in 1702 from Portuguese shippers to the French Guinea Company of the coveted *asiento de negros*, thus giving French merchants an exclusive right to supply black slaves from Africa to Spanish America (Fisher 1997: 112). Shortly thereafter, in 1704, it was agreed to grant French merchant ships permission to sail directly into the Pacific via Cape Horn to trade with Chile and Peru, something they had been doing illegally for several years. In one sense the concession was necessary because the traditional system of supplying Peru with European produce, carried from Cádiz by convoys, the so-called *galeones*, protected by warships to Portobelo and then across the isthmus to Panama, could not function during the war, partly because it was too dangerous for Spanish merchants to put to sea, but primarily because of the volume of contraband trade in the Caribbean. The Portobelo fair of 1708 – the first since 1696, and the only one to be held during the war – was an utter fiasco (Walker 1979: 34–9). That of 1713 was also a flop, mainly because by then the rich Peruvian market was being supplied by French merchant ships, 168 of which entered the Pacific in the period 1698–1726 (Bradley 1989: 182, 187). The convoys for New Spain (the *flotas*), five of which sailed from Cádiz during the war, enjoyed, it is true, rather more success, primarily because it was more difficult for contrabandists to penetrate the well-defended port of Vera Cruz, and contact with other Caribbean ports was maintained by register ships (individual licensed vessels). From 1740, although the convoyed fleets continued to sail for Vera Cruz, the *galeones* system for the viceroyalty of Peru was replaced entirely by register ships sailing directly into the Pacific.

The Treaty of Utrecht of 1713, the international agreement among the participants in the War of the Spanish Succession, formally confirmed the transfer of the Spanish Crown to the new Bourbon dynasty. Together with the subsequent Treaty of Madrid (1721), made necessary by continuing Spanish–Austrian disagreement over territorial claims in Italy, it was seen by its signatories as a definitive peace settlement, which, by recognizing a realistic balance of power between France, England, Portugal, and Spain in the Americas, would establish a period of enduring peace in the European overseas empires, if not in Europe itself (Savelle 1974: 123–4). The undoubted victor in the American sphere was England, which, in return for an agreement that it would respect the territorial integrity of Spanish possessions there, secured the transfer from France of the *asiento de negros*. This concession was valuable even in its own right, but its particular importance was that it provided the newly formed South Sea Company with the opportunity to supply contraband goods to the ports – primarily Buenos Aires – that received its slaves. The supplementary right to send a merchant ship of 500 tons to each of the trade fairs at Portobelo and Vera Cruz attended by the *galeones* and *flotas* respectively was also exploited to the full by the English company, and was a key factor in the lack of success of the Portobelo fairs held in 1722, 1726, 1729, and 1731. That of 1731 was, in fact, the last of these traditional trade fairs. The presence of the English ship was a major factor in their abandonment, partly because of its direct impact in pricing Spanish manufactures out of the market, but primarily because it provided a smokescreen behind which the Peruvian merchants, who traveled up to Portobelo via Panama from Callao, could trade almost openly with the contrabandists who were accustomed to assembling near Portobelo when a fair was due to be held. Consequently, a resigned Spanish Crown decided in 1735 to suspend the dispatch of further convoys to Portobelo, and replace them with register ships sailing to both that port and Cartagena. This less restrictive policy, in its turn, was thwarted by the destruction of Portobelo in 1740 by the English admiral Edward Vernon, and by his even more dramatic attack on Cartagena in 1741, following the declaration in October 1739 of the Anglo-Spanish war ("The War of Jenkins' Ear") which continued until 1748 (Kuethe 1978: 14, 16, 41).

This war, which was precipitated in part by English resentment of zealous Spanish attempts to curb contraband in the Caribbean (hence the cutting off of the ear of the unfortunate captain Jenkins) again demonstrated the capacity of American dis-putes to generate general conflict between the major powers of eighteenth-century Europe (Savelle 1974: 127–8). An important subsidiary factor on this occasion was the willingness of France to intervene in the long-standing Spanish–Austrian territo-rial disputes in Italy by guaranteeing, after the signing of the first Bourbon Family Compact with Spain, the possession of his Italian duchies by Don Carlos (the future Charles III), eldest son of the Spanish Queen, Elizabeth Farnese. The Anglo-Spanish part of the conflict was fought almost entirely as a naval war in the Caribbean, whereas the territorial conflict was diverted to the European mainland in 1740 by the outbreak of the War of the Austrian Succession. During the course of the war, in 1743, France and Spain signed the Second Bourbon Family Compact, one clause of which provided for the mutual guarantee of the integrity of territories "outside of Europe as well as within it" (Savelle 1974: 129). Although this committed France to a war against England, it also guaranteed it Spanish assistance in the ongoing struggle against Austria.

France went on to declare war against England in 1744, with the declared objec-tives in so far as America was concerned, of forcing it to give up the slave *asiento*, and abandon its newly established colony of Georgia, to the north of Florida, which Spain claimed had been founded on territory belonging to the Spanish Crown. The second of these factors reflected an increasing Spanish awareness of the danger of losing to England the vast, unexplored territories in North America to which it claimed title, despite the lack of resources to exploit them. Indications of Spain's more positive intent were provided in the first half of the eighteenth century by the organization of new military governments in Texas (1718), Sinaloa (1734), and Santander (1746). However, a concerted attempt to move into the borderlands of northern New Spain, a process spearheaded by missionaries and soldiers (Moorhead 1975: 86–7), did not come until the second half of the century, with the penetration of California – Los Angeles was founded in 1780 – and the establishment of the military jurisdiction known as the Interior Provinces of New Spain (Navarro García 1964: 131–208). In this latter period expansion beyond San Francisco and Monterey, in Alta California, was checked less by English resistance, although that was significant, notably at Nootka Sound (1789), than by Russian expansion south from Alaska.

Although in the short term the Treaty of Aix-la-Chapelle (1748), which brought to an end the War of the Austrian Succession, did not appear to resolve either of the specific American issues which had helped provoke it (the *asiento*/contraband dispute, and the status of Georgia), it was followed by a brief period of cooperation and goodwill between Spain on one side and England and Portugal on the other. A major contributory factor was the success of negotiations in Madrid in 1750 to terminate the *asiento*, which had been granted for only 30 years in 1713 but had been prolonged because convoys had not sailed in some years, in return for a payment by Spain to the South Sea Company of £100,000. The same year also witnessed the signing of the Treaty of Madrid with Portugal, which attempted to demarcate the boundary between Portuguese and Spanish territory in the Río de la Plata, returning the Portuguese outpost of Sacramento, opposite Buenos Aires, to Spain but granting to Brazil seven Spanish missions north of the newly established boundary. This process was facilitated by the fact that the new Spanish king Ferdinand VI (1746–59) was married to a Portuguese princess, María Barbara de Braganza. A particularly interesting, if idealistic, feature of the treaty was its attempt to deny the logic of international relations in the eighteenth century by invoking "the doctrine of the two spheres": the argument that even in the unfortunate eventuality of war breaking out between Spain and Portugal in Europe, peace would be maintained in South America (Savelle 1974: 132–3). In fact, quite the reverse occurred: when in 1762 Spain and Portugal entered the Seven Years War (1756–63) on opposite sides, Spanish forces not only recaptured Sacramento, which the Portuguese had failed to evacuate despite the 1750 agreement to do so, but also invaded the Brazilian province of Rio Grande, where they remained until the Treaty of San Ildefonso (1777) imposed a boundary settlement which then endured until the Independence period.

The Seven Years War was of crucial importance for the history of Spain's relations with its American possessions in the 50 years before the Napoleonic invasion of the Iberian peninsula. From the trauma and humiliation suffered in the conflict, Charles III, the third of Spain's Bourbon kings, and his ministers derived the sense of purpose and direction required for the formulation and implementation of the all-embracing process of modernization which historians refer to as the "Bourbon reforms." To an even greater extent than the international conflicts that preceded it in the eighteenth century, the Seven Years War was an American conflict (as well as an Indian and African conflict), although on this occasion the principal sources of conflict derived from Anglo-French rivalries, despite continuing Spanish resentment about contraband and English incursions into Yucatán and Honduras. There were two main areas of tension: the Caribbean where, ignoring Spain's feeble claims, the two powers competed to occupy islands including Dominica, Tobago, St. Vincent, and St. Lucia; and, more importantly, the North America mainland, where the French provoked Indian resistance to the westward expansion of the English colonies. Indeed, the formal declaration of war in 1756 was preceded by clashes between English and French forces in the Ohio Valley in 1754, and in Nova Scotia and the Caribbean in 1755.

The conflict went decisively England's way, as its forces took Quebec in 1759, Montreal in 1760, and Martinique in 1761, a process unhindered by Spain's tardy entry in 1762. The new king, Charles III, suffered the appalling humiliation of seeing Havana and Manila fall to English invasion forces. The subsequent Treaty of Paris (1763) restored Cuba to Spain, but confirmed English possession of Florida. France, the main loser, was forced to give all of Canada and the western half of the Mississippi Valley to England, and also gave Louisiana to Spain by the separate Treaty of Fontainebleau to compensate its ally for the loss of Florida. However, despite some attempts to promote the fur trade through New Orleans, neither Charles III nor Charles IV succeeded in establishing more than a token Spanish presence in these vast new territories west of the Mississippi, which were returned to France by the Treaty of San Ildefonso (1801). Soon thereafter (1803) Napoleon Bonaparte sold the Louisiana territory to the USA for $15 million. Portugal, as England's faithful ally, benefited from the 1763 peace settlement, recovering Sacramento. Like England, however, Portugal received a rude shock to its complacency in 1776, following the outbreak of the War for United States Independence (1776–83).

A recent analysis of Spain's intervention in this conflict defines its contribution to the birth of the fledgling nation as "a most intrinsic gift" (Chávez 2003: 212). The question of whether it was wise for Spain to show support for a rebellion of colonial subjects against a European monarchy need not detain us, for, in the short term, at least, there was little indication that Spanish Americans would seek to emulate their example. Moreover, Spain and France entered the conflict on the side of the rebels, in 1778 and 1779 respectively, primarily because of a wish to redress what they perceived as the imbalance of power vis-à-vis England rather than because of any sympathy for the rebellion. For Spain the prize, conferred by the Treaty of Versailles (1783) was the restoration of East and West Florida (and the Mediterranean island of Minorca), in return for some minor concessions to British woodcutters in Campeche and Honduras. Spain emerged from the conflict, therefore, with both the gratitude of the USA for the military assistance provided against English forces in the borderlands, and, more significantly, its own security apparently guaranteed for the first time since the early sixteenth century in the Gulf of Mexico.

The decade that followed – the final five years of the reign of Charles III and the first five of that of Charles IV – was to witness, as we will see in the next section, the high point of Spanish imperial recovery under the Bourbons. The Portuguese viceroyalty of Brazil also enjoyed unprecedented prosperity in this period, partly because of the revival of the sugar industry, especially in the 1790s, as a consequence of both growing world demand and the demise of production in the strife-torn French island of Saint-Domingue, and partly because the loss of the USA impelled Britain to look to Brazil for the supply of raw cotton for its rapidly expanding textile factories.

The period after 1783 saw the American empires of Spain and Portugal expanding their production – in Spain's case in mining as well as agriculture – and their much closer integration into the economic life of Europe. Moreover, it also witnessed, almost imperceptibly at first, the diminution of the strategic importance of the Americas as a source of international conflict between the great European powers. Although England retained Canada and major islands in the Caribbean, its diplomatic and imperial strategy after 1783 came to rely increasingly upon commerce rather than conquest. France, too, remained a significant imperial power in the Caribbean, but the impending loss of Saint-Domingue, coupled with its withdrawal from Louisiana, marked in its case, too, a territorial abdication from American affairs. The USA, for its part, had not yet embarked upon the process of westwards expansion which in the 1830s and 1840s would see it gobble up enormous areas of territory bequeathed to Mexico by Spain in 1821. Like England, in the final decades of the eighteenth century the USA relied upon commercial rather than territorial penetration of Spanish America, effectively turning Havana, the capital of Cuba, into an entrepôt for trade with the whole Caribbean basin by 1800 (Barbier & Kuethe 1984: 112–56). Consequently, Spain and Portugal were left relatively free from direct competition by the other major powers of Europe in their territorial expansion in America, and, until 1796 at least, also enjoyed some success in reasserting their control over imperial commerce.

If the remaining international conflicts of the eighteenth century were caused by American issues to a lesser extent than the wars that preceded them, that does not necessarily mean, of course, that America did not feel their repercussions. On the contrary, the general European conflict which broke out in 1796, continuing with brief interludes until 1815, was fundamentally important, albeit indirectly, in creating the conditions which led to the Spanish American revolutions for independence (1810–25) (Rodríguez O., this volume), and the secession of Brazil from Portugal in 1822 (Bieber, this volume). As a preamble to the wider conflict, Spain briefly reversed the whole thrust of its diplomatic and strategic policies in 1793 by declaring war on France – not, of course, the Catholic, conservative, monarchical France of the Bourbon Family Compacts, but the revolutionary, regicidal France of post-1789. In so doing, Spain had to overcome the novelty of fighting on the same side as England, which, in the course of the conflict, not only occupied Martinique, Guadeloupe, and other French islands, but also attempted, ultimately unsuccessfully, to take control of Saint-Domingue. This invasion cost it the lives of an estimated 13,000 men, victims in the main of disease rather than battle (Geggus 1982: 357–8). It also contributed to the transformation of the French colony into the second new nation in the Americas: Haiti, independent de facto from 1804, and recognized as such by Charles X of France in 1824.

In 1795 Spain saw the Haitian black leader, Toussaint L'Ouverture, abandon his support for Spanish forces in Santo Domingo in favor of an alliance with the French governor of Saint-Domingue against the English forces in the island. Thus Spain, too, in a much broader sense, was unable to resist the temptation to use revolutionary France as a weapon in the much more traditional and deep-seated struggle against England. Following the example of Prussia, Spain made peace with France by the Treaty of Basle in April 1795. The following year, in October 1796, the chief minister of Spain, Manuel de Godoy, emboldened by the award of the title *Principe de la Paz* (Prince of Peace) for negotiating the end of war with France, orchestrated a declaration of war against England, which led immediately to the naval blockade of Cádiz and the consequential collapse of Spain's imperial commercial system.

In many respects America was an observer of the worldwide conflict fought between revolutionary France and its allies, on one side, and the various coalitions of anti-French forces put together by England between 1796 and 1808, on the other. Thereafter, of course, Anglo-Spanish relations took another complex turn, following the French invasion of the Iberian Peninsula in 1807, the flight of the Portuguese royal family to Brazil, the alliance between England and the Spanish *Junta Central*, and, in due course, the dispatch to Portugal of British forces under Arthur Wellesley (future Duke of Wellington) which, after initial setbacks, drove the French out of, first, Portugal and eventually Spain (Esdaile 2002: 407–9). In the meantime America was not entirely immune from the effects both indirect, for example, a massive increase in military expenditure at a time when treasury receipts fell because of the interruption of trade, and direct, mainly English naval attacks in the Caribbean. Although English attempts to take Puerto Rico were beaten off, Trinidad fell to an invasion force in 1797, never to be returned. After capturing the Dutch island of Curaçao in 1798, and subsequently Surinam and Essequibo, English forces went on to occupy Santo Domingo in 1801. In this period there were real fears in Spain, and hopes among the small community of London-based Spanish American revolutionaries, headed by Francisco de Miranda, that England would use Trinidad as a base for supporting revolutionary movements in Venezuela. However, primarily because of other commitments, England gave only token support to the attempted invasion of Venezuela which Miranda mounted in 1806 (Lynch 1986: 196, 199). Far to the south, in the Río de la Plata, a quite different scenario developed in the same year with the capture of Buenos Aires by an English invasion force on June 27, 1806, an event that eventually confirmed statesmen in London in their view that further attempts at conquest on the mainland of Spanish America should be abandoned.

It remains unclear if the naval and military commanders of the English expedition had received express orders for an attack on the Río de la Plata. What is not in doubt is that they had been involved in secret discussions with Miranda in 1804, and that in 1806, having completed the capture of the Cape of Good Hope from the Dutch, they sailed for the Río de la Plata via the Atlantic island of St. Helena. Buenos Aires, capital of the viceroyalty and a city of 50,000 inhabitants, fell easily in June to the small invasion force of 1,600 men, at the cost of one English soldier killed and 12 wounded. Six weeks later, however, a force of 1,000 men, comprising regular troops from Montevideo and *gaucho* light cavalry recruited from the rural districts, appeared before Buenos Aires. In the face of a fierce onslaught, in which the decisive element was an urban guerrilla force within the city that fired on the English from the rooftops, the invaders surrendered with the loss of 200 men killed and 1,200 captured.

Immediately, the inhabitants of Buenos Aires organized defenses against the possibility of a renewed English attack. By October 1806 8,000 men, most of them creoles, were under arms. In the meantime, an astonished English government, which had received news of the initial capture of Buenos Aires in September, had decided to make the best of an unforeseen situation, and dispatched a new force of 6,300 men to the Río de la Plata in October. This expedition captured Montevideo in February 1807 without undue difficulty, and, following the arrival of further reinforcements from the Cape of Good Hope, 9,000 men attacked Buenos Aires on July 5, 1807. Within 24 hours they had lost 400 dead and 650 wounded, and 1,900 men had been taken prisoner. On July 7, 1807 the commander, General John Whitelocke, surrendered to the defenders of Buenos Aires, and agreed to withdraw all his forces from the Río de la Plata. When news of this humiliation reached London the Secretary of State for War, Viscount Castlereagh, resisted the popular clamor to teach the inhabitants of Buenos Aires a lesson. His initial view was that any future British military intervention in Spanish America should be designed to promote movements for independence from Spain, but this approach was abandoned in mid-1808, following the alliance with the Junta Central, and the expeditionary force being assembled in Ireland for an attack upon New Spain was hastily diverted to Portugal. Thereafter, England persisted with a nominal policy of "neutrality" toward the Wars of Independence, which began with the deposition of the Spanish authorities in Caracas and Buenos Aires in April and May 1810 respectively.

The Bourbon Reforms in Spanish America

The traditional interpretation of the history of Spain and Spanish America in the eighteenth century identifies this period as one characterized by, first, French-inspired reform of public administration and economic and cultural life in the Peninsula during the reigns of Philip V (r. 1700–46), Spain's "first enlightened monarch," and Ferdinand VI (r. 1746–59) (Martínez Shaw & Alfonso Mola 2001: 295). Thereafter, the third Bourbon, Charles III (r. 1759–88) concentrated his efforts at reform upon Spanish America, extending to his overseas kingdoms many of the innovations introduced in Spain by his predecessors in a concerted attempt to strengthen imperial defenses, rationalize provincial administration, streamline and expand revenue collection, and liberalize trade – the end result being that his "reign was marked by a remarkable increase in prosperity, both in the Peninsula and the colonies, and for a brief period Spain once more figured as a European power" (Brading 1984: 392). Thereafter, with the pace of imperial reform already slowing following the death in 1787 of José de Gálvez, Minister of the Indies from 1776, the policy of exploiting American resources to underpin a glorious recovery lost direction during the reign of Charles IV (r. 1788–1808), particularly from 1796, when, as noted, hostilities again broke out with England.

Recent scholarship, although confirming that the reign of Charles III embraced a clear policy of seeking to exploit the wealth of Spanish America in a more systematic fashion than before, has begun to question several features of this traditional interpretation. Several scholars, whilst recognizing that the second half of the seventeenth century was, indeed, a period of general decline for Spain in both Europe and America, have argued that the nadir in its weakness – and therefore, the onset of stabilization and recovery – can be identified not in 1700 but in the 1680s, when monetary inflation ended, population and agrarian production began to grow, and new ideas began to penetrate the country, resulting in "the opening of a new era" (Kamen 1980: vii). Others, while still insisting that basic structures remained unreformed until after the War of the Spanish Succession, have stressed that the reform program initiated during the reign of Philip V, although encouraged by France (interested, of course, in having a strong ally), was, to quote Lynch, "Spanish in conception, in leadership, and in its objectives" (Lynch 1989: 317–19; Kuethe & Blaisdell 1991: 579–81).

Further historiographical refinements locate the application of plans to introduce significant reforms in Spanish America firmly in the reign of Philip V, whose ministers succeeded, as already noted, in changing key features of the structures governing American trade. Finally, specialists on the reign of Charles III have gradually reached the conclusion that the depiction of his reign as one characterized by the coherent application of a decisive, seamless reform program might be defined as a "historical myth," albeit one "rooted in not only dogma but also a degree of reality, no matter how distorted or misunderstood" (Fisher et al. 1990: 1). In other words, more attention is now paid to the hesitant, tardy, and incomplete way in which major reforms were introduced in America rather than upon interpreting them through the eyes of Charles III's powerful Secretary of State from 1776, the Conde de Floridablanca. A devoted servant of absolutism, Floridablanca's eulogy of Charles III, written for incoming Charles IV in 1788, but extolling the wide-ranging achievements of his predecessor, first projected the image of "a strong enlightened government actively promoting the prosperity of its subjects" (Brading 1984: 435). If this was the case, scholars now ask, why did the reform of provincial administration in America by means of the introduction of the intendant system, a course of action advocated by José de Gálvez as early as 1768, during his general inspection of the viceroyalty of New Spain, undertaken in 1765–71, not get under way in the mainland viceroyalties until 1782? Similarly, why did the process of reforming the antiquated commercial structure, by gradually introducing "free trade" (that is, permission for the major ports of Spain and America to trade unrestrictedly with each other), begun in 1765, take nearly 30 years to fully implement, with Venezuela and New Spain not feeling the benefits of it until 1789? With these considerations in mind, we now proceed to an analysis of what the Bourbons achieved.

At the macro-level, major administrative reorganization resulted in the separation from the Hapsburg viceroyalty of Peru (which had covered all of Spanish South America except Venezuela) of, first, the viceroyalty of New Granada (modern Colombia, Ecuador, and Panama) in 1738, and, second, the viceroyalty of the Río de la Plata (modern Argentina, Bolivia, Paraguay, and Uruguay) in 1776. In each case the motives were both strategic and fiscal, for it was hoped that the devolution of vice-regal control to Santa Fé de Bogotá and Buenos Aires respectively would increase the efficiency of government and strengthen defenses against foreign intruders. Indeed, the first viceroy of the Río de la Plata, Pedro de Cevallos, arrived in his capital at the head of a large expeditionary force, dispatched to drive the Portuguese out of the Banda Oriental (modern Uruguay) at a time when their English ally was otherwise engaged in North America (Lynch 1958: 39–40). Moreover, in order to ensure that the new viceroyalty would be economically viable, Gálvez ruthlessly brushed aside Peruvian economic and commercial interests by incorporating in it Upper Peru (modern Bolivia), thereby ensuring that tribute and mining revenues collected there would begin to flow into the treasury of Buenos Aires rather than, as previously, that of Lima.

The manner in which the viceroyalty of New Granada was created, by contrast, tends to support the thesis that the Bourbon reforms were hesitant, for the initial decision to separate it from Peru was taken in Madrid in 1718, and the first viceroy, Jorge de Villalonga, actually served in 1719–23. However, following his recall to Spain to answer charges of corruption and involvement in contraband, the experiment was abandoned until 1738 when, facing "the imminent outbreak of international war" in the Caribbean, the Crown appointed an experienced soldier, Sebastián de Eslava, to take charge of the defense of Cartagena, also naming him as the second viceroy of New Granada (McFarlane 1993: 196–7).

The new viceroyalty of the Río de la Plata became in 1782 the first testing ground on the mainland of Spanish America for another of the key features of Bourbon imperial policy: the radical reorganization of provincial government by the creation of intendancies, following the completion in 1749 of the introduction of this system of government throughout peninsular Spain. The aim was to put provincial government in the hands of powerful officials, loyal to a centralizing monarchy, with a mixture of financial, military, and judicial powers. The advisors of Philip V, led by his Minister of Finance José de Campillo, had begun even before that date to advocate similar restructuring in America, as part of a general program of making government more efficient and eradicating fiscal corruption. But it was not until after the Seven Years War that Charles III began, very cautiously at first, to experiment there, appointing an intendant for Cuba. As noted above, Gálvez returned from his general inspection of New Spain convinced of the need to remove from office corrupt local officials, usually American-born, and replace them with peninsular Spaniards, committed to the strengthening of royal authority, and reporting directly to the Ministry of the Indies through a superintendent of the exchequer in the viceregal capital. Viceregal obstruction and procrastination in the city of Mexico, the capital of New Spain, succeeded in delaying the introduction of the system there until 1786, two years after its extension from the Río de la Plata to Peru. Shortly thereafter, the death of Gálvez in 1787 led to the abandonment of plans to extend it further to New Granada, and in the months that followed Charles III was persuaded to recall the superintendents of Buenos Aires, Lima, and Mexico, and transfer their powers to the respective viceroys.

Despite this step backwards, the first generations of intendants were very successful in increasing crown revenues, in part by eradicating fraud from the collection of the tribute paid bi-annually to the Crown by adult male Indians, and the *alcabala*, a sales tax. In the viceroyalty of Peru, for example, tribute revenue rose steadily from 700,000 pesos in 1784 to over 900,000 in 1790, reaching nearly 1,300,000 by the first decade of the nineteenth century (Fisher 1970: 113–14). Similar increases were seen in other viceroyalties, as the zealous new officials tightened the fiscal screws in the interests of providing the Crown with the additional revenue that it needed for improved defenses, by both the construction of massive fortifications at key ports such as Callao, Havana, San Juan, and Vera Cruz, and the recruitment and training of militiamen and regular troops.

The other major element in the Bourbon reform program, which also had a major bearing upon the growth in crown revenues, was commercial reform. Again, as already noted, it is possible to depict this as hesitant and tardy. Having opened the major ports of the Caribbean islands to direct trade with several Spanish ports in 1765, thereby breaching the old monopoly of trade with America enjoyed by the merchants of Cádiz, Spain did not extend the benefits of "free trade" to New Spain and Venezuela until nearly 25 years later. In the meantime, the major reform for other regions came in 1778 when the principal Spanish American ports beyond the excluded zones were granted permission to trade freely with each other and with the 13 principal ports of Spain. Although the entry of Spain into the War of American Independence actually ushered in a commercial decline in 1779–81, trade with America experienced a boom thereafter, with the value of exports dispatched there from Spain (most still went through Cádiz) quadrupling in the period 1782–96, and imports growing by a staggering 1,100 percent, as mining production doubled in Peru and New Spain. Silver and gold remained by far the most important commodities shipped to Spain, representing 56 percent of the value of trade, but sugar from Cuba and New Spain (Mexico), cochineal and dyewoods from Central America, tobacco and cocoa beans from Venezuela, hides from the Río de la Plata, and a whole range of other agricultural goods began to arrive in unprecedented quantities, most of them for re-export to consumers beyond Spain (Fisher 1985: 60–86). The export of hides from Buenos Aires, for example, increased tenfold to 1,400,000 a year in this period, and creoles there (as in other parts of the empire that experienced rapid economic expansion) had a sense of prosperity and well-being that made the more oppressive fiscal and administrative structures tolerable, at least in the short term. However, the virtual collapse of trade with the metropolis after 1796, although alleviated somewhat by the reluctant crown decision in 1797 to permit neutral ships to enter Spanish American ports, a concession withdrawn in 1799, created a new climate in which Spain's American subjects clamored for the right to trade freely with the world at large. In the long term this demand was incompatible with the maintenance of Spanish imperialism.

Portugal and Brazil in the Eighteenth Century

Charles III's measures in Spain and America were part of an overall scheme of imperial reform and reorganization, however dilatory. Brazil, too, experienced such a program during the primacy of the Marquis of Pombal, Chief Minister of José I from 1750 until 1777, whose imperial policies were designed to increase both royal authority and revenues in Brazil. One of the most farsighted of his reforms was the transfer in 1762 of the capital of the viceroyalty from the northern city of Salvador da Bahia to Rio de Janeiro, in recognition of a shift which had taken place in the economic centre of gravity of the colony with the emergence of gold and diamond mining in Rio de Janeiro's hinterland.

The administrative structures established in Brazil during the early colonial period had been less systematic than those of Spanish America, but significant changes had already been made in the pre-Pombaline period with the establishment of the new captaincies of São Paulo in 1709, Minas Gerais in 1720, Goiás in 1744, and Cuiabá (Mato Grosso) in 1748. Increasingly in the eighteenth century, the Crown recruited as captains general or governors individuals who would recognize an allegiance to the interests of the metropolis rather than those of the Brazilian landed elite from which the majority had emerged in the earlier period. Moreover, the shift of the capital to Rio de Janeiro facilitated closer supervision by viceroys, on behalf of the Crown, of these key subordinates, a process made easier by the cancellation of the remaining hereditary captaincies in return for land grants and cash payments. Other important administrative reforms during the Pombaline period included the establishment in Rio de Janeiro in 1751 of a new High Court of Justice, with functions similar to that of Bahia (which continued to exercise jurisdiction over northern Brazil), the codification of Brazilian law in 1754–7, and the creation of provincial courts of justice in 1765. The northern "state of Maranhão and Grão-Pará," which enjoyed a semi-autonomous status before Pombal came to power, was also brought fully under the control of the viceroy. Crown authority was further extended by the expulsion from Brazil in 1759 of several hundred members of the Jesuit Order, following a propaganda campaign waged by Pombal, who succeeded in persuading the king that they were undermining royal authority and using their extensive mission territories to enrich themselves. As in Spanish America, from which 2,000 Jesuits were expelled in 1767 for similar reasons, the expulsion provoked some native revolts, but the discontent of elite families whose Jesuit sons were exiled to Italy was balanced by their satisfaction at having the opportunity to purchase from the Crown the Order's estates, houses, and movable property. In both empires, military reorganization, too, bore striking similarities: of particular importance was the expansion of a militia system, which provided the members of the landed aristocracy who took up commissions with both the social and political prestige that wealth alone could not give.

Like the Caroline reformers, Pombal also implemented a policy of commercial reform, which centered around the abolition in 1765 of convoyed fleets between Lisbon and Brazil. Although they were reestablished temporarily in 1797–1801 to provide defense during wartime from foreign predators, the basic pattern after 1765 was to protect shipping by means of naval patrols. The ongoing alliance with England was obviously beneficial in this respect, although Pombal made strenuous efforts to reduce Portugal's (and Brazil's) economic and commercial dependence upon England by establishing two new monopoly trading companies to promote economic recovery in northern Brazil: the Maranhão and Grão-Pará Company, and the Pernambuco and Paraíba Company, organized in 1755 and 1759 respectively. The former, in particular, like the Caracas Company in Venezuela, was strikingly successful in promoting the production for both domestic and international consumption of non-traditional crops, including rice and cotton. As already noted, the increase in English demand for Brazilian cotton was particularly noteworthy, with the result that by the 1780s Brazilian cotton had replaced gold as the major commodity in Anglo-Portuguese trade. The parallel revival of sugar production in the 1790s began to restore prosperity to the northern provinces of Bahia and Pernambuco. Similarly, the production and export of tobacco and cattle hides grew rapidly, helping to turn Brazil into "the most important economic unit in the worldwide Portuguese empire" (Silva 1984: 508).

Thus, despite the decline of mining in the interior province of Minas Gerais, and the restrictive policies of the Portuguese Crown toward colonial industry and commerce, Brazil by the end of the eighteenth century was increasing in wealth and power. Its population had increased tenfold in the course of the century, and by 1800, at 4 million, was as large as that of Portugal. Although Pombal's removal from office in 1778, following the death of José I in 1777, led to some slackening of the reform program, the vigorous viceroy Luis de Almeida (Marquis of Lavradio), who held office until 1779, maintained the impetus of change a little longer. When Lavradio returned to Portugal Brazil, like Spanish America, was more firmly under the control of the metropolis than at any previous time in its history. However, its economic growth in the eighteenth century, also like that of Spanish America, reflected not just the continued expansion of Iberian imperialism but also spontaneous American growth and integration into the international economy that was paving the way for eventual independence.

Conclusion

The ministers of Charles III of Spain and their agents in America, like their counterparts in Pombaline Portugal and Brazil, hoped and believed that their innovations

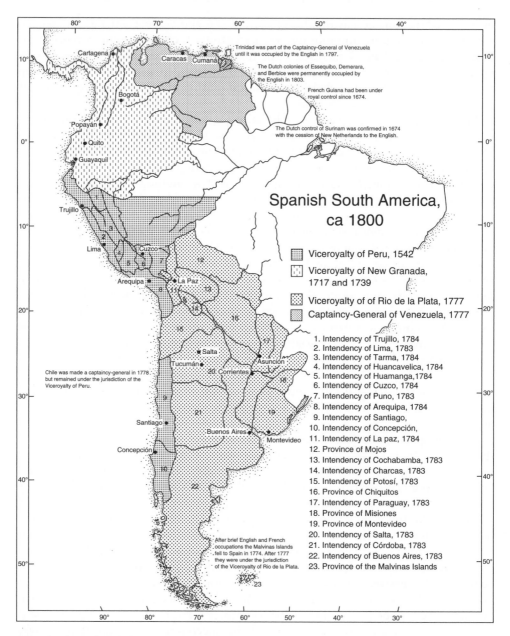

Map 4 Spanish South America, *c.*1800
Source: Cathryn L. Lombardi, John V. Lombardi, and K. Lynn Stoner, *Latin American History: A Teaching Atlas* (Madison, WI: University of Wisconsin Press, 1983). © 1983. Reprinted by permission of The University of Wisconsin Press.

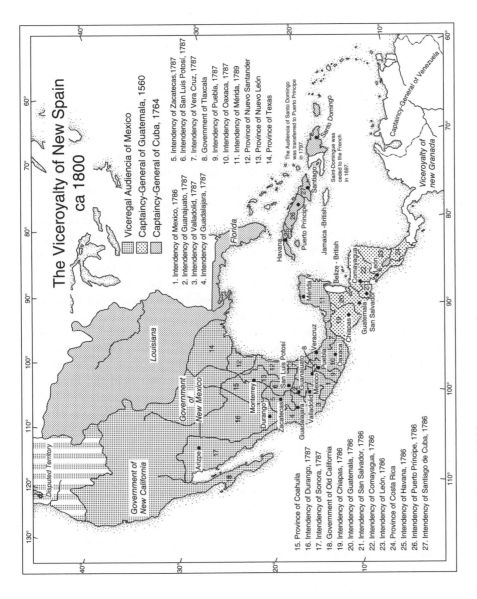

Map 5 The Viceroyalty of New Spain, *c.*1800

Source: Cathryn L. Lombardi, John V. Lombardi, and K. Lynn Stoner, *Latin American History: A Teaching Atlas* (Madison, WI: University of Wisconsin Press, 1983). © 1983. Reprinted by permission of The University of Wisconsin Press.

would promote economic growth, better public administration, and the eradication of fiscal and judicial corruption. They also thought, correctly as it turned out, at least until the closing years of the eighteenth century, that better government would bring in its train the increases in taxation revenue required to underpin the ambitions and the authority of the Braganza and Bourbon dynasties. Obviously these aims embraced a contradiction, for in the long term securing the happiness and prosperity of Americans could not be reconciled with the strengthening of metropolitan authority. There is some evidence of local resistance to the reform programs – the so-called Rebellion of the Comuneros of 1781 in New Granada (Phelan 1978) or the 1788 Tiradentes conspiracy in Brazil (Langfur, this volume), for example. But wherever and whenever insurgency involved significant lower-class and/or indigenous/black participation, it tended to persuade the colonial elites to make common cause with their peninsular masters rather than risk undermining the foundations of colonial society. This was particularly true in the southern Andes, where the prolonged Rebellion of Túpac Amaru (1780–3) in the Cusco region (Walker 1999), and related insurgency led by Túpac Katari in northern Upper Peru, although initially attracting some support from local elites hostile to the centralization of authority in the viceregal capitals, "laid bare contrasts in mentality and material interest between natives and most of the rest of highland (and lowland) society" (Bakewell 2004: 311). Brazil remained politically tranquil during the first decade of the nineteenth century. In Spanish America, by contrast, the first decade of the nineteenth century was one of growing estrangement with Spain, as the prosperity of the late eighteenth century began to fade at the same time as the fiscal demands of the metropolis intensified. However, the failures of both Miranda in Venezuela and of the English in the Río de la Plata indicated that few Americans were willing either to take up arms in support of independence or to exchange Spanish imperial control for that of England. All that began to change, of course, in 1808–10, although in the short term the reaction of most Spanish Americans to the installation of Joseph Bonaparte as king of Spain was to rally to the Junta Central in support of the improvised resistance that held the French at bay in the Peninsula until the end of 1809. In Brazil, events took quite a different course, with the arrival of the royal family and its appendages in Rio de Janeiro apparently strengthening rather than undermining the ties with the metropolitan authorities.

The vast majority of Spanish Americans and Brazilians did not aspire to secure independence in 1808, despite an awareness that the Bourbons and the Braganzas had sought in the second half of the eighteenth century to exploit their American possessions for the first time as genuine colonies administered for the benefit of the metropolitan powers. Moreover, even when creole revolutionaries seized power in 1810 in Buenos Aires, Caracas, Santiago, and other cities, initially in some cases under the guise of loyalty to the deposed Ferdinand VII, the immediate reaction of most Spanish Americans was to try to preserve the ties that bound them to Spain. They did so in part out of intense social and political conservatism, which would be consolidated when premature bids for independence in the viceroyalties of New Spain (the Hidalgo revolt) and Venezuela brought in their train social and ethnic violence, and in part because of the strength of their allegiance to the imperial traditions which had survived the intensification of absolutism in the eighteenth century (Rodríguez O., this volume).

BIBLIOGRAPHY

Alden, D. (1968) *Royal Government in Colonial Brazil, with Special Reference to the Administration of the Marquis of Lavradio, Viceroy 1766–1779.* University of California Press, Berkeley.

Andrien, K. J. & Johnson L. L. (eds.) (1994) *The Political Economy of Spanish America in the Age of Revolution, 1750–1850.* University of New Mexico Press, Albuquerque.

Bakewell, P. (2004) *A History of Latin America.* Blackwell, Oxford.

Barbier, J. A. & Kuethe, A. J. (1984) *The North American Role in the Spanish Imperial Economy, 1760–1819.* Manchester University Press, Manchester.

Brading, D. A. (1970) *Miners and Merchants in Bourbon Mexico.* Cambridge University Press, Cambridge.

Brading, D. A. (1984) "Bourbon Spain and Its American Empire." In L. Bethell (ed.), *The Cambridge History of Latin America. Volume 1. Colonial Latin America.* Cambridge University Press, Cambridge, pp. 389–439.

Bradley, P. T. (1989) *The Lure of Peru: Maritime Intrusion into the South Sea, 1598–1701.* Macmillan, Basingstoke.

Burkholder, M. A. & Chandler, D. S. (1977) *From Impotence to Authority: the Spanish Crown and the American Audiencias, 1687–1808.* University of Missouri Press, Columbia.

Chávez, T. E. (2003) *Spain and the Independence of the United States: an Intrinsic Gift.* University of New Mexico Press, Albuquerque.

Esdaile, C. (2002) *The Peninsular War.* Penguin Books, London.

Fisher, J. R. (1970) *Government and Society in Colonial Peru: The Intendant System 1784–1814.* Athlone Press, London.

Fisher, J. R. (1985) *Commercial Relations between Spain and Spanish America in the Era of Free Trade, 1778–1796.* Centre for Latin American Studies, University of Liverpool, Liverpool.

Fisher, J. R. (1997) *The Economic Aspects of Spanish Imperialism in America, 1492–1810.* Liverpool University Press, Liverpool.

Fisher, J. R. (2003) *Bourbon Peru, 1750–1824.* Liverpool University Press, Liverpool.

Fisher, J. R., Kuethe, A. K., & McFarlane, A. (eds.) (1990) *Reform and Insurrection in Bourbon New Granada and Peru.* Louisiana State University Press, Baton Rouge.

Geggus, D. P. (1982) *Slavery, War and Revolution: the British Occupation of Saint Domingue 1793–1798.* Clarendon Press, Oxford.

Gutiérrez Escudero, A. (ed.) (2000) *Ciencia, economía y política en Hispanoamérica colonial.* Escuela de Estudios Hispano-Americanos, Seville.

Kamen, H. (1980) *Spain in the Later Seventeenth Century, 1665–1700.* Longman, London and New York.

Kamen, H. (2001) *Philip V of Spain: the King Who Reigned Twice.* Yale University Press, New Haven and London.

Kuethe, A. J. (1978) *Military Reform and Society in New Granada, 1773–1808.* University Presses of Florida, Gainesville.

Kuethe, A. J. & Blaisdell, L. (1991), "French Influence and the Origins of the Bourbon Colonial Reorganization," *Hispanic American Historical Review,* 71:3, pp. 579–607.

Latasa, P. (ed.) (2003) *Reformismo y sociedad en la América borbónica.* Ediciones Universidad de Navarra, Pamplona.

Liss, P. K. (1982) *Atlantic Empires: the Network of Trade and Revolution, 1713–1826.* Johns Hopkins University Press, Baltimore.

Lynch, J. (1958) *Spanish Colonial Administration, 1782–1810: the Intendant System in the Viceroyalty of the Río de la Plata.* Athlone Press, London.

Lynch, J. (1986) *The Spanish American Revolutions, 1808–1826.* Norton, London and New York.

Lynch, J. (1989) *Bourbon Spain, 1700–1808*. Blackwell, Oxford.

McFarlane, A. (1992) *The British in the Americas 1480–1815*. Longman, Harlow.

McFarlane, A. (1993) *Colombia before Independence: Economy, Society and Politics under Bourbon Rule*. Cambridge University Press, Cambridge.

McKinley, P. M. (1985) *Pre-Revolutionary Caracas: Politics, Economy, and Society, 1777–1811*. Cambridge University Press, Cambridge.

Martínez Shaw, C. & Alfonso Mola, M. (2001), *Felipe V*. Arlanza Ediciones, Madrid.

Maxwell, K. R. (1973) *Conflicts and Conspiracies: Brazil and Portugal, 1750–1808*. Cambridge University Press, Cambridge.

Moorhead, M. L. (1975) *The Presidio: Bastion of the Spanish Borderlands*. University of Oklahoma Press, Norman.

Navarro García, L. (1964) *Don José de Gálvez y la Comandancia General de las Provincias Internas del Norte de Nueva España*. Escuela de Estudios Hispano-Americanos, Seville.

Phelan, J. L. (1978) *The People and the King: The Comunero Revolution in Colombia, 1781*. University of Wisconsin Press, Madison.

Savelle, M. (1974) *Empires to Nations. Expansion in America, 1713–1824*. University of Minneapolis Press, Minneapolis; Oxford University Press, London.

Silva, A. M. (1984) "Portugal and Brazil: Imperial Reorganization, 1750–1808." In L. Bethell (ed.), *The Cambridge History of Latin America. Volume I. Colonial Latin America*. Cambridge University Press, Cambridge, pp. 441–508.

Walker, C. (1999) *Smoldering Ashes: Cuzco and the Creation of Republican Peru, 1780–1840*. Duke University Press, Durham.

Walker, G. J. (1979) *Spanish Politics and Imperial Trade*. Macmillan, Basingstoke.

Chapter Twelve

THE PROCESS OF SPANISH AMERICAN INDEPENDENCE

Jaime E. Rodríguez O.

The new Iberian nations – both in the Peninsula and in America – emerged from the wars that resulted from Napoleon's invasion of the Iberian Peninsula. In 1807, French troops with the permission of the king of Spain crossed the border to invade Portugal. The king of Portugal fled to Brazil with his entire court. (During the following decade and a half, Rio de Janeiro became the capital of the Portuguese monarchy.) In 1808, Napoleon Bonaparte forced the Bourbon rulers of Spain to abdicate and appointed his brother Joseph king of the Spanish Monarchy. Although the senior Spanish authorities accepted the dynastic change, the people – a new political actor – did not. On May 2, 1808, the residents of Madrid drove the French troops out of the capital. Their temporary victory unleashed a great revolution that transformed the Hispanic world.

The independence of Spanish America was not the result of an anti-colonial struggle; rather, it was a consequence of a great political revolution that culminated in the dissolution of a worldwide political system. The movement was an integral part of the broader process that was transforming *antiguo régimen* societies into modern liberal nation-states. The new countries that emerged from the break-up of the Spanish monarchy reflected the institutions, traditions, and practices of the past. In Spanish America, eight nations – Mexico, the United Provinces in the Center of America, Colombia, Peru, Bolivia, Chile, the United Provinces in South America, and Paraguay – were formed initially from four viceroyalties: New Spain, New Granada, Peru, and the Río de la Plata, and from two captaincies general: Guatemala and Chile. Three of the new countries later fragmented as local and regional groups imposed their particular visions of national boundaries and government structures. The United Provinces in the Center of America divided into five nations: Guatemala, Nicaragua, El Salvador, Honduras, and Costa Rica; Colombia fragmented into three countries: Venezuela, Nueva Granada (later changed to Colombia), and Ecuador; and the United Provinces in South America split into Uruguay and Argentina. Most of the new nations emerged from the territories of former *audiencias* (high courts). The two exceptions were Mexico, which remained one country even though it included two audiencias – Mexico and Guadalajara – and the Audiencia of Guatemala, which shattered into five nations.

The manner in which the process of independence unfolded in the various regions of the Hispanic world shaped the new nations. Several decades of institutional, economic, political, social, and ideological change preceded the transition. Although political ideas, structures, and practices evolved rapidly after 1808, much remained of the antiguo régimen. The nature of social, economic, and institutional relations changed slowly. Throughout this period of transformation, new political processes and liberal institutions merged with established traditions and practices.

Two broad movements emerged in the Spanish world: a great political revolution that sought to transform the Spanish monarchy into a modern nation-state with the most radical constitution of the nineteenth century; and a fragmented insurgency that relied on force to secure local autonomy or home rule. These two overlapping processes influenced and altered one another in a variety of ways. Neither can be understood in isolation. In this essay, the great political revolution of the Hispanic world is examined first to provide a context for the discussion of the New World's multiple armed autonomous movements.

The Political Revolution of the Hispanic World

Throughout most of their history, particularly during the sixteenth and seventeenth centuries, the Spanish possessions in America constituted part of the worldwide Spanish monarchy – a confederation of disparate kingdoms and lands which extended throughout portions of Europe, Africa, Asia, and America (Merriman 1918–34; Kamen 2003). The residents of these kingdoms exercised a high level of political and economic autonomy (Rodríguez O. 2005c: 6–32). Only very late, during the reign of Carlos III (1759–88), did the Crown attempt to centralize the monarchy and create a modern empire with Spain as the metropolis. That effort, widely known as the Bourbon Reforms, was not implemented fully by the time of Napoleon's intervention in 1808. *Americans* – as the people of Spanish America called themselves – everywhere opposed the political and economic innovations that restricted their autonomy and modified many to suit their interests. On the eve of independence, the leaders of the New World retained a significant degree of autonomy and control over their regions (Rodríguez O. 1998: 19–35).

Napoleon's invasion of Spain galvanized Americans to defend the monarchy and expand their rights within the Spanish system. The French invasion of Spain and the collapse of the monarchy triggered a series of events that culminated in the establishment of representative government in the Hispanic world. In Spain, the first impulse after May 1808 was centrifugal – that is, individual provinces formed regional *juntas* (committees) to govern. Each provincial junta, invoking the Hispanic legal principle that in the absence of the king, sovereignty reverted to the people, acted as though it were an independent nation (Artola 1968: 68).

The vast majority of Spaniards and virtually all Spanish Americans opposed the French. After two centuries, we have come to accept the results of the French Revolution as beneficial. However, at the time, the Hispanic people associated the French movement with revolutionary excesses: the terror, atheism, anti-clericalism, and a new and virulent imperialism that had brutally subjugated other European peoples. Far from offering opportunities for democracy and progress, the French epitomized all that the people of Spain and America dreaded. Indeed, French domination implied more centralization and even greater economic exactions than had the Bourbon Reforms.

Although the governing elites in Spain capitulated, the people of the Peninsula and the New World were virtually unanimous in their opposition to the French. The external threat underscored the factors that united them: one monarchy, one faith, one general culture, and one society in crisis. They were members of what soon came to be known as *la Nación Española*, a nation consisting of the Peninsula and the overseas kingdoms. As Simón Bolívar later recalled, "a community of interests, of understanding, of religion; the mutual goodwill; a tender regard for the birthplace and good name of our forefathers; ultimately, all that fulfilled our expectations came from Spain. From these arose a principle of fidelity that seemed eternal" (Bolívar 1977: II, 84). Since all areas of the Spanish monarchy possessed the same general political culture, all groups – including those of America – justified their actions using the same principles and almost identical language. The people of both areas drew upon common concepts and sought similar solutions to the evolving crisis. Inspired by the legal foundations of the monarchy, most agreed that in the absence of the king, sovereignty reverted to the people who possessed the authority and the responsibility to defend the nation.

A sense of *patriotismo*, identification with the locality, existed at the level of *ayuntamientos* (city governments). Based on Roman–Hispanic traditions, the ayuntamientos or *cabildos* of America functioned as provincial capitals; they possessed the voice and vote of their province, which included dependent towns and villages (Bayle 1952; Moore 1966; Miranda 1978). The Bourbon reforms had strengthened regional identification by introducing the intendancy system in the latter part of the eighteenth century. The intendant was a provincial governor whose responsibilities included working with local elites and other groups to foster economic and social well-being within his jurisdiction. The new structure inadvertently contributed to the growth of patriotism or localism (Lynch 1958; Destua Pimentel 1965; Fisher 1970; Rees Jones 1979; Pietschmann 1996). This ayuntamiento–provincial regionalism, while important economically during the antiguo régimen, was dormant as a political force. Regionalism subsequently emerged as a powerful political force during the independence and early national periods. The capitals of viceroyalties and of audiencias considered themselves the leaders of their territories, with the sovereign right to act in the name of their regions. Provincial capitals, however, believed that they too possessed sovereign rights and autonomy. In the absence of the king, the question would ultimately be settled by force.

The creation of the Junta Suprema Central Gubernativa del Reino as a government of national defense on September 25, 1808 appeared to provide a solution to the crisis of the monarchy. That body not only recognized the rights of the Spanish provinces but also acknowledged the Americans' claims that their lands were not colonies but kingdoms, that they constituted equal and integral parts of the Spanish monarchy, and that they possessed the right of representation in the national government, something no other European nation had granted its possessions. The Junta Central was to be composed of two deputies from each province in Spain and one from each of the nine American kingdoms. Many Americans objected to the unequal representation (Rodríguez O. 1998: 59–64).

In 1809, the kingdoms of Spanish America held the first elections for representatives to a monarchy-wide government, the Junta Central. The complicated and lengthy elections constituted a profound step forward in the formation of modern representative government for the entire Spanish nation. Moreover, the process explicitly recognized the ancient putative right of the provincial capitals of America – the *ciudades cabezas de partido* – to representation in a congress of cities. However, the degree of regional representation varied widely since New World authorities differed in their interpretation of the election decree. New Spain, with nearly half the population of Spanish America, granted only 14 cities the right to hold elections, while, in the much smaller Kingdom of Guatemala, an equal number of cities enjoyed that privilege. The situation also varied widely in South America: 20 cities held elections in Nueva Granada, 17 in Peru, 16 in Chile, 12 in the Río de la Plata, and six in Venezuela (Benson 2004: 1–20).

Before the newly elected delegates from America could join the Junta Central, the French renewed their drive to conquer the Peninsula. The decisive French victories of 1809 destroyed the fragile balance established by the Junta Central. When the Junta dissolved itself in January 1810, appointing a Council of Regency in its place, some provinces of Spain and several kingdoms in America refused to recognize the legitimacy of the new government. The Regency's subsequent decision to convene a *cortes* (parliament) to govern Spain and the American kingdoms resolved the concerns of the provinces in Spain and many parts of America. In a few areas of the New World, however, Americans who refused to recognize the Regency formed armed groups to defend their autonomy. Thus, the political revolution of the Spanish world would be carried out within the context of war in the Peninsula and insurgency in America.

In 1810, Americans and Spaniards held elections to select representatives for the monarchy-wide parliament, which possessed the authority to transform the Hispanic world. Sixty-seven New World deputies participated in the Extraordinary Cortes composed of approximately 200 delegates that assembled in the city of Cádiz.[1] The Cortes of Cádiz provided Americans who desired autonomy a peaceful means of obtaining home rule. Moreover, the extensive parliamentary debates, which were widely disseminated by the press during the period 1810–12, significantly influenced those Spanish Americans who supported as well as those who opposed the new Hispanic government (Rodríguez O. 1998: 64–82).

The Spanish and American deputies who served in the Extraordinary Cortes enacted the *Constitución de la Monarquía Española* that transformed the Hispanic world. The American deputies to the Cortes played a central role in drafting the constitution of 1812. Many of the liberal reforms that characterized the Charter of Cádiz are directly attributable to the Spanish American deputies. Their arguments and proposals convinced Spaniards to embrace substantial change in America as well as in the Peninsula. The constitution of 1812, the most radical charter of the nineteenth century, abolished seigniorial institutions, the Inquisition, Indian tribute, forced labor – such as the mita in South America and personal service in Spain – and asserted the state's control of the Church. It created a unitary state with equal laws for all parts of the Spanish monarchy, substantially restricted the authority of the king, and entrusted the legislature with decisive power. When it enfranchised all men, except those of African ancestry, without requiring either literacy or property qualifications, the constitution of 1812 surpassed all existing representative governments, such as Great Britain, the United States, and France, in providing political rights to the vast majority of the male population. François-Xavier Guerra's analysis of the 1813 election census in Mexico City, for example, concludes that 93 percent of the adult male population of the capital possessed the right to vote (Guerra 1999: 45).

The Charter of Cádiz expanded the electorate and dramatically increased the scope of political activity. The new constitution established representative government at three levels: the ayuntamiento (*Ayuntamiento Constitucional*), the province (*Diputación Provincial*), and the monarchy (*Cortes*). When it allowed cities and towns with a thousand or more inhabitants to form ayuntamientos constitucionales, it transferred political power from the center to the localities by incorporating vast numbers of people into the political process (Suanzes-Carpegna 1983; Rodríguez O. 1998: 82–92; Chust 1999). The constitution of 1812 was widely introduced in those regions of the monarchy that recognized the government in Spain. It is striking that New Spain and Guatemala, lands that contained more than half of the population of Spanish America, implemented the new constitutional order more fully than any other part of the Spanish monarchy, including Spain itself. Other areas of America under royal control – the Caribbean, Quito, Peru, and Charcas – as well as in parts of Venezuela, New Granada, and the Río de la Plata also introduced the charter.

Despite confusion, conflict, and delay resulting from the implementation of a new system, the first constitutional elections in Spanish America contributed to the legitimization of the new political culture. Spanish Americans established more than a thousand constitutional ayuntamientos and 16 provincial deputations during 1812–14. In some areas, such as the territories of the Provincial Deputations of Yucatán and Nueva Galicia, as many as three successive ayuntamiento elections were held during the 1812–14 period. Several areas held two elections, first to establish and then to renew their provincial deputations. Americans also elected hundreds of deputies to the Cortes in Madrid. Hundreds of thousands of citizens, possibly more than a million, including Indians, mestizos, castas, and blacks, participated in government both at the local and provincial levels. It is ironic that scholars have tended to ignore this great political revolution and instead have focused almost exclusively on the insurgencies. By any standard, the political revolution was more profound and extensive than the insurgencies, which have primarily occupied historians (Benson 1946: 336–50; Gómez Vizuete 1990: 581–615; Avendaño 1995; Guedea 1997: 39–63; Rodríguez O. 1999, 2005b, 2006; Peralta Ruíz 2001: 105–75; Dym 2005; Almer 2005).

Unlike the elections of 1809 for the Junta Central and those of 1810 for the Extraordinary Cortes of Cádiz, which were conducted by the ayuntamientos, the new constitutional elections of 1812–13 were the first popular elections held in the Hispanic world. Relatively free elections occurred in those areas dominated by the royalists. In contrast, the insurgents either did not hold elections or failed to conduct them in a "democratic" or "popular" manner. Although the elite clearly dominated politics, hundreds of thousands of middle- and lower-class men became involved in politics in a meaningful way and made their presence felt. Most striking, the Indian communities – members of the former *Repúblicas de Indios* – participated actively (Escobar Ohmstede 1996: 1–26; Rugeley 1996; Guardino 2000: 87–114; Rodríguez O. 2005a: 41–64). Ironically, the new Hispanic political system forced many insurgent governments to enhance their legitimacy by drafting constitutions and holding elections. Their constitutions, however, were less revolutionary than the Constitution of Cádiz and restricted suffrage by imposing literacy and property qualifications (Guedea 1991: 20–249; Valencia Llano 1992: 55–101).

The first constitutional era ended in 1814 when Fernando VII returned to the throne. He abolished the Cortes and the Constitution of Cádiz, restoring absolutism. There followed a five-year period in which, unfettered by the Constitution, the royal authorities in the New World crushed most insurgent movements. Only the isolated Río de la Plata remained beyond the reach of a weakened Spanish monarchy.

Civil War in America

A second broad movement, which paralleled the great political revolution, resulted in civil wars in several regions of America. Like the constitutional revolution, the civil conflicts arose in response to the French invasion of the Iberian Peninsula and the removal of the king by Napoleon Bonaparte. The dramatic French victories of 1809, which drove the Junta Central to Cádiz, convinced many in the New World that Spain might not survive as an independent state. Their fears appeared to be justified when the Junta Central dissolved itself at the end of January 1810 and appointed a Council of Regency. Many Americans who questioned that action formed local independent juntas to rule in the name of the imprisoned King Fernando VII.

Supporters of these American juntas based their actions on the same juridical principle that their peninsular counterparts invoked: in the absence of the king, sovereignty reverted to the people. Although that principle justified the formation of local governments in the name of the king, it did not support separation from the monarchy. Those favoring autonomy grounded their arguments on the unwritten American constitution: the direct compact between individual kingdoms and the monarch. According to their interpretation, the king, and only the king, possessed ties with New World kingdoms. If that relationship were severed, for whatever reason, there remained no bond between any American kingdom and Spain or even among individual New World realms. The authorities in Spain found such views unacceptable. The Regency and the Cortes could not constitutionally accede to the separation of the New World kingdoms. Therefore, when reforms and negotiations failed to restore the American juntas to compliance with the government, the authorities in Spain resorted to the use of force.

Disagreement among Spanish Americans concerning the legitimacy of the government in Spain and the locus of sovereignty in the absence of the monarch ignited the subsequent struggle. Spaniards and Americans in the New World, who believed that the Council of Regency and the Cortes were, indeed, the legitimate government, opposed the formation of local juntas. Others believed that the removal of the monarch required the formation of juntas in the Americas. The group favoring the formation of local governments gradually expanded as news reached America of the disastrous defeats of Spanish forces in the Peninsula. The autonomists disagreed among themselves about whether only capital cities of the American kingdoms possessed the right to form local governments or if that right also belonged to the provincial capitals of the various realms. Since the capital cities sought to maintain political control through force, insurgent groups formed to defend provincial autonomy. Divisions among elites within the various provinces also led to intra-elite conflict. In some instances, conflict broke out between the cities and the countryside. Occasionally, these power struggles led to civil wars that pitted the supporters of the Spanish national government against American juntas, the capitals of kingdoms against the provinces, the elites against one another, and urban against rural groups.

In New Spain, an intra-elite conflict heightened divisions and spawned an insurgency. Fearing that the American-born Spaniards would use the crisis in the Peninsula to expand their political and economic influence, the *peninsulares* (those born in the Peninsula) voiced their opposition to the holding of a congress of cities to address the crisis in Spain. When Viceroy José Iturrigaray sided with the *novohispanos* (people of New Spain), the peninsulares overthrew him on the night of September 15, 1808 and assumed control of the government. The novohispano autonomists never accepted the Spaniard's actions. The *golpe* and the subsequent arrogance of the Europeans exacerbated the divisions in New Spain and galvanized the Americans. Some conspired to achieve self-government.

In the fall of 1809, the authorities discovered a serious plot in the Mexican city of Valladolid. The conspirators had supporters in other provincial cities, such as Guanajuato, Querétaro, San Miguel el Grande, and Guadalajara. They prepared an uprising for December 21, 1809, and expected backing from the army and the militia. They hoped to attract thousands of men among the Indians and castas by promising to abolish tribute. The plan differed from the early peaceful autonomy movement in Mexico City only in that the conspirators had to rely on force because the Spaniards had seized the government. When the movement was exposed, the authorities chose to exercise leniency because many important persons openly declared that the conspirators were guilty only of seeking to redress rightful grievances in an inappropriate manner (Rodríguez O. 1998: 71–4).

The Valladolid conspiracy encouraged a similar movement in Querétaro, where militia captains Ignacio Allende and Juan Aldama and *corregidor* Miguel Domínguez began informal talks. By March 1810, the plotters had recruited Father Miguel Hidalgo and other disaffected Americans. They, like the Valladolid group, sought to depose the European Spaniards with the aid of the rural and urban workers of the Bajío and to establish an American junta to govern in the name of King Fernando VII. The conspirators planned the uprising for October 1810, but the authorities exposed the plot and arrested the Querétaro group on September 13, 1810. This preemptive action did not halt the revolt. Conspirators who eluded capture – Hidalgo, Allende, and Aldama – launched the revolt from the prosperous town of Dolores on the morning of September 16, 1810.

The American elite initially received the Hidalgo revolt, which began as a movement for autonomy, favorably. However, the upper classes subsequently withdrew their support when it became evident that the rebel leaders could not control their followers. The sack of the city of Guanajuato constituted the turning point in the revolt. The looting, carnage and destruction of the Bajían city clearly demonstrated that the insurrection promoted uncontrollable class conflict. The elite feared that a revolution would spark a race war, while Indians and campesinos with communal lands feared that the landless poor in Hidalgo's forces might dispossess them. The royal army and most of the militia, which were 95 percent American, remained loyal to the Crown. Ultimately, the royalists defeated the insurgents. Hidalgo was subsequently captured, tried, degraded from the priesthood, and executed (Hamill 1966; Alamán 1985).

His death did not end the insurgency. Ignacio Rayón, a lawyer, assumed leadership of the movement after Hidalgo's execution in 1811. Initially, Rayón attempted to effect reconciliation with the royal authorities. When they rejected his overtures, Rayón and other insurgent leaders organized the Suprema Junta Nacional Americana as an alternative government. In January 1812, royalist forces captured the town of Zitácuaro where the Junta was based. Although Rayón escaped, he gradually lost his position as leader of the rebels. Father José María Morelos, who had been waging a guerrilla campaign in the south, emerged as the most important insurgent chieftain (Alamán 1985: III, 443–580; Guedea 1992: 48–125).

In contrast to the Hidalgo revolt, the Morelos insurgency flourished because he directed an orderly movement that reduced the specter of race and class warfare. During 1811 and 1812, Morelos and his commanders concentrated on cutting the capital's lines of communication and on gaining control of the south. Morelos' greatest success came in 1812 when he captured Oaxaca. The following spring, he initiated a seven-month siege of Acapulco. Despite his military achievements, he could not claim authority merely by force of arms, particularly since the Hispanic Cortes had ratified the notion of popular sovereignty and representative government. After the promulgation of the Hispanic constitution of 1812 and the holding of popular elections throughout New Spain, Morelos' urban supporters urged the convening of a congress to form an alternative government.

In June 1813, Morelos convened elections in the regions controlled by the insurgents for a congress to be held at Chilpancingo, a small, easily defended, friendly town. Elections were held in the insurgent-held areas of Oaxaca, Puebla, Veracruz, and Michoacán; in the insurgent Province of Tecpan; and secretly in Mexico City and possibly in other urban centers. Unlike elections under the Hispanic constitution of 1812, the insurgent elections were less popular and were manipulated by the insurgent leaders (Guedea 1991: 222–48).

Conflict ensued from the outset between the insurgent executive and the legislature. Although congress ratified Morelos' command as generalísimo and declared the independence of América *Septentrional* (North America), the legislative body, like the Cortes in Spain, assumed national sovereignty and attempted to exercise supreme power. On October 22, 1814, congress issued the Constitutional Decree for the Liberty of Mexican America, known as the Constitution of Apatzingán, after the town where it was promulgated. The new charter established a republic with a plural executive and a powerful legislature. Congress rejected Morelos' pretensions to power and stripped him of supreme authority, but it retained his support by appointing him a member of the executive triumvirate. On November 5, 1815, however, royalist forces defeated Morelos. He was captured, tried, degraded from the priesthood, and executed on December 22, 1815. Earlier that month, other insurgent leaders dissolved congress (Macias 1973; Alamán 1985: III, 545–84; Guedea 1991: 203–49). The Constitution of Apatzingán was not implemented and exercised no influence on subsequent constitutional development in New Spain/Mexico. Although the insurgents were successful in waging a guerrilla war and introducing an alternative government, the insurgency did not result in the creation of an independent nation-state.

The kingdoms of South America, like New Spain, reacted with great patriotism when they received the news that the French had invaded the Peninsula and imprisoned the king. They rejected the invaders and supported the new government of national defense, the Junta Central. As time passed, however, and as they learned of the disastrous defeats of Spanish forces, they increasingly favored establishing local governments.

On April 19, 1810, Caracas formed a Junta Suprema Conservadora de los Derechos de Fernando VII. Faced with opposition from other cities and provinces, the Junta Suprema convoked a congress, the Cuerpo Conservador de los Derechos de D. Fernando VII en las Provincias de Venezuela. The body, which met on March 2, 1811, followed many of the precedents established by the Cortes of Cádiz. It arrogated authority to itself and established a weak executive by naming a triumvirate. The situation changed on July 5, when young radicals who favored emancipation used urban mobs to force congress to declare independence; that parliament subsequently wrote a constitution that created a federal system, and, like the charter being drafted in Cádiz, established legislative dominance and retained a weak triumvirate as the executive. However, the Venezuelan charter was more conservative than the 1812 constitution drafted by the Cortes of Cádiz. The Venezuelan constitution decreed legal equality for free men but unlike the Constitution of Cádiz retained property requirements for active citizenship. Drawing on Hispanic traditions, the Venezuelan constitution granted considerable authority to the provinces while seeking to balance their power with that of the state.

Since legislative dominance and executive weakness proved ineffective in times of crisis, the new regime found it necessary to grant extraordinary power to the executive. When royalist forces from the Caribbean joined pro-royalist provinces in opposing the First Venezuelan Republic, the Caracas government appointed Francisco Miranda dictator with full civil and military power. He was unable to defeat the royalists; the Republic collapsed in July 1812. The fall of the First Republic marked the end of widespread political participation in Venezuela. Thereafter, a struggle for political dominance ensued, which pitted ruthless *caudillos* against one another (Stoan 1974: 41–116; McKinley 1996: 161–74).

One of Miranda's former supporters, Simón Bolívar, drew a number of conclusions from the failure of the First Republic that would have wide-ranging repercussions in the subsequent struggle in South America. In his view, the First Republic failed because it adopted a weak federal constitution, because it had been too tolerant of dissenting opinions, because elections had provided the weak and incompetent with too great a voice, and because the government had neither recruited an effective military force nor successfully managed the economy (Bolívar 1939: 11–22). Later, when he gained power, Bolívar preferred to govern as an autocrat, sought to limit civilian participation, and assumed the title of dictator on various occasions.

Neighboring New Granada carried the principles of confederalism and strong legislatures to extremes. There the provinces splintered into three coalitions during 1810–15, a period known as the *Patria Boba* (foolish fatherland). Cartagena de las Indias formed a governing junta on May 8, 1810 upon learning that the Junta Suprema Central in Spain had dissolved and established a Council of Regency. Other provinces followed suit. On July 20, Santa Fe de Bogotá, the capital of New Granada, formed a Junta Suprema del Nuevo Reino de Granada. However, many other provinces, which possessed conflicting economic interests, resented the capital's attempt to dominate them. Cartagena proposed establishing "a perfect federal government," which would grant each province equality and autonomy (Restrepo 1858: I, 88–188; Pompa y Guerra 1986: I, 281–8; Gómez Hoyos 1992: 139–77). Santa Fe countered by convening a congress in the capital. In March 1811, that assembly created the Estado de Cundinamarca, which recognized "Don Fernando VII, by the grace of God and the will of the people, legitimately and constitutionally represented, King of the cundinamarqueses." The new government consisted of a strong legislature and a weak executive. Until the king could come to govern, a president – as viceregent of Fernando VII, associated with two counselors – would exercise executive power. The new "centralist" state consisted of Santa Fe de Bogotá and other provinces of the sierra.

Led by Cartagena, five other provinces formed the Provincias Unidas de la Nueva Granada, a confederation of autonomous provinces with an extremely weak government. Congress received most of the authority in the confederation. The president, "if there were one with separate attributes, or . . . the executive power, if it were created," would be completely subordinate to the congress of the confederation (Pompa y Guerra 1986: I, 389–418). Each of the provinces, which formed part of the confederation, proceeded to write its own constitution. Thus, three contending political blocks existed at the end of 1811 – the provinces such as Santa Marta that remained under royalist control, the State of Cundinamarca, and the Provincias Unidas de la Nueva Granada.

A virulent civil war erupted among the three groups. Most of the conflict, however, occurred between the two autonomous states, Cundinamarca and the Provincias Unidas. After years of warfare, Santa Fe de Bogotá fell to the armies of the Provincias Unidas on December 12, 1814. By that time, however, Fernando VII had abolished the Constitution of Cádiz and dispatched an army under the command of Marshall Pablo Morillo to restore order in northern South America. After a prolonged struggle, the Provincias Unidas collapsed in May 1816.

The centralist–federalist struggle was also a dominant factor in the response of the Viceroyalty of the Río de la Plata to the abdication of the Spanish monarch. The viceroyalty – which was established in 1776 and had not existed long enough to have integrated fully all of its many and distant provinces when Napoleon invaded Spain and deposed Fernando VII in 1808 – provides an extreme example of that struggle. The attempt by the city of Buenos Aires to play a dominant role in the formation and functioning of an autonomous government to address the crisis in the Iberian Peninsula unleashed a period of intense political instability that ended in the creation of four new nations. The response of the residents of the Río de la Plata to events in Spain underscores the tensions between viceregal capitals seeking to maintain their status in the new political context and the determination of provincial cities and their hinterland to assert their autonomy.

On May 13, 1810, news arrived in Buenos Aires that the Junta Central had disbanded after fleeing to Cádiz. The leaders of the city decided not to recognize the Council of Regency. After much heated debate, on May 25 the *porteños* (the people of the port of Buenos Aires) organized the Junta Provisional Gubernativa de las Provincias del Río de la Plata to rule in the name of Fernando VII. The provisional government swore "to conserve intact this part of America for our August Sovereign

Señor Don Fernando VII and his legitimate successors and to observe strictly the laws of this Kingdom" (Varela 1910: I, 214). The following day, the Junta Provisional Gubernativa dispatched a circular letter to the provincial capitals informing them of recent events and requesting that they recognize the body as the provisional government. On May 27, it issued a decree instructing the cities to elect a deputy to the Junta Provisional Gubernativa de Buenos Aires. The change of name from *Río de la Plata to Buenos Aires* clearly indicated that the porteños intended to control the government of the viceroyalty. To ensure its dominance, the Junta organized military forces to impose the authority of the provisional government and its resolutions in all the provinces of the viceroyalty (González 1937–8: I, 269–70, II, 52).

The provinces of the Río de la Plata were not convinced that the Junta Provisional represented their interests. Montevideo and its interior, the Banda Oriental (Eastern Shore), competed with Buenos Aires for control of sea borne trade, including livestock exports. Isolated Paraguay had little in common with the porteños. Charcas, which had fallen under the control of the Viceroy of Peru after the 1809 autonomous movements in La Paz and Chuquisaca, considered Buenos Aires a threat. The interests of the interior provinces of the Río de la Plata, such as Córdoba, Salta, Tucumán, Mendoza, and San Juan also clashed with those of Buenos Aires. Those regions depended on commerce with Upper Peru and Chile and required protection for their manufactures, while the porteños insisted on free trade (Burgin 1940). Thus, the provinces of the Río de la Plata, which resented Buenos Aires' insistence on dominating the region, greeted the pretensions of the Junta Provisional Gubernativa with considerable suspicion. Montevideo, Paraguay, Charcas, Córdoba, and Salta decided to support the Council of Regency in Spain. The Buenos Aires government also was weakened by internal ideological struggles between moderate and radical factions. Porteño radicals favoring harsh anti-Spanish policies competed with moderate provincial deputies for control of the Junta. The moderates supported expanded self-government for the provinces and favored many of the reforms, including freedom of the press that had been adopted by the Cortes in Spain.

The constituent assembly could not resolve the internal divisions. Attempts by the government in Buenos Aires to use military force to maintain control of the provinces frequently failed and hardened separatist sentiments in many regions. The failures of the government in Buenos Aires prompted some provincial leaders to discuss forming coalitions without the port city. Porteño leaders confronted the growing crisis by strengthening the executive and disbanding the assembly before it drafted a constitution and formed a government. In January 1814, they appointed Gervasio Antonio Posadas supreme director and named José de San Martín commander of the Army of the North (Rodríguez O. 1998: 123–30).

The diverse regions that formed the viceroyalty of the Río de la Plata might have united had Buenos Aires been willing to accept the creation of a confederation of equal provinces. It would not. Instead, the porteños sought to impose their rule by force. As a result, three provinces, Charcas, Paraguay, and Uruguay, refused to accept the domination of Buenos Aires and ultimately decided to become the independent nations of Bolivia, Paraguay, and Uruguay (Street 1959; White 1978; Narancio 1992; Siles Salinas 1992). Despite the continuing stalemate between Buenos Aires and the other provinces, the region's isolated geographic position made it relatively safe from royalist forces.

The civil wars engendered by the conflicts between national and provincial capitals raged not only in Venezuela, New Granada, and the Río de la Plata but also in Chile and Quito. These so called federalist–centralist conflicts convinced leaders, such as Bolívar, that only strong united governments would succeed in winning independence and establishing order in South America. Such struggles, however, were difficult to contain; they continued for decades, profoundly affecting governmental stability and constitutional development in Spanish America.

Independence

Fernando VII's return in 1814 provided an opportunity to restore the unity of the Spanish World. Virtually every act that had occurred since 1808 – the struggle against the French, the political revolution enacted by the Cortes, and the autonomy movements in America – was taken in his name. Initially it appeared that he might accept moderate reforms, but ultimately the king opted to rely on force to restore royal order in the New World.

The Crown's repression prompted the minority of the politically active population of America that favored independence to act decisively. They renewed the armed struggle in the southern cone and in Venezuela. The provinces of the Río de la Plata declared independence in 1816 and created *Las Provincias Unidas en Sud América*. Two years later an army under the command of General José de San Martín invaded Chile from the east. He defeated royalist forces by mid-1818 and the local elites created the new nation of Chile. Republicans renewed the struggle in Venezuela in 1817. By 1819 the tide had turned against the monarchy. When a combined force of *neogranadinos* and *venezolanos* defeated the royalists at Boyacá, forcing the viceroy and other officials to flee from Bogotá, it became clear that Fernando VII would have to send more troops if he wished to retain control of América. However, raising an expeditionary force to reconquer the New World increased discontent in the Peninsula. The liberals in Spain exploited the army's disenchantment with war in America, eventually forcing the king to restore the constitution in March 1820. The return of constitutional order transformed the Hispanic political system for the third time in a decade.

The restoration of constitutional government elicited disparate responses from the American regions. New Spain and the Kingdom of Guatemala enthusiastically reestablished the constitutional system. In the months that followed, they conducted elections for countless constitutional ayuntamientos, provincial deputations, and the Cortes. Political instability in the Peninsula during the previous dozen years, however, convinced many novohispanos that it was prudent to establish an autonomous government within the Spanish monarchy. They pursued two courses of action. New Spain's deputies to the Cortes of 1821 proposed a project for New World autonomy, which would create three American kingdoms allied with the Peninsula and governed by Spanish princes under the constitution of 1812. At the same time, fearing that their proposal might be rejected, they organized a movement throughout New Spain to establish an autonomous monarchy under the constitution of 1812. When the Spanish majority in the Cortes rejected their proposal to create autonomous American kingdoms, the leaders of New Spain chose to secede and established the Mexican Empire. Mexico achieved independence not because royalist forces were defeated militarily but because novohispanos no longer supported the monarchy politically. They convinced royalist military officers who were weary of fighting the insurgency to change sides. Central America also declared independence and joined the newly formed Mexican Empire (Rodríguez O. 1994: 97–132; 1998: 169–237; 2003; 2005d; Avendaño Rojas 2001: 321–53).

Like América Septentrional, in the Río de la Plata and Chile the military did not dominate politics. Because autonomists in the southern cone gained control early and did not face major opposition from royalist forces, civilians were not forced to relinquish power to military leaders. Although Buenos Aires and Santiago experienced partisan conflicts and civil wars during the early years, the region escaped the brutal campaigns waged in northern South America. The Río de la Plata obtained its autonomy and ultimately its independence in 1816 by default; the Spanish monarchy lacked the resources to mount a campaign to regain control of the area. Similarly, Chile endured only limited combat in the struggle for emancipation and the military forces that liberated the Andean nation in 1818 quickly departed. Large military contingents left Chile to secure the independence of Peru. As a result, civilians dominated the Chilean government.

In northern South America the restoration of the Hispanic constitution provided insurgents favoring independence the opportunity to press their campaign to liberate the continent. They accepted the armistice offered by the Cortes in order to strengthen their forces, confident that the monarchy would not send a new expeditionary army to restore royal order in the region. However, those favoring independence faced resistance because parts of Venezuela and New Granada and Quito, Peru, and Charcas eagerly implemented the restored constitutional system. They elected hundreds of constitutional ayuntamientos, but were unable to elect provincial deputations or deputies to the Cortes in Madrid because before those complex elections could be completed, the insurgents violated the truce and began a military campaign to bring those areas under their control (Rodríguez O. 1998: 192–204; Almer 2005: 365–95).

In 1820 the republicans renewed the struggle to liberate Venezuela and New Granada. The conflict in northern South America enhanced the power of military men. Self-proclaimed generals like Simón Bolívar and former professional soldiers such as José de San Martín gained immense power and prestige as the leaders of the bloody struggles to win independence. Although civilian and clerical institutions – ayuntamientos, courts, parishes, cathedral chapters – continued to function, and although new governments were formed and congresses elected, military power was dominant. Colombia provides the clearest example of that phenomenon.

Convened by Bolívar in February 1819, the Congress of Angostura legitimized his power and in December created the Republic of Colombia, incorporating Venezuela, New Granada, and Quito. Although Venezuela and New Granada possessed some representation at Angostura, Quito had none. Later in 1821, the Congress of Cúcuta, pressured by President Bolívar and intimidated by the army, ratified the formation of the Republic of Colombia, again without any representation from Quito. In contrast to the Hispanic Constitution of 1812, written by a Cortes composed of elected representatives from all parts of the monarchy – which granted considerable autonomy to the regions via the constitutional ayuntamientos and provincial deputations, restricted the power of the king, and bestowed sovereignty on the legislature – the 1821 Colombian constitution created a highly centralized government and granted vast authority to the president.

Bolívar's actions in the Kingdom of Quito demonstrate his willingness to subjugate other independent governments and impose martial law in his drive to consolidate power and expel royalist forces from the continent. The city of Guayaquil declared independence and formed a republican government on October 9, 1820; in the following months, it attempted without success to free the highland provinces of the Kingdom of Quito. Guayaquil subsequently requested help from San Martín and Bolívar in liberating the highlands. A mixed force consisting mainly of local troops, Colombians, and men from San Martín's army, under the command of General Antonio José de Sucre finally defeated the royalist forces in Quito on May 24, 1822, at the Battle of Pinchincha. Bolívar, who arrived from the north in June with more Colombian troops, incorporated the region into the Republic of Colombia despite opposition from both Quito and Guayaquil. Subsequently, Bolívar imposed martial law in the former Kingdom of Quito to impress men as well as to requisition money and supplies for the struggle against the royalists in Peru, the last bastion of royal power in America (Rodríguez O. 2006: 173–86).

The southern forces led by San Martín landed in Lima in August 1820 with a liberating army composed of Chileans and *rioplatenses*. Although he controlled the coast, San Martín could not overcome the royalists in the highlands. In an effort to win the loyalty of the population, the Spanish liberals forced Viceroy Joaquín de la Pezuela to abdicate on January 29, 1821, implemented the constitution of 1812, and named General José de la Serna captain general. The Spanish constitutionalists reorganized the royal army and nearly drove San Martín's forces from the coast. But divisions within the royalist ranks prevented them from defeating the republican forces.

Unable to obtain the support he needed in Peru and abroad, San Martín ceded the honor of final victory to Bolívar. Although the Colombians arrived in force in 1823, they made little progress. Divisions among Peruvians, shortage of supplies, and strong royalist armies kept them pinned down on the coast. However, the royalists also were divided. In Upper Peru the absolutist general Pedro Olañeta opposed La Serna and the Spanish liberals. After the Constitution of Cádiz was again abolished in 1823, General Olañeta took up arms against the liberals on December 25, 1823. This internecine conflict contributed to the royalists' defeat. For nearly a year, while Bolívar and his men recovered, royalist constitutional and absolutist armies waged war against each other in the highlands. Ultimately, General Sucre defeated the royalist constitutional army in the decisive battle of Ayacucho on December 9, 1824. Olañeta's absolutist forces, however, remained in control of Upper Peru. Political intrigue finally settled the struggle. Olañeta was assassinated in April 1825. The death of the absolutist commander marked the end of royal power in Upper Peru. Subsequently, General Sucre formed the new republic of Bolivia in the territory of the former Audiencia of Charcas. By 1826, when the last royalist forces surrendered, Bolívar dominated northern and central South America as president of Colombia, dictator of Peru, and ruler of Bolivia (Anna 1979).

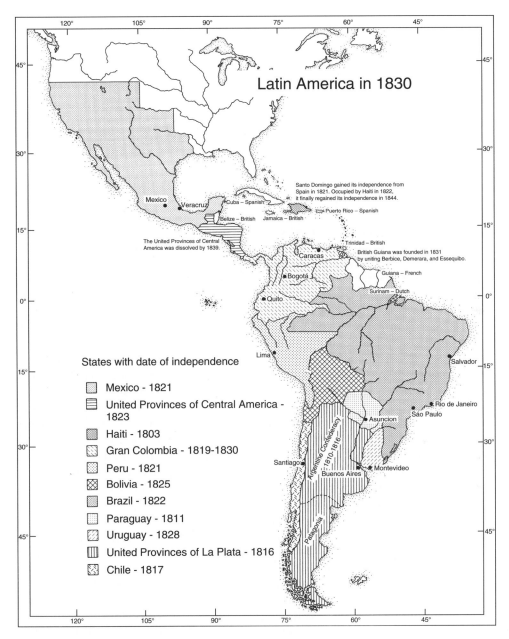

Latin America in 1830

Santo Domingo gained its independence from
Spain in 1821. Occupied by Haiti in 1822,
it finally regained its independence in 1844.

Mexico
Veracruz
Cuba – Spanish
Puerto Rico – Spanish
Belize – British
Jamaica – British

The United Provinces of Central
America was dissolved by 1839.

Trinidad – British

British Guiana was founded in 1831
by uniting Berbice, Demerara, and Essequibo.

Caracas
Guiana – French
Bogotá
Surinam – Dutch
Quito

Lima

Salvador

States with date of independence

Rio de Janeiro
São Paulo
Asuncion

Mexico - 1821

United Provinces of Central America -
1823

Haiti - 1803

Gran Colombia - 1819-1830

Peru - 1821

Bolivia - 1825

Brazil - 1822

Paraguay - 1811

Uruguay - 1828

United Provinces of La Plata - 1816

Chile - 1817

Santiago
Argentine Confederacy 1810-1816
Buenos Aires
Montevideo
Patagonia

Map 6 Latin America in 1830
Source: Cathryn L. Lombardi, John V. Lombardi, and K. Lynn Stoner, *Latin American History: A Teaching Atlas* (Madison, WI: University of Wisconsin Press, 1983). © 1983. Reprinted by permission of The University of Wisconsin Press.

Conclusion

Spanish American political leaders faced two fundamental questions during the early nineteenth century: determining the territory of the nation and selecting the best form of government. Although some subordinate audiencias, such as Charcas and Quito, claimed the right to govern by forming juntas in 1809, many Americans considered the *virreinatos* synonymous with the nation. The capital cities of the viceroyalties, Mexico, Santa Fe de Bogotá, Lima, and Buenos Aires, assumed that they would become the centers of the new countries. Several, most notably Buenos Aires, relied on force to impose their will on the emerging nation. Similarly, although a few leaders spoke of forming a republic, most Spanish Americans, including the large indigenous peasantry in the *república indios*, favored a constitutional monarchy. In addition, most civilians preferred legislative dominance as established by the Constitution of Cádiz and many of the American charters, while military men, such as Bolívar, insisted upon executive dominance.

América Septentrional and *América Meridional* (South America) lived through profoundly different experiences during the years 1810–25. While the Americans in the north participated fully in the political transformation of the Hispanic world, those in the south generally did not. Only the South American areas under royalist control during the two Hispanic constitutional periods (1810–14 and 1820–3) – Quito, Peru, Charcas, and parts of Venezuela and Nueva Granada – held constitutional elections for the Cortes and established provincial deputations and constitutional ayuntamientos. The other regions of South America, those controlled by the autonomists – Río de la Plata and Chile as well as large parts of Venezuela and Nueva Granada – did not share that constitutional experience. While the Hispanic Cortes had introduced popular elections, the autonomists had restricted representation to those men with property and who were literate. Living as they did in a multiethnic society, the leaders of South America sought to form oligarchic regimes, believing it the best way to maintain order. Unlike the Hispanic Constitution of 1812, which defined all men, regardless of race or class, as Spaniards and granted the franchise without property or literacy qualifications to all free men who were not of African ancestry, most South American governments imposed literacy and property qualifications and divided their people into active and passive citizens (Rocafuerte 1971: 419–84). In addition, the South American autonomists failed to resolve the tensions between the capital cities, which insisted upon centralism – a strong national government – and the provinces, which favored confederalism. The two halves of America also followed different paths to emancipation. While the elites of América Septentrional gained independence through a political compromise in which civil and military officials changed sides and supported the decision to separate from Spain, the *independistas* of northern and central América Meridional fought prolonged and bloody wars to defeat the royal authorities. Two pincer movements, one from the south and the other from the north, eventually converged on Peru and Upper Peru, ending Spanish rule in 1826.

By 1826 the overseas possessions of the Spanish monarchy, one of the world's most imposing political structures at the end of the eighteenth century, consisted only of Cuba, Puerto Rico, the Philippines, and a few other Pacific islands. Having achieved independence, the countries of the American continent would henceforth chart their own futures. Most, however, entered a prolonged period of economic decline and political instability. Military strongmen – caudillos but not institutional militarists – dominated many nations, whose shattered institutions no longer functioned. The stable, more developed, and stronger countries of the North Atlantic, such as Britain, France, and the United States, flooded Spanish America with their exports, dominated their credit, and sometimes imposed their will upon the new American nations by force of arms.

As a result of the great political revolution that led to the dissolution of the Spanish monarchy, Spain and the new nations of Spanish America developed a unique political culture based not on foreign models but on their own traditions and experience. After independence in America and after Fernando VII's death in the Peninsula, the old absolute monarchy disappeared. The people of the Spanish-speaking world ceased to be subjects of the Crown and became citizens of their nations. During the nineteenth century, the new political systems of Spain and Spanish America were consolidated on the basis of the liberal traditions that had emerged in the Cortes of Cádiz and its rival regimes in America. Despite power struggles, such as those between monarchists and republicans, centralists and federalists, and parliamentarians and caudillos, a liberal representative, constitutional government remained the political ideal of the Spanish-speaking nations. Indeed, even caudillos and dictators were forced to acknowledge, at least in principle, the supremacy of the rule of law and the ultimate desirability of civilian, representative, constitutional government. That tradition, together with the achievement of nationhood, remains the most significant heritage of Spanish American independence.[2]

NOTE

1 According to Miguel Artola (1959: I, 104), "only 104 [deputies] signed the acta of inauguration. The Constitution contains 184 signatures and the acta ending [the term] of the [General and Extraordinary] Cortes on September 14, 1813, includes 223 names."

BIBLIOGRAPHY

Alamán, L. (1985) *Historia de Méjico desde los primeros movimientos que prepararon su independencia en el año de 1808 hasta la época presente*, 5 vols. Fondo de Cultura Económica, Mexico City.

Almer, C. (2005) " 'La confianza que han puesto en mi': La participación local en el establecimiento de los Ayuntamientos Constitucionales en Venezuela, 1820–1821." In J. Rodríguez O. (ed.), *Revolución, independencia y las Nuevas Naciones*. Fundación MAPFRE-Tavera, Madrid.

Anna, T. (1979) *The Fall of the Royal Government in Peru*. University of Nebraska Press, Lincoln.

Artola, M. (1959) *Los orígenes de la España contemporánea*, 2 vols. Instituto de Estudios Políticos, Madrid.

Artola, M. (1968) *La España de Fernando VII*. Espasa-Calpe, Madrid.

Avendaño, X. (1995) "Procesos electorales y clase política en la Federación de Centroamérica (1810–1840)." PhD thesis, El Colegio de México, Mexico City.

Avendaño Rojas, X. (2001) "El gobierno provincial en el Reino de Guatemala, 1821–1823." In V. Guedea (ed.), *La independencia de México y el proceso autonomista novohispano, 1808–1824.* UNAM & Instituto Mora, Mexico City.

Bayle, C. (1952) *Los cabildos seculares en la América española.* Sapientia, Madrid.

Benson, N. L. (1946) "The Contested Mexican Election of 1812," *Hispanic American Historical Review,* 23:3 August.

Benson, N. L. (2004) "The Elections of 1809: Transforming Political Culture in New Spain," *Mexican Studies/Estudios Mexicanos,* 20:1 Winter.

Bolívar, S. (1939) "Memoria dirigida a los ciudadanos de Nueva Granada por un caraqueño," in *Proclamas y discursos del Libertador.* Litografía del Comercio, Caracas.

Bolívar, S. (1977) "Carta de Jamaica." In J. L. Robero & L. A. Romero (comp.), *Pensamiento político de la emancipación, 1790–1825,* 2 vols. Biblioteca de Ayacucho, Caracas.

Burgin, M. (1940) *The Economic Aspects of Argentine Federalism.* Harvard University Press, Cambridge, MA.

Chust, M. (1999) *La cuestión nacional Americana en las Cortes de Cádiz.* Fundación Historia Social & UNAM, Valencia & México City.

Destua Pimentel, C. (1965) *Las intendencias en el Perú, 1790–1796.* Seville.

Dym, J. (2005) "La soberanía de los pueblos: Ciudad e independencia en Centroamérica, 1808–1823." In J. Rodríguez O. (ed.), *Revolución, independencia y las Nuevas Naciones.* Fundación MAPFRE-Tavera, Madrid.

Escobar Ohmstede, A. (1996) "Del gobierno indígena al Ayuntamiento constitucional en las huastecas hidalguense y veracruzana, 1780–1853," *Mexican Studies/Estudios Mexicanos,* 12:1 Winter.

Fisher, J. (1970) *Government and Society in Colonial Peru: The Intendant System, 1784–1814.* Athlone Press, London.

Gómez Hoyos,R. (1992) *La independencia de Colombia.* Editorial Mapfre.

Gómez Vizuete, A. (1990) "Los primeros ayuntamientos liberales en Puerto Rico, 1812–1814 y 1820–1823," *Anuario de estudios americanos,* 47.

González, J. (1937–8) *Filiación histórica del gobierno representativo argentino,* 2 vols. Editorial la Vanguardia, Buenos Aires.

Guardino, P. (2000) " 'Toda libertad para emitir sus votos': Plebeyos, campesinos, y elecciones en Oaxaca, 1808–1850," *Cuadernos del Sur,* 6:15 June.

Guedea, V. (1991) "Los procesos electorales insurgentes," *Estudios de historia novohispana,* 11.

Guedea, V. (1992) *En busca de un gobierno alterno: Los Guadalupes de México.* UNAM, Mexico City.

Guedea, V. (1997) "The First Popular Elections in Mexico City, 1812–1813." In J. Rodríguez O. (ed.), *The Origins of Mexican National Politics, 1808–1847.* SR Books, Wilmington, DE.

Guerra, F-X. (1992) *Modernidad e independencias: Ensayos sobre las revoluciones hispánicas.* Editorial MAPFRE, Madrid.

Guerra, F-X. (1999) "El soberano y su reino: Reflexiones sobre la génesis del ciudadano en América Latina." In H. Sabato (ed.), *Ciudadanía política y formación de las naciones: Perspectivas históricas de América Latina.* Fondo de Cultura Económica, Mexico City.

Hamill, H. (1966) *The Hidalgo Revolt: Prelude to Mexican Independence.* University of Florida Press, Gainesville.

Kamen, H. (2003) *Empire: How Spain Became a World Power, 1492–1763.* HarperCollins Publishers, New York.

Lynch, J. (1958) *Spanish Colonial Administration, 1782–1810: The Intendant System in the Viceroyalty of the Río de la Plata.* Athlone Press, London.

Macías, A. (1973) *Génesis del gobierno constitucional en México, 1808–1820.* Secretaría de Educación Pública, Mexico City.

McKinley, P. M. (1996) *Pre-Revolutionary Caracas: Politics, Economy, and Society 1777–1811*. Cambridge University Press, Cambridge.

Merriman, R. (1918–34) *The Rise of the Spanish Empire in the Old World and the New*, 4 vols. Macmillan, New York.

Miranda, J. (1978) *Las ideas y las instituciones políticas mexicanas*. Universidad Nacional Autónoma de México, México City.

Moore, J. P. (1966) *The Cabildo in Peru under the Bourbons*. Duke University Press, Durham.

Narancio, E. (1992) *La independencia de Uruguay*. Editorial Mapfre, Madrid.

Peralta Ruíz, V. (2001) *En defensa de la autoridad: Política y cultura bajo el gobierno del virrey Abascal. Perú, 1806–1816*. Consejo Superior de Investigaciones Científicas, Madrid.

Pietschmann, H. (1996) *Las reformas borbónicas y el sistema de intendentes en Nueva España*. Fondo de Cultura Económica, Mexico City.

Pompa y Guerra, M. A. (1986) *Constituciones de Colombia*, 3 vols. Biblioteca Banco Popular, Bogotá.

Rees Jones, R. (1979) *El despotismo ilustrado y los intendentes de la Nueva España*. UNAM, Mexico City.

Restrepo, J. M. (1858) *Historia de la Revolución de la República de Colombia*, 4 vols. Imprenta de José Jacquin, Bensazon.

Rocafuerte, V (1971) "Examen analítico de la constituciones formadas en Hispano-América," *Revista de historia de América*, 72 July–December.

Rodríguez O., J. E. (1994) "The Transition from Colony to Nation: New Spain, 1820–1821." In Jaime E. Rodríguez (ed.), *Mexico in the Age of Democratic Revolutions, 1750–1850*. Lynne Reiner Publications, Boulder.

Rodríguez O., J. E. (1998) *The Independence of Spanish America*. Cambridge University Press, Cambridge.

Rodríguez O., J. E. (1999) "Las primeras elecciones constitucionales en el Reino de Quito, 1809–1814 y 1821–1822," *Procesos: Revista ecuatoriana de historia*, 14.

Rodríguez O., J. E. (2003) *"Rey, religión, independencia y union:" El proceso político de la independencia de Guadalajara*. Instituto Mora, Mexico City.

Rodríguez O., J. E. (2005a) "Ciudadanos de la Nación Española: Los indígenas y la elecciones constitucionales en el Reino de Quito." In M. Irurozqui Victoriano (ed.), *La mirada esquiva: Reflexiones históricas sobre la interacción del Estado y la ciudadanía en los Andes (Bolivia, Ecuador y Perú), Siglo XIX*. Consejo Superior de Investigaciones Científicas, Madrid.

Rodríguez O., J. E. (2005b), "La Antigua provincia de Guayaquil en la época de la independencia, 1809–1820." In J. Rodríguez O. (ed.), *Revolución, independencia y las Nuevas Naciones*. Fundación MAPFRE-Tavera, Madrid.

Rodríguez O., J. E. (2005c) "La naturaleza de la representación en la Nueva España y México," *Secuencia: Revista de historia y ciencias sociales*, 61:6 January–April, pp. 6–32.

Rodríguez O., J. E. (2005d) "'*Ningún pueblo es superior a otro*": Oaxaca and Mexican Federalism." In J. Rodríguez O. (ed.), *The Divine Charter: Constitutionalism and Liberalism in Nineteenth-Century Mexico*. Rowan & Littlefield, Boulder.

Rodríguez O., J. E. (2006) *La revolución política en la época de la independencia: El Reino de Quito, 1808–1822*. Corporación Editora Nacional, Quito.

Rugeley, T. (1996) *Yucatán's Maya Peasantry and the Origins of the Caste War*. University of Texas Press, Austin.

Siles Salinas, J. (1992) *La independencia de Bolivia*. Editorial Mapfre, Madrid.

Stoan, S. (1974) *Pablo Morillo and Venezuela, 1815–1820*. Ohio State University Press, Columbus.

Street, J. (1959) *Artigas and the Emancipation of Uruguay*. Cambridge University Press, Cambridge.

Suanzes-Carpegna, J. V. (1983) *La teoría del Estado en los orígenes del constitucionalismo hispánico (Las Cortes de Cádiz)*. Centro de Estudios Constitucionales, Madrid.

Valencia Llano, A. (1992) "Elites, burocracia, clero y sectores populares en la Independencia quiteña (1809–1812)," *Procesos: Revista ecuatoriana de historia*, 3, II semester.

Varela, L. (1910) *Historia constitucional de la República de Argentina*, 4 vols. Taller de Impresiones Oficiales, Buenos Aires.

White, R. A. (1978) *Paraguay's Autonomous Revolution, 1810–1840*. University of New Mexico Press, Albuquerque.

Chapter Thirteen

New Nations and New Citizens: Political Culture in Nineteenth-century Mexico, Peru, and Argentina

Sarah C. Chambers

In 1833, the official newspaper of Arequipa, Peru, celebrated the large turnout for the first rounds of congressional elections: "We have witnessed the council chambers full of citizens casting their votes: and their patriotic enthusiasm on this occasion is worthy of imitation and praise." Within two months, the people would once again fill the streets to celebrate the decision of the electoral college and then defend their right to gather from attacks by the police. When conservative President Agustín de Gamarra refused to recognize the selection of liberal rival José Luís Orbegoso as his successor, Arequipa was at the forefront of a rebellion to defend the constitutional process. "The barracks became crowded," reported *El Republicano*, "and by some kind of magic spell, the people who have viewed military enlistments with horror, were transformed into a town of soldiers." In gratitude, Orbegoso dubbed Arequipa "The Department of the Law" (Chambers 1999: 224–7).

Readers may be surprised to see an electoral scene open a chapter on politics in nineteenth-century Spanish America. *Caudillos*, military leaders turned governors or presidents, are usually the leading characters in such histories. Political instability, moreover, was a hallmark of early national Spanish America; for example, between 1833 and 1855 the presidency changed 30 times in Mexico, for an average term of less than eight months. Nonetheless, without idealizing the early republics of Spanish America as democracies nor whitewashing the caudillos, we can still take seriously the politics of the era as contests of ideas rather than merely conflicts of personality. A revisionist literature on caudillos depicts them as leaders who represented particular ideologies, appealed to public opinion, and attempted to legitimize their governments through constitutions and elections. And an increasing number of studies are uncovering extensive popular participation in these political processes. This chapter argues that the political cultures of these emerging nations were forged in the three interrelated arenas apparent in the opening scene: electoral campaigns, battlefields, and the courts. Indeed, it was at least partly the very opening of the political system to broad participation and the intensity of the resulting partisan competition that led first to the rise of caudillos and then to increasingly restrictive constitutional regimes in an effort by elites to reestablish order.

Drawing upon recent works about political culture in the new nations, this chapter is written to be a concise consideration of key themes and trends, not a comprehensive narrative of changing regimes. Examples will be drawn from Mexico, Peru, and Argentina; the first two nations emerged from the cores of long-established colonial viceroyalties, whereas Buenos Aires had been designated as a viceregal capital only in the eighteenth century. These countries allow a comparative discussion of common issues – popular participation in elections and military conflict as part of state building – along with a consideration of regional differences. In order to cover approximately 60 years of history, this essay will emphasize different elements of the main theme for each case study: the relatively successful bridge between peasant communities and national politicians in Mexico, the more thorough incorporation of urban workers as compared to rural indigenous peoples into Peruvian politics, and the penetration of politics into everyday life and popular culture in the case of Argentina. These emphases and the choice of particular examples to illustrate them in some depth necessarily simplify more diverse historical experiences. The reader is encouraged to consult works in the bibliography in order to explore some of those complexities.

Military and political leaders attempting to establish stable nation-states would confront at least two major challenges in securing sovereignty over national boundaries and in defining the membership in the new body politic. First, local political communities throughout Spanish America were strong and, having contested colonial authority emanating from Madrid, were not eager to concede much power to new national capitals (Anna 1998). Indigenous villages were prepared to recognize their membership in a larger nation, for example, but claimed a high degree of communal governance. Moreover, the borders of all three nations serving as our case studies shrank between independence and the end of the nineteenth century, owing to both secessions and expansionist neighboring states. Second, the collapse of the Spanish monarchy and the disruption posed by the lengthy wars of independence created a power vacuum in which rival elites courted popular support. In return for their support at both the polls and on the battlefield, the racially diverse rural and urban poor pressed claims for their rights as citizens.

The first prominent national historians were participants in the politics of the period and most identified regionalism and mass mobilization as obstacles to nation-state formation. As their heirs, we still tend to see loyalties to local communities as rooted in the colonial, corporate organization of the Spanish empire and their persistence as a sign of Spanish America's incomplete transition to political modernity. François-Xavier Guerra (1992), in particular, insightfully explored the gradual transformation of citizenship, sovereignty, and nation during this transitional period. But he and other scholars (Annino and Guerra 2003) have tended to identify a small, enlightened elite as a minority embracing modern political ideals in societies where colonial identities and hierarchies persisted well into the nineteenth century. This chapter attempts to nuance that perspective by highlighting the ways in which non-elites negotiated their place in the new republics. Although destabilizing, raucous election campaigns and military revolts were also schools of citizenship, and calls for a degree of local governance were not necessarily incompatible with emerging national identities. Finally, the chapter will expand the boundaries of political culture to consider how politics informed everyday life and how the actions of those excluded from the franchise or military service nevertheless influenced the contours of the emerging nation-states.

Mexico

Of our case studies, Mexico was the scene of the earliest explosions of electoral activity. Indeed, elections in many regions of Mexico began before independence with the implementation of the 1812 Spanish constitution, which many historians regard as the origin of modern politics. This constitution, passed by liberal deputies of the parliament (*Cortes*) in Cádiz while the Spanish king was a captive of Napoleon, had a lasting impact on Spanish American political culture by enfranchising most of the adult male population (including those of indigenous though not African descent) and establishing elected bodies at various levels from the imperial parliament to all towns of at least 1,000 inhabitants. The first independent government in Mexico preserved much of the framework of the 1812 Spanish constitution, but further extended suffrage by eliminating all racial limitations on citizenship. In the city of Oaxaca, those who had been turned away from the polls in 1820 on the grounds of their dark skin returned in 1821 to elect four mixed-race councilmen of humble social origin (Guardino 2005). Mass participation in elections continued throughout the decade; in Mexico City voter turnout reached as high as 70 percent. Competing political philosophies were represented by rival Masonic lodges; the *yorkinos* (York rite) called for federalism, broadly inclusive citizenship, a reduction in the army and the expulsion of Spaniards, while the *escoses* (Scots' rite) advocated a more centralist system with limits on suffrage and a more gradual approach to introducing liberal reforms. Competing dates for independence day also reflected rival political philosophies: celebrating Father Hidalgo's cry for freedom and justice on September 16, 1810, revived the memory of the massive peasant uprising, while marking Agustín de Iturbide's declaration of independence on September 27, 1821 symbolized orderly governance by the respectable classes (Warren 2001).

Mass mobilization and electoral campaigning through the partisan press peaked in the 1828 presidential elections, which pitted the mixed-race independence hero and populist Vicente Guerrero against Manuel Gómez Pedraza, a former royalist officer who, like Iturbide, had thrown his support to independence only after a decade spent repressing the peasant rebellion led by Hidalgo and Morelos. Newspapers, which had proliferated after independence with the lifting of censorship, were filled with partisan attacks on each candidate: Guerrero was depicted as leading mobs of the unwashed and non-white, while Gómez Pedraza was accused of colluding with Spaniards who still hoped to return to power. When national returns indicated a narrow victory for Gómez Pedraza, yorkinos protested fraud, and General Antonio López de Santa Anna led a rebellion that placed Guerrero in the presidency. But it would be a pyrrhic victory. The growing concerns of not just conservatives but also moderate liberals over the consequences of enfranchising the masses were confirmed when a crowd of several thousand rioters celebrated the capitulation of Gómez Pedraza by looting the shops of the wealthy merchants in the Parián market of Mexico City. Within a year, another revolt drove Guerrero from office, and the new government began to restrict suffrage, first by prohibiting the distribution of pre-printed ballots in 1830 and then by imposing income requirements in the centralist 1836 constitution that prevented manual laborers from voting.

The events of 1828 in Mexico set the stage for the country's political culture for the ensuing decades: issues, as well as forceful personalities, mobilized not only elites but a large cross-section of the population, but it would be difficult to limit debates to election campaigns and congressional deliberations. What Will Fowler (1998) calls the era of hope (the first federal republic) gave way to despair by 1853, as Mexicans fought among themselves and lost half of their national territory to the expansionist United States. This period has been depicted as the age of the caudillos, symbolized by the repeated revolts and rule of Santa Anna. Some historians have attributed his success primarily to personality and patronage (Lynch 1992; Costeloe 1993). From a base of support in his home territory of Veracruz, he increasingly built a national clientele, rewarding his followers and reaching out to key sectors of the economic elite. His heroism in battles, especially against foreign invaders, maintained his popu-larity among the masses; the erection of a mausoleum to his leg blown off by a cannon seems the embodiment of a cult of personality. But Santa Anna did not ignore the power of political ideas. Fowler (1996) points out that he saw the need to legitimize his power by courting the support of representative bodies, such as town councils, and calling elections to ratify changes in regimes. Santa Anna worked with civilian politicians to elaborate an ideology that blended elements traditionally seen as either conservative or liberal, but which increasingly appealed to a broad concern among political elites for order. In this period, military might may have determined who held the presidency, but revolts were always accompanied by a *pronunciamiento*, a statement of political principles, to gain support.

While Santa Anna and centralist politicians were building a more conservative and centralized regime in Mexico City, peasants throughout Mexico kept federalism alive as small villages asserted their independence from larger "head towns" as well as Mexico City (Guardino 1996; Rugeley 1996; Ducey 2004). Rival candidates com-peted for municipal office, and those who emerged victorious served as key interme-diaries to broader political and military movements. Such village leaders repeatedly demanded local control of taxation and revenue. In southern Mexico peasant leaders allied with Juan Alvarez, who inherited the mantle of Guerrero in the region that came to carry his name. Although Alvarez acted as a good patron to peasants and served as their intermediary with the central state, their collaboration was primarily based upon a shared political ideology advocating local governance both at the state and municipal levels, broad suffrage, and low taxation. Although the centralist con-stitution of 1836 gave state prefects the authority to appoint local justices of the peace, most in the Guerrero region yielded to pressures to ratify those chosen by communities. These peasant leaders then justified exactions on wealthy landowners and organization of labor for public works in the "name of the Government." At the national level, peasants extended their commitments beyond their villages to support federalist efforts to restore the 1824 constitution and resist the US invasion of Mexico. Although such efforts failed, the government of the newly formed state of Guerrero in 1849 recognized and rewarded the contributions of peasant citizens by lowering taxes, increasing the number of elected municipalities, and broadening the franchise to include even day laborers (Guardino 1996).

[The successful alliance between peasants and political–military leaders in Guerrero resulted in a program of popular federalism. In other regions, such the Yucatán and the eastern region known as the Huasteca, unfulfilled demands from below erupted into violent insurrection. Elites of the period labeled these revolts "caste wars" in an attempt to depict them as atavistic outbursts by isolated indigenous communities largely unchanged since the colonial period. Many historians have emphasized economic grievances, especially the loss of communal lands, as the key trigger. Revisionist studies, however, have demonstrated that rebellious villagers were acting out of raised expectations from the introduction of constitutionalism and were engaging the specific political debates of the early national period (Rugeley 1996; Ducey 2004). In any case, conservative politicians in Mexico City regarded both populist alliances and full-scale rebellions as a threat to national stability and unity, especially when combined with the loss of territory in the war with the United States. An effort by Santa Anna and his conservative allies to repress local movements by abolishing elected town councils backfired, however, by provoking the Revolution of Ayutla (1854–5) and the War of the Reform (1858–61). These revolts brought to power free-market liberals, most notably Benito Juárez. Although remembered as Mexico's first Indian president, Juárez defended individual property rights and rejected demands from the provinces for a decentralization of power and redistribution of land. But liberals owed their victory in great part to local peasant militias and regional leaders like Alvarez, so their 1857 constitution ratified key principles – such as universal suffrage and equality before the law – that kept alive, if not fully implementing, aspirations for local popular sovereignty.

Peasant understandings of their place as citizens, rooted in negotiations over power within communities, developed further through their participation in National Guard units, an experience that bridged local and national politics. The Atlantic tradition of constitutional republicanism, upon which Mexican liberals drew, emphasized military service as a key duty of all citizens (that is, self-supporting male heads of households). Popular nationalism intensified during the war against a French invasion which installed the Hapsburg Archduke Ferdinand Maximilian as Emperor of Mexico (1862–7). In the course of their struggles against the French and their Mexican collaborators, national guardsmen came to see themselves as defenders of the nation as well as of their families and communities, and, once victorious, demanded that military service be rewarded in both collective and individual terms. Although peasants recognized that within a liberal framework property ownership would be private, they demanded that beneficiaries of land grants be loyal and productive members of local communities. The aspiration that their children have access to education similarly reflected liberal ideals but, articulated as village requests for schools, also reinforced communal identities. Finally, national guardsmen claimed that they had fought not to condone a military route to controlling the state, but in defense of their constitutional right to elect their government representatives (Mallon 1995).

Such demands put militia units from the highland region of Puebla in conflict with Juárez's efforts to consolidate central executive authority after the war. In the 1868 elections for the governorship of Puebla, no candidate won a majority but war hero and populist liberal Juan Nepomuceno Méndez came close with 48.5 percent of the vote. The state legislature, however, chose Rafael García, Juárez's handpicked provisional governor, even though he had received only 18 percent of the popular vote.

Petitions from many municipalities protested the manipulative procedure as a violation of the freedom and political guarantees that they had won, in the words of the municipal secretary of Zacatlán, "through the sacrifice of their own blood." When Juárez sent the federal army to Puebla to disarm the militias, many soldiers refused. One national guard unit collectively issued their response that, "understanding it to be their duty to conserve their honor, their glory, their dignity as Citizen-soldiers . . . in honor of their compatriots who were sacrificed while defending republican institutions, they declare: that it is their entirely free will to keep in their possession the weapons they carry" (Mallon 1995: 100–14). The peasant citizen–soldiers lost this particular confrontation with the national state, but their clear articulation of rights resonated with many poor Mexicans and similar political demands would periodically resurface into the next century. In the medium term, Juárez's opposition to Méndez and his supporters rebounded to the benefit of the revolt launched by Porfirio Díaz in 1876. Although by 1910 Díaz symbolized the epitome of authoritarianism, he came to power by claiming to defend the 1857 constitution. Speaking the language of popular liberalism, he successfully mobilized peasant national guard units, many of which had fought under him during the French intervention, and for at least the first years of his rule he honored many claims made on him by those veteran citizens (McNamara 2007).

Peru

Peruvian military and political leaders, like their Mexican counterparts, needed at least moderate levels of popular support, and in exchange indigenous and *mestizo* peasants also asserted the right to govern their own communities. In distinction to Mexico, however, neither elites nor peasants had mobilized as widely in favor of independence and into the early national period both the levels of popular participation and the likelihood that demands from below would be met by the state were lower (Mallon 1995; Thurner 1997; Forment 2003). Peru did not have a political system as federalist as that established by the Mexican constitution of 1824, nor did voter turnout reach comparable levels. Indeed, it appears that in the initial decades after independence, indigenous communities benefited more from benign neglect than state recognition. The Peruvian government continued to rely upon the colonial indigenous head tax for revenue, and although Simón Bolívar had officially decreed the division of communal lands into individual, alienable plots during independence, it was not widely implemented. Therefore, the state implicitly recognized indigenous communities as separate, corporate bodies, even if the constitutions declared Indians to be equal to other Peruvians.

During the first decade after independence, Peru was governed by three constitutions (1823, 1826, and 1828) and few heads of state were in power for more than a year. The 1828 constitution allowed for relatively wide suffrage and decentralized some government functions to elected commissions at the regional level. But the first president to serve a full term, General Agustín de Gamarra (1829–33), came to power after overthrowing his short-lived liberal predecessor José de la Mar. Like Santa Anna, Gamarra was both a caudillo, with a strong regional base of power in his native Cuzco, and a politician who represented the interests of conservatives throughout Peru

(Walker 1999). His championing of economic protectionism served the interests of textile producers in Cuzco and northern landowners who were concerned about having to compete with the sudden flood of European imports. In political terms, Gamarra supported the formation of a centralized and authoritarian state, promoting military officers whom he could count upon as firm allies and appointing subprefects to represent state interests and collect taxes in rural areas. Although Gamarra's home base in Cuzco was surrounded by a predominantly indigenous population, and he appealed in speeches to its glorious Inca past, he did not forge effective alliances with communities as Alvarez did in Mexico. Because a regional economic depression had allowed Indians to hold onto their land in exchange for paying the head tax, there was little Gamarra could offer as an incentive for their political support. Rather than organize local militias, he conscripted Indians into his armies, and Gamarra's defeat by Orbegoso and Bolivian ally Andrés de Santa Cruz in 1835 can be attributed to the soldiers' lack of enthusiasm for the cause and tendency to desert. Orbegoso and Santa Cruz joined the two countries in a confederation until 1839 when Gamarra, with aid from Chile (whose leaders were leery of the potential expansionist aims of a united Bolivia and Peru), managed to overthrow the confederation and serve as president again until 1841. Centralism and executive power were enshrined in the conservative constitution of 1839 that abolished all representative bodies below the national level; hence there were fewer opportunities for peasants to mobilize around elections.

Although there has not been as much research on peasant politics in this period for Peru as for Mexico, studies suggest that the level of mobilization varied significantly by region and that liberal caudillos may have been more effective than Gamarra at garnering support. In the Huanta region of Ayacucho, for example, peasants launched a royalist rebellion immediately after independence (Méndez 2005). Though acting ostensibly in the name of the king, the local government established by the rebels broke with many colonial precedents by abolishing racial caste distinctions and defending the economic interests of small producers. As in the Mexican state of Guerrero, humble farmers and muleteers (identified by outsiders though not themselves as Indians) exercised effective control including collection of tithes and the administration of justice. Although their power was based in military might, they were concerned with legitimating their authority with the vote of communities. Not long after the rebellion was repressed, Orbegoso and Santa Cruz mobilized peasant support in the region. Recognizing local leaders as "citizens so fond of their *Patria's* [fatherland's] happiness" (rather than barbarous Indians and royalists), these liberals called upon them to oppose Gamarra as an unlawful enemy of the republic. In exchange for their support, the Huantinos held these national leaders to their promised "rewards which the Patria grants to those who render it distinguished service," by refusing to pay tribute and again seizing control of local tithes (Méndez 2005: 195–6).

Peruvian peasants, like their Mexican counterparts, were attentive to national politics and adopted the language of republicanism. Nonetheless, owing to a combination of factors – the continuation of a legally distinct status for Indians, the lack of federalism, and possibly greater racial antagonism stemming from late colonial indigenous rebellions – they were not effectively incorporated in significant numbers into national projects during the nineteenth century (Mallon 1995). Urban populations, however,

offered more fertile ground for cross-class political alliances, as suggested by the
anecdote that opened this chapter. In capital cities, such as Lima, artisan guilds initially tended to support politicians who advocated protectionism, but in provincial
cities like Arequipa, guilds were organizationally weak and journeymen might be
attracted by liberal platforms that promoted job creation through economic development and called for the protection of civil as well as economic liberties. José Gregorio
Paz Soldán, for example, opposed the forced conscription of those identified as
vagrants on the grounds that "society does not have the right to obligate a man to
work more time than is necessary to earn his daily bread" (Chambers 1999: 234).
That Paz Soldán entered national politics after serving as a lawyer, judge, and prosecutor in Arequipa is particularly important, because it was in the courts that
members of the lower classes were negotiating their civil rights as citizens in the
new nation.

Elites in Arequipa, like their counterparts throughout Spanish America, had been
alarmed by the potential for popular unrest in the wake of independence and criminal
prosecutions increased dramatically. But defendants and their lawyers appealed to the
language of the constitutions, which were read aloud in the public squares as part of
their ratification, to protest arbitrary arrests. For example, the early constitutions
guaranteed "the good opinion, or reputation of the individual, as long as he is not
declared a delinquent according to the laws." Victoriano Concha, arrested in 1829
on suspicion of being a thief, was among those defendants released when even the
prosecutor acknowledged that the evidence was insufficient "to have persecuted a
man damaging him in his person and honor." Even more defamatory was corporal
punishment; Paz Soldán argued in one case that "with the lashes given to a citizen
all the principles were trampled, the entire public was insulted in [the body of] one
man, the Government, the Constitution and the dignity of the Republic were
violated." The recognition of common men as citizens whose civil rights deserved
protection indicates the impact of workingmen pressuring the state to live up to the
ideals of republicanism. In turn, the authorities demanded that these men fulfill their
duties as citizens by conducting themselves as respectable, hardworking heads of
households. When Enrique Nuñes complained that he had been illegally imprisoned,
the judge countered that he was a "vagrant, ne'er-do-well without an occupation,
and therefore, not a citizen." The constitutions also excluded slaves (prior to abolition in 1854), dependent laborers such as servants, and all women. Indeed working
women neither met increasingly strict criteria for respectability which required them
to remain within the domestic sphere, nor could they, like men, use evidence of their
labor or service to armies to win release from jail or reduced sentences. Instead, the
state prosecutor urged the prefect to take stern measures against "women, who
abandoning modesty, social considerations, and family obligations, have the impu-
dence to present themselves in public as prostituted persons" (Chambers 1999:
182–3, 194, 208–9).

By 1850, during a highly contested presidential campaign, workingmen had
learned to articulate their rights as citizens based upon their fulfillment of the corresponding duties. Most Arequipeños favored liberal Manuel Ignacio Vivanco, but the
supporters of José Rufino Echenique competed actively for votes. The parties used
taverns as their bases of operation from whence they sallied forth to skirmish in
the streets with their political rivals. Among those arrested after a particularly

heated melee were a shoemaker and tailor who indignantly claimed their innocence and protested an order that they be conscripted: "if the Police are authorized to increase their forces, they should do it with vagrants, and not with honorable and married artisans . . . unless it could be considered a crime to have manifested our opinion as free citizens in favor of the candidacy of General Vivanco" (Chambers 1999: 215). Although Echenique won the national vote, by 1854 his administration had been discredited by charges of corruption and General Ramón Castilla, with the support of southern regions such as Arequipa, launched a revolution against his presidency. Like Juárez in Mexico, Castilla successfully forged a coalition between liberals and conservatives whose interest in both order and economic progress increasingly coincided. His administration from 1855 to 1862 provided the first sustained period of political stability in Peru, and with ample state revenues from global sales of the country's bird *guano* fertilizer, he began to build a stronger state infrastructure. A short-lived liberal constitution in 1856 reestablished representative government at the state and local levels under a system of direct elections and universal male suffrage. The 1860 constitution, which endured into the early twentieth century, repealed the more radical of these provisions but did not return to the extremely centralist and authoritarian provisions of Gamarra's 1839 constitution.

The foundation for a liberal state laid by Castilla was built upon by Manuel Pardo, founder of the "Civilist" political party and elected in 1872 as Peru's first civilian president. Pardo, an entrepreneur and economist, called for economic diversification and the construction of railroads to integrate the national market. Although his administration represented the interests of Peru's emerging bourgeoisie, the Civilist party was committed to political as well as economic liberalism. By this time, artisans in Lima had begun to organize themselves in broad mutual aid associations, rather than craft-specific guilds, and to publish newspapers in an attempt to influence public opinion. By basing their identity as citizens based upon a work ethic, they echoed elite liberalism and distanced themselves from poorer urban workers. But artisan spokesmen also articulated an assertive language of political rights and contrasted their civic virtue with the lazy vices of the sons of the wealthy who drank and gambled away their inheritances (García-Bryce 2004). Pardo spoke this language of artisan liberalism as he forged networks of supporters throughout the country who would get voters to the polls by whatever means necessary (McEvoy 1997). After his inauguration, a group of artisans presented him with a petition to take measures to control the escalating cost of living; they reminded him of their "sacrifices and patriotism, thanks to which, with God's protection, we won the most splendid victory over those who trampled upon our laws and committed fraud with the national income" (García-Bryce 2004: 134). Once in office, however, Pardo faced many challenges in implementing his campaign promises. His investment in education earned him the support of teachers, but he faced opposition from the Catholic Church and its supporters. The decline of guano as a source of state revenue made it difficult for the government to meet both the raised expectations of workers and the interests of the economic elite, and popular unrest grew under his successor Mariano Ignacio Prado. Taking advantage of this increasing instability, Chile invaded Peru in 1879. By the time the war ended, Peru had lost its southernmost regions, rich in nitrate mines, and the Civilist party had lost its popular base of support.

Argentina

In both Mexico and Peru, post-independence political movements tended to link centralism and conservatism, on the one hand, and federalism and liberalism, on the other. In Argentina, by contrast, intellectuals who envisioned opening their country to the world market and emulating European-style progress advocated a centralized nation-state and thus called themselves Unitarians, while federalist caudillos defended the interests of local landowners, the Catholic Church, and regional autonomy. The population from which they recruited support also differed significantly from our first two cases. Many native peoples lived beyond the control of the colonial and early national states in the southern reaches of continent. Within areas settled by Europeans and their descendants, the mobile workforce of ranches and farms (the *gauchos*) were of mixed heritage (African as well as indigenous and Spanish). State and village leaders throughout Mexico and Peru advocated for relative local autonomy, but within a national framework. It would take decades, however, to forge a unified Argentine nation out of various provinces within the La Plata region, and large territories of the former viceroyalty remained independent.

As in Mexico, the province of Buenos Aires established virtual universal male suffrage in the 1820s; although some elites tried to negotiate unified lists of candidates, elections became increasingly competitive. Perceiving the raucous campaigns as destabilizing, the provincial legislature granted extensive powers to a governor who would become, from 1829 to 1852, one of the continent's most long-standing and notorious caudillos: Juan Manuel Rosas. In Argentina, even more than in other Spanish American nations, triumphant liberals, such as Bartolomé Mitre and Domingo Faustino Sarmiento, wrote the dominant national histories in the nineteenth century, and their narratives plotted what they saw as the inevitable victory of civilization over the forces of barbarism represented by Rosas. Recent studies, however, nuance our understanding of Rosas and other caudillos: Unitarians and federalists alike resorted to authoritarian, often violent, tactics, but caudillos also constructed a strong basis of popular support.

An alternative version to the official story emerges, for example, from songs and folktales collected in the early twentieth century. Some stories did narrate the omnipresent and arbitrary power of local caudillos. In one, a man whose identity was disguised by his poncho and large hat listened to a group of young Unitarians sing verses that ridiculed Facundo Quiroga; when they finished he revealed himself to be none other than that notorious caudillo and ordered that the singers be shot. But this power was admired as much as feared. Many other tales portrayed federalist leaders as father figures, dispensers of justice, and redistributors of wealth in the style of Robin Hood. One informant recalled the story of a landless peon who helped a stranger cross a river and thus escape the government officials in hot pursuit. As in the first story, the enigmatic figure turned out to be Facundo, but in this case he returned to reward the peon with 10 oxen and 10 cows, enough to start a herd that would lift him out of poverty. These popular stories from the interior provinces yield clues to the ability of local leaders to earn the political support of rural people, offering both material rewards (wages and provisions in wartime and charity in peacetime) and the less tangible benefits of egalitarian sociability. Caudillos expected their authority to be obeyed, but the ease with which they mingled with their followers – playing cards, racing horses, and participating in local religious festivals – blurred the hierarchical distinctions that had characterized colonialism (De la Fuente 2000). Just as languages of republican citizenship had quickly taken hold among the peasants and artisans of Mexico and Peru, the relationships forged between caudillos and gauchos transcended personalities and patronage to embrace the specific political program of federalism.

In the province of Buenos Aires, Rosas similarly built a following by infusing everyday life and popular culture with federalist politics. Civic festivities encouraged popular participation through the renovation of Catholic traditions such as Judas burning, but linking this traitor to contemporary political and class enemies. Rosas also distributed playing cards featuring political figures, an effective means of communication with the working classes. Even the clothes one wore were a political statement. Rosas required all citizens to wear red emblems, the color of the Federalist Party. Urban professionals, often more sympathetic to the Unitarians, would try to deflect suspicion by pinning a scarlet ribbon to the fashionable suit coats that otherwise proclaimed their admiration for European-style progress. By contrast, the rustic clothing of country people symbolized egalitarian ideals, but if too shabby might make them targets for military conscription; to the extent of their means, therefore, they attached gold braid or brass buttons as a sign of distinction (Salvatore 2003).

Whether pressed into the regular army or enrolled in the more prestigious citizen militias, however, military service dominated the lives of many men. Obedience was enforced with corporal punishment and even if a soldier managed to survive a battle and avoid capture by the enemy (both sides routinely executed prisoners), he might easily succumb to illness. But soldiers did not passively accept their fate. They used rumored threats of mass desertion to pressure their commanders for improved benefits and living conditions. Parents also lobbied for exemptions from military service for their sons, and the wives and mothers of those less fortunate petitioned the state for financial support so persistently that they established family rations of meat and other foodstuffs as a virtual entitlement. In their subsequent interactions with political and judicial officials, veterans insistently claimed the rights they had earned through their sacrifices to the nation (Salvatore 2003).

Making politics integral to everyday life helps account for Rosas's longevity in power, but also points to his vulnerabilities. Rosas and other federalist caudillos enlisted the support of entire families, as with the distribution of relief to the wives of soldiers, and petitioners appealed to Rosas's daughter Manuelita to intercede on their behalf. But even Manuelita could not always persuade her father to show clemency, and the Unitarian opposition often played the gender card in their denunciations of federalist cruelty. Juana Manuela Gorriti, a writer from an exiled Unitarian family, wrote stories populated by pure maidens doing moral battle with Rosas's evil henchmen. In one, Clemencia tried to atone for the sins of her father, Roque Black-Soul, by bringing charity to the families of his victims. In the dramatic ending she made the ultimate sacrifice, substituting herself for a Unitarian prisoner; after her father realized that he had mistakenly killed his own daughter "a divine ray of light [shone] down on that man, and it reformed him" (Gorriti 2003 [1865]: 103). But truth could be even stranger than fiction in early national Argentina. When Camila O'Gorman, the daughter of a prominent landowning family, eloped with priest

Ladislao Gutiérrez in 1847, scandal rocked the country. Exiled Unitarian journalists first denounced Rosas for creating a climate of moral depravity in which respectable young ladies could be so easily seduced, and then excoriated the caudillo for ordering the summary execution of not just the priest but also the pregnant Camila (Shumway 2005).

Gender was central to political symbolism, and although women could not vote, they were still active in politics by hosting salons and helping to forge networks. Mariquita Sánchez translated youthful rebellion against colonial arranged marriages into support for independence in 1810 and subsequently leadership of the Society of Beneficence. Although her charitable activities were a suitable extension of domesticity into the public realm, she did not limit herself to presumed women's issues but discussed politics in general with the country's rising intellectuals and politicians. Women like Sánchez actually used their exclusion from formal citizenship to justify an advisory role in politics: less swayed by partisanship, they could mediate between rival factions, an important skill in this turbulent period. As the century progressed, however, men's political activities increasingly occurred in sites where women were rarely present, and girls were educated in schools that emphasized their domestic responsibilities. The next generation of women, therefore, used a maternalist discourse to articulate their political goals (Chambers 2003).

In 1852, an alliance among provincial governors tired of the dominance of the Buenos Aires government (particularly its control of the main port and customs revenues), the Brazilian emperor wary of allowing any neighboring nations from becoming too powerful, and Unitarian exiles in Montevideo defeated Rosas in battle. Weary from years of harsh military service, federalist soldiers put up little resistance. But the defeat of Rosas did not mean the immediate end of federalism as a political force. The victorious provinces drafted a constitution for the new Argentine Confederation in 1853, but Buenos Aires refused to join until 1861. From 1862 to 1880 the administrations of four elected presidents (including Mitre and Sarmiento) repressed recurring federalist rebellions and built a unified national infrastructure – an army, a court system, a central bank, railroads, and an educational system – culminating in the federalization of Buenos Aires as the capital (Adelman 1999). Although the newly unified Argentina was still much smaller than the former Viceroyalty of Rio de la Plata, the national army did secure the northern border during a war against Paraguay in 1865 and expanded effective settlement to the south through campaigns against native peoples. Argentina entered a period of sustained population growth including massive immigration from Europe.

The dominant liberal politicians, having witnessed first the instability of the independence era and then the mobilization of what they regarded as mobs by Rosas, had little faith in the virtue of the citizenry. Although virtually all adult men were enfranchised, voter turnout was low. Some historians, therefore, have downplayed the impact of elections. Paradoxically, however, participation was higher among the working classes than elites, who may have wished to avoid the rowdy activities at the polls. In the political culture of Buenos Aires that emerged in the second half of the nineteenth century, voting was only the tip of the iceberg. Active electoral clubs met to discuss and draw up candidate lists, and the broader population, including women, avidly followed the debates in the press and attended speeches and rallies even if they did not intend to vote. Even between elections, demonstrations over specific issues such as tax laws or the separation of church and state drew large crowds, which political elites watched to measure public opinion. Such actions were often organized by the civic associations – mutual aid societies, immigrant clubs, and Masonic lodges to name only a few – which proliferated in the second half of the nineteenth century (Sabato 2001).

Conclusion

By 1880, both Argentina and Mexico had relatively stable and centralized national states that provided an infrastructure for economic growth based upon a model of free trade and resulting in a growing inequality in the distribution of wealth; Peru had been on a similar path until temporarily derailed by the war with Chile. Most economic and political elites congratulated themselves on having defeated the presumed threats to national order and unity posed by governance rooted in local communities and mass mobilizations. This chapter offers a different perspective on political culture in the aftermath of independence from Spain. Instability, far from reflecting a populace unprepared for modern, republican forms of government, arose from widespread participation in the three arenas of polling places, battlefields, and courtrooms. Recent studies have demonstrated that competitive elections with relatively wide suffrage were more common in Spanish America than previously assumed. Even when military leaders challenged the results, they articulated political platforms to spur supporters to arms. Whether a regime was established by ballots or bullets, peasants and workers came to see themselves as citizens of the nation, and, when challenged, they defended their corresponding civil and political rights in court. It was perhaps liberal elites who were unprepared for the consequences of opening up the political system in diverse societies where, in contrast to North America, indigenous communities were incorporated into the nation and numerous people of color were free rather than enslaved. When military and civilian leaders mobilized supporters in the early years of these republics, they could not always control the direction those movements would take. As the century progressed, elites increasingly set aside their differences; some conservatives abandoned their opposition to a free-market economy and many liberals came to support limits on popular enfranchisement and local governance. A greater degree of unity at the top was forged at the expense of empowerment from below.

This chapter has challenged the depiction of the masses as unruly and unthinking that emerged from victorious nineteenth-century narratives and has continued to influence national historiographies up to our own times. As a counterbalance, it has perhaps verged on idealizing popular participation in politics. Not all Mexican peasants, indigenous Peruvians, or Argentine gauchos embraced republican practices and national identities; similarly, some urban voters were swayed by bribes or drinks to help a particular party seize control of their district polling place by whatever means necessary. Nevertheless, the masses were not simply manipulated or duped. Particularly charismatic politicians and caudillos may have been more successful, but all had to appeal for support based upon political ideas. Historians are increasingly uncovering or reinterpreting sources – proclamations issued by communities or militia units, court testimonies of working people arrested for vagrancy, even folktales and songs

– that reveal widespread popular engagement with modern discourses of citizenship. Rural and urban men from diverse ethnic groups repeatedly claimed rights (variously to local governance, freedom of expression, and protection from arbitrary arrest or conscription) in exchange for fulfilling their obligations to the nation (serving in militias, paying their taxes, and working to support their families). Indigenous communities challenged the classical liberal notion of citizenship defined exclusively in individual terms, but most did not reject outright their incorporation into the nation. These claims from below had an impact on national politics and state formation (albeit limited and less marked in Peru and Argentina than in Mexico). The political regimes consolidated in the 1870s and 1880s were more centralized and suffrage more restricted than in the 1820s, but they were based on constitutions that enshrined popular sovereignty and basic civil rights. There was the potential, therefore, for the resurgence of popular politics in the next century, whether coming from similar sectors, such as Mexican peasants and Peruvian artisans, or from new groups, such as the increasingly immigrant working class of Argentina.

ACKNOWLEDGMENTS

The author thanks John Chasteen, Peter Guardino, Patrick McNamara, Jeffrey Pilcher, Kirsten Fischer, and Lisa Norling for comments on various drafts and apologizes for any suggestions not implemented owing to space constraints.

BIBLIOGRAPHY

Adelman, J. (1999) *Republic of Capital: Buenos Aires and the Legal Transformation of the Atlantic World*. Stanford University Press, Stanford.

Anna, T. E. (1998) *Forging Mexico, 1821–1835*. University of Nebraska Press, Lincoln.

Annino, A. & Guerra, F. X. (eds.) (2003) *Inventando la nación: Iberoamérica, Siglo XIX*. Fondo de Cultura Económica, Mexico City.

Chambers, S. C. (1999) *From Subjects to Citizens: Honor, Gender, and Politics in Arequipa, Peru, 1780–1854*. Pennsylvania State University Press, University Park.

Chambers, S. C. (2003) "Letters and Salons: Women Reading and Writing the Nation in the Nineteenth Century." In J. C. Chasteen & S. Castro-Klarén (eds.), *Beyond Imagined Communities: Reading and Writing the Nation in Nineteenth-Century Latin America*. Woodrow Wilson Center Press and the Johns Hopkins University Press, Washington DC and Baltimore.

Costeloe, M. P. (1993) *The Central Republic in Mexico, 1835–1846: Hombres de Bien in the Age of Santa Anna*. Cambridge University Press, Cambridge.

De la Fuente, A. (2000) *Children of Facundo: Caudillo and Gaucho Insurgency during the Argentine State-Formation Process (La Rioja, 1853–1870)*. Duke University Press, Durham.

Ducey, M. T. (2004) *A Nation of Villages: Riot and Rebellion in the Mexican Huasteca, 1750–1850*. University of Arizona Press, Tucson.

Forment, C. A. (2003) *Democracy in Latin America, 1760–1900: Volume I, Civic Selfhood and Public Life in Mexico and Peru*. University of Chicago Press, Chicago.

Fowler, W. (1996) "The Repeated Rise of General Antonio López de Santa Anna in the So-Called Age of Chaos (Mexico, 1821–55)." In W. Fowler (ed.), *Authoritarianism in Latin American since Independence*. Greenwood Press, Westport.

Fowler, W. (1998) *Mexico in the Age of Proposals, 1821–1853*. Greenwood Press, Westport.

García-Bryce, I. L. (2004) *Crafting the Republic: Lima's Artisans and Nation Building in Peru, 1821–1879*. University of New Mexico Press, Albuquerque.

Gootenberg, P. (1991) "North–South: Trade Policy, Regionalisms, and *Caudillismo* in Post-Independence Peru," *Journal of Latin American Studies*, 23:2, pp. 273–308.

Gorriti, J. M. (2003[1865]) *Dreams and Realities*, trans. S. Waisman and ed. F. Masiello. Oxford University Press, Oxford.

Guardino, P. (1996) *Peasants, Politics, and the Formation of Mexico's National State: Guerrero, 1800–1857*. Stanford University Press, Stanford.

Guardino, P. (2005) *The Time of Liberty: Popular Political Culture in Oaxaca, 1750–1850*. Duke University Press, Durham.

Guerra, F.-X. (1992) *Modernidad e independencias: Ensayos sobre las revoluciones hispánicas*. Editorial MAPFRE, Madrid.

Hale, C. A. (1968) *Mexican Liberalism in the Age of Mora, 1821–1853*. Yale University Press, New Haven.

Jacobsen, N. & Aljovín de Losada, C. (eds.) (2005) *Political Cultures in the Andes, 1750–1950*. Duke University Press, Durham.

Larson, B. (2004) *Trials of Nation Making: Liberalism, Race, and Ethnicity in the Andes, 181–1910*. Cambridge University Press, Cambridge.

Lynch, J. (1992) *Caudillos in Spanish America, 1800–1850*. Clarendon Press, Oxford.

Mallon, F. E. (1995) *Peasant and Nation: The Making of Postcolonial Mexico and Peru*. University of California Press, Berkeley and Los Angeles.

McEvoy, C. (1997) *La utopía republicana: Ideales y realidades en la formación de la cultura política peruana, 1871–1919*. Pontificia Universidad Católica del Perú, Lima.

McNamara, P. J. (2007) *Sons of the Sierra: Juárez, Díaz, and the People of Ixtlán, Oaxaca, 1855–1920*. University of North Carolina Press, Chapel Hill.

Méndez, C. (2005) *The Plebeian Republic: The Huanta Rebellion and the Making of the Peruvian State, 1820–1850*. Duke University Press, Durham.

Peloso, V. D. & Tenenbaum, B. A. (eds.) (1996) *Liberals, Politics and Power: State Formation in Nineteenth-Century Latin America*. University of Georgia Press, Athens.

Posada-Carbó, E. (1996) *Elections before Democracy: The History of Elections in Europe and Latin America*. St. Martin's Press, New York.

Rugeley, T. (1996) *Yucatán's Maya Peasantry and the Origins of the Caste War*. University of Texas Press, Austin.

Sabato, H. (2001) *The Many and the Few: Political Participation in Republican Buenos Aires*. Stanford University Press, Stanford.

Salvatore, R. D. (2003) *Wandering Paysanos: State Order and Subaltern Experience in Buenos Aires during the Rosas Era*. Duke University Press, Durham.

Shumway, J. M. (2005) *The Case of the Ugly Suitor and Other Histories of Love, Gender, and Nation in Buenos Aires, 1776–1870*. University of Nebraska Press, Lincoln.

Stevens, D. F. (1991) *Origins of Instability in Early Republican Mexico*. Duke University Press, Durham.

Thurner, M. (1997) *From Two Republics to One Divided: Contradictions of Nationmaking in Andean Peru*. Duke University Press, Durham.

Tutino, J. (1986) *From Insurrection to Revolution in Mexico: Social Bases of Agrarian Violence, 1750–1940*. Princeton University Press, Princeton.

Walker, C. (1999) *Smoldering Ashes: Cuzco and the Creation of Republican Peru, 1780–1840*. Duke University Press, Durham.

Warren, R. A. (2001) *Vagrants and Citizens: Politics and the Masses in Mexico City from Colony to Republic*. Scholarly Resources, Wilmington, DE.

Chapter Fourteen

Imperial Brazil (1822–89)

Judy Bieber

Prince Regent Dom Pedro's dramatic cry of "Independence or Death" on September 7, 1822 marked the beginning of South America's only enduring constitutional monarchy. The Brazilian empire lasted for just over 67 years, ending with a rapid and nearly bloodless republican coup on November 15, 1889. Traditional historical interpretations highlighted Brazil's unique qualities compared to its contemporaneous Spanish American neighbors – a transition to independence that was swift and relatively peaceful, the perpetuation of crown rule, the preservation of territorial integrity, and an unusual degree of political stability and economic prosperity. Subsequent revisionist literature, however, has emphasized regional cleavages and political rivalries that made Brazil's lauded stability more contingent.

Brazil's successful transition to unified nationhood is all the more surprising given its regional and social heterogeneity. At independence, Brazil was divided into 18 captaincies that maintained more regular and easy communications with Lisbon than they did among themselves. Transportation from interior to coast was limited largely to navigable river systems or primitive trails traversable only by foot or by mule. The population was unevenly distributed, as were the colony's sources of wealth. The slave population, amounting to at least one-third of Brazil's total population of four to five million, was concentrated in the northern captaincies of Maranhão, Pernambuco, and Bahia and the south-central captaincies of Rio de Janeiro and Minas Gerais. The first four of these captaincies produced much of the sugar, cotton, and coffee that dominated Brazil's export earnings; the more diversified economy of Minas Gerais also yielded gold, gems, iron, livestock, and dairy products. The sparsely populated, drought-prone, northeastern interior concentrated on extensive ranching. Indigenous hunter–gatherers still dominated in the far south and west. Urbanization throughout the colony was limited; only the cities of Rio de Janeiro and Salvador da Bahia possessed populations in excess of 50,000. Most provincial capitals had populations of 10,000 or less.

Late colonial Brazilian society was also stratified according to a number of overlapping categories: wealth, lineage, race, education, gender, and slave vs. free status. Plantation owners, merchants, and bureaucrats dominated. Most members of the elite claimed to be white, confirming the Brazilian aphorism that "money whitens." Money, power, and cultural refinement could compensate for racially mixed antecedents, if they were not too obvious. Following independence, new professional groups gained importance. Lawyers trained at one of Brazil's two law faculties, established in 1827 in Olinda in the north (later moved to nearby Recife) and São Paulo in the south, came to dominate political life. Military academies educated technicians who gained prestige in the fields of mining, surveying, and civil engineering. The white population further diversified after 1822 as white Europeans of more humble social origins entered Brazil as small-scale independent farmers, artisans, petty merchants, and, increasingly by the 1870s, as coffee plantation workers. At the empire's beginning, whites constituted no more than one-third of the population; by the period's end, they exceeded 40 percent.

Elite women, particularly in rural areas, were confined mostly to the home and female seclusion was widespread. European naturalists who traveled to Brazil early in the nineteenth century often remarked about how few women they were allowed to meet socially. Girls married young, typically to older men selected by their parents. Sexual virtue was considered central to female honor. The practice of the dowry was still active although it would decline by the end of the imperial period. Over the course of the empire, elite women would make gradual inroads in higher education, particularly as teachers, and in the professions.

Brazil also had a large, heterogeneous population of free people of color. Compared to most slave societies in the Americas, its percentage of freed men and women was unusually high. Approximately half of the colored population of Brazil was free by the mid-nineteenth century and by 1872, that proportion had risen to 70 percent. In that year free people of color comprised 43 percent of the total population of about 10 million, slightly exceeding the white population (42 percent) and vastly outstripping the slave population (just 15 percent). Manumission of slave children at baptism was probably the most significant factor in the growth of the free colored population although manumission of adult slaves through owner beneficence or self-purchase also played a role.

The prestige and fortunes of Brazil's free colored population varied widely. Descendants of slaves could serve as agents of the state as *capitães do mato* (literally "bush captains" but slave catchers in practice) and minor officials. Most occupied the lower socioeconomic echelons as rural dependents (*agregados*), artisans, smallholders, and muleteers. Many led impoverished and insecure lives that represented only a modest material improvement over a life of outright servitude. In the post-independence period, a small minority entered the professions, politics, and the intelligentsia, like engineer André Rebouças, journalist and abolitionist José do Patricinio, and the eminent mulatto novelist Machado de Assis.

Poor women of color led very different lives. They tended to marry later, if at all, and in many locations, up to 40 percent of adult women lived in female-headed households. They also could not maintain the elite ideal of female seclusion because they had to work to survive. In urban areas they entered into domestic service, washed laundry at public fountains, sewed, prepared cooked food for sale, and worked as street vendors, healers, or midwives. Some engaged in prostitution. Despite the realities of working in the public eye, some poor women, regardless of color, internalized and sought to emulate elite ideals of female modesty. For example, in the city of São Paulo, many a poor woman invested her meager savings in the purchase of a single female slave who could work in public on her behalf, thereby allowing her to pursue productive labor in the privacy of her own home. Others wore enveloping clothing when they went into the street. In rural areas, lower-class women often worked outside the household, in the fields, or were engaged in spinning and weaving cloth within.

Slaves constituted roughly one-third of the population at the beginning of the nineteenth century and, like the free colored population, they were a heterogeneous lot. The slave population did not enjoy natural increase through reproduction due to ill treatment, disease, and imbalanced sex ratios. Therefore, Brazil continued to import Africans well into the nineteenth century, and those Africans made enduring contributions to Brazilian culture, religion, music, dance, aesthetics, folklore, and cuisine. African slaves had less status than creoles born in Brazil. Creoles were more likely to be trained in a skill, to be employed in domestic service, or to be manumitted by an owner, particularly if they were female. Urban slaves also enjoyed a greater degree of mobility and relative freedom than did captives who labored on rural plantations. Many urban slaves worked on a *de ganho* basis, paying their owner a fixed sum of their earnings per week and pocketing any surplus as savings or to meet subsistence needs. They were more likely to be able to attain manumission through self-purchase and some even became slave owners themselves. The relative freedoms that urban slaves enjoyed, however, should not be overestimated. They often lacked adequate clothing, food, and shelter, were more susceptible to disease, and came under surveillance and control by emerging police institutions. They did not enjoy legal autonomy and had little or no recourse against mistreatment, corporal punishment, or sexual abuse.

Late colonial Brazil's social and regional divisions seemed to offer poor foundations for the development of a unified imperial state. Indeed, most scholars concur that Brazil's claims to nationhood were not fully consolidated until the mid-nineteenth century. Brazil's transformation from colony to empire owed greatly to external events set in motion by the Napoleonic invasion of Iberia. As Napoleon's troops marched toward the Portuguese border in 1807, Prince Regent Dom João (who would assume the throne in 1816) departed Lisbon with his court of 10,000 to 15,000 followers, the treasury, the archives, and those luxuries fundamental to elite existence. A convoy set sail to Brazil, escorted by a British squadron of warships. Dom João thereby transferred the apparatus of Portuguese metropolitan government to the Brazilian colony.

The removal of the Lisbon court to the city of Rio de Janeiro led to significant economic and political change. The prince regent opened Brazilian ports to foreign shipping and non-Portuguese immigrants. In gratitude for Britain's aid, England received preferential trade tariffs that were lower than those accorded to Portugal itself. Institutions of higher learning, including military and naval academies and medical and law faculties, were established. Restrictions on domestic manufacturing and mining were eliminated, permitting the birth of textile and steel industries. The establishment of Brazil's first public bank, the Banco do Brasil, facilitated investment. By 1815, Brazil's status was elevated to a dual kingdom legally equal to Portugal. A number of state administrative institutions were duplicated, providing bureaucratic opportunities for the Brazilian-born. The prince regent also lavishly distributed titles of nobility to the Brazilian-born elite in exchange for their financial and logistical assistance in reestablishing the Lisbon court on Brazilian soil. Within 10 years of the court's arrival, the population of Rio doubled.

The presence of the royal court served to delay nascent aspirations for political independence. In the late colonial period, few colonists expressed a desire to separate from Portugal. Late colonial revolts emphasized reforms to the colonial system, not its elimination. In particular, Brazilian creoles emphasized economic freedoms. The opening of Brazil to free trade, coupled with expanded access of colonial subjects to the administrative bureaucracy, satisfied the modest political desires of the elite. The colored masses, both free and enslaved, remained largely quiescent.

The growing preeminence of the city of Rio de Janeiro, however, also inspired regional resentment. Elites in the northeastern state of Pernambuco who felt excluded from new political and economic opportunities fomented a short-lived republican revolt in 1817. Leaders came from the elite classes, including the bureaucracy and military officers, liberal professionals, planters, merchants, and the clergy. Many of the rebels were members of Masonic lodges. They formed a provisional government based on the French constitution. Their appeals to regional separatism and anti-Portuguese sentiment failed to gain wide support and the movement was quickly crushed, largely due to elite apprehensions about possible popular political participation. In the words of Brazilian historian Emilia Viotti da Costa, "The democratic intentions of the common people scandalized the upper classes who referred to them as 'explosions of insulting equality' " (Costa in Russell Wood 1975: 67).

Support for Brazilian independence developed in reaction to the 1820 Liberal Revolution of Oporto, Portugal. Bourgeois Portuguese rebels elected a constituent assembly and adopted a charter modeled on the Spanish liberal constitution of Cadiz promulgated in 1812. They also demanded Dom João VI's return to Lisbon. He complied in April 1821 but left his son, Dom Pedro, to rule as regent in Brazil. The Portuguese parliament (*Cortes*) sought to reassert colonial economic restrictions in Brazil in order to rebuild the Portuguese economy. Although Portugal had suffered financially due to successive French and British military occupations, the legislators felt that their economic woes derived largely from loss of revenues from the Brazilian colony.

In 1821 the Cortes invited Brazilian delegates to participate in its deliberations but did not wait for their arrival before drafting policies detrimental to Brazil's autonomy. The Brazilians had only minority representation and were powerless to stop legislative reforms that repealed free trade measures and dismantled institutional and bureaucratic structures in Brazil. The position of the former colony's capital, Rio de Janeiro, was weakened through the establishment of new independent governing councils (*juntas de governo*) and the placement of military governors in each captaincy. On a more personal level, the Brazilian delegates were ridiculed as uncultured rustics by their Portuguese counterparts.

A crisis emerged when, on January 9, 1822, Prince Regent D. Pedro refused to return to Portugal. He barred the arrival of Portuguese troops and reserved the right to reject decrees passed by the Cortes. In so doing, it is believed he had the tacit approval of his father. However, public opinion in Brazil remained divided about independence, especially in provinces that resented the hegemony of Rio de Janeiro. Among the elite, many envisioned continued unity although not in the most flattering terms: "Brazil should lead Portugal 'as a grateful son leads his decrepit father by the hand' " (Costa in Russell Wood 1975: 76). Others offered alternative meanings of constitutionalism, assigning greater weight to popular sovereignty and Brazil's right to dictate its own economic policy. However, the intransigence of the Cortes eventually proved decisive. Its attempts to rescind free trade, its refusal to grant Brazil its own parliament, its dismantling of the Rio government, and the imposition of Portuguese troops to enforce these new policies, met with considerable local resistance. On September 7, 1822, on the banks of Ipiranga creek near the city of São Paulo, Dom Pedro flamboyantly declared "Independence or Death," marking the beginnings of the separate Brazilian nation.

The Portuguese Cortes rejected Brazilian claims to sovereignty and other European nations followed Lisbon's lead. The British mercenary Lord Thomas Cochrane assumed command of the Brazilian navy and ousted Portuguese forces from a number of Brazil's principal ports. A brief war ensued that was limited largely to naval engagements. The northern captaincies of Maranhão, Pará, Piauí, and Ceará refused to recognize the Rio government and remained loyal to Portugal. Moreover, the vital port cities of Salvador da Bahia and Montevideo remained occupied by Portuguese troops. In 1825, Portugal and Brazil finally reached a negotiated settlement, mediated by the British Prime Minister, George Canning. Great Britain's help, however, proved costly. In addition to the payment of a stiff war indemnity to Portugal in the amount of £2 million, Brazil also had to preserve Great Britain's preferential trade status and commit to terminating the transatlantic slave trade by 1830. The Brazilian economy, about which more will be said below, depended heavily upon slave labor in the production of tropical staples like sugar, coffee, cotton, tobacco, and cacao.

The new Brazilian state also had to contend with regional resistance to the hegemony of the former viceregal capital, Rio de Janeiro. In particular, the northern and northeastern provinces resented the centralized control of Rio, as exemplified by the 1817 revolt in Pernambuco. However, regional challenges to national unity were balanced by the actions of an emerging elite political class that was unified in class and education. During the colonial era, young men of good family went to Coimbra University in Portugal for higher education because no universities had been established in Brazil. There, they received uniform educational training and made contacts with their social equals from different regions. These Brazilians, however, came to clash with men of Portuguese birth who held a more traditional/authoritarian notion of the nation-state. Within the Brazilian-born population, a vocal nativist and radical minority called for more democratic institutions and favored the principle of local autonomy.

Coimbra graduates dominated at the constituent assembly of 1823. The one hundred deputies drew their inspiration from the French and British constitutions and a majority favored a moderate and elitist form of liberalism. The national political elite envisioned liberalism as an acceptable means to preserve their socioeconomic privileges and were less concerned with the elimination of traditional privileges and the implementation of democratizing reforms. As debate over the fine points dragged on, Emperor D. Pedro I became increasingly nervous about the likelihood that the proposed constitution would give more power to the General Assembly than to himself. He had the constituent assembly dissolved and wrote his own constitution in consultation with the Council of State and then presented it to the municipal councils for ratification in 1824.

The constitution included many of the central components of European liberalism such as division of powers among the executive, legislative, and judicial branches. It provided for relatively broad suffrage among the free, male population in a system of indirect elections. The franchise was based on a modest income requirement rather than one's race or education. Within the two-tier system voters selected municipal officeholders and members of electoral colleges. Electors, whose income requirement was doubled, were eligible to serve on the electoral colleges that chose provincial and national legislators. Other constitutional guarantees included provision of public education by the state, freer conditions of trade, protection of private property, and formal equality before the law for the free population. However, rights assigned to the individual citizen excluded slaves who then comprised one-third of the Brazilian population, and who were not mentioned in the constitution.

Dom Pedro I's constitution also invested the emperor with extensive political prerogatives under the moderating power (*poder moderador*). This power allowed the emperor to arbitrarily dissolve the Chamber of Deputies, thereby enjoying oversight with respect to nationally elected representatives. The emperor also was empowered to appoint senators from a short list of three candidates who received the most votes in national elections. Those senators enjoyed lifetime tenure in office. The emperor also could veto legislation, name and dismiss at will cabinet ministers, judges, and magistrates, and grant pardons.

The dissolution of the constituent assembly and Dom Pedro I's new charter inspired revolt once again in the northeast. In 1824, Frei Caneca and Manuel Carvalho Paes de Andrade, both veterans of 1817, declared an independent republic, the Confederation of the Equator. Frei Caneca, in particular, objected to the moderating power, lifetime tenure in the senate and the overly centralized state as anti-liberal measures that would serve only to repress the Brazilian population and legitimize a ruling aristocracy. A number of other neighboring provinces joined the Pernambucan rebels but Dom Pedro I's forces defeated the movement within six months. The conspirators were tried in special courts and many, including Frei Caneca, were executed.

Dom Pedro I's autocratic style of government made him increasingly unpopular over the course of the 1820s. His absolutist tendencies, favoritism toward men of Portuguese birth, his erratic and unstable character, and dissolute moral habits alienated Brazilian-born elites and the popular classes alike. Particularly objectionable was the blatant flaunting of his mistress, Dona Domitíla de Castro Canto, the Marquesa of Santos. Economically, Brazil also faced difficulties by the mid-1820s. It had trouble servicing foreign loans and issued excessive amounts of currency, resulting in high levels of inflation. The Banco do Brasil failed and ceased operations in 1829. Further adding to Brazil's economic and political woes was a prolonged, costly, and ultimately unsuccessful war for control over the Cisplatine province (present-day Uruguay), lasting from 1825 to 1828.

Dissent became especially evident in cities and large towns where the urban poor blamed Portuguese merchants and court hangers-on for the declining standard of living. In March 1831, street fighting broke out for several days in what came to be known as the "*noites das garrafadas*," or nights of the broken bottles. The army supported the crowd: the officers in hopes of replacing Portuguese high-ranking officers; the rank and file, in solidarity with civilians that were similar in color, socioeconomic status, and aspirations. Lacking military support, Dom Pedro I abdicated the throne on April 7, 1831 declaring, "I will do everything for the people, but nothing by the people." Strategically, his departure was also motivated by a desire to protect his daughter's succession to the Portuguese throne from usurpation by his brother Miguel.

Pedro I left Brazil in the hands of a regency (1831–40) until his son, Pedro II, then five years old, attained his majority. During the next 10 years, political tendencies and parties emerged, each with competing visions of how the Brazilian nation should develop. At the center were the *moderados* (moderates), dominated by Brazilian-born graduates of Coimbra University. Opposing the moderados were Portuguese-born *caramarús* (restorationists) who called for the return of the exiled Dom Pedro I and defended traditional hierarchies and privileges. Toward the left were the more radical *exaltados*. They became increasingly marginalized due to their extreme nativism, hostility toward the Portuguese, and desire for a political system that approximated republicanism.

During the regency, a series of regional revolts challenged Brazilian national unity. In the northeastern province of Pernambuco, a series of rebellions erupted every few years lasting through the mid-nineteenth century. These included the movements of 1817 and 1824 discussed previously; a series of anti-Portuguese and barracks revolts in 1831; the *Cabanos* war (1832–5); and the *Praieira* revolt of 1849. Other outbreaks of local resistance included the *Sabinada* in Bahia (1837), the *Cabanagem* in Pará (1835–40), and the *Farroupilha* (1835–45) in Rio Grande do Sul. Many of these revolts were grounded in local partisan rivalries while others called for greater regional autonomy. As a group, the post-1835 revolts were federalist and separatist in nature. Initially, most had elite objectives and leadership, but the Cabanos and Cabanagem over time came to incorporate mass participation of racially mixed peasants, Indians, and slaves. These two revolts also suffered sustained repression by the state and great loss of life among the popular participants.

Regional uprisings convinced many among the elite that state centralization was necessary to retain national unity. They argued that Brazil was ill prepared to take effective advantage of democratizing and decentralizing reforms that had been passed in the 1820s–1830s. Politically conservative elites came to oppose practices such as popular election of justices of the peace and jury trials. They claimed that jurors of modest socioeconomic and educational standing were easily manipulated or coerced in the courtroom and that locally elected judges of dubious competence rendered rulings tainted by self-interest. A Criminal Code approved in 1832 further strengthened the powers of these elected justices to arrest and try cases.

The Additional Act to the Constitution, passed in 1834, also reduced the power of the central state. It abolished the hated Council of State, an organ associated with D. Pedro I's autocratic rule, and granted greater legislative autonomy to municipal councils and provincial legislative assemblies. The Additional Act also gave provincial assemblies control over appointment of officers in the National Guard, a citizen's militia that had been created in 1831. The National Guard's low income requirements (the same as for the first level of voters) meant that many free men of color of modest economic means were entitled to serve. The Guard came to perform basic policing functions as well as functioning as a military reserve.

By 1840, a new political party successfully challenged the tendencies toward local autonomy and democratization of power that characterized the regency period (1831–40). In the late 1830s, disillusioned *moderados* like Bernardo Pereira de Vasconcelos moved to the right and initiated the *regresso* (reaction), whose goals were to strengthen the executive, and introduce additional forms of localized social control. Chief among their counterreforms was the "Interpretation" of the Additional Act in 1840, which transferred many of the powers previously granted to the provincial assemblies back to the central government and reintroduced the Council of State. Reforms to the Criminal Code in 1841 transferred powers formerly held by locally elected justices of the peace to police delegates and magistrates appointed by the Minister of Justice. Regresso leaders identified themselves as belonging to the "Party of Order" but also came to be known as the Conservatives. The Liberal party arose from an alternative *moderado* vision. It favored broader voting rights, greater power of elected officials, and increased local autonomy and individual freedoms. The restorationist *caramarús* had disbanded after Dom Pedro I's death in Portugal in 1834.

In 1840, Dom Pedro II prematurely ascended the throne at the age of 15 due to the efforts of the Majority Club, a group of marginalized and nativist politicians who had pushed for his early coronation in hopes of gaining greater political influence. Their aspirations went unrealized; the adolescent emperor quickly turned to the Party of Order. The dissolution of the Liberal-dominated Chamber of Deputies in 1842 led disgruntled Liberals in Minas Gerais, São Paulo, and Rio de Janeiro to foment a short-lived and unsuccessful revolution. Subsequently, the resolution of the Farroupilha revolt in Rio Grande do Sul in 1845 and the Praieira movement in Pernambuco in 1849 brought the era of regional revolts to a close.

Despite his relative youth and inexperience, Dom Pedro II was intellectually prepared to rule. He had been exhaustively trained to assume his responsibilities and demonstrated a life-long passion for learning. Although initially hesitant, by the mid- to late 1840s, he had freed himself from the influence of his royal tutors and began to come into his own politically with respect to domestic and foreign policy. By 1850 both he and the Brazilian nation had achieved a certain degree of maturity.

Yet at mid-century, Brazil still faced a number of challenges. First and foremost was the future of slavery. Slave-based plantation agriculture dominated the Brazilian economy. For much of the imperial period, approximately 80 percent of Brazil's export revenues came from sugar, coffee, and cotton. Over time, the production of sugar and cotton declined with respect to coffee, whose share among national exports rose from 16 percent in 1821 to over 40 percent by 1840. Coffee was first cultivated in the Paraíba valley of Rio de Janeiro province but by mid-century it was expanding into southern Minas Gerais and western São Paulo. Brazil also exported smaller amounts of tobacco, cacao, and hides.

Large landowners relied heavily upon slave labor, especially the expanding coffee elite. However, British diplomatic pressures threatened the longevity of the institution. In 1807, Great Britain outlawed slave trafficking by its nationals and barred slave ships in its territories. Through a variety of diplomatic and extralegal means, England pressured other nations to follow its lead and its navy implemented an aggressive campaign to suppress slaving off the African coast and the high seas. British help in escorting the Portuguese court to Brazil in 1808 and negotiating recognition of Brazilian sovereignty in 1825, and its importance as a trading partner, facilitated that nation's ability to lobby for an end to the Brazilian slave trade.

Consequently, Dom João had agreed in 1810 to limit the slave trade to Portuguese colonies in Africa and to impede Portuguese nationals from engaging in the trade in non-Portuguese territories. In 1815, the combined kingdoms of Brazil and Portugal agreed to cease slaving north of the equator and in 1817 they ratified a search and seizure treaty with England. These measures restricted the trade to Angola and Mozambique. Following independence, Dom Pedro I was pressured to recognize these agreements and to promise a complete halt to the trade by 1830. A law to this effect was passed in 1831 but it was not enforced. Between 1831 and 1846, some 500,000 slaves were imported to Brazil. Formal prohibition actually increased the horrors and abuses of the trade as slavers crammed their holds full of captives, favoring children and women over men.

Despite a lack of will to halt the trade on Brazil's part, Great Britain continued to apply diplomatic and commercial pressure. From 1810 to 1844, Great Britain enjoyed "most favored nation" status in Brazil, including a low 15 percent *ad valorem* tariff on British manufactured goods. However, England maintained high tariffs on Brazilian-grown sugar and coffee to avoid competition with its West Indian producers. When the treaty had come up for renewal in 1827, Britain justified retention of exorbitant tariffs on Brazilian tropical produce because it had been produced by slaves. As trade relations again were renegotiated in the early 1840s, England signaled its willingness to reduce its tariffs on Brazilian sugar and coffee if Brazil would commit to slave emancipation in the near future. Brazil refused, the treaty came to an end, and the Brazilian government modestly increased import duties, largely to expand its base of revenues, 80 percent of which came from customs duties.

Additionally, Great Britain passed the Palmerston Act of 1839 and the Aberdeen Act of 1845. These measures unilaterally gave the British navy the right to arbitrarily search and seize Portuguese and Brazilian ships, even in Brazilian territorial waters. The Brazilian government, then Conservative-dominated, responded by passing the Queiroz bill in 1850 and achieved a definitive end to the trade by the following year. Cessation of the slave trade brought a gain in international respectability but posed a problem for planters, especially those involved in the expanding coffee economy. Labor-hungry landowners resorted to a variety of solutions, including an internal slave trade that drew from economically depressed northern areas of Brazil, the enslavement of unassimilated Indians, the use of dependent tenant farmers and sharecroppers, adoption of vagrancy laws, and the importation of European contract laborers. Owing largely to ideologies of racial inferiority, they expressed little enthusiasm for importing Asian contract workers or free Africans or hiring the "national worker," poor, landless native Brazilians of color.

Ultimately, São Paulo coffee growers relied most heavily on European immigrants while poorer regions such as the declining sugar areas of the northeast relied on tenancy, sharecropping, and debt peonage. The end of the slave trade also caused a dramatic rise in the price of slaves, making other alternatives more attractive. Formal attempts to attract Europeans began in the 1830s and by mid-century some 20,000 had settled in Brazil, although most were more attracted to small-scale agrarian colonies than to laboring alongside African slaves on coffee plantations. The planter and statesman Nicolau Pereira de Campos Vergueiro recruited Swiss and German "colonists" (*colonos*) to work as sharecroppers on his plantation in Rio Claro in the 1840s. The earliest migrants enjoyed the most favorable conditions and often were able to free themselves from debt within a few years. However, as other planters followed Vergueiro's lead, they rewrote contractual terms to further favor their own interests.

The ill-treatment experienced by subsequent migrants was publicized in an account written by a *colono*, Thomas Davatz, in 1850 and this led Germany and Switzerland to prohibit future immigration to Brazil. Paulista coffee growers then looked to southern Europe to meet their labor needs, recruiting from Italy, Spain, and Portugal. In the 1880s they lobbied effectively for subsidies from the provincial government to offset the costs of importing contract laborers. By the late 1880s, tens of thousands of immigrants poured into Brazil annually and Europeans continued to comprise most of the labor force in the coffee sector until the Depression of the 1930s.

The end of the transatlantic slave trade also freed up capital for economic diversification. Slavery, however, was but one of several factors contributing to the limited amount of private entrepreneurship in manufacturing and infrastructure in Brazil. As a slave society, Brazil had a modest consumer base. Slaves and the free colored masses were generally poorly educated and lacked technical skills or scientific training. Brazil faced severe transportation limitations, a lack of industrial fuel, and limited access to capital and banking. The favored status enjoyed by British finished goods also stifled Brazilian industrial production. The ending of England's favored status in 1844 enabled the government to raise tariffs. This was done more for fiscal ends than protectionist motives as taxes on imports comprised about 60 percent of government revenues from 1850 to1875. Nevertheless, it enabled Brazil to make modest gains in small-scale light manufacturing.

In 1850, the Conservatives passed a Commercial Code that laid out state regulations for the creation of joint-stock companies and other forms of business partnerships. Although this legislation has been interpreted as hostile to private entrepreneurship, investors with political connections were able to profit. One such example is the Viscount of Mauá, Irineu Evangelista de Sousa (1813–89). Mauá aggressively invested in infrastructure, utilities, iron foundries, banking, railways, and navigation.

A law regulating land acquisition and title was also passed that served the interests of the planter class. The inspiration for the 1850 *Lei das Terras* derived from E. Gibbon Wakefield's *A Letter from Sydney* (1829), which advocated setting a high price on land in order to ensure a dependent agrarian labor force. By this law people with claims to land through a royal grant, purchase, inheritance, or effective occupation were required to register their titles with the state. Subsequently, all unclaimed land would revert to the state as public land, including lands occupied by non-sedentary indigenous tribes and squatters who failed to register properly the lands that they worked. Although a lack of land surveys and weak enforcement mechanisms hindered the application of this law, the objective of regulating access to public lands was made clear.

At mid-century Brazil also entered a period of national political stability. Separatist regional revolts came to an end. The Liberal and Conservative parties were institutionalized; the Conservatives' leadership base was centered in Rio de Janeiro while Liberal support was concentrated in São Paulo, Minas Gerais, and Rio Grande do Sul. For a time, Liberals and Conservatives assumed greater ideological homogeneity and supported the idea of an effective, centralized state. Partisan compromise peaked during the bipartisan Conciliation cabinet (*conciliação*), which lasted from 1853 to 1857. Beneath the surface, however, smooth political transitions were achieved at a high cost. The counterreforms passed by the Party of Order in the 1840s empowered centrally appointed nominees over locally elected officials. Police delegates and magistrates enforced the laws and supervised electoral boards, thereby playing a vital role in a patronage system that required municipal officials to deliver favorable electoral returns for their patrons. Appointment of National Guard officers also came under centralized control in 1850. Those authorities often resorted to corruption or extralegal force and their political opponents retaliated with violence. Particularly in rural areas, electoral politics became characterized by manipulation, coercion, and fraud.

Liberals and Conservatives again began to diverge ideologically during the War of the Triple Alliance (1864–70), a conflict involving the combined forces of Brazil, Argentina, and Uruguay against Paraguay. The conflict erupted when Francisco Solano López, the Paraguayan head of state, protested Brazilian interference in the internal politics of Uruguay. López proved to be a surprisingly formidable foe, with 80,000 troops mobilized for combat. In Brazil military service traditionally had been viewed as demeaning, and at the outbreak of hostilities the standing army had been reduced to less than 17,000. However, national pride demanded that Brazil demonstrate its capacity to wage and win a modern war against an opponent that was seen as small, indigenous, and mired in barbarous caudillo politics. By 1866, Brazilian troop strength was raised to 60,000 men. Although coerced recruitment of slaves, ex-slaves, and poor men of color made up the bulk of new recruits, idealistic elite youths also responded to patriotic appeals. The war quickly devolved into an expensive stalemate, costing $200,000,000 and at least 24,000 lives of the 83,000 Brazilian combatants, including many from disease. In the war of attrition aimed at eliminating López, Paraguay's demographic losses were catastrophic, losing as much as half of its adult male population.

New political configurations also emerged during wartime. In 1868, Dom Pedro II succumbed to the pressure of the Duke of Caxias, the commander of the Brazilian forces, to use the moderating power to effect a political turnover that brought the Conservatives to power. Shortly thereafter, a group of outspoken Liberals including Joaquim Nabuco and Teófilo Otoni formed the Reform Club in 1869. Their agenda for constitutional reform went beyond that of the Progressive League, a coalition of reform-minded Liberals and Conservatives that had organized in 1864. The Reform Club called for repeal of the centralizing legislation of 1841, limited tenure of senators, a less powerful Council of State, and progress toward emancipation. Later in the year, they issued a Radical Manifesto that additionally called for direct elections including election of provincial presidents and police officials, expanded suffrage, an end to the moderating power and the Council of State, and immediate abolition of slavery.

Some reformist Liberals also defected to form a Republican party in 1870. Their manifesto called for many of the same legislative reforms as well as an end to the empire. Forward-looking Paulista planters, disgruntled by the central government's appropriation of coffee revenues, were at the head of this movement, as were urban professionals who felt marginalized within a political system that privileged rural areas. The Republican Party also attracted members of the military. The Paraguayan War politicized the military, which grew in strength and professional purpose during the prolonged, costly engagement. Some members of the rank and file became politically active, like Candido da Fonseca Galvão, also known as Prince Obá, a black veteran who attended Dom Pedro II's weekly public audiences and published a series of ephemeral newspapers in Rio de Janeiro. Officers who had fought at the front also became keenly aware of the political opportunities afforded to their brothers in arms in the Spanish republics and many became ardent Republicans as a result. Moreover, many came to develop abolitionist sympathies as a result of seeing colored recruits and ex-slaves perform ably in the field of battle.

Abolition became a divisive political issue in the 1870s. By 1872, slaves constituted only 15 percent of the population, mostly concentrated in Brazil's economically dynamic center-south. Although Paulista planters were attempting to shift to free immigrant labor, less affluent coffee growers in Rio de Janeiro and Minas Gerais were more dependent on slaves. Urban slave populations also had grown during the empire, particularly in the city of Rio de Janeiro. As a major port and capital city, it employed slaves in a variety of jobs – gardening and stock raising, fishing and boating, domestic service, laundering, waste disposal, water carrying, construction, and dock work. Many captives occupied more skilled trades as carpenters, masons, metallurgists, barber–surgeons, midwives, healers, dressmakers, cooks, musicians and entertainers, prostitutes, and cooks. They attained a near monopoly in the marketing of produce and cooked food.

Slaves also predominated in the empire's most technologically advanced sectors. The *União e Industria* (Union and Industry) and Mucury companies employed both slave and free labor in the construction of modern roads in the province of Minas Gerais. The British-owned St. John d'el Rey Mining Company employed over 1,400 slaves in its highly capitalized gold mines by the 1860s. The 1845 Aberdeen Act forbade British nationals to own slaves regardless of their place of residence. The company got around this restriction by renting slaves instead of purchasing them outright. However, in 1879 abolitionist lawyer and politician Joaquim Nabuco discovered that the company had reneged on a deal to free a group of rented slaves in 1859. The case drew international attention and, in 1882, Brazilian courts ordered St. John d'el Rey to free the remaining 223 slaves and to pay them back wages (Eakin 1989).

The first significant legal abolitionist measure, the Law of the Free Womb, was approved on September 28, 1871. It granted freedom to slave children born after that date upon reaching the age of 21. Owners could receive some indemnification from the state if they freed slave children at age eight. In addition, the law made provisions for mandatory slave registration, and the creation of an emancipation fund. It also provided legal protection for property accumulated by captives, prohibited the separation of married slave couples, and safeguarded conditional manumission.

In 1880, Joaquim Nabuco established the Brazilian Anti-Slavery Society. Nabuco and other reformers such as José do Patrocinio, the illegitimate son of a planter, André Rebouças, a mulatto engineer, and Luiz Gama, a lawyer and ex-slave, generated enthusiasm for the cause, principally in urban areas. In 1884, the provinces of Ceará and Amazonas, neither possessing a sizable captive population, abolished slavery. The following year, the Saraiva–Cotegipe law freed slaves above the age of 60, while requiring that they work for their former owners for three more years, and those of 65 and older without indemnification. By 1886, slaves had begun to desert coffee plantations in significant numbers, aided and abetted by abolitionist agents. Finally, on May 13, 1888, princess regent Isabel signed the law passed by Parliament freeing Brazil's remaining 750,000 slaves – by then just 5 percent of Brazil's population of over 14 million. Despite widespread elite fears, by the date of final abolition European immigrants were streaming into the São Paulo coffee zone (Holloway 1977), while many ex-slaves continued to labor in other areas, and economic disruption proved minimal. No subsequent social legislation was passed to help the newly freed adjust to their new status or to train them for decent wage employment.

The abolition of slavery also contributed to the currency of new racial ideologies in Brazil. As the Brazilian elite faced slavery's end and sought to attract European immigrants to meet the nation's labor needs, it also was influenced by racial paradigms from abroad. European theorists offered gloomy assessments of Brazil's ability to progress given its racially mixed heritage. Many Brazilian intellectuals came to advocate whitening, aggressively promoting white immigration to lighten (and modernize) the population. Such views were not universally held; for example, military officers looked toward positivism and social engineering as a solution for Brazil's perceived racial woes. However, the linking of blackness to theories of racial degeneration contributed to discrimination in the workplace in the post-emancipation period.

After 1870 the patronage-based, two-party political system could no longer accommodate emergent social groups. Increasing numbers of urban professionals, a glut of law students who traditionally had staffed the imperial bureaucracy and legislatures, newly affluent Paulista coffee growers, and perhaps most importantly, the military, became increasingly frustrated. The army's stature had grown following the War of the Triple Alliance but the central government's gratitude proved to be short-lived. The military budget was downsized and officers and demobilized veterans alike faced limited opportunities for advancement. Universal draft legislation was established in 1874 to broaden the class base of the military but the measure was not enforced due to popular resistance. Draft registration was one of the motives behind the *Quebra Quilos* revolt that broke out in the northeastern backlands in 1874. Although the unrest took its name from popular rejection of metric weights and measures, protesters also destroyed tax and draft lists housed in local notary archives.

Stifled military officers also began to question the corrupt nature of late imperial patronage politics and saw themselves as a morally redemptive force, a sense of national mission that would endure well into the twentieth century. The army found ideological inspiration in the positivist philosophy of Auguste Comte, which soon became part of the curriculum of the military academy. The army's sense of itself as a technocratic elite that was vital to Brazil's future progress was challenged by the "military question" in 1883. At the time, officers resented the civilian minister of war's control over military discipline, appointments, and dismissals. Throughout the 1880s, Pedro II appointed civilians to head the War Ministry. As military spokesmen began to debate the issue in the press, an edict was passed in 1884 prohibiting officers from discussing political or military affairs in print without prior approval of the minister of war, thus curbing military freedom of speech. The ruling was overturned in 1886 but the officers involved in the dispute received no apologies and considered the entire affair an affront to their honor.

A conflict over the relationship of church and state also contributed to the empire's destabilization, albeit to a much lesser extent. The "church question" (1872–5) challenged the Brazilian government's right of patronage, a privilege dating from colonial times that allowed the state to endorse or dismiss papal edicts. A crisis emerged when a European priest, Dom Vital Maria Gonçalves de Olivera, became Bishop of Olinda and attempted to enforce an 1864 encyclical that condemned the Masonic Order. Although the Masons were often associated with anti-clericalism in Europe, they had coexisted peacefully with Catholicism in Brazil. Even the Emperor, Dom Pedro II, and many other prominent statesmen were practicing Masons. Dom Vital, however, took a hard line and began suspending and excommunicating Masons in his diocese. The papacy supported his actions but the Brazilian Council of State did not and sentenced Dom Vital to a prison term. After much wrangling the bishops were granted amnesty and the papacy modified its position on Brazilian masonry. The divisiveness occasioned by the church question had the effect of strengthening those who favored the separation of church and state, namely Republicans, positivists, and the military.

By the mid-1870s, Dom Pedro II was seen as increasingly ineffective and out-moded. His health began to decline due in part to obesity and diabetes. Critics saw him as old-fashioned, an intellectual dilettante, and ever more rigid in his thinking. He became the subject of satires and lampooning in the popular press. He also lacked a viable male heir. His one surviving daughter, Isabel, periodically served as regent but both her gender and her religious inclinations made her unsuitable to succeed him, in the eyes of many. Her French husband, the Conde D'Eu, suffered from stress, ill health, and deafness. Dom Pedro II's grandsons were still too young and four out of the five had been raised in Europe.

Regional economic differentiation added to political dissatisfaction. The center-south continued to benefit most in terms of investment, infrastructure, and popula-tion increase. The city of Rio de Janeiro doubled in size between 1872 and 1890 and São Paulo grew at 5–8 percent per year during the same period. Most of the 9,000 kilometers of railroad track laid by 1889 served Rio and São Paulo. The north-ern provinces of Pará and Amazonas also experienced unprecedented economic growth due to a rubber boom that began in the 1870s. By the late 1880s, rubber comprised 10 percent of Brazil's export revenues. Yet both São Paulo and Pará were underrepresented in the Chamber of Deputies by the empire's end.

The economy also remained largely dependent on export agriculture. This made Brazil vulnerable to price fluctuations in the world market and to international finan-cial crises. The state continued to regulate private enterprise, requiring legislative approval of all joint-stock companies. Internal investment beyond agriculture was minimal, banking remained underdeveloped, and foreigners dominated access to credit. Technical innovation was limited largely to improving processing of sugar and coffee; Brazilian light manufacturing experienced little innovation or growth. The government's failure to enact protectionist legislation displeased nascent industrialists and workers alike. Free urban workers also began to act politically, when they pro-tested increases in streetcar fares in the *revolta do vintem* (penny riot) in 1880.

The *vintem* riot was the catalyst for the passage of electoral reform in 1881 that was long in coming. The traditional parties remained divided over the measure but the system of indirect elections, long associated with electoral corruption, was elimi-nated. Although the new law granted the vote to non-Catholics, thereby favoring immigrants, it imposed a literacy requirement. This had the result of restricting suffrage to just one percent of the population and favoring urban areas, where literacy rates were higher, over rural areas. The 1881 elections were conducted freely and fairly but, within a few years, reverted back to business as usual, suggesting that what was at issue was not the law but the will to enforce it.

In the changing political milieu of the 1880s, the Republicans finally began to make modest gains. Up until the mid-1880s, political representation at the highest levels of government had been limited to a single minister of justice, appointed in 1878, and three deputies to the Chamber in 1884. Its platform was too similar to the Liberals and some Republicans went back and forth between the two parties or ran for office under a Liberal ticket. Party adherents clustered in the center-south, with the greatest base of support in São Paulo, where federalist aspirations were most grounded in economic self-interest. Republican organization solidified later in Minas Gerais and remained somewhat weak in Rio de Janeiro. However, they gained decisively following slave emancipation in 1888, which caused many former slaveholders and their political representatives to withdraw support from the political status quo. A Liberal cabinet under the leadership of Afonso Celso proposed some defensive reforms to satisfy Republican demands, including greater local legislative autonomy, abolition of life tenure in the Senate and the Council of State, and religious freedom. However, it was too little, too late, and was insufficiently federalist in content. The Chamber of Deputies balked and was dissolved.

A Republican military officer, Marshal Manoel Deodoro da Fonseca (1827–92), effected a coup on November 15, 1889, a plan that had been in the making as early as May 1887. In so doing he had the support of Floriano Peixoto, the adjutant general of the army, the officer corps, most of the rank and file, and the Paulista Republicans. The civilian ministers surrendered relatively peacefully and D. Pedro II and the royal family agreed to exile in Paris, where he died two years later in 1891. The Republic (1889–1930) that replaced the Empire achieved the desired goal of decentralized government. But many of the fundamental political, social, and economic characteristics of the Empire remained intact, including a patronage-based, rural-dominated, political system, restricted popular suffrage, socioeconomic hierarchies structured according to race, class, and gender, and excessive economic dependence on export agriculture.

BIBLIOGRAPHY

Barman, R. J. (1988) *Brazil: the Forging of a Nation, 1798–1852.* Stanford University Press, Stanford.

Barman, R. J. (1999) *Citizen Emperor: Pedro II and the Making of Brazil, 1825–91.* Stanford University Press, Stanford.

Barman, R. J. (2002) *Princess Isabel of Brazil: Gender and Power in the Nineteenth Century.* Scholarly Resources, Wilmington, DE.

Beattie, P. M. (2001) *The Tribute of Blood: Army, Honor, Race, and Nation in Brazil, 1864–1945.* Duke University Press, Durham.

Bethell, L. (1970) *The Abolition of the Brazilian Slave Trade. Britain, Brazil and the Slave Trade Question, 1807–1869.* Cambridge University Press, Cambridge.

Bethell, L. (ed.) (1989) *Brazil: Empire and Republic, 1822–1930.* Cambridge University Press, Cambridge.

Bieber, J. (1999) *Power, Patronage, and Political Violence: State Building on a Brazilian Frontier, 1822–1889.* University of Nebraska Press, Lincoln.

Borges, D. (1992) *The Family in Bahia, Brazil, 1870–1945*. Stanford University Press, Stanford.

Caldeira, J. (1995) *Mauá: Empresário do Império*. Companhia das Letras, São Paulo.

Carvalho, J. M. de (1981) *A construção da ordem: A elite política imperial*. Editora Universidade de Brasília, Brasília.

Carvalho, J. M. de (1988) *Teatro de sombras: A política imperial*. Vértice, São Paulo.

Chalhoub, S. (1990) *Visões da liberdade: Uma história das últimas décadas da escravidão na corte*. Companhia das Letras, São Paulo.

Conrad, R. (1972) *The Destruction of Brazilian Slavery, 1850–1888*. University of California Press, Berkeley.

Conrad, R. (1983) *Children of God's Fire: A Documentary History of Black Slavery in Brazil*. Princeton University Press, Princeton.

Conrad, R. (1986) *Worlds of Sorrow: The African Slave Trade to Brazil*. University of Louisiana Press, Baton Rouge.

Costa, E. V. da (1985) *The Brazilian Empire, Myths and Histories*. University of Chicago Press, Chicago.

Dean, W. (1971) "Latifundia and Land Policy in Nineteenth-Century Brazil," *Hispanic American Historical Review*, 51, pp. 606–25.

Dean, W. (1976) *Rio Claro: A Brazilian Plantation System, 1820–1920*. Stanford University Press, Stanford.

Dias, M. O. L. da S. (1995) *Power and Everyday Life. The Lives of Working Women in Nineteenth-Century Brazil*. Rutgers University Press, New Brunswick.

Eakin, M. C. (1989) *British Enterprise in Brazil. The St. John d'el Rey Company and the Morro Velho Mine, 1830–1960*. Duke University Press, Durham.

Eisenberg, P. L. (1974) *The Sugar Industry in Pernambuco, Modernization without Change, 1840–1910*. University of California Press, Berkeley.

Flory, T. (1981) *Judge and Jury in Imperial Brazil, 1808–1871: Social Control and Political Stability in the New State*. University of Texas Press, Austin.

Frank, Z. L. (2004) *Dutra's World: Wealth and Family in Nineteenth-Century Rio de Janeiro*. University of New Mexico Press, Albuquerque.

Graham, R. (1968) *Britain and the Onset of Modernization in Brazil, 1850–1914*. Cambridge University Press, Cambridge.

Graham, R. (1990) *Patronage and Politics in Nineteenth-Century Brazil*. Stanford University Press, Stanford.

Graham, S. L. (1988) *House and Street: The Domestic World of Servants and Masters in Nineteenth-Century Rio de Janeiro*. Cambridge University Press, Cambridge.

Graham, S. L. (2002) *Caetana Says No: Women's Stories from a Brazilian Slave Society*. Cambridge University Press, Cambridge.

Hahner, J. E. (1990) *Emancipating the Female Sex: The Struggle for Women's Rights in Brazil, 1850–1940*. Duke University Press, Durham.

Haring, C. H. (1958) *Empire in Brazil: A New World Experiment with Monarchy*. Cambridge University Press, Cambridge.

Holloway, T. H. (1977) "Immigration and Abolition: The Transition from Slave to Free Labor in the São Paulo Coffee Zone." In D. Alden & W. Dean (eds.), *Essays Concerning the Socio-Economic History of Brazil and Portuguese India*. University Presses of Florida, Gainesville, pp. 150–78.

Holloway, T. H. (1980) *Immigrants on the Land: Coffee and Society in São Paulo, 1886–1934*. University of North Carolina Press, Chapel Hill.

Holloway, T. H. (1993) *Policing Rio de Janeiro: Repression and Resistance in a Nineteenth-Century City*. Stanford University Press, Stanford.

Karasch, M. (1987) *Slave Life in Rio de Janeiro, 1808–1850*. Princeton University Press, Princeton.

Kirkendall, A. (2002) *Class Mates: Male Student Culture and the Making of a Political Class in Nineteenth-Century Brazil*. University of Nebraska Press, Lincoln.

Kraay, H. (2001) *Race, State, and Armed Forces in Independence-Era Brazil: Bahia, 1790's–1840's*. Stanford University Press, Stanford.

Kraay, H. & Whigham, T. L. (eds.) (2004) *I Die With My Country: Perspectives on the Paraguayan War, 1864–1870*. University of Nebraska Press, Lincoln.

Kuznesof, E. (1986) *Household Economy and Urban Development: São Paulo, 1765–1836*. Westview Press, Boulder, CO.

Levi, D. (1987) *The Prados of São Paulo, Brazil: An Elite Family and Social Change, 1840–1930*. University of Georgia Press, Athens.

Lewin, L. (2003) *Surprise Heirs*, Volume 2: *Illegitimacy, Inheritance Rights, and Public Power in the Formation of Imperial Brazil, 1822–1889*. Stanford University Press, Stanford.

Macaulay, N. (1986) *Dom Pedro: The Struggle for Liberty in Brazil and Portugal, 1798–1834*. Duke University Press, Durham.

Marchant, A. (1965) *Viscount Mauá and the Empire of Brazil*. University of California Press, Berkeley.

Mattos, I. R. de (1990) *O tempo saquarema. A formação do estado imperial*, 2nd ed. Hucitec, São Paulo.

Nabuco, J. (1977 [1883]) *Abolitionism: The Brazilian Antislavery Struggle*, trans. and ed. R. Conrad. University of Illinois Press, Urbana.

Nazzari, M. (1991) *Disappearance of the Dowry: Women, Families, and Social Change in São Paulo, Brazil (1600–1900)*. Stanford University Press, Stanford.

Needell, J. (2006) *The Party of Order: The Conservatives, the State, and Slavery in the Brazilian Monarchy, 1831–1871*. Stanford University Press, Stanford.

Nishida, M. (2003) *Slavery and Identity: Ethnicity, Gender, and Race in Salvador, Brazil, 1808–1888*. Indiana University Press, Bloomington.

Reis, J. J. (1993) *Slave Rebellion in Brazil: The Muslim Uprising of 1835 in Bahia*. Johns Hopkins University Press, Baltimore.

Russell-Wood, A. J. R. (1975) *From Colony to Nation: Essays on the Independence of Brazil*. Johns Hopkins University Press, Baltimore.

Schultz, K. (2001) *Tropical Versailles. Empire, Monarchy and the Portuguese Royal Court in Rio de Janeiro, 1808–1821*. Routledge, London.

Schwarcz, L. M. (2004) *The Emperor's Beard: Dom Pedro II and His Tropical Monarchy in Brazil*. Hill and Wang, New York.

Silva, E. (1993) *Prince of the People: The Life and Times of a Brazilian Free Man of Colour*. Verso, London and New York.

Simmons, C. W. (1966) *Marshal Deodoro and the Fall of Dom Pedro II*. Duke University Press, Durham.

Skidmore, T. E. (1993) *Black into White: Race and Nationality in Brazilian Thought*. Duke University Press, Durham.

Stein, S. J. (1957) *Vassouras: A Brazilian Coffee County, 1850–1900*. Harvard University Press, Cambridge, MA.

Toplin, R. B. (1972) *The Abolition of Slavery in Brazil*. Atheneum, New York.

Uricoechea, F. (1980) *The Patrimonial Foundations of the Brazilian Bureaucratic State*. University of California Press, Berkeley.

Weinstein, B. (1983) *The Amazon Rubber Boom, 1850–1920*. Stanford University Press, Stanford.

Chapter Fifteen

ABOLITION AND AFRO-LATIN AMERICANS

Aline Helg

It took almost a whole century for slavery to be abolished in Latin America: from the abolition decree of the French revolutionary commissioner Léger-Félicité Sonthonax in Saint-Domingue in 1793 to the Golden Law signed by the Princess Regent Isabel in Brazil in 1888. Between these two years, revolutions, independences, counterrevolutions, and civil wars upset the region, often putting slavery and the fate of emancipated slaves in the forefront.

The Haitian Revolution (1791–1804) left a long-lasting and contradictory impact on the process of abolition in the Americas. Through massive uprisings, free people of African descent and slaves in Saint-Domingue won two major victories from the French revolutionary legislature. In 1792, on the basis of the 1789 Declaration of the Rights of Man, all free men of color were granted full equality with whites. In 1793, Sonthonax signed a non-official decree abolishing slavery in Saint-Domingue. Then, in February 1794, the French National Convention voted for the complete abolition of slavery in all its American colonies and granted full French citizenship to all former slaves. These decisions, taken shortly after the execution of King Louis XVI, showed for the first time that massive rebellion by people of African descent could force a world power to abolish slavery and racial inequality. There followed then more stunning events: the rise of former slave Toussaint Louverture to the governorship of Saint-Domingue, the destruction of the colony's plantations, the elimination of its whites through exile or massacre, the successful resistance by freedmen and free people of color to Napoleon's attempts to restore slavery and French domination, and finally the independence of the former colony, renamed Haiti, in 1804. Haiti's first constitution, in 1805, confirmed the abolition of slavery, proclaimed all Haitians free, "black," and equal regardless of color, and made it illegal for whites to own land (Geggus 2002: 5–29).

The victory of the Haitian Revolution was a turning point in history that upset the models of modernity established by the US and French revolutions. For slaves all over the Americas, it became a source of hope and inspiration. For planters and ruling elites, it was a source of fear, leading them to bloodily repress any attempt by free and enslaved people of African descent to assert their rights. The Haitian Revolution also tempered the zeal of abolitionists in Europe and the United States, who began to support gradual, rather than immediate, emancipation.

Indeed in the early 1800s, slavery was far from marginal in the Americas. Since the early sixteenth century, all Spanish and Portuguese colonies had depended, in various degrees, on African slavery. Madrid's loosening of the slave trade regulations in 1789 fostered new imports of *bozales*, notably in Cuba, Puerto Rico, Venezuela, and Río de la Plata. Although the Haitian Revolution increased whites' anxieties about people of color, its destruction of the most profitable sugar economy created new opportunities for Puerto Rico and, above all, for Cuba, which became the new Pearl of the Antilles. In Brazil, too, sugar and coffee plantations thrived from the late eighteenth century, thanks to massive importation of African slaves.

By 1800, slaves comprised 37 percent of the total population in Brazil, 35 percent in Cuba, and 29 percent in the Spanish portion of Hispaniola. In Colombia, Venezuela, and Puerto Rico, between 8 and 15 percent of all inhabitants were slaves, whereas elsewhere they were 6 percent or less. However, except in Brazil and Cuba, slaves were largely outnumbered by free people of African descent, with the result that everywhere in Latin America Afro-descended people were an important component of society: between 6 and 10 percent in countries with an indigenous majority, such as Mexico, Peru, and Ecuador; between 23 and 39 percent in Colombia, Argentina, and Uruguay. In Brazil, Venezuela, Cuba, Puerto Rico, Santo Domingo, and Panama, free and enslaved people of African descent were the absolute majority. Only in Chile and Uruguay did whites comprise the majority of the population (Andrews 2004: 41).

The importance of a free population of African descent relative to slaves stemmed largely from Spanish colonial laws that gave slaves the right to purchase their freedom (manumission) – even against their masters' will. In Brazil, self-purchase was also legal but required the consent of slaves' owners. Manumission implied years of extra work in order to progressively accumulate one's value. It was almost inaccessible to plantation slaves, but not to those working in gold mining or to urban slaves living independently from their owners to whom they paid a rent. Thus, women outnumbered men among the free population of color, because most urban slaves were female.

Obviously, the estimated 3,200,000 men, women, and children of African descent living in Latin America around 1800 were far from a homogeneous group. In Brazil and Cuba, where thousands of African slaves forcibly arrived each year, slavery dominated most economic activities, and ties with African cultures were stronger than in Colombia or Venezuela, for example, where the overwhelming majority was American-born and free. "Full" blacks were also more numerous in Brazil and Cuba than elsewhere, where *mestizaje* with Native Americans and Iberians was common. Those who had been brought over from Africa (predominantly Yoruba-speaking peoples and Congos) distinguished themselves from those from families of generations of American residence. Those who had experienced slavery also traveled different paths from those with long-standing free lineage. Among the latter were some artisans, small proprietors, housekeepers, and semi-professionals, who were literate and owned their businesses.

Nevertheless, for the Spanish authorities, all people of African descent fell under the depreciative label of *castas*. Whereas whites, Indians, and their *mestizo* offspring were credited with purity, African slaves and their mixed or unmixed descendants were attributed a permanent "depraved origin." The "stain of slavery" severely reduced their options as it hereditarily excluded them from the *limpieza de sangre* (blood purity) necessary, together with legitimate birth, for most civil, military, and church positions; for admission to secondary and higher education; for the legal exercise of some arts and crafts; and for all kinds of grants and honors.

Yet, in many regions the pool of whites able to prove limpieza de sangre and legitimate birth was too small for racial exclusion to be fully respected, allowing for some castas to accede to positions and trades legally closed to them. After the beginning of the Haitian Revolution, the Spanish monarchy made paradoxical decisions to overcome demographic shortcomings. In particular, it decided to continue to entrust much of the defense of its colonies with a large population of castas and slaves to militiamen of African descent and to grant them the privileges of the military *fuero*. Simultaneously, for fear that they emulate Saint-Domingue's free people of color, Spain issued a series of decrees that conceived of the free castas as hereditarily corrupted in their political ideas by their slave origins. New regulations made marriages between castas and whites of noble status and/or legitimate birth contingent on licenses issued by the viceroyalties (Helg 2004: 100–5).

The abduction of King Ferdinand VII by Napoleon Bonaparte in 1808 marked the beginning of the process of independence in continental Spanish America, with major implications for people of African origin. Until 1814, patriots and royalists fought for the control of regional power in conflicts that resembled civil wars more than anti-colonial struggles. Everywhere, both sides recruited slaves with the promise of freedom. Thousands of mestizos, free castas, and whites also joined the struggle. In some regions, the war took a definitive socioracial dimension. In Mexico, the revolutionary movement initiated by Catholic priests Miguel Hidalgo and José María Morelos (himself of partial African descent), overwhelmingly comprised Indians, mestizos, castas, and runaway slaves, who abolished racial distinctions and slavery and attacked the Spanish and creole elite – prompting the joint reaction of the latter groups. In Venezuela, royalists managed to mobilize *pardos* (free castas) and numerous slaves against the patriots who represented the interests of the creole slave planters. Led by the black José Tomás Boves, the *llaneros* (cowboys) waged a race war reminiscent of the Haitian Revolution against the pro-independence elite and whites in general. At this point, Simón Bolívar, himself a slave-owning aristocrat, realized that Venezuela's independence could not be won without the support of the majority of African descent. He recast the war in new terms: a war to the death between Americans regardless of race and Spaniards. Nevertheless, only with Boves's death and the material support of Haiti did pardos and slaves begin to fight against Spain. In contrast, in Caribbean Colombia most free men of color, including those in the colonial militia, fought for independence. In the south of the continent as well, men of African descent were numerous in the patriot troops. The army of General José San Martín, recruited in Río de la Plata, included not only a majority of castas, but hundreds of slaves, who were joined by hundreds more in Chile and Peru as the liberation army progressed toward Lima (Blackburn 1988: 337–57).

The overrepresentation of men of African descent in the patriot armies had a direct impact on the sociopolitical systems adopted after independence. Most Latin American nations became republics; they abolished the caste system and granted legal equality and qualified suffrage to all adult men *regardless of race*. This pathbreaking racial inclusion erased the "stain of slavery," which for centuries had legally maintained blacks and mulattos in an inferior position. It contrasted sharply with the 1812 Constitution of the Spanish monarchy, which continued to exclude them from the new voting rights it granted to Indians and mestizos. Of course, legal equality regardless of race did not radically modify political and social institutions, which remained almost exclusively in white hands. Nor did it mean universal male suffrage. Up to the mid-nineteenth century, constitutions in general stipulated that all men should defend their homeland but disenfranchised those without property or an independent income – namely, servants and wage laborers, who in their great majority were of partial or full African or Indian descent (Helg 2004: 242–5).

As for Brazil, it achieved independence with little fighting during a phase of rapid expansion of slavery, when in 1822 the son of the king of Portugal crowned himself emperor of Brazil. Earlier, in the 1798 Tailors' Revolt in Bahia and in the 1817 republican uprising in Pernambuco, Afro-Brazilian soldiers and artisans had shown that they were ready to fight for equality. The 1824 imperial constitution granted citizenship to all free male Brazilians, regardless of race. All discriminatory laws vanished, but the constitution excluded *libertos* (free men born in slavery) from voting in secondary elections. Because qualification as a second-degree elector was a prerequisite for almost all high posts, this stipulation de facto discriminated against libertos (Da Costa 2000: 59–62).

Regarding slavery, the record of the new Latin American nations is much less imposing than on the subject of the legal equality of free men. In fact, there was no correlation between independence and abolition. Although pro-independence discourse had often portrayed the colonized homeland as a chained slave, now in the name of private property a majority in the ruling elite refused to grant freedom to the enslaved. Most patriot leaders, often slaveholders themselves, did not perceive slavery as contradictory with a republic. During the early 1810s, they abolished the slave trade, partly on British insistence. However, only the revolutionary movements of Hidalgo and Morelos in Mexico decreed the full abolition of slavery (a decision reversed after their defeat), whereas patriots in Chile and Río de la Plata issued free womb laws (Lynch 1986). In 1816, Bolívar promised President Alexandre Pétion to abolish slavery in the territories he would liberate in return for Haiti's support. Although in 1818 Bolívar issued two edicts that unconditionally abolished slavery in Venezuela, submitting former slaves to the service of arms equally with all male inhabitants, one year later Venezuela's Fundamental Law ignored these edicts and did not mention abolition (Helg 2004: 245–6).

In the early 1820s, with independence achieved, Chile and Central America, where slaves were few, ended slavery as a logical consequence of the principles of liberty and equality. Mexico followed in 1829, under the brief presidency of General Vicente Guerrero, a man of Afro-indigenous ancestry who had been a commander in the Morelos insurgency (Carroll 1991: 110–11). Slavery was abolished in the Dominican Republic in 1822 under Haitian occupation (Sagás 2000: 29–31). In contrast, Venezuela and most other former Spanish colonies issued laws of manumission that only foresaw abolition in the long term. These laws confirmed the ban on the importation of new slaves, but allowed all kinds of transactions within the country. They declared the freedom of the newborn (free womb) but submitted children to unpaid labor for the owner of their slave mothers until they reached adulthood. They stipulated the creation of manumission funds to compensate owners for the freedom of the most "deserving" adult slaves, but these funds were so poor that at best they purchased the freedom of a handful of slaves each year.

Thus, after independence, self-purchase continued to be the principal legal means by which slaves gained their freedom. No legislation aimed at easing the condition of the existing slave population, but new vagrancy laws focused on the repression of flight and assistance to fugitive slaves. Domestic service as well as the mining of gold in the Pacific lowlands of Colombia and Ecuador, of sugar or cocoa in Peru and Venezuela, and of maté in Paraguay still largely depended on slaves. Slavery outlived independence also because no powerful abolitionist movement formed in these new nations – even in those where free people of African descent comprised the majority of the population. When 30 years later, in the 1850s, slavery was finally abolished in Argentina, Uruguay, Venezuela, Colombia, Ecuador, Peru, and Bolivia (Paraguay followed in 1869), it had crumbled as a result of the end of the slave trade, natural death, the upheaval of civil wars, flight, and slaves' self-purchase. By then the British, in 1838, and the French, in 1848, had emancipated all the slaves of their colonies (Lombardi 1971; Blackburn 1988: 358–75). Continental Spanish South America's abolition was, thus, belated.

Despite legal equality, post-independence governments were almost exclusively composed of whites who had had access to higher education under Spain. Few pardo military men became high-ranking officers, and even fewer achieved high political position under the republic they had contributed to forging. Many whites still feared a revolution along Haitian lines and promptly reacted to any attempts by people of African descent to organize and claim a more tangible equality than the one contained in constitutions and laws. Representative of this mindset was Bolívar's concern with what he labeled *pardocracia* (literally, the rule of the pardos – people of color), which would lead, according to him, to the extermination of whites. Bolívar believed that for many blacks and mulattos race was more important than the nation. This belief, added to his thirst for absolute leadership, could turn deadly for those who stood in his way. In 1817, Bolívar had the pardo Manuel Piar executed for challenging his supremacy by allegedly envisioning pardocracia, but he tamed with military advancement two white challengers. In 1828, he also secured the execution of General José Padilla, a pardo who played a decisive role in the liberation of Venezuela and Colombia but protested continuing racial privileges and seized power to defend the 1821 constitution against Bolívar's attempts to impose a semi-monarchical constitution. In Mexico, General Guerrero, who briefly became president in 1829, was not pardoned his lower-class and Afro-Indian origins and participation in Morelos's insurgency, and was executed by the creole aristocracy in 1831.

What sealed the fate of these men was not so much their partial African ancestry, exceptional among top political circles, but the fact that they did not silence it and used it to mobilize lower-class people. In contrast, a handful of Afro-descended leaders who integrated into white aristocratic circles without raising racial issues achieved elite recognition. For example, in Colombia the light pardo Juan José Nieto (1804–66), a merchant, self-taught writer, and Liberal politician of modest origins, became governor of the Province of Cartagena (1851–4) and president of the Sovereign State of Bolívar (1861–4). A few others, such as Bernardo Rivadavia, first president of Argentina in 1825–7, or Vicente Ramón Roca, president of Ecuador in

1845–9, passed for white but were rumored to have some African descent and often ridiculed for that reason (Andrews 1980: 82–3; Helg 2004: 4, 195–218).

As a whole, after independence conditions were particularly difficult in areas devastated by the wars, such as Venezuela and Colombia. In many cities, the white elite, black, pardo, and *zambo* (of mixed African and indigenous ancestry) artisans and leaders had been decimated by war, exile, and repression. Lower-class men of African descent had died disproportionately, leaving women as heads of households and the only wage earners. Employment for domestic servants, day laborers, laundresses, or market vendors was scarce, and beggars and indigents multiplied.

The countryside offered more opportunities, as untitled lands were abundant. The *baldíos* (vacant lands) that had belonged to the Spanish Crown and Spanish properties became national lands. Many plantations and haciendas had been destroyed or had lost part of their slave and free work force, and creole *hacendados* rarely had the necessary capital to rebuild them. Still, most republican governments shied away from distributing national lands to veteran soldiers and freedmen. Instead, they decided to make generous land distribution to European immigrants who would reinforce the white minority, now even smaller after the Spaniards' departure. Only a few European settlers ever materialized, but several members of the postcolonial elite benefited from the colonization scheme. Nevertheless, hacendados remained too few to recover their colonial power. The Catholic Church was too weak to provide enough priests. Thus, in many rural areas, land tenure was relatively open, and people felt little outside domination. Families of peasants and freedmen became squatters on abandoned and vacant lands, living in semi-autonomy and selling their surpluses on local markets. In the Pacific lowlands of Colombia and Ecuador, gold mining too opened up as a result of the postwar crisis. Many slaves ran away; others negotiated less exploitative relations with owners. *Libres* and *libertos*, often female, took possession of abandoned mines, combining cultivation with gold panning (Hudson 1964: 333; Legrand 1986: 6–13; Colmenares 1990).

The weak postcolonial institutional order did not prevent laborers, peasants, and artisans from envisioning of a fair balance between their rights and duties under the republic. Although few lower-class men and women left records of their feelings, no doubt some expected that their lives would improve under the legal equality guaranteed by republican constitutions. When the state, the military, and the Church began to require high contributions from them, they reacted. Up to the 1850s, the state showed its existence outside the main cities principally through its arbitrary and brutal recruitment into the army, which disproportionately fell on the rural poor of African and indigenous descent. People fiercely resisted recruitment, which ruined them. As most Spanish America entered into a period of conflict between regional *caudillos*, forced conscription often became a pattern, and laborers and peasants developed a long-lasting distrust of the state and its institutions (Helg 2004: 175–6, 188–9).

Indeed, by the 1840s politics became increasingly polarized and violent, often turning into civil wars. Although opposing parties drew from all sectors of society, the calls of federalism versus centralism or of liberalism versus conservatism were not meaningless. In general, Liberals (or Federalists) were better represented in provinces that had been marginal under Spain. There, the liberal rhetoric of liberty, equality, democracy, and citizenship echoed well among those still in slavery and those free black and mulattos discriminated because of their race. As for the Conservatives, they tended to be particularly strong in the areas that had concentrated state and church presence under Spain, where the traditional elite was unwilling to renounce its colonial privileges and, thus, championed the preservation of the old order. In Venezuela, these socioracial tensions exploded in the Federal War (1858–63), which pitted rebel armies of pardo peasants, peones, and freedmen under the banner of Liberalism against the Conservative government army (Wright 1990: 35–42). In Colombia as well, the Liberal Party was very strong in the Cauca Valley and the Caribbean Coast where the bulk of the population was black, mulatto, and zambo. Once the Liberals gained power in 1849, lower-class Afro-Colombians pressured for the abolition of slavery and universal male suffrage. Liberal leaders met their demands out of ideology and also to further attach them to the party – which proved crucial in the upcoming civil wars. Similar alignments could also be found in Peru and in Ecuador (Sanders 2004).

In Argentina, in contrast, the Liberal Unitarians failed to attract many blacks and mulattos against Federalist dictator Juan Manuel de Rosas, who recruited and promoted freedmen and free Afro-Argentineans in his armies and encouraged their ethnic societies – while simultaneously maintaining slavery and reauthorizing the slave trade. Only after the Unitarians defeated Rosas and abolished slavery in 1853 were they able to deprive Rosas of his black supporters. In Uruguay too, the long war against Rosas (1839–42) forced the government to deal with slavery in order to attract new recruits into the army: in 1842 slavery was abolished in principle but in reality able-bodied freedmen were forced to immediately enroll in the ranks, while remaining slaves continued in bondage and others were illegally sold to Brazil – extending slavery well into the 1850s. Black and mulattos were also drafted disproportionately in the deadly war that opposed Argentina and Brazil to Paraguay between 1865 and 1870. Although no source clearly demonstrates that Argentina sent its black battalions to fight in order to eliminate part of its Afro-descended population, Paraguay and Brazil, where slavery was still legal, used the old tactic of offering freedom to those slaves who would fight courageously (Andrews 1980: 96–101, 113–37).

Throughout continental Spanish America, the Liberal victory of the mid-nineteenth century ended up carrying bitter rewards for many in the party's lower-class supporters. Liberalism came with the defense of private property and free trade, allowing for manufactured goods from Europe to compete with the local production by artisans, often of mixed African or indigenous descent. These men, who had formed the backbone of many Liberal clubs in the 1840s, found themselves increasingly marginalized and impoverished (Wright 1990: 49–52; Sowell 1992: 54–80). Liberalism came also with the break-up of ecclesiastical, corporate, and communal property, thus with the privatization of land ownership. At the beginning these policies hit mostly religious orders and indigenous communities. But when insolvent governments began to issue certificates of public debt redeemable in public lands to back the national debt, they progressively reached villagers' communal grounds and squatters' untitled lands. As a result, in the 1860s people of African descent – and lower-class people in general – had to negotiate new arrangements to secure their living. Despite their resistance, many artisans were ruined and had to turn to wage labor. Unlike the *libres* and *libertos* in Cauca, who had struggled earlier to obtain the legalization of their settlements, numerous squatters lost the lands they tilled and were forced to become sharecroppers, peones, and day laborers, to migrate to cities in search of a living, or to squat further away in the hinterlands (Colmenares 1990).

If protest against racial discrimination was generally repressed in the name of legal equality, the continuing expression of African-derived alternative cultures encountered diverse reaction from postcolonial elites. In regions or cities in which people of African descent were in the minority, such as Buenos Aires, governments were in a better position to repress them. They passed laws against vagrancy, public disorder, or illegal association to police the lower classes. Especially targeted were black celebrations and street dances as well as black mutual-aid societies, suspected of hiding criminals and political activists (Andrews 1980: 143–52). In nations with an important population of African origin, such as Venezuela and Colombia, white leaders could not exercise hegemony. They tolerated and often sponsored lower-class subcultures. There, popular culture, with its triple – African, indigenous, and European – origins and religious syncretisms, gave meaning to people's lives. If *bailes*, festivals, and carnivals could allow for irreverent, immoral, and unruly conduct, they seldom directly challenged the power of the wealthy. In addition, most public celebrations represented the political system, validating the socioracial hierarchy, and strengthened clientage bonds and the sense of local community, while at the same time offering spaces for enjoyment (Pollak-Eltz 1991: 44–63; Helg 2004: 189–93, 256–60). However, in some enclaves, such as Barlovento in Venezuela or the former slave runaway community of Palenque de San Basilio in Caribbean Colombia, as well as in the Pacific lowlands of Ecuador and Colombia, the population was almost entirely black. Scant church and state presence allowed for several African-derived practices and rituals to thrive under powerful spiritual leaders, among whom women predominated. For example, baptisms of babies were performed long after the eight days following birth prescribed by the Church; funerals involved complex rituals of sorrow and joy; and worshippers associated Catholic saints with African spirits and "brought them down" in ceremonies of trance and possession (Escalante 1954).

In Cuba, Brazil, and, to a lesser extent, Puerto Rico, free blacks and mulattos shared many conditions with their peers in white-dominated Spanish continental America, but they faced an enormous additional handicap. Up to the 1860s, they lived in societies relying extensively on slave labor. This extreme contradiction – slavery in the age of individual freedoms – complicated free blacks' struggle for equal rights and had dramatic consequences for all people of African descent: the ideological construction of scientific racism to mask the falsehood of the liberal republic.

When Brazil became an independent constitutional monarchy in 1822 racial categories vanished from its laws, but in ensuing decades its economy based on slavery took on new life with the expansion of coffee production for export. In 1823 Brazil counted 1,147,515 slaves (about one-third of its population). Although still producing sugar in the northeast, it became the world's top producer of coffee, expanding its cultivation from Rio de Janeiro south and west. Coffee expansion depended on the growth of the enslaved work force which, given the appalling conditions on plantations, required the constant arrival of new African slaves. Despite laws banning the slave trade by 1831, Brazil illegally imported almost 1,000,000 slaves from Africa from the 1820s through the 1840s. At its peak around 1850, Brazil's slave population reached an estimated 1,700,000; slaves then represented half of the population in the coffee-producing southeast. After prohibitions on the transatlantic traffic were finally enforced after 1850 the number of slaves declined, as life expectancy continued very low. Coffee planters turned to internal trade, buying slaves from less demanding areas. By the time of Brazil's first national census, in 1872, slaves numbered 1,500,000, or 16 percent of the total population. With 4,245,428 individuals, free people of color had become the most numerous socioracial category (44 percent of the total), whereas whites represented 40 percent of the population. Yet slave labor continued to dominate in the export sectors (Curtin 1969: 234; Klein 1972: 314; Klein 1986: 124–9).

Throughout these decades, slaves resisted bondage in numerous ways – flight, conspiracy, rebellion (notably the 1835 Malê Rebellion, or Muslim uprising, in Bahia), sabotage, slow labor, and more discrete forms of resistance. In the 1830s slaves and free blacks also joined in regionalist uprisings in Pernambuco, Pará, Maranhão, and Bahia launched by local elites who progressively renounced their claims for fear of the lower classes. The 1837–8 Sabinada revolt in Bahia, in particular, named after its leader, mulatto physician Francisco Sabino, demanded full rights of citizenship and government positions for free individuals of color and attracted many runaway slaves. It ended only after the massacre of at least 1,000 rebels by government forces. After 1840, a precarious calm set in. The continuing arrival of Africans up to the 1850s helped maintain strong bonds among blacks on plantations and in cities, through the African ethnically based *nações* (nations) and Afro-Catholic religious brotherhoods (Reis 1993; Nishida 2003).

Simultaneously the free population of African descent grew and became increasingly diverse. In addition to performing manual trades, Afro-Brazilians were teachers, journalists, and writers. Quite unique in Latin America was the formation of a small Afro-Brazilian elite in some cities. Some mulattos (rather than blacks) studied at the university and became medical doctors, lawyers, and engineers. Some gained national and international fame, such as the mulatto writer and first president of the Brazilian Academy of Letters Joaquim Maria Machado de Assis, or the engineer and abolitionist André Rebouças. Afro-Brazilians were also represented in state and national administrations, in the officer ranks of the army, and in the clergy. Several were elected to the National Parliament and state legislatures. A few mulattos even entered the nobility, such as the Conservative politician Francisco de Sales Tôrres Homem, the illegitimate child of a black laundress and a renegade priest, who graduated in medicine and became senator, minister of finance, and president of the Bank of Brazil before being ennobled as Viscount of Inhomerim by the emperor Pedro II. Needless to say, such a stellar rise was exceptional in a Brazilian society dominated by racial slavery. Despite legal equality for the free, these Afro-Brazilians could not have achieved success without white aristocratic patronage (Klein 1972: 328–9).

In contrast, in Puerto Rico and, above all, Cuba, where slavery also intensified in the nineteenth century, any advancement of free people of African descent along Brazilian lines was unthinkable. There the question of slavery mixed with that of continued colonialism. To Spain and to the creole planters, slavery guaranteed high revenues of sugar production. In the eyes of the elites of both islands, launching an independence war meant risking a revolution along Haitian lines, a risk that Madrid never failed to raise. Indeed, in 1812 black artisan José Antonio Aponte planned a widespread rebellion with other free men of color and some slaves to end slavery and colonialism in Cuba. The conspirators were brutally repressed, yet they left a sense of vulnerability among the island's whites (Childs 2006). Nevertheless, slavery and sugar production continued to thrive. Despite Spain's agreement to ban the slave trade in 1817, planters imported about 550,000 slaves between 1811 and 1866. By 1817, Cuba had about 200,000 slaves who comprised more than one-third of the population. Free people of color were 115,600. For the first time, whites were in the minority (45 percent). By 1841, Cuba had become the world's top sugar producer, with 437,000 slaves in a total population of one million (Curtin 1969: 234; Thomas 1998: 169). One-third of these slaves worked on sugar plantations. As in Brazil, overexploitation, abuse, demographic imbalance (most new African slaves were men), and poor living conditions prevented the natural growth of the slave labor force.

With the expansion of racial slavery, the conditions of free people of African descent deteriorated in the two remaining Spanish colonies. Unlike their peers in independent Latin America, they continued to be submitted to racially discriminatory laws and excluded from suffrage until the 1870s. In Cuba, as whites were outnumbered by blacks and mulattos, the fear of a revolution along Haitian lines increased. In 1844, Spain discovered the alleged Conspiracy of La Escalera, in which thousands of slaves and free persons of color were accused of secretly organizing for abolition and independence. This accusation had some actual basis, as La Escalera revealed the existence of extensive networks linking urban free blacks and mulattos to plantation slaves. But the conspiracy's violent repression and the ever more racist legislation that followed, by further restricting the rights of free people of color, brought them even closer to the slaves under the single label of *raza de color* (race of color). Cuba, unlike the rest of Latin America, began to show a two-tier racial system close to that of the United States, but one that not only preexisted US influence but also distinguished itself from the US "one drop rule" system: in Cuba, the barrier separating blacks and mulattos from whites was based on "visible" African phenotype (skin color, hair structure, and/or facial features). Ironically, Cuba's color bar and two-tier racial system, which prohibited the absorption of some highly educated mulattos into the white planter-dominated elite (as happened in Brazil), favored the relative cohesion of the Afro-Cuban population and facilitated its mobilization in the 1860s (Helg 1995: 3–4; Paquette 1988).

The US Civil War changed everything for Cuba and Puerto Rico. In 1865, the Union navy put an end to the Cuban slave trade and imposed the abolition of slavery on the US South. Simultaneously, Puerto Rican and Spanish Liberals founded the first Spanish abolitionist society in Madrid. Then in 1868 progressive Liberals gained power in Spain. The continuation of slavery in the two Spanish colonies was seriously threatened. In Cuba free Afro-Cubans were recovering from the state terror of 1844 and organizing again. For some white creole elites, independence became an option. In this new context, some planters in the eastern province of Oriente launched the island's first war of independence (1868–78). Under the pressure of their troops, rapidly formed by a majority of free blacks and mulattos and fugitive slaves, in late 1870 the rebel leaders declared the immediate and total abolition of slavery in the territories they controlled. This decision alienated planters in sugar-producing central Cuba and confined the independence movement to the east. In Puerto Rico, too, a group of creoles rebelled against Spain but they were promptly dominated (Scott 1985: 45–62).

In the meantime, in 1870 the Spanish Cortes (Parliament) voted the Moret Law, which gradually emancipated the slaves (free womb, unpaid labor for children until adulthood, freedom for slaves older than 60 years, new manumission procedures). But this law, which would have maintained slavery for another 60 years in the two Caribbean colonies, did not solve the crisis: slaves struggled more than ever to buy their freedom, and in Cuba many also fled to the liberated territories in Oriente. In 1873, Spain's king abdicated, and the short-lived First Republic was proclaimed. A new electoral law ended the exclusion of men of African descent from suffrage. The Republic immediately abolished slavery in Puerto Rico, where slaves were no more than 29,000 (less than 5 percent of the population) – but not in Cuba, where slaves were 288,000 (25 percent of the population) and where the war still raged. In 1874, the monarchy was restored, and, with it, Cuban planters' interests. White insurgent leaders, increasingly worried about black military participation, signed the Treaty of Zanjón with Madrid in 1878. Slaves who had won their freedom in the war remained free, but the Moret Law, and thus slavery, remained untouched. Hundreds of rebels, mostly Afro-Cubans under the leadership of mulatto leader Antonio Maceo, launched a new insurrection to obtain immediate abolition and independence. Spain responded with repression and with a new law that nominally ended slavery but replaced it with the *patronato* (patronage). Slaves, renamed *patrocinados*, were to gain freedom after eight years of "apprenticeship" – in 1888. Slavery rapidly disintegrated as a result of slaves' continuing self-purchase and flight as well as natural death. With only 25,000 patrocinados left in 1886, the Spanish government abolished slavery in that year (Scott 1985: 63–83, 111–72; Schmidt-Nowara 1999: 126–60).

Two years later, in 1888, Brazil, too, ended slavery earlier than stipulated by its own law of gradual emancipation and apprenticeship. Abolitionism there also remained marginal until the US Civil War, which prompted fears of massive slave revolts. In 1871, the imperial government promulgated the Rio Branco Law, or Law of the Free Womb, similar to the Moret Law. At first, the Brazilian law, which theoretically extended slavery until the death of the last slave born before September 28, 1871, was not seriously opposed. Only in 1880 did slaves begin to rebel in several plantations. Simultaneously, large sectors of the intellectual elite (such as deputy Joaquim Nabuco, founder in 1880 of the Brazilian Anti-slavery Society) and the popular classes, regardless of race, mobilized against slavery throughout the country. The movement won its first victory in 1884, with the unconditional abolition of slavery in the northeastern state of Ceará. As a result, secret networks formed that led fugitive slaves to Ceará, like the US Underground Railroad. In response, the planter-dominated parliament declared the freedom of slaves over 60 years old but approved a US-inspired Fugitive Slave Law. Far from slowing abolitionism, the law fostered civil disobedience. The states of Amazonas, Goiás, and Paraná also abolished slavery. Railroad and port workers began to carry runaways free of charge to the liberated states. As the great majority of Brazilians were illiterate, emissaries, transport workers, and peddlers completed the propaganda of the abolitionist press, by popularizing the anti-slavery mobilization. Now not only small groups of slaves escaped to join the free zones, but the whole labor force of some plantations. The movement reached the area of São Paulo; its port of Santos was transformed into a free zone by stevedores, who forced local authorities to shelter 10,000 fugitives. Increasingly, policemen and soldiers refused to arrest runaways, and judges refused to sentence them. The country was on the verge of a civil war. And slavery was collapsing: from 1,346,097 in 1883, the number of slaves had dropped to 723,419 in 1887. By 1887 a program to recruit European immigrants to work in São Paulo's coffee plantations was yielding results. With their labor problem on the way to solution Paulista planters began to see the continuation of slavery as a political hindrance. They then supported the bill in parliament for complete abolition. On May 13, 1888, with her father, Pedro II, sick in Europe, Princess Regent Isabel signed the "Golden Law" that finally ended legal slavery in Brazil – and thus, in the Americas (Conrad 1972; Toplin 1972; Holloway 1977).

Abolition was followed in November 1889 by a military coup overthrowing the Brazilian Empire and the establishment of the First Republic (1889–1930). Tragically, the national abolitionist movement vanished after the Golden Law, leaving freedmen and freedwomen with only the support of black brotherhoods and centers of syncretic worship as well as extended family networks. In addition, the new political system, far from being republican, excluded the majority of the Brazilian people and secured the domination of the planter oligarchy. Moreover, like most Latin American governments at the time, the Brazilian "republic" embraced pseudoscientific racism, social Darwinism, and French philosopher Auguste Comte's positivism. According to these philosophies, non-whites were racially inferior and unfit for free labor, and the best way toward progress was to "whiten" the country's population through massive European immigration. As a result, federal and state governments invested public funds in European immigrants (by paying their transatlantic passage) but refused to make any investment in Brazilians (by developing education and training or subsidizing the transportation of workers from depressed areas to demanding regions). In other words, Europeans were being transported to Brazil to unfairly compete with Afro-Brazilians, and it was assumed that in the contest freedmen and darker Brazilians would lose.

And the planters fulfilled their dream. From 1888 to 1928 four million whites came (primarily Italians, Portuguese, and Spaniards), half of them to the coffee-producing state of São Paulo, where many industries were also created. Immigrants systematically displaced and marginalized Afro-Brazilians. They went to the most prosperous regions and received the most desirable jobs. Blacks were almost entirely excluded from contract work on coffee plantations, as well as from factories and commerce. Black artisans – who had dominated manual production until 1850 – virtually disappeared from the city. They found their opportunities restricted to domestic service and in petty jobs, such as porters, gardeners, newspaper vendors, and day laborers (Holloway 1980; Andrews 1991: 54–85).

After 1886, Afro-Cubans went through a similar process of marginalization. However, some built on the Spanish-imposed concept of *raza de color* to unite blacks and mulattos, Cuban-born and African-born, free and former slaves alike and to foster racial pride. In 1887 mulatto journalist Juan Gualberto Gómez published a newspaper and organized already existing all-black clubs and societies into a federation placed under the leadership of the *Directorio Central de las Sociedades de la Raza de Color* (Central Directorate of Societies of the Colored Race) that successfully co-ordinated anti-discriminatory actions island-wide and challenged Spanish authority.

Afro-Cuban veterans of the previous wars for independence, within Cuba and from exile, also prepared for the renewal of the anti-colonial struggle. After the launching of a new war for independence in 1895, blacks and mulattos joined the Liberation Army against Spain en masse, galvanized by the leadership of General Antonio Maceo and the hope of building a nation founded on socioracial equality. However, the deaths of white anti-racist ideologue José Martí and Maceo in the war led to the marginalization of Afro-Cubans from the leadership of the army and the provisional government, now dominated by socially conservative whites, a few of whom even favored annexation to the United States.

Blacks' marginalization worsened with the 1898 US intervention in the war and military occupation of Cuba (1898–1902). Drawing on Cuba's deeply rooted patterns of racial differentiation, US officials imposed policies that often discriminated against Afro-Cubans. In 1902 the first elected Cuban government, far from making a sharp break with the US occupation, carried on several of the latter's policies. In addition, it promoted the whitening of Cuba through massive subsidized Spanish immigration. It also launched a campaign to repress traditions of African origin under the label of *brujería* (witchcraft) as a means of denigrating all Afro-Cubans. Simultaneously the government claimed that the 1901 constitution, which stipulated the equality of all Cubans and granted universal male suffrage and Cuban citizenship to the African-born, had resolved the "black problem." Thus, it did nothing to desegregate the public sphere and to help Afro-Cubans and the poor in general. No Afro-Cuban served in the upper level of the administration, and the government even publicly offended the few Afro-Cuban congressmen by not inviting their dark-skinned wives to presidential receptions.

Afro-Cubans began to protest marginalization under the republic. In 1908, a group of veterans formed the *Partido Independiente de Color* (Independent Party of Color), which stands out as the first black party in the Americas. The party rapidly achieved nationwide membership, including day laborers, peasants, workers, artisans, and a few middle-class individuals in a program demanding full equality, social reform, and proportional Afro-Cuban representation in public service. Seen as a threat to the new order, the party was banned in 1910 and annihilated in 1912, when hundreds of Afro-Cubans organized an armed protest against that ban in Oriente. The Cuban government sent the army and white volunteers against them. They massacred between 3,000 and 6,000 blacks and mulattos – members and leaders of the Partido Independiente de Color as well as ordinary men, women, and children, killed because of their race. The racist slaughter of 1912 dealt a long-lasting blow to Afro-Cubans, who subsequently struggled within existing political parties and labor unions rather than in their own organizations (Helg 1995).

As in Brazil and Cuba, from the 1880s to the 1920s, positivism and pseudoscientific racism were influential throughout Latin America, drastically limiting the options of people of African descent. The official ideology promoted white superiority and black inferiority as well as various stereotypes denigrating blacks. The population of African descent was universally portrayed as lazy, unfit for democracy, and potentially criminal, and any attempt by blacks to mobilize was qualified as a threat of Africanization or of another Haiti. Like Brazil and Cuba, Argentina and Uruguay were also able to massively attract European immigrants to whiten and "civilize" their population. As a result, in Buenos Aires, Afro-Argentines, who were 25 percent of the capital's population in 1838, had dropped to 2 percent in 1887 (Andrews 1980: 4).

Throughout Latin America, ruling elites masked their racist policies by promoting images of their nations as "racial democracies." Up to the 1960s, they proudly contrasted Latin American legal equality with segregation in the US South. But they redefined equality as "equality based on merits," which conveniently ignored the fact that all individuals, for historical reasons depending on their race, did not originate from equal conditions. Moreover, such a definition implied that merits could be fairly estimated within an ideological framework positing white superiority. Its ultimate function was to place the blame for blacks' continuing lower social position entirely on themselves: if most people of African descent were still poor despite the existence of legal equality, it was because they were *racially* inferior (Andrews 1991; Helg 1995: 105–6; Da Costa 2000: 234–46).

Official discourses of racial equality confronted Afro-Latin Americans with an unsolvable dilemma. If they protested them, they exposed themselves to accusations of being racist and unpatriotic. If they subscribed to them, they had to simultaneously conform to negative views of blacks and remain subordinate. Indeed, such discourses made it blasphemous for people of African descent to proclaim their blackness along with their patriotism.

In general, enfranchised blacks solved this dilemma by conforming to white-dominated multi-party systems and by entrusting their representation to the less elitist party. In Venezuela, blacks traditionally associated themselves with the Liberal (formerly Federalist) party, although successive dictatorships until 1935 made universal male suffrage rather nominal. Similarly, most Afro-Colombians joined the Liberal Party, but a long Conservative rule from the 1880s to 1930 reduced political participation. As for Afro-Brazilians, they had little political say in the first Republic, which allowed only a small fraction of the population to vote and where single parties in each state dominated politics. In the early 1900s, some created class-oriented associations in some cities to offer the recreational activities from which blacks were banned in white clubs. But open struggle for equality began only in the mid-1920s, especially in São Paulo, where one black club publicly protested state discrimination (Wright 1990: 35–43; Andrews 1991: 77, 140–3).

After the Great Depression, suffrage became less restricted, leading to the rise of socialism and populism. People of African descent began to demand racial equality and integration within political parties and unions more forcefully. In Venezuela, after the end of Juan Vicente Gómez's dictatorship in 1935, most pardos, blacks, and indigenous people joined Acción Democrática, a party that advocated racial and class equality (Wright 1990: 98–100). In Colombia, the Liberal Party won the presidency in 1930 and initiated policies that benefited the working class. Liberal populist Jorge Eliécer Gaitán launched a campaign against the oligarchy that earned him broad Afro-Colombian support – as well as the nickname of "*el negro*," despite the fact that he only had partial Indian ancestry (Green 2003). In Cuba, the Communist Party and leftist unions began to champion racial integration, attracting a substantial number of Afro-Cubans in their membership (De la Fuente 2001: 189–99, 215–35). Only in Brazil did a group of blacks from São Paulo attempt to organize separately, by founding the Frente Negra Brasileira in 1931. The Frente protested racial discrimination and European immigration. It forced black admission to some segregated public entertainment places in São Paulo and the enlistment of the first Afro-Brazilian recruits in the state's Civil Guard. But, with Brazil's limited franchise still excluding most Afro-Brazilians from voting, it remained too small to weigh on the Brazilian political system and was allowed to continue until dictator Getulio Vargas's ban on all political parties in 1937 (Butler 1998: 113–28).

If separate black political parties failed throughout Latin America, people of African descent were more successful in maintaining a dissident subculture that permitted collective self-affirmation. This was not a small victory after centuries of attempts by Eurocentric white elites to wipe out all African- (and indigenous-) derived cultures. In the 1930s, facing growing US imperialism, Latin American nations started to search for their roots and identity. In the process, cultural expressions of African origin were recognized as essential parts of the national identity. These include African-derived music and dance, such as the Peruvian *zamacueca* and *marinera*, the *candombe*, ancestor of the Argentinean and Uruguayan tango and *milonga*, the Brazilian *samba* and *capoeira*, the Cuban *rumba* and *son*, the Dominican *merengue*, the Colombian *cumbia*, the Venezuelan *joropo*, the Mexican *son jarocho* – without forgetting the Central American *marimba* – a wooden xylophone introduced by African slaves. However, African-derived counterreligions, such as Cuban santería and palo monte and Brazilian candomblé, were not accepted by the elites before the 1970s (Moore 1997).

Still, the incorporation of African-derived music and dance into Latin American national cultures does not challenge the socioracial order. Up to today, throughout Latin America, people of African descent remain underrepresented in the upper spheres of power and overrepresented in the lower strata of society. Yet any broad movement of black pride or nationwide black political organization would elicit accusations of threatening the integrity of the nation and be strongly resisted. For sure, no government would raise the specter of a revolution along Haitian lines anymore, but it would brandish the banners of racial democracy, legal equality, and cultural inclusion to deny the existence of racism and silence black political voices. *Música sí, política no.*

BIBLIOGRAPHY

Andrews, G. R. (1980) *The Afro-Argentines of Buenos Aires, 1800–1900*, University of Wisconsin Press, Madison.

Andrews, G. R. (1991) *Blacks and Whites in São Paulo, Brazil, 1888–1988.* University of Wisconsin Press, Madison.

Andrews, G. R. (2004) *Afro-Latin America, 1800–2000.* Oxford University Press, New York.

Bergad, L. (1983) *Coffee and the Growth of Agrarian Capitalism in Nineteenth-Century Puerto Rico.* Princeton University Press, Princeton.

Bethell, L. (1970) *The Abolition of the Brazilian Slave Trade: Britain, Brazil and the Slave Trade Question, 1807–1869.* Cambridge University Press, Cambridge.

Blackburn, R. (1988) *The Overthrow of Colonial Slavery, 1776–1848.* Verso, London.

Butler, K. D. (1998) *Freedoms Given, Freedoms Won: Afro-Brazilians in Post-Abolition São Paulo and Salvador.* Rutgers University Press, New Brunswick, NJ.

Carroll, P. J. (1991) *Blacks in Colonial Veracruz: Race, Ethnicity, and Regional Development.* University of Texas Press, Austin.

Childs, M. D. (2006) *The 1812 Aponte Rebellion in Cuba and the Struggle against Atlantic Slavery*. University of North Carolina Press, Chapel Hill.

Colmenares, G. (1990) "El tránsito a sociedades campesinas de dos sociedades esclavistas en la Nueva Granada, Cartagena y Popayán, 1780–1850," *Huellas* (Barranquilla), 29, pp. 8–24.

Conrad, R. E. (1972) *The Destruction of Brazilian Slavery, 1850–1888*. University of California Press, Berkeley.

Curtin, P. D. (1969) *The Atlantic Slave Trade: A Census*. University of Wisconsin Press, Madison.

Da Costa, E. V. (2000) *The Brazilian Empire: Myths and Histories*, 2nd ed. University of North Carolina Press, Chapel Hill.

De la Fuente, A. (2001) *A Nation for All: Race, Inequality, and Politics in Twentieth-Century Cuba*. University of North Carolina Press, Chapel Hill.

Escalante, A. (1954) "Notas sobre el Palenque de San Basilio, una comunidad negra de Colombia," *Divulgaciones Etnológicas*, 3:5, pp. 207–358.

Geggus, D. P. (2002) *Haitian Revolutionary Studies*. Indiana University Press, Bloomington.

Green, W. J. (2003) *Gaitanismo, Left Liberalism, and Popular Mobilization in Colombia*. University Press of Florida, Gainesville.

Guardino, P. F. (1996) *Peasants, Politics, and the Formation of Mexico's National State: Guerrero, 1800–1857*. Stanford University Press, Stanford.

Helg, A. (1995) *Our Rightful Share. The Afro-Cuban Struggle for Equality, 1886–1912*. University of North Carolina Press, Chapel Hill.

Helg, A. (2004) *Liberty and Equality in Caribbean Colombia, 1770–1835*. University of North Carolina Press, Chapel Hill.

Holloway, T. H. (1977) "Immigration and Abolition: The Transition from Slave to Free Labor in the São Paulo Coffee Zone." In D. Alden & W. Dean (eds.), *Essays Concerning the Socio-Economic History of Brazil and Portuguese India*. University Press of Florida, Gainesville, pp. 150–78.

Holloway, T. H. (1980) *Immigrants on the Land: Coffee and Society in São Paulo, 1886–1934*. University of North Carolina Press, Chapel Hill.

Hudson, R. O. (1964) "The Status of the Negro in Northern South America, 1820–1860," *Journal of Negro History*, 49:4, pp. 225–39.

Klein, H. S. (1972) "Nineteenth-Century Brazil." In D. W. Cohen & J. P. Greene (eds.), *Neither Slave Nor Free. The Freedmen of African Descent in the Slave Societies of the New World*. Johns Hopkins University Press, Baltimore, pp. 309–24.

Klein, H. S. (1986) *African Slavery in Latin America and the Caribbean*. Oxford University Press, New York.

Legrand, C. (1986) *Frontier Expansion and Peasant Protest in Colombia, 1850–1936*. University of New Mexico Press, Albuquerque.

Lombardi, J. V. (1971) *The Decline and Abolition of Negro Slavery in Venezuela, 1820–1854*. Greenwood Press, Westport.

Lynch, J. (1986) *The Spanish American Revolution, 1808–1826*, 2nd ed. W. W. Norton, New York.

Moore, R. D. (1997) *Nationalizing Blackness: Afrocubanismo and Artistic Revolution in Havana, 1920–1940*. University of Pittsburgh Press, Pittsburgh.

Nishida, M. (2003) *Slavery and Identity: Ethnicity, Gender, and Race in Salvador, Brazil, 1808–1888*. Indiana University Press, Bloomington.

Paquette, R. L. (1988) *Sugar Is Made with Blood: The Conspiracy of La Escalera and the Conflict between Empires over Slavery in Cuba*. Wesleyan University Press, Middletown, CT.

Pollak-Eltz, A. (1991) *La negritud en Venezuela*. Lagoven, Caracas.

Reis, J. J. (1993) *Slave Rebellion in Brazil: The Muslim Uprising of 1835 in Bahia*. Johns Hopkins University Press, Baltimore.

Sagás, E. (2000) *Race and Politics in the Dominican Republic*. University Press of Florida, Gainesville.

Sanders, J. E. (2004) *Contentious Republicans: Popular Politics, Race, and Class in Nineteenth-Century Colombia*. Duke University Press, Durham.

Schmidt-Nowara, C. (1999) *Empire and Antislavery: Spain, Cuba, and Puerto Rico, 1833–1874*. University of Pittsburgh Press, Pittsburgh.

Scott, R. J. (1985) *Slave Emancipation in Cuba: The Transition to Free Labor, 1860–1899*. Princeton University Press, Princeton.

Sowell, D. (1992) *The Early Colombian Labor Movement: Artisans and Politics in Bogotá, 1832–1919*. Temple University Press, Philadelphia.

Thomas, H. (1998) *Cuba or the Pursuit of Freedom*, 2nd ed. Da Capo Press, New York.

Toplin, R. (1972) *The Abolition of Slavery in Brazil*. Atheneum, New York.

Wright, W. R. (1990) *Café con leche: Race, Class, and National Image in Venezuela*. University of Texas Press, Austin.

Chapter Sixteen

LAND, LABOR, PRODUCTION, AND TRADE: NINETEENTH-CENTURY ECONOMIC AND SOCIAL PATTERNS

Aldo A. Lauria-Santiago

The study of rural production and society in nineteenth-century Latin America experienced a boom during the 1980s and early 1990s. Fueled by the increasing use of local and regional archives and the transition from macro-level conceptualizations of Latin America's dependency and development to more historicized approaches based on class and regional analysis, historians sought in studies of rural social structure, land use, haciendas, communities, plantations, mines, and other contexts more concrete and better documented evidence on how this period established important foundations for the twentieth century. However, the earlier search for the historical origins of twentieth-century problems has become more heterogeneous with more questions connected to the study of local social relations, economies, politics, culture, and race. More recently, the general trend away from so-called structural and economically based arguments in the social sciences and humanities has contributed to a decline in the number of studies that deal with production, work, and land. Still, the important questions about how human and natural resources were organized and their relationship with politics and culture remains one of the fundamental themes in the study of the nineteenth century.

Colonial Legacies

Much of the historiography on socioeconomic development in the nineteenth century addressed the question of Latin America's colonial legacies. Initially these were conceptualized in the context of epochal transformations often inspired by important sweeping interpretations of colonial history published in the late 1970s (Halperín Donghi 1970; Stein & Stein 1970; Cardoso & Faletto 1979). Many of these earlier studies relied on generalizations about late colonial institutions like haciendas, plantations, and communities, based on narrow empirical studies or a myopic empiricism. However, discussions of colonial legacies, often part of larger debates on comparative colonialism, world systems, and dependency theory, acknowledge the critical role of the Spanish colonial state in taxing, distributing resources (especially labor), creating a racial order, and organizing production and trade. We now have a more balanced perspective on the dynamic and more problematic aspects of Spanish colonial rule, and of a regional and institutional heterogeneity in which old generalizations that argued for a stagnant and bureaucratically dominated colonial system simply no longer hold. This more nuanced portrait of the late colonial period as economically, socially, and politically dynamic details the effects of the crisis of the colonial system between the early 1800s and the 1820s, and shows why the period of crisis after 1800 was so disruptive and had such a long-term effect. The conflicted disappearance of the obstacles maintained by the Spanish colonial state did not automatically lead to a period of economic expansion because investment, regional markets, credit and transport systems were disrupted by the transition to independent nation-states.

More peripheral regions, especially those not deeply involved in the large-scale silver mining economies of the Andes and northern New Spain, had greater continuities (rather than the disruptions) between the late eighteenth and early nineteenth centuries. A focus on peasants, slaves and ex-slaves, miners, artisans, and other sub-alterns, especially in less central regions, shows greater diversity in the socioeconomic participation of small-scale producers even as the wars of independence raged, and evidence of extensive non-export commercialization. In some of these regions local producers and small-scale merchants (who often doubled as mule train operators) were quickly able to recreate aspects of the colonial-era trade and production networks, albeit on a smaller scale and not necessarily for export (Mallon 1983; Tandeter 1987; Jacobsen 1993; Larson et al. 1995; Larson 1998). Other regions developed new export products quickly, often stimulated by British or other European investors and merchants, by access to new markets in places without major obstacles to transport, or by strong states that facilitated the expansion of ranches, estates, or estancias. These sectors included hides and salted beef in Buenos Aires province (Adelman 1999), guano in Peru (Bonilla 1984), wheat in Chile's central regions (Bauer 1975), and coffee in Costa Rica (Cardoso & Pérez Brignoli 1977; Gudmundson 1986). In many local production centers traditional commercial and export products recovered quickly with few effects from the larger political transformations. These sectors included indigo in El Salvador (Lauria-Santiago 1999), vanilla and tobacco in western Mexico (Kourí 2004), cochineal in Guatemala (McCreery 1994; Fernández 2003), and coffee, cochineal, and textiles in Oaxaca (Chassen de López 2004). What emerges from the end of the colonial period is a truly mixed portrait of declining central industries (mining and associated regions, battle zones of revolt, civil war and occupation), more modestly prosperous peripheries, and some rapidly rising regions, often associated with coastal port cities and regions that grew in population during the last decades of the eighteenth century.

Falling Behind

Since the 1950s one of the most debated questions among students of Latin American history and development is how and when Latin America "fell behind" the economies of the north Atlantic countries, and the social effects of this process. Theoretical discussions about the origins of development and underdevelopment in the 1970s and early 1980s extended the debates into difficult conceptual and comparative terrain in which the most important colonial-era economic institutions were identified and production, taxation, and trade were quantified. More recently, economic historians have revived the econometric and institutional aspect of these debates, encouraged in part by the accumulation of 30 years of new regional and institutional empirical studies (Coatsworth 1978, 1981; Coatsworth & Taylor 1998; Haber 1989, 1997; Bortz & Haber 2002). The debate points away from the late colonial period and toward the early and mid-nineteenth century as the most important source of the region's "falling behind." There were important obstacles that formed part of the colonial era and its legacy: social (racial hierarchies, church control), economic (internal taxation, state monopolies), technological, and political (divided elites, purchased offices, hierarchical political system). But the timing and depth of the crisis and conflicts of the 1808 to 1850s period in which Latin American nation-states were created were the principal reasons behind Latin America's "falling behind" the United States in terms of per capita production and trade. Most importantly, the post-independence inability of weak or non-existent central states to facilitate or invest in infrastructure and transportation, restore the mining economy, expand large-scale agricultural production and, as in the case of Mexico, protect the territorial integrity of the nation-state, made Latin America fall behind and established the basis for a more subordinate encounter with North American and European markets, technology, and capitals a few decades later in the century.

These debates on the long-term development of Latin American nations in this early period had important effects in the study of agrarian production and social structures. They allowed historians to stop seeing particular institutional forms of land tenure or social organization (especially haciendas and peasant communities) as intrinsically backward, non-market oriented, or inefficient. As a result, haciendas and other rural enterprises are no longer seen as necessarily unprofitable. And in the context of wide-open frontiers for land acquisition large estates were not necessarily involved in a zero-sum economic game with peasants and small-scale producers. Also as a result, peasant communities, large landholding, and production for subsistence or local markets are no longer necessarily seen as a drag on the larger socioeconomic development of the region.

Regional Commercial Agriculture to the 1860s

Until the early 1980s historians of the early post-independence period had missed important evidence on the development of commercial agriculture (not necessarily for export) between the 1820s and 1860s. Until then, because of the nearly automatic identification of small-scale producers with subsistence, and the disruptions assumed to have taken place in these early years, the most noted cases of commercial production were usually those regions that continued to rely on slave labor for export-oriented plantation or mining products. The cases include sugar, and coffee in Cuba and Puerto Rico (Knight 1970; Bergad 1983; Scarano 1984; Figueroa 2005), sugar in northeastern Brazil (Schwartz 1985) or the early export economies of places like central Chile (wheat, nitrates), cattle hides in Buenos Aires province, and guano and nitrates in coastal Peru (Bonilla 1984; Gootenberg 1989). The role of foreign capital and merchants in these activities had made them more visible but eventually historians added many less well-known commercial economies that began in the 1830s and 1840s as incipient but important production centers, including coffee in Costa Rica and Colombia, wool and sugar in coastal and southern Peru, tobacco in Cuba and Mexico, indigo in El Salvador, and cacao in Venezuela.

The older generalization that haciendas and communities had "reverted" back to autarchy and subsistence production after independence has proven to be as mistaken as it was sweeping. In many regions commercial estate production revived, even as the large estates of the colonial period began a process of decomposition and division. The revival of smaller-scale estate production was based on renegotiated terms with workers (often freed slaves), who were granted better terms for land access, wages, and more secure tenancy arrangements than in the more oppressive colonial period. Successful mining, artisanal, and agricultural production for these regional markets could not be large scale almost by definition, given the lack of capital, high cost of internal transportation, political uncertainty, and the social and political strengthening of subaltern groups, many of whom became direct competitors with regional elites for land, labor, and markets. In this context, the local or regional effects of political collapse – including radical federalism, disaggregation or war within nation-states and control by regional warlords, or *caudillos* – established limits to how these regional commercial economies could grow.

These early to mid-century commercial complexes often tied the fate of local landed and commercial elites of modest resources to their ability to negotiate with peasants, local communities, and other subalterns. Sugar economies provide the most common example, as sugar was one of the most important commercial products for local, regional, national, and export markets since before independence. Specific regions often specialized in sugar production by taking advantage of suitable conditions and the proximity to markets. South-central Mexico (Morelos) provides examples of nationally oriented agrarian production that combined industrial, estate, and peasant-based cane production. In Morelos sugar *ingenios* (small, mechanized but not sophisticated sugar mills) benefited for decades from a symbiotic relationship with small-scale peasant producers who provided the seasonal labor for cane cutting or sold their own cane to the mills. By the end of the century, however, the estates consolidated, increased their investment in milling machinery, and, with support from state policies and repression, increased the land under their control, depriving a growing number of peasants and towns of access to land. Morelos's trajectory as the home of the insurgency let by Emiliano Zapata is well known and based on this transition in estate–peasant relations (Womack 1969). Mexico also developed other important regional or small-scale commercial economies in this period: tobacco in the coastal east, cochineal in the south, a modest revival in grain production in the Bajío region, and small-scale, poorly capitalized silver mining in the north (Benjamin & McNellie 1984; Tutino 1986).

In the cotton plantations of coastal Peru a similar transition resulted after the 1830s as peasant producers, squeezed by limited access to land, became sharecroppers and facilitated the transition from slave to tenant labor in the plantations. Complex bargaining, often involving different forms of resistance and patronage, gave tenant sharecroppers a margin for negotiating terms and even hiring outside labor until the plantations completed their transition to wage labor much later in the century. Peasant resistance to planter demands hinged on visions of fair and just labor and land arrangements with the plantation owners but peasants eventually lost out as planters moved to control production directly and thus reduce production costs (Peloso 1999).

Peru's coastal sugar plantations were also socially distant from Peruvian highland peasants. Large numbers of imported Chinese contract workers, working under servile conditions, supplanted Peru's slave labor force and allowed for the survival of this industry despite the lack of technological modernization between the 1830s and 1880s. After the end of the traffic in Chinese workers in the 1870s and the attacks by coolies on the estates during the War of the Pacific (1879–84), the estate owners simultaneously sought to modernize their estates and recruit workers in what became the coercive debt-driven *enganche* of poor peasants from the Andean highlands (Mallon 1983; Gonzales 1985), establishing a pattern of labor migration that expanded dramatically during the twentieth century.

In Costa Rica, the early development of small- and medium-scale coffee production in the context of a frontier-like land settlement economy created a model of small-producer prosperity in which merchants, not landowners, controlled the coffee economy without being able to squeeze small farmers off their land (Hall 1976; Cardoso 1977, 1985; Gudmundson 1986; Samper 1990). As a result, Costa Rica rapidly became a major producer of coffee, providing a basis for relative peasant prosperity into the early twentieth century.

Clearly, the sorts of production that dominated rural Latin America between the 1820s and 1860s did not lay the basis for the region's competition with industrializing Europe or the United States, but neither did it constitute a period of complete stagnation or paralysis even when it came to commercial agriculture and mining. The largest failure of this period was in the state's inability simultaneously to create infrastructure and large-scale investments, and integrate the interests of small-scale and regional elites into more nationally oriented development goals.

Case Study: Community-based Land Tenure, Haciendas, and Agriculture in El Salvador, 1820s–1880s

El Salvador has provided important materials for the study of peasant and rural social structure in this period. After independence haciendas remained important landholding units that controlled around one-quarter of the country's land, but their owners did not have the resources to engage in large-scale commercial or export production, which resulted in extensive tenancy arrangements and the eventual subdivision of estates. Indigo, a rich dark-blue dye used in textile production in Europe and the Americas, was the country's largest export product until the 1880s and was produced mostly in small-scale and community-based units. Even hacienda-based indigo producers were relatively small operators and the country was dotted with dozens if not hundreds of *obrajes* or small workshops in which the leaves of the indigo bush were processed into the powdered dye. Trade in the dye provided for large commercial fairs in which merchants visited the towns and traded manufactured products for indigo bales. The indigo trade engaged thousands of small-scale producers with regional markets in hides, cattle, food products, and textiles that extended to Guatemala, Honduras, and Nicaragua.

Peasant communities, especially the indigenous communities of the central and western regions that had preserved and continued to expand their land resources between the late colonial period and the 1860s, engaged in the individual and collective production of a variety of other commercial products including sugar (most commonly *panela*, or semi-refined sugar), liquor, coffee, manufactured leather, cigars, textiles, and straw goods (hats, mats, and other household items). These communities owned land collectively as an inheritance of colonial-period landholding in which the Spanish king, as a primary obligation of the kingdom, granted possession of the land to indigenous, Spanish, and *ladino* (non-indigenous) communities for their subsistence and use. After a hiatus that lasted into the 1820s El Salvador's economy began to expand, facilitated by low transport costs, internal resources (roads, ports, frequent steamship service, and eventually rails), and the opening of new markets in California and eventually Europe. As a result, local communities experienced a growing differentiation in how their resources were used and distributed, with increasing tensions between rich and poor peasants including within indigenous communities.

In places like mostly-Indian Nahuizalco in the highlands of the west, land ownership and even aspects of production and labor remained collective enterprises until the early twentieth century, governed by councils of elders who protected local resources and traditions from outside influence. In contrast, in nearby Juayua, the indigenous community was largely overrun by entrepreneurial ladinos, many of them newcomers, who overwhelmed the small community and eventually took over many of its unused and uncertainly titled lands, turning them into mid-sized commercial cattle and sugar farms and opening one of the first internal frontiers for coffee expansion. In the central municipalities of Cojutepeque and San Vicente, however, collective land ownership resulted in an earlier process of individual ownership. By the 1850s they had generated an extensive landscape of small farms that combined subsistence and commercial products (sugar, grains, indigo, coffee), which, together with the region's strong, armed peasant militias, delayed the emergence of large-scale commercial farms and haciendas by decades. Izalco, a large mixed-ethnicity municipality in the west, had a more mixed experience with the privatization of lands a few decades later in the century. In Dolores, one of Izalco's indigenous communities, an elite of indigenous entrepreneurs laid claim to the choice unused lands and eventually became identified as ladino as their larger political alliances led them to an implosive conflict in the 1890s that signaled the demise of their collective solidarities. In Asunción, Izalco's other Indian community, a more gradual, and conflicted, process of privatization took place with the survival of a strong faction that sought to defend communal structures against the tide of individual ownership, outside encroachments, and continued internal conflict.

Chalchuapa, a cattle raising, mostly ladino municipality further north in the mountain ranges shared by Izalco, Juayua, and Nahuizalco, had a distinct path. With a rich land and with a strong collective identity (despite its ladino ethnic background), the peasants of mid-nineteenth-century Chalchuapa managed to retain the bulk of their lands, turn them into a plethora of small-scale coffee farms, and still retain sufficient resources to develop paternalistic land rental and labor arrangements with the next generation of settlers and landless workers. Together, these local portraits of agrarian society and of production, trade, and communal organizing show that Salvadoran agrarian history in this formative period was not entirely dominated by a predatory state, large-scale landowners, and estate-based production. Rather, differentiated peasant producers and peasant communities played a critical and active role (Lauria-Santiago 1998a, 1998b, 1998c, 1999).

Peasant Society and Economy

Peasant economy and society, especially peasant commercial agriculture, had been the least studied aspect of nineteenth-century agrarian history in part because of the traditional emphasis on hacienda dominance, mineral production, and long-distance or export production. But if it is not the case that most rural people in nineteenth-century Latin America lived and worked within the regimented structures of the plantation, hacienda, or mine, then what institutions and practices did they rely on? Mexican agrarian studies, fueled by the long-standing interest in understanding the many peasant revolts and insurgencies in Mexico's history but especially the emergence of the revolution of 1910, provide some answers. These studies began by focusing on the effects of haciendas, mines, and other commercial investments on peasant and community land ownership or labor (Tutino 1986). As a result, the Porfirian hacienda was no longer seen as regionally and socially homogeneous and based mostly on rigid conceptions of peonage, let alone debt peonage. Eventually the focus expanded to include other, more internal, aspects of the organization of peasant communities and small producers. In the case of Mexico, this emphasis on peasant society has shifted more recently to studies that focus on peasant politics, culture, and community, paying less attention to the way land, labor, production, and social structure were organized (Guardino 1996; Ducey 2004). However, recent studies on Central America have retained a more balanced integration between resource-based themes and discussions of politics and culture in studies of subaltern life (Gould 1990, 1998; Lauria-Santiago 1999; Grandin 2000; Dore 2006; Wolfe 2007).

An important aspect in the development of nineteenth-century social-agrarian studies has been a dialogue between anthropologists and historians which encouraged important archival studies of local communities and small-scale producers. This dialogue fostered the historicizing of Marxian-based class analysis and a dialogue with European studies about the emergence of capitalism in the countryside with a strong emphasis on commercial production, and the organization of land and labor (Wolf 1959, 1969; Roseberry 1983, 1989). These studies promoted a better understanding of the many ways in which provincial elites, rural middle sectors, and community-based peasantries responded to market opportunities, and began to deconstruct the facile binary opposites that dominated early conceptualizations of the rural world (Roseberry 1993). One important discovery was how heterogeneous regional economies and social structures were; but there was also a more complete understanding of how regions mattered in the formation of nation-states. Most important, these studies began to incorporate careful study of lower classes in ways that often challenged (and continue to challenge – see Dore 2006 for a recent example) accepted conceptualizations of land, labor, class, and production.

During the nineteenth century local producers, including significant indigenous peoples, participated in modest but persistent ways in local and even regional commercial networks involving land, trade, credit, labor, water, and other resources or transactions. They usually did so with a greater level of autonomy and without the restraints and impositions of the colonial-era (or national) state or elites, such as taxes on people, production, and trade, forced purchases, labor drafts, etc. Small-scale producers (best studied so far in Mexico and the central Andes) were involved in commercial production, trade, and resource management that combined market-based with subsistence-oriented goals. Complex and contradictory forces shaped the work of peasant communities, smallholders, and frontier settlers in the tension between individual (usually kin-based) strategies of survival and collective forms of organizations that include municipalities, formal and informal communities, indigenous governments, and factional paramilitary militias. In many cases this tension was expressed as a long, uneven process of peasant differentiation in which even modest changes in power could lay the basis for eventual larger changes in the local distribution of wealth, especially control over land as rich peasants became commercial farmers, labor contractors, or political bosses later in the nineteenth century.

Case Study: Highland Andean Peasant communities, 1800–1870s

Studies of Andean agrarian society provide the materials for the discussion of peasant–hacienda relations in distinct regions of Peru. In Azángaro, in the Peruvian southern altiplano, a relative symbiosis developed between peasant communities and large-scale haciendas until the 1860s (Jacobsen 1993). Wool-producing peasants became increasingly tied to and dependent upon markets and merchants, but managed to retain access to land and control over their labor and resources. After the 1860s market and political conditions allowed for a rapid expansion of livestock-based haciendas as the century ended, resulting in the formation of formidable and stable elite landholdings that slowly turned their focus on securing cheap and manipulable labor from surrounding peasant communities. Initially through labor and *colono* (resident worker) agreements the haciendas used their extensive landholdings as a means of leveraging labor at lower costs, offering these peasants a bargaining position until shifting conditions in the early twentieth century reduced this bargaining power. Life on these estates combined elements of market-based and paternalistic transactions, tying colonos, administrators, and owners in a clientelistic web of reciprocal (even if very unequal) obligations and negotiations.

Mallon's (1983) study of village-based peasants in Peru's central highlands finds similar paternalistic ties but in the context of strong, resource-owning peasant communities undergoing a slow, contradictory, and often halted process of internal differentiation. Haciendas were more static, limited by the lack of capital and the strength of peasant resources. In these communities, small-scale village-based merchants eventually developed the resources to accumulate obligations and debts which eventually (and slowly) led to the concentration of lands and the emergence of village bosses by the end of the nineteenth century. Local elites faced an impasse in their attempt to control and extract resources from the land and peasant communities. Without the capital, markets, technology, political alliances, and other resources that were eventually brought to Peru by the increased presence of foreign capital after the

1890s, their strategies remained uncertain and constantly challenged by peasant resistance, land access, and continued autonomy. The balance broke early in the twentieth century as larger numbers of peasants became seasonal proletarian migrants for longer stretches and at longer distances, eventually forming the basis for the emergence of large working-class nuclei in the mines and coastal plantations (Klein 1993).

The Occupation, Ownership, and Utilization of Land

Demographic expansion and new market opportunities were the most important factors driving the extensive occupation of land across Latin America's many and varied internal frontiers. Frontier expansion, in some cases in conflict with autonomous or sovereign indigenous groups (as occurred in Bolivia, Argentina, southern Chile, northern Mexico, and the interior of Brazil), was important in virtually all the countries of Latin America at some point during the nineteenth century, as the region's population continued a pattern of growth begun earlier in the early eighteenth century, with significant help from large-scale European immigration in some regions after the 1880s. In many cases this frontier expansion was driven by the search for lands suitable for a specific commercial product: coffee in Guatemala, Colombia, Venezuela, Costa Rica, and Brazil; cattle in Argentina, Paraguay, and Honduras; sugar and coffee in Puerto Rico and Cuba. In some regions the expansion was driven initially by subsistence-oriented peasants seeking easier access to state-owned lands, perhaps to escape high rental costs or hacienda dominance in their places of origin (Legrand 1986). Later in the century, rapidly growing export economies such as the Brazilian coffee sector, fueled by expanding markets, infrastructural investments, regional transfer of slaves, technology, and European immigration, encouraged the formation of tenancy and land rental arrangements within newly accessed frontier lands (Stein 1957; Dean 1976; Holloway 1980) in ways that combined elements of smallholding economy with landlord-controlled processes. In many regions (Yucatan, Sonora, Chihuahua, in Mexico; the coastal Andes; Central American and southern Mexican coastal piedmonts) this process constituted a conflicted race toward the land as elites, speculators, and peasants sought scarce fertile land close to transport networks, and irrigation (Aguilar Camín 1977; Gonzales 1985; Wells 1985; McCreery 1994; Grandin 2000). In the most notorious of these cases local elites, allied to foreign capital and national states, established strong enclave and export economies, although these were as likely to be based on coercive or increasingly exploitative labor relations as on the attraction of higher wages.

Before the 1860s and 1870s larger haciendas in many areas were slowly broken up in size while productive units multiplied, in some regions encouraging the emergence of important middle strata (Langer 1989; Tutino 1998; Lauria-Santiago 1999). In regions with strong peasant- or indigenous-based political movements, including regions of Mexico, Guatemala, El Salvador, Colombia, and Paraguay, haciendas were abandoned by their owners because of political turmoil and peasant resistance, and lands were claimed or purchased by peasant settlers or rival peasant communities (Tutino 1986; McCreery 1994). In some regions governments established relatively pro-peasant policies, distributing extensive properties to individual farmers or collectively to communities. Thus relations between haciendas, communities, free-holding peasantries, and wage workers were not necessarily a zero-sum competition for land, but involved different forms of symbiosis and accommodation in contexts in which land was the least scarce resource.

Slave-based plantation agriculture expanded greatly during the early and mid century in Cuban and Puerto Rican sugar, coffee, and tobacco, and Brazilian coffee. In the case of large-scale slave-based sugar production, labor scarcity, abolitionist pressures, war and/or global competition led to decline or consolidation after the 1870s, with final abolition coming in 1886 to Cuba and 1888 to Brazil (Helg, this volume). Plantation slaves in northeastern Brazil, and indentured immigrant workers from south Asia and China in the plantation-controlled regions of the Caribbean, were often given small plots of land in which to grow food within the estates. This often resulted in the marketing of small surpluses and the accumulation of some savings. However, this sort of land access was unstable, and as soon as workers had physical mobility, through individual or collective emancipation or the termination of contracts, they did their best to physically distance themselves from the estates and claim land in the interior.

Community-based landholdings were a legacy of collective land titles granted in the colonial period to many communities and towns, mostly but not only indigenous. But in many places national governments either legally and socially legitimized or extended community-based forms of land tenure. In regions with strong traditions of peasant, and especially indigenous, communal identity and organization, collective land ownership expanded with legal and illegal appropriation of former hacienda and state-owned lands through the 1860s and 1870s. In some cases this occupation of land was not driven by the immediate need for agricultural use but by the desire for community autonomy.

Despite many attempts by local landowners, politicians, and regional or national state policies to break up collective landholding in the 1820s and 1830s, it was only in the later third of the century that collective forms of land ownership began to be transformed from the inside (by internal social differentiation and increased market production among peasants); and by external forces (liberal land policies encouraging or forcing privatization of individual plots). This led to complex and drawn-out processes of privatization of land, mostly after the 1860s. These processes, once seen as the product of despotic appropriation by large landlords under the guise of modernizing liberalism, are now understood as more complicated processes with a variety of outcomes – including, of course, scenarios in which elites came to control vast resources at the expense of native peoples or original settlers. These processes of land partitioning were internally conflicted and not necessarily the result of landlord or state impositions. They took a long time, often resulted in the dissolution of communal organization and solidarity, and could lead to the loss of significant portions of land to outside agents or community leaders. In most places, these processes of land claiming and privatization, either of colonial-era communal landholdings or frontier-like distribution of state-owned land known as *baldíos* by settlers, ex-slaves, and middle strata, led to the formation of freeholding peasantries with differential access to the land and other resources, including a significant sector of smallholders with little land who were highly vulnerable to the processes of commercial expansion which accelerated in the early twentieth century.

In the realm of policies affecting agrarian structures, and the ideologies guiding those policies, most Latin American leaders shared the so-called liberal goals of promoting commercial development, private landholding, foreign investment, and transport infrastructure, but the process of incorporation or negotiation with popular sectors established limits or influenced the dynamics behind state policies, especially when it came to federalism, land, tax and labor policies. In the end, ideology took a back seat to practical considerations and negotiations among interest groups, in determining land, labor, and production policies. The most overriding aspect of these struggles was embedded in debates and conflicts over the relationship between central government and regional political autonomy. All policies relating to land, labor, taxes, and production were refracted through this prism. Many laws and decrees were passed by early liberal-influenced governments in many countries, but these laws were rarely practiced and were often superseded by more negotiated and often contradictory local legislation and practices. National governments had a stronger role in such issues as commercial policy, the opening of ports to "free" trade, or the separation of church and state. But when it came to the distribution of land, taxation, the privatization of collective lands, the implementation of land and public taxes, localities and regional governments reigned supreme. Not until a stronger wave of central government consolidation, as likely to be administered by "conservatives" (as in Colombia and Chile) as by "liberals" (as in Mexico, Guatemala, El Salvador, and Argentina), did central governments, in varying chronologies, gain a stronger hand for the implantation of national economic policies, and even these had an uneven regional application. In the end, the most important lesson from these initially ideologically oriented debates was that the state role, or absence thereof, was a critical component of all economic and agrarian policies, and that this role varied according to the processes of negotiation between classes, regional actors, and other groups embedded in the state itself (Love & Jacobsen 1988; Sowell 1992; Mallon 1995; Guardino 1996, 2005; Peloso & Tenenbaum 1996; Langer & Jackson 1997).

Perhaps the most significant transfer of land took place with the land and other properties owned by the Catholic Church and related institutions. As part of the recurrent and often decades-long conflict between states, national and regional liberal elites, and the Church, hostile policies of privatization were enforced in which Church-owned land or productive estates and farms were sold to tenants or bidders. Most countries in Latin America provide examples of this sort of disentailment, but the most dramatic example was in Mexico during the anti-clerical *Reforma* of 1856–60 led by Benito Juarez, in which large numbers of Church-owned properties were nationalized, auctioned, or otherwise transferred to private owners. The transfer, formally justified in economic (efficiency) and ideological (justice) terms, was driven politically by resentment against the Church for its conservative politics and role in civil wars – a role that continued with Church support for the French invasion of Mexico in 1862 that installed the Austrian Archduke Maximilian as Emperor. In other countries the transfer was not as dramatic, either because it took much longer or because not as many properties were involved. At the local level, many "Church-owned" lands were actually in the hands of Indian- and peasant-controlled religious sodalities, which in most cases continued to control the lands as private holdings (Bazant 1970; Jackson 1997).

Toward the end of the century land was also claimed and occupied through large-scale processes of government concession, capital investment in transportation, irrigation, and drainage, and the establishment of new plantations and large commercial farms. In coastal areas of Guatemala, Ecuador, Colombia, Peru, Honduras, Costa Rica, and Cuba governments granted huge concessions to foreign companies. Under the long authoritarian rule of Porfirio Diaz in Mexico (1876–1910), government-supported land claims in the northern states by US investors, railroad surveyors, large-scale and politically connected commercial ranchers and farmers transferred millions of acres into a few private hands and rapidly created export booms as the frontier became the border (Aguilar Camín 1977; Katz 1981; Wasserman 1984; Nugent 1993). Large-scale cattle raising and cotton, sugar, cacao, coffee, and henequen plantations and processing plants were established in times of high prices through government-facilitated contracts and concessions, sometimes tied to the parallel development of shipping, telegraph, port and rail networks, and the provision of government loans. One land conflict that fueled support for the Villista faction during the Mexican Revolution of 1910 came from the town of Namiquipa in Sonora, where Porfirian-supported wealthy ranchers fought the descendants of earlier "civilized" mestizo Indian-fighting settlers over control of the town's common lands, granted by the king of Spain in the late eighteenth century as recompense for their work in "civilizing" the north. In other parts of northern Mexico, defeated Yaqui Indians lost thousands of acres of their patrimony, with a single company receiving half a million acres in "state lands" (Knight 1986). Peru and Guatemala provide the most extreme examples of these concessions, with multi-million acre concessions of Peruvian land to the Grace Company in 1890 (Mallon 1983) and in Guatemala to United Fruit in 1901 (Dosal 1993).

Case Study: The Privatization of Communal Lands in Papantla, Mexico, 1880s–1890s

The municipality of Papantla in the State of Veracruz, Mexico, provides a detailed look at the relationships between peasants and land. Papantla, a mostly indigenous municipality with deep roots in the colonial and pre-colonial periods, became one of Mexico's specialized producers of vanilla. A mostly Indian-controlled trade well into the nineteenth century, vanilla (like indigo and coffee growing) had no economy of scale, but it required a high level of knowledge of local growing conditions. The commercial economy that emerged by the 1860s and 1870s involved tensions and conflicts between the native producers and collective landowners, the town's Totonac peasants, on the one hand, and the mestizo commercial farmers, merchants, and political officials who had an increasing role in the highly profitable vanilla trade, on the other. In this case, collective land ownership based on ethnic or municipal association was transformed relatively peacefully into large-scale undivided co-ownership units, in which shareholders had relatively conflict-free access to resources in the context of the continued existence of unused lands and high vanilla prices (Kourí 2004).

But taxation increased with privatization, and former competitors were tied together as co-owners who now needed to cooperate. These changes laid the basis not only for protracted conflict and factional violence but an eventual revolt by different Totonac co-owners, as they struggled against a rising tide of corrupt, manipulated, and unfair practices during the state-sponsored conversion of jointly owned lots to individual farms. The end result was not as stark a portrait as has been painted by the older literature on Porfirian agrarian relations, in which a vast majority of landless peasants lost out to market-driven hacendados with state backing, but one that proved to be much more mixed, with large numbers of indigenous peasants holding on to farms but also a large share of Totonac peasants becoming landless and a much smaller upwardly mobile class of mestizo merchant–entrepreneurs forming sizable commercial farms. This is another complex, multi-layered, and surprisingly politicized case of a relatively small although commercially engaged municipality in a slow, contradictory transition from peasant-dominated landholding to commercial farming.

Peasant communities and individual peasants were deeply engaged with powerful outside processes, including the national and regional state, regional elites, and markets, without being passive recipients of history but simultaneously without producing heroic, singular narratives of resistance and victory. What emerges most clearly from these stories is the slow process of erosion and internal fragmentation of the peasantry that, decades later, provided the basis for important political mobilizations of the rural poor.

Labor

Perhaps the most complex aspect of nineteenth-century development and social organization involves rural labor. Because of the documents created by work-related practices, the most studied labor situations involved plantations, commercial farms, and haciendas. In these contexts wage labor, tenancy, sharecropping, debt-management arrangements, or coercive practices left significant paper trails. It is more difficult to recover details of the organization of labor within communities, small-holder kin networks, and laborers only marginally or seasonally connected to estate/commercial farm production. An additional issue related to the study of labor in the nineteenth century is that the need for cheap, pliable labor was the constant mantra of often frustrated elites, who demanded state policies that would facilitate access to the single most important resource they lacked in order to either expand or make more profitable their commercial ventures. Discourses relating to the "scarcity" of labor, dangers from the variously racialized lower classes, and the need for paternal social policies became a confounding trope in many contexts, drawing attention away from actual working conditions and bargaining on plantations, ranches, farms, and estates. The need for cheap labor resulted in efforts to simultaneously control workers and peasants and attract immigrants.

It is also necessary to break down the simple binomial definitions of coerced vs. free labor when looking at labor relations. Slavery and the transitional regimes that followed abolition continued in many countries through the 1830s, and in a few continued into the last third of the century, forming a strong part of the economy in Brazil, Cuba, and Puerto Rico. Plantations often followed the earlier pattern created with slavery and coerced labor from the colonial period, but the conditions became more varied and tied to local patterns of development and state intervention.

In Brazil, state-sponsored European immigration led to a massive influx of southern and eastern Europeans who provided the labor for the expansion of coffee and eventually industrial centers. During the last third of the nineteenth century large-scale European immigration played an important role in the transformation of the pampas of southern South America from extensive pastoralism to an intensive beef and wheat complex, and subsequently the formation of urban working classes in Uruguay and Argentina, as well (Scobie 1964; Solberg 1970). In Peru, Cuba, and Mexico large numbers of Chinese contract workers worked in semi-coerced labor conditions on coastal plantations. In other regions, plantation labor was recruited locally through seasonal arrangements, often in relationship with local peasant communities. In some regions, including portions of highland Nicaragua, Guatemala (McCreery 1994), and southern Mexico (Wells 1985), new and increasingly coercive forms of wage labor were developed mostly as a result of state–planter alliances as agro-export economies expanded late in the century. In these contexts the ability of landlords to coerce workers was highly dependent upon local racial formation and an increased (but still surprisingly regionally circumscribed) state role.

In some contexts, such as cotton in Ecuador, the expansion of plantation agriculture involved sharecropping arrangements with former slaves or their descendants. In other scenarios, in which resource-rich haciendas had little access to capital or markets (usually because of the lack of investment in banking and transport infrastructures), colonos, peons or other forms of resident workers gained access to land within the hacienda in exchange for limited labor or crop-sharing agreements with landlords. For the most part, these complexes were highly stable and often involved haciendas of modest proportions. Still, the slow trend throughout most agrarian contexts was toward the use of wage labor, usually in combination with some form of land access.

Perhaps the most recent although still incipient trend involves attempts by historians at gendering the study of rural social and economic change in this period, although most studies of gender in this context refer to the study of women in the context of male-dominated social and political structures. Studies have begun to incorporate discussions of women in relation to land (their relationship to private or community land use) and labor (their role as slaves, artisans, and seasonal wage workers, part of the peasant kin-based economy). In this area women were extensively involved in land ownership, rural production, and wage labor albeit with important subordinations and limitations to their autonomy. In some contexts communal structures limited their access to resources without men's approval or mediation; it was seen as a willing subordination in which male communal paternalism also provided certain benefits and protections (Mallon 1995; Dore 2006). In some of these contexts the eventual emergence of wage labor provided women with options that made their lives more autonomous, although the opening of this sort of space in the nineteenth century remains debatable.

Late Nineteenth-century Export Booms

During the 1960s and 1970s historians and historically oriented economists devoted much attention to the export booms that began during the 1880s and 1890s (Lewis, this volume). The interest in explaining Latin American underdevelopment, and policies for overcoming that condition, resulted in many studies of the export sector and the emergence (or reemergence) of plantations and export-oriented hacienda production (Duncan & Rutledge 1977; Cortés Conde 1992). From a macroeconomic perspective these booms were critical because they involved many linkages to the world economy, increased state revenues, the enrichment of new national elites, capital formation, and the consolidation of legal and institutional regimes that were conducive to economic modernization (Scobie 1964; Dean 1969; Haber 1997). In some cases, including those of São Paulo in Brazil, Antioquia in Colombia, and the central valley of Chile, these booms facilitated the transfer of wealth from agricultural export to internally oriented early manufacturing.

Hailed as Latin America's solution to its backwardness during the era of free trade and comparative advantage, export-oriented economies came under criticism during the Depression and after, when their "enclave" aspect challenged the expectation that the export sector should serve as an economic engine for internal economic development. But primary (agricultural and natural resource extraction) export activities remained important for most of the twentieth century. In Mexico mining products led the way in the late nineteenth century, with cattle, henequen, and coffee as important secondary commodities. In Chile and Peru nitrates, copper, and guano all had their booms and busts, with copper remaining as Chile's principal export product into the twentieth century. In Brazil the Amazon rubber boom from about 1880 to 1910 transformed class relations and local development in brutal ways. Unlike the longer-lasting coffee boom in southern Brazil, rubber left little "modernization" or progress in its wake (Weinstein 1983). In Peru, an earlier and relatively massive guano export boom of the1860s to 1880s created massive profits but had extremely limited transformative power (Gootenberg 1989, 1993). In Costa Rica, El Salvador, Guatemala, Colombia, Venezuela, as well as Brazil, coffee became the principal export product with varied associated local social structures and economic effects (Roseberry et al. 1995).

The impact of these export-oriented growth spurts were varied, and have been much debated. While acknowledging their positive effects on economic growth (when not in a downward cycle or market collapse), most of these scenarios have been seen as detrimental because of the overspecialization on raw material export or mono-production, which distorted and limited opportunities for more balanced economic development. Their deleterious effects on the acceleration of peasant differentiation or proletarian impoverishment have also been noted, as these enclaves (eventually becoming large-scale mining and oil-extracting sectors in the early twentieth century) encouraged the emergence of new wage-worker sectors with their own demands, politics, and social movements and the blossoming of these sectors as social actors in the early twentieth century. In smaller countries these foreign-dominated export enclaves had a strong impact on the loss of land for peasant settlement and internal food production and limited the options for future development. In coastal areas of sparse settlement the most important conflicts came from the combined effects of reactivated or enhanced commercial linkages in more remote peasant communities that supplied labor and in the emergence of important wage/land demands among emergent wage-based working sectors.

Nonetheless, the export booms, by definition dependent on foreign markets and often driven by either foreign investment or the resources provided by foreign merchants (whether resident or not), transformed important aspects of the national and regional economies and societies of Latin American countries. Mexico was among those most affected by these trends, with huge US investment in railroad construction and mining, British investments in oil production, and European investments in manufacturing. Railroads in particular helped unite Mexico's disconnected and far-flung regions, creating by the 1890s a more integrated national economy (Coatsworth 1981). Large numbers of foreign merchants and émigrés contributed to the modernization of Mexico City.

Other aspects of the export booms of the late nineteenth century that remain relatively understudied are the cultural and economic effects of the import booms that accompanied the late nineteenth-century export economies. Departing from the classic perspective that saw these booms as damaging to artisanal production, these new studies look at changing consumption patterns of the better-off urban workers (Bauer 1975, 2001), or how the export economies created socially and politically important sectors of the working class (Bergquist 1986). In Yucatán after 1902 International Harvester controlled an "invisible or informal empire" through monopoly control of marketing and processing of henequen used for binder twine, while Mexican-owned plantations benefited from extensive debt peonage and coercive controls on large coastal plantations (Wells 1985).

Case Study: Coffee in Brazil, Mexico, and Central America

Coffee was one of Latin America's principal export crops during the nineteenth century. A product that had no significant economies of scale (except in portions of its processing), it lent itself to a great variety of arrangements of land and labor (Roseberry et al. 1995). In southeastern Brazil coffee was initially grown with slave labor imported from Africa and Brazil's stagnant northeastern sugar zone (Stein 1957) but eventually sharecropping and complex annual contracting arrangements incorporated large numbers of European immigrants and some freedmen on São Paulo's large estates (Dean 1976; Holloway 1980). In Costa Rica, Colombia, and the Andean zone of Venezuela (Roseberry 1983; Yarrington 1997) coffee production followed a process of internal frontier land-claiming and settlement in which productive units were initially small and peasant-run and eventually incorporated larger mid-sized farms. In Guatemala, Nicaragua, Puerto Rico, Cuba, and El Salvador mid-sized farms were dominant from the beginning but many small peasant producers also benefited from the high demand and high prices that characterized European markets throughout most of the century (with important declines in the late 1870s and mid to late 1890s). In portions of Guatemala, Nicaragua, El Salvador, and southern Mexico, the expansion of coffee intersected with the presence of long-standing landholding peasant communities, often leading to extensive conflicts, land loss, and internal conflict and differentiation within the communities themselves.

As an important export crop, the study of the coffee-based agrarian economies has raised important questions about the negative effects of mono-crop or overspecialization in exports, the internal effect on the concentration of land and the cheapening of wage labor, the dissolution of indigenous communities, and the emergence of modernizing elites. Within the diversity of scenarios and outcomes, coffee has been an eminently flexible crop that could be adapted and exploited in many varied social configurations. In São Paulo the wealth, infrastructure, and labor supply (through immigration) generated by the coffee boom were of central importance in that region's early industrialization (Dean 1969). In the Antioquia region of Colombia, coffee provided the basis for a more modest process of industrialization that started in the early twentieth century (Bergquist 1978; Palacios 1980; Chassen 1982). However, in other regions with more strictly stratified class relations that pitted emerging coffee oligarchies supported by the state against downwardly mobile peasant communities, coffee generated far more conflicts and even contributed to regimes of coerced indigenous labor, for example in Guatemala and Nicaragua around the turn of the twentieth century (McCreery 1994). In Cuba the initial decline of Haiti as a plantation-based coffee exporter early in the nineteenth century provided the basis (slaves, capital, immigrant planters) to dramatically expand slave-based coffee production in eastern and eventually western Cuba. This stands in contrast with the many regions (eastern Mexico, portions of El Salvador, and portions of Nicaragua, most of Colombia, Costa Rica and Venezuela) in which family farms and small commercial farms predominated and provided the basis for a wider distribution of wealth and land ownership.

At the other end of the coffee trade were processors, merchants, and exporters who controlled the final stages of production, much of which was done in the roasting and packaging plants of European and US port cities where most of the added value of the final market price of coffee was realized. Coffee culture involved complex markets and shifting European and North American tastes (Topik & Wells 1998). Often the merchant nexus that connected Latin American growers to European markets led to extensive European investments, as mostly German (and sometimes English, French, Belgian, Italian, or Spanish) merchants purchased properties, settled frontiers, displaced communal landholdings, and established larger and more complete processing facilities.

At the end of the nineteenth century, through distinct paths and richly diverse social structures, coffee had shown a transformed social order in which more land was settled, privatized, and organized into farms, labor relations shifted toward a increased use of wage labor, and new regional elites became contenders, if not principal players, in the process of national state formation and politics (Pérez Brignoli & Samper 1994; Lauria-Santiago 1999).

BIBLIOGRAPHY

Adelman, J. (1999) *Republic of Capital: Buenos Aires and the Legal Transformation of the Atlantic World*. Stanford University Press, Stanford.

Aguilar Camín, H. (1977) *La frontera nómada Sonora y la Revolución Mexicana*. Siglo Veintiuno Editores, Mexico City.

Bauer, A. J. (1975) *Chilean Rural Society from Spanish Conquest to 1930*. Cambridge University Press, Cambridge.

Bauer, A. J. (2001) *Goods, Power, History: Latin America's Material Culture*. Cambridge University Press, New York.

Bazant, J. (1970) *Alienation of Church Wealth in Mexico: Social and Economic Aspects of the Liberal Revolution, 1856–1875*. Cambridge University Press, Cambridge.

Benjamin, T. & McNellie, W. (eds.) (1984) *Other Mexicos: Essays on Regional Mexican History, 1876–1911*. University of New Mexico Press, Albuquerque.

Bergad, L. (1983) *Coffee and the Growth of Agrarian Capitalism in Nineteenth-Century Puerto Rico*. University of Pittsburgh Press, Pittsburgh.

Bergad, L. (1990) *Cuban Rural Society in the Nineteenth Century: The Social and Economic History of Monoculture in Matanzas*. Princeton University Press, Princeton.

Bergquist, C. (1978) *Coffee and Conflict in Colombia, 1886–1910*. Duke University Press, Durham.

Bergquist, C. (1986) *Labor in Latin America: Comparative Essays on Chile, Argentina, Venezuela and Colombia*. Stanford University Press, Stanford.

Bonilla, H. (1984) *Guano y burgesía en el Perú*. Instituto de Estudios Peruanos, Lima.

Bortz, J. & Haber, S. H. (eds.) (2002) *The Mexican Economy, 1870–1930: Essays on the Economic History of Institutions, Revolution, and Growth*. Stanford University Press, Stanford.

Cardoso, C. F. S. (1977) "The Formation of the Coffee Estate in Nineteenth-century Costa Rica." In K. Duncan & I. Routledge (eds.), *Land and Labour in Latin America*. Cambridge University Press, Cambridge.

Cardoso, C. F. (1985) "Historia económica del café en Centroamérica (siglo XIX)," *Estudios Sociales Centroamericanos*, 4:10.

Cardoso, C. F. S. & Pérez Brignoli, H. (1977) *Centroamérica y la economía occidental (1520–1930)*. Editorial Universidad de Costa Rica, San José.

Cardoso, F. H. & Faletto, E. (1979) *Dependency and Development in Latin America*. University of California Press, Berkeley.

Charlip, J. (2003) *Cultivating Coffee: The Farmers of Carazo, Nicaragua, 1880–1930*. Ohio University Press, Athens.

Chassen, F. R. (1982) *Café y capitalismo: El proceso de transición en Colombia 1880–1930*. Universidad Autonoma del Estado de México, Mexico City.

Chassen de López, F. R. (2004) *From Liberal to Revolutionary Oaxaca: The View from the South, Mexico 1867–1911*. Pennsylvania State University Press, University Park.

Coatsworth, J. H. (1978). "Obstacles to Economic Growth in Nineteenth-Century Mexico," *The American Historical Review*, 83:1 (February), pp. 80–100.

Coatsworth, J. H. (1981). *Growth Against Development: The Economic Impact of Railroads in Porfirian Mexico*. Northern Illinois University Press, DeKalb.

Coatsworth, J. H. & Taylor, A. M. (eds.) (1998). *Latin America and the World Economy since 1800*. Harvard University David Rockefeller Center for Latin American Studies, Cambridge, MA.

Cortés Conde, R. (1992) "Export-led Growth in Latin America: 1870–1930," *Journal of Latin American Studies*, 24 (Quincentenary Supplement), pp. 163–79.

Dean, W. (1969) *The Industrialization of São Paulo, 1880–1945*. University of Texas Press, Austin.

Dean, W. (1976). *Rio Claro: A Brazilian Plantation System, 1820–1920*. Stanford University Press, Stanford.

Dore, E. (2006) *Myths of Modernity: Peonage and Patriarchy in Nicaragua*. Duke University Press, Durham.

Dosal, P. J. (1993) *Doing Business with the Dictators: A Political History of United Fruit in Guatemala, 1899–1944*. SR Books, Wilmington, DE.

Ducey, M. T. (2004). *A Nation of Villages: Riot and Rebellion in the Mexican Huasteca, 1750–1850*. University of Arizona Press, Tucson.

Duncan, K. & Rutledge, I. (eds.) (1977) *Land and Labour in Latin America: Essays on the Development of Agrarian Capitalism in the Nineteenth and Twentieth Centuries*. Cambridge University Press, Cambridge.

Fernández, M. J. A. (2003) *Pintado el mundo de azul: El auge añilero y el mercado centroameri-cano, 1750–1810*. CONCULTURA, San Salvador.

Figueroa, L. A. (2005) *Sugar, Slavery, and Freedom in Nineteenth-Century Puerto Rico*. University of North Carolina Press, Chapel Hill.

Gonzales, M. J. (1985) *Plantation Agriculture and Social Control in Northern Peru, 1875–1933*. University of Texas Press, Austin.

Gootenberg, P. (1989) *Between Silver and Guano: Commercial Policy and the State in Postindependence Peru*. Princeton University Press, Princeton.

Gootenberg, P. (1993) *Imagining Development: Economic Ideas in Peru's "Fictitious Prosperity" of Guano, 1840–1880*. University of California Press, Berkeley.

Gould, J. L. (1990) *To Lead as Equals: Rural Protest and Political Consciousness in Chinandega, Nicaragua, 1912–1979*. University of North Carolina Press, Chapel Hill.

Gould, J. L. (1998) *To Die in This Way: Nicaraguan Indians and the Myth of Mestizaje, 1880–1960*. Duke University Press, Durham.

Grandin, G. (2000) *The Blood of Guatemala: A History of Race and Nation*. Duke University Press, Durham.

Guardino, P. F. (1996) *Peasants, Politics, and the Formation of Mexico's National State: Guerrero, 1800–1857*. Stanford University Press, Stanford.

Guardino, P. F. (2005) *The Time of Liberty: Popular Political Culture in Oaxaca, 1750–1850*. Duke University Press, Durham.

Gudmundson, L. (1986) *Costa Rica Before Coffee: Society and Economy on the Eve of the Export Boom*. Louisiana State University Press, Baton Rouge.

Haber, S. H. (1989) *Industry and Underdevelopment: The Industrialization of Mexico, 1890–1940*. Stanford University Press, Stanford.

Haber, S. H. (ed.) (1997) *How Latin America Fell Behind: Essays on the Economic Histories of Brazil and Mexico, 1800–1914*. Stanford University Press, Stanford.

Hall, C. (1976) *El café y el desarrollo histórico-geográfico de Costa Rica*. Editorial Costa Rica y Universidad Nacional, San José.

Halperín Donghi, T. (1970) *Historia contemporánea de América Latina*. Alianza Editorial, Madrid.

Holloway, T. H. (1980) *Immigrants on the Land: Coffee and Society in São Paulo, 1886–1934*. University of North Carolina Press, Chapel Hill.

Jackson, R. H. (ed.) (1997) *Liberals, the Church, and Indian Peasants: Corporate Lands and the Challenge of Reform in Nineteenth-Century Spanish America*. University of New Mexico Press, Albuquerque.

Jacobsen, N. (1993) *Mirages of Transition: The Peruvian Altiplano, 1780–1930*. University of California Press, Berkeley.

Katz, F. (1981) *The Secret War in Mexico: Europe, the United States, and the Mexican Revolution*. University of Chicago Press, Chicago.

Klein, H. S. (1993) *Haciendas and Ayllus: Rural Society in the Bolivian Andes in the Eighteenth and Nineteenth Centuries*. Stanford University Press, Stanford.

Knight, A. (1986) *The Mexican Revolution*. 2 vols. Cambridge University Press, Cambridge.

Knight, F. W. (1970) *Slave Society in Cuba during the Nineteenth Century*. University of Wisconsin Press, Madison.

Kourí, E. (2004) *A Pueblo Divided: Business, Property, and Community in Papantla, Mexico*. Stanford University Press, Stanford.

Langer, E. D. (1989) *Economic Change and Rural Resistance in Southern Bolivia, 1880–1930*. Stanford University Press, Stanford.

Langer, E. D. & Jackson, R. H. (1997) "Liberalism and the Land Question in Bolivia, 1825–1920." In R. H. Jackson (ed.), *Liberals, the Church, and Indian Peasants: Corporate*

Lands and the Challenge of Reform in Nineteenth-Century Spanish America. University of New Mexico Press, Albuquerque.

Larson, B. (1998) *Cochabamba, 1550–1900: Colonialism and Agrarian Transformation in Bolivia*. Duke University Press, Durham.

Larson, B., Harris, O., & Tandeter, E. (eds.) (1995) *Ethnicity, Markets, and Migration in the Andes: At the Crossroads of History and Anthropology*. Duke University Press, Durham.

Lauria-Santiago, A. (1998a) "La historia regional del café en El Salvador," *Revista de Historia*, (San José, Costa Rica), 38.

Lauria-Santiago, A. (1998b) "Land, Community, and Revolt in Indian Izalco, El Salvador, 1855–1905," *Hispanic American Historical Review*, 79:3 (September), pp. 495–534.

Lauria-Santiago, A. (1998c) " 'That a poor man be industrious:' Coffee, Community, and Capitalism in the Transformation of El Salvador's Ladino Peasantry, 1850–1900." In A. Lauria-Santiago & A. Chomsky (eds.), *Identity and Struggle at the Margins of the Nation-State: The Laboring Peoples of Central America and the Hispanic Caribbean*. Duke University Press, Durham.

Lauria-Santiago, A. (1999) *An Agrarian Republic: Commercial Agriculture and the Politics of Peasant Communities in El Salvador, 1823–1914*. University of Pittsburgh Press, Pittsburgh.

LeGrand, C. (1986) *Frontier Expansion and Peasant Protest in Colombia, 1850–1936*. University of New Mexico Press, Albuquerque.

Love, J. L. & Jacobsen, N. (1988) *Guiding the Invisible Hand: Economic Liberalism and the State in Latin American History*. Praeger, New York.

Mallon, F. (1983) *The Defense of Community in Peru's Central Highlands: Peasant Struggle and Capitalist Transition, 1860–1940*. Princeton University Press, Princeton.

Mallon, F. (1995) *Peasant and Nation: The Making of Postcolonial Mexico and Peru*. University of California Press, Berkeley.

McCreery, D. (1994) *Rural Guatemala: 1760–1940*. Stanford University Press, Stanford.

Nugent, D. (1993) *Spent Cartridges of Revolution: An Anthropological History of Namiquipa, Chihuahua*. University of Chicago Press, Chicago.

Palacios, M. (1980) *Coffee in Colombia, 1850–1970*. Cambridge University Press, Cambridge.

Peloso, V. C. (1999) *Peasants on Plantations: Subaltern Strategies of Labor and Resistance in the Pisco Valley, Peru*. Duke University Press, Durham.

Peloso, V. C. & Tenenbaum, B. A. (eds.) (1996) *Liberals, Politics, and Power: State Formation in Nineteenth-Century Latin America*. University of Georgia Press, Athens.

Pérez Brignoli, H. & Samper, K. M. (1994) *Tierra, café y sociedad: Ensayos sobre la historia agraria centroamericana*. FLACSO Costa Rica, San José.

Roseberry, W. (1983) *Coffee and Capitalism in the Venezuelan Andes*. University of Texas Press, Austin.

Roseberry, W. (1989) *Anthropologies and Histories: Essays in Culture, History, and Political Economy*. Rutgers University Press, New Brunswick.

Roseberry, W. (1993) "Beyond the Agrarian Question in Latin America." In F. Cooper et al., *Confronting Historical Paradigms: Peasants, Labor, and the World System in Africa and Latin America*. University of Wisconsin Press, Madison.

Roseberry, W., Gudmundson, L., & Samper, K. M. (eds.) (1995) *Coffee, Society, and Power in Latin America*. Johns Hopkins University Press, Baltimore.

Samper, K. M. (1990) *Generations of Settlers: Rural Households and Markets on the Costa Rican Frontier, 1850–1935*. Westview Press, Boulder.

Scarano, F. A. (1984) *Sugar and Slavery in Puerto Rico: The Plantation Economy of Ponce, 1800–1850*. University of Wisconsin Press, Madison.

Schwartz, S. B. (1985) *Sugar Plantations in the Formation of Brazilian Society: Bahia, 1550–1835.* Cambridge University Press, Cambridge.

Scobie, J. (1964) *Revolution on the Pampas: A Social History of Argentine Wheat, 1860–1910.* University of Texas Press, Austin.

Solberg, C. (1970) *Immigration and Nationalism, Argentina and Chile, 1890–1914.* University of Texas Press, Austin.

Sowell, D. (1989) "The 1893 *Bogotazo*: Artisans and Public Violence in Late Nineteenth-Century Bogotá," *Journal of Latin American Studies,* 21:2 (May), pp. 267–82.

Sowell, D. (1992) *The Early Colombian Labor Movement: Artisans and Politics in Bogotá, 1832–1919.* Temple University Press, Philadelphia.

Stein, S. J. (1957) *Vassouras, a Brazilian Coffee County, 1850–1900.* Harvard University Press, Cambridge, MA.

Stein, S. & Stein, B. (1970) *The Colonial Heritage of Latin America: Essays on Economic Dependence in Perspective.* Oxford University Press, New York.

Tandeter, E. (1987) *The Market of Potosi at the End of the Eighteenth Century.* University of London, London.

Topik, S. & Wells, A. (1998) *The Second Conquest of Latin America: Coffee, Henequen, and Oil during the Export Boom, 1850–1930.* University of Texas Press, Austin.

Tutino, J. (1986) *From Insurrection to Revolution in Mexico.* Princeton University Press, Princeton.

Tutino, J. (1998) "The Revolution in Mexican Independence: Insurgency and the Renegotiation of Property, Production, and Patriarchy in the Bajío, 1800–1855," *Hispanic American Historical Review,* 78:3 (August), pp. 367–418.

Warren, R. A. (2001) *Vagrants and Citizens: Politics and the Masses in Mexico City from Colony to Republic.* SR Books, Wilmington, DE.

Wasserman, M. (1984) *Capitalists, Caciques, and Revolution: the Native Elite and Foreign Enterprise in Chihuahua, Mexico, 1854–1911.* University of North Carolina Press, Chapel Hill.

Weinstein, B. (1983) *The Amazon Rubber Boom, 1850–1920.* Stanford University Press, Stanford.

Wells, A. (1985) *Yucatán's Gilded Age: Haciendas, Henequen, and International Harvester, 1860–1915.* University of New Mexico Press, Albuquerque.

Wolf, E. R. (1959) *Sons of the Shaking Earth.* University of Chicago Press, Chicago.

Wolf, E. R. (1969) *Peasant Wars of the Twentieth Century.* Harper & Row, New York.

Wolfe, J. (2007) *The Everyday Nation-State: Community, Ethnicity and Nation in Nineteenth-Century Nicaragua.* University of Nebraska Press Lincoln.

Womack, J. W. (1969) *Zapata and the Mexican Revolution.* Knopf, New York.

Yarrington, D. (1997) *A Coffee Frontier: Land, Society, and Politics in Duaca, Venezuela, 1830–1936.* University of Pittsburgh Press, Pittsburgh.

Chapter Seventeen

MODERNIZATION AND INDUSTRIALIZATION

Colin M. Lewis

Introduction

The debate about growth and industrialization has long exercised historians of Latin America. Four distinct approaches dominate the literature: modernization theory; structuralism and neostructuralism; the new institutional economics; and consumption theory. Although quite different in their interpretation of the causes and course of modernization and industrial growth, all focus on a number of critical features. Rostow (1975, 1987), considered to be the father of modernization theory, attributes the process to a combination of science, economics, and politics. He presents industrialization as a central facet – but not the sum – of modernization. Writing in response to Rostow, Gerschenkron (1962) ascribes to government important functions in "late industrialization" in relatively backward economies: the later the onset of industrial growth, the greater the role of the state. North (2003), a proponent of the new institutionalism, similarly stresses the political: economic institutions, he emphasizes, are shaped by political institutions. Focusing explicitly on Latin America from a neostructuralist perspective that acknowledges constraints on the process, Cárdenas et al. (2000) argue that industrialization has been state-led or state-accelerated: the integration of domestic markets was possible only as a result of state action. Consumptionists also attach particular significance to the way in which individuals and households engage with the market, including cultural factors that shaped preferences for locally produced manufactures and imports (Bauer & Orlove 1997: 6–7). Hence, all approaches underscore the interaction of the political and the economic, and acknowledge the centrality of markets in modernization and industrialization.

This chapter considers the extent to which economic and political forces facilitated market formation in Latin America during the 1870–1930 period of global engagement. Economic historians recognize the powerful influence of trade and finance in the consolidation of the world economy. While some would be reluctant to use the term, many also acknowledge the "globalizing" of the international economy during the nineteenth century. Globalization may be defined as the international integration of markets at two distinct levels: the forging of world commodity and product markets; and the internationalization of labor and capital markets. There was also a shared ideology: free trade, and a growing commitment to the gold standard, under-pinned and drove economic openness and internationalization. What distinguishes the nineteenth century from earlier periods of "globalization" is the completeness of the process. Two phenomena, in particular, were peculiar: first, the integration of commodity, product, and factor markets; secondly, the fact that trade grew exponen-tially, considerably faster than output. For the purpose of this chapter, another observation is relevant: if global import and export growth was impressive before 1913, that of Latin America was even more startling.

The World Economy and Latin America: *c.*1870 and beyond

In the "long nineteenth century" (1800–1913), global imports and exports per capita grew by a factor of 25 while total world output increased by a factor of 2.2 only. International trade represented 2 percent of world output in 1800, but 21 percent in 1913. In 1929 the figure had declined to 16 percent, but world trade was still clearly significant (Estevadeordal et al. 2001: i, 3). International trade growth was particularly rapid from about the 1840s to the early 1870s (Kenwood & Lougheed 1999: 78). While world trade growth was sluggish during the two decades following the Great Depression of 1873, the continent was less affected by the slow-down, and rates of growth began to pick up again in the 1890s, with high average rates of international trade expansion being sustained from 1893 to 1913 (Ashworth 1967: 213–14). Critically, most Latin American countries were integrated into the world economy during the surge in global commerce before 1880, and the continent's share of world trade grew by 40 percent in the four decades after the 1873 depres-sion. In the late 1870s, the continent accounted for 5.4 percent of world trade; in 1913, 7.6 percent. Perhaps this was unsurprising in view of the fact that primary commodities accounted for around two-thirds of the total value of international trade between 1876 and 1913, a tendency that explains the strong price performance of many Latin American exports (Kenwood & Lougheed 1999: 80, 83–4). In relative terms, no other region of the world registered a similar increase in its share of world trade, finance, and population: Latin America gained relative presence in the world economy at the expense of other regions.

Between 1850 and 1880 the value of Chilean exports increased by a multiple of 50, and Argentinian by a factor of 10. Although other countries lagged behind these leaders, "export expansion was a notable trait all over the region" (Halperín Donghi 1993: 121–2). Of course, as contemporaries in Latin America understood only too well, trade flows were cyclical, subject to sharp regional and product swings as tastes changed and markets responded to demand, supply, and technology shocks. Such was the degree of global economic integration achieved by some countries toward the end of this first phase of very rapid trade growth that the 1873 international commercial and financial crisis was probably the first modern exogenous shock to afflict Latin America (Ferns 1960: 374–5; Foreman-Peck 1995: 87).

The prominence of commodity trades is associated with the internationalization and industrialization of the world economy after *c.*1870, epitomized by a set of technical and structural changes that assumed a global dimension. Technological improvements in transport and communications, and the mechanization of production (in agriculture as well as manufacturing) triggered demand-side and supply-side changes that effected an outward movement in the world production function, and in the frontier of resource exploitation. Industrialization, urbanization, and rapid population growth in the North Atlantic economies, coupled with declining transport costs, facilitated the emergence of mass markets for such commodities as sugar and coffee – previously considered luxuries – as well a surge in demand for factory inputs like natural fibers (especially wool and cotton) and metals (notably copper and tin by the late nineteenth century), and for farm inputs such as natural fertilizers (guano and nitrates) and grains (wheat and maize). The exponential growth in demand for commodities in the North Atlantic world brought on stream new centers of supply. The steam communications revolution in ocean shipping and railroads was particularly important for Latin America's capacity to respond to rising international demand for primary products, as it had a disproportionate impact on the transport of bulky raw materials and foodstuffs with a high freight/price ratio. The continent hardly featured on the world railway map in 1850. Even in 1870, Latin America accounted for less than 2 percent total world railway mileage. By 1910, however, railways in Latin America made up almost 10 percent of the world total – a proportion somewhat above Asia, and considerably higher than Africa. The Argentine, Brazil, Cuba, and Mexico had extensive networks, and there were near national systems in Uruguay and Chile (Kenwood & Lougheed 1999: 13–14).

Railways spelt more than the communications revolution. In addition, they signaled foreign investment, both borrowing by governments to upgrade social overhead capital, and direct investment by free-standing companies floated to construct and operate public utilities in Latin America. International investment flows further confirm the importance of Latin America in the global order, as well as pointing to the integration of world capital markets and the access of the continent to them. According to Jenks (1963: 13), in 1854, holdings of Latin American securities accounted for between 17 and 18 percent of total British overseas portfolio investment. Stone (1999: 19, 409) argues that this percentage changed little over the ensuing period. Between 1865 and 1914 the continent absorbed 17 percent of new outflows (portfolio and direct) from London. For the whole of this period South America was second only to North America as a recipient of British overseas investment, and often a very near second at that. By the interwar period, the share of the global stock of international capital located in Latin America was similar to the proportion of world investments placed in Canada and the USA, confirming the degree of international integration achieved by the continent between c.1870 and 1930 (Woodruff 1973: 710–11; Regalsky 2002: 44–7; Obstfeld & Taylor 2003: 140–2). Few other regions could demonstrate such consistency of appeal: Latin America was remarkable in that, among non-core economies, it continued to attract a very large proportion of international capital flows for so long.

By the eve of World War I, Latin America was a fully paid-up member of the global commercial and financial system. Overseas trade and foreign finance were critical for Latin America, and the continent was a key region in the international system. No other part of the world experienced the same relative, sustained increased participation in international product and labor markets during the period, and few could match its accelerating integration in the global capital market.

Commodities, Finance, and Migration: Making Markets

Establishing causality between export-led growth and nation-state formation is contentious, but this has not discouraged authors from trying to do so (Halperín Donghi 1993: 115–22; Bushnell & Macaulay 1994: 181, 286–9). Yet, the timing of the surge in exports and the securing of internal order cannot have been coincidental. Before the 1850s, political turmoil had limited the expansion of external commercial and financial relations in many republics. By the 1880s, endogenous institutional developments included more secure constitutional order, monetary and fiscal reform, new commercial codes which facilitated business organization, state action to promote the consolidation of markets, and a general openness to the international economy – all underpinned by the ideology of liberalism (Dye 2006: 177–82, 188–95). Hale and others caution against an uncritical adoption of foreign political and economic ideas by elites in Latin America. Rather, "pragmatic liberalism" may be observed, marked by the ascendancy of positivism (Hale 1985: 387–96; Love 1988: 8–12; Topik 1999: 11–17). Governments sought to create markets and intervened in them. State formation and ideology are important because, as stressed by analysis of modernization and industrialization, centralized, national states have been instrumental in advancing new ideologies, and ideology was often critical to an industrial breakthrough (Rostow 1960: 7; Gerschenkron 1962: 22–6).

If "pragmatic liberalism" was a growth ideology, what sort of progress did export-led growth deliver? Modernization presupposes a combination of market and state initiatives: the transfer (and productive investment) of part of the export surplus in non-export activities; the quantitative growth, and qualitative deepening, of national markets; and state reform – new methods of funding the state and changes in the direction of government expenditure (Lewis 1985: 283–7; 1995: 349–59; Bértola & Williamson 2003: 8–9; Bulmer-Thomas 2003: 15–16). In economies where backward or forward linkages between the export sector and the rest of the economy were weak, where final demand linkages were limited due to restrictive labor practices such as slavery and debt peonage, and where foreign-financed capital-intensive extractive operations siphoned off resources, fiscal linkages (that is, transfers through the state) were crucial to development, provided that governments were able to capture a share of export rents and deploy them productively.

Export commodities are important, but some are more likely to foster modernization (and industrialization) than others. Be that as it may, given the growth in international commodity trades, Table 17.1 shows that exports came to represent a considerable share of economic activity across the continent. Though some may find the figures rather high, Bulmer-Thomas's calculations on the weight of exports in total production are generally well regarded. Yet, despite a general increase in the participation of exports in GDP (gross domestic product) virtually across the continent, growth outcomes varied considerably, as shown in Table 17.2. Endowments (the commodity asset base) in part explain differing performances; institutions were similarly significant, determining the ability of individual Latin American economies to respond to demand/price changes in the global market.

Recalling that global market forces were broadly positive for Latin American commodity prices for most of the nineteenth and early twentieth centuries, the differential

Table 17.1   Value of exports in selected Latin American countries as a share of gross domestic product (percent), c.1850–c.1912

Country	c.1850	c.1912
The Argentine	20	33
Brazil	10	32
Chile	10	32
Colombia	10	14
Cuba	30	44
Mexico	10	14
Peru	10	25
Uruguay	40	26
Venezuela	10	21
Latin America	10	25

Source: Bulmer-Thomas (2003: 420).

Table 17.2   Growth of exports in selected Latin American countries, by value, c.1850–1912 (percent per year)

The Argentine	6.1
Brazil	3.7
Chile	4.3
Colombia	3.5
Cuba	2.9
Mexico	3.0
Peru	2.9
Uruguay	3.4
Venezuala	2.7

Source: Bulmer-Thomas (2003: 62).

growth performance of exports shown in Table 17.2 requires explanation. The critical factor seems to have been a capacity to diversify commodity exports; in other words, flexibility in the face of changing external demand, a capability that presupposes institutional modernization. Countries like the Argentine and Mexico, which demonstrated a remarkable capacity to diversify commodity exports between the 1880s and 1910s, probably experienced the most favorable price profiles.

Other countries were by no means mono-exporters. After the collapse of the guano boom and loss of nitrate territories to Chile, Peruvian export earnings were generated by a shifting basket of commodities that included minerals (silver, copper, and petroleum), natural fibers (cotton and wool), foodstuffs (coffee and sugar), and rubber. Market diversification also had a positive impact on export performance. Of course, for lengthy periods some countries were notoriously dependent on a single commodity and/or a single market. Examples include Bolivia (tin), Brazil (coffee), Chile (nitrates), and Cuba (sugar); and, by c.1900, the USA was absorbing around three-quarters of Cuban and Mexican exports (for some Central American economies the proportions were even higher), and a third of Brazilian exports. Meanwhile, the UK took a quarter of Argentinian exports, a third of Peruvian, and four-fifths of Bolivian. Dependence on a very narrow range of commodities or markets obviously increased the risk inherent in the export model of growth. Contraction of demand in an overseas market, the emergence of a more competitive supplier, or the development of a synthetic substitute could be catastrophic.

Rates of growth, and the longevity of the growth cycle, mattered because they had an impact on state building, and the credibility of the pragmatic liberal growth ideology. With export expansion came imports, which could be taxed to enhance state revenue. Imports, financed by export earnings, appeared to promise a secure source of revenue – one that could be mortgaged to underwrite foreign borrowing. Inflows of foreign funds reduced the cost of state borrowing and weaned some administrations away from dependence on inflation as a means of financing the state (Panettieri 1983; Marichal 1995; Peloso & Tenenbaum 1996). Capacity to borrow and a commitment to repay also implied greater state competence. Thus states were able to expand the supply of public goods. These included political order, economic and social services such as transport and education, and monetary stability. New revenue streams financed the import of Remington rifles and railways, purchased by the state. For proponents of the new institutional economics, "monetary virtue" was also critical to the formation of local capital markets, in part because credible government borrowing might generate additional financial instruments (public bonds) that circulated in local markets alongside commercial paper – yet another indicator of modernization (Bordo & Rockoff 1996; Bordo & Vegh 1998). State formation and market formation were, then, intimately related – though the direction of causality is difficult to fathom.

Land

Factor marketization was a critical prerequisite for modernization or development. How, or to what extent, were national factor markets in land and labor created? The single most striking economic change of the period was a massive increase in the supply of land, "the mainspring for capitalist development" (Glade 1986: 26). Even allowing for modest improvements in yields, the volume growth in exports implied a tenfold increase in land supply (Bulmer-Thomas 2003: 91). Explanations for the increase in land inputs are institutional and technical: private appropriation of public domain, which facilitated a physical expansion of the production function, and railways, which enabled more intense use within the production frontier.

During the middle third of the century there was a massive transfer of land from public and corporate to private hands, a process of privatization that considerably overshadows late twentieth-century disposal of state assets. This involved the disposal of public land, the secularization and distribution of estates held by the Roman Catholic Church, the breakup of communal Indian estates, and the seizure of territory occupied by nomadic Indians. In Mexico, mid-nineteenth-century liberal reformers considered the scale of communal and ecclesiastical landholding a check on production for the market and on the operation of a land market (Weiner 2004: 34–5, 90). In Meso-America and in the Andes, villages retained control of either very large areas, or some of the most productive land. Indian communities held at least one half of all agricultural land in Bolivia in the 1860s. In central Mexico, too, village collectives possessed some of the best-located estates (Bauer 1986: 159). In these areas and elsewhere, landowners anxious to demonstrate modernizing market credentials joined with liberal ideologues to press for disestablishment and individualization of collective holdings. In Chilean and Argentinian Patagonia, and in the Chaco and Amazonia, pressure on nomadic Indian territory increased further after 1870. Evidence points to a fivefold increase in land under cultivation in the Argentine between 1865 and 1873, and a further fivefold increase between 1873 and 1888. Occurring before the massive growth in land exploitation associated with the transport revolution *c*.1890, this expansion was due exclusively to military campaigns on the Indian frontier (Cárcano 1972: 400).

The physical incorporation of new land was accompanied by the application of liberal theories to land legislation. Bauer (1986: 158) describes the fuzziness of rural property rights in much of pre-1870s Latin America: "Haciendas co-existed and overlapped with villages and squatter settlements with whom they carried on a running squabble, now and then erupting into violence, over boundaries and water rights." Institutional changes such as the *Lei da terra* (1850) in Brazil (Dean 1971), the *Ley Lerdo* (1856) in Mexico, and similar projects elsewhere, were designed to remedy these defects and to promote freeholding. In keeping with liberal sentiments, security of tenure and the prohibition of corporate and collective landholding would facilitate the rational use of land, increasing production and productivity. Disposals to latifundistas and merchants resulted in the reallocation of land to export production, though not necessarily to an immediate increase in total output or greater productivity. Despite the liberal rhetoric, landholding became increasingly less "democratic" between the 1860s and 1880s.

From Mexico to the Argentine, large estates monopolized land. Although these estates produced for the market, their history yields little evidence of a flourishing land market. Subdivision was largely the result of biology: according to inheritance law, estates were parceled out amongst all legitimate children on the death of an owner. Yet there is some evidence of a land market emerging after the 1870s. The commercialization of landholdings in northern Mexico, in central Chile, on the coffee frontier in Colombia, and in parts of Ecuador and Peru was associated with an open, active land market (Bauer 1986: 158–9; Glade 1986: 30). Similarly, in regions of massive European colonization, land became a commodity. Holloway (1980) details rising land ownership by former *colonos* in Brazil's coffee sector, and Gallo (1984: 158–78) the diffusion of land ownership among immigrant settlers of the *pampa gringa*. Indeed, the concentration of land ownership, and relatively limited examples of homesteading and medium-scale land ownership, does not necessarily corroborate the anti-market hypothesis, as large estates were traded in an increasingly transparent and active land market (Bulmer-Thomas 2003: 94).

Labor

Land privatization was connected with the marketization of another factor: labor. Three principal sources of labor supply were available to export producers: internal migrants squeezed out of the subsistence sector; selective and massive imports from overseas; and natural population growth. Given that the population of Latin America was overwhelmingly rural through most of the nineteenth century, attacks on corporate and collective landholding consciously sought to separate communards from their means of subsistence, and force them to enter the labor market (Bauer 1986: 159). Albeit subject to haphazard or arbitrary application, vagrancy laws similarly sought to compel workers to sell their labor – in effect, to indenture themselves (Weiner 2004: 26, 36–7). Population growth may have offered a long-run solution, but was of little utility to labor-hungry planters, miners, or even railway contractors in the 1860s, 1870s, and 1880s. Export growth heightened perceptions of a shortage of labor and competition for workers. Did competition mean rural proletarianization and the formation of a wage economy in the countryside?

In the plantation economies of Cuba and Brazil, a massive surge in international demand for sugar and coffee initially strengthened archaic institutions such as slavery. Slaves became an even more sought-after internal commodity when the transatlantic trade closed around the 1850s, but a combination of factors led to its final demise in the 1880s (Helg, this volume). In sugar-producing areas, there were experiments with indentured Asian laborers (Bushnell & Macaulay 1994: 243, 267). The indenturing of Indian and Chinese workers was most pronounced in the Caribbean, the model having been established at the time of abolition in the British West Indies. In the Andes, the Caribbean, and Central America, the contracting of rural free labor (*enganche*) was a common form of labor mobilization. Internal migrant workers were contracted both seasonally and for permanent employment. The system was open to abuse and often compared to slavery (Bauer 1986: 182). Export growth during the middle third of the nineteenth century hardly delivered an immediate switch to a competitive labor market. Employers exhibited a proclivity for coercion rather than market mechanisms to secure scarce labor, and were endowed with the political power necessary to exercise that preference. In many regions, communal land was alienated and villagers displaced, at a time when a rural labor market did not exist: there would be no functioning wage system in the countryside until *c.*1900 (Halperín Donghi 1993: 120). Instead of constituting a rural proletariat, communards perforce drifted toward large estates that offered a garden plot in exchange for labor services. Again, the result was a one-off transfer, not marketization. Former independent producers joined the ranks of "bonded" estate workers (various known as *inquilinos, yanaconas,* and *peones acasillados*), trapped on haciendas by a combination of usufruct, debts, and token wage payments. These arrangements could indicate a lack of employment, or an unwillingness of employers to pay money wages high enough to clear the labor market.

There was substantial variation in regional arrangements, and progress to fully functioning labor markets was slow. Variety and heterogeneity were a function of differing regional factor endowments (in addition to labor), the durability of traditional institutions, and differences in the structure of production in the export sector (Glade 1986: 36). The violent story of henequen plantations of southern Mexico, the life of alcoholism and terror associated with rubber production in Amazonia, and the administration of vagrancy laws by an especially enthusiastic rural gendarmerie in Guatemala provide sufficient evidence of the use of non-market incentive to secure, and hold, labor (Bauer 1986: 182, 183–4). But there is another side to the story. The apparent willingness of Andean contract labor to reengage from year to year, seasonal movements of indigenous workers in central Mexico, and massive annual immigration from Europe to the River Plate and within Southern Brazil and the River Plate, indicate responsiveness to wage signals (Katz 1974; 1980; Blanchard 1980; Bauer 1986; Miller 1990). Of course, these trends could indicate competition for jobs, as much as competition for labor. Nevertheless, wage-labor systems emerged, leading to the fitful consolidation of a labor market.

During the period studied, population growth in Latin America was high by international norms (Kenwood & Lougheed 1999: 17–18, 168–71). Between 1870 and 1930, total population more than doubled. Rates of growth were considerably above the average in formerly lightly populated regions of the Southern Cone, but fairly close to the continental average in relatively densely settled parts of Mexico and the Andes, areas notoriously associated with debt peonage and *enganche*. As demographic historians tend to equate population growth with welfare gains, this would further suggest that such archaic labor institutions were not incompatible with socioeconomic progress (Komlos 1995).

Voluntary international migration is probably one of the most effective indicators of labor market formation, and of welfare. Mass immigration effected thoroughgoing changes in labor relations. Between the mid-nineteenth and the mid-twentieth century, the Argentine received around seven and a half million immigrants and Brazil something less than five million, concentrated in the center-south of the country (Sánchez-Albornoz 1974; Merrick & Graham 1979). These countries were, respectively, the second and third most favored destinations of European emigrants, after the USA. Other countries, notably Uruguay, Chile, and Cuba, also received substantial numbers of immigrants. Indeed, virtually every country attracted some (Bailey & Headlam 1977; Denoon 1983). Given that these countries were "competing" with the USA and other areas of recent settlement, the mass movement of people implies economic opportunity, reasonable political order, and the existence of functioning labor markets. Immigration of this magnitude had a significant demographic, social, and political impact.

Mass migration, supported by policies designed to attract immigrants, and related institutional changes – including the abolition of slavery, legislation prohibiting the payment of wages in kind, modest paternalistic efforts after 1900 to regulate the employment of women and children and limit the length of the working day, and a very gradual acceptance of collective bargaining (invariably counterpointed by state violence and massacre at the hint of worker autonomy and solidarity) – all point to the modernization of labor markets. The market was the principal, near dominant, mechanism of labor recruitment for employers in the Argentine, Uruguay, central Chile, and southern Brazil. Regional (or seasonal) labor markets probably functioned elsewhere, not least in central and northern Mexico, in coastal Peru and parts of Colombia. In other regions, pre-capitalist institutions of labor mobilization coexisted alongside waged employment.

Population growth, urbanization, and the hesitant emergence of national (or regional) labor markets were part of a broader process of societal modernization. New middle sectors associated with urbanization arose with the formation of civic and mutual societies, and an increase in the supply of such public goods as education. The university reform movement rapidly spread across the continent from the Argentinian city of Córdoba after 1918. There was hesitant action by worker associations. These events appear to indicate a thickening of associational life. The most potent forces working for change were nationalism and demands emanating from largely urban classes for greater access to power (Hall & Spalding 1985: 346–65; Hale 1985: 422–8; Halperín Donghi 1993: 168–9, 180, 186–94; Annino 1995; Munck 1998). Nationalism and populism became especially pronounced in Cuba, the Southern Cone, and Brazil. Perhaps because they were articulated earlier, populist programs seemed to have been most easily accommodated in Uruguay. There were, of course, limits to the transforming effects of marketization and monetization, illustrated by archaic social relations of production in areas like Amazonia, the northeast of Brazil, the Andean altiplano, and large parts of Central America. The persistence of arcane institutions in large swaths of rural Latin America pointed to the strength of resistance to market forces and represented a check on development.

Capital

If land was an endogenous factor, and labor supply became progressively domestically available with population growth, liquid capital was substantially an imported factor. As shown above, Latin America attracted a large and relatively stable share of international capital flows. Export sector activities were consistently supported by international capital markets, though the form of savings inflow changed over time, moving broadly from portfolio finance to direct investment. But even toward the end of the period, local capital markets, where they existed, are usually depicted as small and shallow. This does not mean that institutional credit was totally absent, nor that the situation was static. How could it be, given the rate of economic growth? Admittedly, until massive injections of foreign savings generated greater liquidity, local capital tended to be relatively immobile, represented by physical assets such as land and slaves or (relatively more liquid) livestock and crops. Institutional, impersonal forms of long-term credit were virtually unknown during the early part of the nineteenth century. For many decades thereafter, working capital was only available from merchants who made short-term advances, secured on crops. Longer-term funding was obtained though family and social networks. Moreover, during the immediate post-independence decades, the demands of the state crowded out private borrowers. Governments either commandeered the limited supplies of funds available, or resorted to inflation financing, which compromised the consolidation of local money markets.

Foreign capital markets were largely responsible for financing basic infrastructure, making possible such lumpy investment as railways, gas and water plants, and a wide range of public utilities. This has led structuralists to argue that a scarcity of domestic credit acted as a check on development: foreign banks focused narrowly on the requirements of the overseas trade sector, and official banks favored friends of the regime. But export sector savings flowed into a broad range of businesses dependent on the internal market. Antônio da Silva Prado exemplified the type of *fazendeiro*–entrepreneur who channeled coffee profits into corporate initiatives such as railways, ports, meat-packing, and glass and shoe manufacture. Another example from Brazil, that of the Matarazzo clan, demonstrates how well-located immigrants were able to plug into informal and formal credit networks associated with the overseas trade sector to create one of the largest industrial complexes in South America (Stein 1957: 133; Dean 1969: 30–1, 45, 49–66). Several business clusters emerged between the 1880s and 1920s involving planters, merchants, and immigrants. These groups, families, or networks of families were responsible for promoting several lines of Brazilian manufacturing (Suzigan 1986: 126–56). The importance of networks of families in the history of modern manufacturing has been stressed for other countries. For example, several nineteenth-century industrial consortia in Mexico included immigrants, merchants, and politically well-connected land-owners. These groups often emerged from short-term partnerships which, once trust had been established, were strengthened by ties of marriage, and the diversification of activities (Trujillo Bolio 1997: 245–74). Networks of families were able to draw on extended credit chains and had access to larger pools of entrepreneurial talent.

Credit chains were by no means all informal. The proliferation of banks and the emergence of local stock exchanges indicate the institutionalization of finance. The first modern banks emerged in the late 1850s or early 1860s, a process principally associated with the arrival of foreign firms. By the 1880s, foreign banks were operating alongside a growing number of domestic official and private firms (Joslin 1963: 53, 108–9; Jones 1987: 127–40; Young 1995: 97, 104–7). At least in capital cities, something like a competitive market for short-term credit may already have existed by c.1900. Not all foreign banks confined their activities to overseas trade. Even some nominally British overseas banks were prepared to break with the conservative orthodoxy usually associated with London-registered houses, and lend to businesses operating largely within the confines of host economies (Joslin 1963: 109, 176–7; Jones 1987: 40–3, 129–32).

In the Argentine, large, diversifying processing and manufacturing enterprises were precisely those that secured credit from official banks and foreign institutions. The Tornquist group used banking and financial links with European money markets to secure funding for sugar refineries and textile production. Similarly, Bunge y Born, ultimately a large multinational conglomerate, utilized lines of credit with official and private banks to diversify from grain dealing into production, milling, and storage. By the turn of the century, European–River Plate banking consortia were transforming the credit market and the nature of banking business. Immigrant penny capitalists, notably Italians, were also able to draw upon "ethnic" banks to finance commercial and manufacturing ventures. The Banco de Italia y Río de la Plata and the Banco Francés e Italiano para la América del Sud appeared to be dependable sources of funding for would-be immigrant industrialists (Guy 1982: 361–5; Barbero 1990: 329–31; Regalsky 2001: 236–42; 2002: 140–57). In Brazil, too, overseas banks played a significant role in the development of local money markets and made term advances to manufacturers (Saes & Szmrecsányi 1995: 240–1). Perhaps latecomer foreign banks were compelled to look for business beyond traditional areas of activity, such as international trade. Alternatively, as the Latin American export economies grew and diversified, and as political order became more secure, new lucrative opportunities for domestic lending were presented to all banks – foreign and national, private and official.

Modernization, Urbanization, and Industrial Growth

Did the consolidation of factor markets (albeit partial and imperfect), urban growth, and the rise of a social order based on class rather than caste, facilitate industrial growth? And, how big was manufacturing?

Latin America in 1930 was neither an urban nor an industrial continent. Rapid and sustained urbanization lay in the future. Yet there had been some solid urban and industrial growth prior to 1930. In parts of southern South America, large primate cities had already emerged, as had clusters of manufacturing. In core North Atlantic economies, the emergence of modern cities was triggered by industrialization; hence the assumption, or expectation, that industrialization and urbanization represented economic and societal modernization, and the political processes that accompanied these transformations.

If growth was export-led between c.1870 and 1930, it follows that expansion in manufacturing and in urban populations must be broadly explained by the same process. It also follows that, as with the performance of export sectors, there were wide variations in rates of urban and industrial growth. National integration and urbanization were critical to the development of markets, for local manufacturers as much as for importers. Initially associated with the production of commodity exports, railways changed the geography, character, and composition of local output. Investment in rail networks and public utilities like power-generating plants undermined obstacles to domestic factory production, facilitating the integration of domestic consumer markets (Bauer 2001: 141–4; Bulmer-Thomas 2003: 133–5). Local entrepreneurs were not slow to seize opportunities. National textile mills, breweries, and food-processing plants appeared. Steam power and electricity represented an energy revolution that transformed production in many sectors, including the local manufacture of items that had previously been imported. Modern factories displaced imports and artisan production. Economic openness, macroeconomic stability, and lightly regulated markets were good for national industry. In addition to these factors, new economic institutionalists also attach special importance to the securing of property rights and access to formal channels of credit in explaining the growth of manufacturing before 1930. Structucturalists and neostructuralists devote more attention to active policies. Scholars of all persuasions search for evidence of the emergence (or otherwise) of an industrial entrepreneurial class, and its capacity to organize.

Domestic markets in Brazil and the River Plate republics grew as a result of natural population growth and mass immigration. Before 1914, employment in the export and public sectors stimulated the growth of home demand in Chile. European immigration to these republics and the movement of people across national frontiers and provincial boundaries indicate the operation of regional labor markets and labor responses to differing wage levels. Qualitative changes in the composition, as well as the expansion, of aggregate demand may be observed in the Argentine between the 1890s and 1914. A breakdown of consumption data reveals a rising trend of domestic supply, and a concomitant restructuring in the import schedule (Díaz Alejandro 1970: 40–4; Cortés Conde 1979: 211–40; Vázquez-Presedo 1979: 135–7). Changes in the structure of Argentinian imports before World War I corroborate the extent of industrial diversification. Imports of basic wage goods fell relatively after the 1880s as imports of capital goods and intermediate products rose and registered a shift toward industrial machinery (away from transport equipment) and supplies of fuel and industrial materials. A similar expansion in the absolute and relative weight of imports of industrial capital goods took place in Brazil and Chile (Kirsch 1977; Suzigan 1986). For Mexico the evidence is more equivocal. Metal working was probably more advanced there than in any other part of Latin America, and the textile industry was second only to that of Brazil. Yet, for Mexican manufacturers, domestic market conditions were probably less dynamic. Real wages declined after the end of the nineteenth century (Gómez-Galvarriato 1998: 351, 365). This increase of misery is partly explained by the capital-intensive form of much activity in the export sector, the nature of the Porfirian model that facilitated foreign penetration, and an exceptionally skewed pattern of wealth distribution.

As shown, Brazil's industrial entrepreneuriat was diverse, coming from the coffee planter elite and immigrant communities (Dean 1969; Cano 1981). But not all rural producers investing in manufacturing were connected with the export sector (Birchal 1999). Colombia and Mexico offer similar examples of diversity in the origin of industrial entrepreneurs along with distinct regional differences in the composition of business elites (Dávila 1986, 1991; Cerruti 2000). However, while studies on Brazil, Colombia, and Mexico applaud national and regional entrepreneurial achievement, observing domestic as well as immigrant contributions, the literature on other areas is less convinced about the engagement of domestic capitalists in manufacturing. The Chilean industrial entrepreneuriat seems to have been largely immigrant and/or mercantile in origin (Kirsch 1977; Ortega 1991; Bauer 2001). For the Argentine and Uruguay, too, enduring consensus points to the overwhelmingly immigrant or expatriate origin of the industrial entrepreneuriat before the 1920s (Cornblit 1967: 641–91; Finch 1981: 163; Guy 1982; Lewis 1987: 85–9; Barbero 1990). Irrespective of the origin of industrialists, there was a further key development: by the turn of the century, manufacturers were organizing. In a few countries, the influence of the business lobby may have been considerably greater than previously supposed (Schvarzer 1991; Quiroz 1993; Ridings 1994). The proliferation of business associations and industrial clubs evidence the enhanced social status and the growing confidence of manufacturers. Before World War I, associations such as the *Sociedad de Fomento Fabril* in Chile, the *Sociedad Nacional de Industrias* in Peru, and the *Unión Industrial Argentina* were recognized channels for the articulation of manufacturer opinions. During the 1920s the *Unión Industrial Argentina* and the Brazilian *Associação Industrial* organized industrial expositions and mounted sophisticated campaigns in favor of tariff reform which stressed national security and job creation, playing upon deficiencies in these economies revealed by World War I. Even if lobbying rarely achieved the desired objective, these bodies certainly represented a significant addition to the organizational setting.

Whether resulting from pressures for tariff protection from emerging industrial groups, from perspicacious policies, or from the vagary of world price movements, tariffs facilitated the growth of infant industries. After the 1880s industrialists in Brazil, Chile, and Mexico could count on a significant degree of protection even if the tariff was still primarily fiscal (Kirsch 1977; Suzigan 1986; Topik 1987; Haber 1989; Birchal 1999). As customs codes became more discriminatory, backward linkages fostered a deepening of the industrial process: entrepreneurs vertically integrating distinct stages of the manufacturing process and new suppliers emerged, stimulated by a demand for industrial inputs. Less consistent tariff protection was available to manufacturers in Peru and Colombia (Ospina Vásquez 1955; Thorp & Bertram 1978). Unsurprisingly, the ability of industrialists to influence what might be described as macroeconomic policy depended on connections with the dominant export oligarchy and a capacity to press conjunctural or strategic advantage. Governments were invariably more responsive to the clamor for protection when short of cash.

Changes in the external value of a currency had an impact upon domestic incomes, directly affected the price of imports (not least of inputs required by manufacturers), and influenced rates of domestic inflation and the incidence of tariff protection. Manufacturers were acutely aware of the relationship between exchange rates and the tariff in determining levels of protection. Industrialists knew that while tariff protection offered safeguards against a fall in the price of imported manufactures or a rise in domestic production costs, the exchange rate influenced both. There was a tendency for industrial investment in Brazil to grow at a faster rate in periods of exchange stability and output during periods of currency depreciation. The steady depreciation of the Chilean peso following the decision to abandon convertibility in 1878 is likewise argued to have internalized demand and, as it was accompanied by loose monetary policies, promoted domestic manufacture. There were similar trends in Peru and Mexico when those countries' currencies were based on a silver standard. Local production of silver ensured both an expanding monetary base and a fall in the external value of the sol and peso against gold, which secured domestic producers against the general decline in import prices. Conversely, Peru's access to the gold standard in 1897 set the process into reverse. In the Argentine and Brazil, manufacturers viewed with unease occasional appreciations in the external values respectively of the peso and milreis during the 1920s, tendencies that, it was feared, might induce the "dumping" of imports to the detriment of local factories. The result was often a renewed campaign for tariff protection – special pleading that new institutionalists depict variously as the hallmark of the inefficient or of the rent seeker.

Greater formality – and transparency – ensured that manufacturing firms in Brazil obtained considerably easier access to institutional credit than their counterparts in other parts of Latin America. With the development of an equities market, Brazilian firms grew in size and reaped efficiency gains associated with large-scale operations (Haber 1989: 287–9; 1991: 559–80). Hanley (1998: 128–30) also finds increasing formality in the São Paulo capital market, with considerable growth in the size and outreach of the Stock Market in the pre-1914 period: investor interest rose, financial instruments proliferated, and the Exchange accommodated a widening spectrum of enterprises. The early history of the Buenos Aires Stock Exchange shows how money markets could emerge even in the most inhospitable environments, in this case one hobbled by persistent monetary and political turmoil in the 1850s. The Bolsa, banks, and commercial and financial associations "contributed to the emerging publicness of business affairs . . . [and] . . . helped nurture an emerging market for capital itself" (Adelman 1999: 238). Recognizing its limits, Nakamura and Zarazaga (1998: 296) point to the vibrancy of Argentinian financial market development in the decades leading to 1930. This involved the growth of bank credit and market capitalization of domestic firms. In Brazil, the Argentine, and elsewhere, companies enjoying access to institutional credit, either through the stock exchange or from banks, tended to be larger, to grow faster, and were more profitable than privately owned firms (Guy 1982; Barbero 1990).

Historians of consumption observe yet another socio-organizational development around 1900: the emergence of a "mass" consumer society and accompanying business responses. Contingent on the consolidation of domestic demand, the consumer revolution entailed not only national market integration and national production; it also involved a transformation in retailing. By the early twentieth century, department stores were appearing in capital cities. Shopping arcades and such modern emporia as Gath y Chaves, El Palacio de Hierro, and Harrods at first offered only the "best goods" direct from Paris or London. By the interwar decades they were also purveying items marked *industria mexicana* or *industria argentina* (Rocchi 1998: 533–58; Bauer 2001: 156–62). Such retail palaces could not have existed without modern urban agglomeration. By 1914, Buenos Aires was already an international metropolis and, according to national census classification, half the Argentinian population was urban. Beyond the Southern Cone, only around a quarter of population was urban. Yet, by 1910, at the end of the *porfiriato*, with its broad avenues and glittering shopping arcades illuminated with modern electric lighting, Mexico City similarly aspired to be the Paris of Latin America. Quantitative and qualitative domestic market expansion induced changes in the composition of industrial output and the scale and organization of production and distribution.

By *c.*1930, there was a manufacturing base in many economies, although with marked variations among countries, as illustrated in Table 17.3. Representing more than a fifth of total economic activity by 1930, the sectoral weight of industry was greatest in the Argentine. The data, however, needs to be treated with caution. For example, even at mid-twentieth century, meat packing represented the single largest subsector of "manufacturing," measured by the value of output. Elsewhere, export processing similarly featured in data on industrial activity. In Brazil and Mexico, the manufacture of cotton textiles probably constituted the largest branch of manufacturing *c.*1900. Textiles, footwear, and processed food – basic wages goods – overwhelmingly dominated schedules of industrial output, notwithstanding the manufacture of some capital equipment, often in the workshops of the larger railway and public utility companies. Perhaps the distinction between processing and manufacture is semantic, though it needs to be acknowledged, not least due to likely linkage affects.

A stylized schema of industrial growth for the period may be traced, confirming that export-led growth created preconditions for the rise of industry, and triggered

Table 17.3 Share of industry in GDP in selected Latin American countries, *c.*1930 (percent)

The Argentine	22.8
Brazil	11.7
Chile	7.9
Colombia	6.2
Mexico	14.2

Source: Statistical Abstract of Latin America, elaborated from ECLA(AC) data.

an expansion of modern, factory-based manufacture. Export-led growth increased the availability of key factors, including capital, entrepreneurship, and labor. Export-led growth monetized large parts of the continent and increased the supply of essential public goods, such as railways and banks. Investment in manufacturing grew, closely correlated with upswings in the export cycle. Crisis in the external sector, however, was not always inimical to domestic manufacture. Import scarcity enabled modern firms to obtain a larger share of smaller home markets. These firms were then well placed to take advantage of the next exports surge when accumulated profits could be used to import capital equipment in response to anticipated recovery in domestic demand. Post-crisis shakeouts resulted in increases in the scale and capital intensitivity of manufacturing, with larger, modern factories capturing a greater share of home markets. Credit market consolidation also contributed to the growing presence of corporate businesses in the manufacturing sector. Size mattered, as did policy. Corporate players were more effective lobbyists.

Conclusion

A signal transformation occurred in the society and economy of Latin America between 1870 and 1930. Barely within the space of a couple of generations, the "first" era of globalization witnessed the integration of the continent into the prevailing world economic system. No other part of the world experienced a more profound institutional shock during the period. Modernization, represented by the formation of markets and monetization, was underwritten by the production of commodities for the world economy. The commodity trades valorized domestic assets and facilitated factor flows: exports and the concomitant growth in imports – of goods, capital, labor, and ideas – made domestic markets, and consolidated political order. These developments were neither linear nor hazard-free. Structuralists and neostructuralists sensibly draw attention to the volatility of pre-1930 growth. Making markets involved winners and losers. Even long-term welfare gains, implied by population growth, the thickening of civil society suggested by the proliferation of associative organizations like business lobbies, mutual societies, and worker unions, and the dynamics of such market-making agents as banks and railways, did not mean that the consequences of modernization were not dire for some groups. The lot of dispossessed *campesinos* and people left out of the model testifies both to the violence of making markets, and to imperfections in the process. Yet, there was growth and technological change. Arguably, a mark of the transformations achieved in Latin America before 1929 is provided by the capacity of the former export economies to recover from the dislocation of the 1930s. It is generally recognized that Latin America recovered earlier and faster from the effects of the global crisis than most other regions (Díaz-Alejandro 1984; Thorp 1998: 107–25; Maddison 2001: 262). Despite marked variations in state and market performance, this points to the capacity of institutions and organizations forged during the phase of export-led growth.

The manner in which gains resulting from incorporation into the international economy were employed and distributed, and the extent to which they promoted domestic growth was, to a very large extent, shaped by endogenous institutions. Institutionalists, not least social science historians, admit that relations between Latin

America and the western world were stormy, but insist that because most countries had, by the 1870s, developed institutions and organizations capable of coping with trade on a large scale and because competition rather than monopoly was the rule, the continent tended to gain more from international economic insertion that most regions of Africa and Asia (Obstfeld & Taylor 2003: 120–6). Historians of culture similarly point to the importance, and the durability, of national institutions. While shocks to the international system (for example, financial crises, recession, and war) played a contributory role, endogenous processes like demographic growth, nationalism, and the democratization of consumption formed a filter through which imported ideas were absorbed, and external opportunities negotiated (Bauer 2001: 13–14).

Two further points are worth reiterating. First, while the pre-1914, or pre-1920s, period was one of industrial growth, the export sector remained the main force for economic modernization, not industrialization. Along with growth in industrial output, in some of the larger economies, there was also a change in the composition of domestic industrial output to include the production of some basic capital goods. Qualitative changes in the scale and organization of manufacturing also occurred. Nevertheless, industry did not become a Rostovian lead sector, driving structural change in the economy at large. Neither was there an industrial "spurt." Secondly, and as these remarks imply, industrial growth was not a function of government action. While such policy initiatives as tariff reform may have assisted growth, government action was not designed to promote manufacturing. Industrialization was not a Gerschenkronian objective of state policy. During the period covered here the policy environment may have been less inimical to industrial growth than sometimes is argued, but it remained largely neutral. Conscious, consistent, state-directed sponsorship of industrialization did not become the dominant policy model until the developmentalist era following World War II (Wolfe, this volume).

BIBLIOGRAPHY

Adelman, J. (1999) *Republic of Capital: Buenos Aires and the Legal Transformation of the Atlantic World*. Stanford University Press, Stanford.

Annino, A. (ed.) (1995) *Historia de las elecciones en Iberoamérica, siglo XIX*. Fondo de Cultura Económica, Buenos Aires.

Ashworth, W. (1967) *A Short History of the International Economy since 1850*. Longman, London.

Bailey, J. P. & Headlam, F. L. (1977) *Immigration from Overseas to Latin America: Comprising a Bibliography of Works Mainly in English*. La Trobe University Press, Bundoora.

Barbero, M. I. (1990) "Grupos empresarios, intercambio comercial e inversiones italianas en la Argentina, 1910–20," *Estudios Migratorios Latinoamericanos*, 25/26.

Bauer, A. (1986) "Rural Spanish America, 1870–1930." In L. Bethell (ed.), *The Cambridge History of Latin America: Volume IV, c.1870–1930*. Cambridge University Press, Cambridge, pp. 151–86.

Bauer, A. (2001) *Goods, Power, History: Latin America's Material Culture*. Cambridge University Press, New York.

Bauer, A. J. & Orlove, B. (1997) "Giving Importance to Imports." In B. Orlove (ed.), *The Allure of the Foreign: Imported Goods in Postcolonial Latin America*. University of Michigan Press, Ann Arbor, pp. 1–29.

Bértola, L. & Williamson, J. G. (2003) *Globalization in Latin America before 1940*. NBER Working Paper No. 9687, Cambridge, MA.

Birchal, S. de O. (1999) *Entrepreneurship in Nineteenth-Century Brazil: The Formation of a Business Environment*. Macmillan, London.

Blanchard, P. (1980) "The Recruitment of Workers in the Peruvian Sierra at the Turn of the Century: The Enganche System," *Inter-American Economic Affairs*, 33:3.

Bordo, M. D. & Rockoff, H. (1996) "The Gold Standard as a 'Good Housekeeping Seal of Approval,'" *Journal of Economic History*, 56:2, pp. 389–428.

Bordo, M. D. & Vegh, C. A. (1998) *What if Alexander Hamilton Had Been Argentinean [sic]? A Comparison of the Early Monetary Experience of Argentina and the United States*. NBER Working Paper No. 6862, Cambridge, MA.

Bulmer-Thomas, V. (2003) *The Economic History of Latin America since Independence*. Cambridge University Press, Cambridge.

Bulmer-Thomas, V., Coatsworth, J., & Cortés Conde R. (eds.) (2006) *The Cambridge Economic History of Latin America*. Cambridge University Press, Cambridge.

Bushnell, D. & Macaulay, N. (1994) *The Emergence of Latin America in the Nineteenth Century*. Oxford University Press, New York.

Cano, W. (1981) *Raízes da concentração industrial em São Paulo*. Difusão Europeia do Livro, Rio de Janeiro.

Cárcano, M. A. (1972) *Evolución histórica del régimen de la tierra pública, 1810–1916*. EUDEBA, Buenos Aires.

Cárdenas, E., Ocampo, J. A., & Thorp, R. (eds.) (2000) *An Economic History of Twentieth-Century Latin America*. Palgrave, London.

Cerruti, M. (2000) *Propietarios, empresarios y empresa en el norte de México: Monterrey de 1848 a la globalización*. Siglo Veintiuno Editores, Mexico City.

Cornblit, O. (1967) "Inmigrantes y empresarios en la política argentina," *Desarrollo Económico*, 6:24, pp. 641–91.

Cortés Conde, R. (1974) *The First Stages of Modernisation in Spanish America*. Harper & Row, New York.

Cortés Conde, R. (1979) *El progreso argentino, 1880–1914*. Ed. Sudamericana, Buenos Aires.

Dávila, C. (1986) *El empresariado colombiano: Una perspectiva histórica*. Universidad de los Andes, Bogotá.

Dávila, C. (1991) *Historia empresarial de Colombia: Estudios, problemas y perspectivas*. Universidad de los Andes, Bogotá.

Dean, W. (1969) *The Industrialization of São Paulo, 1880–1945*. University of Texas Press, Austin.

Dean, W. (1971) "Latifundia and Land Policy in Nineteenth-Century Brazil," *Hispanic American Historical Review*, 51:4, pp. 606–25.

Della Paolera, G. & Taylor, A. M. (eds.) (2003) *The New Economic History of Argentina*. Cambridge University Press, Cambridge.

Denoon, D. (1983) *Settler Capitalism: The Dynamics of Dependent Development in the Southern Hemisphere*. Clarendon Press, Oxford.

Díaz Alejandro, C. F. (1970) *Essays on the Economic History of the Argentine Republic*. Yale University Press, New Haven.

Díaz Alejandro, C. F. (1984) "Latin America in the 1930s." In R. Thorp, *Latin America in the 1930s: The Role of the Periphery in World Crisis*. Macmillan, London, pp. 17–49.

Dye, A. (2006) "The Institutional Framework." In V. Bulmer-Thomas, J. H. Coatsworth, & R. Cortés Conde (eds.), *The Cambridge Economic History of Latin America*. Cambridge University Press, Cambridge, pp. 169–207.

Estevadeordal, A., Frantz, B., & Taylor, A. M. (2001) "The Rise and Fall of World Trade," (October 2001) mimeo.

Ferns, H. S. (1960) *Britain and Argentina in the Nineteenth Century*. Clarendon Press, Oxford.

Finch, M. H. J. (1981) *A Political Economy of Uruguay since 1870*. Macmillan, London.

Foreman-Peck, J. (1995) *A History of the World Economy: International Economic Relations since 1850*. HarvesterWheatsheaf, London.

Gallo, E. (1984) *La pampa gringa: La colonización agrícola en Santa Fe, 1870–1895*. Sudamericana, Buenos Aires.

Gerschenkron, A. (1962) *Economic Backwardness in Historical Perspective*. Harvard University Press, Cambridge, MA.

Glade, W. P. (1986) "Latin America and the International Economy, 1870–1914." In L. Bethell (ed.), *The Cambridge History of Latin America: Volume IV, c.1870–1930*. Cambridge University Press, Cambridge, pp. 1–56.

Gómez-Galvarriato, A. (1998) "The Evolution of Prices and Real Wages in Mexico from the Porfiriato to the Revolution." In J. H. Coatsworth & A. M. Taylor (eds.), *Latin America and the World Economy since 1850*. Harvard University Press, Cambridge, MA.

Gootenberg, P. (1993) *Imagining Development: Economic Ideas in Peru's "Fictitious Prosperity" of Guano*. University of California Press, Berkeley.

Guy, D. 1982 "La industria argentina, 1870–1940: Legislación comercial, mercado de acciones y capital extranjera," *Desarrollo Económico*, 22:87, pp. 361–5.

Haber, S. (1989) *Industry and Underdevelopment: The Industrialization of Mexico, 1890–1940*. Stanford University Press, Stanford.

Haber, S. (1991) "Industrial Concentration and the Capital Market: A Comparative Study of Brazil, Mexico and the United States, 1830–1930," *Journal of Economic History*, 51:3, pp. 559–80.

Haber, S. (ed.) (1997) *How Latin America Fell Behind: Essays on the Economic Histories of Brazil and Mexico, 1800–1914*. Stanford University Press, Stanford.

Hale, C. A. (1985) "Political and Social Ideas in Latin America, 1870–1930." In L. Bethell (ed.), *The Cambridge History of Latin America: Volume IV: c.1870–1930*. Cambridge University Press, Cambridge, pp. 367–441.

Hall M. M. & Spalding, H. A. (1985) "The Urban Working Class and Early Latin American Labour Movements, 1880–1930." In L. Bethell (ed.), *The Cambridge History of Latin America: Volume IV: c. 1870–1930*. Cambridge University Press, Cambridge, pp. 367–441.

Halperín Donghi, T. (1993) *The Contemporary History of Latin America*. Duke University Press, Durham.

Hanley, A. G. (1998) "Business Finance and the São Paulo Bolsa, 1886–1917." In J. H. Coatsworth & A. M. Taylor (eds.), *Latin America and the World Economy in the Nineteenth and Twentieth Centuries: Explorations in Quantitative Economic History*. Harvard University Press, Cambridge, MA, pp. 115–38.

Holloway, T. H. (1980) *Immigrants on the Land: Coffee and Society in São Paulo, 1886–1934*. University of North Carolina Press, Chapel Hill.

Jenks, L. H. (1963 [1927]) *The Migration of British Capital to 1875*. Nelson, London.

Jones, C. A. (1987) *International Business in the Nineteenth Century: The Rise and Fall of a Cosmopolitan Bourgeoisie*. Wheatsheaf Books, London.

Joslin, D. (1963) *A Century of Banking in Latin America*. Oxford University Press, London.

Katz, F. (1974) "Labor Conditions on Haciendas in Porfirian Mexico," *Hispanic American Historical Review*, 54:1, pp. 1–47.

Katz, F. (ed.) (1980) *La servidumbre agraria en México en la época porfiriana*. Ediciones Era, Mexico City.

Kenwood, A. G. & Lougheed, A. L. (1999) *The Growth of the International Economy, 1820–2000*. Routledge, London.

Kirsch, H. W. (1977) *Industrial Development in a Traditional Society: The Conflict of Entrepreneurship and Modernization in Chile.* Universities of Florida Press, Gainesville.

Komlos, J. (ed.) (1995) *The Biological Standard of Living on Three Continents: Further Explorations in Anthropometric History.* Westview Press, Boulder, CO.

Lewis, C. M. (1985) "Industry in Latin America before 1930." In L. Bethell (ed.), *The Cambridge History of Latin America: Volume IV: c.1870–1930.* Cambridge University Press, Cambridge, pp. 267–323.

Lewis, C. M. (1987) "Immigrant Entrepreneurs, Manufacturing and Industrial Policy in the Argentine, 1922–28," *Journal of Imperial and Commonwealth History,* 16:4, pp. 77–108.

Lewis, C. M. (1995) "Industry Before 1930: A Bibliography." In L. Bethell (ed.), *The Cambridge History of Latin America. Volume XI: Bibliographical Essays.* Cambridge University Press, Cambridge, pp. 349–58.

Lewis, W. A. (1978) *Growth and Fluctuations, 1870–1913.* George Allen & Unwin, London.

Love, J. L. (1988) "Structural Change and Conceptual Responses in Latin America and Romania, 1960–1950." In J. L. Love & N. Jacobsen (eds.), *Guiding the Invisible Hand: Economic Liberalism and the State in Latin American History.* Praeger, New York, pp. 1–33.

Maddison, A. (2001) *The World Economy: A Millennial Perspective.* Organization for Economic Cooperation and Development, Paris.

Marichal, C. (1995) "Introducción." In C. Marichal (ed.), *Las inversiones extranjeras en América Latina, 1850–1930: Nuevos debates, y problemas en historia económica comparada.* El Colegio de México/Fondo de Cultura Económica, Mexico City, pp. 1–25.

Merrick, T. & Graham, D. H. (1979) *Population and Economic Development in Brazil: 1808 to the Present.* Johns Hopkins University Press, Baltimore.

Miller, S. (1990) "Mexican Junkers and Capitalist Haciendas, 1810–1910: The Arable Estate and the Transition to Capitalism Between Insurgency and the Revolution," *Journal of Latin American Studies,* 22:2, pp. 229–63.

Munck, R. (1998) "Mutual Benefit Societies in Argentina: Workers, Nationality, Social Security and Trade Unionism," *Journal of Latin American Studies,* 30:3.

Nakamura, L. I. & Zarazaga, C. (1998) "Economic Growth in Argentina in the Period 1900–1930: Some Evidence from Stock Returns. In J. H. Coatsworth & A. M. Taylor (eds.), *Latin America and the World Economy since 1850.* Harvard University Press, Cambridge, MA.

North, D. C. (2003) *The Role of Institutions in Economic Development: Gunnar Myrdal Lecture.* United Nations Publications, New York.

Obstfeld, M. & Taylor, A. M. (2003) "Globalization and Capital Markets." In M. D. Bordo, A. M. Taylor, & J. G. Williamson (eds.), *Globalization in Historical Perspective.* University of Chicago Press, Chicago, pp. 121–83.

Orlove, B. (ed.) (1997) *The Allure of the Foreign: Imported Goods in Postcolonial Latin America.* University of Michgan Press, Ann Arbor.

Ortega, L. (1991) "Economic Policy and Growth in Chile from Independence to the War of the Pacific." In C. Abel & C. M. Lewis (eds.), *Latin America, Economic Imperialism and the State.* Athlone, London, pp. 147–71.

Ospina Vásquez, L. (1955) *Industria y protección en Colombia, 1810–1930.* ESF, Bogotá.

Panettieri, J. C. (1983) *Devaluaciones de la moneda (1822–1935): Debate nacional.* Centro Editorial de América Latina, Buenos Aires.

Peloso, V. & Tenenbaum, B. (eds.) (1996) *Liberals, Politics and Power: State Formation in Nineteenth-century Latin America.* University Georgia Press, Athens.

Platt, D. C. M. (ed.) (1997) *Business Imperialism, 1840–1930: An Inquiry Based on British Experience in Latin America.* Clarendon Press, Oxford.

Quiroz, A. W. (1993) *Domestic and Foreign Finance in Modern Peru, 1850–1950: Financing Visions of Development.* Macmillan, London.

Regalsky, A. M. (2001) "¿Una experiencia de banca industrial en la Argentina exportadora?: El Banco Francés del Río de la Plata, 1905–1914," *Anuario del Centro de Estudios Históricos* (Córdoba), 1:1, pp. 236–42.

Regalsky, A. M. (2002) *Inversores y elites: Las inversiones francesas en la Argentina, 1880–1914.* EDUNTREF, Buenos Aires.

Ridings, E. (1994) *Business Interest Groups in Nineteenth-century Brazil.* Cambridge University Press, Cambridge.

Rocchi, F. (1998) "Consumir es un placer: La industria y la expansión de la demanda en Buenos Aires a la vuelta del siglo pasado," *Desarrollo Económico*, 148, pp. 533–58.

Rostow, W. W. (1960) *The Stages of Economic Growth: A Non-Communist Manifesto.* Cambridge University Press, Cambridge.

Rostow, W. W. (1975) *How It All Began: Origins of the Modern Economy.* McGraw-Hill, New York.

Rostow, W. W. (1887) *Rich Countries and Poor Countries: Reflections on the Past, Lessons for the Future.* Westview Press, London.

Saes, F. A. M. & Szmrecsányi, T (1995) "El papel de los bancos extranjeros en la industrialización inicial de São Paulo." In C. Marichal (ed.), *Las inversiones extranjeras en América Latina, 1850–1930: Nuevos debates, y problemas en historia económica comparada.* El Colegio de México/Fondo de Cultura Económica México City, pp. 230–43.

Sánchez-Albornoz, N. (1974) *The Population of Latin America: A History.* University of California Press, Berkeley.

Schvarzer, J. (1991) *Empresarios del pasado: La Unión Industrial Argentina.* La Planeta, Buenos Aires.

Stein, S. (1957) *The Brazilian Cotton Manufacture: Textile Enterprise in an Underdeveloped Area, 1850–1950.* Harvard University Press, Cambridge, MA.

Stone, I. (1999) *The Global Export of Capital from Great Britain, 1865–1914.* Macmillan, London.

Summerhill, W. R. (2003) *Order against Progress: Government, Foreign Investment and Railroads in Brazil, 1854–1913.* Stanford University Press, Stanford.

Suzigan, W. (1986) *Indústria brasileira: Origem y desenvolvimento.* Editora Brasiliense, São Paulo.

Thorp, R. (1998) *Progress, Poverty and Exclusion: An Economic History of Latin America in the Twentieth Century.* IDB, Baltimore.

Thorp, R. & Bertram, G. (1978) *Peru, 1890–1977: Growth and Policy in an Open Economy.* Macmillan, London.

Topik, S. C. (1987) *The Political Economy of the Brazilian State, 1889–1930.* University of Texas Press, Austin.

Topik, S. C. (1999) "The Construction of Market Societies in Latin America: Natural Process or Social Engineering?" *Latin American Perspectives*, 26:1, pp. 3–21.

Triner, G. D. (2000) *Banking and Economic Development: Brazil, 1889–1930.* Palgrave, New York.

Trujillo Bolio, M. (1997) "La fábrica de La Magdalena Contreras (1836–1910): Una empresa textil precursora en el valle de México." In C. Marichal & M. Cerruti (eds.), *Historia de las grandes empresas en México, 1850–1930.* Fondo de Cultura Económica, México City, pp. 245–74.

Vázquez-Presedo, V. (1979) *El caso argentino: Migración de factores, comercio exterior y desarrollo, 1875–1914.* EUDEBA Buenos Aires.

Weiner, R. (2004) *Race, Nation, and Market: Economic Culture in Porfirian Mexico.* University of Arizona Press, Tucson.

Woodruff, W. (1973) "The Emergence of an International Economy, 1700–1914." In C. M. Cipolla (ed.), *The Fontana Economic History of Europe,* Volume IV: *The Emergence of Industrial Societies* (Part 2). Collins/Fontana, London, pp. 656–737.

Young, G. (1995) "Los bancos alemanes y la inversión directa alemana en América Latina, 1880–1930." In C. Marichal (ed.), *Las inversiones extranjeras en América Latina, 1850–1930: Nuevos debates, y problemas en historia económica comparada.* El Colegio de México/ Fondo de Cultura Económica, México City, pp. 96–124.

Chapter Eighteen

PRACTICAL SOVEREIGNTY: THE CARIBBEAN REGION AND THE RISE OF US EMPIRE

Mary A. Renda

Venezuela and the Olney Doctrine

Christmas, 1895, witnessed the capital of Venezuela alive with celebration, not only for the holiday, but also for the recent message of US President Grover Cleveland, declaring that the United States was resolute in its determination to preserve the Monroe Doctrine. At issue was the location of Venezuela's boundary with British Guiana, and the cheers of thousands greeted the US minister who announced Cleveland's words of December 17 from the legation: he insisted on arbitration and warned Lord Salisbury that if necessary "it would be the duty of the United States to resist" British appropriation of Venezuelan territory "by every means in its power" (Perkins 1937: 192). A holiday procession made its way through the streets of Caracas, and, in striking contrast to the crowds that would greet US Vice President Richard Nixon with swinging sticks and spit in 1958 (McPherson 2003: 29), these Caraqueños bestowed "crosses, flags, flowers, and floral emblems" upon a statue of George Washington to express gratitude at the fulfillment of their hopes for action by the North American power (Robertson 1920: 4).

Since at least 1876, Venezuelan leaders had appealed to the United States to enlarge upon James Monroe's 1823 doctrine against further European colonization in the Americas, specifically to assist in the ongoing border dispute with British Guiana.[1] Originally issued in opposition to French and Spanish threats against the new Latin American republics and the possibility of Russian designs on the Pacific coast of North America, the Monroe Doctrine had not yet been transformed into a cornerstone of US expansionist policy. Venezuelan elites could still look to the emerging wealth and power of the United States and see, not a threat to their independence, but a model of progress, a kindred racial vision of civilization, and a rising power with the ability to fend off British advances in the Orinoco Delta.

Expanding economic and cultural connections established the context for the Venezuelans' pragmatic diplomatic appeal to the Monroe Doctrine. Notwithstanding strong cultural ties to France (Diaz 2004), in 1872 Ramón Paez admired "the vigor of the Anglo-Americans who dominated their vast deserts and mountains and mined the gold of California" (Ewell 1996: 85). The influential liberal leader Antonio Guzmán Blanco, who cultivated a North American presence in the 1870s and 1880s, commissioned the statue of George Washington for an international exposition to celebrate the centennial of Simon Bolívar's birth, to encourage "the popular view of the historical parallels between the two American liberators" (Ewell 1996: 67–8). In the liberal view, US Americans with capital and engineering expertise could develop railroads, steam travel, and mining operations; Protestant influence would help to limit the backward pull of the Catholic Church; and immigrants from the north would "whiten" the population, enhancing Venezuela's claim to civilized status in the community of nations (Diaz 2004).

Ultimately, Protestant missionaries did not get far and US immigrants were few, but Venezuela succeeded in attracting North American capital and entrepreneurial activity. Venezuelan asphalt, for example, would literally pave the roads to urban and suburban development in the United States. To some Venezuelans, however, the outcome of asphalt operations and other US activities (including no small amount of corruption) were not quite so satisfactory. A veritable industry of US claims against the Venezuelan government occasioned critical readings of the Monroe Doctrine and the United States' pretense of guarding "America for the Americans." "Monroe's compatriots," read an 1870 article in *La Opinion Nacional*, "far from protecting the *Americans* (if those of the *South* are even Americans) . . . believe that a scandalous fraud can be converted into a legal claim, even to the point of supporting it with the logical arguments of gunboats" (Ewell 1996: 87). In 1873, Venezuela established legal limitations to impede the seemingly endless parade of claimants, foreshadowing the more famous Calvo Clause and Drago Doctrine. And Simón Camacho, Venezuelan consul in New York during the 1850s and 1860s and later Minister to the United States, resented Washington's presumptuous attitude with regard to his nation's chosen paths toward economic development. "To pretend that we would refuse" to rely on French capital "to bring out the natural resources of this country," Camacho wrote, "and that we could shut our door to progress because it happens to suit your 'Monroe Doctrine' or any other idea of a protection you wish to exercise at a distance of 2,000 miles, would be the height of folly on our part" (Ewell 1996: 87–8). Poor and working-class people had their own ways of expressing their rejection of US impositions, such as refusing to work for US mining companies and supporting political leaders who opposed the overweening influence of the United States and its elite partners in Caracas. Frances B. Loomis, US Minister to Venezuela from 1897 to 1901, complained of anti-Americanism "among the 'unenlightened,'" but discounted the significance of this unpleasantness in so far as he discounted their relevance to policy matters (Ewell 1996: 97).

Social, cultural, and political dynamics such as these – in Venezuela, and across the Caribbean region – were essential to the emergence and career of United States empire. I use the term "empire" to describe the effective, albeit contested, phenomenon of US rule over an expanding geographical area, through formal and informal means. US empire proceeded, from 1776 onward, both within national boundaries (e.g., where Native Americans continued to assert or aspired to regain sovereign status) and across them (as in the United States' search for control over the Caribbean region in the period under consideration here). Many scholars acknowledge a key distinction between formal European empires and the range of informal mechanisms of control employed by the United States beyond its borders. To be sure, the institutional forms of European rule in Asia, Africa, and the Caribbean may be distinguished in some important respects from US rule in the Americas. Nonetheless, the present argument rejects the opposition between formal and informal empire precisely in order to explore the continuum of imperial mechanisms and forms that has characterized US rule and to emphasize that the variety and interaction of such mechanisms itself evolves over time. A growing literature on the cultural and social dimensions of the US presence in circum-Caribbean (as well as in Latin America more generally) now makes clear that the push and pull of social and political forces in the region contributed to the emergence of US national wealth and molded the contours of North American power as it emerged in the late nineteenth century and grew in the twentieth. Empire was never simply a policy emanating from Washington and received, happily or not, in the region's capitals. Nor did it emerge solely out of the halls of North American industry and finance. Divergent histories of conquest, genocide, slavery, resistance, revolution, and independence conditioned the scope and impact of US action and the evolving nature of US power – as did competing ideas about the relationship between race and gender in civilized society. In response to changing social contexts and power relations in the Caribbean as well as in North America, US empire developed a shape-shifting resilience that accounts, in part, for its persistence and force.

This chapter begins with Venezuela because it was in response to repeated Venezuelan invitations that a US secretary of state articulated one of the boldest policy statements of US empire, ostensibly as a clarification of the Monroe Doctrine. Five months before Cleveland's good news reached Caracas, Richard Olney penned a now famous memorandum to be conveyed to Lord Salisbury. The Olney Doctrine, as that memorandum came to be known, asserted US supremacy and authority over the Americas, based in the seemingly "infinite resources" and "isolated position" of the North American power. "Today the United States is practically sovereign on this continent," wrote the former railroad lawyer and steel-fisted Attorney General-turned-Secretary of State, "and its fiat is law upon the subjects to which it confines its interposition" (Olney 1895; Holden & Zolov 2000). How did Olney's brusque assertion rise out of the transnational realities of the nineteenth century? And how would it square with the complex social and political dynamics of Venezuela and the Caribbean region in the ensuing decades?

"Infinite Resources"

Before turning to relevant patterns of inequality and transnational Caribbean realities, let us first consider the North American springs that fed US imperial power. The accumulation of wealth in North America was at the heart of US empire's rise, and here, too, as in the Caribbean, myriad social, cultural, and political processes shaped and limited the empire's range of action. At base, US wealth sprang from the physical resources of the vast North American continent and the equally vast population that worked to exploit them, with slavery and the early conquest of Native American lands and peoples setting the process in motion. Cotton picked and cultivated by enslaved Africans and their descendants built mercantile fortunes and founded US manufacturing. Paper and lumber mills ate up trees felled across a continent seized and settled by immigrants and their children, with assistance from the US Army. Copper for wire and piping made its way to the cities on railroads built by Chinese and European Americans, having been mined in Bisbee and Morenci by Mexicans and Mexican Americans. And wheat, raised by men and women of many nationalities, made flour one of the nation's leading nineteenth-century exports.

Industrialists, bankers, engineers, and aspiring entrepreneurs also played key roles in the production of the United States' seemingly "infinite resources," backed by the power of the US state both on and beyond the continent. In the Great Uprising of 1877, the United States turned its military forces against its own citizens and workers; in 1894 it was none other than Richard Olney calling out the troops for the Pullman Palace Car Company. When capitalists looked to build their wealth farther from home – whether they sought asphalt in Venezuela, gold-rush railroad business across Panama and Nicaragua, or sugar in Cuba – the "logical argument of gunboats" played an important role. Panama alone (then part of Colombia) saw the arrival of US military forces at least eight times between 1856 and 1895, all prior to the more profoundly transformative interventions of the twentieth century (Lindsay-Poland 2003: 16–17). By the 1880s, leading naval strategist Alfred Thayer Mahan's vision of a new navy to support the imperial future of the United States was under construction; soon the Caribbean would be fairly blanketed with US warships, each and all busy with patrols, escorts, exercises, geographical surveys, intelligence gathering, diplomatic errands, plainly targeted missions of intimidation, and, of course, ferrying troops. By the 1890s, moreover, the US Marine Corps, the Navy's infantry, emerged as a dedicated colonial landing force.

The productive and political processes that built US wealth fueled the nation's imperial will on many levels (and fragmented it as well, but that is beyond the scope of this essay). Industrialization created demand for raw materials available beyond US borders and the prospect of fortunes to be made through access to foreign markets. But commerce in consumer goods produced in the Caribbean, and later, direct investment, also linked pressure for US control of Caribbean societies to the needs of a growing industrial population, as the banana trade illustrates. Even before the merger of the Boston Fruit Company with the interests of Minor C. Keith in Central America to form the soon-to-be notorious United Fruit Company in 1899, bananas offered a low-cost, high-calorie "fast food" – affordable to an ever-growing population of US workers with less time for food preparation in the face of new practices of industrial labor discipline (Soluri 2003). Demand for such goods in turn fueled US investment and created pressure for more extensive North American control. Moreover, as Lori Merish has argued, with the advent of consumer capitalism, product advertising appealed to racialized and gendered constructions of selfhood among working-class consumers to constitute and expand new forms of imperial subjectivity. If bananas were "the poor man's luxury" at mealtimes, the after-dinner Cuban cigar came to be figured as a masculine status marker bound up with imperial significance and broadly available to working-class men in the United States after 1900 (Merish 2000: 283).

But long before the five-cent cigar drew working-class US men more fully into the circuit of imperial desires, the evolution of racism set up whites of all classes to claim the supremacy of their nation over their neighbors to the south, often in gendered terms. Over the course of the nineteenth century – from racist antebellum ideals of domesticity, scientific justifications for slavery, and notions of Anglo-Saxon manifest destiny, to the rage for lynching, rape, and other forms of violent intimidation that swept the US South in response to Reconstruction – ideas and practices of racial supremacy shaped US perceptions of Latin America and the Caribbean. Racism divided US opinion with regard to traditional forms of colonization – fueling opposition to annexationist designs on Cuba, the Dominican Republic, Hawaii, and the Philippines for fear of inundation by peoples of color – but it pervaded the whole range of schemes for US domination in the Caribbean region.

”Practically Sovereign”

As in Venezuela, so too in Cuba, Puerto Rico, Central America, and Colombia: Caribbean resources and social dynamics contributed to the consolidation of US wealth and power, and the demand for continued access to the region's wealth-producing capacity directed US policy. This is not to say that Washington's policy makers merely genuflected before capital; the negotiation of power was often far more complicated than that. But in the decades surrounding the turn of the twentieth century, sugar directed US attention to Cuba and Puerto Rico; bananas drove US policy in Honduras and elsewhere in Central America; and the prospect of access to Asian markets pointed to the importance of control over Panama. For Presidents Grover Cleveland, William McKinley, and Theodore Roosevelt, notions of civilization and national–imperial competition, linked to an assumption of Anglo-Saxon superiority, oriented US policies toward the advance of what Thomas O'Brien (1996) has called "the revolutionary mission" of US companies to transform Latin America. For all three presidents, in different ways, corporate ventures constituted the leading edge of "America's" rise to power.

In Cuba and Puerto Rico, the United States benefited initially from Spain's open trade policy and later from the nature of the struggle for national independence. The Cuban case illustrates the interplay between US interests and Caribbean realities especially well. By the third quarter of the nineteenth century, the mercantile fortune that Moses Taylor had built on the Cuban sugar trade was feeding the rise of City Bank (which as First National City Bank later played an important role in "dollar diplomacy" arrangements, particularly in Haiti, 1915). Taylor's fortune also helped fuel the rage of land speculation that claimed western US lands, and the growth of core industrial sectors in the United States such as railroad construction, coal mining, and iron production (O'Brien 1996). Cuban sugar augmented the fortunes of William A. Rockefeller, John Jacob Astor, and J. P. Morgan as well. Cuban forests, mining possibilities, and of course tobacco also interested US investors. North Americans also had their eyes on Cuba to strengthen the political force of slaveholding before the US Civil War, and to draw off the population of former slaves after it. A long line of US presidents and secretaries of state had imagined that one day, near or far, Cuba would be annexed to the United States, though racism prevented that dream from being fulfilled. In 1869, Ulysses Grant went as far as negotiating a treaty to that end (LaFeber 1993: 66). The "Ten Years War" for Cuban independence (1868–78) then saw the deliberate destruction of sugar plantations in the eastern part of the

island, which weakened not only Spain's hold on Cuba, but also that of Cuban planters on their own estates. In this way, the war precipitated an enormous expansion in
US control over Cuban sugar production, with 94 percent of the industry's output
reportedly headed for the US market by 1886 (Pérez 1983: 28). In turn, the Cuban
independence movement probably received a boost, whether intended or not, from
US trade policy, when tariff legislation shifted in 1894 during a period of profound
economic depression, with devastating effects on the Cuban economy.

But the evolution of Cuban projects for independence and the racial and class
dynamics of Cuban society had troubling implications for the United States. Beginning in the middle of the nineteenth century, Cuban sugar planters migrated to the
United States and established themselves in New York City as a lobbying force
seeking to suture US national interest to the cause of Cuban separation from Spain.
Early on, planters saw annexation as a means to strengthen their hold over an enslaved
population of cane workers. During the Ten Years War, while calls for annexation
revived, New York also became a center for the conservative wing of the independence movement. By the 1890s, New York was home to a substantial set of Cuban
planters, with many now adopting US citizenship and calling on Washington to
intervene in Cuba (Pérez 1983: 391, n.56).

Meanwhile, other forces pushed Cuban *independentistas* in a more radical direction. The need to recruit forces for the Ten Years War moved the nationalists to a
more inclusive racial and class politics, resulting in the abolition of slavery in 1886
and the articulation of an explicitly anti-racist independence politics. Moreover,
Cuban émigrés from the tobacco sector established factories in Key West, New York,
and later Tampa, and these cities became centers of Cuban working-class and labor
organizing. Labor migration between Cuba and these tobacco centers in the United
States also served both to strengthen the Cuban labor movement and move it closer
to the cause of independence, from which it had earlier held itself apart (Casanovas
1998) By 1891 José Martí's anti-racist politics and critique of US imperialism found
a ready audience in these urban US settings, enabling him to build a broad base of
support for independence and providing necessary funding for the cause (Poyo 1989:
114; Martí 1999). By 1895, when the second war for independence began, the
movement to liberate Cuba was more than a call for national self-determination; it
was a fight for broad social transformation, built on a fragile alliance between elites
seeking independence from Spain and former slaves and working people seeking social
and political inclusion. This was provocation indeed to US elites, now in control of
the Cuban economy (de la Fuente 2001).

The United States' turn to war with Spain in 1898, though egged on by a variety
of circumstances, was at base a reflex of growing US imperial ambitions and a means
to transform the mechanisms of US control in Cuba in the face of revolutionary
challenge. For three full years prior to the entry of the United States, Cubans had
waged their second war for independence carrying the banner of a martyred José
Martí, whose ringing call for a revolution "with all, and for the good of all," echoed
beyond his death in 1895 (Martí 1999 [1891]: 144). In the United States, in contrast, a popular image figured Uncle Sam as the gallant savior of female Cuba, ravaged
by a Spanish brute – a figure that reflected the significance of manhood as part of
the hawkish ideology that pushed for war, "any war," but also rendered the Cubans
helpless victims and thus served to elide the active agency of the Cuban independence

movement (Johnson 1993; Hoganson 1998: 39). The explosion of the battleship *Maine* in Havana Harbor famously sparked the fire, freeing Washington to pursue its policy objective to keep Cuba on course as a crucial part of the emerging enterprise of "American empire."

Cuban racial and class politics, seen through the lens of prevailing US racial codes, seemed to present both the necessity of US guidance for Cuba, once freed from Spain, and the impossibility of incorporating it into the United States as a territorial acquisition. The latter concern, combined with the interests of the United States' domestic beet sugar lobby, contributed to passage of the Teller Amendment to the war appropriations bill, in which Congress foreswore any intention to prevent or to breach Cuban sovereignty. Yet the racial dynamics of combat provided a better gauge of what was to come: the exclusion of Cubans themselves from decision making (and the racism that shaped African American soldiers' experiences of the battlefield) foretold the exclusion of Cubans from negotiations to settle the peace, and the tone and texture of US imperial design in Cuba. The Teller Amendment had made provision for circumstances in which US rule would be required, and, on the heels of victory, Senator Orville Platt sponsored a second famous amendment on Cuba, stipulating a wide range of limitations on Cuban decision making: Cuba could not enter into treaties with any nation other than the United States, could assume no debts, could cede no land. The United States alone could approve such measures, could intervene militarily, and would henceforth have title to the important deep-water port and naval base at Guantanamo Bay. With the initial US military occupation of Cuba from 1899 to 1902 under General Leonard Wood, and the inclusion of the Platt Amendment in the Cuban constitution, US policy formalized Richard Olney's view of the United States' "practically sovereign" position – at least in Cuba.

Also as a result of the war with Spain, Puerto Rico became a US colonial holding, and there the United States asserted its sovereignty more directly – both due to the absence of a constraining prewar promise and because local relations of power facilitated the assertion of US rule. Puerto Ricans had also fought for independence from Spain with a series of uprisings dating back to the 1820s, the most famous of which was *El Grito de Lares* in 1868, and secured the abolition of slavery in 1873, 13 years before Cuba. The movement thereafter developed rather differently. In the 1890s, during the second Cuban war for independence, Puerto Ricans won autonomy from Spain, and a liberal, nationalist elite exercised power, as Eileen Findlay (1999) has shown, based on a politics of sexual respectability that effectively repressed Puerto Rico's African heritage and politically subordinated the island's popular classes. With the arrival of US colonialism at the conclusion of the war of 1898, Puerto Rico was not without anti-imperialist defenders. Puerto Ricans in New York, led by Eugenio Maria de Hostos, organized *La Liga de Patriotas Puertoriqueños* (Foner 1988), but prevailing local relations of power on the island rendered the US presence useful in too many ways to too many people for de Hostos' organizing to take root at home. Thus even as the concentration of capital and the process of proletarianization produced additional hardships over the course of the next two decades, Puerto Rican workers looked to their alliance with organized labor in the United States; Afro-Puerto Ricans looked to the legacy of Lincoln and US commitment to democracy; and women of the popular classes made use of US-imposed changes in divorce law – each seeking, in the resources and policies of the United States, remedies to the hardships already felt at the hands of Puerto Rican elites. In these ways, local social dynamics smoothed the road for US colonial power in Puerto Rico, which was eventually formalized with limited citizenship rights by the Jones Act of 1917.

In the decades surrounding the turn of the twentieth century, US power established itself in other forms in Central America, Colombia, Haiti, the Dominican Republic, and even in the European colonies that persisted in the Caribbean region (Moberg 2003). In Central America, the basic process leading to US imperial oversight would be familiar, starting with local elite invitations to US capital. As in Venezuela and Cuba, railroad construction (in some cases begun by the British) was an important stage in the consolidation of control over the local economy. Where Cuba and Puerto Rico had sugar, tobacco, and coffee, Central America had sugar, coffee, lumber, silver, gold, and bananas. An increasing measure of control over local politics followed the acquisition of major transportation, communications, and agricultural holdings, and US military power underwrote increasing economic and political influence.

Yet, differences are also evident in this part of the Caribbean region. The Central American republics had gained independence from Spain in the early 1820s, so national elites there could proceed with liberal development projects without the constraints imposed in Cuba by nationalist revolutionary struggle, although a powerful British presence certainly loomed large in Central American politics. And as US investments in coffee, mining, communications, and especially bananas grew, the social configuration of power proceeded in relation to the region's very different racial and class terrain, characterized by the persistence of indigenous populations, but also by internal variation across national borders and regional patterns of ethnic concentration (Gould 1998; Grandin 2000). In Caribbean coastal areas of Honduras, Nicaragua, and Costa Rica, for example, ethnic divisions tended to limit possibilities for effective organizing against domination by US fruit companies, a dynamic that was explicitly exploited at least by United Fruit (Euraque 2003). The evolution and particularities of racism and ideas about civilization in these settings had profoundly different effects on US power. And the absence of formal US political oversight could allow companies more room to maneuver the challenges of worker resistance and local opposition because Washington would not be held accountable in the same ways – at least at this stage.

Yet the resources and markets of Cuba, Puerto Rico, and Central America, in themselves, while all economically significant to the United States, paled in comparison to dreamed-of Asian markets to be made accessible by an isthmian canal – and the strategic advantages of exclusive US control over it. As early as 1846, US President Polk had secured the right to build a canal across Panama, and in 1851 Cornelius Vanderbilt commissioned a survey of Nicaragua for the same purpose (McCullough 1977). In 1850 the Clayton–Bulwer Treaty committed the United States and Britain to a joint and neutral canal project, if either was to proceed with one. In the middle of the 1880s, when a French company under the direction of the engineer Ferdinand de Lesseps had put years of work into the construction of a canal, one US commentator referred to this Anglo-American pact as a "covenant of national disgrace" (LaFeber 1984: 32). By the end of 1901, the hobbling treaty was superseded by one that gave the United States free rein to build and defend an American canal, and –

despite widespread preference for a Nicaraguan route among Washington's canal dreamers and planners – Theodore Roosevelt set his sights on Panama (McCullough 1977).

As US engineers readied themselves to accomplish the extraordinary technical feat, Roosevelt undertook to engineer the political circumstances US dominance would require. "I took Panama," Roosevelt proudly claimed, looking back on his role in the events that followed his decision. When the Colombian government rejected a treaty granting to the United States a 100-year lease of territory for the canal, Roosevelt turned to Colombian supporters of the project with assurances of military and financial support for Panamanian independence. In little over two weeks, the feat was accomplished and the United States had gained control of the new canal zone, along with additional territory as needed and the right to use its armed forces to protect its new holdings, "in perpetuity," in exchange for a financial sum and the promise to serve as guarantor of Panamanian independence (LaFeber 1979). With the protectorate in place, Panamanian independence from Colombia and the use of US military power to engineer that "independence" thus ironically placed another brick in the foundation of the United States' "practically sovereign" position in the Americas. The canal opened in 1914, and Panama was central to all US goals in the Caribbean henceforth.

"Its Fiat Is Law"

Richard Olney's assertion that the United States was "practically sovereign" in the Americas did not, of an instant, make it so, but the train of events that followed from that 1895 pronouncement, through the "taking" of Panama and beyond, effectively transformed the Monroe Doctrine into a powerful imperial reflex. Washington invoked it repeatedly for over three decades following Olney's memorandum – essentially enforcing its law of "fiat" with a train of military abuses – until that bedrock of US policy was repudiated, within the US State Department by Undersecretary of State J. Reuben Clark in 1928 and publicly by Secretary of State Henry L. Stimson in 1930. Although the Clark Memorandum repudiated the Roosevelt Corollary's interpretation of the Monroe Doctrine, which had rendered it a justification for intervention, neither Clark nor Stimson repudiated the Monroe Doctrine itself. In the meanwhile, US troops landed over 30 times from Cuba to Panama, the Dominican Republic, Nicaragua, Haiti, and Mexico; ruled each through extended and sometimes repeated military occupation; established client military forces; stood in the aisles of legislative halls with guns cocked, to control the outcome of elections; menaced other nations (e.g., Venezuela, Honduras, El Salvador, and Costa Rica) from nearby waters; and stepped in at times to back up companies facing striking workers.

Yet even as the United States seemed to reach new heights of imperial influence and power, "the subjects to which it confine[d] its interposition" did not merely accept US imperial rule. As with all empires, the emerging US empire was a contentious affair, and contention in one part of the empire could have far-reaching consequences partway around the world. Thus even as the newly reinvented Monroe Doctrine seemed to limn the boundaries of a uniquely "American" sphere of control from Venezuela to Panama, events in the Philippines worked to limit and shape outcomes in the Caribbean region. Since coming into US possession after the 1898 war, US rule in the Philippines had proceeded in the face of intense military resistance under the nationalist leadership of Emilio Aguinaldo. The US war against Filipino independence was ruthless, with heavy resistance, high casualties, and news of torture coming back to the States. This news, in turn, fomented widespread resistance in the United States, including fears about the degeneration of US manhood and the undermining of US democracy, both mixed with racial anxieties. By 1902 a US congressman could ask how American generals in the Philippines could have adopted "the notable and brutal methods" that the Spanish had employed in Cuba (Hoganson 1998: 184–5). In short, the war in the Philippines gave imperialism a bad name in the United States.

This made matters worse for Teddy Roosevelt in the Caribbean, and particularly in Venezuela. In 1899, the year Aguinaldo's forces dug in, United Fruit united, and Leonard Wood set up shop as Governor General in Cuba, arbitration results came in for Venezuela and British Guiana – and the Venezuelans reacted. There were no wreaths for George Washington's statue this time around. The United States had proceeded with the border arbitration, all the while excluding Venezuela from negotiations (just as it excluded Cuba, the Philippines, Puerto Rico, and Guam from postwar negotiations with Spain). In the end much of what the South American nation sought, it lost (Schoultz 1998: 123). That same year, Cipriano Castro, an outraged anti-imperialist from the mountainous Táchira State, claimed the presidency of Venezuela from Caracas liberals bent on attracting US capital – on US terms.

Holding the presidency through 1908, Cipriano Castro was a source of profound frustration and provocation to Theodore Roosevelt – and the original inspiration for his "big stick" policies in the Caribbean region. Theodore Roosevelt's friends and subordinates were also a source of profound challenge for Cipriano Castro. Between January 1901 and November 1902 the New York and Bermudez Company, an asphalt concern closely tied to the US legation in Caracas in part because of ties between Roosevelt and one of the company's officers, helped to fund a revolution against Castro, costing Venezuela dearly in both financial and human terms, with 20,000 deaths in the course of the war (Ewell 1996: 101). Having inherited the outsized European loans his predecessors had taken on in the 1880s and 1890s, and faced with his country's inability to repay them, Castro expressed "his outrage at the excesses of foreign companies and their governments" and referred his nation's creditors to the Venezuelan courts for redress of their grievances, following the principle laid out in the Calvo Doctrine (Ewell 1996: 98, 100). In the face of Castro's refusal to pay, British and German forces seized Venezuelan ships and set up a blockade in 1902–3, leading to a second "Venezuela crisis" for the Monroe Doctrine. Washington stepped in to arbitrate once again, and Castro was forced to accept harsh measures to repay the debts. But afterward the Venezuelan president looked for ways to limit the damage and restrict foreign economic activity in his country, particularly in the mining sector, so important to US investors (Ewell 1996: 102). Through to the end of Castro's and Roosevelt's presidencies, the US leader chafed at his inability to persuade the people of the United States that this "unspeakably villainous little monkey," as he privately referred to Castro, deserved a military lesson. "If I started to deal with him as he deserves," TR wrote in October 1908, "the enormous majority of my countrymen would be so . . . absolutely out of sympathy with me as if I undertook personally to run down and chastise some small street urchin who yelled some epithet of derision at me while I was driving" (Ewell 1996: 105–6).

The lessons that Roosevelt took from his dealings with Cipriano Castro became the basis for his famous corollary to the Monroe Doctrine, which he first put into effect in the Dominican Republic in 1905. A nation that "knows how to act with reasonable efficiency and decency in social and political matters," Roosevelt stated in his annual message to the US Congress in December 1904, "need fear no interference from the United States." On the other hand, Roosevelt continued, "Chronic wrong-doing, or an impotence which results in a general loosening of the ties of civilized society, may in America as elsewhere ultimately require intervention by some civilized nation." The Monroe Doctrine, Roosevelt continued, could as a consequence, "force the United States, however reluctantly, in flagrant cases of such wrongdoing or impotence, to the exercise of an international police power." Whereas in 1895 Richard Olney had rested his assertion that US "fiat is law" on the claim that the will of the United States needed no more justification than US military and financial strength and geographical separation from Europe, by 1904, in response to mounting resistance, Roosevelt couched his assertion more carefully. By opposing "efficiency and decency" to "chronic wrongdoing and impotence," the leader of the rough riders and champion of "the strenuous life" invoked deeply felt meanings associated with race, gender, and sexuality to establish the righteousness and necessity of US oversight in the Caribbean (Bederman 1995; Rosenberg 2003: 39). The Dominican Republic, reeling with revolutionary "wrong-doing" since the fall of its longtime dictator Ulises Heureaux in 1899, and impotent to repay its European and North American debts, was the first candidate for correction under the United States' newly articulated international police power – no less so for the fact that Dominican leaders themselves called for assistance in meting out such correction.

Despite the high-handed language of the Roosevelt Corollary, the actual working out of a new relationship with the Dominican Republic continued to require a measure of responsiveness to the push and pull of politics in both countries. Even the hint of protectorate status readied for protest a Dominican population poised to revolt against the usurpations of the capital, where the US-based Santo Domingo Improvement Company had been a central player in Dominican affairs for over 10 years already. Roosevelt called on financial experts and investment bankers in the United States to devise a sufficiently modest but workable plan: for starters, a customs receivership administered by an appointee of the US president would garner 55 percent of Dominican customs for repayment of the nation's debts, leaving 45 percent for the needs of the Dominican government and population (Rosenberg 2003: 43). It took another three years to work out the full plan which, by treaty, lodged supervisory authority over decisions about the Dominican national debt in the president of the United States and required the Caribbean nation to consolidate its outstanding debts through a private loan contract with a New York bank. As Emily Rosenberg explains, "this model of government–bank cooperation, using what would be called a 'controlled loan' brokered by a professional consultant in international finance, seemed to offer the possibility of guiding a dependent state through a process of fiscal reform without the United States having to assume the burdens and risks of political sovereignty" (Rosenberg 2003: 46).

This arrangement, inaugurated under Roosevelt, was the heart of the policy most often associated with his successor, William Howard Taft. The chief architects of the model, economists Charles Conant, Edwin Kemmerer, and Jeremiah Jenks, saw it as a beneficial form of imperialism geared toward integrating poor nations into the dominant capitalist economic system, but the evolving political climate led elected leaders away from such frank language. To Roosevelt, it was benevolent supervision enforced by "international police power"; to William Howard Taft's Assistant Secretary of State for Latin American affairs, F. M. Huntington Wilson, it was "the substitution of dollars for bullets," and it came to be known as "dollar diplomacy" (Schoultz 1998: 208–9). Despite the evolution of its rhetorical clothing, this program became increasingly tainted with the charge of imperialism, and policy makers were forced to tweak the mechanism repeatedly to obscure the involvement of the US government in overseas banking ventures requiring supervision of "client" nations. Roosevelt secured a treaty to guarantee the exchange of financial advisors for a bank loan in the Dominican case, but not so his successors. The Taft administration turned to private loan contracts (stipulating mandatory advisory missions) to avoid congressional scrutiny, and worked out alternative means to extend "government backing" to raise the value of the bonds (Rosenberg 2003: 73).

In the Caribbean region, the Roosevelt Corollary and dollar diplomacy exacerbated the very problem they were designed to address, a seemingly pervasive political instability that plagued regional governments and weakened the ground for capitalist activity across the region. As in Venezuela and the Dominican Republic, prior to the severe economic depression of the 1890s, regional elites had taken out substantial loans made available by European and North American banks, counting on the imperial tradition of gunboats coming in to protect the "lives and property" of nationals – and to collect their debts. Regional liberal elites had attempted to modernize their countries by attracting this capital, but, among other obstacles, local populations often refused to accept the levels of privation and social dislocation that resulted from these economic and social programs. In the aftermath of the 1890s depression, many regional governments found themselves caught between foreign military power and domestic opposition.

As a result, governments either entrenched themselves with repressive measures or fell quickly, sometimes in rapid succession, and often facing insurrections funded by foreign concerns and peopled by angry citizens. Cipriano Castro came to power in one such confrontation, then fought off the populist José Manuel "El Mocho" Hernández as well as an insurrection funded in part by the New York and Bermudez Company. In the Dominican Republic, Heureaux fell to an assassin's bullet in 1899, followed by a series of revolutionary challenges to his successors. In Honduras, at least seven revolutions proceeded in succession between the early 1890s and 1909, when the Taft Administration began its failed attempt to work out a controlled loan treaty there. In that case, fruit company machinations, with US diplomatic and military assistance, resulted in yet another change in government, this time more favorable to US concerns (LaFeber 1984: 44–5). In Nicaragua, the Liberal José Santos Zelaya took power in 1893, originally on good terms with Washington due to mutual hopes for a Nicaraguan canal, but over the course of next 17 years (and especially after 1903) his nationalist policies, in some cases directly targeting US concerns, and his attempt to entrench his own rule over a wider swath of Central

America, created a significant challenge for Washington. The United States supported a successful conservative revolution against him led by Emiliano Chamorro and Juan Estrada, from the US stronghold in Bluefields on the Miskito Coast. Under the direction of Smedley Darlington Butler, US Marines stayed on to micro-manage the new government (Schmidt 1987: 45) and in 1911 faced down another revolutionary challenge, this time resulting in the installation of a US mining company employee, Adolfo Diaz, as the new president. Revolutionary activity continued, and US troop commitments reached 2,700 in September 1912, before being scaled back to a "legation guard" of 130 in November (Schoultz 1998: 218–19). The Marines stayed on almost continuously until 1933.

In Haiti, as governments changed ever more rapidly after 1910, this pattern worsened a situation already made difficult by the original circumstances of national independence. In 1825 France extorted from Haiti an indemnity – payment for former French plantation owners who lost their fortunes in the Haitian Revolution – as a condition for recognition of Haitian independence. Hobbled by this debt, and facing a peasantry deeply committed to refusing plantation labor or any other arrangement that resembled slavery, the nation's political elite increasingly regarded the great powers as resources to be played off one against another in order to maintain a fragile state of independence – and the profitability of government service (Plummer 1988). The political house of cards collapsed finally in late July 1915, when the Marines disembarked.

In Woodrow Wilson's hands, the search for stability occasioned frequent deployment of the Marines, repeated invasions, and extended military occupations. Wilson sought to cleanse government-sponsored lending policies and financial oversight of their money-grubbing associations and to reject the imperialism endorsed by his predecessors. In a speech to the Southern Commercial Congress in Mobile, Alabama, in 1913, he foreswore "degrading" policies based on the promotion of "material interests" foreign to the real needs of Caribbean and Latin American peoples. A more selfless version of US leadership would presumably guide weaker nations into harmonious and beneficial commerce with the United States, while strengthening their financial and democratic practices.

But longtime and ongoing regional experience with US capital and local elites – both backed by US arms – continued to kick up revolutionary opposition, and Wilson's resort to force engendered even greater instability. In Mexico Wilson saw military intervention as a means to "teach Mexicans to elect good men." Wilson ordered the military occupation of Tampico in 1914 and a punitive expedition into northern Mexico in 1916, but his gambit failed (Link 1960: 479). Article 27 of the 1917 Mexican Constitution challenged his paternalist program by providing for nationalization of subsoil mineral resources. The Mexican Revolution, moreover, with its profound anti-imperialist sentiment, served as an inspiration to others across the region. In the Dominican Republic, US Marines faced the united opposition of peasantry and elites, which together with protest in neighboring Haiti, forced the US Congress, by 1922, to launch an investigation of the two occupations. The occupation of Haiti lasted through 1934, engendering years of military resistance, not only by its initial abrogation of Haitian independence and heavy-handed insistence on "electing" a pliant figurehead president, but also by forcing through constitutional revision removing the long-cherished prohibition on foreign land ownership and through untold violence associated with a corvée to support road building. The brutalities of the occupation also contributed to a growing anti-imperialist movement in the United States and occasioned international criticism when the Haitian puppet president, Sudre Dartiguenave, appealed to Wilson at the Versailles conference, where the US leader was ostensibly defending the rights of small nations. Under Wilson, US military forces also hovered in Honduran waters at least four times (1913, 1915, 1916, 1919) and seized "domestic police powers" in Panama twice (Schoultz 1998: 233–4).

World War I and the Russian Revolution transformed the terrain of the United States' Caribbean empire in ways that both strengthened the law of fiat and challenged it. On the one hand, US wealth grew during the war, especially relative to other nations. Also US citizens' experiences with liberty bonds helped to expand credit markets, facilitating dollar diplomacy arrangements at the same time that Latin American governments found themselves even more needful of funds (Rosenberg 2003). In all, the war brought about a transition from British to US leadership in the world economy. On the other hand, the carnage of war led to doubt about the value of Euro-American civilization and a sense among US Americans of having been betrayed by Wall Street bankers who supposedly led the United States into war for profit alone. These developments fed the anti-imperialist movement in the States and precipitated growing links to anti-imperialists in the Caribbean and Latin America generally. At the same time, the Russian Revolution offered a model, an inspiration, and concrete resources for challenging US imperialism. Communist parties, founded in the early 1920s, devoted significant energy to this goal, and helped to bring widespread attention to the atrocities accompanying US power in the Caribbean region (Renda 2001a). In the 1920s, the Mexican Revolution, while drawing on long-standing internal opposition to the sway of US corporate power, also turned to relations with Moscow as ballast against the colossus of the north (Spenser 1999).

Practical Sovereignty

In the aftermath of World War I, then, the architecture of US imperial interest and strategy shifted. It had always been constructed out of many distinct motivations and investments (in both economic and psychological senses). To name only some of the forces that added up to the seeming monolith of US imperial relations in the region: On the part of North Americans there were entrepreneurial excitement, professional aspiration, paternalist and maternalist condescension, reformist zeal, and assimilationist striving, as well as pure profit seeking. On the part of Caribbean peoples there were liberal development schemes, elite political maneuvering, indigenous opposition to liberal nationalism, and the need for resources available from the United States. After the war, the fractious quality of US empire came to the fore both in the Caribbean and in North America. Political opposition to imperialism, the valuing of indigenous culture, growing awareness of racism, revulsion against Americanization schemes, divergent projects for remaking and making use of US wealth and power, and more widespread suffering associated with the Great Depression pointed policy makers, citizens, and activists in new directions in the 1920s and 1930s. It is not that US empire ended during this period. Instead, the sometimes solid and sometimes tentative alliances that had constituted the transnational phenomenon of US empire shifted, showed their fault lines, and in some cases broke apart, while new ones formed. Even "Washington," which had never actually been a monolith to begin with, showed its fault lines more fully in this period, with the emergence of an influential peace party raising objections in Congress to the role of Wall Street and the reflexive use of military power in US relations with Latin America and the Caribbean (Johnson 1995).

But, as we have seen, opposition to US empire was not born in the halls of the United States Congress. More widespread resistance simmered for years in the fields, mines, and mills of the Caribbean region within US corporate culture and creative deployment of US imperial agendas. People around the region adapted pragmatically to conditions of employment which included racist disrespect, lack of mobility across job classifications, stringent forms of worker control, company towns extending that control beyond the workplace, radical challenges to values of family and community, and in many cases severe dangers on the job, most notably in the mining sector.

In the 1910s and 1920s, more forceful and visible protests emerged. Major strikes in Guatemala (1914 and 1923), Mexico (1916), Honduras (1920 and 1924), and Cuba (1924) as well as further south in Peru and Argentina called up strenuous responses from US corporations and the military forces that backed them up, with varying degrees of success in putting down protests and rejecting the strikers' demands (O'Brien 1999: 81–5). Socialism deepened the critiques articulated in these contexts, and Lenin's arguments about the inevitability of imperialism under capitalism resounded through much anti-imperial discourse. In 1920, Henry Catlin of General Electric had to be escorted by US Marines out of Guatemala; challengers to longtime dictator Manuel Estrada Cabrera made much of secret deals between the president and the Yankee capitalist (O'Brien 1999: 76). In El Salvador, Communist organizers found fertile soil as critics took issue with US dominance over the food industry and the role of US capital in the entrenched power of the nation's "forty families" (LaFeber 1984: 71). In Costa Rica, *El Repertorio Americano* became a mouthpiece for anti-imperialist sentiment from across the region and Latin America generally (Rosenberg 2003: 235). In Haiti, signs asking "Shall Haiti Be Your Belgium?" greeted the US Senate investigating committee in 1921 and 1922; dissident editors faced jail sentences for speaking out in the middle years of the decade; and a general strike involving students and workers brought daily business to a halt in the summer of 1929. In Nicaragua, US dictation came in diverse forms, at the hands of diverse US actors, and with unintended outcomes for different sectors of the Nicaraguan population (Gobat 2005). And it gave rise to Augusto Sandino's influential and seemingly intractable revolt between 1927 and the final withdrawal of US marines in 1933. Indeed following the onset of the Great Depression, protest extended across the region.

One dimension of protest emphasized pride in local culture in opposition to the pervasive racial denigration of Caribbean and Latin American peoples. Indigenism as an idiom of resistance and anti-imperial opposition flourished in the postwar context but varied widely across the region. In Mexico, José Vasconcelos' 1925 volume *La raza cósmica* asserted the power of *mestizaje* in opposition to the sterile rigidity of the Anglo-Protestant culture of the capitalist North. Vasconcelos looked to the celebration of Mexican identity and history as a means to mute the power of *El Norte*

(McPherson 2003: 15). In Haiti, the 1920s and 1930s saw an upsurge of interest in folklore, ethnology, and literature emphasizing Haiti's unique folk culture and proud African heritage – developments which formed the roots of *noirisme*, with implications for anti-imperial opposition well beyond the Caribbean region and US empire (Renda 2001b). But some iterations of indigenism could also reinforce exclusions within Latin American nations. In Honduras, indigenist opposition to the power of United Fruit (highlighting an Indo-Latin national identity) contributed to the targeting of the black population of the Caribbean coastal region, including longtime Garifuna residents and more recent West Indian migrants who dominated the workforce of the powerful *frutera* (Euraque 2003). In Nicaragua, liberalism had long excluded indigenous groups, a fact which helped to create an opening for US power in 1909. Subsequently, as Jeffrey Gould (1998) has shown, Sandino's resistance to Yankee imperialism cultivated a discourse of mestizaje that allowed for the marginalization of indigenous communities' needs and views. And, in some cases, indigenism fired up populist discourses that contributed to the rise of dictators. Anastazio Somoza in Nicaragua, Raphael Trujillo in the Dominican Republic, and eventually François "Papa Doc" Duvalier in Haiti (elected in 1957, after building his *noiriste* populist following initially in the 1930s) rode to power on the strength of state structures consolidated by US military occupations and populist discourses fired up in opposition to those occupations (Trouillot 1990).

Meanwhile, regional politicians, both in response to popular resentment and based on their own agendas, increasingly articulated their rejection of the logics of US rule. Latin American leaders and scholars meeting in Havana in 1925 and Rio de Janeiro in 1927 made clear their rejection of the Monroe Doctrine and the Roosevelt Corollary. In Costa Rica, Honduras, Guatemala, and Mexico (as well as in Argentina) politicians condemned US intervention in Nicaragua in their respective legislatures, in some cases passing resolutions against it (Rosenberg 2003: 235). At the Sixth Inter-American Conference in Havana in 1928, representatives of the Latin American nations pushed for a resolution against intervention, to the great embarrassment of the United States. Former Secretary of State Charles Evans Hughes mounted a defense of the principle of intervention, but retreat from that stance was already in the offing back in Washington.

Transnational connections brought all this and more to the attention of US citizens, who were primed to listen with a more open mind now that convictions about the superiority of Euro-American civilization were coming apart at the seams. The Pan American movement, progressive missionaries, African American civil rights leaders, peace activists, and journalists cultivated links across national boundaries, increasing the flow of information from US protectorates and other spaces of imperial rule, despite US schemes to limit the flow of such information (Rosenberg 2003: 236). By these routes, the entrenched occupation of Haiti, intervention in Nicaragua, and the continued activities of the State Department in negotiating dollar diplomacy arrangements became subjects of deep concern to activists and politicians in the United States. Growing cultural interest in Mexico and sympathy with Augusto Sandino's nationalist army in Nicaragua, in particular, drew widespread comment in the United States.

Pan African and other transnational black activism also challenged US empire. W. E. B. Du Bois' immediate criticism of the US occupation of Haiti led the way in

1915, and his subsequent leadership of Pan African conferences facilitated further critical analysis of US "interposition" in the region. Marcus Garvey's profoundly popular Universal Negro Improvement Association, established in the United States in 1917 (having been founded several years earlier in Jamaica) created an even more powerful vehicle for black resistance, reaching a far wider population and linking people of African heritage with one another through the travels of the Black Star Line (Stephens 2005). Like Du Bois, Garvey connected analyses of domestic US racism to North American power in the Caribbean.

The United States' pragmatic assertion of its imperial rule in the Caribbean region shifted in the face of this multi-pronged opposition, building on a pattern of adaptability already well established. The State Department tried to step farther back from the controlled loans it brokered, though at times bankers betrayed US government involvement, setting cabinet members' nerves on edge (Rosenberg 2003). The US Navy and its adjunct Marine Corps reined in much of the freewheeling military deployment that had characterized the administrations of Roosevelt, Taft, and Wilson, though some military projects persisted, as we have seen. President Harding ended the occupation of the Dominican Republic in 1924 and reorganized the occupation of Haiti after the Senate's investigation; however, continued pressure to end that occupation failed until the protests of 1929 – and the US massacre of Haitian citizens at Aux Cayes that ensued – made their mark in the press and US public opinion.

Diplomacy also relied increasingly on financial rather than military power. The Department of Commerce, in the influential hands of Herbert Hoover from 1921 to 1928, took the lead in formulating US foreign policy, in keeping with a shift from military to economic instruments for asserting US power. An important example is provided by the diplomatic work of Dwight Morrow in Mexico in 1924. The year before, the United States had succeeded in negotiating with Mexican President Alvaro Obregón the Bucareli Accords, which limited the impact of the 1917 Mexican constitution by establishing a retroactive exception to the rule, known as "the doctrine of positive acts." When Plutarco Elías Calles succeeded Obregón, he refused to follow the doctrine. Morrow used the "loss of future loans" as a leverage point to blunt Calles' nationalist program (Gilderhus 2002: 64). Seeking and maintaining access to key raw materials was high on Hoover's list of priorities. Oil figured importantly in this program, not least due to the restrictions imposed by the Mexican constitution of 1917 and, after 1924, nationalist action against a US company in Colombia (Rosenberg 1982: 130–1). A close and long-standing relationship with Venezuelan dictator Juan Vicente Gomez paved the way for legislation authored by US companies in that oil-rich country (Ewell 1996: 134).

Repression of dissent within the United States, in US protectorates, and in other spaces of imperial rule also formed a part of the United States' imperial adaptability in the 1920s – a development linked to US support for dictatorships in the post-colonial nations of the region. Laws restricting interstate commerce were used to oppose the All-America Anti-Imperialist League (Rosenberg 2003: 236) organized by members of the Communist Party, which played key roles in publicizing US repression in Haiti and established organizing links between the United States and Mexico (Shipman 1993). In 1925, the State Department unsuccessfully attempted to prevent *Atlantic Monthly* from publishing an article by the longtime missionary and Pan American organizer Samuel Guy Inman, entitled "Imperialistic America"

(Rosenberg 2003). The Department redoubled its efforts during Sandino's rebellion, putting enormous pressure on Costa Rica, Honduras, and El Salvador to silence dissent by targeting outspoken leaders (including some who had played key roles at the Inter-American Conference at Havana) and succeeding in significant ways in Honduras and El Salvador (Rosenberg 2003: 236). From time to time, pressure to impose or condone censorship elicited queasy reactions from US diplomats (Ewell 1996), but in the face of 1920s resistance, such hesitations did not prevail, and censorship was routine (Renda 2001a: 33, 267). The consolidation of state power under US occupation and in US client states was an extension of repressive domestic policies, unfettered by the bill of rights. It laid the foundation for the rise and entrenchment of dictators such as Juan Vicente Gomez, Rafael Trujillo, Anastasio Somoza, and Fulgencio Batista, whose regimes, in turn, served important ends in the evolving program of US rule – notwithstanding US diplomats' attempts to prevent or to soften fascistic authoritarianism.

The military occupations of the Dominican Republic, Haiti, and Nicaragua (as well as the protectorate status of Cuba and Panama and the colonial status of Puerto Rico), provided opportunities for pioneering other practical mechanisms for US rule – mechanisms that would serve the needs of US empire well beyond the 1930s and the Caribbean. The occupations became testing grounds for training client military forces (constabularies, in name), practicing aerial maneuvers and bombing, and devising approaches to covert operations. From Panama to Nicaragua to Haiti, USMC General Smedley D. Butler played a key role in these innovations; "undershirt diplomacy" was his term for disreputable and clandestine strong-arm tactics that later came to be known as "covert ops" (Schmidt 1987; Renda 2001a: 125). When Augusto Sandino refused to cave in to US demands in 1927 – in the midst of intense pressure for US withdrawal from Nicaragua – Washington devised a plan to wage its war against the recalcitrant general by proxy, building on what the Marine Corps learned in the Dominican Republic and Haiti to develop and train the new Nicaraguan *Guardia Nacional*.

In the context of these innovations – bureaucratically supported economic leverage, client military forces, repression of dissent, and backroom strong-arm tactics – Washington accepted the necessity of foreswearing direct and open military intervention. These mechanisms formed the new arsenal of force that would replace Marine landings and formal occupations in the region once J. Reuben Clark's 1928 memorandum, repudiating interventionism in the name of the Monroe Doctrine, began to hold sway in the minds of leading policy makers. Herbert Hoover made a goodwill tour in 1928. By 1933, the last Marines withdrew from Nicaragua, and a year later, from Haiti. The year 1934 also saw the abrogation of the Platt Amendment, new levels of home rule in Puerto Rico, the promise of independence to the Philippines, Secretary of State Cordell Hull signing onto the principle of non-intervention at the Seventh Inter-American Conference at Montevideo, and a victorious FDR expounding the Good Neighbor policy as the basis for relations with Latin America. Until Lyndon Baines Johnson ordered the invasion of the Dominican Republic in 1965, in the context of the war in Vietnam, this approach held: US rule required the outward renunciation of force and other overt signs of practical sovereignty.

The US policy reversal summarized by the term "good neighbor" negated Richard Olney's 1895 assertion, reinforced by the Roosevelt Corollary, that US fiat could be enforced in the Americas at the point of a gun. It recognized the weakening of US power in the context of the Great Depression and in the face of concerted opposition in Latin America. But the narrow scope of this reversal left much in place. It called attention to military arrangements and protectorates but elided the significance of continuing financial arrangements and the influence of US companies backed by quieter or localized military support. Also, and perhaps more fundamentally, the seeming rejection of "imperialism" rested on a set of nationalist assumptions that very poorly represented the actual functioning of US imperial power by the 1920s. As Eric Roorda (1998) has shown in the case of the Dominican Republic, the gendered culture of the military helped forge transnational ties between men who served in the Dominican *Guardia Nacional* (later known as the *Policía Nacional*) and the US Marine Corps. A brotherhood of gold braid and epaulets continued to function beyond the withdrawal of the United States in 1924 and, after Rafael Trujillo seized power in 1930, served to strengthen his regime in crucial ways. Trujillo's manipulations presented significant obstacles to Washington, as he defied US will, courted the Third Reich for a time, and constructed his own mechanisms of power (Roorda 1998: 203–8). But the Dominican loose cannon still answered to Washington on numerous levels and still served the ends of US empire. Not least, the customs receivership continued in the hands of the Foreign Bondholders Protective Council (Roorda 1998: 89, 217). Trujillo's regime maintained an open door to US capital, fell in line (ultimately) with Fortress America in opposition to European fascism, and stood firmly against Communism in this hemisphere – the emerging priority of US empire in the years to come.

Like Trujillo in the Dominican Republic, Anastasio Somoza García in Nicaragua came to power by paths laid down by US imperial rule and proceeded to walk a fine line between embracing and thumbing his nose at the United States. It was not that Washington picked Somoza or placed him in office, as Michel Gobat (2005) has shown, but rather that he capitalized on the centralization of power in the *Guardia Nacional*, and benefited from the weakening of his rivals and the flourishing of his supporters under US occupation. Like Trujillo, Somoza turned away from the lessons in liberal democracy espoused by representatives of the northern power, while embracing the law of fiat they had modeled in practice in the name of James Monroe.

Conclusion

Venezuela was significant not only as the site of the United States' assertion of the Monroe Doctrine and its transformation of that doctrine into a tool of imperial power, but also as a site of the sorts of social complexity with which Washington and US Americans had to contend in the process of asserting their power. The springs of that power came from the dynamics of US growth and development as a wealthy nation born of a world of empires and imperial ambitions, but the US empire took its shape from all the complex interactions of the Americas, with their layered legacies of empire and varied patterns of inequality. The Venezuelan invitation as well as critiques of *Monroismo*, the scrappy maneuvering of Cipriano Castro, US hesitations over pushing censorship in the early Gómez years, and the emergence of the co-operative, repressive state of Gómez, whose dictatorial rule, fueled by oil, lasted well into the 1930s – these factors, along with others across the region, shaped and directed the career of US empire.

In the first Venezuela crisis, Richard Olney set forth an unusually bald assertion of US power: US "fiat is law" for no other reason than that, as a practical matter, US might makes it so. His emphasis on the "practical" dimension of US sovereignty in the hemisphere seems prescient now in light of the pragmatic resilience of US imperialism since that time. But his use of the phrase "practically sovereign" also points to the limitations placed on US imperial power (as on all imperial power, in my view) by local and transnational developments beyond its control. US empire did not saturate the region evenly or consistently: there were always places where national governments and groups of people either successfully resisted or went their own way.

By the time Franklin Roosevelt took office, Olney's conceit seemed wildly inappropriate to the realities of the moment. Yet, the long-term US project of seeking to establish and maintain effective sovereignty over the Americas, and especially in its Caribbean "sphere of influence," persisted both beyond and by means of the Good Neighbor policy. While uneven over time and space, and stunted at times by various forms of opposition, this was and continues to be sovereignty of a practical, functioning nature, traveling under whatever name and guise seem to serve the exigencies of the moment.

NOTE

1   According to Schoultz (1998), the first appeal to the Monroe Doctrine specifically in relation to the border question was 1876, but Harris (1999) argues that the appeal to the Monroe Doctrine began earlier, at least with the Civil War-era offer of a cavalry unit in exchange for a pact of confederation.

BIBLIOGRAPHY

Bederman, G. (1995) *Manliness and Civilization: A Cultural History of Gender and Race in the United States, 1880–1917.* University of Chicago Press, Chicago.

Bourgois, P. I. (1989) *Ethnicity at Work: Divided Labor on a Central American Banana Plantation.* Johns Hopkins University Press, Baltimore.

Calder, B. J. (1984) *The Impact of Intervention: The Dominican Republic During the U.S. Occupation of 1916–1924.* University of Texas Press, Austin.

Casanovas, J. (1998) *Bread or Bullets: Urban Labor and Spanish Colonialism in Cuba, 1850–1898.* University of Pittsburgh Press, Pittsburgh.

De la Fuente, A. (2001) *A Nation for All: Race, Inequality, and Politics in Twentieth-Century Cuba.* University of North Carolina Press, Chapel Hill.

Delpar, H. (1992) *The Enormous Vogue of Things Mexican: Cultural Relations Between the United States and Mexico, 1920–1935.* University of Alabama Press, Tuscaloosa.

Diaz, A. J. (2004) *Female Citizens, Patriarchs and the Law in Venezuela, 1786–1904.* University of Nebraska Press, Lincoln.

Euraque, Darío A. (2003) "The Threat of Blackness to the Mestizo Nation: Race and Ethnicity in the Honduran Banana Economy." In S. Striffler & M. Moberg (eds.), *Banana Wars: Power, Production, and History in the Americas.* Duke University Press, Durham, pp. 145–70.

Ewell, J. (1996) *Venezuela and the United States: From Monroe's Hemisphere to Petroleum's Empire*. University of Georgia Press, Athens.

Ferrer, A. (1999) *Insurgent Cuba: Race, Nation, and Revolution, 1868–1898*. University of North Carolina Press, Chapel Hill.

Findlay, E. S. (1999) *Imposing Decency: The Politics of Sexuality and Race in Puerto Rico, 1870–1920*. Duke University Press, Durham.

Foner, P. S. (1988) *U.S. Labor Movement and Latin America: A History of Workers' Response to Interventionism, Volume I, 1846–1919*. Bergin and Garvey Publishers, South Hadley, MA.

Gatewood, W. B. (1971) *"Smoked Yankees" and the Struggle for Empire: Letters from Negro Soldiers, 1898–1902*. University of Illinois Press, Champaign.

Gilderhus, M. T. (2002) *The Second Century: U.S. Latin-American Relations since 1889*. Scholarly Resources, Wilmington, DE.

Gobat, M. (2005) *Confronting the American Dream: Nicaragua Under U.S. Imperial Rule*. Duke University Press, Durham.

Gould, J. L. (1990) *To Lead as Equals: Rural Protest and Political Consciousness in Chinandega, Nicaragua, 1912–1979*. University of North Carolina Press, Chapel Hill.

Gould, J. L. (1998) *To Die in This Way: Nicaraguan Indians and the Myth of Mestizaje, 1880–1965*. Duke University Press, Durham.

Grandin, Greg (2000) *The Blood of Guatemala: A History of Race and Nation*. Duke University Press, Durham.

Green, D. (1971) *The Containment of Latin America: A History of the Myths and Realities of the Good Neighbor Policy*. Quadrangle Books, Chicago.

Greenberg, A. S. (2005) *Manifest Manhood and the Antebellum American Empire*. Cambridge University Press, Cambridge.

Harris, W. L. (1999) "Venezuela: Wars, Claims, and the Cry for a Stronger Monroe Doctrine." In T. Leonard (ed.), *United States–Latin American Relations, 1850–1903: Establishing a Relationship*. University of Alabama Press, Tuscaloosa.

Hoganson, K. L. (1998) *Fighting for American Manhood: How Gender Politics Provoked the Spanish-American and Philippine American Wars*. Yale University Press, New Haven.

Holden, R. H. & Zolov, E. (eds.) (2000) *Latin America and the United States: A Documentary History*. Oxford University Press, New York.

Jacobson, M. F. (1998) *Whiteness of a Different Color: European Immigrants and the Alchemy of Race*. Harvard University Press, Cambridge, MA.

Jacobson, M. F. (2000) *Barbarian Virtues: The United States Encounters Foreign Peoples at Home and Abroad, 1876–1917*. Hill and Wang, New York.

Johnson, J. J. (1993) *Latin America in Caricature*, 2nd ed. University of Texas Press, Austin.

Johnson, R. D. (1995) *The Peace Progressives and American Foreign Relations* Harvard University Press, Cambridge, MA.

Joseph, G. M., et al. (eds.) (1998) *Close Encounters of Empire: Writing the Cultural History of U.S. Latin American Relations*. Duke University Press, Durham.

Kaplan, A. (2002) *The Anarchy of Empire in the Making of U.S. Culture*. Harvard University Press, Cambridge, MA.

LaFeber, W. (1963) *The New Empire: An Interpretation of American Expansion, 1860–1898*. Cornell University Press, Ithaca.

LaFeber, W. (1979) *The Panama Canal: The Crisis in Historical Perspective*. Oxford University Press, New York.

LaFeber, W. (1984) *Inevitable Revolutions: The United States and Central America*. Norton, New York.

LaFeber, W. (1993) *The Cambridge History of American Foreign Relations, Volume II: The American Search for Opportunity, 1865–1913*. Cambridge University Press, Cambridge.

Lindsay-Poland, J. (2003) *Emperors in the Jungle: The Hidden History of the U.S. in Panama.* Duke University Press, Durham.

Link, A. S. (1960) *Wilson: The Struggle for Neutrality, 1914–1915.* Princeton University Press, Princeton.

Martí, J. (1999 [1891]) "With All, for the Good of All" [Speech, November 26, 1891, Tampa, Florida]. In D. Shnookal & M. Muniz (eds.), *José Martí Reader: Writings on the Americas.* Ocean Press, Melbourne.

May, E. R. (1975) *The Making of the Monroe Doctrine.* Harvard University Press, Cambridge, MA.

McCullough, D. G. (1977) *The Path between the Seas: The Creation of the Panama Canal, 1870–1914.* Touchstone, New York.

McPherson, A. (2003) *Yankee No! Anti-Americanism in U.S.–Latin American Relations.* Harvard University Press, Cambridge, MA.

Merish, L. (2000) *Sentimental Materialism: Gender, Commodity Culture, and Nineteenth-Century American Literature.* Duke University Press, Durham.

Moberg, M. (2003) "Responsible Men and Sharp Yankees: The United Fruit Company, Resident Elites, and Colonial State in British Honduras." In S. Striffler & M. Moberg (eds.), *Banana Wars: Power, Production, and History in the Americas.* Duke University Press, Durham, pp. 145–70.

O'Brien, T. (1996) *The Revolutionary Mission: American Enterprise in Latin America, 1900–1945.* Cambridge University Press, Cambridge, MA.

O'Brien, T. (1999) *The Century of US Capitalism in Latin America.* University of New Mexico Press, Albuquerque.

Olney, R. (1895) "Memorandum to Thomas F. Bayard, 20 July 1895." In *The Foreign Relations of the United States,* 1895, Vol. 1, pp. 542–76.

Palmer, S. (1998) "Central American Encounters with Rockefeller Public Health, 1914–1921." In G. M. Joseph, et al. (eds.), *Close Encounters of Empire: Writing the Cultural History of U.S.–Latin American Relations.* Duke University Press, Durham, pp. 311–32.

Pérez, Jr., L. A. (1983) *Cuba between Empires, 1878–1902.* University of Pittsburgh Press, Pittsburgh.

Pérez, Jr., L. A. (1998) *The War of 1898: The United States and Cuba in History and Historiography.* University of North Carolina Press, Chapel Hill.

Pérez, Jr., L. A. (1999) *On Becoming Cuban: Identity, Nationality, and Culture.* HarperCollins, New York.

Perkins, D. (1927) *The Monroe Doctrine, 1823–1826.* Harvard University Press, Cambridge, MA.

Perkins, D. (1937) *The Monroe Doctrine, 1867–1907.* The Johns Hopkins University Press, Baltimore.

Perkins, D. (1963) *A History of the Monroe Doctrine.* Little, Brown, and Co., Boston.

Plummer, B. G. (1988) *Haiti and the Great Powers, 1902–1915.* Louisiana State University Press, Baton Rouge.

Plummer, B. G. (1992) *Haiti and the United States: The Psychological Moment.* University of Georgia Press, Athens.

Poyo, G. E. (1989) *"With All, and for the Good of All": The Emergence of Popular Nationalism in the Cuban Communities of The United States, 1848–1898.* Duke University Press, Durham.

Renda, M. A. (2001a) *Taking Haiti: Military Occupation and the Culture of U.S. Imperialism, 1915–1940.* University of North Carolina Press, Chapel Hill.

Renda, M. A. (2001b) "Sentiments of a Private Nature," *Journal of American History,* December, pp. 882–7.

Robertson, W. S. (1920) "Hispanic-American Appreciations of the Monroe Doctrine," *Hispanic American Historical Review,* 3:1 (February), pp. 1–16.

Roorda, E. P. (1998) *The Dictator Next Door: The Good Neighbor Policy and the Trujillo Regime in the Dominican Republic, 1930–1945*. Duke University Press, Durham.

Roseberry, W. et al. (eds.) (1995) *Coffee, Society, and Power in Latin America*. Johns Hopkins University Press, Baltimore.

Rosenberg, E. S. (1982) *Spreading the American Dream: Economic and Cultural Expansion, 1890–1945*. Hill and Wang, New York.

Rosenberg, E. S. (2003) *Financial Missionaries to the World: The Politics and Culture of Dollar Diplomacy, 1900–1930*. Duke University Press, Durham.

Salisbury, R. V. (1989) *Anti-imperialism and International Competition in Central America, 1920–1929*. Scholarly Resources, Wilmington, DE.

Schmidt, H. (1987) *Maverick Marine: General Smedley D. Butler and the Contradictions of American Military History*. University Press of Kentucky, Lexington.

Schoultz, L. (1998) *Beneath the United States: A History of U.S. Policy toward Latin America*. Harvard University Press, Cambridge, MA.

Schroeder, M. J. (1998) "The Sandino Rebellion Revisited: Civil War, Imperialism, Popular Nationalism, and State Formation Muddied Up Together in the Segovias of Nicaragua, 1926–1934." In G. M. Joseph, et al. (eds.), *Close Encounters of Empire: Writing the Cultural History of U.S.–Latin American Relations*. Duke University Press, Durham, pp. 208–68.

Scott, R. J. (2000) "Fault Lines, Color Lines, Party Lines: Race, Labor, and Collective Action in Louisiana and Cuba, 1862–1912." In F. Cooper, et al., *Beyond Slavery: Explorations of Race, Labor, and Citizenship in Postemancipation Societies*. University of North Carolina Press, Chapel Hill, pp. 61–106.

Shipman, C. (1993) *It Had to Be Revolution*. Cornell University Press, Ithaca, NY.

Smith, P. (1996) *Talons of the Eagle: Dynamics of U.S.–Latin American Relations*. Oxford University Press, New York.

Soluri, J. (2003) "Banana Cultures: Linking the Production and Consumption of Export Bananas, 1800–1980." In S. Striffler & M. Moberg (eds.), *Banana Wars: Power, Production, and History in the Americas*. Duke University Press, Durham, pp. 48–79.

Spenser, D. (1999) *The Impossible Triangle: Mexico, Soviet Russia, and the United States in the 1920s*. Duke University Press, Durham.

Stephens, M. A. (2005) *Black Empire: The Masculine Global Imaginary of Caribbean Intellectuals in the United States, 1914–1962*. Duke University Press, Durham.

Striffler, S. & Moberg, M. (eds.) (2003) *Banana Wars: Power, Production, and History in the Americas*. Duke University Press, Durham.

Trouillot, M.-R. (1990) *Haiti: State Against Nation: The Origins and Legacy of Duvalierism*. Monthly Review Press, New York.

Chapter Nineteen

THE MEXICAN REVOLUTION

Adrian A. Bantjes

Though declared dead on at least three occasions, the memory of the Mexican Revolution, the first great social revolution in Latin American history, continues to exert a fundamental influence on Mexican society (Ross 1966; Meyer 1992; Barrón 2002). Even after the political system that emerged from the revolution finally collapsed in 2000, President Vicente Fox still sought to bolster the legitimacy of Mexico's first post-revolutionary, democratically elected government by identifying it as heir to the revolutionary movement of Francisco I. Madero. Of course, Fox did so in a highly selective fashion, ignoring or disavowing most revolutionary currents. Such selective borrowing is nothing new. The revolution never was a unified movement, despite officialist assertions to the contrary, and its meaning has always been contested. Likewise, though authoritative academic interpretations abound – officialist, Marxist, social, political, revisionist, post-revisionist, culturalist, or otherwise – they fail to find common ground. Making sense of the revolution remains a daunting task. In this essay, I offer a narrative of the revolutionary process as well as analysis of causation and outcome, while focusing on classic social interpretations and alternative political readings. I conclude that although recent scholarship has altered our understanding of the revolution in important aspects, a social reading remains the most compelling approach to this complex historical process.

The Problem of Causation

In 1910, a range of factors combined to spark a massive, highly heterogeneous revolutionary movement, a movement that barely unified long enough to topple longtime dictator General Porfirio Díaz (1876–1911) before disintegrating into internecine warfare. This does not mean that the revolution was no revolution at all, nothing more than a Hobbesian free-for-all, with power and wealth as spoils. Such a cynical perspective fails to explain the motivations that inspired revolutionaries to strive toward a new society. However chaotic and contradictory the process may have been, revolutionary actors pursued clearly articulated aims, though they frequently lost sight of these in the heat of battle.

Historical interpretations locate the roots of the revolution in the social and political conditions that prevailed during the Porfirian era. After Mexico achieved independence in 1821, political instability, foreign intervention, and economic stagnation plagued the young republic until Díaz, the liberal military hero, came to power in 1876. Fueled by foreign investment, Díaz's modernization project sparked a boom in commercial agriculture, mining, and industry, but also caused rapid, unbalanced demographic expansion, urbanization, internal migration, and, most detrimentally, large-scale alienation of communal landholdings. While growth initially benefited broad sectors of society, the peasantry, which made up the majority of the population, lost much of its land due to the acceleration of liberal disentailment, i.e., the privatization of communal village lands or *ejidos*. An increasingly autocratic president and a small coterie of elite officials, entrepreneurs, and intellectuals, the *científicos*, centralized power, trampling on states' rights and local autonomy. Thus, far from generating balanced development, Díaz's agenda of "Order and Progress" created profound tensions that would explode in 1910.

Distinct schools of thought have identified either social or political factors as paramount causes of the revolution. The agrarian school, pioneered by Frank Tannenbaum (1933) and forcefully revived by historian Alan Knight, argues that the revolution was a "fully fledged social revolution," based on a "genuinely . . . popular and agrarian movement. . . . The key to the social revolution lies in the countryside" (Knight 1986a: ix, 78). As commercial haciendas and railroads expanded, village-based peasants, tenants, and peons endured a massive loss of land, higher contributions, proletarianization, and declining living standards. Liberal disentailment and the surveying of "vacant" lands were the main tools for peasant dispossession. While disentailment became national policy with the passing of the Lerdo Law in 1856, legislation was not implemented on a national scale until the Porfiriato (Escobar Ohmstede 2001: 179–81). Knight (1986a: 95) argues that, "the 1880s and 1890s . . . witnessed a land-grab of unprecedented proportions." Demographic growth exacerbated the problem, as Mexico's population expanded from 9.6 million in 1877 to 15.1 in 1910 (Hernández Chávez 1993: 128–9).

Dramatic examples of land alienation and agrarian conflict can be found in many regions, notably the sugar-producing state of Morelos, the mountain communities of Chihuahua, and the Laguna region. In his classic, *Zapata and the Mexican Revolution*, John Womack portrayed rural Morelos as "the perfect plantation," a land where expanding haciendas devoured entire villages, expelled tenants, and forced indebted *campesinos* to hire themselves out as estate workers. These "country people . . . did not want to move and therefore got into a revolution" (Womack 1968: ix, 43–7, 50, 54). Captained by Emiliano Zapata, the *presidente municipal* of the town of Anenecuilco, the campesinos of Morelos launched the most tenacious of all revolutionary movements.

Chihuahua, another key revolutionary *foco*, experienced a similar conflict. By the 1880s, public lands used by communities for grazing were surveyed by private companies, fenced in, and often sold or traded to large cattle haciendas owned by the Porfirian elite or foreign companies, while traditional grazing rights on haciendas were abruptly abolished, adversely affecting villagers and smallholders, who now faced deprivation and proletarianization (Katz 1998: 11–56, 794).

While the agrarian interpretation retains much of its persuasive power, it may be in need of revision. Our understanding of the agrarian history of Porfirian Mexico remains sketchy, and recent research should at least caution us not to extrapolate from a limited number of cases. The nineteenth-century agrarian transition was devil-ishly complex. In fact, Porfirian Mexico sustained a "range of agrarian rationalities" that belies generalization (Hernández Chávez 1993: 125). Disentailment actually started haltingly in some states not long after independence. In some cases, commu-nities were initially able to use disentailment to their advantage. The subdivision of communal lands in the form of *condueñazgos*, private agricultural associations consist-ing of shareholders with usufruct rights but no individual title, at first functioned as a defense mechanism for the reproduction of village-based social relations before succumbing to alienation through sales to outsiders and concentration after 1894 (Escobar Ohmstede 2001: 183–6, 192; Haber et al. 2003: 294). Frequently, internal village dynamics, not external pressures, drove disentailment. Far from considering privatization an alien concept that clashed with community solidarity, to be resisted at all costs, in some cases (e.g., the Papantla region) villages embraced disentailment and the transformation of communal lands into condueñazgos. However, by the 1890s, village notables of Papantla succeeded in privatizing the condueñazgos after bitter internal conflicts. Thus, many regions witnessed a dramatic reconfiguration of land tenure and social diversification that highlighted the crucial role of an aggressive rural middle class (Kourí 2004: 158, 280).

Even in Morelos hacienda encroachment on communal lands may not have been the main cause of revolutionary unrest. Horacio Crespo (2000: 71–2) argues that land concentration by sugar haciendas pre-dated the Porfiriato, and that disentailment focused on establishing title to lands already held by peasant families within a com-munal context, not on transferring communal lands to the haciendas. In northern and eastern Morelos, and in neighboring Zapatista regions of Tlaxcala, México state, Puebla, Guerrero, and Oaxaca, land tenure patterns varied, and tenants and small-holders featured as prominent actors while the hacienda was less prevalent. Thus, the social makeup of the Zapatista movement was much more diverse than its *campesino* base, and included peons, sharecroppers and renters, smallholders, artisans, workers, and middle-class elements. The tenantry, in particular, which lost access to land on a massive scale during the Porfiriato, likely played a key role in rural resistance (Avila Espinosa 2000: 33–4, 38, 42–3; Hart 2005: 196, 216, 266–7).

A conclusion that disentailment was more complex, the hacienda less dominant, and rural society more diverse than previously thought hardly invalidates an agrarian interpretation; it merely shifts the burden from the large estate to a range of actors. Even in regions where disentailment was the product of internal pressures, the process was still caused by the commercialization of agriculture. A widespread, messy, at times violent disentailment process, driven by both external and internal factors, combined with the Porfirian boom in commercial agriculture to alter land tenure patterns pro-foundly by the eve of the revolution.

While rural tensions were a key contributing factor to rising unrest, industrial workers and urban artisans also voiced their grievances, though few would argue that they spearheaded a proletarian revolution (Hart 1987: 52). Workers were largely influenced by liberalism and sought reform, not revolution (Knight 1986a: 127–50). The diverse working class of Mexico City, for example, addressed a rapidly deteriorat-ing situation (poor working conditions, declining wages, squalid tenement housing, high rents, the repression of workers' associations, and foreign control of industry) through mutualist societies and nascent unions. Yet despite outbursts of unrest in the streets of the capital, Mexico City workers failed to play a prominent role in the revolution of 1910–11 (Lear 2001: 123–42). There is more evidence of militancy and revolutionary participation among industrial workers in the mining, textile, and railroad sectors. The influence of the anarchist *Partido Liberal Mexicano* (PLM) was significant in some locations, especially the northern mining zones, though elsewhere it succumbed to repression. The strikes that erupted in 1906–7, notably at the Cananea copper mine in Sonora and the textile mills of Río Blanco, demanded wage hikes, labor reform, and union rights, but cannot be considered revolutionary precursor movements (Anderson 1976). However, the brutal suppression and massacre of striking workers contributed mightily to the radicalization of labor and provoked nationwide condemnation. Miners later joined the ranks of the northern revolutionaries, and textile workers staged attacks on federal forces. More importantly, labor later established a radical partnership with the revolutionary state, and struggled for improved working conditions and the nationalization of the railways and the mineral and petroleum industries during the 1920s and 1930s. Workers' actions on the eve of the revolution prefigured the radical reshaping of post-revolutionary labor relations (Gonzales 1994; Gonzales 1996; Anderson 1997: 681–6; Katz 1998: 43–4, 212).

Political analysts have recently attempted to downplay or even completely replace the social interpretation with an essentially political reading. François-Xavier Guerra (1986: vol. 2, 307–12), for example, depicted the revolution as the result of a breakdown of "traditional" organic politics in the face of liberal modernization. As the Díaz regime became increasingly authoritarian, paternalistic links with a range of traditional actors broke down, generating rising opposition.

Recent research indicates that nineteenth-century Mexican political culture may have been more "modern" and broad-based than previously thought. As Peter Guardino (2005: 1) argues, "[b]y the 1850s, society and state were idealized through images of popular sovereignty and republican citizenship. . . . [T]he cultural transformation of politics did not affect only elites. Spanish America's impoverished majorities also experienced and participated in the dramatic revolution in political culture." Nineteenth-century Mexican politics was not just the realm of a small minority, nor was popular political culture entirely dominated by "traditional" loyalties and praxis.

Alicia Hernández Chávez (1993: 9–14) takes this line of thought to extremes by depicting the revolution as just another episode in a long-term, almost teleological, cross-class struggle to forge a liberal, democratic republic. She argues that modern Mexican politics emerged in response to the Spanish liberal Constitution of 1812 and had begun to mature during the liberal Reform and the Restored Republic (1855–76), but was dismantled during the Porfiriato, sparking a broad-based revolutionary effort to restore constitutional rights. Liberal ideals (personal freedoms, popular sovereignty, constitutionalism, federalism, municipal autonomy) and practices (elections and patriotic civic ritual) held meaning for many Mexicans. Both rural and urban lower classes, including indigenous groups, mobilized enthusiastically for electoral contests, defended citizenship rights, served in the National Guard, and contributed to military victories, notably the glorious defeat of the French at Puebla in 1862. By mid-century, many states had witnessed a "significant political *apertura*" based on direct suffrage for governorships, state legislatures, and municipal councils (Hernández Chávez 1993: 86–90; Guardino 2003: 248–71). Thus, new concepts of citizenship had taken root in the popular imagination, generating at least a "democratic fiction" that inspired popular sectors to mobilize in defense of perceived rights.

Political interpretations contend that, far from resulting from social pressures, the revolution was caused by the eruption of a range of dissident political movements that shared the conviction that Díaz and the Porfirian elite had broken a perceived compact with the citizenry, whether a paternalistic alliance with "traditional" sectors or one based on modern notions of citizenship. The 1880s and 1890s marked a shift in the nation's political culture. The ties that Díaz, on coming to power in 1876, had established with a range of political actors, including popular sectors, began to erode. Díaz's authoritarian regime infringed on established rights guaranteed by the liberal Constitution of 1857, which provided for federalism, municipal autonomy, individual freedoms, free elections, and the separation of powers. Díaz reinstated indirect elections for governors and state legislatures in most states. Governors, *jefes políticos* (district heads), and mayors increasingly served as appointees of the president and the oligarchy. Porfirian politics corrupted electoral colleges and rendered Congress powerless. Díaz abolished the National Guard, a source of civic pride for an "armed citizenry" nostalgic for the glories of Mexico's struggle against the French. The gap between Porfirian political reality and this shared liberal republicanism became ever more glaring. The bonds between elite and people, whether "traditional" or "modern," were sundered, society was depoliticized, and a marked "oligarchization" took place. Yet liberal political culture persisted as an ideal to be rekindled. In response to authoritarian rule, the revolution sought a restoration of popular sovereignty and constitutional rights and the creation of a truly democratic regime.

Anti-Díaz political leadership has traditionally been associated with the ascendant middle class. Middle-class Jacobins and liberal constitutionalists loathed the exclusive, positivist *científicos*. Across the country, they established cross-class liberal clubs that decried church–state détente, and sought to restore the neglected 1857 Constitution and establish a democratic, secular (anti-clerical), liberal republic (Knight 1986a: 43–5, 63–4). A small anarcho-syndicalist branch headed by Ricardo Flores Magón split off from the liberal constitutionalists, radicalized the PLM, and developed an agenda for direct action and revolution that was widely disseminated. Catholic social reformers and Protestant dissidents added their voice to the generalized call for change.

However, the anti-Díaz movement had a much broader base than the middle class. Artisans, workers, and rural folk all employed the discourse of liberalism to attack the sclerotic Díaz administration. Even marginalized regional elites, the victims of Porfirian centralization and crony capitalism, became increasingly hostile to the regime and, in some cases, the foreign interests allied to it. Anti-foreign sentiment was widespread and deeply rooted among broad segments of the population (Hart 1987: 352; 2002: 271–304; Katz 1998: 43; Haber et al. 2003: 52). As conditions deteriorated, marginalized elites felt emboldened to attack the entrenched positions of state and local authorities.

Liberal discourse certainly held meaning for the popular movements. Zapatismo, for example, did not focus exclusively on the land conflict. Actually, a degree of social stability prevailed in the countryside of Morelos well into the Porfiriato, until overproduction finally caused the sugar economy to decline after 1903. Politics also featured prominently on the Zapatista agenda. The 1909 gubernatorial elections, in which a popular candidate was eliminated by a Porfirian outsider, represented a last-ditch effort to retain a semblance of popular representation. Steeped in traditional liberal discourse that evoked the memory of Benito Juárez, the Constitution of 1857, and the heroic struggle against the French, the inhabitants of Morelos demanded municipal autonomy, citizenship rights, and democracy. Zapata himself stemmed from a rural middle-class family with strong liberal credentials. In addition, unfair taxation featured as a bone of contention. The 1909 Revaluation Law placed drastic new tax burdens on the rural middle class while decreasing rates on large haciendas (Womack 1968: 53; Brunk 1995: 8–11, 66–7; Avila Espinosa 2000: 34; Crespo 2000: 85; Hart 2005: 151, 181, 190, 192).

Likewise, Chihuahuans lost control of local governance as previously elected jefes políticos and mayors became appointed officials. Village notables were ousted, and their economic resources usurped by outsiders and foreigners. This shattered the illusion of democracy that had survived in Chihuahua well into the Porfiriato. The economic crisis of 1907–8 caused rising resentment among the working class, especially mineworkers, who proved receptive to anarchist proselytizing. Here too, the middle class was targeted for dramatic tax increases, while hacendados remained exempt. Taken together, mass peasant dispossession, political closure, and economic crisis united Chihuahuans in opposition to the hated Díaz regime. Once proud of the prominent role they had played in the struggle against the Apaches and as liberal militias, Chihuahuan villagers now felt abandoned and betrayed (Katz 1998: 17–44, 48–50, 797–8). As Friedrich Katz (1998: 32) demonstrates, social and political grievances were closely interrelated: "[i]n the years between 1884 and 1910, the state's free villages lost most of their lands and their traditional rights and suffered an attack upon their sense of dignity, which was based on their economic independence and freedom from outside interference."

Political interpretations have the merit of stressing continuities between nineteenth-century liberalism and the revolution. However, the "modernity" of popular politics should not be exaggerated, while the prevalence and praxis of a liberal political culture, especially among popular sectors, is still poorly documented. Guardino (2005: 18) cautions that "[p]opular political culture in the middle of the century did not fulfill the 'modern' expectations of liberal politicians . . ." Instead, popular politics displayed a high degree of syncretism. Peasants and plebeians used an array of traditional and novel political discourses and practices, ranging from *caciquismo* to popular liberalism, in defense of land and autonomy. As Knight (2005: 48) reminds us, "Mexico has lived with an 'articulation of modes of politics' as contrasting political ideologies and procedures have coexisted in a loose, shifting ensemble . . ."

Threatened municipalities and pueblos became the locus of resistance and mobilized in defense of constitutional rights, effective suffrage, land rights, fair taxation, and local "patrimony," bridging the interests of local elites, the middle classes, and peasants and workers (Hernández Chavez 1993: 91, 97, 109–11). Liberalism provided a shared discursive framework that rural and urban communities used to address political closure and mounting social tensions. As the economy slipped into a recession in 1907–8, causing falling wages and rising unemployment, mounting discontent with an hermetic, aging elite exploded into widespread opposition. Social grievances intertwined with demands for the restoration of political rights, thus explaining the widespread appeal of Madero's call for local and national democracy.

The Madero Revolution, 1911–13

By 1909, Díaz had destroyed what remained of Mexico's liberal, republican political culture. Yet, to everyone's surprise, he publicly declared that the presidential election of 1910 would be free and democratic – a novelty, given that Díaz, who would turn 80 in 1910, had been "reelected" seven times, perpetuating his dictatorship for 34 years. The elite divided between *científicos*, who favored a Díaz–Ramón Corral ticket, and *reyistas*, supporters of populist General Bernardo Reyes, who attracted an expansive cross-class following. After Díaz eliminated Reyes's candidacy, opposition congealed around Francisco Madero, a wealthy Coahuilan landowner, who called for "effective suffrage" and "no reelection," i.e., the establishment of a classic liberal democracy.

Taking advantage of the nationwide network of liberal clubs, Madero launched his campaign in 1910 under the Anti-Reelectionist banner. His powerful political message offered hope for all Mexicans, not just the middle class, though it lacked a concrete agenda for social reform. The textile workers of Veracruz, Tlaxcala, Mexico City, and Puebla overwhelmingly backed Madero's candidacy, and in Mexico City Maderista workers rallied en masse during the chaotic days before Díaz's resignation (Lear 2001: 123–42). Even in rural Morelos, where Anti-Reelectionist organizations were weak, Madero's crusade galvanized the population (Womack 1968: 57–8). Mounting opposition reflected the frustration and hopes of a diverse, tenuous coalition of Mexicans desirous of change.

Predictably, Díaz won the fraudulent contest and jailed Madero, who fled to the United States and from there exhorted his fellow Mexicans to rise up against the illegitimate regime. While urban areas remained quiescent, largely autonomous popular movements responded by staging localized uprisings in the countryside, especially in northern and central Mexico, but also in the Gulf region (Portilla 1995). In Chihuahua, Pascual Orozco headed a rebellion that spread into the Laguna and beyond. In Morelos and adjacent regions, the Zapatista rebellion, only loosely allied to Maderismo, sought to settle long-standing local agrarian and political conflicts. The stunning success of these revolts rapidly undermined Díaz's credibility and brought about his resignation on May 25, 1911.

Madero won the nation's first democratic elections by a landslide and was triumphantly inaugurated as president in 1911. Yet the euphoria was ephemeral, and his heterogeneous coalition rapidly disintegrated. Madero's vacillating administration focused on establishing a democracy but failed to tackle Mexico's profound social problems, alienating allies in Chihuahua, Morelos, and elsewhere. Conservatives and Catholics gridlocked Congress, elements of the *ancien régime* conspired, President Taft in the USA grew disenchanted, and rebellions broke out across the country. In his *Plan de Ayala* of 1911, which would become an enduring manifesto of peasant politics and laid the foundation for future agrarian reform, Zapata denounced Madero as a tyrant who had betrayed the revolution and called for the restoration of pueblo lands, the redistribution with indemnization of one-third of all hacienda lands, the confiscation of enemy properties, the restoration of state sovereignty, and federal elections. "Mexican people, support this plan with arms in hand and you will make the prosperity and well-being of the fatherland" (full text in Womack 1968: 400–4). Madero's doomed presidency ended in tragedy in 1913, when counterrevolutionary forces, allied with his traitorous military advisor General Victoriano Huerta, staged a coup that cost him his life.

Counterrevolution and Civil War, 1913–15

Huerta established a counterrevolutionary government (1913–14) that sought to restore the old regime. However, Madero's death and the violent suppression of the liberal democratic project sparked a series of regional uprisings. In the north, the Coahuila-based Constitutionalist movement, headed by *primer jefe* Venustiano Carranza, a wealthy landowner, represented the ideals of Maderista liberal constitutionalists. Carranza was joined by Sonoran militias captained by Alvaro Obregón, a politically astute farmer and military genius. In response to the breakdown of the federal pact between the states and the central government, the Constitutionalists reclaimed state sovereignty in anticipation of the restoration of a legitimate national government (Hernández Chavez 1993: 175).

The popular movements in Chihuahua and Morelos continued their struggle. Loosely allied to Constitutionalism, Francisco "Pancho" Villa, a poor and uneducated but brilliant and charismatic rebel leader, organized the *División del Norte*, a powerful army that consisted of a heterogeneous following of villagers, smallholders, peons, ranchers, miners, cowboys, and middle-class elements. In Morelos and neighboring states, Zapata's guerrillas fought a brutal war against the federal army.

As fighting spread throughout Mexico, US President Woodrow Wilson compounded Huerta's problems by rejecting his government and ordering Marines to occupy the port of Veracruz. When federal forces proved unable to stop the rebel offensive, Huerta's position became untenable, and he resigned in the summer of 1914.

Yet Mexico would see no peace. With Huerta eliminated, the revolutionary factions turned against each other. The Villistas and Zapatistas established a short-lived alliance against the Constitutionalists and briefly occupied Mexico City. In Morelos, Zapata initiated a land reform program that involved the surveying, redistribution, and titling of hacienda lands. Inspired by "the utopia of a free association of rural clans," Zapata's followers established "democratic municipalities, country neighborhoods where every family had influence in the disposition of local resources" (Womack 1968: 224, 228–41). In Chihuahua, Villa expelled the oligarchy, established a state government, and managed confiscated enemy ranches to finance arms procurements and a welfare program providing the poor, especially veterans' widows and orphans, with subsidized food, free health care, and education. Though he contemplated a future division of hacienda lands and the establishment of military colonies for veterans, his dreams were never realized. Nor did Villa establish anything akin to liberal democracy. As Katz (1998: 429–30) affirms, "Villista society was not democratic. There were no elections, the press did not criticize the government, and criticism of Villa was unheard of." Instead, Villa's charismatic *caudillo* rule prevailed.

The Villista and Zapatista movements were, however, doomed. After an all too brief honeymoon, during which it considered Villa a serious contender for national leadership, the United States abandoned him and threw its weight behind the more reliable Constitutionalists. Obregón's machine-gun emplacements cut down Villa's cavalry during the spring of 1915, annihilating the famed Division of the North. In an attempt to embarrass Carranza and damage his relationship with the Wilson administration, in 1916 Villista *guerrilleros* launched a cross-border attack on Columbus, New Mexico, provoking a futile US punitive expedition. In Morelos, stubborn resistance continued until 1919, when Zapata fell victim to a Constitutionalist assassination plot at the Hacienda de Chinameca. Government agents gunned down Villa in 1923 (Katz 1998: 780–2). After their deaths, both Zapata and Villa were exalted as icons of popular resistance.

It has been argued that the popular revolutionary movements were incapable of establishing a stable, reformist national government due to their parochial, personalist nature. Knight (1986b: 29, 301, 526) contends that without effective external advisors Villismo would have produced a "faitnéant Mexico City regime weakly presiding over dozens of local, largely independent fiefs. . . . The same was a fortiori true of Zapata and many other popular leaders. . . . [P]olicies of reconstruction, demilitarization, centralization, state-building, bureaucratization and mass political mobilization would all run into the brick walls of entrenched *caudillaje.* . . ."

Others offer a more sanguine assessment of the popular movements' administrative capabilities. Villa's biographer reasons that if a Villista–Zapatista coalition had triumphed, land reform along Zapatista lines would have been implemented throughout Mexico, including Chihuahua. A more egalitarian society would have emerged, based on Zapatista organic village democracy, which was compatible with the northern frontier tradition. Ultimately, the eternal threat of the Colossus of the North would have forced Villistas and Zapatistas to embrace a stronger, centralized government (Katz 1998: 814–16).

Likewise, students of Zapatismo argue that the movement was not doomed by its peasant makeup and remind us that the Zapatistas developed plans for national administrative reform, including municipal autonomy, a unicameral Congress, an independent judiciary, and free elections. They established an effective administration in Morelos and neighboring states, and during 1914–15 in Mexico City, where they collaborated closely with labor and anarchist intellectuals to outline an agenda for social reform (Womack 1968: 215; Brunk 1995: 235; Avila Espinosa 2000: 38–9). This coherent Zapatista project was capable of "articulating in a typical liberal-democratic fashion social and political rights" (Hernández Chavez 1993: 186–7).

Though not devoid of merit, this argument has its limitations, certainly in the case of Villismo. Villa made no attempt to forge a liberal democracy, relying instead on personalism, militarism, and patronage. Even the Constitution of 1857 seems to have meant little to Villa and his generals. When Villa asked him what he thought of the document, one of his generals replied: "I know very little about constitutions, but since Carranza abolished the Constitution of 1857, it means that it must be good" (Katz 1998: 700).

Be this as it may, both movements proved incapable of withstanding the Constitutionalist *military* onslaught. The battered remnants of Villa's forces retreated to the mountains of Chihuahua, while the death of Zapata orphaned a weakened and compromised peasant movement. Whether Villa and Zapata were capable of creating a new, more egalitarian Mexico is, ultimately, a moot point.

The Triumph of Constitutionalism, 1915–20

By the fall of 1915, the Constitutionalists had gained the upper hand. Carranza's warlords established power bases throughout Mexico by forging alliances with business groups, peasant leagues, and unions. They now controlled regional economies and transport systems, manipulated local politics, and initiated reform. Tax revenues poured in from occupied customs offices and railways, and the economy rebounded markedly (Haber et al. 2003: 345–7). Carranza, recognized by the United States in 1915 and elected president in 1917, began to reconstruct Mexico's government and finances, which had virtually ceased to exist, in the process laying the foundations for future statism.

However, unlike some of his fellow Constitutionalists in the provinces, Carranza was reluctant to implement sweeping social reform. True, he enacted legislation to restore illegally alienated pueblo lands, abolish debt peonage and company stores, provide tax relief, and initiate labor reform. Foreign oil companies and the US government were outraged when Carranza, a fervent economic nationalist, attempted to tax their landholdings retroactively (Hernández Chavez 1993: 188–9, 197). But he responded to increased social demands too late and with too little. The actual acreage the state granted peasant villages was minimal, and to mollify the elite Carranza reinstated lands confiscated from "enemy" landowners.

Carranza's administration soon confronted rising popular impatience with the disastrous social effects of civil war and economic dislocation. The anarcho-syndicalist *Casa del Obrero Mundial*, established in 1912, staged a wave of successful strikes, collaborated with the Zapatistas, and contributed Red Battalions to the Constitutionalist cause. Cities such as Veracruz, Mexico City, Puebla, and Mérida produced militant labor and renters' movements (Lear 2001: 355–8; Wood 2001: 24–33). Elsewhere, however, cross-class urban movements were primarily inspired by pre-revolutionary liberal notions of citizenship and municipal freedom, and sought to further the goal of urban modernization (Jiménez 2004). Carranza only tolerated workers' mobilization up to a point. He dissolved the Casa and suppressed labor mobilization in 1916. A more pliant organization, the *Confederación Regional Obrera de México* (CROM), assumed supremacy soon after its establishment in 1918.

Carranza's main achievement was the revolutionary Constitution of 1917, which, drafted by a convention at Querétaro, became the legal foundation of modern Mexico. While Carranza was concerned with adapting the hallowed Constitution of 1857 to new circumstances, younger delegates pushed through a radical blueprint for social reform. Mexico's new Magna Carta provided for national control of subsoil wealth and the expropriation and redistribution of private property, especially hacienda lands (Art. 27); a labor code addressing minimum wages, working conditions, the eight-hour work day, labor contracts, debt peonage, the right to unionize and strike, and female and child labor (Art. 123); the regulation of religious worship, and the elimination of clerical influence in education and politics (Arts. 3 and 130).

Finally, in 1920, disenchanted followers of General Obregón, as well as defeated Zapatistas and Villistas, and labor and peasant organizations (CROM), backed a brief rebellion that toppled Carranza's government, claimed his life, and brought to power Obregón's popular, progressive coalition.

The Sonoran Regimes, 1920–34

Sonoran revolutionaries dominated government from 1920 to 1934, under Presidents Obregón (1920–4) and Plutarco Elías Calles (1924–8), as well as a succession of presidential figureheads during the so-called *Maximato* (1928–34), when Calles ran the country from behind the scenes as *Jefe máximo*. The Sonorans forged a revolutionary state, garnered institutionalized support from peasants and workers, rebuilt a shattered economy, and launched a veritable cultural revolution.

In 1929, in an effort to avert continued factional violence in the wake of Obregón's assassination at the hands of a Catholic militant, Calles created a loose party structure that unified as a "revolutionary family" the quarrelsome generals, peasant leaders, union bosses, and regional *políticos*. The *Partido Nacional Revolucionario* (PNR) was the forerunner of the *Partido Revolucionario Institucional* (PRI), which would dominate Mexican politics until 2000. However, Madero's democratic ideals were forgotten as the pragmatic Sonorans struggled to achieve political consolidation.

The contours of a future corporatist arrangement became evident when Obregón established a close association with CROM and its political arm, the *Partido Laborista Mexicano*. In return for CROM's pledge to unify and control Mexico's workers, government offered labor enhanced wages and working conditions, recognition of the right to strike, sympathetic arbitration, and representation in Congress and government (CROM leader Luis Morones became Labor Minister). This mutually beneficial relationship lasted until 1928 and set an important precedent for state–labor relations. Likewise, limited land reform – Obregón and Calles distributed over four million hectares – served to reward peasant revolutionaries, the Zapatistas in particular, and the burgeoning regional peasant leagues, which established a *Partido Nacional Agrarista*, but also provided government a tool with which to mobilize land reform petitioners and beneficiaries (*agraristas* and *ejidatarios*) in armed and electoral support of the regime (Wilkie 1967: 188).

However, the northern revolutionaries envisaged an economic future that would rely heavily on the contributions of commercial agriculture and were loath to dismantle the haciendas. In 1929, the government went so far as to halt land distribution temporarily. In an impressive attempt to rebuild and modernize a tattered economy and confront the disastrous effects of global depression, Calles launched infrastructural projects, established a Central Bank, and developed a network of agricultural banks. Despite US opposition to Mexico's continued efforts to enhance national control of the foreign-owned petroleum and minerals industries, which provided the bulk of the nation's tax income, Obregón's administration received US recognition in 1923 after lengthy negotiations on the foreign debt and the indemnization of US citizens. The prolonged conflict with the United States over subsoil rights temporarily subsided in 1927–8 when Mexico pledged not to retroactively require confirmatory government concessions (Smith 1972: 231–57).

To establish a new nation, Mexico also required a cultural revolution. Rationalist rural education, revolutionary art, anti-clerical and anti-religious campaigns, Indian assimilation, and moralization drives all served to refashion an "ignorant," "superstitious," often indigenous peasantry and forge a patriotic, modern, secular, productive, and moral culture for all Mexicans (Knight 1994a). The Muralist Movement, represented by artists such as Diego Rivera, José Clemente Orozco, and David Alfaro Siqueiros, sought to develop a new, popular, truly Mexican art. Government created an anthropological establishment to Mexicanize the indigenous population. However, despite the fact that women had taken advantage of societal openings presented by the revolution, whether as *soldaderas*, members of popular associations, or feminist organizers, there was no concerted effort to experiment with new gender roles or shape a New Mexican Woman. Women would not receive the vote until 1953.

Many revolutionaries considered the Catholic Church and popular religion obstacles on the path to modernity. Taking up the old liberal theme of anti-clericalism, Calles cracked down on the clergy and Catholics by enforcing constitutional articles calling for secular education, the disentailment of what remained of church property, the enforcement of state limitations on the clergy, and the regulation of worship. This provoked the suspension of services in 1926 and the eruption of the Cristero revolt, a bloody Catholic rebellion that wracked much of central Mexico and ended in a military stalemate and a US-brokered *modus vivendi* in 1929. However, the conflict would fester until the late 1930s.

By 1934, the Sonorans had forged a new polity, subjugated the Church, and eliminated rival factions. Though the economy was still mired in a stubborn recession, the regime had drawn up a blueprint for future development. The revolutionaries had learned to acknowledge powerful non-revolutionary actors, notably the private sector, foreign bankers and investors, and the US government, and established an enduring property rights regime (Haber et al. 2003: 350). Yet social reform still lagged. It was only a matter of time before the revolution would veer to the left under the leadership of a new generation of progressive revolutionaries.

Cardenismo, 1934–40

In an attempt to perpetuate the *Maximato*, Calles chose as president yet another figurehead, General Lázaro Cárdenas (1934–40). But Cárdenas turned against his master and ended Sonoran hegemony by establishing a populist power base of progressive politicians and officers, workers and *agraristas*, and assorted anti-Callistas. He mobilized his newfound allies to enhance presidential powers, construct a corporatist state, and push through long overdue social reforms.

The Great Depression galvanized a disoriented labor movement. Renegade unions led by Vicente Lombardo Toledano and Fidel Velásquez seceded from CROM and in 1936 constituted what became Mexico's hegemonic, official labor confederation, the *Confederación de Trabajadores de México* (CTM). The CTM forged a dynamic alliance with the Cárdenas government, which intervened on its behalf in numerous labor conflicts, bestowing wage hikes, supportive arbitration, and experiments in workers' administration. Unions boldly pushed for workers' control of industry. In 1938, Cárdenas responded to labor unrest in the oil industry by nationalizing the

US and Anglo-Dutch companies and establishing a state monopoly, *Petróleos Mexicanos* (PEMEX), which became a symbol of economic nationalism.

Agrarian reform was the keystone of Cardenismo, both a means to achieve social justice and a tool for social engineering, economic development, and political control. The redistribution of 18 million hectares to 810,000 peasants changed the face of rural society by eliminating the Porfirian landed estate and creating an *ejido* sector that came to control half the nation's arable land, including prosperous agricultural zones such as the Yaqui Valley, the Laguna, and Yucatán (Wilkie 1967: 188, 194). The state assumed control of agro-industrial plants and agricultural banks.

The cultural revolution deepened. Cárdenas's "socialist education" sought to instill a modern, secular, collectivist, and patriotic ethos among peasants, Indians, and workers. This effort met strong, sometimes armed, Catholic resistance where, as was often the case, anti-clericalism and secularization were its objectives. Yet when respectful of local cultures, teachers were received with open arms and succeeded in radicalizing local politics and social relations (Vaughan 1997).

An acute financial crisis in 1937, caused by extravagant government expenditure, combined with renewed recession and labor unrest to spark rising opposition from foreign actors, industrialists, conservative revolutionaries, Catholics, the middle class, and neglected labor sectors. Social experimentation waned in anticipation of the contested 1940 presidential election (Schuler 1998). Cárdenas faced the challenge with the aid of a revamped, more durable political system, the corporatist *Partido de la Revolución Mexicana* (PRM). Founded in 1938, the party institutionalized the revolution by organizing into four party sectors the military, organized labor, the peasantry, and "popular organizations" (state workers, women's and youth groups, and small merchants). Cárdenas threw his weight behind the centrist official candidate, General Manuel Avila Camacho, who, with the aid of machine politics, repression, and "electoral alchemy," defeated a popular conservative independent. Avila Camacho's triumph demonstrated the effectiveness of the new machine politics, which endured for the rest of the century, but also augured the demise of revolutionary experimentation.

The Fruits of Revolution

The Mexican Revolution was a true social revolution that fundamentally transformed society and politics. Naturally, it did not appear *ex nihilo* and exhibited continuities with the liberal past. However, Maderista democratic ideals were ultimately abandoned in light of the day-to-day exigencies of Hobbesian strife, barely surviving at the rhetorical level or as the dream of isolated opposition politicians. Thus, a purely political interpretation would seem to offer at best only a partial explanation of the dynamics of revolution.

Instead, the new, civilian, social-authoritarian regime was highly centralized, presidentialist, and bureaucratized (Otero 2004). Tellingly, in 1946 the official party assumed the name *Partido de la Revolución Institucionalizada* (PRI). Yet the system still exhibited markedly "pre-modern" modes of informal politics, such as *caciquismo* and patrimonialism, which functioned well to link the central bureaucracy with the regions (Knight 2005).

Despite the defeat of Zapatismo and Villismo, the popular agenda produced profound, long-term societal change. Post-revolutionary leaders were obliged to maintain a populist style and discourse. In deference to its origins, the regime over the years strategically enacted agrarian reforms and provided favored labor sectors with significant benefits. The petroleum workers became a labor elite with close ties to the ruling party. Union bosses, in particular perpetual CTM leader Fidel Velásquez, who headed the confederation until his death in 1997 at the age of 97, remained influential. However, the corporatist system ultimately served to bind workers and peasants to the regime, repress independent mobilization, sometimes with brutal force, and create a pliant electorate for ritualistic sham elections.

The revolution opened up venues for social mobility. A revolutionary elite displaced the Porfirian oligarchy. However, despite the rise to power of peasants and proletarians during the armed revolution, it was in the end the middle class that prevailed in the new, bureaucratized polity. Though a new bourgeoisie absorbed revolutionary elements, it was largely the product of a fusion of old and new money, and political and economic elites never merged.

Mexico's development strategy changed as policy makers abandoned the export-led model based on minerals and commercial agriculture and focused on industrial development and modernization instead. Despite its statist proclivities, even the populist Cárdenas administration never seriously questioned the capitalist nature of Mexico's economy (Schuler 1998: 200). US investment grew rapidly after 1940, becoming essential for the nation's economic expansion.

The main socioeconomic transformation wrought by the revolution was the destruction of the old hacienda-based economy and its replacement by the large *ejidal* sector and private capitalist farms. Agrarian reform may have dramatically altered land tenure patterns; in the end it failed to improve the lot of Mexico's rural poor. By the end of the century, the *ejido*s were mostly bankrupt, and hundreds of thousands of *ejidatarios* had abandoned their plots for the cities or the United States. In 1992, government enacted legislation aimed at privatizing the moribund ejidal sector, thus acknowledging the dismal failure of revolutionary reform in the countryside.

The cultural revolution's impact was ambiguous. Education, civic ritual, and new institutions and practices (the party, unions, elections) forged a lasting sense of patriotism and spawned a flowering of national culture, establishing unity in a once fragmented society. However, the state was less successful in overcoming cultural inertia. Although it succeeded in relegating the Church to a subordinate position, Mexico remained devoutly Catholic. Popular and indigenous cultures remained rooted in tradition, though the state became quite adept at manipulating "tradition" for its own purposes. Structural factors (urbanization, migration, globalization) played an important role in changing Mexican culture (Knight 1994a: 441). The society that emerged from the ashes of the revolution, the product of both revolutionary reform and structural change, endured for the rest of the twentieth century.

Eternal Revolution: The Future of the Revolution

Mexico's first post-*priísta* administration, headed by President Vicente Fox, struggled to define its relationship with the revolution. While denouncing the authoritarianism and corruption of the old regime, it attempted to retain elements of the revolutionary mystique. Fox identified his administration with Madero, Mexico's signifier for liberal democracy. As Fox's Interior Minister, Santiago Creel, put it, Madero was "the man who initiated our revolutionary feats and established the political ideals of the modern Mexico of [the twenty-first] century." Madero features as a messianic figure, the herald of modernity, a man ahead of his times. His tragedy was to be "the hinge, the intermediate point between the barbarous Mexico that refused to die and the democratic Mexico that longed to live. . . . [A]ll of us who have been fighting for democracy since 1913 consider ourselves his heirs" (Creel Miranda 2005).

The Foxista interpretation crafted a powerful teleology that legitimized the democratic overthrow of the post-revolutionary regime as a return to Mexico's true, liberal, revolutionary roots. Fox's party, the centrist *Partido Acción Nacional* (PAN) could now claim a central role in that heroic legacy. It allowed Fox to co-opt discursively most anti-PRI movements as elements of a nationwide pro-democracy movement. In his acceptance speech before Congress, the president included in his pantheon of illustrious democrats Maderista intellectuals, Catholics, communist labor leaders, socialist intellectuals, conservative PANistas, and even the PRI's conveniently assassinated presidential candidate, Luis Donaldo Colosio (Fox Quesada 2000). Thus, Fox portrayed himself as a latter-day Madero who had led all Mexicans, irrespective of ideology, in the final battle for a truly democratic nation, fulfilling Madero's prophecy.

Yet Fox's liberal, political reading of the revolution seems narrow at best. What of the rest of the revolutionary legacy, forged after Madero's death in 1913? During this era the just ideals of 1910 were abandoned and "barbarous Mexico" was plunged into violence, corruption, hunger, pillage, rape, and disease. A "political cannibalism" that devoured the revolution's leaders overtook democratic ideals (Rosas 2005a). Villa is dismissed as little more than a vain caudillo, "an assassin contemptuous of the civilian population" (Rosas 2005b). In a nod to the left-wing *Partido de la Revolución Democrática* (PRD), Lázaro Cárdenas, the father of PRD leader Cuauhtémoc Cárdenas, is heralded as a virtuous and honorable man who broke the cycle of repression that characterized the Sonoran regimes and, most importantly, defended Mexico's national sovereignty by expropriating foreign petroleum companies (Rosas 2005c). Despite his neoliberal leanings, during the 2001 commemoration of the anniversary of the expropriation Fox felt obliged to reiterate his pledge to defend Mexico's national sovereignty and not privatize PEMEX: "this is the wish and the mandate of the Mexican people . . ." (Fox Quesada 2001). Yet it had to be acknowledged that Cárdenas had created the nefarious ejido system, "a failure and a terrible instrument for social control," as well as the authoritarian system that for so long stymied Mexico's attempts to realize the dreams of Madero (Rosas 2005c).

In his dynamic but ill-fated 2006 presidential campaign, populist PRD candidate and former Mexico City mayor Andrés Manuel López Obrador (2006) offered a different interpretation of the revolution's legacy. He distanced himself from foreign models, e.g., Venezuelan President Hugo Chávez, instead claiming as his inspiration not only Madero, but also Villa, Zapata, and Cárdenas, thus moving back to the old, powerful official interpretation of a unified revolution. López Obrador's discursive attempt to evoke the popular tradition once again demonstrated the social revolution's enduring allure.

Thus, while post-*priísta* politicians struggle with the discursive legacy of the revolution, one thing is clear: as Mexicans approach its hundredth anniversary, they still cannot disassociate themselves from the revolutionary past as they seek to construct a new future. The Mexico of the twenty-first century will inevitably remain a product of the revolution.

BIBLIOGRAPHY

Anderson, R. D. (1976) *Outcasts in Their Own Land: Mexican Industrial Workers, 1906–1911.* Northern Illinois University Press, DeKalb.

Anderson, R. (1997) "Industrial Labor: 1876–1910." In M. S. Werner (ed.), *Encyclopedia of Mexico: History, Society and Cultura*, vol. 1. Fitzroy Dearborn, Chicago, pp. 681–6.

Avila Espinosa, F. (2000) "La historiografía del zapatismo después de John Womack." In L. Espejel (ed.), *Estudios sobre el zapatismo.* INAH, Mexico City, pp. 31–55.

Barrón, L. (2002) *La tercera muerte de la Revolución mexicana: Historiografía reciente y futuro en el estudio de la revolución.* CIDE, Mexico City.

Bethell, L. (ed.) (1991) *Mexico since Independence.* Cambridge University Press, Cambridge.

Brunk, S. (1995) *Emiliano Zapata: Revolution and Betrayal in Mexico.* University of New Mexico Press, Albuquerque.

Creel Miranda, S. (2005) http://presidencia.gob.mx. February 22.

Crespo, H. (2000) "Los pueblos de Morelos. La comunidad agraria, la desamortización liberal en Morelos y una fuente para el estudio de la diferenciación social campesina." In L. Espejel (ed.), *Estudios sobre el zapatismo.* INAH, Mexico City, pp. 57–120.

Escobar Ohmstede, A. (2001) "La estructura agraria en las Huastecas, 1880–1915." In A. Escobar Ohmstede & T. Rojas Rabiela (eds.), *Estructuras y formas agrarias en México. Del pasado y del presente.* CIESAS, Mexico City, pp. 177–96.

Fox Quesada, V. (2000) "Mensaje del Licenciado Vicente Fox Quesada." http://presidencia.gob.mx. December 1.

Fox Quesada, V. (2001) "Palabras del Presidente Vicente Fox." http://presidencia.gob.mx. March 18.

Gonzales, M. J. (1994) "United States Copper Companies, the State, and Labour Conflict in Mexico, 1900–1910," *Journal of Latin American Studies*, 26:3, pp. 651–81.

Gonzales, M. J. (1996) "U.S. Mine Companies, The Mine Workers' Movement, and the Mexican Revolution, 1910–1920," *Hispanic American Historical Review*, 76:3, pp. 503–34.

González, L. (ed.) (1977–95) *Historia de la revolución mexicana*, 23 vols. El Colegio de México, Mexico City.

Guardino, P. (2003) "Postcolonialism as Self-Fulfilled Prophecy? Electoral Politics in Oaxaca, 1814–1828." In M. Thurner & A. Guerrero (eds.), *After Spanish Rule: Postcolonial Predicaments of the Americas.* Duke University Press, Durham, pp. 248–71.

Guardino, P. (2005) *The Time of Liberty: Popular Political Culture in Oaxaca, 1750–1850.* Duke University Press, Durham.

Guerra, F. (1986) *Le Mexique: De l'Ancien Régime à la Révolution*, 2 vols. L'Harmattan, Paris.

Haber, S., et al. (2003) *The Politics of Property Rights: Political Instability, Credible Commitment, and Economic Growth in Mexico, 1876–1929.* Cambridge University Press, Cambridge.

Hart, J. M. (1987) *Revolutionary Mexico: The Coming and Process of the Mexican Revolution.* University of California Press, Berkeley.

Hart, J. M. (2002) *Revolution and Empire: The Americans in Mexico since the Civil War.* University of California Press, Berkeley.

Hart, P. (2005) *Bitter Harvest: The Social Transformation of Morelos, Mexico, and the Origins of the Zapatista Revolution, 1840–1910.* University of New Mexico Press, Albuquerque.

Hernández Chávez, A. (1993). *La tradición republicana del buen gobierno*. Fondo de Cultura Económica, Mexico City.

Jiménez, C. M. (2004) "Popular Organizing for Public Services: Residents Modernize Morelia, Mexico, 1880–1920," *Journal of Urban History*, 30:4, pp. 495–518.

Joseph, G. & Nugent, D. (eds.) (1994) *Everyday Forms of State Formation: Revolution and the Negotiation of Rule in Modern Mexico*. Duke University Press, Durham.

Katz, F. (1998) *The Life and Times of Pancho Villa*. Stanford University Press, Stanford.

Knight, A. (1986a) *The Mexican Revolution*, Vol. 1, *Porfirians, Liberals and Peasants*. Cambridge University Press, Cambridge.

Knight, A. (1986b) *The Mexican Revolution*, Vol. 2, *Counter-revolution and Reconstruction*. Cambridge University Press, Cambridge.

Knight, A. (1994a) "Popular Culture and the Revolutionary State in Mexico, 1910–1940," *Hispanic American Historical Review*, 74:3, pp. 393–444.

Knight, A. (1994b) "Cardenismo: Juggernaut or Jalopy?," *Journal of Latin American Studies*, 26:1, pp. 73–107.

Knight, A. (2005) "*Caciquismo* in Twentieth-century Mexico." In A. Knight & W. Pansters (eds.), *Caciquismo in Twentieth-Century Mexico*. Institute of the Americas, London, pp. 3–48.

Kourí, E. (2004) *A Pueblo Divided: Business, Property, and Community in Papantla, Mexico*. Stanford University Press, Stanford.

Lear, J. (2001) *Workers, Neighbors, and Citizens: The Revolution in Mexico City*. University of Nebraska Press, Lincoln.

López Obrador, A. M. (2006) "Comunicado de prensa, 0083/06." http://www.prd.org.mx. March 24.

Meyer, L. (1992) *La segunda muerte de la Revolución mexicana*. Cal y Arena, Mexico City.

Otero, G. (ed.) (2004) *Mexico in Transition: Neoliberal Globalism, the State, and Civil Society*. Zed Books, London.

Portilla, S. (1995) *Una sociedad en armas: Insurrección antireeleccionista en México, 1910–1911*. El Colegio de México, Mexico City.

Rosas, A. (2005a) "Réquiem por la revolución mexicana." http://presidencia.gob.mx. November 17.

Rosas, A. (2005b) "Siniestra emboscada: Pancho Villa." http://presidencia.gob.mx. July 21.

Rosas, A. (2005c) "El hombre de Jiquilpan, Lázaro Cárdenas." http://presidencia.gob.mx. May 20.

Ross, S. (ed.) (1966) *Is the Mexican Revolution Dead?* Knopf, New York.

Schuler, F. (1998) *Mexico between Hitler and Roosevelt: Mexican Foreign Relations in the Age of Lázaro Cárdenas, 1934–1940*. University of New Mexico Press, Albuquerque.

Smith, R. (1972) *The United States and Revolutionary Nationalism in Mexico, 1916–1932*. University of Chicago Press, Chicago.

Tannenbaum, F. (1933) *Peace by Revolution: An Interpretation of Mexico*. Columbia University Press, New York.

Vaughan, M. K. (1997) *Cultural Politics in Revolution: Teachers, Peasants, and Schools in Mexico, 1930–1940*. University of Arizona Press, Tucson.

Vaughan, M. K. & Lewis, S. (eds.) (2006) *The Eagle and the Virgin: Nation and Cultural Revolution in Mexico, 1920–1940*. Duke University Press, Durham.

Wilkie, J. (1967) *The Mexican Revolution: Federal Expenditure and Social Change since 1910*. University of California Press, Berkeley.

Womack, J. (1968) *Zapata and the Mexican Revolution*. Vintage, New York.

Wood, A. (2001) *Revolution in the Street: Women, Workers, and Urban Protest in Veracruz, 1870–1927*. SR Books, Wilmington, DE.

Chapter Twenty

Populism and Developmentalism

Joel Wolfe

The Great Depression brought lasting change to Latin America by bringing to an end the long nineteenth century of classic liberal export economies. Throughout the region, export-led growth had fueled urbanization and some early industrialization. New groups, from urban workers to middle-class professionals, had been pressuring the landed elites and commercial interests who held sway over Latin American nations from the late nineteenth through the early twentieth century for a greater voice in local and national politics. With the collapse of the US and Western European economies and the concomitant impact on Latin American exports, economic and political issues no longer dealt with questions of which segment of the agricultural or mining elite would govern and whether or not they might bring some members of the emerging middle class into their coalitions. New styles of governing with new groups and their new economic interests came to dominate Latin American politics in the era after the Great Depression. Those new trends were further modified by the opportunities available in the aftermath of World War II.

No two Latin American countries experienced the same politics or economic realities, but the region's larger nations, especially those that had had some initial period of industrialization in the early twentieth century, shared several characteristics in the three decades following the advent of the Great Depression. This essay focuses on Argentina, Brazil, and Mexico, which all had a period in which populism dominated politics. In the Latin American context, populism refers to cross-class coalitions of workers and industrialists who coalesced around a charismatic, usually nationalistic, leader to promote redistributive, reformist policies. In the aftermath of the populist era, each of these countries had periods of developmentalist governance led by politicians who, although very different from their populist predecessors, relied on populist-era coalitions. In Argentina and Brazil, the failure of developmentalism led to eras of military dictatorship; in Mexico, the developmentalist politicians ruled through a more benevolent authoritarian regime and so did not suffer the same fate as their colleagues in South America. In addition to these three cases, the example of Chile from the mid-1930s through the 1960s reveals important similarities in developmentalist politics without the presence of a Latin American populist-style leader. These four countries share a history of attempts to peacefully navigate the political changes fostered by new economic realities. These nations' leaders then attempted to use politics to reshape their economies to be more independent of international forces and less dependent on the export of commodities.

The periods of populism and developmentalism dissolved into eras of violent dictatorship in Argentina, Brazil, and Chile. Mexico avoided this fate perhaps because its governing coalition was born out of the nation's extremely violent 1910–17 Revolution. Despite these differences, all four countries shared important political and economic trends in the mid-twentieth century. Their common histories, along with the significant ways they differed, demonstrate some of the ways in which these disparate nations share a Latin American identity.

Economic Nationalism and the Prebisch–ECLA Thesis

The 1948 founding of the Economic Commission for Latin America (ECLA or CEPAL for *Comisión Económica para América Latina*) by the United Nations seemed to signal the beginning of a new era for the region. Headquartered in Santiago, Chile and staffed by a group of young economists and bankers, under the leadership of the Argentine Raúl Prebisch, ECLA quickly became both a catalyst and a clearinghouse for ideas about how to spur Latin American economic development. Its founding also symbolized what many in the region hoped would be a new era not only of economic growth, along with its associated political stability and social peace, but also of an increasingly pan-Latin American identity in policy making. ECLA's ties to the newly inaugurated United Nations gave it further prestige and, at least symbolically, further distanced economic policy making from North American influence (Hodara 1987; Love 1996; Lora & Mallorquin 1999).

ECLA's policy prescriptions and the steadily increasing power of nationalist forces in Latin America challenged the long-dominant place of economic liberalism among political and business elites. Those ideas also created a challenge to many in the United States who supported unfettered free trade in the region. The policies articulated by ECLA's economists and their allies came to be known as "developmentalism." From the mid-1940s through the consolidation of the Cuban Revolution in the early 1960s, developmentalism dominated policy making in much of Latin America. Although broadly similar, each country's policies reflected its history and traditions (Sikkink 1991).

Before the 1930s several Latin American governments made some small efforts to encourage domestic industrial production in the late nineteenth and early twentieth centuries. They did so without a broad plan for national development, and they did not seek to challenge the power of agricultural and mining elites and their allies in commerce and finance who dominated the region's politics and economies. Indeed, the growth of Latin America's textile industries was often linked to the region's agricultural sectors (Stein 1957).

The advent of World War I brought the first coordinated spurt in national industrial development in Latin America. Light industries (textiles, food processing, light metalworking) grew dramatically during the war as local manufacturers filled the void left by the cut-off in imports from Europe and later the United States (Dean 1969; Albert & Henderson 1988). Although industries in Argentina, Brazil, and Chile grew dramatically at this time, the end of the war ushered in an era of renewed free trade with the United States, which was now dominant throughout the hemisphere. North American cars, radios, telephones, and other advanced manufactured goods flooded Latin American markets, and raw materials flowed to the United States to pay for these consumer goods (O'Brien 1996; Bauer 2001). This era of intense economic liberalism was followed by the Great Depression, which did much more harm to the economies of the United States and Western Europe than to those in Latin America. After recovering from the initial shocks brought on by the collapse in commodity prices, the major Latin American economies turned inward. Once again, industrial production grew dramatically in the second half of the 1930s. The advent of World War II, when the region was again cut off from imported manufactured goods, furthered domestic industrial development and ushered in an era of high commodity prices (Baer 1983; Díaz Fuentes 1994).

The two world wars and the Great Depression had shown how the Latin American economies could grow when protected from the competition of international markets. During the 1930s and 1940s Argentina, Brazil, Chile, and Mexico all experimented with some form of government intervention in the economy to bolster broad economic development. These experiments in planning and even state ownership of some key industries helped to create a policy vocabulary and set of experiences that informed the articulation of the Prebisch–ECLA thesis of Latin American developmentalism in the post-1945 era. Simply put, the ECLA economists argued that classical free trade based on a system of comparative advantage had disadvantaged Latin America. Exchanging commodities for finished products, they argued, left Latin American economies lagging behind those of the industrial nations. Commodities, by definition, are interchangeable. A manufacturer of electric motors can use copper mined in Chile, Peru, Mexico, or the United States, leaving the producing countries little pricing power. Indeed, commodity prices often reflect world supply and demand. Moreover, many Latin American commodities were produced by multinational corporations that could manipulate their rate of profit more easily by coordinating their far-flung production than by operating as part of a cartel to drive up commodity prices (Moran 1974).

ECLA's economists argued further that Latin American nations suffered from an inherently unequal exchange with North American and European producers. The value added to manufactured goods imported to Latin America made the return of its commodities in those goods a costly exchange for the region, and over time the value of Latin American primary products would stagnate relative to the cost of imported manufactured goods (Cardoso & Faletto 1978). The answers to this embedded set of problems seemed obvious to Prebisch and his colleagues: the Latin American nations should attempt to form producer cartels to drive up commodity prices, and they should industrialize through a public–private partnership, sheltering infant industries with protective tariffs, and promoting infrastructure development. Although it was an innovative and *sui generis* response to the region's economic woes, the ECLA program mirrored the experiences of several Latin American economies during the two world wars. High commodity prices – in response to demand by the warring nations – and the growth of domestic industry when imports were restricted, had demonstrated the feasibility of such proposals. Moreover, the internal growth many Latin American economies experienced during the 1930s provided evidence that such industrialization was possible even in an era of weak commodity prices.

Beyond the economic efficacy of such proposals, ECLA's policies also meshed with the political realities and mood of the post-1945 period. The success of many Latin American export economies had led to increasing urbanization and early industrial development. These trends presented challenges to political systems throughout the region that were dominated by agricultural elites and their allies in commerce and finance. ECLA's developmentalism, in theory, would bolster both the agricultural and industrial sectors. It also promised to increase urban employment in the new factories. In addition, this program was consistent with the growing sense of nationalism many in Latin America felt at this time. In other words, ECLA's policy prescriptions were in practice a powerful set of reformist ideas that promised to diminish the influence of both the United States and the increasingly assertive Marxist left in the region.

Argentina: Populism and Developmentalism

When Juan Perón burst on the political scene in Argentina, the economy was dominated by the agricultural sector. Beef and wheat exports made up the bulk of foreign exchange earnings and those industries that had developed during the first three decades of the twentieth century produced light consumer goods for Argentina's growing population (Díaz Alejandro 1970). Perón and the other officers who seized power in 1943 had an ill-defined set of nationalist ideas for governing the nation. They rejected the extreme economic liberalism of their predecessors, especially the 1933 Roca–Runciman Agreement that reserved the bulk of foreign trade for Great Britain, and they worried about the growing potential for social conflict as more and more people migrated from the agricultural interior to Buenos Aires looking for employment and generally improved lives (Waisman 1987). Perón's embrace of urban labor in late 1943 was both opportunistic and prophetic. With the enthusiastic backing of Argentina's expanding working class, Perón easily won the 1946 presidential election (James 1988).

Once in office, Perón inadvertently embraced a version of ECLA's developmentalism. For most of its modern history, a series of Manichean divides defined Argentina, building on a tradition of social and political polarization by dividing the nation between his coalition of urban workers and new industrialists, on the one hand, and the agricultural elites, on the other. Perón's government sought to reorganize society through a corporatist framework. Workers' unions and industrialists' associations would use state institutions to settle wage and other disputes. Agricultural producers were required to sell their wheat, beef, and other products through the Argentine Trade Institute (*Instituto Argentino de Promoción del Intercamio* or IAPI). This state agency bought low and sold high, because international commodity prices (especially for foodstuffs) were high as Europe sought to recover from the devastation of World War II. Perón used the surplus generated by the IAPI to build infrastructure and schools, provide social welfare, subsidize industry, and for graft (Page 1983).

Perón referred to his use of corporatism to promote industrialism and the fortunes of the nation's workers as *Justicialismo*, which he saw as a third way between capitalism and communism. This use of the state to direct the economy and promote social justice for the popular classes were hallmarks of Perón's emerging populism. Latin American populism is characterized first and foremost by its emphasis on reform over revolution. Moreover, populism often involves the incorporation of new groups into the polity by responding to their demands in ways the old political style did not. Perón focused on mobilizing workers who had no, or weak, ties to existing labor organizations; many of these workers had recently arrived from the rural sector or had gained their first industrial jobs (Horowitz 1990a). Perón elevated the status of these workers not only by providing real increases in workers' incomes, while at the same time increasing GDP, but also culturally by enshrining the recent arrivals from the countryside, "the shirtless ones" (*los descamisados*) as the authentic representatives of the nation. This populism also relied on charismatic leadership. Juan Perón could stir the passions of los descamisados with both his words and deeds, but his wife Eva Duarte de Perón (or Evita) occupied a unique cultural and political space in 1940s Argentina. Her beauty and humble origins, along with the real benefits distributed to the poor through the Eva Perón Foundation, made her the embodiment of the benevolent state (Plotkin 1994; Fraser & Navarro 1996).

Perón had also mastered one more key component of Latin American populism: the demonizing of the opposition. In Perón's case, he used nationalism as a key component of his politics and he relied on traditional Argentine Manichaeism in his treatment of his domestic opponents, particularly large landed interests. He used national pride as campaign issue in 1945, capitalizing on the ham-fisted opposition to his candidacy by the US ambassador Spruille Braden. Nationalism became policy when Perón nationalized British-owned railroads, the US-owned telephone system, and the French-owned docks. Although extremely popular, in each case the Argentine treasury woefully overpaid for the undercapitalized facilities. Moreover, such hostility to foreign capital limited foreign investment just as Argentina's main regional rival, Brazil, was welcoming direct foreign investment in its heavy industries. The regime's domestic opponents suffered economically and politically during the entire first era of Peronist governance (1946–55). Rural producers consistently received payments for the goods well below market prices and they had no political mechanism to correct this. The regime did not, however, challenge their ownership of the land and other productive resources, and so did not destroy their ultimate source of power. Like its attack on foreign capital, the government's treatment of the rural sector antagonized agricultural elites without eliminating their power base. In both cases, Perón eventually paid a steep price for how he demonized his opponents.

In the short term, however, Peronism seemed to be a great success. The Argentine economy grew at an annualized rate of 8.6 percent in 1946, 12.6 percent in 1947, and 5.1 percent in 1948. Workers' real incomes grew 25 percent in 1947 and 24 percent in 1948 (Lewis 1990). Moreover, Peronism granted workers a greater sense of citizenship in Argentina. Their higher wages, access to better food and other consumer goods, and their ally in the Casa Rosada (presidential palace) were signs that the new Argentina was a forward-looking nation flourishing through its embrace of the Third Way. These rights and sense of citizenship were extended to women in 1948 when Perón granted them the franchise. Argentina's sense of self-importance was further stoked at this time by a series of unrelated, but culturally significant developments. The first was the design, manufacture, and testing of the Pulqui jet aircraft in 1947. While most of the industrial development fostered by the regime focused on labor-intensive light manufacturing, government support for the aeronautics industry put Argentina, for a brief time, in the forefront of modern technology. Then, in 1951, Perón publicly declared Argentina's intention to develop nuclear energy (Mariscotti 1996). Such projects created great prestige for Perón and the nation. The international success of Juan Manuel Fangio (1986), considered by many to be the greatest automobile racer of all times, simply added to the growing sense of national pride many Argentines felt at this time.

Much of Perón's political success and its accompanying cultural changes were fueled by the robust post-World War II world economy. When European agricultural producers came back on line and the initial US postwar pent-up demand for goods played out a bit, Argentina faced declining prices for its agricultural exports. Moreover, the regime's policy of antagonizing rural elites through the IAPI without taking control of their land eventually had serious economic consequences for the nation. Rural producers, rather than continue to receive under-market prices for their goods, simply decreased or ceased production. They kept cattle on the hoof rather than sell them for slaughter and let fields lie fallow. This producers' strike cost the regime a great deal of foreign exchange, reduced employment in the important meat-packing sector, and drove up domestic food prices. By 1949, Perón reacted to this reversal of fortune by embracing an orthodox economic stabilization program, inviting in foreign capital and denying workers' wage demands. Despite his political pivot, Perón failed to garner support among his former enemies. He did, however, succeed in alienating his political base. Only four years after his 1951 reelection, Perón was removed from office through a military coup. Despite workers' passionate support for the regime, there was little opposition to Perón's ouster.

The military government that followed allowed free elections in early 1958. Arturo Frondizi, an economist and leader of the middle-class Radical party, won the presidency. Frondizi responded to the debacle of Peronist economic policy making by embracing a modified ECLA-style developmentalism. He proposed decreasing the government's role in the economy, stimulating agricultural production, welcoming foreign investment, and solving the nation's balance of payments and domestic budget crises. Frondizi made this difficult set of policies even harder to achieve by having allied himself with the Peronists in the 1958 election. Decreasing social spending, working with multinational corporations to increase energy production and expand industrial capacity, and devaluing the currency as a component of a radical shock therapy to the economy quickly undermined his alliance with populist labor (James 1988; Brennan 1994). Frondizi's grand developmentalism was severely constrained by both his fiscal and political room to maneuver.

Frondizi's policies had their intended effects. The stabilization program dramatically affected workers' real incomes in 1959, but helped attract direct foreign investment. That foreign participation in the economy helped develop a national steel industry and increase domestic oil production, but alienated those segments of domestic capital that did not benefit from the presence of the multinational corporations. So, when the economy began to recover in the early 1960s, Frondizi had to face an increasingly assertive group of political opponents. He fulfilled a campaign promise by legalizing the Peronist party for the 1962 elections, and when they won more votes than either part of the divided Radical party, the military intervened to force the expunging of the electoral results. When Frondizi refused the military's demands, they removed him from office on March 29, 1962, thus ending Argentina's attempts at developmentalism through either charismatic populism or electoral reformism.

Brazil: Nationalist and Multinationalist Developmentalism

When Getúlio Vargas took office as Brazil's provisional president in November 1930, his ascension to power seemed to be one more squabble among the powerful agricultural interests that had dominated Brazil throughout the Empire (1822–89) and ruled during the First Republic (1889–1930). Vargas, the governor of Rio Grande do Sul state, had run for the presidency in an alliance with elites from Minas Gerais against the interests of São Paulo state. When the Paulista won, Vargas and his allies went into revolt, gained the support of the military, and took power. There was little in his background or campaign program that suggested he would challenge the nation's economic reliance on agricultural production or political orientation of extreme federalism (Abreu 1997). Once in power, however, Vargas unveiled a program to strengthen central state power and deepen industrial development (D'Araujo 1999). He first replaced most of the existing state governors with appointed "Interventors." Next, he began the initial phase of a corporatist program to bolster industrial development by creating the Ministry of Labor, Industry, and Commerce in 1931. A series of strikes in São Paulo, Brazil's largest city and industrial hub, in 1931 revealed the promise and pitfalls of Vargas's new system. The city's workers used their new unions to negotiate through the new national Ministry of Labor. Although Vargas's government did little for the strikers, São Paulo's industrialists worried about the consequences of the federal government's role in settling a local dispute. Those and other fears of the creeping power of Vargas's government soon brought on the 1932 Civil War, which pitted the state of São Paulo against the national government (Wolfe 1993; Weinstein 2003).

Although Vargas's government defeated the rebels in only three months, the conflict had broad implications for Brazilian developmentalism. Vargas quickly recognized the national government's limited ability to control powerful regional elites and so pulled back from his centralizing project, especially in São Paulo. Within the rebellious state, new experiments with Fordist policies to spur production of materiel not only revealed the efficacy of such practices for the maintenance of social peace, they also pointed the way to entire new areas of production. São Paulo, Brazil's industrial heartland, quickly turned its metalworking shops into armament and vehicle factories. Like the cut-off in world trade caused by World War I, the advent of the Great Depression and then the 1932 Civil War demonstrated the latent power of Brazilian industry and the significant domestic market for its goods (Leff 1968). São Paulo's war against the national government helped to define more precisely what that market was. Brazilian industry now needed reliable and affordable supplies of steel, for example, and would soon turn its attention to its woefully inadequate energy supplies (Wirth 1970; Brannstrom unpublished). By the mid-1930s, Vargas had completely shifted away from providing workers with some governmental support through the corporatist Ministry of Labor and began to focus on providing industrialists with the inputs they needed to deepen economic development.

Vargas consolidated his power by declaring the *Estado Novo* (New State) dictatorship in 1937. Although nominally embracing a centralizing program to attempt again to limit the states' autonomy from the national government, the dictatorship did much more to advance industrial development with state aid, and often at the expense of the nation's workers, than to unify Brazil politically (Wolfe 1993; Williams 2001). Vargas used the corporatist system he had put in place in the early 1930s to keep workers' wages low in order to deepen capital formation among industrialists. The government then moved to eradicate a series of economic bottlenecks affecting industry. Vargas traded his support for US strategic interests in the late 1930s for US government financing of a new steel industry to be located in Volta Redonda, halfway between the cities of São Paulo and Rio de Janeiro (McCann 1973). Vargas further spurred industrial development by supporting the early stages of the nation's alternative energy program (primarily through state support for the domestic manufacture of the gasogene, a wood- or charcoal-fueled gasification reactor for cars and trucks) and by building the National Motors Factory, which began producing airplane engines, but after World War II produced trucks under license from Italy's Alfa Romeo (Wolfe forthcoming). The government also promoted the marketing cartels for many of Brazil's agricultural exports during this era of increasing demand for commodities. These moves, along with the suppression of workers' independent organizing and strike activities, which in turn depressed wages, deepened development through state intervention in the economy.

Vargas's Estado Novo rule contrasted sharply with Juan Perón's first term as president. Whereas Perón had governed as a populist, using controlled mobilization of the popular classes to achieve his political ends, Vargas suppressed labor activity and ruled as a dictator. He did so while Brazilian troops fought under the command of US General Mark Clark in Italy and the citizenry suffered shortages and high prices as a consequence of the nation's declaration of war against the Axis powers (Cytrynowicz 1998). Belatedly, Vargas tried to turn to labor for support, but after years of declining real wages, the nation's workers had little interest in supporting the dictator. The many contradictions of Vargas's long rule, along with pressure from the US government and a sense of exhaustion with the regime, led to his ousting by the military in October 1945. The next president, Army general Eurico Gaspar Dutra, treated labor as Vargas had during the darkest days of the Estado Novo and did little to foster economic development. Such classical economic liberalism seemed out of place to many intellectuals, politicians, and workers. So, when Vargas declared his intention to run for the presidency in 1950 he did so as a developmentalist populist. He won handily and took office in 1951 (Skidmore 1967).

Serving for the first time as Brazil's elected chief executive, Vargas tried to balance the competing components of his constituency – nationalist business interests, bureaucrats and members of the middle class, and urban workers – by attempting to deepen national development. Many of the disconnected ideas about national unification and economic growth from the Estado Novo were given a systematic structure by the recommendations of the Joint US–Brazil Economic Development Commission. This massive study had been initiated in 1949 with the explicit goal of determining the extant bottlenecks to Brazil's ongoing industrial and agricultural development. The report highlighted transportation infrastructure and energy production as areas that prevented Brazil from moving forward with its development.

Vargas responded by redoubling road-building efforts and, more significantly, creating a mixed public–private entity to control oil exploration and production. PETRO-BRAS, founded in 1951, was the centerpiece of Vargas's nationalist developmentalism. He hoped it would spur further economic growth with some state direction, but without alienating the private sector. As is often the case, PETROBRAS's mixed nature failed to satisfy many of the nationalist left and yet still worried conservative businessmen (Miranda 1983; Randall 1993).

Throughout his political career, Vargas had deftly avoided becoming a captive of one political extreme or the other. Even as his government in the 1930s and 1940s declared itself on the side of Brazil's working people and promulgated the nation's first comprehensive labor code, labor's share of national income fell. Vargas co-opted formal unions and attempted to suppress independent workers' commissions. As an elected president, Vargas had considerably less room to maneuver politically. Massive strikes in the industrial heartland of São Paulo in 1953 challenged Vargas to put into practice the populist promises of his political campaigns (Moises 1978; Wolfe 1993). In June 1953, three months after workers had paralyzed the city of São Paulo with a six-week long general strike, Vargas finally appointed a pro-worker politician to head the federal Ministry of Labor. João Goulart was a young PTB activist from Vargas's home state and he sought to use the national government to support workers' demands, particularly in the face of the high rates of inflation Brazil experienced in the early and mid-1950s. Goulart's presence was highly significant because the corporatist labor system Vargas had put in place in the 1930s and codified with the 1943 labor code gave the federal government the ultimate authority in wage and other disputes. All wage demands, for example, were supposed to be settled by a tripartite labor court with one representative from the Ministry of Labor, one from industry, and one from workers' unions. Labor's representative would vote in favor of labor, and industry's for industry, leaving the government official to settle the dispute (Mericle 1974).

Goulart had few opportunities to deliver on Vargas's populist promises. The administration was torn between forces attempting to bolster its standing with workers and the poor, and Vargas's old-line allies who attempted to bring the budget under control. The latter group seemed to win this internal struggle in February 1954 when Vargas removed Goulart from the Ministry of Labor, but then the president quickly changed course and proposed on May 1, 1954 a 100 percent increase in the national minimum wage. Vargas's administration was in disarray and faced increasingly vocal and credible claims that it was also a hotbed of corruption. Vargas responded to his critics by committing suicide on the night of August 24, 1954. His suicide note, read on nationwide radio broadcasts the following day, blamed his demise on both foreign and domestic "hidden forces." The end of Vargas's regime had much in common with Juan Perón's ouster, although the military was not directly involved in the Brazilian episode. Still, both regimes shared a number of characteristics that helped define both Latin American populism and its associated form of developmentalism.

In Argentina and Brazil, the multi-class nature of Perón's and Vargas's political coalitions and their reliance on controlled popular mobilization paid short-term dividends but had long-term costs. Perón could satisfy both workers and their employers by funding industry with agricultural-sector profits. The accumulated foreign reserves earned during the war and continued high commodity prices in its aftermath provided the means for papering over the contradictions in the Peronist movement. Vargas's coalition was more complex. Rural interests and many industrialists opposed his government, while labor, segments of the middle class, and the bureaucracy, which had grown significantly since 1930, supported him. Vargas, though, could not easily balance deepening Brazilian development and satisfying workers' wage demands in an inflationary environment. Just as Perón depended on beef and wheat exports, Vargas was ultimately a captive of the international price for coffee, Brazil's largest export. Even with high coffee prices, Brazil's appetite for imported manufactured goods, particularly automobiles, drained foreign reserves in the post-1945 period. The economics of this trade deepened Brazilian suspicion of foreign economic interests and so led to Vargas's use of nationalist rhetoric in the creation of PETROBRAS (Miranda 1983). Still, Vargas's nationalism was tempered by his understanding of the important role of foreign capital in the Brazilian economy. In the final analysis, none of Vargas's policies seemed to go far enough: domestic political coalitions and international trade relationships were maintained and so the limits of his reformism were quickly reached. His suicide seemed to mark the end of populist developmentalism in Brazil.

Juscelino Kubitschek, the former governor of Minas Gerais and a classic PSD politician, won the 1955 election with just 36 percent of the vote. Despite his seemingly uninspiring background, JK (as he was widely known) became one of Brazil's most effective and popular chief executives. He seized on the same latent desire for development Vargas had tapped into, but he did so without his predecessor's political liabilities and history. He was able to mobilize broad segments of Brazilian society without pitting one against another; moreover, he crafted a highly nationalist message of Brazilian-based economic growth that not only avoided demonizing foreign capital but depended upon it. His political message was extremely popular and cut across class, regional, and party lines. One reason was that Kubitschek carefully crafted his policies and rhetoric through the extensive use of public opinion polls. Using a private firm to contact and interview carefully identified segments of the population was necessary at this time because Brazil still had an extremely weak party system and a severely limited franchise. Polling therefore provided the most accurate measure available to determine popular reception of policy.

JK summarized his developmentalism in the slogan "Fifty Years of Progress in Five." Soon after taking office, Kubitschek formed a commission to create the program that would propel Brazil forward during his five-year presidency. JK's team included most of the proposals of the Joint US–Brazil Economic Development Commission in their detailed Target Plan (*Programa de Metas*). In all there were 30 numbered targets broken down into five sectors (Energy, Transportation, Food, Basic Industries, and Education). Only one concerned a consumer good: Target 27, "The Automobile Industry," called for the manufacture of 170,000 Brazilian vehicles by 1960. The others concerned classic developmentalist goals, such as calling for increased rubber production, the construction of cold-storage warehouses, and increases in cement production (Brazil 1958; Sikkink 1991). JK deftly melded these broad economic goals with popular sentiment by proposing that Brazil emulate the US and Western European economies by manufacturing automobiles, trucks, and buses. He next combined developmentalist thinking about opening Brazil's vast territorial spaces to development with long-held national beliefs about the importance of gaining control over the entire nation. JK did that by including one more "synthesis goal" in his Target Plan: the building of a new, inland capital, Brasília.

JK's program had several unique features. Unlike other developmentalist schemes, Kubitschek's policies included a strong geographical focus. In addition to building a new capital far inland, he proposed that an extensive highway system link every state to Brasília. The new auto industry would provide the vehicles for this more integrated nation. Kubitschek's program provided for regions with special needs by creating a separate development agency for Brazil's impoverished northeast. SUDENE (*Superintendência para o Desenvolvimento do Nordeste*) used a variety of tax incentives and direct government investment to promote industrialization in the northeast, to provide expanded opportunity to its residents and to diminish the ongoing concentration of industrial development in Brazil's center-south region (Page 1972). These policies not only reflected Brazilians' aspirations to be a modern, developed nation on a par with the USA and Western Europe, they also touched on important political and cultural strains in the country's history. By finally fulfilling a long-held hope of a new capital city in the country's interior, and by doing so quickly and with futuristic modernist architecture and urban planning, Kubitschek seemed to be finally meeting the promise of the Brazilian Republic, which embraced the motto, "Order and Progress" (Holston 1989; Maxwell 2004).

JK also balanced his nationalism with economic pragmatism. In addition to this broad development program, he was elected with the populist stalwart João Goulart as his vice presidential running mate. Yet, much of his development program was predicated on the active support of foreign capital. Beyond the debt used to finance the construction of Brasília, road building, and other targets, JK invited foreign auto companies to build integrated factories in Brazil. Ford and General Motors had been assembling cars and trucks from kits manufactured in the USA since the early 1920s. Going forward, they and other foreign companies would have to manufacture 90 percent of their vehicles' content in Brazil. A great number of European and North American companies opened manufacturing facilities for auto production and its associated backward and forward linkages. During Kubitschek's administration Willys-Overland (a subsidiary of Kaiser Industries) and Volkswagen soon dominated car production, while Ford and GM initially chose to concentrate on truck and bus manufacture. Rather than fuel resentment, the presence of the foreign factories boosted Brazilian national pride. Brazilians now built advanced industrial products and even exported some cars and auto parts to the USA and Western Europe (Shapiro 1994; Addis 1999; Wolfe forthcoming).

Kubitschek was certainly a talented politician who balanced Brazil's place in the international economy with a nationalistic development program. He satisfied elites, helped to expand the middle class, and provided industrial training, employment, and high-paying jobs to auto workers. Kubitschek was also able to use Vargas's corporatist state structure to his advantage. The expanding economy, especially in the new, well-financed auto industry, brought new workers into state-sponsored unions. Moreover, Goulart's presence in the administration mollified the more activist segments among labor leaders. Expanding the economic pie in a seemingly sustainable way was a key ingredient in JK's success. The other was his reliance on foreign financing. Kubitschek's debt financing of development no doubt had positive long-term implications for the Brazilian economy, but its short-term impact was seen in an ever-escalating rate of inflation.

JK's formula for successful developmentalism was put to the test by his successors. Jânio Quadros, an erstwhile reformer from São Paulo, won the 1960 presidential election. He proved himself to be one of the most artless chief executives in the nation's history and in August 1961 resigned the presidency only seven months after his inauguration, hoping to promote a broad popular appeal to stay in office. His vice president, João Goulart, assumed the presidency after accepting the military's demands that he serve with diminished powers. Goulart not only lacked Kubitschek's political skills, but he also inherited all the deferred costs of JK's policies. Inflation increased steadily from 1960 through 1964, reaching 78.4 percent in 1963 and 89.9 percent in 1964 (Baer 1983). Neither workers nor members of the middle class could sustain any reasonable purchasing power in such an inflationary environment. Rural workers and peasants, who had been largely ignored in Kubitschek's developmentalism, gained unionization rights in 1963 and increasingly mobilized for access to land and better wages. They also used land invasions in the northeast in 1963 and 1964 to press their demands. All these factors, along with long-standing opposition to Kubitschek and Goulart – who were seen as Vargas's heirs – and the belief by many in the military hierarchy that only they could guide Brazil forward by providing the order necessary to ensure progress, brought an end to Brazilian democratic developmentalism (Skidmore 1988). The April 1, 1964 coup led to 21 years of military dictatorship.

Mexico: The Developmentalist Regime

Mexico's twentieth-century history has been largely shaped by its bloody and transformative revolution (1910–17), but populism, corporatism, and developmentalism were nonetheless dominant themes from the 1930s through the 1960s (Bantjes, this volume). When Lázaro Cárdenas assumed the presidency in 1934 there was little sense that he would begin the transformation of the Mexican economy by significantly deepening its internal markets and building state capacity in ways that would have long-term implications (Hamilton 1982). Cárdenas's agrarian reform distributed 44 million acres of land to 800,000 recipients through reconstituted peasant communities known as *ejidos*. Moreover, Cárdenas created the governmental infrastructure both to redistribute the land and to support the new ejidos. The government formed *Banco de Crédito Ejidal* to help finance both individual and community needs in the countryside. The bank made loans for everything from seed and fertilizer to hospital construction (Aguila M. & Enríquez Perea 1996). Although politically a successful populist gesture to the peasant sector so important in the course of the Mexican Revolution, Cárdenas's redistribution of agricultural land had mixed results economically. The ejidos never received the levels of financial support they required and these smaller units were often inefficient producers of foodstuffs for the cities. Still, Cárdenas's agrarian reform bolstered Mexico's internal market by transferring wealth and productive capacity to so many in the rural sector. He also expanded state institutions and their reach throughout the countryside.

Cárdenas also nationalized foreign railroads and oil holdings. The latter move, creating *Petróleos Mexicanos* or PEMEX, stoked Mexican nationalism and earned the ire of foreign capital. These moves further deepened the state's presence in the economy and were also important components to Cárdenas's populism. Like Perón and Vargas, Cárdenas followed a reformist and redistributive course without challenging the underlying principles of capitalism. Cárdenas, like Perón and Vargas, relied on controlled mobilizations of the popular classes (Basurto 1983). Unlike these other leaders, Cárdenas was able to mobilize Mexicans in both agriculture and industry (Becker 1995). He used the ruling party (*Partido de la Revolución Mexicana*, PRM) and its corporatist structure to manage these political sectors by creating four divisions: agrarian, labor, military, and popular (a catchall that included government bureaucrats and other members of the middle class). The final component of Cárdenas's populist orientation, his nationalism, had an obvious and potent target in the United States. He was fortunate that Franklin Roosevelt's Good Neighbor policy and the growing conflict in Europe and Asia muted the US response to the oil nationalization.

In these ways, Cárdenas was yet another example of a mid-twentieth-century Latin American populist leader. What set him apart from Perón, Vargas, and others was the fact that he presided over an institutionalized populism, which was clearly expressed in the structure of the political party that dominated the government. As popular and charismatic a figure as he was, Lázaro Cárdenas was constitutionally limited to serving only one six-year term, and he turned the presidency over to the minister of war, General Manuel Avila Camacho in 1940. Avila Camacho slowed agrarian reform and dampened the activism of urban labor, whose leaders cooperated with the regime as it limited workers' rights to strike in the 1940s (López Villegas-Manjarrez 1983). Much of this turn away from progressive politics was overshadowed by World War II, which had profoundly positive effects on Mexican economic development. The government's close cooperation with the USA eased the tensions that remained from the Cárdenas-era expropriations. This rapprochement with the United States paid dividends in the postwar years. Like other larger Latin American countries, Mexico experienced a spurt of industrialization with the slowdown or even cut-off of manufactured imports from the USA and Western Europe. Avila Camacho responded by shifting the government's focus away from the agrarian sector toward industry. In 1940, he created the *Nacional Financeira* to provide credit for such enterprises and in 1944 the Mexican government even allowed foreign capital in to participate as minority shareholders in manufacturing businesses (Medina 1979). With labor under more conservative control and trade with and investment from the USA growing throughout his term, gross domestic product increased over 230 percent from 1940 to 1946, while industrial production increased by 73 percent.

When Miguel Alemán became president in 1946 he was the first Mexican leader who had not served in the military since Venustiano Carranza (1917–20). He represented the transition from revolutionary-era heroes to professional politicians in Mexican governance. His administration and that of Adolfo Ruiz Cortines (1952–8) embraced the broad tenets of developmentalism by investing heavily in Mexico's infrastructure, continuing to promote social peace through corporatist institutions, and deepening domestic industrial capacity (Sherman 2000). Alemán built a series of important dam projects to control flooding, provide reliable water supplies to agriculture and urban populations, and, perhaps most significantly, to generate electricity for industry. He also dramatically expanded Mexico's highway system and completed the section of the Pan-American Highway that connected the United States with Central America. Ruiz Cortines did not initiate new public works; instead, he focused his energy on reforming the bloated and corrupt bureaucracy and deepening the role of primarily US-based multinational corporations. Even more than his predecessor, Ruiz Cortines represented the shift from the heritage of the Revolution to an institutionalized developmentalism in politics. Unlike their contemporaries, such as Kubitschek and Frondizi, this generation of Mexican leaders lacked charisma. They also did not operate within a democratic polity or face the specter of military intervention if popular mobilization seemed to go too far. The PRI contained most social and political conflict within the party. In doing so, it became the backbone of a remarkably durable one-party state.

Chile and the Legacy of Central State Planning

There is some irony in the fact that Chile, which had embraced broadly developmentalist goals and methods by establishing a government agency to promote development in 1939 (the *Corporación de Fomento*, known as CORFO) and was the home to ECLA itself, eschewed the Prebisch–ECLA policy prescriptions throughout the 1950s and early 1960s. Only with the election of the Christian Democrat Eduardo Frei (1964–70) in the midst of the US-sponsored Alliance for Progress did Chile openly adopt ECLA-style developmentalism (Latham 2000). Frei was elected with significant assistance from the US government, which feared that the Socialist candidate, Salvador Allende, would improve on his 1958 electoral showing and win the presidency. With clandestine financial backing from the USA and an agreement with the Conservatives to support his candidacy, Frei easily won a majority of the vote (Rabe 1999). His administration was to be a showcase for the Alliance for Progress programs even as US policies under Lyndon Johnson moved away from Kennedy's support for reformers.

In office, Frei adopted policies that were mildly developmentalist. He brokered a middle path regarding the nationalization of foreign-owned copper mines by creating a process of "Chileanization," through which the state became a minority partner with the Anaconda Copper Mining Company and a majority shareholder of the Kennecott Copper Corporation. Frei's election raised expectations that a program of nationalist developmentalism would be implemented with few problems. Even though the Christian Democrats easily won the 1965 congressional elections, the government was constrained on the right and left politically. Moreover, Frei was seen by many in Chile as too closely allied with the USA. His agrarian reform was approved by Washington and the Chileanization of copper was considered by conservatives and the left as a halfway measure that left the North American companies with too much. Frei also encouraged significant infusions of foreign capital through profit remittance and other arrangements that made investment in Chile even more profitable for multinational corporations (Moran 1974).

In some ways, Frei's government was similar to those of Kubitschek and Frondizi. On closer examination, though, the significant differences between the Chilean regime and those in Brazil and Argentina tell us much about the nature of Latin American politics in the 1950s and 1960s. Kubitschek and Frondizi were self-consciously developmentalist in their thinking. They both followed populist politicians who had promoted nationalist industrialization in haphazard ways. They set out to bring order and planning to an identifiable process of industrialization and the transformation of agriculture. Likewise, Mexican presidents after Cárdenas sought to institutionalize many of the populist advances of an earlier era. Frei, on the other hand, confronted a much more complicated political environment. He was elected in no small measure to prevent the left from gaining power electorally in the aftermath of Fidel Castro's proclamation that the Cuban Revolution was indeed Marxist. With the backing of the conservatives, middle groups, and the US government, but faced with a broad-based leftist coalition in opposition, Frei's policy making had to be more overtly political than that of Kubitschek, Frondizi, or the Mexican presidents. With so little room to maneuver, Frei's government disappointed its supporters and alienated its former allies on the right. It is perhaps not surprising that the left, organized as the *Unidad Popular*, won the 1970 election and put Socialist Salvador Allende in the presidency. Chilean politics became increasingly polarized and tense, and Allende's "bloodless road" to socialism could not be sustained in the face of internal and international pressure. The violent military coup led by General August Pinochet on September 11, 1973 ended Chile's long history of electoral politics for some time thereafter.

Conclusion

Developmentalism and populism ultimately failed to provide smooth and enduring transitions from export-oriented oligarchies to democratic, industrialized states. Populism itself, as a reformist and redistributive system, was inherently weak. Industrialists in São Paulo and Argentine landowners were challenged by Vargas and Perón, but they never lost control of their property and hence their power. Cárdenas succeeded in large measure because his program was part of the resolution to the violent and destructive Mexican Revolution in which the power and property of the old elite had been at the very least dramatically altered. Developmentalism seemed to offer a different path. ECLA's policies and the politics of Kubitschek, Frondizi, and post-1940 Mexican presidents sought to expand Latin American economies by earning more from commodity exports and through industrialization. Their leaders hoped that their economies would generate enough wealth to alter their nation's polities. Smallholders and workers, they believed, would have a large enough stake in the system to participate in democratic politics without intimidating elites and segments of the middle class. In the cases reviewed here, however, the extant political and economic systems prevented the rural and urban poor from participating fully in the fruits of developmentalism. Their high expectations were soon dashed by the increasingly authoritarian responses of Latin American militaries and their civilian allies in the 1960s and 1970s (Mares, this volume).

BIBLIOGRAPHY

Abreu, L. A. de (1997) *Getúlio Vargas: A construção de um mito, 1928–30*. EDIPUCRS, Porto Alegre.

Addis, C. (1999) *Taking the Wheel: Auto Parts Firms and the Political Economy of Industrialization in Brazil.* Pennsylvania State University Press, University Park.

Aguila M, M. T. & Enríquez Perea, A. (eds.) (1996) *Perspectivas sobre el cardenismo: Ensayos sobre economía, trabajo, política y cultura en los años treinta.* Universidad Autónoma Metropolitana, Azcapotzalco.

Albert, B. & Henderson, P. (1988) *South America and the First World War: the Impact of the War on Brazil, Argentina, Peru, and Chile.* Cambridge University Press, New York.

Baer, W. (1983) *The Brazilian Economy: Growth and Development,* 2nd ed. Praeger, New York.

Basurto, J. (1983) *Cárdenas y el poder sindical.* Ediciones Era, Mexico City.

Bauer, A. J. (2001) *Goods, Power, History: Latin America's Material Culture.* Cambridge University Press, New York.

Becker, M. (1995) *Setting the Virgin on Fire: Lázaro Cárdenas, Michoacán Peasants, and the Redemption of the Mexican Revolution.* University of California Press, Berkeley.

Bojunga, C. (2001) *JK o Artista do Impossível.* Objetiva, Rio de Janeiro.

Brannstrom, C. (unpublished) "Was Brazilian Industrialization Fueled by Wood? Evaluating São Paulo's Energy Hinterlands, 1900–1960."

Brazil (1958) Presidência da República, Conselho do Desenvolvimento, *Programa de Metas. Tomo 1: Introdução.* Gráfica Editora Jornal do Comércio, Rio de Janeiro.

Brennan, J. P. (1994) *The Labor Wars in Córdoba, 1955–1976: Ideology, Work, and Labor Politics in an Argentine Industrial City.* Harvard University Press, Cambridge, MA.

Camp, R. A. (1999) *Politics in Mexico: Democratizing Authoritarianism,* 3rd ed. Oxford University Press, New York.

Cardoso, F. H. & Faletto, E. (1978) *Dependency and Development in Latin America,* translated by M. M. Urquidi. University of California Press, Berkeley.

Cytrynowicz, R. (1998) "Guerra sem guerra: A mobilização do 'Front Interno' em São Paulo durante a Segunda Guerra Mundial, 1939–1945." PhD dissertation, Universidade de São Paulo.

D'Araujo, M. C. (ed.) (1999) *As instituições brasileiras da era Vargas.* Editora FGV, Rio de Janeiro.

Dean, W. (1969) *The Industrialization of São Paulo, 1880–1945.* University of Texas Press, Austin.

Díaz Alejandro, C. F. (1970) *Essay on the Economic History of the Argentine Republic.* Yale University Press, New Haven.

Díaz Fuentes, D. (1994) *Crisis y cambios estructurales en América Latina: Argentina, Brasil y México durante el periodo de entreguerras.* Fondo de Cultura Económica, Mexico City.

Drake, P. (1978) *Socialism and Populism in Chile, 1937–1952.* University of Illinois Press, Urbana.

Fangio, J. M. (1986) *Fangio: Cuando el hombre es más que el mito.* Sudamericana/Planeta, Buenos Aires.

Fraser, N. & Navarro, M. (1996) *Evita.* W. W. Norton, New York.

Hamilton, N. (1982) *The Limits of State Autonomy: Post-Revolutionary Mexico.* Princeton University Press, Princeton.

Hodara, J. (1987) *Prebisch y la CEPAL: Sustancia, trayectoria y contexto institucional.* Colegio de Mexico, Mexico City.

Holston, J. (1989) *The Modernist City: An Anthropological Critique of Brasília.* University of Chicago Press, Chicago.

Horowitz, J. (1990a) *Argentine Unions, the State and the Rise of Peronism, 1930–1945.* Institute of International Studies, Berkeley, CA.

Horowitz, J. (1990b) "Industrialists and the Rise of Perón, 1943–1946: Some Implications for the Conceptualization of Populism," *Americas,* 47:2, October, pp. 199–217.

James, D. (1988). *Resistance and Integration: Peronism and the Argentine Working Class, 1946–1976.* Cambridge University Press, Cambridge.

Latham, M. (2000) *Modernization as Ideology: American Social Science and "Nation Building" in the Kennedy Era.* University of North Carolina Press, Chapel Hill.

Leff, N. (1968) *The Brazilian Capital Goods Industry, 1929–1964.* Harvard University Press, Cambridge, MA.

Lewis, P. (1990) *The Crisis of Argentine Capitalism.* University of North Carolina Press, Chapel Hill.

López Villegas-Manjarrez, V. (1983) *La CTM vs. las organizaciones obreras.* Ediciones El Caballito, Mexico City.

Lora, J. & Mallorquin, C. (eds.) (1999) *Prebisch y Furtado, el estructuralismo latinoamericano.* Benemerita Universidad Autonoma de Puebla, Instituto de Ciencias Sociales y Humanidades, Puebla.

Love, J. (1996) *Crafting the Third World: Theorizing Underdevelopment in Rumania and Brazil.* Stanford University Press, Stanford.

Mariscotti, M. (1996) *El secreto atómico de Huemul,* 3rd ed. Estudio Sigma, Buenos Aires.

Maxwell, K. (2004) *Conflicts and Conspiracies: Brazil and Portugal, 1750–1808.* Routledge, New York.

McCann, F. D. Jr. (1973) *The Brazilian–American Alliance: 1937–1945.* Princeton University Press, Princeton.

Medina, L. (1979) *Civilismo y modernización del autoritarismo.* El Colegio de México, Mexico City.

Mericle, K. S. (1974) "Conflict Regulation in the Brazilian Industrial Relations System." PhD dissertation, University of Wisconsin-Madison.

Miranda, M. A. T. (1983) *O Petroleo É Nosso: A luta contra o "entreguismo" pelo monopolio Estatal, 1947–1953.* Vozes, Petrópolis.

Moisés, J. A. (1978) *Greve da massa e crisis política: Estudo de Greve de 300 Mil em São Paulo, 1950–54.* Polis, São Paulo.

Moran, T. H. (1974) *Multinational Corporations and the Politics of Dependence: Copper in Chile.* Princeton University Press, Princeton.

Nozoe, N. H. (1984) *São Paulo, economia cafeeira e urbanização: Estudo da estrutura tributária e das atividades econômicas na capital paulista, 1889–1933.* IPE-USP, São Paulo.

O'Brien, T. F. (1996) *The Revolutionary Mission: American Enterprise in Latin America, 1900–1945.* Cambridge University Press, New York.

Ortega, L. (ed.) (1993) *La guerra civil de 1891: 100 años hoy.* Universidad de Santiago de Chile, Santiago.

Page, J. (1972) *The Revolution That Never Was: Northeast Brazil.* Grossman Publishers, New York.

Page, J. (1983) *Juan Perón: A Biography.* Random House, New York.

Plotkin, M. B. (1994) *Mañana es San Perón: Propaganda, rituales políticos y educación en el régimen peronista, 1946–1955.* Ariel Historia Argentina, Buenos Aires.

Rabe, S. (1999) *The Most Dangerous Area in the World: John F. Kennedy Confronts Communist Revolution in Latin America.* University of North Carolina Press, Chapel Hill.

Randall, L. (1993) *The Political Economy of Brazilian Oil.* Praeger, Westport, CT.

Rock, D. (1993) *Authoritarian Argentina: The Nationalist Movement, Its History, and Its Impact.* University of California Press, Berkeley.

Rosemblatt, K. (2000) *Gendered Compromises: Political Cultures and the State in Chile, 1920–1950.* University of North Carolina Press, Chapel Hill.

Shapiro, H. (1994) *Engines of Growth: The State and Transnational Auto Companies in Brazil.* Cambridge University Press, Cambridge.

Sherman, J. W. (2000) "The Mexican 'Miracle' and Its Collapse." In M. Meyer & W. Beezley (eds.), *The Oxford History of Mexico*. Oxford University Press, New York.

Shumway, N. (1991) *The Invention of Argentina*. University of California Press, Berkeley.

Sikkink, K. (1991) *Ideas and Institutions: Developmentalism in Brazil and Argentina*. Cornell University Press, Ithaca.

Skidmore, T. E. (1967) *Politics in Brazil, 1930–1964: An Experiment with Democracy*. Oxford University Press, New York.

Skidmore, T. E. (1988) *The Politics of Military Rule in Brazil, 1964–1985*. Oxford University Press, New York.

Stein, S. J. (1957) *The Brazilian Cotton Manufacture: Textile Enterprise in an Underdeveloped Area, 1850–1950*. Harvard University Press, Cambridge, MA.

Waisman, C. H. (1987) *Reversal of Development in Argentina: Postwar Counterrevolutionary Policies and Their Structural Consequences*. Princeton University Press, Princeton.

Weinstein, B. (1996) *For Social Peace in Brazil: Industrialists and the Remaking of the Working Class in São Paulo, 1920–1964*. University of North Carolina Press, Chapel Hill.

Weinstein, B. (2003) "Racializing Regional Difference: São Paulo versus Brazil, 1932." In N. P. Appelbaum, A. Macpherson, & K. Rosemblatt (eds.), *Race and Nation in Modern Latin America*. University of North Carolina Press, Chapel Hill.

White, R. A. (1978) *Paraguay's Autonomous Revolution, 1810–1840*. University of New Mexico Press, Albuquerque.

Williams, D. (2001) *Culture Wars in Brazil: the First Vargas Regime, 1930–1945*. Duke University Press, Durham.

Wirth, J. (1970) *The Politics of Brazilian Development, 1930–1954*. Stanford University Press, Stanford.

Wolfe, J. (1993) *Working Women, Working Men: São Paulo and the Rise of Brazil's Industrial Working Class, 1900–1955*. Duke University Press, Durham.

Wolfe, J. (forthcoming) *Autos and Progress: The Brazilian Search for Modernity*. Oxford University Press, New York.

Zeitlin, M. (1984) *The Civil Wars in Chile, or, the Bourgeois Revolutions That Never Were*. Princeton University Press, Princeton.

Chapter Twenty-One

THE CUBAN REVOLUTION

Luis Martínez-Fernández

This chapter addresses the Cuban Revolution, a highly controversial subject that has suffered the deformation of polarized and highly politicized perspectives, the concomitant mythologies generated by the so-called right and left, and a cacophonous chorus of voices which have romanticized, demonized, caricaturized or otherwise distorted the last half century of Cuba's convulsed history. Notwithstanding the outpouring of numerous serious scholarly works over the past few decades, perceptions of the Cuban Revolution are still captive to polarized views; plagued with silences that fail to mention, on the one hand, the revolution's shortcomings or, on the other, its accomplishments.

Almost half a century has elapsed since Castro rose to power and subsequently established a socialist regime. It is, therefore, problematic to generalize about the entire period as many students of the revolution insist on doing. To avoid such generalizations, this chapter is organized chronologically with attention to major themes within the following periodization: Rebellion (1952–8); Laying of the Revolution's Foundations (1959–62); Radicalization, Internationalism, and Soviet Hegemony (1963–70); Institutionalization, Sovietization, and Military Intervention in Africa (1971–84); Crisis and Rectification (1985–9); The Long Special Period (1990–2001); and The Revolution Approaches Fifty (2002–).

Rebellion (1952–8)

While the roots of the Cuban Revolution run deep into the island's past, its most immediate trigger was the coup d'état of March 10, 1952 in which Fulgencio Batista deposed democratically elected President Carlos Prío Socarrás. Corruption and political violence, however, had marred Cuba's short-lived democratic experience. The coup cancelled the general elections scheduled for June 1, 1952 in which Ortodoxo Party candidate Roberto Agramonte and Auténtico Party candidate Carlos Hevia held the lead, followed by Batista as a distant third candidate.

Opposition to Batista's dictatorship surfaced immediately, mainly from established opposition parties and various action movements. Fidel Castro led the most dramatic and significant opposition attack, an armed assault against the Moncada army barracks and other strategic targets in and around Santiago, Cuba's second-largest city. The attack took place on July 26, 1953, hence the name of the revolutionary movement it inspired, the 26th of July Movement.

Castro was born in 1926 into a wealthy landowning family in Birán, Oriente Province. He received a privileged education, including high school at the prestigious Jesuit-run Colegio Belén. Later he pursued a law degree at the University of Havana, where as student leader he joined one of several violent political gangs. Castro's political ideology drew from various sources, including the ideas of Cuban patriot José Martí and the thinking of Ortodoxo politician Eduardo Chibás, whose suicide in 1951 left a leadership vacuum among Cuban progressives (Szulc 1986).

The Moncada attack forces consisted of around 150 untrained and poorly armed combatants, mostly young, poor and working-class individuals and a handful of university students. Nine rebels and 19 soldiers died in the battle. The aftermath was far bloodier with an estimated 68 rebels tortured and executed. Survivors, including Castro and his brother Raúl, were pursued, captured, tried, and sent to prison.

Although failing to accomplish their military objectives, the attacks were successful in many other ways. For one, they demonstrated the vulnerability of Batista's army; they also catapulted Castro to a position of prominence within the opposition and produced dozens of martyrs, victims of the government forces' mounting cruelty and brutality. The Moncada trial also provided Castro with a platform from which to launch a scathing critique of Cuba's economic, social, and political ills and to outline a reform program. His lengthy self-defense speech, later published with the title *History Will Absolve Me* (Castro 1968), painted a grim picture of an impoverished island, trapped by sugar monoculture and languishing under the corrupt, brutal, and illegitimate government of Batista; tens of thousands of landless peasants and agricultural workers; chronic unemployment and underemployment; inadequate housing that for many consisted of huts and hovels; a disease-ridden population with little access to medical and educational services.

Geographer Leví Marrero (2005) and others, however, have convincingly argued that Cuba's economic and social indicators at the time compared very positively with those of Latin America's most prosperous nations and in some cases with those of industrialized countries. Cuba's per capita production ranked third among Latin American nations. Its literacy rate was the fourth highest in Latin America at 75 percent, while its higher education rate was surpassed worldwide only by that of the United States. With one physician per 980 inhabitants, it ranked second in Latin America. Cuba also had a rather large and comfortable middle class consisting of 22–33 percent of the population.

By Latin American standards, class differences between the upper and lower classes were not abysmal but still significant. Sharp distinctions were also evident between regions and between urban and rural areas. Havana, once described as a First World capital of a Third World country, was the wealthiest and most privileged part of Cuba. Havana's opulence and favorable social and economic indicators distorted national averages. Illiteracy was four times higher in rural areas than in cities. While there was one physician per 227 people in Havana, the ratio was one per 2,423 in Oriente Province, the nation's poorest. There were, arguably, really two Cubas: one poor, one wealthy; one eastern, one western; one rural, one urban; one black, one white.

The rebellion, thus, pitted the two Cubas against each other and the ensuing revolution fed upon those differences.

A growing, prosperous, and increasingly national economy and relative social peace made the Batista dictatorship's assault on democracy and atrocities somewhat tolerable for many; and further solidified the support of US interests, national elites, and large segments of the middle class. Economic progress included the expansion of sugar exports and the development of other sectors of the economy such as manufacturing and tourism, with gambling, prostitution, and organized crime as byproducts. The Cold War context also made Batista a valuable anti-communist ally of the United States.

With the help of the state's repressive apparatus, including the Military Intelligence Service (SIM) and CIA-created Bureau of Repression of Communist Activities (BRAC), the government cracked down on clandestine armed groups. By the end of 1954 Batista's forces had neutralized all major opposition movements, including Castro's.

After spending 19 months in prison in the Isle of Pines, the Castros and other rebels were released under the provisions of the amnesty of May 1955. By July, the 26th of July Movement had regrouped and expanded its membership. When the Castro brothers left for Mexico in July to train for another attack against Batista, they left behind a well-organized movement whose leadership included: Faustino Pérez, Raúl Chibás, Carlos Franqui, Armando Hart, Frank País, and Haydée Santamaría.

Other revolutionary movements resurfaced, such as Justo Carillo's Agrupación Montecristi and Prío's Organización Auténtica (OA). In February 1956 a new Havana-based revolutionary movement, Directorio Revolucionario (DR), emerged under the leadership of charismatic student leader José Antonio Echevarría. Yet another anti-Batista movement brewed within the ranks of the military, Los Puros, led by Colonel Ramón Barquín, who scheduled a coup for April 2. It failed because details about the conspiracy had been leaked; the plotters were immediately arrested and imprisoned. Later that month, OA's leader Reynold García launched an attack on the Goicuría army post in Matanzas. Government forces received the rebels with heavy gunfire; all survivors were summarily executed.

Castro's quixotic armed landing aboard the *Granma*, with another 81 revolutionaries including Raúl Castro, Che Guevara, Camilo Cienfuegos, and Juan Almeida was 1956's most significant anti-Batista armed action. Scheduled for November 30, the landing was meant to coincide with rebel military operations in and around Santiago under the leadership of Frank País, a courageous 21-year-old Baptist school teacher. The landing was delayed, however, until December 2, and Batista's forces fired upon the vessel. The 17 or so surviving expeditionaries later established a rebel foothold in the Sierra Maestra highlands, a haven where they received provisions, recruits, and intelligence.

The year 1957 saw an intensification of violent confrontations between the military and police forces and an increasingly radicalized opposition. Highland guerrilla actions increased, as did sabotage activities in the lowlands. In March the DR staged a daring – arguably suicidal – assault on the Presidential Palace with the intention of assassinating Batista. Echevarría and 29 other rebels were killed either during the attack or in the violent clean-up operation that followed. Later in the year DR rebels regrouped in the Escambray mountains under the command of Eloy Gutiérrez

Menoyo, establishing the Second National Front of El Escambray. On July 30, Frank País was killed in battle in Santiago. In early September, Batista smashed the short-lived naval insurrection staged in the naval station of Cienfuegos. By the end of 1957, Castro remained standing in the relatively secure context of the Sierra Maestra as the most viable revolutionary leader.

Batista's regime began to crumble in 1958. It received a severe blow in March, when the United States imposed an arms embargo against it because of its increasingly brutal military and police tactics; this sanction had a profoundly demoralizing effect because it demonstrated that US support for Batista was not unconditional. At the same time, Cuba was enduring a profound economic crisis, partially fueled by the 26th of July Movement's offensive against economic targets such as US-owned mines, plantations, and refineries. The army's defeat and surrender at El Uvero on May 28 was the first major rebel victory; two months later, the guerrilla victory at El Jigüe marked the war's turning point.

By the fall of 1958 both US economic interests and the US government realized that Batista had become a dangerous liability and that he had to be replaced. A glimmer of hope was placed on the presidential elections scheduled for November 3, which Batista's hand-picked successor, Antonio Rivero Agüero, won through fraud. Since Batista refused to yield power, US diplomats proceeded to negotiate a third option under a military–civilian junta led by General Francisco Tabernilla. Che Guevara's troops struck the decisive victory in Santa Clara on December 31, 1958. A few hours later, Batista, his family, and a small group of close associates fled Cuba on an airplane bound for the Dominican Republic.

Laying of the Revolution's Foundations (1959–62)

On January 1, 1959 Castro and his troops marched triumphantly into Santiago, where euphoric crowds greeted them with jubilation. Throughout the island masses celebrated the end of civil war, the fall of Batista, and the advent of a new, reformist government.

Castro designated former judge Manuel Urrutia and Bar Association President José Miró Cardona as president and prime minister, respectively. The original revolutionary cabinet included other respected men, such as Roberto Agramonte, Raúl Cepero Bonilla, Raúl Chibás, Armando Hart, Felipe Pazos, and Manuel Ray. These were middle- and upper-middle-class individuals with liberal and moderate political views. Their presence helped calm the anxieties of domestic and US economic interests as well as those of the US government because they represented the promise of a reformist and democratic, rather than revolutionary and autocratic, process of social and economic transformation.

Castro found a political and military vacuum, the result of Batista's dismantling of the democratic political system and the implosion of his military and police apparatus. The only standing political and military forces were the victorious Rebel Army, the 26th of July Movement, and a few smaller organizations such as the DR and the Popular Socialist Party (PSP, Soviet-aligned communist party).

Doubtless, Castro had become the most powerful – perhaps undisputedly so – military and political leader. In mid-February, following Miró Cardona's resignation, he became prime minister. The masses venerated him as the *líder máximo*, a larger-than-life, inspiring, and charismatic leader. *Fidelismo* became the ideological foundation of Castro's rule as the masses supported whatever initiatives he embarked upon.

The Revolution's first order of business was the elimination of all remnants of the defunct dictatorship. Batista's men were hunted down and imprisoned; they became the targets of mob violence; their properties, the object of sacking and confiscation. By January 20, around 200 hundred *Batistianos* had been executed; two months later the number of executions approximated 500. Many others fled, mostly to Miami.

The next casualties of the revolutionary government were the democratic institutions that had survived Batista's dictatorship – dormant and mangled as they may have been – namely, the Constitution of 1940, the electoral process, an elected legislative branch, and an independent judiciary. President Urrutia was reduced to a figurehead while Castro held actual executive power as prime minister, presiding over, and controlling, the cabinet, through which he also dominated the legislative branch. Castro's dominance over the judiciary was made evident by his authority to order retrials of individuals that he did not want to see absolved. Castro also banned the old political parties, except the PSP, and postponed elections for 15 months. In April he stated: "Revolution first, elections later"; a year later he announced that there would be no elections. Castro ousted President Urrutia by mobilizing *Fidelista* mobs. In September he replaced most of the remaining liberal and moderate cabinet members. The judicial branch underwent a similar cleansing with 21 of 32 judges resigning between November 1960 and February 1961.

Cuban communists were instrumental in the displacement of the moderate revolutionary leadership. The PSP membership was well disciplined; and its leaders had not been marred by scandal and corruption. It also enjoyed Soviet support, an increasingly valuable asset as relations between Cuba and the United States soured. While not affiliated with the PSP, Raúl Castro and Guevara were known for their communist ideology and both played a major role in appointing communists as officers of the newly formed Revolutionary Armed Forces (Franqui 1980).

By the fall of 1959, just holding anti-communist views had become a dangerous liability. Major Huber Matos, for example, was sentenced to 20 years in prison for denouncing communist infiltration within the armed forces; another popular and charismatic revolutionary, Major Camilo Cienfuegos, disappeared soon thereafter under mysterious circumstances. As liberals were being purged from the revolutionary government, communists received key appointments: Lázaro Peña (secretary general of the Confederation of Cuban Workers [CTC]); Antonio Nuñez Jiménez (executive director of the National Agrarian Reform Institute [INRA]); Raúl Roa (minister of foreign relations); Juan Marinello (president of the University of Havana), Aníbal Escalante (coordinator of Integrated Revolutionary Organizations [ORI]) and others.

Organized opposition to Castro's regime emerged early on with the formation of the *Movimiento Rescate Revolucionario* (Revolutionary Rescue Movement), led by 27-year-old Manuel Artíme, and the emergence of several underground movements engaging in sabotage activities. Opposition guerrilla movements also brewed in various rural locations, most notably in the highlands of El Escambray. Many of the regime's most vocal opponents sought exile in Miami. The growing list of exiled political leaders included Artíme, Carrillo, Rolando Masferrer, Manuel "Tony"

Varona, and Miró Cardona, who became president of the anti-Castro umbrella organization, Cuban Revolutionary Council.

The revolutionary government treated opponents and dissenters with a heavy hand. The state's political police, the G2, identified, monitored, and imprisoned members of the opposition, employing brutal tactics and torture in an effort to eradicate counterrevolutionary activities. Some estimate the number of political prisoners in mid-1959 to have reached 75,000 (López Vilaboy 1973: 430). Only 90 miles away, the United States played once again the role of haven for the opposition and dissenters. An estimated 200,000 Cubans fled the island, mostly to South Florida, between 1959 and mid-1962, among them over 1,400 unaccompanied minors through Operation Pedro Pan (Conde 1999).

Castro proceeded to centralize power by assuming control over civil society: the media, professional organizations, and churches. In January 1960 the regime began to censor various independent print media by imposing "coletillas," brief government-produced comments and refutations that followed editorials and news stories. Editors and newscasters deemed uncooperative endured harassment and were eventually forced to resign. Before long, Castro's dictatorship had taken over or shut down all independent media. In mid-1960 the regime secured control of the previously autonomous University of Havana, imposing a new president and governing board; later that year, armed government operatives stormed the offices of the Bar Association and closed it down. The Catholic Church was the only major non-governmental institution left standing at the end of 1960. Clashes between church and state intensified in 1961 and outright confrontation exploded in the aftermath of the failed Bay of Pigs invasion, when the regime nationalized Catholic schools and expelled most priests and nuns.

The government's most important allies in the process toward political and economic centralization were the poor and peasant and worker masses that had been mobilized by civil war, general strike, and mass rallies. The Revolution demobilized and/or co-opted all existing mass organizations. Simultaneously, society was re-mobilized under new mass organizations created by the government, among them the Federation of Cuban Women (FMC) under the leadership of Vilma Espín, Raúl Castro's wife; the militias; the Association of Rebel Youth; neighborhood watchdog organizations known as Committees for the Defense of the Revolution (CDRs); and the National Association of Small Farmers (ANAP).

The social and economic agenda of the revolutionary government aimed at reducing the island's historical dependence on sugar and its evil concomitants: latifundia, landlessness, seasonal unemployment, poverty, and extreme dependence on trade with the United States. The battle against king sugar included plans for the diversification of agriculture and industrialization as efforts to reduce dependence on imported foodstuffs and manufactured goods.

The Agrarian Reform Law of May 17, 1959 was the most far-reaching and comprehensive reform enacted by the revolutionary government during its first year. The law limited individual landholdings to 402 hectares and to a maximum of 1,340 hectares for land units whose productivity exceeded the national average by 50 percent or more. Before the end of the summer of 1959 the agrarian reform had nationalized a total of 2.5 million acres. The reform did not end latifundia but rather turned vast extensions of formerly private land into government-owned farms; and mid-size farms came under government-controlled cooperatives.

Laws and decrees raised workers' salaries, reduced utility bills substantially, and cut rents by 30–50 percent under the provisions of the Urban Reform Law of March 1959. The government also focused on the expansion of education, by increasing school enrollments. The most ambitious and successful educational effort was the literacy campaign of 1961, when an estimated 271,000 Cubans including teachers and even students as young as 10 were mobilized to eradicate illiteracy. According to government statistics, by the end of 1960, illiteracy had fallen below 4 percent. The campaign, however, also served as an indoctrination tool. The expansion of health services became another social priority. The cost of medicines dropped and new health-care facilities were created in poor, rural, and remote locations. Of all social concerns, housing received the least attention. An already insufficient supply of housing units shrank further as demand grew.

During 1960 and 1961 Castro's regime continued to expand its grip over the economy. This was a gradual process with foreign oil companies – Texaco, Sinclair, Shell, among others – becoming the first targets. Cigar and tobacco companies followed. A broader nationalization process began in October 1960, including banks, factories, department stores, and cinemas. Such widespread nationalizations further alienated the middle and upper middle classes but were welcomed and supported by the government-controlled unions and mass organizations. Before 1961 was over, the Cuban state directly controlled 85 percent of all domestic production.

The years 1961 and 1962 witnessed an economic downturn resulting from the manifold economic and social transformations brought on by the Revolution, including the socialization of the means of production, the application of income redistribution measures, the imposition of a trade embargo by the United States, and the flight of thousands of professional and skilled workers, including managers, technicians, engineers, and agronomists. Contrary to the Revolution's economic objectives, dependence on imports increased, as did the island's trade deficits. Lower productivity levels coupled with the government's redistributive agenda forced the government to impose a rationing system for food and clothing; even sugar was rationed.

The United States government was quick to protest the early measures of the Revolution having a direct impact on US economic interests. In response to the nationalization of US corporate landholdings, the United States retaliated by slashing Cuba's quota of sugar imports to the United States. Economic war between the United States and increasingly radical Cuba escalated quickly during 1960 (Welch 1985). At the same time, Cuba moved closer to the USSR both economically and politically as the Soviets filled in the trade gaps created by the cutting of Cuba's sugar quota and the US trade embargo. In February 1960 Soviet First Deputy Premier Anastas Mikoyan visited Cuba; an agreement was reached then whereby the USSR would purchase sugar, provide loans, and sell crude oil at reduced prices. When the first Soviet crude oil shipments arrived, Castro instructed US oil companies to refine them. They rejected the order and Castro proceeded to nationalize their facilities. The United States then retaliated by cutting Cuba's sugar quota much further; to which Castro responded by nationalizing the assets of remaining US-owned companies.

The next round in the economic war against Cuba brought the imposition of a trade embargo on October 19, 1960. In December the United States cut the sugar quota down to zero. Both nations broke diplomatic relations in January 1961. The trade embargo had the effect of further pushing Cuba into the Soviet orbit and making it dependent on the USSR and other socialist nations as markets for sugar and providers of oil, chemicals, industrial equipment, manufactured goods, and foodstuffs. Change happened so quickly that within a matter of two years the Soviet Union and other socialist nations completely replaced the United States as Cuba's premier trading partner. In 1961 socialist nations received the same proportion of Cuban exports (74 percent) as the US received in 1959. During the same period socialist imports to Cuba (70 percent in 1961) replaced and outpaced US imports (64 percent in 1959).

At the same time more direct forms of confrontation brewed, accompanied by increasingly belligerent rhetorical exchanges. The CIA began to train Cuban exiles to carry out anti-Castro covert operations; it also developed Operation Mongoose, which included sabotage, economic warfare, and multiple assassination attempts on Castro. The Soviets responded with a promise to defend Cuba in case of any attack from the United States and deployed tens of thousands of Soviet troops and large amounts of military equipment.

The first armed confrontation over Cuba was the Bay of Pigs invasion of April 15–19, 1961. The attacking exile force, named Brigade 2506, consisted of nearly 1,500 CIA-trained Cuban exiles. One hundred and forty members of the brigade died in combat and another 1,180 were captured by the Cuban armed forces. An estimated 2,200 Cuban soldiers died in battle. The invasion failed for a number of reasons: it was poorly planned; Castro expected the invasion and ordered a preemptive arrest of nearly 100,000 domestic opponents; the CIA took charge over the coordination with disregard for the exile leadership; supply vessels were unable to land with the necessary weapons and ammunition; and President John F. Kennedy ordered the withdrawal of the promised air support (Wyden 1979; Kornbluh 1998). The victory of the Cuban troops demonstrated the strength of the Revolution and further solidified Castro's rule. Later that year, Castro declared himself and the Revolution to be Marxist–Leninist.

An increase in Soviet military presence, including 40,000 soldiers and the deployment of nuclear missiles to the island, led to the next confrontation, the Missile Crisis of October 1962, which brought the world close to a nuclear conflagration (Kennedy 1969; Chang & Kornbluh 1998). In contrast with his indecisive handling of the Bay of Pigs, Kennedy now acted firmly, declaring a naval blockade of the island on October 22 to stop further shipments of weapons and to force the Soviet Union to withdraw the missiles already on the island. Following six more days of mutual threats and tense negotiations, Washington and Moscow reached an agreement to end the crisis when the Soviets promised to remove their nuclear weapons in exchange for a US pledge to not invade the island. Castro felt personally humiliated for being left out of the negotiations and the Soviet Union's unilateral decision to withdraw the weapons.

Cuba's mounting hostilities with the United States and increasingly close relations with the Soviet Union had global reverberations in the highly polarized Cold War context of the early 1960s. The nations of the Americas, with the exception of Mexico and Canada, broke diplomatic and trade relations with Cuba. The rebel island was expelled from the Organization of American States (OAS) in January 1962. Cuba's hemispheric isolation, however, was counterbalanced by new and expanding trade and diplomatic relations with the European socialist bloc as well as with China, Vietnam, and North Korea.

Radicalization, Internationalism, and Soviet Hegemony (1963–70)

By 1963 the Revolution had succeeded politically. Castro had formed a solid government structure buttressed by the support of mass organizations created during the first years of revolution. Through exile, mass incarcerations, and violent repression of the opposition, he managed to rid the island of all viable forms of resistance, with the exception of a few thousand peasant guerrillas operating in El Escambray. In sharp contrast, however, the Revolution had failed economically. The initial goals of economic diversification and development through import-substitution ended disastrously. And the production of sugar, Cuba's historic cash crop, suffered from neglect and inept management. The 1963 harvest reached only 3.9 million tons, the lowest output since 1945. General agricultural productivity levels fell almost 50 percent from an all-time high in 1960–1 to the low-point year 1963–4. These abysmal economic circumstances threatened national sovereignty and the long-term survival of the Revolution.

In the aftermath of the disappointing 1963 harvest the government shifted back its resources toward sugar with the hope that increased sugar revenues would generate the necessary capital for a now postponed industrialization process. The timing proved auspicious as world sugar prices rose sharply. Cuba's return to sugar dovetailed with the Soviet Union's agenda of subjecting the island to a relationship of economic dependence similar to that which it previously endured with the United States: a supplier of raw materials (i.e., sugar) and importer of oil, machines, and manufactured goods. In the spring of 1963 Castro paid his first visit to the Soviet Union where he secured sugar trade agreements at highly subsidized prices. The following year both nations negotiated the price at six cents a pound, twice the international market price. Soviet loans and technology were also instrumental in the modernization of sugar mills.

Cuban–Soviet relations during the 1960s, while collaborative, were plagued by tensions. Moscow and Havana did not see eye to eye on many international matters and Cuban revolutionaries forged their own version of socialism according to Cuban values and circumstances as well as Castro's personalistic rule and whim. The first major disagreement occurred during the Missile Crisis, when the United States and the Soviets left Cuba out of the negotiations. Later in the decade, tensions mounted over Cuba's insistence on exporting revolution to Africa and South America. The Soviets took advantage of Cuba's economic dependence, holding back from purchasing 20 percent of the agreed 1967 sugar quota to force the regime to halt its export of guerrillas to Latin America. Economic coercion worked. The following year Cuba was compelled to defend the Soviet invasion of Czechoslovakia, as payback for Soviet subsidization of the Cuban economy (Karol 1970).

Che Guevara, who had pro-China rather than pro-Soviet sympathies, was the point man in the efforts to export revolution through guerrilla warfare. Born in Argentina on June 14, 1928, Guevara joined Castro in Mexico in 1955 and became a top rebel officer. He was instrumental in the implementation of major economic restructuring during 1959–63, when he held several key posts such as president of the National Bank and Minister of Industries. Guevara believed that the *foco* guerrilla model (building an armed movement from an isolated rural starting point) that had succeeded in the Cuban highlands could be replicated elsewhere (Guevara 1985). At Castro's urging, Guevara resigned from all of his government appointments to avoid any connections between Cuba and Guevara's guerrilla activities. Guevara's guerrilla activities took him to Bolivia, where he was captured by US-trained Bolivian soldiers and executed on October 9, 1967 (Anderson 1997).

Domestically, the firmly entrenched revolutionary government became increasingly radical in its goals to eradicate the remnants of capitalistic institutions, values, and behaviors. During the mid- to late 1960s the state worked hard to instill socialist values among the population through education, indoctrination, and legislation. The government devised mechanisms to discourage individualism and personal profit, and to reduce class inequalities, while promoting an ideology of hard work and sacrifice: the creation of a so-called "New Man" that would give himself fully in service of the Revolution (Bunck 1994). Chronic consumer goods shortages in the 1960s did not permit the regime to reward hard work and sacrifice with material incentives such as higher salaries and bonuses. Besides, the distribution of material incentives would have run counter to the Revolution's redistributive goals, as such incentives threatened to reestablish social and economic inequalities. Instead, the Revolution offered so-called moral incentives such as public recognition and honors symbolized by medals, plaques, scrolls, and the like.

Castro's success in the centralization of power and the symbiotic relation that his government established with the masses allowed the Cuban state to further radicalize its socialist agenda during the balance of the 1960s. In 1963 it imposed a far-reaching second agrarian reform that included the nationalization of all but the very smallest (67 acres or less) landholdings remaining in private hands. The final blow to capitalism and private employment came in March 1968 when the so-called Revolutionary Offensive nationalized all remaining private businesses and banned self-employment. These measures affected around 57,000 small businesses, ranging from TV repair shops and beauty salons to cab drivers and street fruit vendors. Thus, by the end of 1968, the government controlled 100 percent of industry, construction, retail, wholesale, and international trade, transportation, banking, and education; only 30 percent of agricultural production remained in private hands; its distribution and sale, however, was also monopolized by the state.

Other redistributive efforts entailed the compression of salaries to reduce income differences. By 1970 unemployment had virtually disappeared, further reducing income differentials. The expansion of free social and public services, including health care, education, childcare, bus transportation, and various utilities also helped erode class differences. In 1967 primary education was made compulsory and educational efforts increasingly focused on the expansion of middle school enrollment and retention. Although student numbers rose, graduation rates made only modest gains. Medical services continued to expand during the balance of the 1960s through the creation of rural clinics and regional hospitals.

Castro continued to confront dissent and opposition with a heavy hand. Cuba's notorious jails housed an estimated 20,000 political prisoners in 1965 (Pérez 1995:

349). The state also continued to export its opposition, namely through exile to the United States. Following the United States' ban on flights from Cuba in the aftermath of the Missile Crisis, the flow of exiles dwindled to about 3,000 per year. In the fall of 1965 Castro once again opened the escape valve of exile, when he allowed some 7,500 Cubans to be picked up by boats at the port of Camarioca. The Lyndon B. Johnson administration took steps to control the brewing exodus crisis. Both governments negotiated the establishment of an air bridge (Liberty Flights) that allowed disaffected Cubans to resettle in the United States. These flights, which lasted until 1971, transported approximately 200,000 Cubans to the United States (Masud-Piloto 1988).

The sugar-based development strategy begun in 1963 was scheduled to peak triumphantly during the1970 sugar harvest with a target of 10 million tons. In pursuit of this goal, the revolutionary government channeled its resources toward sugar at the expense of other sectors of the economy. A total of 1.2 million Cubans (14.5 percent of the population) worked the harvest. This included 300,000 regular sugar-cane workers, 100,000 military troops, hundreds of thousands of volunteers and so-called volunteers, as well as thousands of political prisoners conscripted through the infamous Military Units to Aid Production (UMAP). In the end, the 1970 sugar harvest fell short of its goal, reaching, according to official statistics, 8.5 million tons; other estimates placed the harvest at only 7.5 million tons. Because the revolution's leadership had hinged so much on the 10 million ton harvest, turning it into a matter of national honor, the failure to reach the goal represented a moral defeat and the failure of the "New Man." The extreme focus on sugar had serious long-term consequences. The fact that other sectors of the economy were woefully neglected during the 1970 sugar frenzy further debilitated other agricultural, mining, and manufacturing activities.

Institutionalization, Sovietization, and Military Intervention in Africa (1971–84)

The aftermath of the 10 million ton harvest fiasco brought about major changes to the orientation of the Revolution. Several of its original foundations were sacrificed. Autonomous, self-sustained economic development and national sovereignty were replaced by a model of economic growth dependent on the Soviet Union and Eastern Europe (Mesa-Lago 1974). Likewise, wealth redistribution and egalitarianism, as well as the use of moral incentives to motivate productivity, were reversed by instituting material incentives that contributed to growing income inequalities. Furthermore, during the 1970s Cuba embarked on a process of political institutionalization both of its relationship with the Soviet Union and of its domestic government structures. Cuban sociologist Marifeli Pérez-Stable claims that such changes marked the conclusion of the Revolution: "Indeed, the year 1970 poignantly marked the end of the revolution" (Pérez-Stable 1999: 120).

At the heart of the national effort to expand productivity was the desire to incorporate the vast majority of the able-bodied population to the workforce. The year 1971 was declared the "Year of Productivity." Anti-vagrancy laws were enacted to expand the labor base. Special efforts were also made in coordination with the FMC to incorporate a higher percentage of the female population to the workforce. These proved successful as the proportion of women of working age climbed rapidly from 24.9 percent in 1970 to 44.5 percent in 1979.

The revolutionary leadership recognized that expanding the labor base was not sufficient; higher productivity required material motivations. The 1960s Guevarist model of self-sacrifice and volunteerism, which had seemingly failed, gave way to so-called material incentives associated with capitalist practices and mechanisms that rewarded individual workers and particular production units for increasing productivity. Managers of successful factories and farms received bonuses; workers earned extra pay as well as material rewards such as TV sets and resort vacations. In 1973 the Cuban Workers Central (CTC) agreed to tie salaries to productivity, and a new pay scale in 1980 further widened the income gap. Individuals were also allowed to engage in limited, independent economic activities that provided opportunities for economic gain. In 1980 peasants were permitted to sell their excess production in Peasant Free Markets. In the same vein, artists and craftspeople could now sell their works to the public. Moreover, the government partially opened the real estate market, allowing individuals to trade houses and apartments. Such measures, while conducive to increased productivity, had the effect of widening the income gap. Growth of expendable income also led to increased consumerism that fueled the emergence and expansion of black market activities.

The economy turned around during the 1970s and continued to expand during the first half of the 1980s. GDP grew every year between 1970 and 1984, with the exception of 1980. The rate of economic growth averaged 5.75 percent per year between 1971 and 1980; and 7.3 percent from 1981 to 1985. While labor productivity grew sharply, several other factors helped economic growth. For one, it was a period of high sugar prices: from 3.2 cents per pound in 1969 they rose to 4.5 cents in 1971 and to 9.59 cents in 1973, peaking at a dizzying 29.6 cents in 1974. When world sugar prices plummeted after 1975, Cuban sugar trade agreements with the Soviet Union for 1976–80 guaranteed a stable Soviet market at a subsidized price of 30 cents a pound. Cuba also benefited by its formal incorporation to the socialist economic system when it joined the Council of Economic Mutual Assistance in July 1972. All in all, more intimate trade relations with the Soviet Union based on the sugar mono-export translated into greater dependence on, growing trade deficits with, and deeper indebtedness to the Soviet Union. In 1975 sugar accounted for 90 percent of all Cuban exports, up from 80 percent on the eve of the Revolution.

The political institutionalization of the Revolution followed Soviet models. The Cuban Communist Party had been established in 1965 as a single party but held its first congress a decade later in 1975. By then party membership had reached just over 200,000. The First Congress's most important accomplishment was the drafting of a new constitution. The 1976 constitution established the functions of the various components of the revolutionary government. These included a national legislative body, the National Assembly of People's Power. Its power, however, remained mostly symbolic because it met only twice a year for just a few days. Moreover, because the various lower bodies of the legislative structure served as filters, it excluded opposing or dissenting voices. Executive functions were to be carried out by the State Council and the Council of Ministers, whose leadership was ostensibly selected by the National Assembly. Within the new structure, Castro presided over the Council of State and assumed the prime ministry of the Council of Ministers; his dictatorial powers also included being commander-in-chief of the Revolutionary Armed Forces, first secretary of the Communist Party, as well as member of its Political Bureau.

At the same time, the FMC became more widely participatory and expanded its influence within society. The Federation played a key role in the creation of the Family Code of 1975, which intended to end discrimination against women and reformed laws pertaining to maternity leave, divorce, alimony and child support, and abortion. Access to free abortion services expanded and the proportion of pregnancies ending in abortion rose to 40 percent in 1979 and 49 percent in 1989. Divorce rates also grew, reaching 44 divorces per 100 marriages in 1989 (Smith and Padula 1996).

In 1980 a large and dramatic wave of exiles left Cuba in what came to be known as the Mariel Boatlift. In all, 125,000 people left between April 21 and September 26, 1980, bound for Key West, Florida. The massive size of the exodus reflected the growing dissatisfaction with the Revolution. Significantly, the composition of this migratory wave included a dominant proportion of working-class individuals, mostly young, single males, a substantial proportion of whom were black or mulatto. While the Mariel exodus exposed widespread disaffection with the regime, thus a source of embarrassment for the revolutionary leadership, Castro used the opportunity to rid the island of those deemed undesirable by the regime: criminals, lazy individuals, Jehovah's Witnesses, mental patients, and gays and lesbians, among others (Fernández 2002).

The 1970s witnessed dramatic transformations in Cuba's foreign relations and international standing. Its hemispheric isolation began to dissipate as a few left-leaning governments reached power in Latin America. Peru under General Juan Velasco Alvarado reestablished trade and diplomatic relations with Cuba in 1968. Chile followed in 1971, after the election of socialist president Salvador Allende. Two years later, anticipating the return of Juan Perón, Argentina followed suit. In 1975 the OAS reopened its doors to Cuba. Later in the decade, Cuba found a strong regional ally, as Sandinista guerrillas reached power in Nicaragua with Cuban support. Cuba's standing among Third World nations peaked late in the decade when Castro was elected chair of the Non-Aligned Movement (1979–82). The regime's unabashed support of the Soviet invasion of Afghanistan later that year, however, eroded its credibility among the non-aligned nations.

Beginning in the second half of the 1970s, Cuba carried out large-scale military interventions in Africa. In October 1975, some 500 military advisors arrived in newly independent Angola to support the People's Movement for the Liberation of Angola (MPLA) against the opposing National Front for the Liberation of Angola and National Union for the Total Independence of Angola (UNITA). The latter had the support of Zaire, South Africa, and the United States. In all, nearly 400,000 Cubans served in Angola between 1975 and 1991 in either military or civilian capacities. Cuban soldiers and weaponry were instrumental in the defeat of Zairian and South African troops. Cuban soldiers also fought on the side of Ethiopia against Somalia. In September 1977 15,000 combatants, under the leadership of General Arnaldo Ochoa along with the Soviet-supported Ethiopian army, repelled Somali invading forces (LeoGrande 1980; Mesa-Lago & Belkin 1982).

While Cuban military incursions in Africa became a primary bone of contention between Cuba and the United States, Jimmy Carter's election in 1976 signaled the arrival of an era of rapprochement. First, in 1977 diplomatic interest sections were opened in each country; soon thereafter, the United States relaxed restrictions on travel to Cuba. The juncture was also favorable for a dialogue between the Cuban government and certain segments of the Cuban exile community. As a result of the dialogue of 1978, Cuba released some 3,600 political prisoners and began to allow exiles to visit their relatives. In 1979 alone, over 100,000 traveled to the island. When Ronald Reagan became president in 1981, US policy toward Cuba became increasingly hostile. That year US forces conducted threatening military training operations near Cuba. Travel to Cuba was banned in 1982. On May 20, 1985, Radio Martí, sponsored by the US government, began broadcasting anti-Castro programs to Cuba.

Crisis and Rectification (1985–9)

The year 1985 brought a new economic crisis and the beginning of significant transformations in the orientation of the Revolution. Mikhail Gorbachev was elected Soviet Premier and began a radical process of reforms that included *glasnost* (political openness) and *perestroika* (economic restructuring). These dramatic changes eventually contributed to the collapse of the socialist bloc in 1989 and the disintegration of the Soviet Union two years later. Because of its profound dependence on the Soviet Union and Eastern Europe, Cuba's relations with the socialist bloc became increasingly distant. The fact that sugar prices fell sharply to only 4 cents per pound in 1986 further aggravated the situation, producing a foreign exchange crisis that led to severe import cuts and to the nation's default on its foreign debt. In May 1986 Cuba stopped payments of principal and interest on its medium- and long-term foreign loans. The Soviets demanded that Cuba make its trade payments in US dollars and, during a visit to Cuba in April 1989, Gorbachev announced the end of Soviet subsidies.

Going against the grain of developments in the Soviet Union, Castro rejected both perestroika and glasnost. Actually, the Revolution moved in the opposite direction, its leaders launching an offensive against capitalist influences that had penetrated Cuba during the previous decade and a half, when material incentives had increased income and standard of living differences. For one thing, the new economic crisis made it hard for the government to continue providing material incentives. For another, the use of material incentives had had a demoralizing effect on those who worked in non-incentive areas such as education and health.

In 1986 Castro launched the so-called Rectification of Past Errors Campaign in which material incentives were replaced by moral incentives reminiscent of the 1960s. Among the targets of rectification were independent merchants, hustlers, black marketers, and others who had profited from past economic opportunities. Representative of the new changes was the closing in 1986 of farmers' markets that had been authorized earlier in the decade. The state once again promoted the values of volunteerism and sacrifice; not coincidentally, Che Guevara was resurrected and used as symbol of a revolutionary ethic of hard work and austerity. The regime reintroduced volunteer and communal efforts such as the mobilization of construction microbrigades.

Contrary to the tenets of perestroika, the government's response was the state's expansion into, and monopolization of, all economic activities. In 1986 the state set up special "dollar stores" in order to collect much-needed hard currency. The government also increased its attention to foreign exchange-generating export crops at the expense of food production, and began investing in the expansion of the tourist industry, deemed a promising source of hard currency income.

In the late 1980s several high-ranking officials participated in smuggling activities, including African ivory and diamonds as well as drug trans-shipments from Colombia. In June 1989 General Ochoa, who a few years earlier had led victorious troops in Africa, was arrested and charged with drug trafficking. His status as Hero of the Revolution, his popularity, and his reformist inclinations made Ochoa threatening to the Castro brothers. Also accused of drug trafficking were Ministry of the Interior Colonel Antonio de la Guardia and his twin brother Ministry of the Interior Brigadier General Patricio de la Guardia. Ochoa, Antonio de la Guardia, and two others were executed by firing squad. The Castros used the occasion to purge and reduce the numbers of both the Revolutionary Armed Forces and the Ministry of the Interior. Minister of the Interior José Abrantes and other high-ranking officials were also removed from their posts (Oppenheimer 1993).

The Long Special Period (1990–2001)

In light of the looming economic debacle, in December 1989 Castro uttered the ominous phrase "Socialism or Death," defiantly expressing his resolve to remain in power and maintain the island's socialist system. The following year, Castro announced the beginning of a "Special Period in Times of Peace," requiring emergency measures of sacrifice and austerity to confront the shocks produced by the loss of Soviet subsidies. In 1991 the crumbling Soviet Union cut Cuba's lifeline by abruptly ending its yearly subsidies of around 5 billion dollars; oil shipments from the former Soviet Union dropped to only 6 million tons in 1992, less than half of 1990 levels (Mesa-Lago 1993; Azicri 2000).

The ensuing economic crisis was catastrophic. Various indicators dramatize the economy's free fall between 1989 and rock-bottom year 1993. GDP fell by 35 percent. Trade volume fell 75 percent (imports) and 79 percent (exports). Foreign debt grew 42 percent. Sugar, the economy's traditional backbone, dropped precipitously: the 1994–5 harvest produced only 3.5 million tons.

The social consequences of the economic crisis proved severe. As a result of falling revenues, the government curtailed social expenditures. The number of surgeries, for example, fell from 885,790 in 1990 to 486,067 in 1993. Food rations were significantly reduced as well, bringing down the average daily caloric consumption level from 2,908 in the 1980s to 1,863 in 1993, short of the required minimum of 2,400. As a result of the impoverished diet, average birth weight fell and nutrition deficit diseases augmented, most notoriously an epidemic of optic myelo-neuropathy. The sudden 50 percent drop in oil imports forced daily electricity blackouts and sharp reductions in public transportation. Unemployment peaked in 1995 at 7.9 percent.

The government pursued drastic measures, including numerous economic re-forms to prop up the embattled system. Thirty-nine-year-old physician Carlos Lage spearheaded the reformist program as president of the National Commission for the Special Period. Cuba moved decisively toward market-oriented reforms, a path similar to the Chinese model, whereby the state opened up spaces within the economy but maintained rigid political and social control over the population.

With the Soviet Union rapidly vanishing from the equation, the economy desperately required new sources of hard currency to be generated through the restructuring of its foreign trade – namely, replacing the Soviet Union and other socialist nations with new markets. Thus, the Soviet Union's share of Cuba's foreign trade fell sharply from 69 percent (1988) to only 20 percent (1993); at the same time trade with Western Europe and Latin America shot up from 7 percent and 4 percent to 30 percent and 30 percent, respectively.

Cuba also embarked on an aggressive campaign to attract foreign capital. These efforts lured significant investments from major international corporations such as Canada's Sherritt International (nickel), Spain's Grupo Sol Meliá (tourism), Telecomunicaciones Internacionales de México (phone service), and France's Pernod Ricard (rum). Foreign capital also came in the form of mixed ventures, in which the state held at least 51 percent of the ownership of several hundred business, including supply and management services. The state's participation in the market economy also included the managing of diverse production, business, and banking enterprises, particularly by the armed forces, which ran a variety of economic activities such as sugar production and fisheries as well as hotel chains, airlines, banks, and cigar store chains.

Of all the sectors of the economy, tourism received the most attention; the regime invested heavily in the construction of an adequate tourism infrastructure in partnership with foreign capital. Tourism became the primary engine behind Cuba's economic recovery, surpassing sugar in 1994 as the main generator of hard currency. The number of tourists visiting the island grew consistently and sharply from 340,000 in 1990 to 546,000 in 1993 to 1,004,000 in 1996 to 1,600,000 in 1999.

Among the most important and far-reaching of the Special Period's reforms was the legalization of the US dollar in 1993. This move, embraced reluctantly by the "old guard" revolutionary leadership, allowed the government to increase its revenues and, furthermore, stimulated the inflow of remittances by Cubans living abroad. Remittances soon became the second most important source of hard currency with an estimated $800 million to $1 billion per year during the balance of the decade.

The reforms paid off. After hitting its lowest point in 1993, the economy began to rebound in 1994: the GDP increased 2.5 percent in 1995 and grew by a sharp 7.8 percent in 1996. Over the next few years the economy continued to grow, albeit at a slower rate. Other economic indicators, meanwhile, pointed in the direction of a highly vulnerable economy resting on a poor trade, financial, and social base. While the level of foreign investment had risen substantially to around $5 billion in 2000, Cuba's debt mounted to $11 billion plus another $24 billion to the former USSR. Trade deficit also towered with $1.66 billion in exports and $4.3 billion in imports.

The economy's recovery did not touch the lives of most Cubans. Since most individuals did not have access to dollars, the reforms produced growing inequalities between state employees, whose income remained stagnant, and dollar-earning individuals. In 1999 mean state salaries ranged between 150 and 200 pesos per month (the equivalent of 7 to 10 US dollars). Those individuals being hired out by the state to mixed ventures earned somewhat higher wages and had access to bonuses but were also the most exploited: the state charged employers in dollars and paid workers in pesos. State workers with access to tips, such as bartenders, also earned considerably more. Black marketers, prostitutes, and others operating on the margins of legality earned several times what a teacher or physician made. Other Cubans, perhaps 20 percent of the population, supplemented their income with remittances sent by relatives living abroad; due to the racial composition of the Cuban diaspora, remittances favored white Cubans disproportionately. Thus, one of the legacies of the dollarization of the economy was the growth of social and racial inequalities, which had been aggressively targeted during the 1960s.

The first organized human rights movement dates to 1976 when former University of Havana professor and political prisoner Ricardo Bofill and physician Martha Frayde began to document human rights abuses and make that information available to the international community. Both were eventually imprisoned by the regime. Along with other former political prisoners they later formed the Cuban Human Rights Committee. In 1982 political prisoner Armando Valladares was released after serving 22 years; he published *Against all Hope* (1986 [1985]), a scathing denunciation of the horrors taking place inside Cuba's prisons.

In 1987, Elizardo Sánchez Santacruz formed his own organization, the Cuban Human Rights and National Reconciliation Commission. When Bofill left Cuba in 1988, Moncada attack veteran Gustavo Arcos replaced him as the movement's leader. Yet another emerging opposition group was the Christian Liberation Movement, founded in 1989 by Oswaldo Payá. Over 100 dissident groups joined the umbrella organization, Cuban Council, in 1996. One of the most important documents to come out of the dissident movement was "The Fatherland belongs to all of us." Signed by Valdimiro Roca, Felix Bonné, René Gómez Manzano, and Marta Beatriz Roque, it offered a critique of a document produced by the Cuban Communist Party (Martínez-Fernández et al. 2003: vol. 2, 652–3). Pope Paul John II's January 1998 visit raised the hope of many Cubans for a better future. His words, "Do not be afraid," energized Payá's Varela Project, which collected over 11,000 signatures to petition the government for a referendum.

The early to mid-1990s also witnessed the emergence of numerous non-governmental organizations that ended the government's monopolistic control over the island's civilian associations, thus establishing the bases for the formation of civil society. Some of these organizations grouped professionals: lawyers, physicians, teachers, writers and artists, economists, etc. Journalists established various groups of independent journalists, such as Raúl Rivero's CubaPress. Independent libraries also emerged as alternative sources of information. Independent journalists, librarians, and other dissidents endured continuous harassment and periodic incarcerations. One of the most notorious episodes of governmental repression was the arrest of 75 dissidents in 2003; their sentences ranged between 12 and 28 years. Later that year the international organization Journalists without Borders ranked Cuba second to last in terms of press freedoms.

Dissatisfaction with conditions on the island was also manifested through flight. On July 13, 2004 a group of individuals seeking to escape the island hijacked the *13 de Marzo* tugboat; the coastguard sank the vessel killing 41 people, 20 children among them. On August 5 riots broke out in Havana and a few days later Castro ordered the Cuban Coast Guard not to interfere with *balseros* (rafters) seeking to leave the island; as a result, an estimated 36,000 rafters left.

The United States government saw the Special Period as an opportunity to further debilitate the Cuban government. In 1990, the United States began to broadcast TV Martí from South Florida with strong anti-Castro messages. Two years later President George H. W. Bush signed into law the Torricelli Act that, among other things, strengthened the US trade embargo by extending its restrictions to subsidiaries of US companies and by prohibiting the arrival of foreign ships that had called in to Cuban ports in the previous six months.

The Bill Clinton administration faced other challenges. The rafters crisis of 1994 forced the United States to negotiate with the Castro government, resulting in a promise by the United States to accept 20,000 Cubans per year as long as Cuba clamped down on illegal boat departures. On May 2, 1995, Clinton put into effect the so-called wet feet/dry feet policy, whereby Cuban rafters would be returned home unless they had touched US soil. Two years later, another crisis erupted, when Cuban MiGs shot down two US-based planes piloted by members of the *Hermanos al Rescate* (Brothers to the Rescue) exile organization; four pilots died. Less than three weeks later, Clinton responded by signing the Helms–Burton bill which became the US–Cuban Liberty and Democratic Solidarity Act. The new law offered assistance in the transition toward democracy as long as Cuba met a number of requirements, such as the Castro brothers stepping down and the liberation of all political prisoners.

One of the most intense confrontations between the Cuban government and Miami Cubans to date was the custody battle over five-year-old Elián González, who survived the sinking of the raft in which he, his mother, and 12 others had fled Cuba in November 1999. The US Immigration and Naturalization Service granted provisional custody of Elián to one of his uncles living in Miami. The child's father, with the help of the Cuban government, demanded and eventually accomplished the return of Elián to Cuba in June 2000.

The Revolution Approaches Fifty (2002–   )

The new century brought with it new global and geopolitical realities, salient among them the ascendancy of China as an industrial powerhouse and worldwide investor. Chinese economic activity in Cuba has risen since 2002 in terms of increased trade levels and investment in mining and biotechnology. By 2005 China had become Cuba's third largest trading partner. Geographically closer to Cuba, Venezuela's leftist president, Hugo Chávez, developed a close relationship with Castro. Beginning in 1999 both nations established special trade relations and within a few years Venezuela became Cuba's new source of subsidized oil and trade credits; by mid-decade, yearly subsidies reached about $2 billion and Cuba's debt with Venezuela surpassed the $1 billion mark. In return, Cuba deployed to Venezuela an estimated 50,000 professionals, technicians, and military advisors, a third of them physicians and dentists.

During the same period, although hostility between Cuba and the United States did not dissipate, the United States relaxed its 40-year-old embargo by allowing shipments of agricultural and pharmaceutical products and medical equipment to the rebel island. Sales to Cuba, however, were restricted to cash-only transactions. The first shipments arrived in Havana in December 2001. Cuban purchases reached $139 million in 2002 and surpassed $500 million in 2005, making the United States the third largest exporter to Cuba behind Venezuela and Spain.

The end of the Special Period was codified in law by a 2002 constitutional amendment that promised never to return to capitalism and declared Cuba's political and social systems "irrevocable." Government officials began a rectification of the errors of the Special Period, which in turn had rectified the rectification of errors of 1986–9. It was yet another swing of the pendulum that had shifted for decades between two formulas: rigid centralization of the economy with moral incentives, and limited economic openness with material incentives. Numerous measures and laws were instituted to reverse the economic openings of the Special Period. Opportunities for self-employment, for example, fell as the state reduced the number of permissible economic activities and raised taxes and fees on the self-employed.

Another component of the concerted plan to return to pre-Special Period economic practices was the removal, in 2004, of US dollars from circulation; convertible pesos and euros took their place. In the process the government devalued US dollars by setting an exchange rate of 1 convertible peso = US$0.93. Dollar remittances were taxed further, discounted 20 percent.

Sugar, an industry whose subsidies had dried up with the collapse of the Soviet Union, became a major casualty of the early 2000s. With such subsidies gone, sugar production became an unprofitable venture that did not justify the repair – let alone modernization – of the sugar mills in operation. In 2002, the government made a concerted effort to restructure the sugar industry, shutting down 85 of the island's 156 mills. Production fell accordingly until it dropped to a token amount of 1.3 million tons in 2005, the lowest output since 1908. Castro proudly wrote sugar's epitaph: "Sugar will never return to this country; it belongs to the time of slavery."

Social conditions did not improve parallel to the economy's recovery; rather, the ranks of those depending on social assistance swelled to half a million in 2005, a 250 percent growth from 2002. After over a decade of opportunities for individual entrepreneurship and market activities, it was hard to convince the population to return to a centralized, fully socialized economy, where hard work was once again recognized with medals and scrolls. Black market activities and corruption actually increased. A 2003 study by the *Centro de Investigaciones Psicológicas y Sociológicas* (CPIS, Center for Psychological and Sociological Research) demonstrated that more than 90 percent of the population was involved in illegal activities, which could be as innocent as purchasing powdered milk from someone who in turn "steals" it from his or her workplace.

Few outside observers had thought that the Revolution would survive the crisis prompted by the collapse of socialism in the Soviet Union and Eastern Europe, let alone continue under Castro's leadership for over a decade and a half more. In July 2006 Castro surprised the world by announcing that he was temporarily yielding power to his younger brother due to illness; a few days later, the ailing Castro turned 80. The year 2009 will mark the 50th anniversary of the triumph of the Revolution; if still in power, Castro's rule will become the longest in the history of Latin America, surpassing the 49-year reign of King Dom Pedro II of Brazil.

Will Castro's death signify the Revolution's demise? While history, as a discipline, has broadened beyond the old emphasis on history's leading figures – the so-called "great men" – there is much to be said about the larger-than-human role that Castro has played in the past half century, not just within Cuba but around the world. Besides the fact that Castro has centralized power around himself and has single-handedly made the island's big – and not so big – decisions, he has become a continuous presence in the lives and minds of Cubans on the island and abroad, an ominous presence that generates hatred and admiration, fear and contempt, hope and despair. Even those who disagree with the equation Castro = Revolution should recognize the fact that Castro = stability. In an island with a long history of political instability and political violence, Castro has managed to provide stability and create the conditions for political peace.

As far back as 1959, Castro selected his younger brother, Raúl, as his heir. While lacking Fidel Castro's charisma, intelligence, and mythical stature, Raúl Castro appears to be the ideal transition leader, given his brother's blessing, his 40-odd-year experience as minister of the Armed Forces, his pragmatism and relative flexibility. The younger Castro's rule will have to be one of shared power, perhaps as head of a civilian–military junta; and will have to offer a transition strategy leading to free elections and a market economy. Other transition scenarios would present higher risks of chaos, violence, and foreign economic subordination, a scenario similar to that of 1898, when US troops and US monopoly capital marched and poured onto a desolate, impoverished island, which soon thereafter became a protectorate of the United States. Arguably, there would have been no 1959 without an 1898.

BIBLIOGRAPHY

Anderson, J. L. (1997) *Che Guevara: A Revolutionary Life*. Grove Press, New York.
Azicri, M. (2000) *Cuba Today and Tomorrow: Reinventing Socialism*. University Press of Florida, Gainesville.
Bunck, J. M. (1994) *Fidel Castro and the Quest for a Revolutionary Culture in Cuba*. Penn State Press, University Park, PA.
Castro, F. (1968 [1954]) *History Will Absolve Me*. Cape, London.
Castro, F. (1959–96) Castro Speech Database, <http://lanic.utexas.edu/la/cb/cuba/castro.html> (accessed November 10, 2006).
Chang, L. & Kornbluh, P. (eds.) (1998) *The Cuban Missile Crisis, 1962: A National Security Archive Documents Reader*, 2nd ed. The New Press, New York.
Conde, Y. M. (1999). *Operation Pedro Pan: The Untold Story of 14,048 Cuban Children*. Routledge, New York.
Domínguez, J. I. (1978) *Cuba: Order and Revolution*. The Belknap Press, Cambridge, MA.
Eckstein, S. E. (2003) *Back from the Future: Cuba Under Castro*, 2nd ed. Routledge, New York.
Fernández, G. (2002) *The Mariel Exodus Twenty Years Later*. Ediciones Universal, Miami.
Franqui, C. (1980) *Diary of the Cuban Revolution*. A Seaver Book, New York.
Guevara, E. (Che) (1985). *Guerrilla Warfare*. University of Nebraska Press, Lincoln.
Karol, K. S. (1970) *Guerrillas in Power: The Course of the Cuban Revolution*. Hill and Wang, New York.
Kennedy, R. (1969) *Thirteen Days: A Memoir of the Cuban Missile Crisis*. W. W. Norton, New York.

Kornbluh, P. (ed.) (1998) *Bay of Pigs Declassified: The Secret CIA Report on the Invasion of Cuba*. The New Press, New York.

LeoGrande, W. M (1980) *Cuba's Policy in Africa, 1959–1980*. Institute of International Studies, Berkeley.

López Vilaboy, J. (1973) *Motivos y culpables de la destrucción de Cuba*. Editora de Libros, San Juan, PR.

Marrero, L. (2005 [1966]) *Cuba en la década de 1950: Un país en desarrollo*. Carta de Cuba, San Juan, PR.

Martínez-Fernández, L., Figueredo, D., Pérez, Jr., L. A., & González, L. (eds.) (2003) *Encyclopedia of Cuba: People, History, Culture*, 2 vols. Greenwood Press, Westport, CT.

Masud-Piloto, F. R. (1988) *With Open Arms: Cuban Migration to the United States*. Rowman & Littlefield, Totowa, NJ.

Mesa-Lago, C. (1974) *Cuba in the 1970s: Pragmatism and Institutionalization*. University of New Mexico Press, Albuquerque.

Mesa-Lago, C. (ed.) (1993) *Cuba after the Cold War*. University of Pittsburgh Press, Pittsburgh.

Mesa-Lago, C. & Belkin, J. (eds.) (1982) *Cuba in Africa*. University of Pittsburgh Press, Pittsburgh.

Oppenheimer, A. (1993) *Castro's Final Hour*. TouchStone Books, New York.

Pérez, L. A., Jr. (1995) *Cuba between Reform and Revolution*, 2nd ed. Oxford University Press, New York.

Pérez-Stable, M. (1999) *The Cuban Revolution: Origins, Course and Legacy*, 2nd ed. Oxford University Press, New York.

Smith, L. M. & Padula, A. (1996) *Sex and Revolution: Women in Socialist Cuba*. Oxford University Press, New York.

Sweig, J. (2002) *Inside the Cuban Revolution*. Harvard University Press, Cambridge, MA.

Szulc, T. (1986) *Fidel: A Critical Portrait*. Morrow, New York.

Thomas, H. (1977) *The Cuban Revolution*. Harper & Row, New York.

Valladares, A. (1986) *Against All Hope*. Knopf, New York.

Welch, R. E., Jr. (1985) *Response to Revolution: The United States and the Cuban Revolution, 1959–1961*. University of North Carolina Press, Chapel Hill.

Wyden, P. (1979) *Bay of Pigs: The Untold Story*. Simon and Schuster, New York.

Chapter Twenty-Two

The National Security State

David R. Mares

Governments created by military coups and run brutally by individual military officers have not been strangers in Latin American history. But the aftermath of military coups in Ecuador in1963 and Brazil in 1964 ushered in a new era of authoritarian governments in which the military as an institution ruled directly or indirectly, using military-generated doctrines concerning security and development as guides. And though the Ecuadorian (1963–6 and 1972–9) and Peruvian (1968–80) military governments were not particularly egregious violators of human rights (Fitch 1992: 63; Palmer 1992: 304–5), Brazil's horribly systematic use of torture to limit opposition (1964–85) was repeated by military governments in Argentina (1976–82), Chile (1973–89), and Uruguay (1973–85).

The phenomenon has been labeled variously, each highlighting a distinct aspect. The most widely used and known is Guillermo O'Donnell's "Bureaucratic-Authoritarian Regime" (1979), which highlights the institutional and technocratic side of the political regime's approach to governing. But Alain Rouquié's "Terrorist State" (1987) also attracts adherents because of its emphasis on the human misery inflicted upon its own society by these governments. And Jorge A. Tapia Valdés's "Stratego-cratic State" (1986) as well as Frederick Nunn's "Professional Militarism" (1992) concept insist upon the military nature of these regimes. Because of the key role that the doctrine of national security played in these regimes, however, the nomenclature of "National Security State" (NSS) is particularly apt. Scholars agreed on the basic outlines of these new forms of governing, but soon came to disagree on the most useful characterization of them, their origins, and their dynamics (Collier 1979). In this chapter we will review the characteristics of these governments that placed an ideology of national security above all other considerations across the gamut of human interactions and briefly explain their origin and demise. This chapter will not present the histories of individual NSSs; readers can peruse the attached bibliography for histories of the particular countries' experiences with the phenomenon. The key argument here is that political crises, economic crises, and social stratification were not sufficient to produce the National Security States of Latin America; it was only in combination with a professionalized military institution wielding a specific doctrine of national security that the subjugation of the citizenry to the state could be attempted.

Defining the National Security State

Two key characteristics define the National Security State: the military institution itself is intimately involved in leading the political system, and its goals are to transform the country's political and economic institutions. This distinguishes military rule in the NSS from previous regimes in which military officers seized power for personal benefit (e.g., General Anastasio Somoza García and his family dynasty in Nicaragua, 1936–79; General Fulgencio Batista in Cuba, 1952–9; and General Luís Garcia Meza in Bolivia, 1980–1); for the protection of the economic interests of a particular group in the country (e.g., the Salvadoran military [Stanley 1996]); or to throw out one set of politicians and let other politicians compete in new elections (the "moderating pattern" of military intervention).

The development of a perspective within the military that it should run the country for a period of time while it transforms the political and economic institutions that it expects will produce national development is the result of both the military's professional development and the adoption of a particular doctrine of national security, which began to evolve in the late 1950s. In the National Security State (Tapia Valdés 1980) the professional military only rules for reasons of national security. To rule when national security is not at stake would divert the military from its job, thereby endangering national security; hence, a professional military would reject the call or the temptation to govern in these circumstances.

In the National Security State the military governs as an institution, not as the followers of a particular military leader. This distinction allows for a personalist General to assume the office of President, as in the cases of Augusto Pinochet Ugarte (Chile, 1973–89), Juan Velasco Alvarado (Peru, 1968–75), and Guillermo Rodríguez Lara (Ecuador, 1972–5). The link between the personalist military leader and the military institution in these cases is philosophical, ideological, and systematic, rather than being based on personal enrichment or to defend the particular interests of any particular group, including those of the military. (Supporting this perspective, military spending as a percentage of the total government budget tends to decrease in almost all of the NSSs [Fitch 1992: 28].) The military and the military president respond to what they see, through the lens of the national security doctrine, as their *obligation* to the nation.

The other distinguishing element of the National Security State is its system-transforming orientation. Instead of attempting to defend the existing political and economic institutions of the country, the military see them as aggravating the problems confronting the nation because they are inefficient, corrupt, and designed to benefit one group of society at the expense of another. The result of these old institutions, the professional military have come to learn, is subversion and underdevelopment. Consequently, the defense of national security requires system transformation (Stepan 1973; Rouquié 1987). This goal stands in great contrast philosophically from those of other military governments that seek personal or corporate enrichment, or to defend the class interests of a particular group in society, or who see themselves as temporary caretakers during transitions from one civilian government to another.

It is important to note that three elements commonly ascribed to the National Security State – gross violation of human rights, neoconservative economics, and intelligence paranoia – are not distinguishing characteristics. The violation of human rights, either in terms of its depravity or its volume, is not peculiar to the NSS, nor even a necessary characteristic (the Peruvian and Ecuadorian NSSs were not particularly horrific violators of human rights). Argentina, Chile, Uruguay, and Brazil were certainly gross violators of human rights, but in the 1970s so were Paraguay, Bolivia, Guatemala, El Salvador, and Nicaragua. The repression in these latter cases was exercised in the name of the elite and against the people, whereas the national security doctrine insists that its use of repressive tactics is for the benefit of the people and the nation.

Nor does a particular economic policy distinguish the National Security State. As discussed below, the NSS usually becomes viable when citizenry, elite, and the military agree that current economic development policy is simply reproducing economic and political crises. The Argentine, Uruguayan, and Chilean NSS pursued radical economic liberalization policies to free up the market in the expectation that the country would prosper simply by assuming its appropriate place in the worldwide division of labor (Foxley 1983; Ramos 1986). But Brazil adopted a mixed strategy in which the government remained a key player in markets deemed important for national development (Evans 1979), while Peru under General Juan Velasco Alvarado (1968–75) and Ecuador (1972–5) were very interested in guiding economic forces to meet the needs of those at the lower ends of the socioeconomic strata (McClintock & Lowenthal 1983; Isaacs 1993).

Though intelligence and spying are very important to the NSS (see below), again they are not uniquely characteristic. The Cuban communist government is equally paranoid about independent thinking, unauthorized political gatherings, and opposition to the government. But the repression and spying engaged in by the Castro government is carried out in the name of defending class revolution, not in the name of the nation of Cuba.

While military rule and system transformation distinguish the NSS they do not imply a united military institution nor policy coherence of the government. These are behavioral outcomes and thus questions for empirical examination rather than proof-by-assertion. Making decisions about the allocation of resources among legitimate claimants (however legitimacy has been defined by the NSS) necessarily creates competing advocates. Hence once the military as an institution has to make those decisions, disagreements will develop and call into question the unity of the military in defense of its self-identified "national security." Another factor undermining military unity is how those disagreements are resolved. Since national security is at risk, and the military has imposed discipline and punishment upon those in civil society who do not accept the military's definition of the threat and appropriate response, can it act with less vigor against those within the government and military that also disagree? Finally, these threats to the national security can give rise to powerful intelligence forces that threaten to undermine the hierarchy that is so fundamental to the military institution. Autonomous intelligence groups strike fear and resentment among military officers because military hierarchy is set aside, and the very ambiguity of "threat to national security" that allows the government to "legally" move against a civilian of questionable loyalty can also be used within the military institution to silence dissenters.

All of the NSS governments experienced important disagreements within the high commands of the armed forces concerning the installation, development, and retreat of the NSS. Analysts identify these divisions as representing legalists (they want a quick return to democracy), moderates (they are willing to turn politics back to the civilians after moderate purging of the politicians and some tinkering with political institutions), and hardliners (they see a need for a "deep cleansing" of social and economic structures, not just politics, and have no timetable for a return to democracy). The tension is always there, but usually obscured by press censorship. Still, sometimes the disagreements are too deep or too consequential to hide. The Ecuadorian junta expelled the Air Force commander in 1965 and in Chile Pinochet moved against his Air Force commander in 1978. Argentine factions engaged in armed combat against each other in 1962 and 1963, Ecuador's NSS confronted a military revolt in 1975, and the Uruguayan Navy went into the streets in 1972 to prevent an overt coup. During the first year of the Brazilian military government 1,200 officers were purged (Moreira Alves 1985); the 11-year ebb and flow of the Brazilian *distensão* and *abertura* to "guided democracy" reflected the relative standing of the hardliners and softliners (the latter were a group around the first military president, General Humberto Castelo Branco, and became known as *castelistas* [Skidmore 1988]).

Another empirical variation among National Security States is their degree of inclusiveness of social groups into their policy-making circles. Some analysts have made a distinction between inclusionary and exclusionary NSSs. These are authoritarian governments, so the difference lies in who is represented, not in to whom the government is accountable. Inclusionary governments (Peru and, to a lesser degree, Ecuador) wanted the "popular sectors" (workers, peasants, and students) mobilized to receive the benefits of the system transformation carried out by the NSS. Exclusionary governments (Brazil, Argentina, Uruguay, and Chile), on the other hand, did not.

My reading of history and the scholarly literature leads me to stress three common elements that give rise to the military deciding to rule as an institution in order to transform the nation's political and economic institutions: the ideology of national security; the belief that national security professionals should lead; and a perception of intelligence as a key defense mechanism. These elements produce structures and behavior that vary roughly in accordance with the historical and conjunctural distinctiveness of each country, as well as the personal proclivities of key military leaders.

The Ideology of National Security

The ideology of the military as the founder of the nation and the ultimate guarantor of legality, order, Christianity, and "national essence" is as old as independence and has roots in Spanish colonialism (Loveman 1993; 1999). In those earlier times the military had not yet professionalized, and thus their intervention in politics responded to either personal or class interests. It was not until militaries encountered a specialized paradigm that emphasized their unique role as professionals in diagnosing the threats to the nation and giving them pride of place in addressing them that the National Security State became possible.

The study of geopolitics provided the underpinnings of that paradigm, beginning in the late nineteenth and early twentieth century. It was imported from Europe (geopolitical thinking could not prosper in the USA because of its self-conception as simply abiding by its "Manifest Destiny") and had its greatest impact in South America (Arriagada Herrera 1986a; Kelly & Child 1988). Geopolitics is about the implications of geography on foreign and security policy as well as the relationship between national power and geography. It provided an interpretation of the territorial conflicts and rivalries that developed in the wake of Latin American independence and a vision of what a nation must do to prosper. The key characteristics of geopolitics as it was adopted in South America are: the nation perceived in organic terms (it lives and dies); a zero-sum view of international relations because growth and power come at the expense of others' territory and influence; the concept of strategic territory; and a phobia about lines of territorial projection into the seas and the security of lines of communication. Although geopolitics lost its expansionist rationale in South America, one can still see the impact of these ideas in continued concerns about national control over Antarctica and the Amazon.

Geopolitical analyses emphasize the internal elements of national power. The "interior frontiers" emphasized by many military and civilian advocates of geopolitics encompassed an extremely broad range of factors: morality, intellectuality, esthetics, religion, tradition, sociopolitical fashions, and lifestyle, as well as technology, production processes, and economic systems (Guglialmelli 1977). A nation's population becomes an instrument for the power policy of the state, not just as soldiers but as economically active people (Arriagada Herrera 1986a: 137). In line with this focus on interior frontiers, one of the greatest threats to the state is internal decay, including civil war.

Nunn (1992) demonstrates that military journals throughout Latin America had been discussing the links among social and economic development and political stability since the 1930s. An interest in civilian–military integration to address these issues was thus topical long before the development of the doctrine of national security. Varas & Agüero's (1984) study of Chilean military writing demonstrates that, while concerned with these issues in the earlier period, military writers thought about them as economic, political, or administrative issues, not as military ones.

Before the doctrine of national security, geopolitics was seen as providing its sophisticated users with the "ability to create political systems and practice the art of statesmanship in the same manner that the General dominates the art of war" (Medina Parker 1944: 408). Professor of Military Geography Colonel Augusto Pinochet Ugarte explained in his textbook, written five years before the Chilean coup, that geopolitics "is a political science," by which he meant that it is the scientific study of the dynamic development of the state, and thus "serves as a guide to the statesman for the political leadership of the State" (Pinochet Ugarte 1984: 49–50).

One of the problems that geopolitics – and later national security doctrines – pose for those who would be guided by it, is its ambiguous methodology and the contradictory proposals that could follow from them. For example, distinct Argentine geopoliticians have seen Brazil as a "subimperialist" threat and as a potential partner against threats from powers outside of the South Atlantic (Arriagada Herrera 1986a: 139; Pittman 1988: 30–54). A more pertinent question for our topic concerns the relationship between the people and the state. On the one hand, one can perceive the population as merely an instrument for state policy and thus argue that leaders must have a free hand in ruling over society; this was the position taken by hardliners.

But one of the major Brazilian geopoliticians, General Golbery do Couto e Silva, argued in the 1950s that national security required democracy because the people could not play their proper role in national development if they were "slaves" (Tapia Valdés 1989: 199).

The study of geopolitics was most developed and innovative in Brazil. Peruvian and Chilean military academies produced a consistent line oriented toward applications rather than theory. The Argentine military was divided about the utility of a geopolitical paradigm with the result that it never dominated the military institution, as was the case in Brazil and Chile. Geopolitical analysts of the Argentine situation were prolific, but their work was contradictory and confused, and largely elaborated outside of official military channels. It became intimately linked with the political sentiments of civil society groups that wished to garner military backing for their political projects. Writers placed great emphasis on distancing geopolitics from Nazism and, after the overthrow of Juan Perón in 1955, from Peronismo (Arriagada Herrera 1986a: 140).

When Peru's *Centro de Altos Estudios Militares* (CAEM, Center for Higher Military Studies) and Brazil's *Escola Superior de Guerra* (ESG, Superior War College) began developing national security doctrines for their countries in the 1950s (Stepan 1973: 47–65), the link between national development and security resonated easily with officers already familiar with geopolitical thinking. The Superior War Colleges took up the challenge of integrating geopolitical analysis with French and US counterinsurgency doctrine in the late 1950s and early 1960s (Stepan 1973: 64–8, 172–87; Arriagada Herrera 1986a: 146; Tapia Valdés 1989: 375–8). Given world events, particularly Chinese and Vietnamese modification of Marxism to incorporate peasant-based People's War and the emergence of the Guevarist *foco* strategy with Castro's victory in Cuba, it was not strange that Latin American militaries would be concerned with the possibility of domestic subversion. A focus on counterinsurgency fit in well with geopolitics' concept of "interior frontiers" and the domestic sources of power. Although counterinsurgency led each of these professional militaries to conclude that fundamental changes in their countries' social, political, and economic systems were necessary to avoid revolution, it did not determine how those changes were to occur. Hence both left- and right-wing National Security States emerged.

The close ties of Latin American militaries with the USA and France also affected the evolution of national security doctrines at this time. The US foreign policy establishment had been emphasizing the importance of planning in order to make the most efficient use of a nation's resources for development and security since its elaboration of the Marshall Plan and the North Atlantic Treaty Organization (NATO) in the late 1940s. France articulated a concern with internal subversion in the 1950s as its colonial empire began slipping out of its hands in Southeast Asia and Algeria, while US experiences in Southeast Asia and Cuba also refocused its concerns in the developing world from traditional military conflicts like Korea to revolutionary war. National planning and counterinsurgency both received a big push from the militaries that the South American professional militaries emulated. For example, General Golbery in 1952 had noted, "It should not be thought that the sacrifice of liberty will always lead to an increase in security. On the contrary, beyond certain limits, the loss of liberty will create a vital loss of security." By the 1960s he was articulating the view that internal subversion constituted the greatest threat to security in the region and the world (Tapia Valdés 1989: 199–200). Golbery became a chief architect of the Brazilian NSS, though as a moderate.

Because throughout the region US anti-communist counterinsurgency doctrine was taught to military officers and used to pursue "subversives," that doctrine by itself cannot be what distinguishes the NSS. The uniqueness lies in the link between counterinsurgency and geopolitics. That connection facilitates the incorporation of a counterinsurgency perspective for creating a new political system, one that would be used to further the interests of the nation and not simply the class interests of the national elite or US Cold War interests.

The national security strategy, in both its left- and right-wing versions, entailed intervening in the organizations which citizens "mis-used" in the workplace and in politics to articulate and defend what NSS thinkers considered "selfish" interests. But the National Security State was not totalitarian, so there were no sustained efforts to create their own mobilization strategy at work and in politics in the manner of fascist, corporatist, or communist regimes. Even the Peruvian NSS, which mobilized significant sectors of the lower classes to implement policy at the local level, did not organize them into a political party that could support the government (Mauceri 1996: 15–39). Instead, NSSs chose to reorganize unions and political parties, at times forbidding them, at other times creating very limited and defined spaces for their existence. The goal of the NSS was to remake the manner in which societal interests were articulated and the distribution of influence in policy making. Success for the NSS would depend upon getting society to accept the national security doctrine, thereby legitimately leaving society with only a marginal ability to alter the military's strategy for defending national security.

Now that we have defined the NSS, it is important to note a significant difference from many analysts. These analysts of the NSS in Latin America claim that the militaries adopted counterinsurgency perspectives because their countries had no external threats for which military power would be relevant (Rouquié 1987: 98–9). In this view, the USA kept extra-hemispheric powers at bay, no Latin American military could defeat a US invasion, and Latin American countries have enjoyed a long peace amongst themselves since World War II, except for the One Hundred Hours War between El Salvador and Honduras in 1968.[1]

But with the exception of Uruguay, all of the countries that experienced National Security States had military disputes with their neighbors. Border disputes have erupted in violent confrontations involving Ecuador and Peru; Bolivia, Peru, and Chile; Chile and Argentina. Argentina did fight a war with Great Britain over the Malvinas/Falkland Islands in 1982. Also, Argentine and Brazilian nuclear weapons programs in the 1970s were indicators of their recognition that military power is part of the currency of international power (Mares 2001).

Some analysts claim that the development of an internal mission is not consistent with a military force that can be used in traditional state–state confrontations (Fitch 1992: 22). If that were true, and given the record of militarized interstate conflict mentioned in the previous paragraph, these professional militaries would be de facto derelict in their first responsibility to defend the nation. Some militaries were aware of this tension between internal and external threats. For example, the military in Peru, after failing to defend the Leticia territory against Colombia in 1932, decided to resist generals who wanted to use them to support a dictatorship (Villanueva 1971:

100–7); in Ecuador in 1975 one of the arguments for the transition out of the National Security State was the need to focus on the disputed territory with Peru (Mares 1996–7). But the tension doesn't come just from having an internal mission. In the USA the Army was used to quell industrial disputes and social and racial tensions in the period 1877–1945 and even developed a civil disturbance doctrine that contemplated the harsh use of force when necessary (Laurie & Cole 1997). Rather, the question is to what degree the military can do both; the US military was able to successfully balance those roles, and Chile's performance in 1977–82 standing up to Peru, Bolivia, and Argentina at the same time demonstrates that it is possible even for a non-great power.

In summary, the national security doctrine identified the goals a nation should have and the factors that would determine its success. The doctrine itself required implementation and thus the other two characteristics of the National Security State became key.

National Security Professionals Must Lead

Professionalization entails creating a sense of identity linked to one's profession and an appreciation of the skills required to perform one's task; one becomes the "expert" whose responsibility is to provide society with the benefits of that expertise. Along with the development of those skills emerges a set of values concerning the importance of the military's tasks, and hence of their unique contribution. The military becomes the expert in utilizing violence to defend the nation; that use of violence requires understanding how potential enemies plan to use violence in order to devise military strategies and tactics to deter or defeat them, thereby defending the nation.

It is this skill building in the analysis of threat and the employment of violence that separates some Latin American militaries from their contemporaries in places like Haiti, Guatemala, and the armies of their own nations in the nineteenth century. Civilians were interested in using the military to infuse values of patriotism and the social skills of the modern man (hygiene, education, time discipline, etc.). But the modern professional military is not about building citizens; it is about building experts in the defense of the nation.

The advanced training provided by military educational institutions stimulates two aspects of military leadership. First, such specialized education increases the officer corps' sense of professionalism. And it provides an institutional philosophy and methodology for the analysis of national defense. In the NSS, that philosophy was the doctrine of national security and the methodology was based on geopolitics.

Professionalization of the military becomes perverse and undermines both political democracy and traditional forms of authoritarian government when officers perceive that their skills and values permit them to identify threats to the nation that, while imminent, either remain unseen by self-interested politicians or cannot be effectively addressed because self-interested classes or social groups refuse to sacrifice to save the nation. The advanced training, combined with the national security doctrine, provides a basis for military officers to see themselves as possessing specific "scientific" knowledge that civilians do not have; they are consequently the only ones who can truly appreciate the requisite expertise required to defend the nation. It is for this reason that once they take control of the government their "goals [are] more ambitious than those of the coups undertaken by less professional armed forces" (O'Donnell 1976: 212).

Professionalization did not proceed at the same pace among the countries that established National Security States, nor only among militaries that later overthrew elected governments. The early professionalizers in Peru and Brazil wanted key civilians to understand the central concepts and collaborate with the military in implementing the doctrine of national security and development. Hence, in Brazil civilians constituted about half the students in the courses at the Superior War College, which also offered civilians extension courses (Stepan 1988: 47). Peru invited prestigious civilian instructors from Europe and officers attended UN centers that studied development issues (Stepan 1973: 63; Rouquié 1987: 320). Professionalization of the Argentine military made important advances in the mid-1960s (O'Donnell 1976: 206–10).

Ecuador, Uruguay, Bolivia, and Paraguay did not have specialized military academies that provided training in national security doctrines (Nunn 1992: 230–1; Isaacs 1993: 102). The Uruguayan, Paraguayan, and Bolivian militaries, however, were very tied in to their Argentine and Brazilian counterparts and made efforts to follow them into NSS. In the "moderately professionalized" Uruguayan Army the hard-line faction was known as the "Brazilianists" and those who advocated more social reforms were labeled "Peruvianists." An interesting result of the lower level of confidence the Uruguayan military had in their rationale for establishing a National Security State is that they preferred to rule with a civilian figurehead in the presidency (Handelman 1981: 22–3; Fitch 1992: 9). In Paraguay and Bolivia pre-professional armies had long dominated politics and in the 1970s the Stroessner and Banzer regimes, respectively, developed closer links with the NSSs in Argentina, Brazil, and Chile, but could not themselves transition into a NSS. Chile and Argentina had weaker educational traditions than Peru and Brazil, but experiential learning helped close the gap. Chilean military success in two wars with Bolivia and Peru, plus Prussian military training and the strength of the Chilean political system and the militarized National Police Force (*Carabineros*), produced a military that, except for a difficult period from 1924 to 1932, eschewed involvement in politics. But as the political system weakened in the face of economic crisis and growing class conflict in the 1960s, the military got drawn into politics (North 1986). At this point the Chilean military, like the Argentine, benefited from experiential learning in their adoption of national security doctrine. The political advances of the radical left, hypermobilization, and, in Argentina, urban guerrilla terrorism all provided on-the-ground education for the military.

The national security ideology recognizes that security and development require the institutionalization of a political and economic system, not just arbitrary "cleansing" and commanding. Military leadership and the new regime, therefore, require legitimacy; they cannot be established simply by force, even when it was the force of arms that created the opportunity. This is not just an institutional efficiency argument. The geopolitical strain in their national security doctrine required an expression of legitimacy, at some point, from outside the military, by making either the population at large or the national elite fundamental players in national development. Thus although the military-led "revolutions" in the NSS looked to their own actions in saving the nation to legitimate their takeover of national power, their continued rule required some expressed support by either the elite or the population.

Once the military sought that legitimacy, it was very difficult to turn back the pages if the group solicited refused to bestow it. The Brazilians were cautious in their search for legitimacy. In Institutional Act No. 1 they declared that it was the Revolution itself that provided legitimacy, rather than the people or the constitution, and they never subjected the Institutional Acts that were the fundamental underpinnings of the NSS to a direct vote. Instead, the elections they held were to determine who would participate in government within those rules. Since people voted, the rules seemed to have legitimacy; consequently, when the vote didn't provide the "correct" results in 1965 or the right-wing party voted against the government in Congress in 1968, initially even the *castelistas* and *legalistas* within the military supported tinkering with the new rules. Since the Revolution was still in its early stages, students were mobilizing against the NSS and guerrilla activity was appearing, the NSS had some residual legitimacy from the crisis that had provoked the Revolution, and the hardliners were able to steer the NSS into an increasingly repressive period. But by 1974 only the hardliners within the military were willing to argue that, despite the successes of the government against the overt subversives, rapid economic growth, and the creation of multiple new institutions (including voting rules and participation requirements), national security required continued unilateral military rule.

The Uruguayan NSS confronted its defining moment in 1980 when the electorate rejected the proposed new constitution. Since the Institutional Acts themselves were part of the proposed constitution, its rejection eliminated any façade of their legitimacy as well; as a result, the hardliners within the Uruguayan military couldn't block the decision to seek a transition back to democracy (González 1983; Gillespie 1991: 50–78). The Chilean military took their authoritarian constitution to a plebiscite in 1980, seven years after their bloody coup, and their electoral victory was successful enough that it took almost two decades after the return of democracy to begin passing major amendments to it. But General Pinochet also suffered a huge loss when the 1988 plebiscite provided an overwhelming "NO" to the continuation of his rule and the junta members insisted that he accept that judgment. In each of these three cases the majority of the key officers within the military refused to accept the continuation of the military government as a legitimate expression of the National Security State after the nation had been asked and had rejected it. Instead, the officers sought transition toward civilian government while retaining key institutions believed necessary to national security.

A legal framework not only helps to create a sense of legitimate order and rule, it also provides a basis for responding to demands of the opposition without turning to ad hoc, and hence arbitrary, measures. This is true even outside authoritarian situations: law provides guidelines that limit internal conflict and oppositions' claims for greater changes. Chile's 1980 constitution provided a timetable for a plebiscite, making Pinochet's refusal to resign and hold elections in response to post-1982 mobilizations by the opposition seem reasonable to his supporters and to some in the middle; the opposition wound up playing by these rules (Agüero 1998: 383–404).

The specific manner in which NSS governments dealt with the question of institutionalizing military leadership varied across them, but all sought to retain a key role in politics through wide-ranging national security laws and councils. Brazil also attempted to create a two-party system privileging a right-wing party that they erroneously expected would naturally accept indirect leadership from the military (Skidmore 1988). In Argentina a number of generals, including Presidents Generals Roberto Viola (1981) and Leopoldo Galtieri (1981–2) believed that their "cleansing" of society and economic restructuring made it possible to slowly reintroduce elections in which generals would be the leading candidates – Galtieri expected to win himself.

Although the national security-oriented professional military expected to lead, military officers disagreed significantly over *how* they could best lead. *Legalists* continued to favor the old "moderating coup," which could keep civilians within very tight bounds. These tended to be the first officers purged by the national security doctrine-influenced officers. *Moderates* wanted to redesign institutions, then allow competition across a fairly wide spectrum, excluding only a few individuals who had the potential to wield enough political influence to undermine the new institutions. The Ecuadorian transition begun after 1976 was guided by these officers, as they vetoed the presidential candidacy of Assad Bucaram. *Hardliners* insisted upon deep cleansing of society, not just of the political and economic systems, and were willing to rule by arbitrary force for an indefinite period of time. Disagreements among factions within the military were so great that armed confrontations occurred between them, as in Argentina in 1962 and 1963 (O'Donnell 1976: 206), and the leaders among dissenting officers were murdered, as in the case of Chile's ex-Minister of Defense General Carlos Prats, shot down in the streets of Buenos Aires along with his wife, and General Alberto Bachelet Martínez, who died in his cell after months of being tortured.[2]

Though the national security ideology resonated with the military officer corps and some high-level technocrats, it was not as attractive to the state bureaucracy, which would be responsible for much of the policy implementation. Many military officers, including those who wrote for the Superior War Colleges, believed that national development, and hence national security, simply entailed a leadership identifying solutions, giving orders to implement policy, and evaluating the outcomes for any necessary adjustments (Nunn 1992). In the absence of party and totalitarian ideologies that could indoctrinate them, however, the lower levels of the bureaucracy did not necessarily accept the military government's paradigm. Because of this, the coherence of the regime, particularly as regards implementation of policy, was never as complete as expected by the high command (Cardoso 1979: 48–9).

Intelligence as a Key Defense Mechanism

Just like various versions of its Marxist competitor, the national security doctrine highlighted the ability of the internal threat to hide among the population and spread the revolutionary message among students, within unions, and to landless peasants. In this context, intelligence became an important tool in the fight against subversion. French and US counterinsurgency doctrines emphasized the fundamental importance of timely intelligence to defeat the internal threat. Secret US CIA and Army training manuals were revealed which advocated and trained in the use of abduction and assassination as well as medical, chemical, and electrical techniques during interrogation (Cohn et al. 1997; McSherry 2002: 41–2).

Recognition of the need for intelligence, evenly timely intelligence, does not necessarily produce widespread and vicious violations of human rights. While it is true that the pre-professional military and the police have historically murdered and beaten people from the lower classes who they saw as threatening the dominant political, economic, and social systems, this does not explain such behavior by the NSS, for a number of reasons. One of the defining characteristics of the NSS is its domination by a professional military institution. Hence, first, the deviant behavior of non-professional military and police is not expected to persist in the new institution. Second, not all of the NSSs engaged in widespread and brutal violations of human rights (the two Ecuadorian and the Peruvian did not). Third, the NSSs that did engage in vicious human rights violations devised new and horrific means of torture. Fourth, the NSSs subjected people from the middle and upper classes to torture, murder, and "disappeared" them along with the perennial targets from the lower classes. It is important, therefore, to distinguish among the development of an intelligence capability, its transformation into a power center, and the deterioration of its function in the National Security State into a moral abyss even within that state.

Before detailing some of those horrors, it is important to recognize that they were not simply conceived of and carried out by sadists, sociopaths, and other societal misfits. Instead, we must understand these actions as the deliberate strategy of professional military officers who saw themselves engaged in a war for nation and God.[3] Brazilian President Ernesto Geisel (1974–9), by no means one of the hardliners within the military, justified the use of torture with reasoning that attempts to place it within the Just War tradition: "there are circumstances in which a person is forced to engage in [torture] for obtaining confessions and, thus, to avoid a greater harm [to society]" (cited in Huggins 2000: 74). All of the military officers interviewed by Huggins (2000: 74) also argued that it was their professional duty, and not an issue of morality, to sometimes torture and murder.

The supreme irony, however, is that in the defense of Christendom and the nation they engaged in behavior that egregiously violated modern Christian doctrine and the constitutions of their nations (Loveman 1999b: 227–52). Because of NSS efforts to ensure amnesty once the discussion of a transition to democracy occurred, the Chilean case is illuminating. The Chilean military government's decree of an amnesty for itself in 1978, long before they contemplated returning power to a "protected democracy," suggests that they realized that the states of emergencies and civil war that they were engaged in to defend national security did *not* make these actions legal or moral.

There was a tendency for intelligence services to act independently in the early days of the establishment of the NSS. Torture and repression are instrumental tools for the NSS and thus their use corresponds to the evolution of the relationship between the goals sought by those with the potential to wield those tools and the targets against whom, from their perspective, it would make sense to employ such measures. The Chilean and Argentine militaries took control in a period when they and their civilian supporters feared that the left was poised for a civil war; quick action to destroy mobilized groups and root out their supporters seemed to be called for (from their perspective). In Uruguay the military had already defeated the *Tupamaros* when they effectively seized power from President Bordaberry. To implement the National Security State they sought to keep the level of fear in the population up while they created the institutions of the NSS and negotiated a transition to a protected democracy. Brazil saw its highest levels of repression in the period after the decision was made to transition to a protected democracy, as the hardliners sought to terrorize those in society who were negotiating, and convince the military that subversives continued to conceal themselves in society (Skidmore 1988: 125–35; Stepan 1988: 27–8).

The search for a process to begin the transition out of overt military rule can be associated with more repression, particularly violations of human rights, as the hardliners seek to convince their moderate to soft-line colleagues that the danger of subversion remains and to provoke civilian negotiators into more intransigent positions against the military. Since the hardliners tend to be overrepresented among the intelligence forces, they have the best information about the decreased threat from subversion at the time that every transition out of a NSS begins. Their obstructionist behavior, consequently, is an indication that they are clearly aware that society has not been remade into the form that the national security doctrine had postulated was necessary for the nation to develop and be secure. They realize, consequently, that transition means that the national security mission is not completed and will be undermined in the years to come. Despite much of the bemoaning of *democraduras* (democracies with strong authoritarian features) in the post-transition scholarly literature, only in the Chilean and Brazilian cases (for very different reasons) did the NSS survive even five years out.

The Brazilian intelligence institution (*Serviço Nacional de Informações*, SNI) was the most autonomous of the NSSs. General Golbery developed the plans for the SNI before the coup, and it installed branches in every government ministry with "veto power over top-level and secondary-level appointments." It created its own school to train personnel, gaining such a monopoly on the intelligence function that the intelligence courses of the Superior War College were eliminated. Indicative of its influence, two of its chiefs, Médici and Figueiredo, became Presidents during the NSS. The SNI was not directly involved in physical repression and torture; they left that to the intelligence services of the branches of the armed forces, the state police, and the paramilitaries (Moreira Alves 1985: 48–50; Dassin 1986; Skidmore 1988: 56–7; Stepan 1988: 14–20, 25–9).

During the first few months of the Chilean military government the various branches of the armed forces and the Carabineros carried out intelligence functions in an uncoordinated fashion (Arriagada Herrera 1986b: 130–2). The *Dirección Nacional de Inteligencia* (DINA) was created in January 1974 to centralize intelligence gathering and analysis; it operated beyond all legal bounds. By 1977 the growing power of DINA and its leader, General Manuel Contreras, as well as international pressure to improve its human rights performance, led General Pinochet to replace DINA with the *Central Nacional de Inteligencia* (CNI). This move was part of an effort to transition into institution building, including a new legal regime, which would provide legitimacy for continued military rule (the project for a new constitution was begun shortly after). Nevertheless, the military and CNI continued to violate human rights into the 1980s whenever they perceived it "useful" (Garretón 1986: 160–3) or even in revenge, as when there was an assassination attempt on Pinochet.

Uruguay institutionalized human rights violations within the regular military rather than creating a specialized intelligence service. The function was seen as operational, and thus under the control of combat units; military officers, consequently, rotated through intelligence duties (Stepan 1988: 13–29). This normalization of intelligence functions probably explains the Uruguayan NSSs extensive use of incarceration: one in six Uruguayans was imprisoned during its reign (Barahona de Brito 1997).

Argentina has the bloodiest and most sordid legacy of the National Security States, perhaps partially due to the fact that, like Uruguay, it never created a centralized intelligence service. During the *Proceso*, power was divided among the three branches of the military. The President was an agent of the Military Junta, made up of the Commanders in Chief of each service. But the high commands of each branch met separately to discuss the issues of the day. The service Commanders thus had a politicized and mobilized group of officers overseeing them. In this context it was difficult for an autonomous intelligence agency to arise and concentrate power (Stepan 1988: 24–5; Russell 1990). Instead, each of the military branches repressed as they saw fit, producing not only uncoordinated intelligence but also probably contributing to the far greater levels of execution and disappearance inflicted upon civil society.

The list of violations of human rights engaged in by the Chilean NSS is also indicative of what happened in Brazil, Argentina, and Uruguay: "arbitrary arrest, imprisonment, torture, forced disappearances, summary executions, collective executions, the negation of the right to appeal War Council sentences, homicide, exile, internal exile, abduction, intimidation, attempted homicide, death threats, raids, dismissal from jobs and surveillance. Such treatment violated the following rights: the right to life, the right to personal integrity, the right to personal liberty, the right to personal security and the right to live in one's country" (Human Rights in Chile 2006). To this list survivors have added rape, psychological torture through witnessing the torture, murder, and rape of family and loved ones, and, in the case of Argentina, the theft of the children of those they murdered, whom they placed for adoption in "good" military homes (Argentina 1986).

In violating human rights these four NSS behaved similarly, though they varied in their reliance on one means over another. Chile is the leader in the percentage of its population killed by the military in the seizing of power and its immediate aftermath (1973–4). Uruguay had the NSS that detained, interrogated, and intimidated the greatest percentage of its population. The security forces of the Argentine version of the NSS "disappeared" the greatest percentage of its population in the period just before and after creating the NSS. The magnitude of the Argentine and Chilean horrors can be appreciated in the following statistic for dead/disappeared per 100,000 people: Brazil 0.1, Uruguay 1.0, Chile 31.2, and Argentina 32.[4]

The right-wing NSSs (Argentina, Brazil, Chile, Uruguay, and their satellites Bolivia and Paraguay) shared with the left-leaning NSSs (Peru, Ecuador) the perception that internal revolutionaries were philosophically and materially supported by communists outside of the country (Rouquié 1987: 331–2). But only the right-wing NSSs decided to work together to gather and share intelligence concerning the transnational nature of the threat as well as collaborate in addressing it across national borders. In 1974 Argentina, Uruguay, Bolivia, Chile, and Paraguay met to discuss intelligence and operations cooperation against people considered subversives, including those within the military who disagreed with the installation of a National Security State. The following year Brazil joined the group and it formally became "Operation Condor" (McSherry 2002: 45). Four features characterized Operation Condor: it was a secret but official operation; it focused on international operations; it was multinational; and it chose its targets very selectively, rather than engaging in the more general terror designed to inspire fear in society (Martorell 1999; McSherry 2005: 1–10).

With this background in the definition, ideology, and key characteristics of the NSS we turn now to a brief discussion of their origins and demise.

Origins of the National Security State

The origins of the National Security States that reigned from 1963 to 1989 were similar and their militaries shared important perceptions and goals. A perverse process of military professionalism and the doctrine of national security are not sufficient to create the National Security State. Civil society needed to provide a context for its development and the initial demand for the coup that, much to the chagrin of the majority of the civilian coup supporters, opened the door to the NSS. But the specific institutional structure developed for the NSS as well as the intensity with which its development was pursued reflected the specifics of their institutions, their domestic societies, the nation's distinct vulnerabilities and advantages in the international political economy, and the personalities of those generals who successfully maneuvered internal military politics and rose to the top.

By the 1960s perverse military professionalism and national security ideology had attracted numerous adherents within the military, but a catalyst was needed for the ideology to translate to action. That catalyst came from civilian behavior in rejecting the political system and creating threats against the military itself (Stepan 1988: 123–71). By making officers overtly dependent upon political criteria for advancement, politicians and civilian groups subverted professionalism, and when civilian radicals called for the lower ranks to rise up against the officers or armed workers, peasants, and students, they challenged the military's monopoly over the legitimate use of force.

The path to this catalyst was constructed by economic crises and societal praetorianism – that is, the politicization and mobilization of a significant number of the institutions of society, including the Church. Economic crises were endemic in Latin America during the 1960s and early 1970s. This was a period of frustrated efforts to advance the country's development beyond the rapid industrialization many countries experienced in the 1940s and 1950s. Some scholars refer to these earlier decades as the "easy phase" of Import Substitution Industrialization (ISI), one in which countries largely imported intermediate and capital goods for assembly at home behind high-tariff walls on finished goods. This generated an industrial labor force and new capitalists as the multinational companies that had previously exported their product to Latin America now found that they needed to produce the product internally.

The political bargains bringing labor and domestic capital into association with state-owned enterprises produced highly subsidized industries and state-provided infrastructure. Imported intermediate and capital goods were the economic life-blood of the process, but the exchange rate could not decline in reflection of the economic inefficiencies running rampant through the economy because devaluation would make the necessary imports more expensive. Agricultural exports declined as the overvalued exchange rate made them less competitive on world markets, producing a disinvestment in the agricultural economy. For some countries, dramatic negative fluctuations in the world price for their dollar-denominated primary product exports (e.g., coffee for Brazil, copper for Chile) contributed to inflation and stop-go cycles of economic growth. Governments also pressured agricultural producers to provide for a growing internal market, especially for meat and dairy products demanded by unionized labor in the cities, which then induced many producers of basic foodstuffs to shift into production of animal feed. Shortage of basic foodstuffs led many governments to increase subsidies to poor urban consumers and to import wheat, corn, and beans, creating a new draw on already limited foreign exchange. Balance of payments crises ensued, devaluations became more painful as they were put off until the last minute, inflation climbed, and members of the ISI coalition blamed each other rather than question the model itself.

The political economy of the social coalitions that supported ISI was more to blame for the stagnation of the industrialization process than was a "general crisis of capitalism" or any "exhaustion" of the late dependent development process (Hirschmann 1979). Economic crises (even severe ones like that of 2001 in Argentina which produced riots in the streets that forced President Fernando De la Rua to resign) can be addressed without destroying the political system if civilians believe that the system can generate new leaders who will address the problems. But in the NSS cases, many civilians, including traditional political parties, were demanding a military coup because they had lost confidence in the political system's ability to successfully confront the challenges of development (Stepan 1988: 147–52; Rial 1990).

Latin American societies were already praetorian, but the loss of confidence took an already mobilized society to dysfunction. A significant number of groups became veto groups – that is, they could and would stop the machinery of government and the economy if their demands were not immediately met. In this context of hyper-mobilization and radical politics, the military was as legitimate a target as was a housing ministry. Consequently, a growing number of officers perceived their professionalism threatened through contagion in the ranks or political interference in the institution by demagogic politicians. Defense of the institution that had the self-assumed responsibility to save the nation, therefore, required eliminating that societal praetorianism. The threatening actors could be urban guerrillas or middle-class housewives banging pots in the streets; the point was that the political system's channels for dissent and the expectation that one could wait for an election had lost legitimacy. Into this vacuum stepped those military officers with, in some cases, an incipient understanding of the national security doctrine (the *castelistas* in Brazil), and in others, a total commitment to the national security doctrine (Ecuador, Peru, Chile, Argentina, and Uruguay).

The End of the National Security State

None of the National Security States survived, though liberal democracies were not their successors. Two disappeared after a long and arduous transition (Brazil and Uruguay); one collapsed (Argentina); one faded away after a short negotiated transition (Ecuador); and another became dormant, to be resuscitated for a period as a civilian-dominated version of the NSS (Peru under President Alberto Fujimori, 1992–2000). The Chilean NSS was the most durable: the military handed over the government after 17 years to a civilian government that accepted the military's 1980 constitution as well as its basic economic strategy and proclaimed "Mission Accomplished." Fifteen years after the transition to a "protected democracy," however, it is being dismantled under a left–center coalition.

We can point to specific problems faced by the NSSs which produced a revitalization of political parties and social organizations: military defeat in the Malvinas/Falklands War for the Argentine NSS, economic crises for the Peruvian version, and internal disunity for Ecuador's NSS. But ultimately, it was the inability of the National Security State to legitimize and institutionalize itself that guaranteed its demise. For the National Security States could never eliminate the economic and social inequalities that characterize Latin America and thus they could never convince sufficient numbers of people that the expression of conflicting views over where the nation should go and how it should get there was illegitimate. The national security doctrine could only maintain primacy as long as a significant portion of the politically active citizenry feared instability *and* believed that the military could provide security.

Fear is not the same as legitimacy. The professional military that internalized the national security doctrine could never see that they were doomed from the start: to the degree that they eliminated the specter and reality of violent anti-system forces, they were not needed. And if they insisted (as the hardliners were wont to do) that those forces lurked in private spaces, waiting for a chance to return, then pursued them with fury, the National Security State became a threat to more and more citizens who had looked to the military to defend them. Ultimately the growth in the number of people who saw the military themselves as the threat brought an end to the National Security State.

NOTES

1   Sometimes called the "Soccer War." The implication that the war had anything to do with the soccer riots is demeaning to the 4,000 Hondurans who died when Salvadoran forces invaded and diverts our attention from the migration and territorial issues that underlay the conflict (Durham 1979).

2   Air Force General Alberto Bachelet Martínez was the father of Michelle Bachelet Jeria, who was elected President of Chile in early 2006.

3   One might hypothesize that it is this belief in defending Christendom that explains why the four right-wing National Security States engaged in terrifying human rights violations far beyond what the more left-leaning NSSs in Peru and Ecuador committed. Given Stalin's gulags, Mao's Cultural Revolution, and the North Vietnamese abuse of US prisoners of war, one would not want to postulate that it is simply a matter of the morality of the right versus that of the left.

4   Stepan (1988: 14, 70). Chilean data on disappeared and dead is from "Desaparecidos": www.desaparecidos.org/chile/eng.html; and population data from: www.library.uu.nl/ wesp/populstat/Americas/chilec.html (accessed March 10, 2006).

BIBLIOGRAPHY

Agüero, F. (1998) "Legacies of Transitions: Institutionalization, the Military, and Democracy in South America," *Mershon International Studies Review*, 42:2, November.

Argentina [Comisión Nacional sobre la Desaparición de Personas] (1986) *Nunca Más – Never Again: a Report by Argentina's National Commission on Disappeared People*. Faber & Faber, London.

Arriagada Herrera, G. (1986a) *El Pensamiento Político de los Militares*, 2nd ed. Aconcagua, Chile.

Arriagada Herrera, G. (1986b) "The Legal and Institutional Framework of the Armed Forces in Chile." In J. S. Valenzuela & A. Valenzuela (eds.), *Military Rule in Chile*. Johns Hopkins University Press, Baltimore.

Barahona de Brito, A. (1997) *Human Rights and Democratization in Latin America: Uruguay and Chile*. Oxford University Press, Oxford.

Cardoso, F. H. (1979) "On the Characterization of Authoritarian Regimes in Latin America." In D. Collier (ed.), *The New Authoritarianism in Latin America*. Princeton University Press, Princeton.

Cohn, G., Thompson, G., & Matthews, M. (1997) "Torture was taught by the CIA: declassified manual details the methods used in Honduras; agency denials refuted," *Baltimore Sun*, January 27.

Collier, D. (ed.) (1979) *The New Authoritarianism in Latin America*. Princeton University Press, Princeton.

Constable, P. & Valenzuela, A. (1991) *A Nation of Enemies: Chile Under Pinochet*. Norton, New York.

Dassin, J. (ed.) (1986) *Torture in Brazil: A Report by the Archdiocese of São Paulo*. Vintage Books, New York.

Durham, W. (1979) *Scarcity and Survival in Central America: Ecological Origins of the Soccer War*. Stanford University Press, Stanford.

Evans, P. (1979) *Dependent Development: The Alliance of Multinational, State, and Local Capital in Brazil*. Princeton University Press, Princeton.

Fitch, J. S. (1992) *The Armed Forces and Democracy in Latin America*. Johns Hopkins University Press, Baltimore.

Foxley, A. (1983) *Latin American Experiments in Neo-Conservative Economics*. University of California Press, Berkeley.

Garretón, M. A. (1986) "Political Processes in an Authoritarian Regime: The Dynamics of Institutionalization and Opposition in Chile, 1973–1980." In J. S. Valenzuela & A. Valenzuela (eds.), *Military Rule in Chile*. Johns Hopkins University Press, Baltimore.

Gillespie, C. G. (1991) *Negotiating Democracy: Politicians and Generals in Uruguay*. Cambridge University Press, Cambridge.

Gonzalez, L. (1983) "Uruguay, 1980–1981: An Unexpected Opening," *Latin American Research Review*, 18:3, June.

Guglialmelli, J. (1977) "Geopolítica en la Argentina," *Estrategia*, 46–47, May–June, p. 5, as cited in G. Arriagada Herrera (1986), *El Pensamiento Político de los Militares*, 2nd ed. Aconcagua, Chile.

Handelman, H. (1981) "Military Authoritarianism and Political Change." In H. Handelman & T. Sanders (eds.), *Military Government and the Movement toward Democracy in South America*. Indiana University Press, Bloomington.

Hirschmann, A. O. (1979) "The Turn to Authoritarianism in Latin America and the Search for Its Economic Determinants." In D. Collier (ed.), *The New Authoritarianism in Latin America*. Princeton University Press, Princeton.

Huggins, M. (2000) "Legacies of Authoritarianism: Brazilian Torturers' and Murderers' Reformulation of Memory," *Latin American Perspectives*, 27:2, March.

Human Rights in Chile (2006) *The Legacy*: www.chipsites.com/derechos/dictadura_victimas_eng.html (accessed February 2, 2007).

Isaacs, A. (1993) *Military Rule and Transition in Ecuador, 1972–92*. University of Pittsburgh Press, Pittsburgh.

Kelly, P. & Child, J. (eds.) (1988) *Geopolitics of the Southern Cone and Antarctica*. Lynne Rienner, Boulder, CO.

Laurie, C. D. & Cole, R. H. (1997) *The Role of Federal Military Forces in Domestic Disorders, 1877–1945*. US Army Center of Military History, Washington, DC.

Loveman, B. (1993) *The Constitution of Tyranny*. University of Pittsburgh Press, Pittsburgh.

Loveman, B. (1999) *For la Patria: Politics and the Armed Forces in Latin America*. Scholarly Resources, Wilmington, DE.

Mares, D. (1996–7) "Deterrence in the Ecuador–Peru Enduring Rivalry: Designing Around Weakness," *Security Studies*, 6:2, Winter.

Mares, D. (2001) *Violent Peace: Militarized Interstate Bargaining in Latin America*. Columbia University Press, New York.

Martorell, F. (1999) *Operación Cóndor, el vuelo de la muerte: La coordinación represiva en el Cono Sur*. Lom Ediciones, Santiago, Chile.

Mauceri, P. (1996) *State Under Siege: Development and Policy Making in Peru*. Westview Press, Boulder, CO.

McClintock, C. & Lowenthal, A. (eds.) (1983) *The Peruvian Experiment Reconsidered*. Princeton University Press, Princeton.

McSherry, J. P. (2002) "Tracking the Origins of a State Terror Network: Operation Condor," *Latin American Perspectives*, 29:1, January.

McSherry, J. P. (2005) *Predatory States: Operation Condor and Covert War in Latin America*. Rowman & Littlefield, Lanham, MA.

Medina Parker, H. (1944) "La Geografía y la Política," *Memorial del Ejército de Chile*, May–June, p. 408, as cited in Arriagada Herrera (1986a).

Moreira Alves, M. (1985) *State and Opposition in Military Brazil*. University of Texas Press, Austin.

North, L. (1986) "The Military in Chilean Politics." In A. Lowenthal (ed.), *Armies and Politics in Latin America*. Holmes & Meier, New York.

Nunn, F. (1992) *The Time of the Generals*. University of Nebraska Press, Lincoln.

O'Donnell, G. (1976) "Modernization and Military Coups: Theory, Comparisons, and the Argentine Case." In A. Lowenthal, *Armies and Politics in Latin America*. Holmes & Meier, New York.

O'Donnell, G. (1979) *Modernization and Bureaucratic-Authoritarianism: Studies in South American Politics*. Institute of International Studies, University of California Berkeley, Berkeley.

Palmer, D. S. (1992) "The Armed Forces in Society and Politics." In R. Hudson, *Peru: A Country Study*. Federal Research Division, Library of Congress, Washington DC.

Pinochet Ugarte, A. (1984) *Geopolítica*, 4th ed. Editorial Andrés Bello, Santiago, Chile.

Pittman, H. (1988) "Harmony or Discord: The Impact of Democratization on Geopolitics and Conflict in the Southern Cone." In P. Kelly & J. Child (eds.), *Geopolitics of the Southern Cone and Antarctica*. Lynne Rienner, Boulder, CO.

Ramos, J. (1986) *Neoconservative Economics in the Southern Cone of Latin America, 1973–1983*. Johns Hopkins University Press, Baltimore.

Rial, J. (1990) "Los Partidos Políticos Uruguayos en el proceso de transición hacia la democracia." Working Paper #145, October. Kellogg Institute for International Studies, University of Notre Dame, South Bend, IN.

Rock, D. (1993) *Authoritarian Argentina: The Nationalist Movement, Its History, and Its Impact.* University of California Press, Berkeley.

Rouquié, A. (1987) *The Military and the State in Latin America.* University of California Press, Berkeley.

Russell, R. (1990) "El Proceso de toma de decisions en la política exterior argentina." In R. Russell, (ed.), *Política exterior y el proceso de toma de decisiones en América Latina.* Grupo Editorial Latinoamericano, Buenos Aires.

Schneider, R. M. (1971) *The Political System of Brazil: Emergence of "Modernizing" Authoritarian Regime, 1964–1970.* Columbia University Press, New York.

Skidmore, T. (1988) *The Politics of Military Rule in Brazil, 1964–85.* Oxford University Press, New York.

Stanley, W. (1996) *The Protection Racket State.* Temple University Press, Philadelphia.

Stepan, A. (1971) *The Military in Politics: Changing Patterns in Brazil.* Princeton University Press, Princeton.

Stepan, A. (1973) "The New Professionalism of Internal Warfare and Military Role Expansion." In A. Stepan (ed.), *Authoritarian Brazil: Origins, Policies, and Future.* Yale University Press, New Haven.

Stepan, A. (1978) *The State and Society: Peru in Comparative Perspective.* Princeton University Press, Princeton.

Stepan, A. (1988) *Rethinking Military Politics: Brazil and the Southern Cone.* Princeton University Press, Princeton.

Tapia Valdés, J. (1980) *El terrorismo de estado: La doctrina de la seguridad nacional en el cono sur.* Editorial Nueva Imagen, Mexico City.

Tapia Valdés, J. (1986) *Estrategocracia: El gobierno de los generales.* Ediciones del Ornitorrinco, Santiago, Chile.

Tapia Valdés, J. (1989). "National Security: The Dual State and the Rule of the Exception." PhD dissertation, Erasmus University, Rotterdam, Netherlands.

Varas, A. & Agüero, F. (1984), *El Proyecto Político Militar.* FLACSO, Santiago, Chile.

Villanueva, V. (1971) *100 años del ejército peruano: Frustraciones y cambios.* Editorial Juan Mejía Baca, Lima.

Chapter Twenty-Three

CENTRAL AMERICA IN UPHEAVAL

Julie A. Charlip

The year 1960 was a pivotal one for Central America. In Nicaragua, President Luis Somoza Debayle declared a state of siege. Military officers revolted in Guatemala. A new junta promising free elections briefly held power in El Salvador but was overthrown by a right-wing coup. And the governments of El Salvador, Guatemala, Nicaragua, and Honduras agreed to form the Central American Common Market (CACM).

The last event may seem the most prosaic, but in many ways it was the most indicative of problems that would explode into bloody warfare in the 1970s and 1980s. The CACM was an attempt to increase trade by linking the region's thin markets, comprising the tiny group of elites with spending power. Central American leaders preferred to seek new consumers in neighboring countries rather than carry out programs to help their impoverished majorities.

Families who made their fortunes in agricultural exports, primarily production of coffee and sugar, starting in the nineteenth century, dominated Central America. They invested little in manufacturing, preferring to import goods. Their workers, therefore, were never viewed as consumers, needing at least enough money to buy the products their bosses manufactured. They were seen only as a cost, and owners sought to keep costs to a minimum. Much of the population worked for the big landowners at meager wages or eked out a living on insufficient plots of land.

Despite highly unequal land distribution, there were still many small and medium-sized landholdings and subsistence farms. The smaller farmers, however, had little political voice. Their marginality was guaranteed by exclusive political systems controlled by the elites, or dictators who ruled in their stead, limiting freedoms for workers and ensuring consolidation of wealth by a few.

The elites found new sources of wealth in the 1960s by responding to increased US demand for cotton, sugar, and beef. The USA reoriented its cotton imports to the Southern hemisphere during the Korean War and sought new sources of sugar after cutting Cuba's quota in 1960. Rapid expansion of US fast-food restaurants created demand for inexpensive beef.

But new exports came at the expense of poor *campesinos*.[1] The elites used economic and political clout to take over their properties. Some campesinos were pushed onto marginal lands; others swelled the ranks of landless workers. They found limited employment in the new export sector, since cattle raising requires little labor, and the use of machines and pesticides reduced labor demand in cotton and sugar. Campesinos who moved to the cities found the new industries created by the CACM provided few, low-wage jobs. As gross domestic product grew, so did unemployment and hunger. Exports displaced food production, and the newly landless and unemployed could not afford high-priced imports. Many began to migrate in search of seasonal work, as families and communities fell apart.

The illusory prosperity of the 1960s was quickly eroded by the international economic crises of the 1970s. Governments borrowed to pay for oil after price hikes in 1973 and 1979, but the oil crises sparked a recession in the developed world, depressing the demand and price for Central American exports. The reduced income had to satisfy elite profits and repay the debt. The cost was paid by the lower classes. Central America might have weathered the economic storm were it not for the refusal of ruling elites to respond to the needs of the majority. Political intransigence coupled with economic crisis fueled an explosive situation.

The explosion came in the geopolitical context of the United States' sphere of influence. Central America represented the US southern flank and access to the Panama Canal, largely symbolic, since supertankers could not fit through the canal. More importantly, it was a region historically dominated by the USA. As the Cold War intensified, control was seen as essential. The pivotal year 1960 was also when US reservations about the Cuban Revolution hardened into implacable opposition – the trade embargo began, along with planning for the Bay of Pigs invasion in 1961. The invasion was modeled on a more successful one – the 1954 CIA coup that overthrew Guatemala's reformist president Jacobo Arbenz, ushering in decades of dictatorship.

The Bay of Pigs invasion, in turn, highlighted Central America's strategic importance. The invasion force was trained in Guatemala, and launched from Puerto Cabezas on Nicaragua's Atlantic Coast. The role of Guatemala and Nicaragua was indicative of what the USA expected from its clients. They were joined in the Cold War struggle, and any pressure for social, economic, and political change would be viewed in that context. Central American elites, eager to maintain their wealth and power, labeled any movement for change as communist, an epithet sure to win US support. The United States provided training, arms, and ammunition to help Central American governments maintain the highly unequal status quo.

New social actors, the product of economic changes of the 1950s and 1960s, challenged that inequality in the 1960s. An expanded working class organized labor unions, bargained for better wages and working conditions, and called strikes. A new middle class aspired to a role in government. They created new political parties, most notably the Christian Democrats, and sought an end to military rule. Their children were university students swept up in the international youth movement that protested imperialism in Vietnam. Inspired by Cuba, they took to the streets to call for change.

Perhaps the greatest challenge came from the Catholic Church, long a bastion of conservative support. The Second Vatican Council (1961–5), convoked by Pope John XXIII and continued by Pope Paul VI, gave the Church a new mission. The Pastoral Constitution on the Church in the Modern World urged Catholics not to shirk their responsibility to the poor and oppressed. In Latin America, theologians responded with a new doctrine, liberation theology, drawing on Jesus' first sermon in Luke (4:18–21), in which the gospel says Jesus came "to liberate those who are oppressed."

Faced with a shortage of religious, the Latin American church organized lay Bible groups called Christian Base Communities (*Comunidades de Base*). Priests trained "delegates of the word" to lead the communities in reading the Bible through the lens of social justice. The Second Latin American Bishops Conference in Medellín, Colombia, ratified these changes in 1968, where the bishops accepted the "preferential option for the poor."

But moderate forces for change met intransigence from Central American elites and the military governments that protected them. Democratic openings ended in bloodshed. With peaceful change blocked, Central Americans resorted to armed warfare, forming guerrilla groups in Nicaragua, Guatemala, and El Salvador. The elites' worst fears were realized when Nicaragua's Sandinistas defeated the Somoza dynasty in 1979. The United States responded by waging a proxy war against the Sandinistas and funding the governments of El Salvador and Guatemala to prevent "another Nicaragua."

The military responded with stunning viciousness. In Nicaragua under Somoza and in El Salvador, brutalized remains of torture victims were dumped in plain view as a warning. In Guatemala, entire villages were destroyed under scorched-earth policies. By the time the wars ended, the death toll was 75,000 in El Salvador, 80,000 in Nicaragua, and 200,000 in Guatemala.

The inconceivable brutality was fueled in part by class and ethnic animosities that enabled elites to see the majority as "others," in the same way that troops characterize foreign enemies. Guatemala's indigenous majority were incorporated into society only as workers forced to leave their villages and labor on coffee and cotton estates. El Salvador's Pipil indigenous communities abandoned any markers of ethnic difference after a 1932 massacre killed as many as 30,000 (Anderson 2001). Nicaragua claimed to be a *mestizo* country, but supposed *mestizaje* did not give the poor majority equal status. Dictator Anastasio Somoza García aptly summed up the Nicaraguan elite attitude. When someone suggested educating his workforce, Somoza famously replied, "I don't want an educated population; I want oxen" (Lernoux 1980: 85). The dehumanization of the population throughout the region led to a policy of slaughter.

This combination of factors – economic, social, and political; domestic and international – led to the upheavals in Central America that devastated the region in the late twentieth century.

Nicaragua: Victory and Defeat

Nicaragua's active volcanoes are a frequently used trope to characterize the long-simmering explosiveness of the country's history. In a region characterized by imperialism and dictatorship, Nicaragua stands out for the longevity and durability of its subjection.

United States interest in Nicaragua began when gold prospectors discovered it would be easier to cross Nicaragua than Panama to get to California. In 1848, the

USA and England signed the Clayton–Bulwer Treaty, agreeing that neither power would build a Nicaraguan canal without the other's approval. Nicaraguans were not consulted. In 1857, US President Franklin Pierce quickly recognized the regime of William Walker, a US filibuster invited to Nicaragua by the Liberal Party to defeat their Conservative rivals. Walker turned on the Liberals, became president, instituted slavery, and made English the official language. Central American forces overthrew him, and no Liberals held power again until José Santos Zelaya in 1893.

An ardent nationalist, Zelaya was a tough negotiator when the United States sought a canal across Nicaragua. The USA opted for the more pliant Panamanians, but Zelaya sparked concern when he consulted Germany and Japan about building a rival canal. The USA helped Conservatives overthrow Zelaya in 1909 and spent the next 70 years propping up leaders friendly to the USA, including occupation by US troops, with brief exceptions, from 1912 to 1933.

The last great Liberal–Conservative struggle shaped Nicaragua's modern history. General José Maria Moncada led Liberal troops against the Conservatives, but in 1927, Moncada agreed to a US-brokered truce in exchange for his turn in the presidency. His venality prompted one commander, Augusto C. Sandino, to attack the real power: the US Marines.

Sandino gathered his "crazy little army" among workers on US-owned banana plantations and gold mines, and among poor campesinos. The Marines pursued him without success through the rugged Segovia Mountains, as Sandino became an international *cause célèbre*: China's Kuomingtang army in 1928 boasted a Sandino brigade. Salvadoran communist organizer Farabundo Martí joined Sandino, but he left when Sandino maintained his ardent nationalism against Martí's communist internationalism.

In 1933, the United States withdrew, but in their place they left the *Guardia Nacional* under the compliant leadership of Anastasio Somoza García, whose first act was to order the assassination of Sandino, his only potential rival. Somoza's formula for rule was to maintain the Guardia as a corrupt, repressive force, cultivate the US, and co-opt rivals with political and economic favors. A clever politician, he weathered democratic trends in 1944 by using populist measures to win labor support, while using the Guardia to repress democratic movements. He viewed Nicaragua as his own estate, and he parceled its rule out to his sons: Luis headed Congress, Anastasio the National Guard. Somoza García remained in power until 1956, when a young poet, Rigoberto López Pérez, assassinated him. He was succeeded by his son Luis Somoza Debayle, who first ruled directly, then through René Schick (1963–7). Luis has usually been described as the more moderate Somoza, but it was during his presidency that the Sandinista guerrilla movement was formed, and his response was violent.

The *Frente Sandinista de Liberación Nacional* (FSLN) was founded in 1961 by university students Carlos Fonseca, Tomás Borge, and Silvio Mayorga. Fonseca resurrected Sandino, transforming him from the bandit of Nicaraguan history books into a symbol of resistance to imperialism and dictatorship. Like most Central American revolutionary groups, they were few in number and believed in Che Guevara's *foco* strategy – the idea that a small group fighting in the isolated countryside could spark a larger, successful war. But the Guardia defeated the short-lived "*foco* on the Río Coco" in 1963. From 1963 to 1967, the FSLN focused on campus agitation at the National University at León, while quietly working with campesinos in the mountains.

Although the Sandinistas were not a serious threat, Luis Somoza availed himself of counterinsurgency training offered by the USA under the Alliance for Progress, launched by President John F. Kennedy in 1961 to counter Cuba's appeal. The program publicly offered economic assistance to ameliorate conditions that cause revolution. Quietly, it provided training to help the military fight revolutionaries. The Guardia, run by Luis's brother, Anastasio Somoza Debayle, who by 1966 was poised to run for president, tortured captured Sandinistas.

In 1967, Nicaraguan politics took a dramatic turn. In January, the Guardia attacked a rally of 60,000 supporting presidential candidate Fernando Agüero. Luis Somoza died of a heart attack in April, and Anastasio became president in May. In August, Sandinistas were massacred in the battle of Pancasán. Both peaceful and violent attempts at change seemed to end, and little was heard from the Sandinistas from 1967 to 1974, the period of "the silent accumulation of forces" (Black 1985: 82).

The last Somoza lacked Luis's moderation and their father's political finesse. His brutality toward opposition politicians and revolutionaries sowed hatred. His remarkable venality turned even many of the upper class against him. By the time of his overthrow, the Somoza family owned 20 percent of the country's arable land, 40 percent of rice production, 51 percent of the cattle ranches, 65 percent of commercial fishing, three of six sugar refineries, the only two meat-processing plants licensed to export, the country's only pasteurized milk facility, the national airline, a newspaper, a cement company, a textile mill, six breweries, rum distilleries, the Mercedes Benz dealership, and the merchant marine lines.

It was, in fact, Somoza's greed that helped bring his downfall. In 1972, most of Managua was destroyed by a rapid series of three earthquakes that killed 20,000 and left 250,000 homeless. The $772 million in damage included the destruction of 75 percent of the city's housing and 90 percent of its commercial capacity. Somoza called the earthquake "a revolution of possibilities." He took control over the $250 million in international aid, while the Guardia sold stolen property and donations of medicine and food on the black market. Somoza cornered the market for reconstruction, controlling demolition, real estate speculation, concrete, building materials, metal structures, roofing, asbestos, and plastics.

New construction in the aftermath of the earthquake increased the size of the urban working class, leading to a strike in 1973. Coincidentally, a two-year drought reduced food crops, leading to higher food prices, land invasions, and campesino migration to the city. In this tense atmosphere, the Sandinistas dramatically reappeared on the national stage.

In December 1974, José María "Chema" Castillo, a wealthy cotton exporter who had served in Somoza's Office of Security and as Minister of Agriculture, was hosting a reception for US Ambassador Turner B. Shelton. Minutes after Shelton left, 13 Sandinistas stormed the house and held hostages until their demands were met: the release of 18 political prisoners; $1 million in ransom; and publication and broadcast of communiqués calling for wage increases for workers, including enlisted men in the Guardia. Somoza capitulated and, for the first time, the dictatorship looked vulnerable.

Somoza responded with a state of siege that lasted for 33 months. The Guardia launched search-and-destroy missions in the northern mountains, accompanied by the Air Force using bombs, napalm, and defoliant. They killed thousands of campesinos, and, in November 1976, wiped out a small guerrilla group that included FSLN founder Carlos Fonseca.

His death coincided with increasingly bitter Sandinista debates about the proper strategy to win the revolution. In 1977 they split into three tendencies: *Guerra Prolongada Popular*, which focused on rural warfare; *Tendencia Proletaria*, which concentrated on the small but militant working class; and *Tendencia Insurreccional*, more commonly known as the *Terceristas*, which opted for a broad multi-class alliance for rapid overthrow of the dictatorship.

Fonseca's death also coincided with the election in the United States of Jimmy Carter, who promised a foreign policy focused on human rights. Carter pressured Somoza to lift the state of siege. Hoping to find a more moderate force than the Sandinistas, Carter supported the *Unión Democrático de Liberación* (UDEL), founded by *La Prensa* editor Pedro Joaquín Chamorro, a longtime Somoza foe who used *La Prensa* to report on repression and resistance.

Throughout 1977, the Terceristas organized training schools for young revolutionaries who flocked to their ranks, many from Christian youth groups influenced by liberation theology. By October, Somoza's indiscriminate violence prompted a group of prominent Nicaraguans known as *Los Doce* (The Twelve) to declare their support for the Sandinistas. Even Archbishop Miguel Obando y Bravo condemned the regime's violence and said people had a right to resort to armed struggle.

Somoza responded with more violence. In January 1978, Pedro Joaquín Chamorro was assassinated. Enraged Nicaraguans took to the streets. Businessmen went on strike, hoping to force Somoza to resign. But within weeks, the strike sputtered out. Somoza remarked cynically, but accurately, "This was a strike of millionaires who have forgotten that my government assured them the social peace necessary to build up their fortunes" (Black 1985: 111). The collapse of the strike left the Sandinistas as the only potential leaders.

From February 1978 on, Nicaragua was in full insurrection. The indigenous community of Monimbó exploded with contact bombs, made with whatever chemicals, nails, and rocks they could assemble. Managuans dug up Somoza's paving bricks and built barricades.

By June, Somoza's human rights violations were so severe that the Organization of American States launched an investigation. Despite the supposed commitment to human rights, however, Carter was more concerned with stopping the Sandinistas. Hoping to moderate the regime, Carter sent a private letter congratulating Somoza on human rights improvements. Somoza publicized the letter as proof of US support. The Terceristas responded with a spectacular action: on August 22, 26 Sandinistas disguised as Guardia seized the National Palace and held 2,600 hostages until winning their demands, including release of 58 political prisoners (another 27 whose release they sought were already dead).

The Sandinistas launched their final offensive in September 1978, and full-scale war ensued. The three tendencies, which had been negotiating throughout 1978, reunited in January 1979. On July 17, Somoza fled the country, taking with him the bodies of his father and brother and most of Nicaragua's treasury. Before he left, he ordered the bombing of Nicaragua's cities.

On July 19, 1979, the victorious Sandinistas took power after 18 years of struggle for the FSLN founders and a frenetic 18 months that defeated Latin America's longest-running dictatorship. The cost was high: 50,000 dead, or 1.6 percent of the population (an equivalent percentage of the US population would have been four million people).

The Sandinistas pledged a mixed economy, political pluralism, and national sovereignty. They set out to rebuild the country with $3 million in the treasury and foreign debt of $1.6 billion. Seizing Somoza property gave the government 20 percent of the nation's arable land, and the Sandinistas began to redistribute it. By 1989, the campesino share of landholding had grown from 3.4 percent to 35 percent. Sandinista social programs reduced illiteracy from 60 to 20 percent, and health programs eliminated malaria and polio.

However, the United States was implacably opposed to the Sandinistas. Carter set the tone, trying to remove Somoza, maintain the Guardia, and eliminate the Sandinistas. When those efforts failed, Carter gave the CIA $1 million to support opposition political parties, labor unions, and the media. In January 1981, just before turning the White House over to Ronald Reagan, Carter suspended all aid to the Sandinistas.

The Reagan administration came to power vowing to reestablish US dominance after the humiliation of Vietnam. The Sandinista victory, in Reagan's eyes, was the triumph of Soviet and Cuban communism. Reagan ordered the CIA to organize remnants of the Guardia into a counterrevolutionary force, called the *contras* (short for *contrarevolucionarios*). The contras waged a campaign of terror in the countryside, targeting Sandinista schools, clinics, and cooperatives. Under relentless attack, the Sandinistas allocated an increasing share of their budget to defense.

The contra war was part of a new US strategy – low-intensity conflict (LIC) developed because of "Vietnam syndrome," reluctance on the part of the US public to support foreign wars. Rather than send US troops, the plan was to use foreign nationals funded and equipped by the USA in long-term struggles. The cost to the USA was low, but the intensity of the war was high for people in Central America.

In 1984, the United States increased pressure with an economic blockade, cutting off US trade and blocking loans from multinational organizations. Between 1979 and 1984, the Nicaraguan economy grew 22 percent overall, while the rest of Central America declined by 5.7 percent (Conroy 1985: 220). But the blockade sent the Nicaraguan economy into a nosedive. The results were shortages of basic goods and soaring inflation, rising by 1987 to 1,347 percent (Ricciardi 1991: 261).

The Sandinistas hoped to legitimate the revolution in US eyes with elections in 1984, which international observers certified as free and fair. Sandinista Daniel Ortega became president with 67 percent of the vote. But the exercise did not change US policy. The Reagan administration instead planted stories in US newspapers claiming that Soviet MiG fighter planes were en route to Nicaragua. The fabricated story supplanted news of the election.

The disinformation campaign was just one US strategy, in addition to contra terror and the mining of Nicaragua's harbors and bombing of fuel supplies by CIA operatives. In self-defense, the Sandinistas instituted a military draft in 1983, which became increasingly unpopular as the war dragged on. The combination of war and economic devastation eroded Sandinista social programs and popular morale.

In 1990, Nicaraguans headed to the polls again. US President George H. W. Bush backed a coalition of 21 parties, the United Nicaraguan Opposition, which nominated Violeta Chamorro, widow of the martyred *La Prensa* editor. Violeta campaigned as a mother who could gather all four of her children peacefully at the dinner table, although two were Sandinistas and two were contras. She pledged to do the same for Nicaragua, and the USA pledged to help her. Furthermore, Bush said a Sandinista victory would be a sure indication of fraud, and the USA would continue to fund the war. Weary Nicaraguans voted for Violeta, while still giving the Sandinistas 41 percent.

The revolution that began with gunshots ended with ballots. Its rise and fall had significant consequences for Nicaragua's neighbors.

El Salvador

At 8,124 square miles, El Salvador is the smallest country in Latin America. But its people have lived an outsized history, marked by one defining event: the *matanza* of 1932. The massacre was the reaction of the Salvadoran ruling class to unrest that grew out of the 1929 Great Depression. Export profits plummeted, and workers lost jobs or suffered wage cuts. Economic disaster led to strikes, protests, and the rise of opposition parties.

In 1930, activists founded the *Partido Comunista de El Salvador* (PCS) and the *Socorro Rojo Internacional* (SRI), led by Farabundo Martí, the student radical and labor organizer who fought with Sandino. They were supported by the labor group, *Federación Regional de Trabajadores de El Salvador* (FRTS), but found less support in the countryside, where urban, mestizo leaders had little understanding of the rural realities for mostly indigenous campesinos.

The Communists organized in the space opened by President Arturo Araujo's election in January 1931. As the candidate of the *Partido Laborista*, Araujo ran on intellectual Alberto Masferrer's doctrine of *vitalismo*, calling for a "vital minimum" of housing, health care, education, and land. But plunging coffee prices kept Araujo from keeping his vague promises. As strikes spread, Araujo was overthrown in December 1931 by troops led by vice president and minister of war, General Maximiliano Hernández Martínez.

Within weeks of the coup, in January 1932, the Communists learned that campesinos were planning to revolt. They may have questioned the wisdom of an uprising, but the Communists decided they had no choice but to support it. The plan was compromised, however, when Martí was arrested. The party tried to warn the campesinos to stop the uprising, but it is not clear that they had a sufficient network to do so, or that the campesinos would have listened. The revolt began on January 21 and, three days later, the government counterattacked.

In San Salvador, the military targeted unionists and Communists. But in the countryside, there was indiscriminate slaughter. Any campesino with a machete was suspect. Families were told to report for safe conduct, then were forced to dig their own graves before being shot. Some 30,000 people died; most were indigenous. Survivors stopped speaking Nahuatl and put away distinctive clothing, determined not to be targeted again. Salvadoran elites, terrified by armed campesinos, willingly ceded political control to the military.

Hernandez Martinez's rule (1931–44) was characterized by forcefulness and eccentricity – a spiritist, he was called *El Brujo* (the warlock) because he held séances in the presidential palace and hung colored lights across the streets in San Salvador to stem a smallpox epidemic. He resigned under pressure in 1944 when his attempts to stay in office without elections triggered a coup by junior officers.

But the end of the dictatorship did not mark a democratic opening – the military stepped in to keep populist Arturo Romero from winning the presidential election. The military, however, also had its internal divisions. In 1948, the majors' coup brought in a new generation of officers, committed to modernizing the country. Modernization, however, was not equated with civilian rule, which would not return to El Salvador until 1984. The presidents who followed the 1948 coup (Colonel Carlos Osorio, 1950–6; Colonel Jose Maria Lemus, 1956–60) were eager to promote economic development, including public works and diversification of agriculture. They advocated limited social reform, providing social security and allowing unions to organize and bargain. But there was no consideration of such fundamental changes as agrarian reform.

The regimes of the 1960s coincided with the Alliance for Progress, which provided investment that stimulated industrialization. El Salvador was the chief beneficiary of the new CACM. The share of manufactures in exports rose from 5.6 percent in 1960 to 28.7 percent in 1970; industrial employment jumped from 85,038 in 1961 to 248,165 in 1971 (North 1985: 52–3). The result was an expanded working class, which organized unions, and an expanded middle class, which formed the *Partido Demócrata Cristiano* (PDC).

The other side of the Alliance for Progress, of course, was counterinsurgency training. Salvadoran generals created the *Organización Democrática Nacional* (ORDEN) with input from the US State Department, CIA, and Green Berets. ORDEN tried to indoctrinate campesinos against communism. Suspected subversives were executed by an elaborate security system that included ORDEN, the army, the Guardia, and such newly formed paramilitary groups as *Mano Blanca* (Montgomery 1992: 55–6).

Despite military domination, the Christian Democrats were popular. In 1964 they won 14 seats in the Legislative Assembly and 37 mayoralties. Most significant was the election of José Napoleon Duarte as mayor of San Salvador. Duarte's local self-help projects to renovate schools, build parks, and provide adult education earned him reelection in 1966 and 1968. Because of San Salvador's importance, Duarte became a national figure.

El Salvador weathered the dislocations of 1960s export expansion by using neighboring Honduras as a safety valve. But as coffee, cattle, and cotton began to displace Honduran campesinos, the 300,000 Salvadorans in Honduras became targets of violence and deportation. In May 1969, thousands of Salvadorans headed home to an economy unable to support them. Tensions in June during a three-game elimination match between the two countries for the World Cup in soccer led to violence, and in July, El Salvador attacked Honduras. The appeal to Salvadoran nationalism created a temporary distraction from the country's growing economic problems, but the "Soccer War" made the economic situation worse. The government spent one-fifth of its annual budget, $20 million, in just four days, and the CACM was destroyed. The Honduras safety valve no longer existed, and the country had to absorb the returned immigrants.

General Fidel Sánchez Hernández responded by indicating that some reforms might be needed. A National Agrarian Reform Congress convened in January 1970, and to the shock of the elites, criticized land concentration and called for agrarian reform. The elites responded by abandoning progressive parties and supporting the military. In the next elections, the Christian Democrats lost 70 of their 78 mayoralties (Montgomery 1992: 61–2).

Progressive parties hoped to counter military dominance by uniting for the 1972 presidential campaign behind the popular Duarte. Election returns showed the countryside voting for Colonel Arturo Armando Molina, but Duarte won overwhelmingly in San Salvador. In an obvious fraud, Molina was declared the winner by a slim margin. The controversy led to an abortive coup, led by Colonel Benjamin Mejía. Duarte reluctantly joined, calling on people to support the coup. Guardia units streamed into San Salvador from garrisons in Sonsonate and San Miguel, and the Air Force received support from the dictators of Nicaragua and Guatemala via the Central American Defense Council (CONDECA) (Armstrong & Shenk 1982: 95–6). Duarte sought refuge in the Venezuelan embassy, where Salvadoran armed forces ignored diplomatic tradition and arrested him. Before deporting him, they broke Duarte's cheekbones and cut the tips from three of his fingers. Molina then cracked down on dissent: the National University was attacked, 800 were arrested, and the university closed for two years.

For many, the events of 1972 showed that peaceful change was impossible. A group of young Communists left the party and, joined by young Christian Democrats and children of the bourgeoisie, formed the *Ejercito Revolucionario del Pueblo* (ERP). It was El Salvador's second guerrilla group. In 1970, Salvador Cayetano Carpio had resigned from the Communist Party when it refused to back armed struggle and founded the *Fuerzas Populares de Liberación* (FPL).

The Salvadoran left was characterized from the outset by sectarianism. The FPL believed in a prolonged popular struggle in the countryside; ERP subscribed to the *foco* theory. Both believed more in armed struggle than political organizing. When one ERP faction, the *Resistencia Nacional* (RN), encouraged political action through the *Frente de Acción Popular Unificada* (FAPU) in 1974, the ERP split. Divisions reached their nadir with the 1975 assassination of poet Roque Dalton, an active supporter of political struggle. The RN then left ERP to form the *Fuerzas Armadas de Resistencia Nacional* (FARN). In 1976, a fourth armed group emerged from the Communist Party – the *Partido Revolucionario de los Trabajadores Centroamericanos* (PRTC), which envisioned a regional struggle, and, in 1979, the *Fuerzas Armadas de Liberación* (FAL) was formed.

Each armed group also had popular organizations working with campesinos and trade unions. Even the reluctant ERP formed the *Ligas Populares 28 de Febrero* in 1978. And each group believed that its own analysis, strategy, and tactics were the only way to achieve victory. The divisions made the left more vulnerable to the Salvadoran armed forces.

The 1970s were characterized by a surrealistic swirl of popular organizing and violent repression. For example, in 1975, El Salvador hosted the Miss Universe pageant. University students at the Santa Ana campus protested such use of scarce resources and were attacked by the Guardia Nacional. When students in San Salvador marched in solidarity, they were encircled and attacked by Guardia.

As the Molina government considered the idea of a mild agrarian "transformation" – the word "reform" carried the taint of communism – the oligarchy made it clear that more force was needed to maintain order. They were rewarded in February 1977 with fraudulent elections that brought to power General Carlos Humberto Romero, Molina's minister of defense. His election opened the floodgates to a wave of repression, much of it aimed at the Catholic Church and Christian base communities, which had been demanding land reform and political change.

In 1977, flyers appeared proclaiming, "Be a patriot – kill a priest." Among the many murdered was Father Rutilio Grande, killed just two months after his friend Oscar Arnulfo Romero was named archbishop of San Salvador. Romero was a scholarly cleric whom Vatican officials had hoped would be a moderating influence, but Grande's death sparked Romero's activism. In weekly homilies, broadcast on radio, Romero deplored government repression.

The archbishop was briefly encouraged when Jimmy Carter took office. Carter delayed naming a new US ambassador, sent human rights investigators, and withheld a $90 million loan from the Inter-American Development Bank (Armstrong & Shenk 1982: 956). But Carter was afraid his actions would strengthen the left. When General Romero lifted a 10-month state of siege, Carter immediately approved the loan and named a new ambassador.

When the Sandinistas triumphed in Nicaragua, Salvadoran elites feared they were next. Young officers, believing that hard-line military measures had become counter-productive, overthrew General Romero in October 1979 and replaced him with a civilian–military junta. But by January 1980, it was clear the old guard was still in control. The civilians resigned, only to be replaced by others who were equally powerless. One of the new members, Héctor Dada, resigned after Attorney General Mario Zamora, who favored negotiations with the left, was murdered by gunmen who burst into a party at his home, dragged him to the bathroom, and shot him in the head. Dada was replaced by the erstwhile Duarte.

Duarte initiated moderate change – a limited agrarian reform, bank nationalizations – but he could not control the armed forces. The situation was so desperate that Archbishop Romero spoke directly to the armed forces in his Sunday homily on March 23: "I beseech you, I beg you, I order you, in the name of God, stop the repression." The next day, he was assassinated while saying Mass. Crowds of mourners at his funeral were greeted by gunfire.

The assassination motivated the fragmented left to unite their political forces in the *Frente Democrático Revolucionario* (FDR, Democratic Revolutionary Front); in October, the armed groups formed a united command, *Frente Farabundo Martí para la Liberación Nacional* (FMLN). Like the Sandinistas, the FMLN rooted their unity in national history, reaching back to a martyr of the *matanza* of 1932.

The 1980s marked several changes in the Salvadoran conflict. The united revolutionaries were far more effective, and by the end of the decade a third of the country was FMLN territory. However, they had lost the Catholic Church as a strong ally. Archbishop Arturo Rivera y Damas was cautioned to be more circumspect by the Vatican, since 1978 under the control of the more conservative Pope John Paul II, who challenged liberation theology.

Furthermore, the Salvadoran military had a strong backer in Ronald Reagan. Despite evidence of atrocities, his administration issued a white paper assuring people that the situation had improved. US aid doubled from 1982 to1987, and arms, training, and support were provided. The Salvadorans were also encouraged to provide at least the façade of democracy. In 1984, Duarte was elected president in "demonstration elections," staged to give the appearance of democracy when none actually existed (Brodhead & Herman 1984).

Despite US support, the Salvadorans could not defeat the guerrillas, whose forces grew from a few hundred in 1981 to 12,000 in 1984 (Montgomery 1992: 169). By 1985, the FMLN used highly effective lightning strikes against such targets as electricity plants, and all combatants were trained as political officers to educate campesinos. In 1989, the war was at an impasse, and popular opinion favored negotiations. The war expense was a heavy burden to an economy reeling from worldwide recession and the debt crisis of the 1980s, which became Latin America's lost decade.

In June 1989, newly elected President Alfredo Cristiani called for negotiations, and the FMLN agreed. Talks ended after two meetings, however, when the headquarters of the largest trade union federation was bombed. The FMLN returned to arms and launched the November offensive, bringing the war to San Salvador. The attacks shook urban elites and took the US Embassy by surprise. Cristiani's limited power over the military was clear on the fourth day of the offensive, when the elite US-trained Atlcatl battalion went to the Jesuit-run *Universidad Centroamericana* and killed six priests, their housekeeper, and her daughter.

The final offensive failed to bring down the government, but it succeeded in prompting the United Nations to help negotiate a ceasefire and set conditions for peace talks in 1990. The FMLN embraced the idea of negotiations after the Sandinistas were defeated in the November 1990 elections, casting doubt on the wisdom of continuing armed struggle for state control that could be fleeting. Peace accords were signed on January 16, 1992 and, like the Sandinistas, the FMLN became a political party.

Guatemala's Guerrilla War

Guatemala is a hauntingly beautiful country of green mountains where the majority of people are indigenous, descendants of the Maya. In the late twentieth century, many still dressed in traditional, colorful woven textiles and spoke 22 different indigenous dialects. In the nineteenth century, it was the goal of modernizing elites of Spanish descent to build coffee farms on the lower slopes of those green hills, displacing the indigenous population farther north to the *altiplano*. But, paradoxically, the modernizers needed the indigenous in significant numbers as workers during the harvest.

Elites turned to the government to guarantee the workforce, and President Justo Rufino Barrios (1873–85) established the *mandamiento*, a form of forced labor. Manuel Estrada Cabrera (1898–1920), whose military guaranteed a supply of cheap labor, reinforced the model. The price was the forfeiting of elite political participation to Estrada's personalist dictatorship, immortalized by Nobel laureate Miguel Angel Asturias in *El Señor Presidente*. Part of Estrada's legacy was the relationship he formed with the United Fruit Company (UFCO), which dominated banana production and owned Guatemala's railroad and port facilities.

The overthrow of Estrada in 1920 briefly opened a political space, quickly filled by a new labor movement and Communist Party. But the 1932 uprising in El Salvador served as a warning for General Jorge Ubico. Like his Salvadoran counterpart, Ubico ruled from 1931 to 1944. His regime repressed opponents, massacred rebels, and killed labor leaders and intellectuals. Unlike in El Salvador, Ubico's overthrow came via civilian protest. Prominent lawyers and businessmen convinced him to resign after the cavalry charged a peaceful protest by teachers, killing 200. Ubico turned power over to General Federico Ponce, but an army revolt led by Major Francisco Arana and Captain Jacobo Arbenz guaranteed elections and opened the 10-year Guatemalan Spring.

It began with the election of Juan José Arévalo, a former schoolteacher who had been exiled in Argentina. Arévalo's reforms were mostly political: the secret police were disbanded; a constitutional assembly wrote a new constitution, and a new National Assembly was elected. Economic change was left to the next government, headed by Arbenz, who pledged to convert Guatemala to a modern, capitalist country and raise the standard of living of the masses. His blueprint was a World Bank report calling for government regulation of energy companies, higher wages, regulation of foreign business, industrialization, a capital gains tax, and public spending on transportation, communications, education, and health care. The plan put the government on a collision course with Guatemala's dominant economic groups: coffee producers and UFCO.

In 1952, Arbenz adopted an agrarian reform aimed at the expropriation of idle land on large plantations. Left untouched were farms smaller than 233 acres and those from 223 to 670 acres with at least two-thirds of the land cultivated. Fully cultivated estates of any size were permitted. Confiscated land was paid for in 25-year bonds at 3 percent interest, with compensation pegged to the declaration of taxable worth filed in May 1952. The government confiscated 1.5 million acres, paid $8.3 million in bonds, and distributed land to 100,000 (Jonas 1991: 27).

The landowning elite called the reform a Communist plot, a charge guaranteed to get US attention. The state department watched apprehensively but said nothing until 1953, when the Guatemalan government seized 413,573 acres of idle UFCO land. UFCO enjoyed unusually close connections to the US government: The law firm of Secretary of State John Foster Dulles drafted UFCO's 1930 and 1936 agreements with Guatemala. His brother, CIA director Allen Dulles, had served as president of the United Fruit Company. John Moors Cabot, assistant secretary of state for Interamerican affairs, owned UFCO stock. However, it was not unusual for the government to intervene on behalf of US corporations. Such intervention had, in fact, been US policy for many years. Furthermore, Guatemalan coffee producers applauded US opposition to Arbenz and would have asked for such help had it not already been forthcoming.

A steady stream of propaganda in the United States claimed that Communists influenced the Arbenz government. By late 1953, Arbenz feared intervention and sought arms in defense. When the USA embargoed arms sales, Arbenz turned to Czechoslovakia. The arms shipment, arriving in May 1954, became the state department's proof of Communist control.

In the Honduran capital Tegucigalpa, the USA equipped a small army under the command of Guatemalan army exile Colonel Carlos Castillo Armas. In June 1954,

Castillo Armas and 150 men penetrated about 25 miles into Guatemala but engaged in no significant action. They did not need to – the army refused to defend Arbenz, and the workers were not armed. US pilots flew raids over Guatemala City, terrorizing the population. Arbenz resigned.

Castillo Armas ruled without elections for three years. He abolished all opposition parties, and the police jailed, tortured, exiled, and executed political opponents, claiming they were Communists. The land reform was reversed, and the land returned to its previous owners. Castillo was assassinated by one of his own guards in1957, but that did not put an end to the country's political repression. He was followed by a series of military-dominated regimes: General Miguel Ydígoras Fuentes (1958–63), Julio Cesar Mendez Montenegro (1966–70); Colonel Carlos Arana Osorio (1970–4); General Kjell Laugerud (1974–8), General Romeo Lucas García (1978–82), General Efraín Rios Montt (1982–3), and General Oscar Humberto Mejía Victores (1983–5).

The dictatorial regimes did not rule without challenge. In 1960, more than a third of the army tried to overthrow Ydígoras, a coup sparked by the president's decision to let the USA train the Cuban invasion force in Guatemala. The rebellion was quashed, but it led to the 1962 formation of the first guerrilla organization, *Movimiento Revolucionario 13 de Noviembre*. Later that year, the *Partido Guatemalteco del Trabajo* (PGT) also formed a guerrilla front, and the two groups merged into the *Fuerzas Armadas Rebeldes* (FAR) in December 1962.

The FAR, based in the primarily ladino (non-indigenous) regions of eastern Guatemala, gained substantial campesino support. In addition to rural operations, FAR assaulted army and police stations and staged bank robberies and kidnappings. Ideological differences led to a split in 1964, reunion in 1967, and division again in 1968. One of the divisive issues was whether to support the electoral process of 1966. The PGT convinced the others to suspend armed action and support the civilian candidate Méndez Montenegro. The military took advantage of the truce to launch a brutal counterinsurgency campaign under the control of Colonel Carlos Arana Osorio. By 1970, thousands of campesinos had died, and FAR was defeated.

In early 1972, FAR survivors regrouped in Guatemala's western highlands. They were armed with new ideas: not just Marxism, but also liberation theology and race consciousness. The *Ejército Guerrillero de los Pobres* (EGP) built a support base by working with indigenous campesinos. Their first action was in 1975, when they assassinated Luis Arenas Barrera, an abusive landowner who had served in both the Castillo Armas and Arana Osorio regimes. The assassination triggered a wave of repression against the campesinos.

The 1970s were marked by the emergence of a strong labor movement and strikes, starting with teachers in 1973, then spreading through the public sector in 1974. The most significant strike came at the Coca Cola plant, *Embotelladora Guatemalteca*. The struggle went on for years and resulted in the murder of most of the union leaders, but it also led to the formation of the first labor federation since 1954, the *Comité Nacional de Unidad Sindical* (Jonas 1992: 123–4).

An earthquake in 1976, resulting in 25,000 dead, 70,000 injured, and more than 1.25 million homeless, exacerbated the problems (Jonas 1992: 95). Damage was greatest in the poorest neighborhoods, and the ranks of the homeless increased by some 50,000 people who arrived from the countryside. Out of this chaos emerged such popular organizations as the *Movimiento Nacional de Pobladores*.

In the countryside, displaced campesinos organized into cooperatives, Christian base communities, and finally into the *Comité de Unidad Campesina* (CUC). CUC gained national attention in May 1978, when army troops fired in broad daylight on 700 Kekchí protesting eviction from land at Panzós in Alta Verapaz, known as the "Zone of the Generals," a region where military officials had been buying land (Lucas García owned 78,000 acres). More than 100 people were killed and dumped into mass graves (Jonas 1992: 128).

Throughout the 1970s, new guerrilla groups formed. Another FAR faction regrouped in 1971 as the *Organización Revolucionaria del Pueblo en Armas* (ORPA), which worked clandestinely until 1979, when it began operating openly around Lake Atitlán and the southern coast. Rodrigo Asturias, son of the Nobel laureate, headed ORPA. The FAR reemerged in 1978, and another group split from the workers' party to take up arms in the late 1970s as the *Núcleo de Dirección*, working mostly in Guatemala City and on the southern coast.

The Lucas regime was effective at repressing unarmed urban popular movements and urban guerrillas, but the rural insurgency spread. By 1981 there was growing concern about the army's inability to defeat the revolutionaries. After a fraudulent election in 1982, junior officers staged a coup, bringing to power General Efraín Rios Montt. The coup coincided with a new politico-military project to create a counter-insurgency state, beginning with wholesale slaughter, followed by the creation of institutions interlinking military and society, and ending with apparent democratization under continued military control (Schirmer 1998).

Ríos Montt carried out the bulk of the scorched-earth policy: "in eighteen months, 446 villages were razed, an estimated 50,000 to 75,000 people were massacred, and more than a quarter of the rural indigenous population was displaced" (Schirmer 1999: 94). The devastation did more than deny the guerrillas a support base; it tore apart the rural social fabric, destroying autonomous indigenous communities. When this phase was finished, so was Ríos Montt; a coup in 1983 brought General Oscar Humberto Mejía Victores to power.

The holocaust was followed by creation of military–civilian institutions – survivors were relocated to development poles, new communities created and controlled by the military. The army provided food, work, and shelter, supposedly winning campesinos' hearts and minds. Violence against those who did not comply was still an option, a formula that the military called 30–70. General Hector Alejandro Gramajo, chief architect of the plan, explained: "Rather than killing 100 percent, we provided food for 70 percent . . . while killing 30 percent" (Schirmer 1999: 96). The complement to development poles was civilian patrols, *Patrullas de Autodefensa Civil* (PAC). Refusal to serve in the PACs was a death sentence. PACs patrolled villages, rooted out suspected guerrillas, and sometimes carried out massacres, making more than 900,000 indigenous campesinos complicit in counterinsurgency (Vilas 1995: 153).

The 1983–5 period culminated in a new constitution, which clearly made the army the guardian of national interests, charged with preserving the balance when the state appeared vulnerable and protecting the state from enemies, both foreign and domestic. The democratic veneer was completed in 1985, when Christian Democrat Vinicio Cerezo became president. He had no more power to control the armed forces than did Duarte in El Salvador.

Despite the devastation of the early 1980s, the guerrillas were not fully defeated. The groups united in January 1982 as the *Unidad Revolucionaria Nacional Guatemalteca* (URNG). From 1987 to 1989, army counteroffensives inflicted casualties but failed to eliminate the threat. The URNG repeatedly called for negotiations, to no avail.

But the 1990 electoral defeat of the Sandinistas, followed by the negotiated settlement in El Salvador in1992, helped lead to peace talks in Guatemala. After protracted negotiations beginning in 1990, a peace agreement was signed in 1996. Lasting peace, however, was more elusive: in 1998, Auxiliary Bishop Juan Gerardi was beaten to death two days after presenting a report blaming the army and PACs for nearly 80 percent of human rights abuses in the civil war.

Conclusions

From the 1960s to the 1990s, Central America was riven by violence provoked as guerrilla groups resorted to armed struggle to confront an entrenched elite willing to resort to brutal military repression in order to keep their privileges. The left's greatest success was the triumph of the Nicaraguan Revolution in 1979, but the electoral defeat of the Sandinistas in 1990 in the aftermath of US aggression signaled to Guatemalans and Salvadorans that the winning of state power was no guarantee. The guerrillas negotiated settlements to their conflicts and formed political parties, which met with varying degrees of success: in El Salvador, the FMLN won governorships, Legislative Assembly seats, and the important office of mayor of San Salvador; the presidency, however, eluded the party. After three failed attempts, Daniel Ortega regained Nicaragua's presidency in 2006, though he now promised that he was no longer the fiery revolutionary of old. In Guatemala, the URNG candidates made weak showings in elections, in large part a reflection of the massive violence that did so much to destroy their base of support. But URNG weakness also reflected the ongoing ethnic divisions that kept many of Guatemala's poorest from joining the left-wing organizations in the first place. As the twenty-first century began, reports were still emerging from Guatemala about disappearances of activists, while poverty throughout the region remained intractable. Clearly, Central America's deep-rooted problems had yet to be solved.

NOTE

1   The Spanish word *campesino* literally means a person from the countryside. It is frequently translated as *peasant*, a word that refers historically to medieval serfs and other dependent categories of agricultural producers, or that is frequently used to refer to subsistence farmers, who supposedly are not interested in commercial production. Neither category is accurate for modern *campesinos*, many of whom aspire to be small commercial producers, and many of whom are landless but still identify as agrarian producers. For these reasons, the term *campesino* will be used here, rather than its more common English translation.

BIBLIOGRAPHY

Anderson, T. (2001) *Matanza*. Curbstone Press, Willimantic, CT.

Armstrong, R. & Shenk, J. (1982) *El Salvador: The Face of Revolution*. South End Press, Boston.

Black, G. (1985) *Triumph of the People: The Sandinista Revolution in Nicaragua*. Zed Books, London.

Booth, J. & Walker, T. (1989) *Understanding Central America*. Westview Press, Boulder, CO.

Brodhead, F. & Herman, E. (1984) *Demonstration Elections: U.S.-Staged Elections in the Dominican Republic, Vietnam, and El Salvador*. South End Press, Boston.

Bulmer-Thomas, V. (1988) *The Political Economy of Central America since 1920*. Cambridge University Press, Cambridge.

Charlip, J. (2003) *Cultivating Coffee: The Farmers of Carazo, Nicaragua, 1880–1930*. Ohio University Press, Athens, OH.

Ching, E. (1998) "In Search of the Party: The Communist Party, the Comintern, and the Peasant Rebellion of 1932 in El Salvador," *Americas*, 55:2, pp. 204–39.

Conroy, M. (1985) "Economic Legacy and Policies: Performance and Critique." In T. W. Walker (ed.), *Nicaragua: The First Five Years*. Praeger Publishers, New York.

Dunkerley, J. (1982) *The Long War: Dictatorship and Revolution in El Salvador*. Verso, London.

Dunkerley, J. (1988) *Power in the Isthmus: A Political History of Modern Central America*. Verso, London.

Gleijeses, P. (1991) *Shattered Hope: The Guatemalan Revolution and the United States, 1944–1954*. Princeton University Press, Princeton.

Gould, J. (1998) *To Die in This Way: Nicaraguan Indians and the Myth of Mestizaje, 1880–1965*. Duke University Press, Durham.

Handy, J. (1984) *Gift of the Devil: A History of Guatemala*. Between the Lines, Toronto.

Handy, J. (1994) *Revolution in the Countryside: Rural Conflict and Agrarian Reform in Guatemala, 1944–1954*. University of North Carolina Press, Chapel Hill.

Jonas, S. (1991) *The Battle for Guatemala: Rebels, Death Squads, and U.S. Power*. Westview Press, Boulder, CO.

LaFeber, W. (1983) *Inevitable Revolutions: The United States in Central America*. W. W. Norton, New York.

Lernoux, P. (1980) *Cry of the People: The Struggle for Human Rights in Latin America – The Catholic Church in Conflict with U.S. Policy*. Penguin Books, New York.

Montgomery, T. S. (1992). *Revolution in El Salvador: From Civil Strife to Civil Peace*. Westview Press, Boulder, CO.

North, L. (1985) *Bitter Grounds: Roots of Revolt in El Salvador*, 2nd ed. Lawrence Hill & Co, Westport, CT.

Ricciardi, J. (1991) "Economic Policy." In T. Walker (ed.), *Revolution and Counterrevolution in Nicaragua*. Westview Press, Boulder, CO.

Schirmer, J. (1998) *The Guatemalan Military Project: A Violence Called Democracy*. University of Pennsylvania Press, Philadelphia.

Schirmer, J. (1999) "The Guatemalan Politico-Military Project: Legacies for a Violent Peace?" *Latin American Perspectives*, 26:2, March, pp. 92–107.

Vilas, C. (1995) *Between Earthquakes and Volcanoes: Market, State, and the Revolutions in Central America*. Monthly Review Press, New York.

Walker, T. (ed.) (1982) *Nicaragua in Revolution*. Praeger, New York.

Walker, T. (ed.) (1985) *Nicaragua: The First Five Years*. Praeger, New York.

Walker, T. (ed.) (1987) *Reagan versus the Sandinistas: The Undeclared War on Nicaragua*. Westview Press, Boulder, CO.

Walker, T. & Armony, A. (eds.) (2000) *Repression, Resistance, and Democratic Transition in Central America.* Scholarly Resources, Wilmington, DE.

Walter, K. (1993) *The Regime of Anastasio Somoza, 1936–1956.* University of North Carolina Press, Chapel Hill.

Williams, R. (1986) *Export Agriculture and the Crisis in Central America.* University of North Carolina Press, Chapel Hill.

Chapter Twenty-Four

CULTURE AND SOCIETY: LATIN AMERICA SINCE 1900

Robert McKee Irwin

La Belle Époque

The twentieth century began in a moment of relative political stability and economic prosperity for the ruling classes throughout most of Latin America. It was an era in which elite culture looked to Europe – particularly to France, sometimes to Spain or Germany, and often to European classic antiquity – for artistic inspiration. Poets such as Nicaraguan Rubén Darío, Argentine Leopoldo Lugones, Uruguayan Julio Herrera y Reissig, and Mexican Amado Nervo boldly defied Latin American literature's customary preoccupation with nation building and social critique, producing poetry for poetry's sake with a focus on aesthetics and exercising a will to experiment with traditional poetic form. Themes of the mythological, the pastoral, the exotic, the spiritual, and the boldly erotic abound in their works. While much of the most groundbreaking poetry of their generation was published in the last decades of the nineteenth century, early twentieth-century publications of note include Darío's *Cantos de vida y esperanza*, Herrera y Reissig's *Los éxtasis de la montaña*, Nervo's *Los jardines interiores*, and Lugones's *Lunario sentimental*. Books and journals of these poets were often illustrated by fellow bohemians such as Mexican Julio Ruelas, whose dark, erotic, and sometimes bloody drawings challenged Latin America's conventional aesthetic traditions in a parallel fashion.

The celebration of the aesthetic, however, drew a limited audience, even to the most acclaimed works of the era. The literary production of these poets was erudite, frequently anti-Catholic, and elitist. Though a few attained wide acclaim, for the most part their readership was miniscule, and most writers made their living in other ways, often as diplomats or *cronistas*. The genre of the *crónica*, which offered newspaper readers erudite commentaries on anything from street brawls to coronations of European royalty, covered both the quotidian and the bizarre, with reports also coming from abroad (typically Paris or Madrid), where these cronistas often lived. The crónica, an important quasi-literary genre for decades in many parts of Latin America, was in its heyday in the early twentieth century. The very literary, sometimes autobiographical, and often boldly elitist writings – i.e. writings that not only identified with European high culture, but also frequently expressed disdain for poor, non-white classes of

Latin Americans – of such writers as Brazilian João do Rio and Guatemalan Enrique Gómez Carrillo established the figure of the *literati* as something of a nomadic dandy with a keen *flaneur*'s eye for the titillating and outlandish, and a fascination with both local popular culture and the evolving everyday life of urban modernity.

While many of these poets and cronistas often strove to aestheticize sensuality, exoticism, paganism, crime, violence, and even death, other writers, inspired by popular French novels of the era, focused on similar themes, but depicted them in their most lurid forms. Authors such as Bolivian Alcides Arguedas (*Pueblo enfermo*), Brazilian Euclides da Cunha (*Os sertões*), and Mexican Federico Gamboa (*Santa*) explored themes of racial degeneration, religious fanaticism, and urban prostitution in nationally acclaimed texts that aspired to help modern society begin to understand its major social problems by dissecting and portraying them in sordid detail, often finding inspiration in the positivist doctrines popular in the era. Latin American positivist scientists such as Argentine José Ingenieros (*La simulación de la locura*), Mexican Carlos Roumagnac (*Los criminales en México*), Brazilian Nina Rodrigues (*Os africanos no Brasil*), and Cuban Fernando Ortiz (*Los negros brujos*) themselves were studying Latin American society beyond *la ciudad letrada*, focusing their attention on its most marginalized classes: immigrants, criminals, racial minorities, sexual deviants, and the mentally ill. The positivist writings of Latin American elites blamed urban social ills on the increasingly visible urban poor.

The popular press, too, with greater distribution than ever, sought out scandalous news stories on themes such as murder, suicide, adultery, and transvestism, competing for readers' attention with strident headlines and, increasingly, photos and illustrations. Some of these visual images, most notably the distinctive engravings of Mexican José Guadalupe Posada, including his famed *calaveras* (skeletons), would later be recognized as major works of popular art and national consciousness.

1898 Aftermath

While many of the most prominent artists and writers of the day rejected the nation-building projects of the nineteenth century, preferring a largely Eurocentric cosmopolitanism, late nineteenth-century imperialist gestures by the United States, particularly toward Cuba and Puerto Rico, reinvigorated nationalist discourse, even among some elite poets. The poetry of Peruvian José Santos Chocano, as well as the latter works of Darío and Lugones, took on a decidedly New World consciousness that at times reversed the dominant trend of form over content to the point of turning decidedly political in major collections such as Lugones's *Odas seculares*, Chocano's *Alma América*, and Darío's *Cantos de vida y esperanza*.

Darío, the most accomplished and world-renowned Latin American poet of his generation, was forced to respond when Uruguayan José Enrique Rodó proclaimed that Darío was "not the poet of América." Inspired by the Latin Americanist rhetoric of José Martí's classic essay, "Nuestra América," Rodó continued, in his own now classic essay *Ariel*, to promote the notion of Latin American identity and pride. Rodó identified Spanish American culture as "Latin," characterized by a superior spirituality and humanism, which he opposed to coarse "Anglo-Saxon" American culture, utilitarian and greedy.

Revised Nationalisms

By the century's second and third decades, artistic refinement was swept aside by a new literary realism that took up themes of social justice and national identity. The Mexican revolution of the 1910s inspired a whole generation of novels, the first and best of which was Mariano Azuela's *Los de abajo*. These novels explored themes of class struggle and the plight of uneducated rural laborers, adopting a social realist style, frequently informed by Marxist doctrine. Major literary works elsewhere in Latin America often turned to rural life, as well, reassuming the nineteenth century's obsessive pitting of civilization against barbarism, but this time locating the heart of the nation in the Argentine pampa (Ricardo Güiraldes's *Don Segundo Sombra*), the dusty Venezuelan plains (Rómulo Gallegos's *Doña Bárbara*), or the devouring Amazon jungle (Colombian José Eustacio Rivera's *La vorágine*). These novels often expressed an ambiguous attitude toward modernization by, for example, paying homage to the nearly extinct *gaucho* or exposing the barbarity of industrialization through the experience of rubber harvesters in the Amazon, while they also marked tradition and nature itself as distinctly barbarous.

While Uruguayan Horacio Quiroga also set many of his works in the jungle or among animals (*Anaconda*), the greatest Latin American short-story writer of the early twentieth century ended his career with a collection of stories that focused on human tragedy (*Los desterrados*). Quiroga's often grotesque characterizations rival those of the anti-heroes of Argentine Roberto Arlt's colorful novels. The latter's works, such as *Los siete locos*, retained a focus on the barbarous underbelly of a rapidly modernizing urban life. Arlt's critique of urban modernity, atypical of Latin American literature of his generation, was perhaps ahead of its time. Another important early twentieth-century writer whose comic novels (*O triste fim de Policarpo Quaresma*) express discomfort with urban modernization is Brazilian Alfonso Henriques de Lima Barreto, a mulatto whose caricatures of Rio de Janeiro society are especially critical of class hierarchies and mechanisms of social control.

By the 1920s, as Mexico consolidated its revolution, it (and other Latin American governments as well) began to become broadly and formally involved in national cultural production, subsidizing, commissioning, and promoting carefully chosen images of national culture. A surge of populist politics (exemplified by José María Velasco Ibarra in Ecuador, Lázaro Cárdenas in Mexico, and, later, Juan Perón in Argentina, and, in his later phase, Getúlio Vargas in Brazil) fueled – in defiance of Eurocentric elitism of previous generations – a move toward the incorporation of the mixed-race, often illiterate masses into national culture. Mexico's José Vasconcelos, himself author of a key essay entitled *La raza cósmica*, in which he fomented the self-esteem of Latin Americans as a *mestizo* race, played a major role in providing state sponsorship for Mexico's muralist movement as Secretary of Public Education. Painters such as Diego Rivera, José Clemente Orozco, and David Alfaro Siqueiros earned commissions to depict images of Mexican history and identity in huge murals on major public buildings. The Mexican muralist movement attained world renown for its mission of bringing socially conscious art (and nationalist propaganda) to the masses. This highly influential movement inspired muralist art throughout Latin America. Ecuador's Oswaldo Guayasamín, for example, a student of Orozco, developed his own style by building on Orozco's brutally expressive social realism.

In a similar vein, Latin American composers such as Colombian Antonio María Valencia (*Chirimía y bambuco sotareño*), Argentine Juan José Castro (*Sinfonía argentina*), Cuban Amadeo Roldán (*Obertura sobre temas cubanos*), Mexican Carlos Chávez (*Sinfonía india*), and Brazilian Heitor Villa-Lobos (the *Choros* series) began studying indigenous and popular musical styles prominent in their respective countries, incorporating these elements into their own nationalist symphonies. While each of these composers followed his own trajectory (Valencia, for example, was schooled in France, and rose up through the Colombian music academy, while Villa-Lobos was mostly self-taught, making a living initially playing cello in Brazilian cafés prior to his excursions into the Brazilian rainforests and hinterlands to learn about popular music traditions), they shared similar goals, combining training in classical European styles with self-study in regional ethnomusicology in order to bring the folk traditions of their nations into a symphonic repertoire.

This broad reaction against the elitism and Eurocentrism of turn-of-the-century Latin American art resulted in a nationally identified cultural production much more deeply connected with a wider range of Latin Americans than ever before. Yet its scope remained limited by masculinist convention. Woman writers, for example, were largely excluded from the scene, although a few managed to establish themselves and publish highly memorable and innovative works, including poets Uruguayan Delmira Agustini and, later, Argentine Alfonsina Storni. These rebellious women were discouraged at every turn by their male peers, and often expressed their resentment, directly or indirectly, in their works. Their writings often feature female characters in complex roles as thinkers and rebels, as opposed to their usual positions in Latin American letters of the era as idealized objects of desire, saintly matrons, or vulgar whores. An excellent example of these more complex female protagonists is that of Venezuelan Teresa de la Parra's *Ifigenia*, a young woman from a wealthy family who, as an independent thinker, is repeatedly confronted by the weight of social convention. Another novel, *Parque industrial* by Brazilian Patrícia Galvão (best known by her pseudonym of Pagú), represents the plight of female laborers from a communist perspective.

Music Industries

The 1920s and 1930s also saw the rise of two key modern cultural industries in Latin America: that of music and its corollary, dance. Radio gave birth to a whole new industry of recorded music, permitting the promotion of popular songs and artists at both national and international levels. Regional genres were transformed as they gained attention on the world stage. The traditional dances associated with these genres also traveled, inevitably changing form as they did so, to audiences throughout Latin American and beyond.

Tango, once confined to the streets, bordellos, and other public spaces of urban *barrios* in Argentina and looked down upon by elites because of its roots in African music and its popularity with working-class immigrants, became Argentina's national music and dance form after it was a hit in Paris. Cuban *rumba* was transformed from a genre based entirely on percussion, played only by Afro-Cubans and disdained by Cuban *letrados*, into a major national export, co-opted by Havana's greatest orchestras such as that of Don Azpiazu, featuring Antonio Machín (*El manisero*, known in English as *The Peanut Vendor*, the hit song that launched the rumba craze internationally), which added European-style instrumentation and often mocked the Afro-Cuban culture they represented. Indeed the "rumba" that became an international sensation was more akin to the less African-influenced Cuban folk genre known as *son*. In Mexico, the regional *son jaliscience* was transformed into the *ranchera* ballads that were played by large *mariachi* bands as the music of Mexico's national heritage, while the traditional dance known as the "Jarabe tapatío" from the same region (Jalisco) was performed and taught all over the country. Some forms of music with roots in popular tradition (Cuban son, Brazilian samba) entered mass culture through radio, and folk dance patterns were formalized into social dance genres; other forms (Mexican son jarocho, Peruvian huayno, Venezuelan joropo) were not embraced by international mass culture, but were instead promoted nationally as part of a local heritage. By mid-century, folk dance was being incorporated into government-subsidized programs of education and performance, promoting national identity in countries like Mexico, Peru, and the Dominican Republic.

By the second quarter of the century, major stars emerged in the fledgling recording industry, many of whom became hugely popular throughout Latin America and beyond, including Argentines Carlos Gardel and Libertad Lamarque; Mexicans Agustín Lara, Trío los Panchos, Toña la Negra, and Jorge Negrete; Cubans Sonora Matancero, Beny Moré, and Trío Matamoros, among many others. Some classic popular hits such as Cuban Rita Montaner's rumba "Ay Mamá Inés" (composed by Eliseo Grenet) and Brazilian Francisco Alves's samba "Aquarela do Brasil" (composed by Ary Barroso) borrowed extensively from Afro-American (i.e. Afro-Cuban and Afro-Brazilian) popular music. Although control of the music industry remained in the hands of light-skinned elites, radio brought this music to diverse and massive audiences whose collective tastes for popular musical genres of autochthonous flavor began to change the composition of the national imaginary far more than liberal artists, writers, and musicians could. Mass media gave a new voice to consumers of culture, who no longer needed to be literate or wealthy to participate actively in shared national tastes.

The Avant-garde

Latin American poets of the avant-garde also celebrated popular culture and folk traditions. Cuban Nicolás Guillén (*Motivos de son*) incorporated Afro-Cuban dialect and speech rhythms into a poetry that brought to life scenes of both day-to-day life and the mythology of Afro-Cubans. Brazilian Oswald de Andrade (*Pau Brasil*) redefined national identity by seeking out a revised multicultural history, in a quest shared by Mário de Andrade (no relation), whose greatest work, the fantastic but very Brazilian novel *Macunaíma*, uses multiethnic folklore as a major inspiration for playful artistic experimentation.

While non-conformist poets such as Colombian Porfirio Barba Jacob had begun moving beyond the confines of poetic tradition prior to the 1920s, the strident self-promotion of European avant-garde movements exhibited a powerful influence on Latin American poetry, for example in the works ·of Europe-based poets such as Chilean Vicente Huidobro. Complete with manifestos and public happenings, *vanguardismo* injected excitement into the new generation of Latin American poets; works by such poets as Argentine Oliverio Girondo were playful and innovative, radical in their experimentation with language and form, presenting an imagery not of idyllic mythological gardens or exotic islands, but of the modernizing city with its rapid pace and unruly crowds, and the encroaching presence of industry. Peruvian César Vallejo's complex and original poetry confronted modernity by liberating itself from tradition, exhibiting an often disconcerting freshness with form and language in dramatic and innovative works such as those collected in *Trilce*.

Poets of the era often banded together with visual artists who experimented with similar themes in painting. Brazilian avant-garde writers and painters launched themselves simultaneously in São Paulo's highly controversial Semana de Arte Moderna of 1922, in which both Mário and Oswald de Andrade participated along with several prominent names among Brazil's new generation of artists, including Anita Malfatti, Emiliano di Cavalcanti, Tarsila do Amaral, and Vicente do Rego Monteiro, whose art incorporated elements of Afro-Brazilian, indigenous, and popular culture. In Cuba, at the First Exhibition of New Art of Havana in 1927, in an era of political repression and a crisis in sugar markets that allowed US interests accelerated access to the economy, Cuban avant-garde art showed a distinctly nationalist character in Víctor Manuel's primitivist revolt against conservative artistic tradition and Amelia Peláez's trademark still lives featuring the succulent fruits and rich palette of the tropics.

Argentine avant-garde painters, too, allied themselves with poet contemporaries through the journal *Martín Fierro*. But unlike Brazil's "anthropophagists" (Oswald de Andrade, "Anthropophagist Manifesto") who devoured foreign influences only to transform them by reworking them through Brazilian autochthonous cultural forms and images, the so-called Florida group (whose writer members included Jorge Luis Borges and Ricardo Güiraldes, and which was named for a street in Buenos Aires where they gathered) took a less radical stance, promoting modernization and cosmopolitanism, albeit in works that often exhibited a distinctly national character. While Florida artist Emilio Pettoruti did depict scenes of everyday life in Buenos Aires barrios, the "criollismo" of the group's best-known artist Alejandro Xul Solar looks to modern graphic design and not local folk art for its inspiration.

Defining National Cultures

The new obsession with defining a deep-rooted and (usually) multiracial national culture went beyond the realm of the arts. Essayists combined historiography, ethnography, and psychoanalysis in producing what became highly influential treatises aimed at defining national culture and identity. These works sought out national types, often marked by race or social class, and linked defining personality traits of national identity to circumstances of geography, climate, colonial history, and immigration patterns. Important examples include Peruvian José Mariátegui's *Siete ensayos de la interpretación de la realidad peruana*, Argentine Ezequiel Martínez Estrada's *Radiografía de la pampa*, Brazilian Gilberto Freyre's *Casa grande e senzala*, Cuban Fernando Ortiz's *Contrapunto del tabaco y el azúcar*, and Mexican Octavio Paz's *Laberinto de la soledad*. These texts were highly influential, often beyond the context of the nation. For example, the concept of "transculturation," as defined by Ortiz, became an important tool of social analysis.

For his part, Octavio Paz, also a major poet and literary critic, went on to win the Nobel Prize for Literature in 1990. However, he was not the first Latin American to receive this honor. Chilean Gabriela Mistral, known to many as "*la maestra de América*," a rural schoolteacher who rose to fame as an internationally acclaimed poet and diplomat, was the first (1945). Aside from her public role as teacher, Mistral's poetic voice was often that of a mother (despite the fact that Mistral never married or gave birth) in acclaimed collections such as *Ternura* and *Tala*.

Guatemalan Miguel Ángel Asturias was the second Latin American Nobel Prize winner (1967). His complexly written novels such as *El señor presidente* explored themes of social oppression under dictatorship that were implicitly critical of political leadership in his country, from which he lived many years in exile. That Guatemala (and indeed much of Central America) was in the midst of decades of civil war – much of it provoked by US commercial and political intervention, which devastated many rural indigenous communities – attached to his work an undeniable social significance. The new visibility of Latin American writers on the world literary scene by mid-century served to bring international attention to important domestic problems of small countries like Guatemala.

In a similar vein, Peruvian José María Arguedas (*Los ríos profundos*) – who grew up among indigenous peasants, spoke fluent Quechua, became an anthropologist, and dedicated himself passionately to the plight of indigenous peoples – and Mexican Rosario Castellanos (*Balún Canán*) – who was born into a landholding family in Chiapas that was driven into poverty by post-revolutionary land reform policies – produced critically acclaimed works of enduring importance that gave new insight into Latin America's indigenous cultures to readers worldwide. While nationalist cultural policies to rescue indigenous traditions, often under the banner of "*indigenismo*," tended to focus on past glories of great civilizations such as the Inca or the Maya, while dedicating great efforts to education campaigns designed to sever living indigenous men and women from their "backwards" traditions and assimilate them into the national mix, these novels drew attention to the contemporary indigenous cultures as vibrant and complex, revealing to readers that these peoples had much to teach the Eurocentric mainstream (Arguedas), and that the will to modernization carries with it a painful destructiveness (Castellanos).

From a different angle, the constructivist movement in the arts linked ancient Latin American tradition to quintessentially modern geometric forms. Uruguayan artist Joaquín Torres García was this school's leading promoter in Latin America, while its most visible mark can be seen in the continent's highest-profile architectural project of the century, the construction of Brasília, a new ultramodern national capital city built deep in the sparsely populated Brazilian hinterland, a collaborative project headed by urban designer Lúcio Costa and architect Oscar Niemeyer.

Golden Age of Film

However, literature and art from the 1930s through the 1950s were in many ways overshadowed by the new form of cultural production that could bring the riveting stories of literature and the visual appeal of painting to massive audiences, including not only the urban literate elite, but also the semi-literate and illiterate masses, as cinema became widely popular throughout Latin America. From film's first exhibitions in Latin America in the 1890s, this new technology's ability to capture what seemed to be reality made a huge impression on Latin Americans.

Burgeoning film industries in Argentina, Brazil, and Mexico began to draw huge audiences by the mid-1930s. Argentina and Mexico were able to export films to other Spanish-speaking countries. Although during World War II the United States worked behind the scenes through its "good neighbor" policy to bolster the Mexican and Brazilian film industries and to impair that of Argentina, all three countries continued production at a significant pace through the 1950s.

Early landmark films such as the artistically acclaimed *Limite* by Brazilian director Mario Peixoto, and the early commercial success, *Allá en el Rancho Grande*, directed by Mexican Fernando de Fuentes, set the scene for what became known as the Golden Age of Latin American cinema. Major Mexican directors included Emilio "el Indio" Fernández, whose so-called Mexican school of cinema (in which the role of cinematographer Gabriel Figueroa was also key) won accolades at Cannes with *María Candelaria*; de Fuentes, who also made waves with a series of films depicting events of the Mexican revolution, such as *Vámanos con Pancho Villa*; and Alberto Gout, who specialized in lurid musical melodramas set in cabarets, including *Aventurera*. Argentina's most successful early directors were José Agustín "el Negro" Ferreyra, best known for his *arrabal* dramas such as *Calles de Buenos Aires*; and Lucas Demare, whose *La guerra gaucha* looked back nostalgically to nineteenth-century icons of national culture. Adhemar Gonzaga, director of musical comedies (known as *chanchadas*) such as *Alô, Alô Brasil*; Humberto Mauro, whose films, including *Ganga bruta*, were more artistically conscious dramas; and Vitor Lima Barreto, who directed the stylish adventure story of social bandits, *O cangaceiro*, were a few of the major directors of early Brazilian film.

Other countries did not develop major film industries in these years, but a handful of directors were active. Cuba's Ramón Peón worked mainly in Mexico, but back home became a pioneer of Cuban cinema, managing to produce a few films celebrating major themes in Cuban popular culture. *Romance del palmar*, for example, contrasts city and country life in very recognizably Cuban terms. German-born Chilean José "Che" Bohr, a popular singer, made dozens of films, including some highly entertaining gangster musicals such as *¿Quién mató a Eva?* in Mexico, Argentina, and Chile.

Early films defined national cultures for their audiences through key archetypes portrayed by their stars, including Mexicans Dolores del Río (always virtuous and elegant, even when portraying an indigenous heroine as she did in *María Candelaria*), María Félix (*"la devoradora de hombres"* in films such as Fernández's comic masterpiece, *Enamorada*), Jorge Negrete (the noble *charro* in films such as Joselito Rodríguez's *Ay, Jalisco no te rajes*), Pedro Infante (the lovable macho, as in Ismael

Rodríguez's *barrio* melodrama, *Nosotros los pobres*), and Mario Moreno (better known as Cantinflas, *el pelado*, a lower-class urban clown, a role he repeated in countless films including Juan Bustillo Oro's classic *Ahí está el detalle*); Brazilian comic actors (Spanish-born) Oscar Lorenzo Jacinto de la Imaculada Concepción Teresa Diaz and Sebastião Prato (better known respectively as Oscarito and Grande Otelo, a pair of comic vagabonds, the former white, the latter black, stars of *chanchadas* such as José Carlos Burle and Carlos Manga's *Carnaval Atlântida*); and Cuban *rumbera* bombshells María Antonieta Pons (star of Mexican Raúl de Anda's *La reina del trópico* as well as Brazilian *Carnaval Atlântida*) and Ninón Sevilla (*Aventurera*).

It is notable that larger, wealthier nations such as Mexico not only disseminated national ideals nationally, but exported them to neighboring countries whose own national projects did not benefit from the power or influence of a major industry. Thus, to this day Mexico's national archetypes are much better known in Venezuela than are the latter's in Mexico, and without the audiovisual impact of cinema, many smaller countries' cultural policies of mid-century were less successful than in countries like Argentina or Brazil.

Additionally, major artists of the music business such as Argentine Carlos Gardel; Cuban Rita Montaner; German-born Chilean José Bohr (who directed and starred in movies in Mexico and Argentina, as well as in Chile); Argentine Libertad Lamarque (who spent her later career in exile in Mexico); Mexicans Agustín Lara, Pedro Vargas, and Toña la Negra (Antonieta del Carmen Peregrino); and Portuguese-born Brazilian Carmen Miranda enhanced their superstar status through their work in film. Music and dance were frequently key elements in Latin American films, promoting the popularity of what became several widely recognized national musical genres including the tango in Argentina, the rumba in Cuba, and the samba in Brazil. As artists such as Carmen Miranda moved to Hollywood, "Latin" music reached an even wider audience. The rumba craze of the 1940s became the mambo craze of the 1950s, although Cuban artists such as "Mambo King" Damaso Pérez Prado did not necessarily become as successful as US-based performers such as New York-based Spanish/Cuban orchestra leader Xavier Cugat.

Cultural Roots

While most film was light in content, entertainment oriented, and geared toward making money, its use of music and dance, as well as character types and familiar locations, served to promote national identity in those countries with major film industries. Visual arts, on the other hand, in these same years, assumed a fervently anti-colonial posture, celebrating Latin America's indigenous past and autochthonous heroes. Peru's José Sabogal assumed a Messianic stance in fomenting an artistic indigenismo that incorporated indigenous Peruvian culture into the heart of the national imaginary.

Surrealist conventions were also readily incorporated into Latin American art of the first half of the twentieth century, combining with foundations in indigenous and Afro-American cultural production. In this way, the works of such figures as Cuban Wilfredo Lam, Chilean Roberto Matta, and Mexican Frida Kahlo foreshadowed Latin American literature's trademark "magical realism." Lam, part Chinese, part

Afro-Cuban, and Kahlo, the outspoken wife of Diego Rivera, became major national icons themselves. While Kahlo's work, characterized by haunting self-portraits and a marked influence of traditional *retablo*-style folk art, did not attract immediate attention, Lam's did. Artists such as Lam and Matta, who spent most of their lives abroad, defined Latin American art for world markets as surrealistic, rooted in the "primitive" (Lam depicted an African imaginary set in the jungle; Matta studied the style of Preconquest codices), and sensually colorful.

Latin America received additional promotion abroad as sensual and fun in the 1950s and 1960s as Latin American popular music continued to evolve, with the aforementioned mambo craze, and Brazilians João Gilberto and Antônio Carlos Jobim bringing *bossa nova* to a global audience. Much Latin music became popular by passing first through New York, as was the case with, for example, mambo and cha-cha-chá. New York-born Puerto Rican band leader Tito Puente and Cuban exile vocalist Celia Cruz were perhaps the two figures most associated with the rise of salsa, a music style that fused Caribbean rhythms with jazz and drew from different Afro-Caribbean dance traditions, but found its home in Latino New York.

The World Stage

Another massively popular cultural expression in Latin America has been sports, particularly soccer. Uruguay was a football powerhouse in the first half of the century, winning Olympic gold medals in 1924 and 1928. When Uruguay captured the inaugural World Cup in 1930, and then repeated the win in 1950, over Argentina and Brazil, respectively, Latin America as a region consolidated its position as a major world presence in football. Brazil then took over by winning successive World Cups in 1958 and 1962, regaining the title in 1970 (led all three times by superstar Pelé), essentially dominating the sport during these years. Sports also became a means of promoting national unity among different social classes as fans, primarily but not exclusively men, rallied behind their compatriots in international competitions. Latin American men and women also took pride in young Latin American women's competition in the Miss Universe pageant, which has seen 17 title holders from Latin America since its inception in 1952, including early winners from Peru, Colombia, Argentina, and Brazil.

Latin America took on prominence in global affairs not just for its soccer prowess and beauty pageant triumphs in the 1950s and 1960s, but also for the global impact of the Cuban Revolution of 1959. On the one hand, the victory of the Cuban guerrillas under the leadership of Fidel Castro and Ernesto "Che" Guevara gave great hope to the Latin American left. Cuba's defiance of the United States seemed to fulfill a Latin American dream of autonomy as articulated by Martí in the nineteenth century. On the other hand, Cuba's alliance with the Soviet Union made Latin America a key strategic locus for Cold War maneuverings, ensuring US involvement in all kinds of contests for political power, ranging from elections to guerrilla warfare and military coups. US intervention in the political affairs of countries such as Guatemala, El Salvador, Nicaragua, and Chile was notorious during the Cold War.

Much Latin American literature of this period took on a decidedly leftist political stance, glorifying the common people, indigenous groups, and workers, and vociferously defending cultural and political autonomy. No one better represents this socially committed art than Chilean poet Pablo Neruda. His most celebrated collection of poetry is *Canto general*, an epic work whose scope spans the history, geography, and culture of all Latin America. While his overt communist politics made him unpopular with right-wingers during the Cold War, he nonetheless was awarded the Nobel Prize for Literature in 1971.

The Boom

Neruda had already gained international prominence long before the Cuban Revolution, but became even more of a celebrity when the world turned to Latin America in the 1960s, sparking an international boom in interest in Latin American literature. Novelists in particular rose to the occasion, experimenting boldly with literary form like their peers in countries with well-established international literary reputations, but bringing to the fore elements of local tradition and cultural idiosyncrasy. At the same time, boom writers dared to locate Latin American characters on a contemporary international stage, for a contemporary world audience, conscious that for the first time their readers were not limited to their own national elite, and that their best novels would be translated into many languages.

Paraguayan Augusto Roa Bastos's masterpiece, *Yo el supremo*, parodied national history in order to critique contemporary Latin American politics, both in Paraguay, which was then under the dictatorship of Adolfo Stroessner, and abroad (post-revolutionary Cuba). In contrast, Argentine Julio Cortázar set his greatest novel, *Rayuela*, between Buenos Aires and Paris, focusing on the tribulations of privileged youth. Many boom novelists had already been publishing for decades prior to their rise to worldwide celebrity in the 1960s and 1970s. Brazilian Jorge Amado, for example, saw national recognition turn international with the boom. His most successful titles in global markets were less political than sentimental and picaresque, with novels such as *Gabriela, cravo e canela* playing to First World (heterosexual male) fantasies of an exuberant, voluptuous, and bountiful (female) Latin America. Peruvian Mario Vargas Llosa is well known for his complex social and psychological dramas set in the Amazon rainforest, contemporary Lima, and the Peruvian highlands, among them *La casa verde*, while Mexican Carlos Fuentes brings elements of ancient Aztec tradition into the backdrop of the ultramodern megalopolis of Mexico City in *La región más transparente*.

However, the boom is best remembered for a particular style that came to define Latin American literature for many international readers: magical realism, a complex technique that expands on realist mimesis (from a mainstream occidental point of view) by incorporating elements of alternate belief systems of Latin American culture, most with roots in indigenous or African cultures, in oral history and local legend. The many writers who have been lumped together by global marketers as magical realists experiment with language, narrative structure, local tradition (often in confrontation with modernity), and the fantastic, with objectives that are not escapist, but profoundly political. This erudite (but generally not elitist) literature readily incorporated a full spectrum of race and class categories into its national imaginary. In an era in which political authoritarianism was on the rise (and repressive dictatorships were in fact well established in some countries), this newly empowered literature served as a means of intellectual resistance.

The works that have been classified as magical realism are quite diverse. Mexican Juan Rulfo's *Pedro Páramo* plays with Aztec mythology of death and the underworld and contemporary myths of rural Mexican machismo, creating a dreamlike purgatory in which his protagonists are trapped in their own illusions. Cuban Alejo Carpentier's most acclaimed work, *Los pasos perdidos*, employs his trademark baroque style to contrast empty and alienating capitalist modernity with the richness of the unspoiled nature of multiracial Latin America. The most highly acclaimed boom novel of all, Colombian Gabriel García Márquez's *Cien años de soledad* incorporates elements of oral history, folk medicine, and non-Western concepts of time. This revised and expanded vision of reality startled and excited readers worldwide, and earned García Márquez a Nobel Prize in 1982.

García Márquez, of course, like most great boom writers, was a committed leftist, whose writing clearly demonstrated his opposition to colonialism, imperialism, and invasive capitalist growth. For many, García Márquez is Latin America's greatest writer, not only because he is a master storyteller, but also for the innovative style, and the committed humanism and charged content of his literature. His greatest competition is perhaps Argentine Jorge Luis Borges, who also saw many of his works translated in the wake of the Latin American literary boom, although he is often considered separately from it, and in fact had earned a certain international acclaim well before the boom. Borges's best works are his short stories (*Ficciones*), witty and ingenious creations that question how knowledge is produced and circulates. The philosophical complexity of his work does not affect its accessibility, particularly due to Borges's wry humor. However, its lack of overt political commitment (along with Borges's own occasional rightist interventions, such as his dedication of a translation of Walt Whitman to US President Richard Nixon) and the infrequency of its focus on the particularities of Latin American thought and tradition set it apart from most boom writing. As wise and appealing as Borges's writing may be, it is not what the world has sought from Latin America, and that, for many, is the reason he never won the Nobel Prize.

New Cinema

If Borges's writing was not socially and politically committed like that of Neruda, neither was it frivolously lowbrow like much of the most successful early Latin American cinema. With the energetic return of mostly frivolous Hollywood movies to international film markets following World War II, Latin American filmmakers rejected not only movies whose sole goal was entertaining the masses, but also so-called *auteur* cinema, product of the existential and artistic preoccupations of bourgeois filmmakers. The new generation of Latin American film directors promoted a new style of realistic cinema committed to social protest and anti-imperialism.

Directors such as Brazilian Nelson Pereira dos Santos (*Rio Zona Norte*), Argentine Leopoldo Torre Nilsson (*La casa del ángel*), Brazilian Glauber Rocha (*Deus e o diabo na terra do sol*), Argentine Fernando Solanas (*La hora de los hornos*), Cuban Tomás Gutiérrez Alea (*Memorias del subdesarrollo*), and Chilean Miguel Littín (*Acta General de Chile*) treated tough social themes in grave and gritty films. One of the most interesting projects to come out of this movement was Bolivian Jorge Sanjinés's *Yawar Mallku*, a film criticizing intervention of international "aid" organizations into indigenous communities, whose actors are the indigenous people themselves, acting in their own language (Aymara).

Few Latin American films achieved commercial success in the 1960s and 1970s, and although many earned critical acclaim, distribution remained limited to art houses, even in home markets, and many of even the best films saw little or no international distribution. One exception was the work of exiled Spaniard Luis Buñuel (*Los olvidados, Viridiana*), whose experimental, highly conceptualized and often outrageously ironic films, best known for their critique of social convention, gave Mexican cinema one last jolt of success as its golden age faded out. Another was the Brazilian cinema of the 1970s which pitched sexy, colorful comic dramas to world audiences in the work of directors Bruno Barreto (*Dona Flor e seus dois maridos*), Nelson Pereira do Santos (*Como era gostoso o meu francês*), and Carlos Diegues *(Xica da Silva)*. Latin American intellectuals looked down on cheaply produced "B" movies such as those featuring Mexican icons Santo, the professional wrestler otherwise known as Roberto Guzmán Huerta (*Santo contra la invasion de los marcianos*) and la India María, creation of comedienne María Elena Velasco (*Sor Tequila*), that were among the few profitable locally produced films of the 1970s and 1980s.

Repression and Resistance

Similarly, in the world of music, music of social protest, rooted in folk traditions, became a major trend. Artists such as Argentine Atahualpa Yupanqui, Chileans Violeta Parra and Víctor Jara, Argentine Mercedes Sosa, and the Chilean group Inti Illimani celebrated indigenous traditions while promoting anti-imperialist messages. In Brazil, music of social and political protest emerged as a response to authoritarian rule and in opposition to a national rock and roll phenomenon. The late 1960s iconoclast movement Tropicália, led by Caetano Veloso and Gilberto Gil, sought to transcend divisions, fusing or juxtaposing traditional forms of Brazilian music with rock and other international styles while offering a nuanced, ambiguous picture of nationality and modernity. Later, Panamanian Ruben Blades and Nuyorican Willie Colón would bring social and political themes to salsa music. Meanwhile, more popular artists such as Brazilians Sergio Mendes and Brasil 66, Mexican Juan Gabriel, Cuban American Gloria Estefan, and Dominican Wilfredo Vargas continued – despite their roots in Latin American musical styles including Cuban son, Mexican ranchera, and Dominican merengue – to forge Latin America's image as passionate but lightweight because their music was geared more toward sentimental themes and social dancing.

Socially committed art became more important than ever in the 1970s and 1980s as military dictatorships became the norm in many parts of Latin America (Brazil, Peru, Chile, Uruguay, Argentina, Bolivia, etc.), and long-term guerrilla wars raged between leftist revolutionaries and right-wing forces (El Salvador, Nicaragua, Guatemala, Colombia), the latter often funded by the United States as part of a Cold

War obsession with stamping out communism. The rise to power of Nicaragua's Sandinistas in 1979 was a rare victory for Latin America's left. Under the conditions of warfare and repressive military dictatorship, many artists were unable to produce overtly political images.

Visual artists meanwhile struggled to get beyond what had become Latin American art's trademark: the muralism movement, which by the 1970s had been criticized as dogmatic and heavy-handed. The equally well known primitivist-surrealist style of Latin American art continued to be popular, as seen in such works as the expressionist monsters of Benjamín Cañas of El Salvador, or the explorations of tropical lushness and primitive wisdom of Venezuelan Jacobo Borges. Brazilian artists such as Rubens Gerchman, famous for his representations of soccer stars, appropriated some of the techniques associated with pop art, adapting them to a local context, while his compatriot, Hélio Oiticica, proposed an "environmental" art that demanded a high degree of participation from the spectator. His installation "Tropicália," which provided the name for the movement associated primarily with popular music, revived the metaphor of anthropophagy in its attempt to locate Brazilian artistic practice within the context of the international avant-garde.

Performance

More politically committed art would often not be seen in galleries, but might take more ephemeral forms. In the years of the Pinochet dictatorship, Chilean Raúl Zurita produced corporal mutilations in public acts of protest. Las Yeguas del Apocalypsis (Pedro Lemebel and Francisco Casas) staged scandalous events, often dressed in drag, protesting the violent abuses suffered by homosexuals under the Pinochet regime. In Mexico, actress Jesusa Rodríguez and her partner, Argentine exiled musician Liliana Felipe, staged performances of biting political and social critique in Mexico (including their highly publicized marriage) for decades at a small cabaret theater in Mexico City.

However, scandalous protest, with its elements of entertainment value, has not been produced by artists alone. The public protests of las Madres de la Plaza de Mayo in Buenos Aires, mothers who demanded investigations of the disappearances of their sons and daughters, brought worldwide attention to the abuses of Argentina's military dictatorship. In the 1990s, the armed uprising of the Zapatistas in Chiapas, Mexico, was accompanied by an internet-based publicity campaign including a certain degree of theatrics as the group's most visible spokesperson, known as Subcomandante Marcos (later identified as leftist intellectual Rafael Guillén), and later several indigenous leaders of the group such as Comandantes Tacho and Ramona, their faces concealed behind black ski masks and bandanas, staged a media-friendly revolution.

Literature and Dictatorship

In the realm of literature, writers such as Argentine Rodolfo Walsh (*Operación masacre*), Chilean Ariel Dorfman (*Para leer al Pato Donald*), Uruguayan Eduardo Galeano (*Las venas abiertas de América Latina*), Cuban Miguel Barnet (*Biografía de un cimarrón*), and Mexican Elena Poniatowska (*La noche de Tlatelolco*) took on themes of social justice, racism, colonialism, and government oppression in books that moved beyond the high literary forms of the boom generation, working from genres of historiography, autobiography, journalism, and *testimonio*. The works of Reinaldo Arenas (*Antes que anochezca*) complicate old-school leftist ideology by drawing attention to social repression of gays in post-revolutionary Cuba.

In the 1980s, the publication of *Me llamo Rigoberta Menchú y así me nació la conciencia*, the testimonial account of an indigenous woman from Guatemala (Menchú) who had survived the violent oppression of the Guatemalan government, made a huge international impact. The testimonio genre received great attention as it appeared to give a voice to the most marginalized of Latin Americans, bringing the stories of illiterate *campesinos* and urban poor to receptive audiences, and Menchú went on to win the 1992 Nobel Peace Prize.

Cultures of the Masses

Meanwhile, Latin American authors began drawing more and more from popular and mass culture in their works. Argentine Manuel Puig's novels (*El beso de la mujer araña*) explored themes of everyday social relations (among family, neighbors, friends, lovers, etc.) in novels that drew openly from popular genres such as movie tearjerkers and romance novels. In Mexico, Carlos Monsiváis injected new life into the crónica genre, bringing his biting wit to bear on everyday cultural phenomena such as rock concerts, social dance, devotional practices of popular religion, and sporting events.

Mass culture, far removed from high art forms, took on ever greater prominence within the realm of Latin American cultural production as the century progressed. Comic strips such as Lino Palacio's *Ramona* (popular as early as the 1940s) and Joaquín Salvador Lavado (Quino)'s *Mafalda* (from the 1960s) interpret Argentine society and culture through the eyes of a female servant (Ramona) and a precocious little girl (Mafalda). Mexico gave birth to a huge comic book industry, whose most popular titles include *Kaliman* (created by Rafael Cutberto Navarro and Modesto Vázquez González) and *Memín Pinguín* (Yolanda Vargas Dulché and Sixto Valencia Burgos), the former being an exotic orientalesque superhero, the latter a little loveable Afro-Mexican rascal. Along with Chile's long-running *Condorito* (René Ríos aka "Pepo") and Brazil's phenomenally popular *Mônica* (Maurico de Sousa, "the Brazilian Walt Disney"), these popular comics direct their simple social messages not to intellectual elites, but to children and to the impoverished, sometimes semi-literate masses.

Similarly, television industries including especially TV Globo in Brazil, Televisa in Mexico, and Univisión in the United States came to reach massive audiences and have played a huge role, especially since the 1970s, in disseminating and shaping culture. Latin American *telenovelas*, a melodramatic genre usually aired daily for a period of several months, have been especially popular – and the most successful series have been exported not only throughout Latin America, but also in translation to world markets (countries such as Kenya or Serbia). Some of the biggest hits include Mexico's *Los ricos también lloran* (Fernando Chacón), Brazil's *Escrava Isaura* (Milton

Gonçalves and Herval Rossano), Venezuela's *Kassandra* (Grazio D'Angelo and Olegario Barrera), and Colombia's *Café aroma de mujer* (Pepe Sánchez). Variety shows such as Televisa's long-running *Siempre en domingo* and TV Globo's *Xou da Xuxa* have played a huge role in generally disseminating popular culture and communicating shared values to the masses. The growth of the television industry and the accessibility of television programming to an ever wider range of the populace have given these media giants immense power to mold public opinion and ideology. These conglomerates manage multiple television channels, produce and export programming, and run vast publishing empires, exerting an influence that goes well beyond what literature or cinema had ever attained.

Television has also brought sports to wide audiences. Soccer has continued through the century to be the most popular Latin American sport and World Cup victories by Argentina in 1978 and 1986 (led by superstar Diego Maradona) and Brazil in 1994 and 2002 (led by Ronaldo) further solidified Latin American prominence in the sport. Most recently, Argentina won the Olympic gold medal in football in 2004. Sports, especially football, have served as a rallying point for national and sometimes Latin American unity on a massive scale and various leagues and tournaments appear daily on Latin American television.

Baseball has also been an important sport in some parts of Latin America, mainly Mexico, the Spanish-speaking Caribbean, and Central America. Cuba, in particular, has been dominant in the sport, winning Olympic gold medals in 1992, 1996, and 2004. Additionally, several Latin Americans have become major tennis stars, beginning in the 1950s and 1960s with Mexican American Pancho González, Peruvian Alex Olmedo, and Brazilian María Bueno, and continuing with Argentines Guillermo Vilas and Gabriela Sabatini, Brazilian Gustavo Kuerten, and Puerto Rican Gigi Fernández, to name a few. Although an elitist sport in Latin America, tennis has produced a steady supply of Latin American stars.

Finally, Latin American women have continued to win international beauty pageants, which are inevitably given substantial coverage on Spanish- and Portuguese-language television. Puerto Rico and Venezuela, in particular, have become well known for their repeat (five and four, respectively) victories in the Miss Universe pageant between 1970 and 2006.

Globalization and Neoliberalism

The late twentieth century also saw a resurgence in Latin American cinema as directors sought to make films with sometimes serious messages more appealing to mass audiences, often working with bigger budgets and obtaining greater distribution by collaborating with foreign production companies. Economic policies of neoliberalism, and an end to repressive dictatorships and guerrilla wars, gradually made it easier for foreign investors to work in Latin America, and for Latin Americans to collaborate across national boundaries in the last quarter of the century. Mexican Arturo Ripstein (*El lugar sin límites*), Argentine María Luisa Bemberg (*Camila*), Argentine-born Brazilian Héctor Babenco (*El beso de la mujer araña*), Mexican María Novaro (*Danzón*), Brazilian Walter Salles (*Central do Brasil*), Mexican Alejandro González Iñárritu (*Amores perros*), Mexican Alfonso Arau (*Como agua para chocolate*), and

Mexican American Gregory Nava (*El norte*) are among the most successful directors of recent decades. Argentine Luis Puenzo won Latin America's only Best Foreign Film Oscar for *La historia oficial* in 1985. Foreign directors such as US-born Joshua Marston (*María, llena eres de gracia*, produced in Colombia) have also achieved major hits with Spanish-language films. Latin Americans Sônia Braga of Brazil, Salma Hayek and Gael García Bernal of Mexico, Colombian American John Leguizamo, Benicio del Toro of Puerto Rico, and Nuyorican Jennifer López have become international film stars.

Likewise, since the boom, it has become much easier for Latin American writers to gain international prominence and see their books translated into other languages. Some contemporary authors have continued to present themselves as political activists, dealing with issues of marginalization in its multiple forms (Chilean Diamela Eltit, *Lumpérica*), political repression and abuse (Argentine Luisa Valenzuela, *Cola de lagartija*), gender and sexuality (Chilean cronista Pedro Lemebel, *Loco afán*), race (Cuban poet Nancy Morejón, *Parajes de una época*), everyday urban violence (Colombian Fernando Vallejo, *La virgen de los sicarios*), social marginalization and drug-related bloodshed (Brazilian Paulo Lins, *Cidade de Deus*), or postdictatorial memory and mourning (Argentine Tununa Mercado, *En estado de memoria*), and these writers, particularly those who manage to connect into global academic circuits, have achieved international fame. On the other hand, Latin America's best-selling novelist of the late twentieth century, expatriate Chilean Isabel Allende (*La casa de los espíritus*), writes romantic historical novels that avoid explorations of social problems that go beyond the superficial. Celebrated for following the trend of magical realism, her novels are rapidly translated into multiple languages and are instant international bestsellers.

Meanwhile, US Latino/a writers, many of whom became successful by publishing in English in the United States, have increasingly had their work translated into Spanish to take advantage of the huge global market in that language. Writers such as Puerto Rican Esmeraldo Santiago (*Cuando era puertorriqueña*) and Mexican American Sandra Cisneros (*La casa en Mango Street*) have been able to use the power of their wealthy US publishing houses to attain a distribution unimaginable to many Latin American writers. Latino/a writers who do write in Spanish, such as Chicano Tomás Rivera (*. . . y no se lo tragó la tierra . . .*), still depend on English translations to reach much of their readership, as Latino/a literature has become a popular genre in the USA, but mainly in English. However, the innovative work of Latino/a intellectuals such as Gloria Anzaldúa (*Borderlands/la frontera*), who wrote in a mix of English, Spanish, and Nahuatl, has helped legitimize the hybridized language spoken by many recent immigrants to the United States.

Music, however, is the sector of cultural production that had become most globalized by the century's end. Stars of pop (Puerto Rican Ricky Martin, Colombian Shakira), rock (Colombian Juanes, Argentines Los Fabulosos Cadillacs), "tropical" Caribbean dance music (Dominican Juan Luis Guerra, Cubans Los Van Van), updated traditional music (Mexican American Lila Downs, Colombian Carlos Vives, Peruvian Susana Baca), and Brazilian popular music (Maria Rita, Daniela Mercury) sold their music throughout the Americas and beyond on international record labels that categorized them all as "Latin," with much of the music business operating through multinational companies located in the United States.

Latin American visual artists, on the other hand, have not entered mass culture, with a few notable exceptions. The best-known works of a few Latin American artists including José Guadalupe Posada, Frida Kahlo, and Diego Rivera, as well as Colombian Fernando Botero, best known for his parodic portraits of chubby subjects, have been widely merchandized through posters and *tchotchkes*. However, most artists have little name recognition even in their home countries, except among specialists.

Century's End

The twentieth century ended with both a cultural empowerment, as Latin American cultural production reached ever-wider audiences, and a cultural dilution, as global centers of culture such as the United States, France, and Spain achieved ever-greater penetration and influence in Latin American markets. The neoliberal politics of many Latin American regimes, elected in increasingly democratic systems, has encouraged these inevitable effects of globalization. Meanwhile, Latin American emigration to wealthy countries such as the United States, Canada, and Spain has established an ever-stronger presence of Latin Americans, many of whom continue to identify strongly with their heritage nations and languages (whether Spanish, Portuguese, or indigenous languages) well beyond the first generation, outside the geographic bounds of what has been traditionally understood as Latin America. The local comes to mingle ever more with the global, and the power of mass culture makes elite forms of culture production ever less influential. Meanwhile, the global intellectual project of Latin American Studies, often referred to as "Latinamericanism," in reference to Edward Said's renowned study on the European colonial construction of an Asian imaginary, *Orientalism*, has drawn ever-greater attention to Latin American culture as an object of study, both in Latin America and around the world, earning it an academic status once reserved only for Europe. Thus, even as the weight of global markets encroaches more and more into Latin American cultural terrain, autonomous Latin American cultural production continues to flourish.

ACKNOWLEDGMENTS

I am indebted to Marisol de la Cadena, Christopher Dunn, and Marilyn Miller for their insightful comments on an earlier draft of this chapter.

BIBLIOGRAPHY

Note: The authors and titles discussed in this chapter appear in many overview texts and reference works focusing on Latin American culture, and the titles are often available in multiple editions, including many in translation. It would be both limiting and duplicative to list those titles here again in specific editions. The works listed below constitute suggestions for readers who might wish to explore the themes of this chapter further.

Aparicio, F. R. & Jaquez, C. F. (eds.) (2002) *Musical Migrations: Transnationalism and Cultural Hybridity in Latin/o America*. Palgrave Macmillan, New York.

Beezley, W. & Curcio-Nagy, L. (eds.) (2000) *Latin American Popular Culture: An Introduction*. Scholarly Resources, Wilmington, DE.

Darder, A. & Torrese, R. D. (eds.) (1998) *The Latino Studies Reader: Culture, Economy, and Society*. Blackwell, Malden, MA.

Del Sarto, A., Ríos, A., & Trigo, A. (eds.) (2004) *The Latin American Cultural Studies Reader*. Duke University Press, Durham.

Franco, J. (1985) *La cultura moderna en América Latina*, trans. Sergio Pitol. Grijalbo, Mexico City.

García Canclini, N. (1989) *Culturas híbridas: Estrategias para entrar y salir de la modernidad*. Grijalbo/Consejo Nacional para la Cultura y las Artes, Mexico City.

Hinds, H. Jr. & Tatum, C. (eds.) (1985) *Handbook of Latin American Popular Culture*. Greenwood Press, Westport, CT.

King, J. (2000) *Magical Reels: A History of Cinema in Latin America*. Verso, London.

King, J. (ed.) (2004) *The Cambridge Companion to Modern Latin American Culture*. Cambridge University Press, Cambridge.

López, A. M., King, J., & Alvarado, M. (eds.) (1992) *Mediating Two Worlds: Cinematic Encounters in the Americas*. British Film Institute, London.

Lucie-Smith, E. (2004) *Latin American Art of the 20th Century*, 2nd ed. Thames & Hudson, London.

Martin, G. (1989) *Journeys Through the Labyrinth: Latin American Fiction in the Twentieth Century*. Verso, London.

Olsen, D. A. & Sheehy, D. E. (eds.) (2000) *The Garland Handbook of Latin American Music*. Garland, New York.

Rowe, W. & Schelling, V. (1991) *Memory and Modernity: Popular Culture in Latin America*. Verso, New York.

Schechter, J. M. (1999) *Music in Latin American Culture: Regional Traditions*. Schirmer Books, New York.

Taylor, D. (2003) *The Archive and the Repertoire: Performing Cultural Memory in the Americas*. Duke University Press, Durham.

Traba, M. (1994) *Art of Latin America, 1900–1980*. The Johns Hopkins University Press/Inter-American Development Bank, Baltimore.

Yúdice, G. (2003) *The Expediency of Culture: Uses of Culture in the Global Era*. Duke University Press, Durham.

Chapter Twenty-Five

ENVIRONMENTAL HISTORY OF MODERN LATIN AMERICA

Lise Sedrez

When the Portuguese Prince Regent João de Braganza arrived with his court in Rio de Janeiro in 1808, the colonial capital, with a population of some 50,000 people, was surrounded by forested hills. Half a century later, his grandson Pedro II, the emperor of an independent Brazil, promoted a daring reforestation project for the same hills, then dominated by coffee plantations or simply cleared of their native forest. Pedro II hoped that reforesting the Tijuca hills would protect the water supply for the almost 200,000 residents of the city, from which 90 percent of the Brazilian coffee crop was exported. Although the reforestation project was quite unique, Rio de Janeiro's deforestation problem was not isolated. Nineteenth-century agricultural and urban demands placed such pressure on the environment of Latin America that they effectively changed the landscape, watercourses, and the population distribution to an extent unforeseen in the colonial period.

The Iberian conquests of the sixteenth century brought what Alfred Crosby (1972, 1986) termed "the Columbian exchange" – the large-scale exchange of animals, plants, and diseases between the Old World and the New World. The introduction of European livestock – horses, donkeys (and their hybrid offspring, mules), cattle, pigs, sheep, goats, and chickens – as well as Eurasian domesticated plants – importantly wheat, barley, oats, and rice – transformed both the food supply (Super & Wright 1985; Super 1988; Diamond 1997) and land use in many regions of the Americas. Elinor Melville (1994), building on the concept of ecological revolution developed by Carolyn Merchant (1987), applied it to the environmental consequences of the Spanish conquest of Mexico. Large-scale mining operations, especially in north central Mexico and at Potosí in upper Peru (Bakewell 1971, 1984), brought massive ecological changes in their wake, including deforestation for fuel and timbers. In many areas of colonial Latin America conflict over water resources reflected changing patterns of agriculture and population distribution (Lipsett-Rivera 1999).

In the nineteenth century landscapes in Latin America were transformed on a newly expanded scale. Historians sometimes refer to this period as the "second conquest" for the influence that global economy had in Latin America (Morse & Hardoy 1992: 20). It also constituted the largest environmental transformation in the region since the conquest. Like the Columbian exchange, it represented an ecological revolution. Two distinct and interrelated trends characterized the transformation of nature in modern Latin America: first, the conversion of forests and local ecosystems into areas of production of goods for the international market; and second, the drastic urbanization of Latin America in the twentieth century.

Transformation of nature in Latin America during the nineteenth century followed patterns established in colonial times, led by large plantations and monoculture. New transportation technology, particularly railroads, and new markets for Latin American agricultural commodities supported the expansion of this pattern into hinterland hundreds of miles away from seaports. In Brazil, where sugar cane agriculture had already consumed most of the one million square kilometers of the coastal rainforest cleared by 1850 (Dean 1997), the pace accelerated with the growth of the international demand for coffee. In the early nineteenth century, coffee claimed the hills Pedro II would reforest, which had escaped the voracity of sugar cane cultivation that favored coastal lowlands. Coffee also expanded into the Paraíba River Valley (Stein 1956), and then the purple soil of São Paulo's western plateau (Dean 1976; Holloway 1980). It claimed the inland regions of Antioquia and Cundinamarca in Colombia (LeGrand 1986), the highlands of Chiapas, Mexico, and large areas of Guatemala, El Salvador, and Costa Rica. As long as more fertile soils in forested areas were available, the so-called "itinerant coffee" often left behind soils destroyed by erosion and deprived of nutrients. Likewise, when Argentina's beef, mutton, and wool entered the global economy, the small forests native to the pampas soon vanished to the endless sheep and cattle herds tended by gauchos, the trees turned into fuel for the *estancias* and paddocks for the livestock (Scobie 1964; Garavaglia 2002: 110). In both Colombia and Argentina, the new export commodities set the pace for a myriad other enterprises that converted forest land into new economic activities.

Energy demands of the ever-growing cities also greatly affected the surrounding forests. By 1910, traditional fuel-wood removal for city residents cleared large patches around Lima, Bogotá, and other urban centers. After the 1950s, the Brazilian state sponsored the construction of many hydroelectric dams, from the São Francisco River to the giant Itaipu Dam in the Paraguay River, and millions of hectares of forest were lost to deforestation or flooding. By the end of the twentieth century, less than 8 percent of the Brazilian Atlantic coastal rainforest remained (Dean 1997; McNeill 2001: 233). From the Araucania forests in southern Chile to the Lacandón forest in Chiapas, Mexico, much of the forest cover in Latin America has been cleared for agricultural activities or industrial production. The loss of biodiversity in this process is impossible to estimate. Costa Rica's forests and the Brazilian Atlantic rainforest have some of the highest indexes of endemic species; destruction of habitat in these ecosystems means the extinction of these species.

Cities in Latin America generated their own urban environmental dilemmas, equally related to the changes in the natural landscape. From Mexico City to Buenos Aires, air pollution, inadequate sanitary systems, and insufficient access to clean water have plagued Latin America's urban population, combining problems of a postindustrial society with historical legacies of inequality. Partly as a response to this process, Latin America also developed a thriving popular environmental movement, promoted some of the world's earliest experiences in reforestation, and created a large network of protected areas. The environmental history of modern Latin America shows a challenging combination of ecological degradation and environmental awareness.

Mapping Latin America's Ecology

Interest in Latin America's nature mounted with the independence process. Throwing off the yoke of colonial absolutism meant the end of many restrictions for foreign travelers in most Latin American nations. Scientists and naturalists were eager to follow in the steps of Alexander von Humboldt and Aimé Bonpland, who studied Latin America nature from 1799 to 1805 and returned to Europe with enviable collections of fauna and flora as well as important new geological and geographical information. Beyond advancing scientific knowledge in several disciplines, including new classifications and new biological and geological concepts, von Humboldt's Latin American expedition had the practical effect of initiating new studies on the use of guano (historically accumulated deposits of bird dung, rich in phosphates and other chemicals) as agricultural fertilizer. Thus, the study of nature in Latin America had a double and diverse perspective. On the one hand, it belonged with the larger expansion of scientific knowledge in the nineteenth century: for example, Charles Darwin's travels to the Galapagos islands, visiting Brazil, Argentina, and Chile on the way, led to the basis for his theory of evolution by natural selection and represented a benchmark in the history of western science. On the other hand, European and Latin American scientists sought to identify among the native species what could become the new prized commodity, new source of national income and basis for economic development. Or, at the very least, they sought the secrets for the best acclimation of exotic plants and tropical crops, for which European and US markets showed an increasing hunger and willingness to pay (McCook 2002).

Thus the independent Latin American states sponsored local scientific expeditions, botanical gardens, centers for experimental agriculture, and the elaborations of ambitious national flora directories. This scientific mapping of nature was as much a part of Latin American nation building as the formation of governments and constitutions. Venezuela founded its Economic Society in 1836, which promoted the first national scientific surveys (McCook 2002). The Brazilian Institute of History and Geography was instituted in 1838, and had several distinguished naturalists – such as the German Carl Friedrich Philipp von Martius – among its members.

Forests and Agriculture

Despite scientific advances in zoology and botany, the agricultural expansion of the late nineteenth century did not imply significant efforts to modernize soil conservation techniques. The benefits of guano and other chemical soil nutrients were sufficiently well known to sustain a good part of the Pacific Latin America's export economy (Gootenberg 1989), but there was little interest in using them in the local plantations. Coffee growers sometimes instructed slaves to leave fallen leaves and stems of the coffee as "green manure" for the soil – but just as often they did not. Thus Peruvian guano was sold to enrich European soils, while the expanding coffee industry compensated for the loss of productivity in exhausted soils by claiming more forest area. José Bonifácio de Andrada, a leading political figure of post-independence Brazil, cursed the plague of slavery for the loss of Brazilian forests, resulting from the combination of "the murderous broadax of the black and the devastating flames of ignorance" (Pádua 2002: 124–50). As historians Steven Topik and Mario Samper write, "The Brazilian coffee boom was financed by the inheritance of planters' future descendents and the destruction of other creatures' habitats" (2006: 127).

If export crops led to large-scale deforestation, subsistence farmers also kept a constant if less aggressive pressure on forest resources. Rather than the crop rotation long practiced in Europe, antiquated slash-and-burn techniques of forest clearing in frontier areas was the most common strategy for maintaining or increasing production. Soil exhaustion was not the only threat for small farmers. Roaming cattle and pigs, no longer hindered by dense forests, often invaded manioc or corn fields (Dean 1997: 186–95). Once abandoned or turned into pastures, sometimes limited patches of forest regenerated; sometimes, however, rain and wind hit the exposed soil hard, and erosion scars (*voçorocas*) became part of the natural landscape.

Cocoa, coffee, bananas, rubber, and sugar cane dominated the export market, and the export market dominated the landscape. From the island of Cuba to Venezuela to Brazil to Argentina, landowners expected to find the most efficient variety of sugar cane and the most fertile land, in order to extract the maximum value per hectare. One of the costs of large-scale monoculture was vulnerability to plant disease. The continuous search for the most productive seeds around the world brought parasites as well as the desired species to the sugar plantations in Cuba, Puerto Rico, and Brazil. Soon states found they needed to invest in pest control research, as much as in seed improvements. Sugar cane in Puerto Rico succumbed to cyclical pests such as the Mosaic, which arrived with a new species of sugar cane imported from Asia in 1917 – and the Center for Agricultural Research was hard pressed to save the crop responsible for 47 percent of the island's exports.

Sometimes, technological research was not enough. From 1928 through World War II the Ford Motor Company tried to grow natural rubber in a plantation system in the Brazilian Amazon – the natural habitat of the *Hevea brasiliensis*. Widely dispersed in natural stands, rubber trees can fend off parasites and other natural pests. When the trees are brought together in monocultural plantations, however, the pests also become concentrated, devastating the plants. These natural barriers, along with the inability to impose rigid labor regulations upon Amazonian workers, doomed *Fordlândia* to failure. Large monocultures of *Hevea brasiliensis* thrived in Asian and African plantations. But in its native forest, surrounded by native pests, the rubber had to be extracted in the time-honored extractive technique, locating and harvesting the latex from wild trees separated by life-saving distances (Dean 1987).

Armies were often the first clear presence of the state in densely forested areas. Chile's campaign against the Mapuches in the south (1860s), the Paraguayan war (1865–70), Argentina's so-called Conquest of the Desert in the 1870s, the negotiation between Bolivia and Brazil over the territory of Acre (1904), the war of Chaco (1932–5), reminded Latin American states of the limits of modernity's grasp over a large portion of the continent. Military officers wrote home about the environmental conditions they encountered, the diseases, the uncharted rivers, and the presence of indigenous people with little or no relationship to the modern states other than contention. The contrast between these conditions and the European-inspired societies of the Latin American elites fired the imagination of many Latin American writers in the creation of "romances of the jungle," which depicted an impenetrable, strong, and vengeful nature – a far cry from the Eden-like narratives of a bountiful nature that were common in colonial times. Hoping to strengthen their claim over remote territories, governments invested more in official surveys of the hinterland, both to confirm the demarcation of borders and to assert active sovereignty. Telegraphs, roads, and military outposts were established in the jungle (Diacon 2004). Successes were mixed. These state-sponsored initiatives did open new forest areas for settlers, farmers, and sometimes industrialization. But international borders within Latin America remained very permeable. In the 1920s a group of young officers challenged the Brazilian oligarchies by leading the rebel Costas–Prestes Column in a long march through the Brazilian hinterland, and by crossing the Paraguayan borders whenever it was convenient to avoid persecution (Macauley 1974). For rural guerrillas in Colombia, and coca or gold smugglers in the late twentieth century, the combination of permeable borders and dense forest created a virtual autonomous territory.

The Amazon, the world's largest remaining tropical rainforest, is a dominant feature in the Latin American environmental map. Although river-borne expeditions had traversed the region from colonial times, the interior of the Amazon forest and the transitional biomass remained sheltered from much permanent settlement until the middle of the twentieth century. By 1962, it was estimated that only 2 percent of the Brazilian Amazon rainforest had been converted to other uses, although many of the region's environmental resources had been exploited earlier. Amazon turtle eggs had been hunted almost to extinction by mid-nineteenth century. The manatee population had already decreased considerably by 1905. By the 1910s the search for rubber had encouraged migration to the Amazon, led to the transfer of the territory of Acre from Bolivia to Brazil, and caused violent clashes between rubber tapers and indigenous populations (Weinstein 1983; Dean 1987). But it was only in the 1970s that most countries invested more aggressively in the occupation of the Amazon, seeking funding from the World Bank for large-scale projects. In Brazil, Amazonian development in this period was also central to the drive to "national integration" and resource exploitation carried out by the military-dominated government (Moran 1981; Bunker 1985).

The World Bank development programs in the post-World War II era had a clear concept of what was a beneficial project. Biotechnology, large mechanization and mining, export crops, opening of new areas for agriculture, dams, and large-scale irrigation systems were part of this model; conservation techniques were not. Thus in the 1970s logging operations, particularly for valuable mahogany, opened a large part of the Amazon forest for settlers and cattle ranchers. Large-scale mining of bauxite and iron ore added to environmental degradation. In 20 years, by the early 1980s, some 16 percent of the Brazilian Amazon had been cleared, eight times as much deforestation as in the four preceding centuries.

Urbanization

Cities also extracted a heavy toll on natural resources both near and far. They consumed charcoal and firewood, in the residences, in bakeries, coffee roasters, sugar refineries, and early industries of all kinds. Ancient man-made shell mounds (*sam-baqui*) left by pre-Columbian settlements provided the raw material for lime used for mortar and plaster in the modern city construction (Dean 1997: 197).

Urbanization slowed during the disruption of independence and the following years of political strife and economic stagnation in the first half of the nineteenth century. But cities were essential in international trade as the terminals from where export commodities were shipped to the world. They grew along with Latin America's integration into international trade. They were also the ports by which hundreds of thousands of forced and free immigrants reached Latin America. Cuba and Brazil received large numbers of African slaves until 1850 (Helg, this volume). In the late nineteenth century, Italian and other southern European immigrants energized the coffee industry in São Paulo and the wheat cultivation in Argentina (Scobie 1964; Holloway 1980). Newcomers from Japan revolutionized the fisheries and the cuisine in Peru. It was not only foreign labor that moved across the land; as agriculture moved plants, opened roads, imported new seeds, and grew new crops, masses of rural workers followed. If work was to be found in the cities, as well as better health conditions, migrants would seek better opportunities in the urban areas. At the same time, health improvements both in the countryside and in the cities improved the life expectancy of the Latin American population; in particular, child mortality rates decreased. Where population growth was not combined with growth of economic opportunity, it increased the masses of internal migrants. Studies in Mexico, for example, showed that by the 1980s 50 percent of the Mixteca population would leave their original area, either permanently or to become temporary workers (Wright 2005: 133).

This immense mass of new people fed the urban structure in Latin America in the twentieth century. Latin America went from 7 percent urban population in 1910 to circa 80 percent by 2000. Mexico City's population jumped from 350,000 to more than 20 million in 100 years (McNeill 2001: 421). São Paulo and Mexico City are among the 10 largest megacities in the world, with over 20 million people. Rio de Janeiro and Buenos Aires are not far behind, with around 10 million each. The growth of the cities is closely connected to Latin America's insertion in the global economy, but state-sponsored industrialization from the 1930s, particularly after World War II, accelerated this process (Wolfe, this volume). As cities grew, their residents and industries needed more land, more energy, more fuel-wood, more water. On the eve of the Mexican Revolution, sanitation was a challenge for Mexico City; on the eve of the twenty-first century, it was a disaster. As with many other phenomena, urbanization mirrored the social and economic inequality of Latin American development. In 1940, access to clean water for the population in Lima was celebrated as a conquest of modernity; but the poor neighborhoods still fight for this particular marker of modernity in the early twenty-first century.

Since the 1960s, some governments have offered fiscal incentives for the establishment of industries in remote territories, seeking to alleviate the pressure on the older cities while developing new urban areas. In 1965, Mexico signed an agreement with the USA to allow the construction of US-owned assembly factories, *maquiladoras*, along its northern border, while in 1970 Brazil's military government created the Manaus Tax-Free Zone in the heart of the Amazon forest. With no real urban or industrial planning, both cases generated labor and environmental disasters. Industrial effluents contaminated parts of the Rio Grande along the USA–Mexico border and the Negro river where Manaus is located, and governmental agencies report considerable health and environmental impact (Roberts & Thanos 2003).

Health risks associated with industrial pollution did not alarm Latin American leaders until the 1980s – and not for the lack of critical events. In 1960, for example, air pollution produced by a copper smelter near Ilo, in southern Peru, affected people, vegetation, and crops in a range of 200 miles (McNeill 2001: 85). But pollution seemed a small price to pay for progress, and Brazilian officers agreed with Indira Gandhi, at the 1972 UN Conference on the Human Environment at Stockholm, that, "the worst pollution was poverty" (Duarte 2005: 145). The dominant ideology in the age of developmentalism was: grow first, clean up later.

In the 1980s, however, urban pollution rose to critical levels. Ozone alerts were frequent in Mexico City, where much of the country's industry was concentrated. Inefficient cars and a bowl-shaped topography only added to the crisis. The government took draconian measures to address the problem, with only partial success. In the 1980s the Brazilian city of Cubatão, a center of petrochemical refineries located on the São Paulo coast near hydroelectric power sources, became a symbol of air and groundwater pollution, with high levels of infant mortality and birth defects. By the early 1990s, however, the city could boast of having dealt with the most critical aspects of industrial pollution and had shown rapid improvements in environmental quality (McNeill 2001: 77–83).

Modern Agriculture and Biotechnology

The drive for higher productivity and economic growth added a new urgency to agricultural expansion in the second half of the twentieth century. Although native communities had improved seed and plants for millennia, modern biotechnology was hailed as a major contributor to Latin American development. Agricultural centers developed a very pragmatic research agenda focused largely on the improvement of the major export crops in the early twentieth century – with the exception of Mexico, where most biotechnological research since 1923 dealt with maize, an important domestic staple. Biotechnology research increased dramatically after World War II, particularly in Mexico, where President Manuel Ávila Camacho personally promoted Green Revolution technologies. Ávila Camacho largely abandoned his predecessor Lázaro Cárdenas's commitment to land reform and the *ejidos* (collective landholdings) as the basis for Mexican agriculture, and invested instead in the development of several high-yielding corn varieties, with the support of the Rockefeller Foundation. The new agricultural techniques, including biotechnology and massive irrigation projects, made large-scale agricultural units highly profitable in the 1980s and 1990s. The expansion of large landholdings, criticized in the 1960s as inefficient and backward *latifundia*, was by the 1980s celebrated by most governments. In the 1990s, agribusiness in Chile, Uruguay, Argentina, Brazil, and Mexico, including large multinational conglomerates, wielded considerable political power in environmental regulations. In the case of Brazil, this led to the rapid expansion of extensive soybean farms in the vast savanna stretching south from the Amazon forest. Genetically modified seeds of soy, corn, and wheat were widely planted in Argentina and Brazil, despite initial regulations. In the case of Mexico, modern agricultural issues were heavily contemplated in the NAFTA (North American Free Trade Agreement) negotiations, particularly regarding pesticides and fertilizers.

The Green Revolution – a combination of improved crop varieties, heavy inputs of fertilizers and pesticides, and mechanized cultivation and harvests, all heavily dependent on petroleum-based products – has had an uneven impact in Latin America. Many countries, such as Paraguay, Bolivia, Peru, Ecuador, and the Central American countries, could not generally afford the necessary investments in research, fertilizers, pesticides, and high-yielding seeds that were part of the full package. The countries that did invest in biotechnology discovered that genetically identical hybrid high-yielding seeds could be even more vulnerable to plant diseases than the traditional monocultures, and therefore needed even more pesticides. Small farmers who could not keep pace with the modern agribusinesses were often forced to abandoned their lands and migrate to the cities or become seasonal rural workers. Based on the increase in the use of pesticides in Latin America, biotechnology, and modern irrigation projects, the Green Revolution represented the loss or displacement of indigenous agricultural patterns. For example, irrigation experts had recognized since 1917 the success of the Papago Indians in Mexico in carefully using all available moisture and organic matter to fertilize and water their desert soils. Fifty years later, however, this recognition had been lost under the centralized planning of agricultural development that had little time or resources to adapt to the diverse ecosystems and cultures (Wright 2005: 143–84).

The rise of agribusiness in Latin America overlapped with the beginning of Cuba's "Special Period," i.e., the collapse of the Soviet Union and the loss of Cuba's privileged relationship with the former Eastern Bloc after 1990 (Martínez- Fernández, this volume). Without its market for sugar and its supplier of subsidized petroleum, agriculture in Cuba had to adapt to the new conditions. In the mid-1990s, sugar and tobacco plantations received most available fuel and pesticides; food crops, on the other hand, underwent a radical conversion to organic agriculture, combining traditional techniques, such as the use of ox-driven plows, with sophisticated biological pest control and large-scale production of compost fertilizer (Rosset & Cunningham 1994). As the price of sugar fell, workers in the sugar industry were retrained to work in the new national industry, tourism, while many of the mills and plantations that supported what had been the island's most important crop for 300 years were converted for other uses.

Organic agriculture or agro-ecology also emerged in other areas. Although natural rubber was no longer the major economic sector it had been in the early twentieth century, rubber tappers were able to strike alliances in the 1980s with indigenous groups and environmentalists to protect the natural stands of brazil nut trees and rubber trees in the Amazon. The high visibility of the rubber tappers' campaign exposed to the world the violence implicit in the conversion of forest into pastures or agricultural land; the death of their leader Chico Mendes in 1988 had international repercussions (Revkin 1990). The campaign provided enough political leverage for the rubber tappers to advance their proposal for a new kind of conservation unit that allowed economic extractivism and organic agriculture within the protected forest. More significant economically, cocoa growers invested in agro-ecological research to fight a fungal disease called witch's broom that plagued plantations in Guatemala,

Ecuador, Colombia, Venezuela, and Brazil in the 1990s. In some regions, witch's broom could cause the loss of up to 100 percent of the crop. Threatened with a possible shortage of chocolate in the world market, cocoa growers obtained some success in controlling the disease by cultivating smaller units and planting other species among the cocoa trees (Dand 1999).

Mineral Resources

Just as gold and silver flowed to the Old World during the Colonial period, the second industrial revolution of nineteenth-century Europe and the USA required growing supplies of copper and other raw materials. Prices of copper and oil defined much of the economic trajectories of Mexico, Venezuela, Chile, and Peru in the early twentieth century. The allure of mining and the uncovered secrets of the Latin American subsoil resources did not fade. Vestiges of gold had attracted migrants to the Tapajós River in the Brazilian Amazon since the 1960s, but the old images of Eldorado reemerged strongly in 1980 when the rich deposits in Serra Pelada were discovered. The gold rush in the Serra Pelada and elsewhere in the Amazon not only created violent land conflicts with local communities, but also produced mercury residues that traveled far beyond the gold fields. In 1985 health agents identified symptoms of mercury poisoning in all age groups in indigenous tribes located hundreds of miles to the north of the Tapajos River.

Petroleum, more essential for modern societies than gold, loomed large in the Venezuelan and Mexican economies in the twentieth century, facilitated by their proximity to the world's largest oil consumer, the USA. Oil fields near traditional communities were a blessing and a curse. Populations agonized between the loss of culture and control over their natural resources, and the economic opportunities offered by the industries. The Huastecs in Veracruz, Mexico, faced with the oil boom in the 1920s, pressed their government for collective landholdings (ejidos) in an effort to keep their agricultural way of life and avoid further ecological degradation. Although not completely successful, at the end of the Mexican oil boom they still had sufficient community identity to cling to their now sadly polluted, but still productive ancestral lands (Santiago 2006). With the nationalization of oil in Mexico in 1938 and the increased activity by US-owned oil companies in Venezuela, oil became the most important commodity for that country, around which national politics and economics revolved. Some indigenous communities, such as the Motilones of Lake Maracaibo, resisted the oil industries from 1914 to 1930, often driving oil prospectors away with arrows and spears. Eventually the Motilon Indians lost to more heavily armed men, as well as to the contamination of the ground and the dwindling of hunting grounds (Kozlof 2002). The dispute between local communities and the exploitation of underground resources provided the state of Venezuela with a valuable income, and a recurring precedent. In the 1990s, the extraction of coal and oil deposits at the borders between Colombia and Venezuela in the Sierra de Perija displaced the Wayuu and Yupka peoples. The new 1999 constitution pledged that the Venezuelan government would no longer support the extraction of natural resources without previous consultation with indigenous groups, but it represented a daring (and untested) departure from tradition. The Ecuadorian Amazon has also been the site of contention between indigenous groups and multinational petroleum companies (Sabin 1998; Sawyer 2004).

As Latin America grew to be more dependent on the oil economy – producing or importing – oil spills became more common in the region. In 1979, 600,000 tons of oil spilled from the Ixtoc I offshore well in the Gulf of Mexico. The impact on the entire Caribbean Sea was acute, and in 1983 the Caribbean countries signed an agreement of cooperation for combating oil spills in the wider Caribbean region. For a vulnerable ecosystem, even a small oil spill like the one off the Galapagos Islands in 2001 could have devastating ecological consequences – in this case killing off 60 percent of the marine iguanas. More common was the case of Guanabara Bay, in Rio de Janeiro, Brazil. In addition to two large oil spills in 1975 and 2000, ordinary amounts of oil spilled from normal maritime traffic, badly maintained underwater pipes, or maritime gas stations and refineries. Cartagena Bay in Colombia has a similar history of occasional disaster and everyday spill-off.

Water Resources

Water – or drought – has been an important factor in the occupation of Latin America's territory. South America contains large supplies of fresh water – 10 times as much per person as Asia – as well as large dry, desert areas (McNeill 2001: 119). The northern half of Mexico is also characterized by semi-arid conditions, even as large-scale agribusiness has expanded in the region. Control over water, through dams, reservoirs, and irrigation in the twentieth century became one of the more significant and resource-consuming tasks for local and national governments.

European settlers first reached Latin America by water routes and for three centuries most of the Latin American population stayed close to the coasts. Fisheries constituted an important element in the food supply for the urban centers. The Humboldt Current in the Pacific, extremely rich in marine life, benefited Chile, Peru, Ecuador, and Colombia with an extensive maritime biota – including guano-producing sea birds. Governments often supported fishing development as part of national security, as traditional fishermen were perceived as the basis for a national navy. Overall, artisanal fishing prevailed on the Pacific coast until the 1930s, with small fishing communities supplying the internal market. After World War II, the industry grew rapidly. By the late 1960s, Peru was responsible for 20 percent of the world harvest of anchovies, which represented a third of its foreign exchange earnings. Overfishing from Peruvian and Californian boats since the 1950s, combined with a harsh El Niño in 1972, reduced the catch from 12 million tons in 1971 to just 1.5 million tons in 1982 (McNeill 2001: 249).

Coastal whaling represented an important industry in Argentina and Brazil in the eighteenth century. However, due to overhunting and an increase in maritime traffic, by the nineteenth century it had all but disappeared. Whalers had to travel far from the coast to find whales, and they competed with large ships from the USA and Northern Europe. In northern Peru, New England whalers supported significant local development from 1830 to 1860, but the industry was clearly dominated by the US operators. By the mid-twentieth century, only Peru and Mexico still had significant whaling industries.

Away from the coasts, dams and large-scale irrigation schemes changed the flow of rivers, created lakes where forests existed, displaced communities, and made the industrialization of Latin America possible. Irrigation projects had been common in Latin America since the Inca Empire. Modern irrigation schemes, however, privileged mostly export crops, mobilizing a considerable population of seasonal workers who lived at the edge of such projects. For example, a federal irrigation project in the valley of Culiacán, Mexico, begun in 1948, by 1981 supplied water to circa 600,000 acres of land, and attracted a population of some 140,000 migrant farm workers living in *campamentos* – overcrowded, unhealthy open-sided sheds (Wright 2005: 13).

As many water basins covered more than one country, irrigation projects, dams, or other water uses often had environmental impact across borders. For instance, the withdrawals in the USA from the Colorado River in the last half of the twentieth century diminished the amount of fresh water flowing into the ocean and affected the quality of water of the Sea of Cortés. Herbicide sprayed on illegal crops of coca in Colombia raised concerns about the safety of the water supply in the Amazon basin, as the chemicals drained into the Amazon River and its tributaries. Shared water resources led governments and local movements to collaborate when they perceived common interests. Brazil and Paraguay joined forces for the construction of the gigantic Itaipu hydroelectric dam in the Paraná River, begun in 1970, and the resulting energy was split between the two countries. A product of two authoritarian regimes, the construction of Itaipu also caused the obliteration of the magnificent Seven Falls of the Paraná, damage or flooding of 700 square kilometers of forests (mostly on Paraguay's side), and the displacement of some 10,000 families, with little hope of compensation.

In 1992, in more democratic times, indigenous leaders from around the Amazon basin established a transnational forum to pressure their governments regarding their environment and social agendas. Following their lead, in the late 1990s eight countries of the Amazon basin agreed to regular meetings to address problems of transboundary pollution, smuggling, guerrilla groups on the borders, as well as common policies for the native populations in the Amazon.

Epidemics and Environmental Change

Expansion of the agriculture frontier, large public works in the tropical forests, and the transfer of thousands of immigrants to these new areas created a favorable environment for epidemics. Malaria was known in Latin America since early in the colonial period, and yellow fever was a common urban tragedy in many cities from the 1850s to the 1930s. As new diseases expanded their range in a transformed environment, governments took action to control them. In particular, malaria, yellow fever, and hookworm disease were targeted by governments and international organizations such as the Rockefeller Foundation in the early twentieth century. These diseases threatened the labor force committed to the construction of the Panama Canal, in the United Fruit plantations in Central America, in the Rockefeller Standard Oil coastal oil fields in Mexico, and Venezuela. A large number of US and Latin American scientists were mobilized to identify and control the disease vectors (McNeill 2001: 421).

Local governments also supported and created national scientific institutes to eliminate yellow fever. In 1904, physician Oswaldo Cruz was given free rein to change Rio de Janeiro's reputation of being a dangerous city – which he did, with the use of draconian measures. Forced vaccination, quarantine, and mandatory inspection of houses (including breaking any water recipient believed to facilitate mosquito reproduction) drastically reduced yellow fever cases in the Brazilian city in 1906 (Stepan 1976). As happened in other areas of Latin America, "*cientificos*" and hygienists often found resistance by the poor population regarding their public health policies, since many of these plans were associated with larger modernization processes of Latin American cities. In the case of Rio de Janeiro, the vaccination campaign was the trigger for a popular riot in 1904 against the imposition of urban reforms that eventually replaced low-income, unsanitary residences in downtown Rio with large, European-style boulevards for the wealthier population (Meade 1997).

Disease control policies included many drainage projects, drastically altering wetlands and other vulnerable ecosystems. In Brazil, Argentina, and Chile, a large part of the budget for public works was dedicated to draining swamps and straightening river courses near urban areas. In Panama, Costa Rica, Honduras, and Guatemala, the United Fruit Company manifested the same concerns. Faster transportation technology, however, helped pathogens and their vectors to move quickly from infected to virgin areas, faster than public health plans could counteract the spread of disease. In the 1930s, a new malarial mosquito species arrived in Latin America by plane from West Africa, causing some 20,000 deaths. From then on, malaria and yellow fever control combined with drainage and insecticide campaigns (McNeill 2001: 421). Heavy use of DDT and drainage also favored the urbanization trends in Latin America after World War II, with significant loss of wildlife, wetlands, and mangrove forests.

Yet malaria has continued to be a concern in the Latin American tropical zones. As governments sought to develop the Amazon region or expand irrigation projects, malarial outbreaks kept surfacing, and eradication campaigns were only partially successful. In the 1970s, Brazil's military government invested heavily in the opening of a network of roads in the Amazon rainforest, with a workforce of poor northeastern immigrants and peasant farmers. With no access to anti-malaria drugs and little resistance to the disease, these workers were victims to endemic malaria. In the early 1990s, malaria cases peaked in Peru with over 121,000 confirmed cases in Loreto, after eradication campaigns had reduced malaria to some 1,500 cases in 1965 (Guarda et al. 1999).

Droughts, Floods, and Earthquakes: Redefining Natural Disasters

Plants, animals, and people in Latin America adapted to the widest range of climates: from the extreme dryness of the Atacama desert of northern Chile to the wet season in the Amazon forest to the west winds in the Patagonia and the high slopes in the Andes. These climate patterns have suffered continuous slow alteration by human action, through deforestation, resource extraction, and pollution. They also have suffered the drastic impact of El Niño and La Niña – global anomalies in the air and ocean temperature that occur on average every two to eight years. When both man-made and natural factors overlap, consequences have often been disastrous.

Geological and archeological records of cyclical droughts in Mexico, Peru, and Chile attest to the influence of El Niño in arid regions since before colonial times, an influence made more acute as new settlements mined out vegetation and water resources. In 1825, the drought-prone Brazilian northeast experienced a famine that killed at least 30,000 people, uncovering the environmental vulnerability of the cattle and subsistence-agriculture economic base (Davis 2001). It was a modest preview of the Great Drought 50 years later. In late 1876, a major El Niño occurrence changed climatic conditions in Asia, Africa, and Latin America. Because it coincided with a global economic crisis, the resulting drought and inability (or unwillingness) of governments to react to the crises brought about the most disastrous famine of the nineteenth century over three continents. In 1877, the drought scorched the already thirsty interior *sertão* in the Brazilian northeast, or about one-tenth of the territory of Brazil. Cotton harvests dried up, cattle perished, and hungry working people left their homes in huge migrant waves. They ate palm hearts, cactus, and cassava – sometimes poisonous cassava – and anything else they could find. Late and incompetent intervention by the federal government did not help, as relief was wasted in far-fetched and inefficient schemes. In the meantime, the desperate refugees moved to areas not yet destroyed by the drought, increasing the pressure on the remaining vulnerable resources. The *sertão* lost, in those two years, 90 percent of its population. The city of Fortaleza received over 100,000 refugees, four times its normal population. Recife and other cities on the coast were likely destinations and suffered similar invasions of migrants. The government tried to deport the refugees from the drought to the Amazon, but there were not enough ships to board that many people. Smallpox, caused by unsanitary conditions, followed the huge agglomerations of refugees. One-third of the population of Fortaleza died in two months in 1878, according to one author; 100,000 people died in Ceará alone, according to another (Davis 2001). The Great Drought ended in 1880, but it left deep marks on the Brazilian memory. It defined, for instance, the responsibility of the federal government to address disaster situations; it promoted the first plans for the transposition of the San Francisco River as a definitive solution for the cyclical droughts; and it proved that the "drought industry," the management of government assistance by private companies, could be as profitable as any agricultural enterprise.

Local climatic changes, less dramatic, left permanent scars in the landscape. In Venezuela, the expansion of cocoa plantations from 1850 to 1930 took over the humid lowlands from the lake of Maracaibo to the Barlovento, near the Tuy River. With cocoa arrived also settlements of poor blacks and mulattoes (slaves until 1854 and free peons after that), and the damages of torrential floods in deforested land (Grau 2002: 147). Erosion and flooding become "natural" features in the region. In Rio de Janeiro, the rainstorms of 1966 and 1967 provoked deadly landslides in the deforested hills where the poorest population lived. It paralyzed the city with floods caused less by the volume of rain precipitation than by the clogged and overtaxed runoff and sewage systems. Along with the fear of water-borne epidemics, those exceptional floods bared the very ordinary inadequacy of the urban structures.

Likewise, the earthquakes in Lima in 1974, and in Mexico City in 1985, more than cyclical disasters, exposed the uneven vulnerability of Latin American cities.

Latin American history has recorded earthquakes, mostly on the Pacific Coast, and hurricanes in the Caribbean since long before Columbus's arrival. The urbanization of the late twentieth century, however, turned natural disasters into urban catastrophes. The 1970 earthquake in southern Peru, one of the world's worst in the twentieth century and the deadliest in Latin America, caused over 66,000 deaths; 200,000 homes and buildings were destroyed and approximately 800,000 people were left homeless. Most of the victims were urban dwellers in insecure houses around the cities of Chimbote, Trujillo, and Huaraz. The earthquakes of 1972 in Nicaragua and 1976 in the Guatemalan highlands caused also mostly urban victims. The Nicaragua earthquake, in which the city of Managua had 80 percent of its buildings destroyed, was aggravated by the rampant corruption of Anastasio Somoza's dictatorship, which included embezzlement of the international aid sent to Nicaragua and looting of the city by the National Guard. The natural disaster, in this case, triggered a crisis in Somoza's government, its alliance with Washington and with the country's elite, and helped set the stage for the Sandinista victory in 1979 (García-Acosta 1997).

There were thus some new repercussions in these modern natural disasters. First, while earthquakes, droughts, and floods were natural events, the calamities and mortality that resulted from these events also involved human failures of omission and commission. Second, their impact was greater in urban Latin America, due to the larger concentration of people and the environmental vulnerability of the poorest sectors of the urban populations. Finally, particularly in the second half of the twentieth century, natural disasters assumed a political profile, and the populations held their governments accountable, if not for preventing the disaster itself, at least for mitigating the direst consequences.

Environmentalism in Latin America

The earliest organizations for environmental conservation in Latin America were mostly urban-based and inspired by the American model of national parks. In fact, since the 1920s campaigns for national parks have surged in Mexico, Costa Rica, and Brazil, with considerable support from government officials (Evans 1999). The parks were usually located in areas with particular aesthetic appeal and usually with little economic attractiveness. By 1950, societies for the conservation of nature were created in several countries, usually with a more ambitious agenda, and took part in several conflicts with industries and landowners. Even for these societies, the focus was on the conservation of a certain concept of pristine nature threatened by economic interests and population pressure. By the late 1960s, however, a new sort of "environmental movement" appeared in some low-income urban neighborhoods. Resulting from the inordinate growth of Latin American cities, it demanded better living conditions, which included clean water, sewage systems, and solutions to urban pollution. These movements were not necessarily connected to traditional political channels, since several countries in Latin America were under authoritarian regimes. Their agendas were quite pragmatic and urgent, and evolved into more sophisticated environmental movements in the 1980s (Hurrell 1992).

Latin America participated in the worldwide increase in environmental awareness in the 1980s in several different ways. On the one hand, the increase in economic activity and forest clearing by burning in the Amazon was captured in satellite pictures and ignited a strong response. On the other hand, local groups seized the opportunity to reframe their traditional struggles for access to natural resources and land within a modern environmental perspective. Rubber tappers and Indians joined forces with local and international non-profit organizations to launch international campaigns against World Bank-funded and government-sponsored development projects that threatened their livelihood. In Ecuador's Amazon, Huaorani tribes used modern technology and environmental advocacy in alliance with environmental groups to negotiate with oil companies and their government (Sabin 1998; Sawyer 2004). Wherever democratic access was blocked locally, international visibility worked to create indirect pressure on local governments, in a "boomerang effect" (Keck 1995). The movement was successful in creating a debate on the destiny of the Amazon forest, although more permanent policy changes remain to be seen. Local organizations, however, often complained that while a sustainable agenda for the Amazon forest was important, it somehow monopolized international solidarity when many other environmental crises affected Latin American populations with more urgency.

One consequence of the campaign was the selection of Rio de Janeiro to host the United Nations Conference on Environment and Development in June 1992. The event offered a unique opportunity for the local environmental organizations to create articulations at the regional level, and for human rights, labor, and women's organizations to incorporate common environmental issues in their traditional agendas.

Conclusion

Global economic integration was an essential factor in the transformation of Latin America's environment. From the sugar plantations in the Caribbean and Brazil to the banana plantations in Honduras, from the coca fields in Bolivia to the implantation of *maquiladoras* in northern Mexico or Costa Rica, Latin American environmental history is closely integrated with its history of international trade, unequal access to natural resources, and dependency. It is not a homogenous history – the connection to the global economy was different from country to country and from time to time, the internal social structure varied hugely, and so did the specific conditions of the diverse Latin American ecosystems. But both the global economy and local environmental conditions shaped much of the social and environmental history of Latin America. The large lowlands in the Argentine and the international demand for meat created the basis for the gaucho culture in the nineteenth century, as the presence of guano in Peru and the need for fertilizer in Europe wrote a page of Peruvian history (Gootenberg 1989; Slatta 1983), among many possible examples.

In both urban and rural aspects, environmental degradation has had an uneven impact in Latin America. Forest and biodiversity loss, coastal water pollution, soil erosion, desertification, and air pollution are the prices paid by the present generation for the promises of economic development in the past. At the same time, environmental changes were part of the accelerated development and industrialization process of Latin America in the twentieth century. Inequality in enjoying the fruits of this development ironically mirrors the inequality in bearing its costs: the populations who least benefited from economic growth are also those more vulnerable to the hazards of concomitant environmental degradation.

BIBLIOGRAPHY

Bakewell, P. J. (1971) *Silver Mining and Society in Colonial Mexico: Zacatecas, 1546–1700.* Cambridge University Press, Cambridge.

Bakewell, P. J. (1984) *Miners of the Red Mountain: Indian Labor in Potosí, 1545–1650.* University of New Mexico Press, Albuquerque.

Bunker, S. G. (1985) *Underdeveloping the Amazon: Extraction, Unequal Exchange, and the Failure of the Modern State.* University of Illinois Press, Urbana.

Crosby, A. W. (1972) *The Columbian Exchange: Biological and Cultural Consequences of 1492.* Greenwood Publishing, Westport, CT.

Crosby, A. W. (1986) *Ecological Imperialism: Tthe Biological Expansion of Europe, 900–1900.* Cambridge University Press, New York.

Dand, R. (1999) *The International Cocoa Trade.* CRC Press, Boca Raton, FL.

Davis, M. (2001) *Late Victorian Holocausts: El Niño Famines and the Making of the Third World.* Verso, London.

Dean, W. (1976) *Rio Claro: A Brazilian Plantation System, 1820–1920.* Stanford University Press, Stanford.

Dean, W. (1987) *Brazil and the Struggle for Rubber: A Study in Environmental History.* Cambridge University Press, New York.

Dean, W. (1997) *With Broadax and Firebrand: The Destruction of the Brazilian Atlantic Forest.* University of California Press, Berkeley and Los Angeles.

Diacon, T. (2004) *Stringing Together a Nation: Candido Mariano da Silva Rondon and the Construction of a Modern Brazil, 1906–1930.* Duke University Press, Durham.

Diamond, J. (1997) *Guns, Germs, and Steel: The Fates of Human Societies.* W. W. Norton, New York.

Duarte, R. H. (2005) "Por um pensamento ambiental histórico: O caso do Brasil," *Luso-Brazilian Review,* 41:2, pp. 144–61.

Evans, S. (1999) *The Green Republic: A Conservation History of Costa Rica.* University of Texas Press, Austin.

Gade, D. (1999) *Nature and Culture in the Andes.* University of Wisconsin Press, Madison.

Garavaglia, J. C. (2002) "La pampa como ecosistema." In B. García Martínez & M. del Rosario Prieto (eds.), *Estudios sobre historia y ambiente en America II: Norteamérica, Sudamérica y el Pacífico.* Instituto Panamericano de Geografía e Historia, Mexico City, pp. 103–24.

García-Acosta, V. (1997) *Historia y desastres en América Latina, Vol. II.* La Red/Ciesas, Lima.

Garcia Martinez, B. & González Jácome, A. (eds.) (1999) *Estudios sobre historia y ambiente en América I: Argentina, Bolívia, México, Paraguay.* Instituto Panamericano de Geografía e Historia, Mexico City.

Gootenberg, P. E. (1989) *Between Silver and Guano: Commercial Policy and the State in Postindependence Peru.* Princeton University Press, Princeton.

Grau, P. C. (2002) "Movimientos pioneros y deterioro ambiental y paisjístico en el siglo XIX venezolano." In B. García Martínez & M. del Rosario Prieto (eds.), *Estudios sobre historia y ambiente en America II: Norteamérica, Sudamérica y el Pacífico.* Instituto Panamericano de Geografía e Historia, Mexico City, pp. 141–60.

Guarda, J. A., Asayag, C. R., & Witzig, R. (1999) "Malaria Reemergence in the Peruvian Amazon Region," *Emerging Infectious Diseases,* 5:2, pp. 209–15.

Holloway, T. (1980) *Immigrants on the Land: Coffee and Society in São Paulo, 1886–1934.* University of North Carolina Press, Chapel Hill.

Hurrell, A. (1992) "Brazil and the International Politics of Amazon Deforestation." In A. Hurrell & B. Kingbury (eds.), *The International Politics of the Environment: Actors, Interests, and Institutions.* Clarendon Press, Oxford, pp. 396–420.

Keck, M. E. (1995) "Social Equity and Environmental Politics in Brazil: Lessons from the Rubber Tappers of Acre," *Comparative Politics,* 27:4, pp. 409–24.

Kozlof, N. (2002) *Maracaibo Black Gold: Venezuelan Oil and Environment during the Juan Vicente Gómez Period, 1908–1935.* Oxford University Press, Oxford.

LeGrand, C. (1986) *Frontier Expansion and Peasant Protest in Colombia, 1850–1936.* University of New Mexico Press, Albuquerque.

Lipsett-Rivera, S. (1999) *To Defend Our Water with the Blood of Our Veins: The Struggle for Resources in Colonial Puebla.* University of New Mexico Press, Albuquerque.

Macauley, N. (1974) *The Prestes Column: Revolution in Brazil.* New Viewpoints, New York.

McCook, S. G. (2002) *States of Nature: Science, Agriculture, and Environment in the Spanish Caribbean, 1760–1940.* University of Texas Press, Austin.

McNeill, J. R. (2001) *Something New under the Sun: An Environmental History of the Twentieth-Century World.* W. W. Norton, New York.

Meade, T. A. (1997) *"Civilizing" Rio: Reform and Resistance in a Brazilian City, 1889–1930.* Pennsylvania State University Press, University Park.

Melville, E. G. K. (1994) *A Plague of Sheep: Environmental Consequences of the Conquest of Mexico.* Cambridge University Press, Cambridge.

Merchant, C. (1987) "The Theoretical Structure of Ecological Revolutions," *Environmental Review,* 11:4, pp. 265–76.

Moran, E. (1981) *Developing the Amazon.* Indiana University Press, Bloomington.

Morse, R. M. & Hardoy, J. E. (1992) *Rethinking the Latin American City.* Johns Hopkins University Press, Baltimore.

Nations, J. (2006) *The Maya Tropical Forest: People, Parks, and Ancient Cities.* University of Austin Press, Austin.

Pádua, J. A. (2002) *Um sopro de destruição: Pensamento político e crítica ambiental no Brasil escravista, 1786–1888.* Jorge Zahar, Rio de Janeiro.

Radding, C. (2005) *Landscapes of Power and Identity. Comparative Histories in the Sonoran Desert and the Forests of Amazonia.* Duke University Press, Durham.

Revkin, A (1990) *The Burning Season: The Murder of Chico Mendes and the Fight for the Amazon Rain Forest.* Houghton Mifflin, Boston.

Roberts, J. T. & Thanos, N. D. (2003) *Trouble in Paradise: Globalization and Environmental Crises in Latin America.* Routledge, New York.

Rosset, P. & Cunningham, S. (1994) *The Greening of Cuba: Organic Farming Offers Hope in the Midst of Crisis.* Institute for Food & Development Policy, Oakland, CA.

Sabin, P. (1998) "Searching for Middle Ground: Native Communities and Oil Extraction in the Northern and Central Ecuadorian Amazon, 1967–1993," *Environmental History,* 3, pp. 144–68.

Santiago, M. (2006) *The Ecology of Oil: Environment, Labor, and the Mexican Revolution, 1900–1938.* Cambridge University Press, New York.

Sawyer, S. (2004) *Crude Chronicles: Indigenous Politics, Multinational Oil, and Neoliberalism in Ecuador.* Duke University Press, Durham.

Scobie, J. (1964) *Revolution on the Pampas: A Social History of Argentine Wheat, 1860–1910.* University of Texas Press, Austin.

Slatta, R. W. (1983) *Gauchos and the Vanishing Frontier.* University of Nebraska Press, Lincoln.

Soluri, J. (2005) *Banana Cultures: Agriculture, Consumption, and Environmental Change in Honduras and the United States.* University of Texas Press, Austin.

Stein, S. (1956) *Vassouras, a Brazilian Coffee County.* Harvard University Press, Cambridge, MA.

Stepan, N. (1976) *Beginnings of Brazilian Science: Oswaldo Cruz, Medical Research and Policy, 1890–1920.* Science History Publications, New York.

Super, J. C. (1988) *Food, Conquest, and Colonization in Sixteenth-century Spanish America.* University of New Mexico Press, Albuquerque.

Super, J. C. & Wright, T. C. (eds.) (1985) *Food, Politics, and Society in Latin America.* University of Nebraska Press, Lincoln.

Topik, S. & Samper, M. (2006) "The Latin American Coffee Commodity Chain: Brazil and Costa Rica." In S. Topik, C. Marichal, & Z. Frank (eds.), *From Silver to Cocaine: Latin American Commodity Chains and the Building of the World Economy, 1500–2000.* Duke University Press, Durham, pp. 118–46.

Weinstein, B. (1983) *The Amazon Rubber Boom, 1850–1920.* Stanford University Press, Stanford.

Wright, A. (2005) *The Death of Ramón González: The Modern Agricultural Dilemma*, 2nd ed. University of Texas Press, Austin.

Chapter Twenty-Six

WOMEN, GENDER, AND FAMILY IN LATIN AMERICA, 1820–2000

Nara Milanich

The history of women and gender has proven one of the most dynamic fields of Latin American history in recent years. Taking stock of this explosion of scholarship, Gilbert Joseph (2001: 445–6) commented, "gender analysis not only invites us to bring new questions to our data and explore new or woefully understudied problems . . . but also compels us to rewrite the history of more commonly studied issues and institutions . . ." Yet in spite of this intellectual promise, women and gender have been unevenly incorporated into standard narratives of modern Latin American social, political, and economic development.

Textbooks are diagnostic in this regard. One popular survey of modern Latin America (Chasteen 2001) peppers the narrative with "women worthies." The pageant of Latin American history is graced by La Malinche and Sor Juana; various independence-era heroines, nineteenth-century intellectuals, and twentieth-century feminists; Frida Kahlo, Carmen Miranda, Rigoberta Menchú. The *dramatis personae* are brave and feisty during their brief forays onto the public stage. But they are also starkly one-dimensional and, other than refracting a familiar tale of oppression and rebellion, they do not tell us much about historical change in Latin America and women's relationship to that process. They tell us even less about gender. Other texts (Burns & Charlip 2002; Keen & Haynes 2004) devote more attention to ordinary women, but the parry and thrust of domination and resistance tends to frame these portrayals as well. What is more, the texts tend to privilege women's political activism or publicly visible labors, thereby reinforcing the impression that domestic roles and labors, informality, and "private" life are largely irrelevant to historical understanding. And once again, gender is missing from these accounts.

By "gender" I refer to "a constitutive element of social relationships based on perceived differences between the sexes" (Scott 1988: 25) that is also "a primary way of signifying relationships of power" (Scott 1986: 1067). The present essay takes as its organizing thread a fairly standard chronicle of social, political, and economic change over 200 years of Latin American history. With an eye to the shortcomings of the textbooks, it then shows when and how gender matters to this narrative as well as when this interpretive approach challenges the narrative. The crucial point is that the histories of women and gender do not constitute a story separate from and parallel to other accounts of social change. Rather, they are threads that, inextricably intertwined with others, constitute that narrative. The historical experiences of women, and the historical meanings of gender, are conditioned by, and also impact, other chronicles we might construct of change over time.

Following the intellectual and political commitments of women's history, this essay pays particular attention to women's roles and experiences. At the same time, gender necessarily assumes that male and female experience and identity are defined in relational terms and that male roles are as socially constructed as female ones. Thus, to the extent possible given the limitations of a nascent scholarship, the essay also explores masculinity and men's roles. Finally, the essay looks at how changing social relationships or power dynamics in modern Latin America have been expressed through, or "signified by," gender.[1]

Men, Women, and Families in the New Republics

Accounts of early republican Latin America commonly stress the search for order in the chaos following independence. With the collapse of imperial authority and corporate colonial hierarchies, Spanish American societies grasped for new ways of organizing political and social power. Standard narratives dwell on *caudillismo* as a key strategy for doing so. Another institution that took on heightened significance in this context was the family. As Elizabeth Dore (2000a: 15) has suggested, "the family became the bulwark of the new society." Long a unit basic to social organization, the family was imbued with new functions and meanings reflecting a changed political and social context.

On a symbolic level, family metaphors were central to the republican political imaginary (Felsteiner 1983). On a practical level, patriarchal authority became a precondition of republican citizenship. As the Colombian constitution declared, "no one can be a good citizen who is not a good father, good son, good brother, good friend, and good husband" (Earle 2000: 140). Similarly, in Mexico, Central America, and Brazil, men became citizens at a younger age if they married. Thus, citizenship was not just limited to propertied men; it was defined in relationship to one's status as family patriarch. In turn, women's relationship to the state was mediated through male relatives; in this sense, the new republics did not just exclude women, but in their foundational essence were "constructed against" them (Landes in Earle 2000: 137).

Civil codes promulgated across the hemisphere strengthened the hands of husbands and fathers in an effort to consolidate the family unit. Women, particularly married ones, suffered a clear loss of authority over property and children. Mandatory partible inheritance was abolished in many (though not all) countries, a reform that both reinforced fathers' power over their children and also undermined women's economic status in so far as sons were favored in the distribution of property (Dore 2000a). Finally, with the prohibition of paternity investigation, fathers gained absolute freedom to recognize or reject offspring born out of wedlock. This latter reform was clearly inspired by the Napoleonic code, but it had uniquely far-reaching effects in Latin American societies where a quarter, a third, or more of births were illegitimate (Milanich 2002). The establishment of the new republics had terminated once and for all the quintessential patriarchal authority, that of the king. But jurists resurrected his likeness in the heart of the family.

If legal codification implied a deterioration of women's position, the concomitant expansion of judicial systems may well have had a countervailing effect. Women, particularly poor ones, were active litigants in domestic disputes in nineteenth-century courts. Their frequent recourse to law may reflect the fact that they simply had myriad grievances to air. But it could also indicate that they found the courts to be a useful tool for negotiating, even tempering, patriarchal power (Cicerchia 1998; Rodríguez 2000; Putnam 2002: 212).

The gendered struggles that played out in nineteenth-century courts involved not just men and women but also nascent states as contenders. Through a newly enhanced legal apparatus, the Costa Rican state, for example, sought to impose on litigants upper-class ideals of companionate marriage between breadwinner husbands and homemaker wives (Rodríguez 2000). Similarly, in mid-nineteenth-century Venezuela, "in contradiction to their liberal agenda, the state intervened in the private sphere by ruling over courtship, marriage, child custody, and divorce" (Díaz 2001: 72). The Argentine state interceded in custody disputes even to the detriment of fathers, usurping for itself the role of patriarch (Guy 2000). In light of such evidence, much recent scholarship has posited that a heightened regulatory impetus vis-à-vis gender and the family was central to the consolidation of Latin American states: that is, that "state formation is intimately tied up with the regulation of gender" (Dore 2000a: 155).

Yet state rhetoric and action could be manifestly less determinant of quotidian realities than the dictates of labor markets, demographic patterns, and grinding poverty. One study of poor women in São Paulo argues that beneath the vociferous moral pontification of authorities, there existed a thick stratum of popular experience largely untouched by these disciplinary efforts. If there was any top-down initiative that impacted poor women's lives and livelihoods, it was a rather banal one: the municipal regulation of bread sales (Dias 1995). A similar conclusion is reached in a study of a very different context, the communities of late nineteenth-century Caribbean Costa Rica. There, "changes and continuities in everyday life" tended to be "unconnected to attempts by rulers to intervene, educate, moralize, or reform." Instead, "the structure of markets, population, and settlement were consistently important . . . The impact of top-down projects was far more circumscribed" (Putnam 2002: 212).

Gender and Capitalism in the Nineteenth Century

Indeed, this observation reminds us that liberalism was as much an economic project as a political one, and many of the most important changes in nineteenth-century Latin America were economic in nature. What is more, the family rhetoric of liberal authorities and the economic consequences of liberal policies could work in direct opposition to one another. In the community of Diriomo, Nicaragua, municipal authorities sought to regulate sexuality and impose gender norms in ways parallel to initiatives elsewhere. Yet the growth of an agro-export coffee economy had what can only be characterized as a countervailing impact. Land privatization resulted in a surprising number of female property holders, and the commercialization of the economy apparently engendered new economic opportunities for women. The coffee revolution also resulted in increased female headship and lower rates of marriage. Whether these developments resulted in greater gender parity or in the social or economic empowerment of women is an open question (Dore 2000b). What *is* clear is that while liberal authorities espoused a particular normative vision of gender relations, their economic policies could unwittingly encourage very different realities.

Liberal political and economic projects were of course interrelated. Yet recent scholarship on gender has shed much greater light on the former issue – the relationship of gender to nation building and state formation – than on the latter – the gendered nature of liberal capitalist expansion.[2] The emergence of agro-export economies and the region's integration into global markets are processes fundamental to the making of modern Latin America. It therefore seems crucial to attend to the relationship of these developments to gender regimes, even if, given the dearth of scholarship, this overview is necessarily cursory.

Not surprisingly, it is impossible to make any categorical statements about the relationship between gender and capitalism in late nineteenth-century Latin America because capitalist expansion itself hardly constituted a single, unified process. How it played out at the local level varied widely across the hemisphere, according to prevailing land and labor systems, the degree of integration of a given area or region into wider markets, local political configurations, and myriad other factors. What we can say is that while these were macro-processes initiated from above, they were always mediated by "preexisting social and cultural relations that reconfigure[d] and localize[d]" that which was externally imposed (Roseberry 1989: 515). Among these "preexisting social and cultural relations," gender ideologies, gender practices (not least of which was the sexual division of labor), and household structures figure prominently. Thus, men and women of the same social stratum had very different relationships to the emerging export economies, to commercialization, and to the dislocations and opportunities they generated. Several historical vignettes will illustrate both the diversity of scenarios as well as some recurring patterns.

One scenario is the displacement of women's traditional occupations. In the provinces of Argentina, as in many other places, skilled female artisanal crafts such as spinning and weaving were important productive enterprises. But the importation of textiles from abroad wiped out these cottage industries. Alternative employment for women as domestics and in piecework did not compensate for the loss of skilled labors. As a consequence, female unemployment rose, and statistics indicate a "drastic reduction in the percentage of adult women who either claimed a profession or received remuneration for their labor" (Guy 1981: 66).

A very different story, one less of displacement than of a gendered reorientation around new economic activities, played out in late nineteenth-century Costa Rica. There, field workers and stevedores who labored in the banana economy were overwhelmingly male, but the export boom also catalyzed the growth of a parallel economy comprised of women workers and concerned with social reproduction. This informal sector produced the "food, clean clothes, shelter, sex and companionship that sustained the regional workforce" of the export sector (Putnam 2002: 7). Informal and invisible, women's labor was nonetheless crucial to the banana economy.

A third scenario involves the reinscription of the preexisting gendered division of labor in the face of technological advances and intensifying commercialization. In Córdoba, Veracruz, Mexico, coffee production had always been characterized by distinct roles for women and men. After the mechanization of parts of the production process, men performed the higher-paid, skilled labor of operating the machines, whereas women continued to be in charge of the low-skill, low-wage, seasonal picking and sorting of beans. At the same time, the growing immiseration of peasant households that resulted from land concentration meant that more family members were sent out to work for wages. Even though women were relegated to undervalued tasks and paid less for them, their wages became a crucial component of household income. The significance of their economic contribution may in turn have enhanced women's status both within and beyond the household (Fowler-Salamini 1994: 64–8).

As processes of socioeconomic change interacted with gendered labor patterns, they also affected household structure. In some communities, from Brazil to Chile to Venezuela to Nicaragua, one result of the transition from a subsistence economy to a market-oriented one was a significant increase in the numbers of female-headed households. Studies suggest women headed as many as 25 to 45 percent of households in some communities, making this household form much more common than in Europe or the USA (Johnson 1978; Kuznesof & Oppenheimer 1985: 224). Given the contrast that widespread female headship presents both with the "paradigmatic" Euro-North-American cases, as well as with conventional "wisdom" about how patriarchy has operated historically in Latin America, it is worth exploring the causes and consequences of this phenomenon in some detail.

The best-studied case is that of São Paulo, Brazil, where female headship increased by about 50 percent (to almost 45 percent of all households) between 1765 and 1802. The increase was a result of new commercial opportunities that arose with the emergence of market-based exchange. Female-headed households were often production units; more than half were engaged in home-based textile production and involved the co-residence of multiple women, related and unrelated, who worked together. By 1836, the commercial opportunities that had given rise to female headship had all but disappeared as local textile production was obliterated by the arrival of cheap British imports. But while households headed by women were in serious economic straits, their numbers declined only slightly. This is because no new economic opportunities emerged that would have sustained households based on the stratification of male–female labor (as had been the case with the subsistence economy, and as would eventually be the case with factory production). In other words, female-headed households arose as a direct result of new commercial opportunities associated with the rise of the market, but they persisted, albeit in an impoverished condition, when these opportunities dried up and were not replaced by alternatives. The proto-industrial phase of home-based production that gave rise to female headship was very prolonged in São Paulo, where it lasted into the early twentieth century, and probably in many other communities in Latin America as well.

We know female headship was widespread and persistent in Latin America, and we can generate explanations for why this was so, but we know much less about the significance of this fact for the gender order. The fact that female-headed households in São Paolo were impoverished suggests they were an adaptation based more on "necessity than choice" (Kuznesof 1980: 606) and that their ubiquity should not be interpreted as reflecting the autonomy, much less the empowerment, of women. However, it should be noted that female headship, while sustained by poverty, first arose as a response to economic opportunity. Similarly, in Diriomo, Nicaragua, where

40 percent of households were female-headed in the late nineteenth century, it was associated with the expansion, not the contraction, of economic opportunities for women (Dore 2000b).

Moreover, whatever its *causes*, female headship may have had important *consequences* for the practice of patriarchy. How are male and female honor constructed when men are not always the breadwinners and women's labor and sexuality are not necessarily subject to the control of a husband or father? It is worth thinking about issues of autonomy and empowerment in historically comparative, rather than absolute, terms. For example, the status of poor women in the nineteenth century may appear more favorable when viewed against the increased economic subordination of working-class women occasioned by protective legislation and welfare programs in the early twentieth century. The renewed proliferation of female-headed households in the final decades of the twentieth century provides still another opportunity to assess their meaning. I return to these issues below.

A phenomenon related to headship was migration. Men and women moved in response to stratified economic opportunities, and the resulting geographies were unmistakably gendered. While men disproportionately found employment in agriculture and mining, female employment was often concentrated in urban locales. As a result, many late nineteenth-century cities – Caracas, Mexico City, São Paulo, Santiago, and others – were in a very real sense cities of (poor) women, in which women outnumbered men.[3] Female migrants concentrated in informal activities, including domestic service, petty commerce, and prostitution. After the turn of the century, as the pace of industrialization quickened, they entered the industrial workforce in increasing numbers, particularly such sectors as textile manufacturing (Wolfe 1993). Their public labors – washing at fountains, plying their wares in the market, soliciting clients on the street (Graham 1988), and, slightly later, toiling on the factory floor – became a subject of considerable concern to observers. One common response was to associate women's waged labor with sexual exploitation, prostitution, and promiscuity. In the pages of the labor press, lascivious bourgeois overseers stalked working women on the shop floor. "Labor's flesh . . . prostitution's flesh . . . the same misfortune," intoned one Puerto Rican anarchist periodical, articulating the link between economic and sexual exploitation that was a hallmark of this period (Suárez Findlay 1999: 150).

Gender, Modernity, and Civilization in the Twentieth Century

The turn of the twentieth century witnessed the genesis of new, increasingly politicized social groups, namely, the working class and the middle class. Much recent scholarship has argued that new class identities were intimately intertwined with gender and sexuality, as moral distinctions came to differentiate between social groups and demarcate class and racial hierarchies. For example, in mid-nineteenth-century Chile, public discussions of illegitimacy focused on the cross-class liaisons of poor women and wealthy men. But by the late nineteenth century, commentators portrayed out-of-wedlock birth as an attribute specific to, even constitutive of, plebeian status, in spite of ample evidence that men of all social classes fathered children outside of marriage (Milanich 2002: chap. 2). In Porfirian Mexico, meanwhile, the juxtaposition of (poor) prostitutes and (bourgeois) guardian angels, both recurring symbols in middle-class discourse, simultaneously implied moral distinctions as well as social demarcation.

Anxieties about a changing social order and aspirations for national progress were often telescoped into concerns about families and gender roles. As Sueann Caulfield (2001: 475) has noted, "gender played a primary role in defining and representing modernity and civilization, and . . . women were primary targets for reformers" seeking to promote progress while containing disorder. One recurring trope that characterized political discourse across the hemisphere during the first half of the twentieth century was the cult of working-class domesticity and the attendant ideology of the family wage. From Puerto Rico to Mexico to the Southern Cone, the rationalization, moralization, and modernization of the working-class family became touchstones of national progress and development. According to this vision, the family should properly consist of a male breadwinner and a dependent wife schooled in modern maternal skills, scientific hygiene, and state-of-the-art domestic know-how (Weinstein 1996; Klubock 1998; Suárez Findlay 1999; Rosemblatt 2000a; Vaughan 2000; Hutchison 2001). With this modern wife and mother at its helm, the working-class household would both domesticate working-class males and rear healthy and moral future workers. At different times and places, Catholics and liberals, labor leaders and multinationals, leftists, state authorities, and some feminists all propounded this family model.

A good example of this impetus to "rationalize domesticity" is rural development policy in post-revolutionary Mexico (Vaughan 2000). Teachers, nurses, and social workers participated in campaigns to reform the *campesino* household, introducing the corn mill, instructing women how to sanitize living quarters and prepare nutritional foods, distancing them from traditional healers, and schooling them in the virtues of modern medicine. Meanwhile, male campesinos were encouraged to embrace new roles as upstanding breadwinners who rejected violence and drunkenness. Ultimately, the purpose of such reforms was not to eliminate patriarchy but to modernize it. At the same time, even as this model of gender relations implied the economic subordination of wives to husbands, it could provide a wedge against male violence and irresponsibility. What is more, the "morally upstanding" and "properly constituted" household – when it was achieved – could accord a degree of social respectability to non-elite families.

This fixation on the household as a pillar of stability and a site for the inculcation of new social norms is on one level nothing new; it echoes similar discourses a century earlier in the aftermath of independence. The difference is that now ideas about family and gender order were linked to aspirations for modernity and development, and conservative political projects as well as populist and leftist ones espoused these gender ideals as part of broader developmentalist discourses. Another difference is that twentieth-century states, often in concert with the private sector, now had the wherewithal to promote their visions of gender through means other than just ideological suasion. They did so through educational programs (Weinstein 1996) but also through material incentives – namely, through the family wage and the creation of myriad other benefits contingent on formal marriage and legitimacy. The emerging industrial sector associated with mid-century Import Substituting Industrialization provided some male workers with the wages and benefits that allowed them to support dependent wives and children in keeping with the ideological prescription (Rosemblatt 2000a; Farnsworth-Alvear 2000). The result was evident in places like Chile, where marriage rates began to rise and illegitimacy rates to decline in the 1930s.

Ultimately, however, enduring cultural visions of household and family as sites of domestication, while ideologically powerful, could prove of limited efficacy in practice. In Chile's El Teniente copper mine, company officials sought to impose male-headed nuclear families among miners as a means of rooting and pacifying a transient and unreliable labor force. On one level, they succeeded: marriage became more prevalent and miners' households came to resemble more closely the model propounded by company officials. Yet in the end, such transformations did not lead to the pacification of the labor force. On the contrary, mining families became sites of a combative labor activism (Klubock 1998).

How, ultimately, should we evaluate the significance for women and men of this twentieth-century turn to domesticity? Both contemporaries and historians alike have tended to regard these gender prescriptions as "traditional." Yet such a characterization is misleading, in so far as patriarchal households of male workers and dependent females were not historically the only, and often not the most common, family form.[4] As discussed above, female headship was widespread in the nineteenth century. Another household role has also been associated with poor women: that of domestic servant (Graham 1988; Kuznesof 1989). If female headship may at times have accorded or reflected some measure of autonomy, and the role of working-class housewife and mother could garner a degree of social respectability, none of these attributes accrued to domestic service. Historically, service was symbolically and materially marked by baseness and dependence. Yet in Chile, much nineteenth-century prescriptive literature emphasized that poor women's proper destiny was not as wives and mothers but as domestics. In other words, poor women were first marked as servile dependents in others' households; only in the twentieth century were they exhorted to become housewives and mothers in their own right. Viewed from this perspective, the twentieth-century cult of domesticity, retrograde in its gender implications, appears progressive in terms of its class implications. "Wife" and "mother" have been privileged roles to which women of all social ranks could only recently aspire.[5]

Women Organizing: From Beneficence to Feminisms

If gender helped demarcate class, it also figured centrally into elite responses to growing class tensions and to the social disorder that appeared to stem from rapid social and economic change, immigration, the politicization of labor, and the spread of leftist political doctrines. Middle- and upper-class women became protagonists of charitable initiatives to improve the moral and material condition of the poor. This was of course true in other parts of the world as well, but female voluntarism was never generic; it reflected the felt needs of the particular social and political contexts in which it developed. In Argentina, elite women made the socialization of foreign immigrants and, especially, of their children an important focus of their charitable activities (Mead 2000). In the wake of increasingly violent labor strife in Chile, meanwhile, some elite women's organizations couched their mission in terms of the pressing need to assuage class tensions. One organization in the 1920s called for charitable initiatives that "generate rapprochement . . . between the different social classes, placing the rich person before the poor one, not as an enemy but as an older sibling, who can protect him and raise him up" (Larrain de Vicuña 1924: 9–10). In both instances, women tied their beneficent activities to the unity of the nation, whether across cultural or class divides.

Ironically, just as the ideology of domesticity became an increasingly hegemonic prescription for working-class women, groups of educated middle- and upper-class women began to question the legal and social bases of the patriarchal household and their own subordination within it. In the nineteenth century, women's social roles had come under scrutiny by individual authors – intellectuals such as the notable Peruvians Flora Tristán and Clorinda Matto de Turner, as well as the many authors who wrote for nascent women's presses in places like Puerto Rico and Brazil (Hahner 1990; Suárez Findlay 1999). But feminism as a distinct political movement associated with a specific reform agenda emerged in Latin America after the turn of the century. Thus, the early twentieth-century massification of politics incorporated not only new middle- and working-class constituencies but also female political activists, the so-called "first-wave feminists," who voiced critiques of the gender order. How these reformers understood "feminism" often varied widely, a point addressed below. This first wave waned after the first decades of the twentieth century, to be revived in the 1970s and 1980s, in the perhaps unlikely context of Cold War authoritarianism.

Feminist movements in Latin America were decisively marked by the national political contexts in which they evolved. If in the USA the women's rights movement was forged in the crucible of abolition, in Cuba feminism was indelibly marked by the struggle against Spanish colonial domination (a struggle in which women were active participants) and the tensions engendered by US imperialism. While Cuban feminists' goals were moderate compared to some ideas circulating at the time, their movement was linked to the "the revolutionary ferment" that characterized contemporary Cuban politics (Stoner 1991: 11). In Brazil, meanwhile, the founding of the republic in 1889 constituted the backdrop for the emergence of feminist activism. Debates about women's rights were framed through the familiar dialectics of "order and progress": where advocates equated female emancipation with modernity, their adversaries opposed it on the grounds that it was "anarchic" (Hahner 1990). The Mexican feminist movement came to fruition in the ideological ferment of the post-revolutionary period. Yet, ironically, revolutionary ideology may have made it harder, not easier, for feminists to make their voices heard. Virulent anti-clericalism and the belief that women were conservatives in thrall to the Catholic Church produced some particularly misogynistic popular representations of women's rights activists. Such characterizations were ironic indeed, given women's active participation on behalf of the revolutionary state as well as feminists' tendency to highlight, in keeping with prevailing nationalist currents, the distinctly Mexican nature of their movement (Olcott 2005). Finally, even as women's rights movements across the hemisphere bore the distinct imprints of national politics, Latin American feminists gained strength from transnational alliances consolidated in periodic pan-American reunions beginning in the 1920s (Miller 1991; Lavrin 1995).

Early twentieth-century women's rights activists organized around several recurring issues. One was opposition to the nineteenth-century legal reforms that had deprived married women of authority over their children and property and stripped illegitimate offspring of basic legal rights. In some countries, such as Cuba, legal reform was the principal focus of feminists' efforts. But elsewhere, other crucial areas of activism gained attention as well, including women's social and economic rights, educational and employment opportunities, and the welfare and protection of working women and children. Maternalism – cultural convictions about the special aptitudes and interests of women as mothers – constituted a politically and culturally palatable raison d'etre for female political involvement and constitutes one of the defining characteristics of Latin American women's activism, feminist and otherwise.

Notably, and in contrast to the United States and Great Britain, female suffrage was not initially a priority of feminist activism. This was likely because in political environments characterized by very limited suffrage and corrupt or unstable electoral processes, the vote had less practical and symbolic import. When Brazil became the second Latin American country to grant women the vote in 1932, property and literacy restrictions meant that just 5 percent of the population, male or female, was eligible to cast a ballot. Moreover, five years later, in 1937, Getúlio Vargas established the Estado Novo and suspended open elections. Neither men nor women voted again until 1946 (Miller 1991). When women ultimately did acquire the vote – a process that spanned more than three decades, from 1929 when Ecuador granted female suffrage to 1961 in Paraguay (Chaney 1979: 169) – the process followed very different patterns. In some countries, female suffrage resulted from a synergistic coalition of feminists and labor activists for whom it was one component of a broader project of enfranchisement. Elsewhere, as in Ecuador, it came at the behest of conservatives who wagered that women's supposed traditionalism would enhance conservatives' electoral prospects. Finally, female suffrage could reflect a largely non-ideological bid to enhance an authoritarian leader's own power, as was the case in Trujillo's Dominican Republic (Miller 1991).

To what female constituencies did feminism ultimately respond? This question highlights the complex class and racial politics of Latin American women's rights movements. The leadership of early twentieth-century feminist movements was almost always drawn from the upper rungs of society, and, in some countries, feminism was essentially a movement of an educated elite. In Cuba, for example, Afro-Cuban and working-class women were apparently absent from feminist cadres. However, such exclusivity did not characterize all movements in the hemisphere. Bourgeois, white feminists in Puerto Rico drew assiduous boundaries between themselves and their plebeian and Afro-Puerto Rican counterparts, but some working-class feminists in Puerto Rico nevertheless elaborated alternative feminist critiques. In the Southern Cone, working-class feminists also generated conversations about women and labor, gender, economics, and sexuality. Indeed, from its inception, feminism in Latin America was never a single, coherent doctrine or movement but was characterized by an eclectic range of ideological positions – liberal, Catholic, anarchist, socialist, etc. – leading scholars to refer to Latin American "feminisms." Thus, the recurring accusation lodged by the left that "feminism" is a bourgeois distraction ignores both the eclecticism of feminism as an intellectual project and its social diversity as a movement.

But however inaccurate, the assertion raises the important fact that from their origins to the present day, women's rights movements in Latin America have been indelibly marked by the politics of class. Indeed, if there is anything distinctly "Latin American" about Latin American feminisms it is perhaps this: that political movements for women's emancipation have developed in the context of profound, pervasive socioeconomic inequalities and that feminism as an intellectual project has evolved in dialogue with Marxism and its progeny. Socialist feminists first posed questions about the roots of female oppression. Was it patriarchy and men that were the central issue, or capitalism and the bourgeoisie? Was subordination primarily economic or social in nature? Such debates presaged the close but conflictual relationship between feminism and the left in twentieth-century Latin America; they would become even more pressing and pervasive in the context of feminism's second wave. Such tensions are intellectual, reflecting enduring debates over the primacy of gender versus class. They are also strategic and organizational, posing questions about the proper relationship of feminist movements to male-dominated partisan politics, especially those of the left (Saporta Sternbach et al. 1992). If class has long been a flashpoint of feminist politics in Latin America, race and ethnicity have had a much more muted presence in these debates and dialogues, though this situation is changing.

Gender, Revolutions, and Reactions

If feminism in Latin America has developed in a close but conflictual relationship with the left, progressive and populist movements and governments have long been attuned to women as constituents and to the political significance of gender. In attempting to remake the social, economic, and political order, these movements – whether the Mexican, Cuban, or Nicaraguan Revolutions or the governments of Perón or Allende – have espoused changes to the gender order. Fidel Castro famously proclaimed women's emancipation to be "a revolution within the revolution." Yet, as one scholar has noted, the "implicit meanings" of self-styled progressives' gendered messages "at times contradicted the explicit message." Indeed, "their manipulation of gendered concepts for political ends leads one to question the revolutionary character" of such regimes (Deutsch 1991: 261, 305). When viewed from the perspective of gender politics, in other words, the revolutionary experiments of twentieth-century Latin America appear rather less radical.

From the Cuban *mambisas* who opposed Spanish colonialism to the schoolteachers who worked on behalf of a revolutionary Mexican state to the women's groups that organized against the human rights violations and economic policies of Cold War authoritarian regimes in Central America and the Southern Cone, women in modern Latin America have long mobilized in the service of self-styled progressive and populist projects. Women's involvement in the Peronist movement in Argentina is just one notable example. The *Partido Femenino Peronista*, created in 1949, was in principle independent from and equal to other branches of the Peronist government, in contrast to the subordinate position that characterized women's sections of most Latin American political parties. In just three years, the party attracted some 500,000 members, most of them working-class women with no prior political experience (Deutsch 1991: 273).

Yet Peronism's posture vis-à-vis women mirrored its posture toward workers: the idea was to mobilize previously disenfranchised sectors strategically under the tutelage of the Peronist state, not to empower them as autonomous political subjects. Peronism's tactical stance toward its female constituency is hardly unique in this regard. One Chilean commentator likened women's presence in politics to a Greek chorus: ushered onto the stage at strategic moments, once their bit part is over they are hustled unceremoniously back into the wings (Winn 1995: 343). Indeed, while progressive political movements at times resulted in very real gains for women – whether suffrage under Perón or the sweeping educational, social, and economic reforms benefiting women in Castro's Cuba – there may still be reason to scrutinize the motives of self-styled reformers. The scholarly consensus seems to be that the mobilization of women and the use of egalitarian rhetoric have tended to reflect as much calculated political strategy as genuine commitment to gender parity or women's emancipation.

The cultivation of female constituencies and the use of gendered rhetoric have hardly been the exclusive prerogative of the left. Women have mobilized on behalf of right-wing movements and causes as well: they participated in fascist and Nazi movements in the Southern Cone, constituted an important Somocista constituency, and subsequently comprised a significant proportion of demobilized Contras, to give just a few examples (González and Kampwirth 2001). And in perhaps the best-studied instance, right-wing women's mobilization became a galvanizing milestone for opposition to the leftist government of Salvador Allende in Chile (Power 2002).

Examining right- and left-wing social movements through the lens of gender reveals otherwise invisible commonalities and overlaps between ideological camps that on the surface appear diametrically opposed. Perhaps the most pervasive feature shared by many social movements involving women in Latin America is the invocation of maternalism. In the early twentieth century, women were deemed uniquely qualified stewards of charitable initiatives due to their maternal sentiments; the objects par excellence of these charitable endeavors were poor mothers and children. Maternalism has also been a recurring attribute of Latin American feminisms, which have tended to emphasize "difference" over "equality." That is, they have often invoked women's superior moral status as justification for their entry into public fora and their social roles as necessitating compensatory and protective measures. First-wave feminists sought to grant mothers concrete legal rights consistent with the cultural veneration of motherhood. More recently, maternalism has been in evidence in the resurgence of women's political activism in the 1970s and 1980s, when the political repression and economic hardships associated with Cold War dictatorships and structural adjustment catalyzed a wave of protest among both second-wave feminists and the *movimientos de mujeres* (women's groups that address the concerns of poor women but do not identify gender equity as a primary objective of their activism).

Perhaps the best-known, and most successful, iteration of maternalism in this context was that deployed by the *Madres of the Plaza de Mayo* in response to the human-rights violations of the Argentine dictatorship. At a moment when civil society had been paralyzed by repression, a group of 14 women appeared in April 1977 in the historic Plaza de Mayo in central Buenos Aires to ask the simple yet politically momentous question, *¿Dónde están?* (Where are they?) Cloaked in the maternalist mantle, they could plausibly maintain that they merely wished to locate their disappeared family members. While by no means immune to the repression – several Madres themselves became victims of the regime – there is little doubt that their status as self-styled apolitical mothers accorded them some measure of protection. It was simply not politically tenable for the dictatorship to pursue middle-aged matrons with the same ruthless brutality it had employed against other sectors of the opposition. In addition, at least initially the regime failed to recognize the political content of the women's actions because it could not fathom housewives spearheading a serious challenge to its power. Subsequently the Madres universalized their protest, presenting themselves as mothers not just of their own disappeared children but of all Argentine young people, indeed of a suffering Argentine nation writ large.

Thus, maternalism is a persistent feature of women's political activism – and of the discursive landscape of modern Latin American politics more generally. It characterizes political rhetoric on both the right and left, among both self-identified feminists and activist women who do not identify as feminists. It has been marshaled by both female and male political actors to justify public activism by women, to advance political goals promoted by them, and to garner their support for predominantly male-led political movements. Maternalism has surely proven so powerful and so persistent because of its ideological plasticity and its cultural resonance. At the same time, it is not some timeless and uncontested cultural discourse, a sort of *marianismo* (cult of the Virgin Mary) for the public sphere. Both scholars and activists continue to debate whether maternalist rhetoric reflects more strategy or conviction on the part of those who invoke it, and the extent to which it may challenge or merely reinscribe deeply rooted constructions of public and private.

Gender at the Turn of the Twenty-first Century: Liberalism Redux

Ironically, while maternalism retains its ideological resonance, the material reality of full-time motherhood is an increasingly exceptional one for many women in the region, due in no small part to contemporary neoliberal policies. The gendered impact of the Pinochet dictatorship illustrates this contradiction between prescription and reality. While the regime touted self-sacrificing domesticity as the highest calling of Chilean womanhood, its economic program ultimately contravened such prescriptions. Under Pinochet, female labor-force participation increased, as did male abandonment and female household headship.

Such patterns are in evidence throughout the hemisphere today. The numbers of women entering the labor market more than quadrupled from 1950 to 1980. It seems particularly appropriate to conclude an essay on women, family, and gender in Latin America with a brief discussion of contemporary economic trends because so many critiques of neoliberalism are refracted through the lens of gender. Critics have argued that the dismantling of social welfare nets, the feminization of poverty, and the exploitation of female workers demonstrate that neoliberal economic policies are particularly detrimental to women. Indeed, perhaps the most potent symbol of a rapacious global capitalism, the *maquiladora* assembly plants along the US–Mexican border, are quintessentially gendered. As critics have noted, two-thirds of the maquila labor force is female, comprised primarily of very young women who labor in terrible conditions for low wages. Gendered forms of labor control – pregnancy tests, sexual harassment – keep workers in line (Fernández-Kelly 1983). Exploitation within the factory is further linked, on a conceptual level, to the unsolved murders of hundreds of women, many of them maquila workers, in the vicinity of Ciudad Juárez since the early 1990s.

There is no arguing the gendered impact of neoliberal economic policy or the particular toll it has taken on poor women in Latin America. At the same time, as Heidi Tinsman (2000) has argued, such critiques can devolve into a simplistic "paradigm of the suffering woman," which rests on assumptions about the peculiar iniquity of exploiting *female* workers and, on a broader level, about the undesirability of female waged labor. Such critiques further assume that capitalist exploitation and patriarchy are "mechanically related," such that "their intensities necessarily rise and fall together." Rural women's experiences under Pinochet, to cite just one example, suggest otherwise. Even as policies that pushed women into rural waged labor engendered "new forms of labor exploitation, political repression and personal suffering," they also catalyzed "the erosion of male dominance, an increase in women's political agency, and the emergence of gender equality as an ideal" (Tinsman 2000: 147, 155). The impact of neoliberalism on women, and on men, is thus multifaceted and potentially contradictory.

These patterns are not without historical precedent. Latin America's late twentieth-century neoliberal experiment recapitulates an economic model first implemented a century before. To what extent has contemporary neoliberalism reproduced the gendered patterns described above? The social-scientific scholarship on women and contemporary economic development and, more recently, on gender and neoliberalism, have hardly addressed this question. This conclusion will no more than suggest some initial points of historical comparison.

Economic restructuring at the end of the twentieth century has clearly had a profound impact on women's work, household structure, and gender relations, as it did in the nineteenth century. Perhaps most obviously, contemporary trends have generated new, though circumscribed, employment opportunities for women. Today key export sectors, from agro-industry to garment and electronics manufacturing, exhibit a predilection for young, female workers. In low-wage export sectors across Latin America, as in other parts of the developing world, women workers are considered nimble, flexible, docile, and unpoliticized – and may be paid less than men. Female employment in the formal export sector contrasts both with the nineteenth century, when women were often, though not always, relegated to the informal periphery of the export economy, as well as with mid-twentieth-century industrialization, when the industrial workforce was (or became) overwhelmingly male (Farnsworth-Alvear 2000).

Yet even as women are more likely to be employed in formal-sector jobs, this fact matters less due to the casualization of this employment. Because of subcontracting, the seasonal nature of agro-industrial labor, the routine use of temporary labor contracts, and their definition as unskilled, formal-sector jobs no longer imply security or benefits. They contrast in particular with the relatively well-paid jobs that benefited male workers employed in capital-intensive industrial production at mid-century. In other words, if in the past there usually existed a clear distinction between formal and informal labor, with women concentrated disproportionately in the latter sector, today the distinction has lost much of its salience. What is more, even as they enter the formal economy in greater numbers, women continue to be heavily concentrated in the informal and service sectors – employment that is often, as in the case of the informal periphery of the nineteenth-century Costa Rican banana economy, generated by the export sector itself.[6] For these reasons, despite superficial differences, it is probably important not to overstate women's changing structural location within labor markets.

Meanwhile, the declining ability of male workers to support a family and the increasing significance of women's wages have resulted in distinct, though again by no means predictable, effects on gender relations within and beyond the household. For example, these economic patterns have apparently been associated with an increase in female-headed households, at least in some countries or regions: today, some 20 percent of all households in Latin America are headed by women, while in the Caribbean the figure is 26 percent. Gendered patterns of labor migration are also part of these processes. Both female headship and gendered migration are, of course, not new; yet they are often treated as such in the social-scientific literature.

Meanwhile, the ideological frameworks within which these material processes are couched also echo the past. The paradigm of the suffering woman worker has a long historical genealogy. As part of this paradigm, contemporary critics of liberalism draw conceptual links between economic and sexual exploitation, as they did a century ago. Today as yesterday, women's wage labor is frequently associated with sexual harassment (as with the maquila workers) and with promiscuity (as in the anxieties of men who fear wage-earning wives are cheating on them) (Tinsman 2002). And contemporary critiques of neoliberalism often fault it with no less than the "breakdown of the family" – an assessment that mirrors the social panic over working-class families and women at the turn of the last century.

Viewed from a historical perspective, patterns of "family breakdown" – widespread female employment, gendered migration, female headship, and the like – are hardly anomalous in either their late nineteenth- or late twentieth-century renditions. Rather, what appears historically exceptional is what comes in between: the nuclear family models undergirded by a male breadwinner's family wage in the industrial sectors of the mid-twentieth century. Much more systematic analysis would be required to substantiate such an interpretation. Here is yet another example of how attentiveness to gender can help to tease out threads of social, economic, and political change and continuity in modern Latin America.

NOTES

1 There are some conspicuous omissions in this survey, which reflect the uneven coverage of scholarship on the modern period. For example, while class is a key concept, race and ethnicity make all too fleeting appearances. While Suárez Findlay (1999), Caulfield (2001), and Martinez-Alier (1974) deal with race, ethnicity, and gender in the modern period, it is hard to avoid the conclusion that, as a field, colonial history has dealt much more thoroughly with these issues. Another omission is the Catholic Church and religion in general, an ellipsis that once again reflects the available scholarship.

2 This is perhaps ironic given that a thick vein of early scholarship on women in Latin America in the 1970s dealt with the relationship between capitalism and patriarchy. Authored

primarily by social scientists, it focused on the contemporary context. See Caulfield (2001) for an overview of this literature.

3   In Santiago in 1907, for example, there were 118 women for every 100 men (Hutchison 2001: 25). This pattern was not necessarily new; women outnumbered men in some late colonial cities, such as Mexico City. However, nineteenth-century economic processes appear to have made it more widespread.

4   Dore (1997) discusses the persistence of this "imagined household" in political rhetoric, historical scholarship, and popular opinion.

5   This point is made in Milanich (2005). More work clearly needs to be done not only on prescriptive discourses but also on the actual prevalence of these different roles – household head, servant, wife – and the meanings that accrued to them in different places at different times.

6   Talcott (2004) discusses how the employment of women in the Colombian flower industry creates a demand for the informal employment of older women as child-care workers. As in Putnam's (2002) account of the Costa Rican banana industry, the formal sector generates and is subsidized by informal female labor.

BIBLIOGRAPHY

Besse, S. (1996) *Restructuring Patriarchy: The Modernization of Gender Inequality in Brazil, 1914–1940*. University of North Carolina Press, Chapel Hill.

Burns, E. B. & Charlip, J. (2002) *Latin America: A Concise Interpretive History*, 7th ed. Prentice-Hall, Upper Saddle River.

Caulfield, S. (2001) "The History of Gender in the Historiography of Latin America," *Hispanic American Historical Review*, 81, pp. 3–4, pp. 449–90.

Chaney, E. (1979) *Supermadre: Women in Politics in Latin America*. University of Texas Press, Austin.

Chasteen, J. C. (2001) *Born of Blood and Fire: A Concise History of Latin America*. W. W. Norton, New York.

Cicerchia, R. (1998) *Historia de la vida privada en la Argentina*. Editorial Troquel, Buenos Aires.

Deutsch, S. M. (1991) "Gender and Sociopolitical Change in Twentieth-Century Latin America," *Hispanic American Historical Review*, 71:2, pp. 259–306.

Dias, M. S. O. (1995) *Power and Everyday Life: The Lives of Working Women in Nineteenth-Century Brazil*. Rutgers University Press, New Brunswick.

Díaz, A. (2001) "Women, Order and Progress in Guzmán Blanco's Venezuela, 1870–1888." In R. Salvatore, C. Aguirre, & G. Joseph (eds.), *Crime and Punishment in Latin America*. Duke University Press, Durham.

Dore, E. (1997) "The Holy Family: Imagined Households in Latin American History." In E. Dore (ed.), *Gender Politics in Latin America: Debates in Theory and Practice*. Monthly Review Press, New York, pp. 101–17.

Dore, E. (2000a) "One Step Forward, Two Steps Back: Gender and the State in the Long Nineteenth Century." In E. Dore & M. Molyneux (eds.), *Hidden Histories of Gender and the State in Latin America*. Duke University Press, Durham, pp. 3–32.

Dore, E. (2000b) "Property, Households, and the Public Regulation of Domestic Life: Diriomo, Nicaragua, 1840–1900." In E. Dore & M. Molyneux (eds.), *Hidden Histories of Gender and the State in Latin America*. Duke University Press, Durham, pp. 147–71.

Dore, E. & Molyneux, M. (eds.) (2000) *Hidden Histories of Gender and the State in Latin America*. Duke University Press, Durham.

Earle, R. (2000) "Rape and the Anxious Republic: Revolutionary Colombia, 1810–1830." In E. Dore & M. Molyneux (eds.), *Hidden Histories of Gender and the State in Latin America*. Duke University Press, Durham, pp. 127–46.

Farnsworth-Alvear, A. (2000) *Dulcinea in the Factory: Myths, Morals, Men, and Women in Colombia's Industrial Experiment, 1905–1960*. Duke University Press, Durham.

Felstiner, M. L. (1983) "Family Metaphors: The Language of an Independence Revolution," *Comparative Studies in Society and History*, 25, pp. 155–80.

Fernández-Kelly, M. P. (1983) *For We Are Sold, I and My People: Women and Industry in Mexico's Frontier*. SUNY Press, Albany.

Fowler-Salamini, H. (1994) "Gender, Work, and Coffee in Córdoba, Veracruz, 1850–1910." In H. Fowler-Salamini & M. K. Vaughan (eds.), *Creating Spaces, Shaping Transitions: Women of the Mexican Countryside, 1850–1990*. University of Arizona Press, Tucson, pp. 51–73.

French, J. & James, D. (eds.) (1997) *The Gendered Worlds of Latin American Women Workers: From the Household and Factory to the Union Hall and Ballot Box*. Duke University Press, Durham.

French, W. (1992) "Prostitutes and Guardian Angels: Women, Work, and the Family in Porfirian Mexico," *Hispanic American Historical Review*, 72:4, pp. 529–53.

González, V. & Kampwirth, K. (eds.) (2001) *Radical Women in Latin America: Left and Right*. Pennsylvania State University Press, University Park.

Graham, S. L. (1988) *House and Street: The Domestic World of Servants and Masters in Nineteenth-Century Rio de Janeiro*. Cambridge University Press, New York.

Graham, S. L. (2002) *Caetana Says No: Women's Stories from a Brazilian Slave Society*. Cambridge University Press, New York.

Guy, D. (1981) "Women, Peonage and Industrialization: Argentina, 1810–1914," *Latin American Research Review*, 16, pp. 65–89.

Guy, D. (2000) "Parents Before the Tribunals: The Legal Construction of Patriarchy in Argentina." In E. Dore & M. Molyneux (eds.), *Hidden Histories of Gender and the State in Latin America*. Duke University Press, Durham, pp. 172–93.

Hahner, J. (1980) "Feminism, Women's Rights, and the Suffrage Movement in Brazil, 1850–1932," *Latin American Research Review*, 15:1, pp. 65–111.

Hahner, J. (1990) *Emancipating the Female Sex: The Struggle for Women's Rights in Brazil, 1850–1940*. Duke University Press, Durham.

Hutchison, E. (2001) *Labors Appropriate to Their Sex: Gender, Labor, and Politics in Urban Chile, 1900–1930*. Duke University Press, Durham.

Johnson, A. H. (1978) "The Impact of Market Agriculture on Family and Household Structure in Nineteenth-century Chile," *Hispanic American Historical Review*, 59:4, pp. 625–48.

Joseph, G. (2001) "A Historiographical Revolution in Our Time," *Hispanic American Historical Review*, 81:3–4, pp. 445–7.

Keen, B. & Haynes, K. (2004) *A History of Latin America*, 7th ed. Houghton Mifflin, Boston.

Klubock, T. (1998) *Contested Communities: Class, Gender, and Politics in Chile's El Teniente Copper Mine, 1904–1951*. Duke University Press, Durham.

Kuznesof, E. (1980) "The Role of the Female-headed Household in Brazilian Modernization: São Paulo, 1765–1836," *Journal of Social History*, 13, pp. 589–613.

Kuznesof, E. (1989) "A History of Domestic Service in Spanish America, 1492–1980." In E. Chaney & M. Garcia Castro (eds.), *Muchachas No More: Household Workers in Latin America and the Caribbean*. Temple University Press, Philadelphia, pp. 17–35.

Kuznesof, E. & Oppenheimer, R. (1985) "The Family and Society in Nineteenth-century Latin America: An Historiographical Introduction," *Journal of Family History*, 10:3, pp. 215–34.

Larrain de Vicuña, M. (1924) "Seamos cristianos de verdad," *Almanaque del Patronato de la Infancia*. Año V. Imprenta Cervantes, Santiago, pp. 9–10.

Lavrín, A. (1995) *Women, Feminism and Social Change in Argentina, Chile and Uruguay, 1890–1940*. University of Nebraska Press, Lincoln.

Lavrín, A. (1998) "International Feminisms: Latin American Alternatives," *Gender and History*, 10:3, pp. 519–34.

Martínez-Alier, V. (1974) *Marriage, Class and Colour in Nineteenth-century Cuba: A Study of Racial Attitudes and Sexual Values in a Slave Society*. Cambridge University Press, New York.

Mead, K. (2000) "Beneficent Maternalism: Argentine Motherhood in Comparative Perspective, 1880–1920," *Journal of Women's History*, 12:3, pp. 120–45.

Milanich, N. (2002) "The Children of Fate: Families, Class and the State in Chile, 1857–1930." PhD dissertation, Yale University.

Milanich, N. (2005) "From Domestic Servant to Working-class Housewife: Women, Labor, and Family in Chile," *Estudios Interdisciplinarios de América Latina y el Caribe*, 16:1, pp. 11–39.

Miller, F. (1991) *Latin American Women and the Search for Social Justice*. University Press of New England, Hanover.

Molyneux, M. (1986) "No God, No Boss, No Husband: Anarchist Feminism in Nineteenth-century Argentina," *Latin American Perspectives*, 13:1, pp. 119–45.

Olcott, J. (2005) *Revolutionary Women in Post-Revolutionary Mexico*. Duke University Press, Durham.

Power, M. (2002) *Right-Wing Women in Chile: Feminine Power and the Struggle Against Allende, 1964–1973*. Pennsylvania State University Press, University Park.

Putnam, L. (2002) *The Company They Kept: Migrants and the Politics of Gender in Caribbean Costa Rica*. University of North Carolina Press, Chapel Hill.

Rodríguez, S. E. (2000) "Civilizing Domestic Life in the Central Valley of Costa Rica, 1750–1850." In E. Dore & M. Molyneux (eds.), *Hidden Histories of Gender and the State in Latin America*. Duke University Press, Durham, pp. 85–107.

Roseberry, W. (1989) *Anthropologies and Histories. Essays in Culture, History, and Political Economy*. Rutgers University Press, New Brunswick.

Rosemblatt, K. (2000a) *Gendered Compromises: Political Cultures and the State in Chile, 1920–1950*. University of North Carolina Press, Chapel Hill.

Rosemblatt, K. (2000b) "Domesticating Men: State Building and Class Compromise in Popular-Front Chile." In E. Dore & M. Molyneux (eds.), *Hidden Histories of Gender and the State in Latin America*. Duke University Press, Durham, pp. 262–90.

Saporta Sternbach, N., et al. (1992) "Feminisms in Latin America: From Bogotá to San Bernardo," *Signs*, 17:2, pp. 393–434.

Scott, J. (1986) "Gender: A Useful Category of Historical Analysis," *American Historical Review*, 91:5, pp. 1053–75.

Scott, J. (1988) "Women's History." In J. Scott, *Gender and the Politics of History*. Columbia University Press, New York, pp. 15–27.

Stern, S. (1995) *The Secret History of Gender: Women, Men, and Power in Late Colonial Mexico*. University of North Carolina Press, Chapel Hill.

Stoner, K. L. (1991) *From the House to the Streets: The Cuban Woman's Movement for Legal Change, 1898–1940*. Duke University Press, Durham.

Suárez Findlay, E. (1999) *Imposing Decency: The Politics of Sexuality and Race in Puerto Rico, 1870–1920*. Duke University Press, Durham.

Talcott, M. (2004) "Gendered Webs of Development and Resistance: Women, Children, and Flowers in Bogotá," *Signs*, 29:2, pp. 465–89.

Tinsman, H. (2000) "Reviving Feminist Materialism: Gender and Neo-liberalism in Pinochet's Chile," *Signs*, 26:1, pp. 145–88.

Tinsman, H. (2002) *Partners in Conflict: The Politics of Gender, Sexuality, and Labor in the Chilean Agrarian Reform, 1950–1973*. Duke University Press, Durham.

Vaughan, M. K. (1997) *Cultural Politics in Revolution: Teachers, Peasants, and Schools in Mexico, 1930–40*. University of Arizona Press, Tucson.

Vaughan, M. K. (2000) "Modernizing Patriarchy: State Policies, Rural Households, and Women in Mexico, 1930–1940." In E. Dore & M. Molyneux (eds.), *Hidden Histories of Gender and the State in Latin America*. Duke University Press, Durham, pp. 194–214.

Weinstein, B. (1996) *For Social Peace in Brazil: Industrialists and the Remaking of the Working Class in São Paulo, 1920–1964*. University of North Carolina Press, Chapel Hill.

Winn, P. (1995) *Americas: The Changing Face of Latin America and the Caribbean*, 2nd ed. University of California Press, Berkeley.

Wolfe, J. (1993) Working Women, Working Men: São Paulo and the Rise of Brazil's Industrial Working Class, 1900–1955. Duke University Press, Durham.

Chapter Twenty-Seven

IDENTITY, ETHNICITY, AND "RACE"

Peter Wade

Background

The assertiveness of indigenous and Afro-Latin peoples in Latin America has a long history. Rebellions, escape from enslavement, the maintenance of indigenous and African cultural practices in religious and other domains, struggles to retain land and form new communities – all this forms part of the background to Afro-Latin and indigenous identity formation from the mid-twentieth century. The background also includes the process of indigenous and black people becoming *mestizos* (mixed people); of slaves becoming free (and in some cases acquiring their own slaves); of communities of escaped slaves (*palenques* and *quilombos*) seeking work on nearby haciendas and asking Catholic priests to administer rites for them; of slave, free black, and indigenous people forming lay brotherhoods attached to the Church; of struggling for rights as citizens of the new republics, with no assertion of ethnic identity but rather a claim to equality and, if anything, disavowal of black or indigenous culture – or at least a view that such culture needed modernizing.

Take the case of indigenous people of the Cauca region of Colombia in the late nineteenth century (Sanders 2003: 35–7). In their struggle for land against liberal depredations, they deployed both a discourse of equality for all citizens and a discourse that pointed up their particular status as *indios*. The latter included references to their own wretchedness, lack of sense, and helplessness. This is a complex mixture of self-assertion and self-denigration. Take again the case of the *Frente Negra Brasileira* (FNB) of 1930s Brazil (Andrews 1991). This was an early example of black political protest, already being aired in the burgeoning black-owned press, against immigration policies that favored Europeans, the de facto disenfranchisement of many blacks, and the domination of the trade unions by white immigrants. Yet the FNB was elitist, avowed a civilizing mission for Afro-Brazilians, and ended up in an alliance with quasi-fascist tendencies in Brazilian politics. Or take the case of Cuba in the early 1900s when some Afro-Cuban leaders formed the *Partido Independiente de Color* (PIC) (Helg 1995). They were fighting for the inclusion of Afro-Cubans into the political and economic structures of the new republic, after their huge contribution to the wars of independence. The PIC's name suggested an explicit assertion of black identity, yet this was very contested. Other Afro-Cuban leaders opposed the PIC, many ordinary Afro-Cubans did not vote for it, while the Conservative Party formed alliances with the PIC in order to split the Liberal vote. Overall, the main project of the PIC – and other Liberal Afro-Cuban leaders – was one of integration not separation. The goal was equality of liberal-style citizenship, a society where race really did not matter. These examples alone show the complexity of indigenous and Afro-Latin ethnic assertiveness.

Much analysis of Latin American ethnic mobilization, especially with regard to Afro-Latins, has emphasized its historic weakness (Field 1994; Hanchard 1994; Winant 1994; Brysk 1996). Comparisons are drawn with the USA and the successes of ethnic social movements there. It is argued that Latin American societies were typically formed around the idea of *mestizaje* (racial and cultural mixture) as the basis for nation building and that definitions of ethnic and racial identity are highly subjective and shift according to context. This was more so in some nations than others. In Guatemala and Peru, for example, discourses of mestizaje were at times subordinate to discourses that emphasized the separation of indigenous people from mestizos (or *ladinos*, the term used in Central America for non-indigenous people). The concept of mestizaje allows a certain fluidity around ethnic identity: intermediate categories between white and indigenous and black are socially recognized and this defuses clear oppositions between these three polar categories (De la Cadena 2000). Mixed people who have links to the black and/or indigenous ends of the spectrum also have links to the white category, links that are socially recognized and quite possibly more highly valued. This leads to a lack of clear boundaries between categories and the possibility that lighter-skinned blacks or indigenous people who can re-identify as mestizo will not feel any political solidarity with those they see as lower down the socioracial scale than themselves. All this underwrites the widespread idea in Latin American countries that racial identity and racism are not important issues: the myth of racial democracy acts as a hegemonic ideology that undermines ethnic consciousness. Instead, class has often been seen as the most important dimension of inequality and identity, both by scholars and by lay Latin Americans, with ethnic identities either being subsumed by or struggling against class. The examples cited above show that, while ethnic mobilization can and has occurred in these conditions, it is often riven with contradictions and tensions and does not necessarily resonate with the bulk of Afro-Latin and indigenous populations. Approaches that emphasize inherent structural obstacles to ethnic mobilization in Latin America are not entirely displaced by, but still have to confront, the evident rise of black and indigenous movements. These are linked to changing national and transnational dynamics, rather than being permanently blocked by particular features of Latin American socioracial structures.

The Emergence and Shape of Ethnic Movements

Indigenous and Afro-Latin movements took off from about the 1960s (Kearney 1996; Wade 1997; Warren 1998; Warren & Jackson 2003). The Bolivian *Movimiento Indio Tupac Katari* dates from 1962, while in Mexico, the National Council of Indigenous Peoples was formed in 1975, and in Colombia, the Regional Indigenous Council of Cauca, formed in 1971, drew on local Paéz and Guambiano indigenous populations. The Central American pan-Maya movement dates from about the mid-1980s, although with roots in the early 1970s, when educated Mayas, who were often the beneficiaries of 1950s Church-based educational programs, began to come of age; the Council of Maya Organizations of Guatemala was founded in the late 1980s. It is worth noting that these movements tapped into a global phenomenon: in the USA, the National Indian Youth Council was established in 1961 and the American Indian Movement in 1968. Meanwhile, in Australia, the Federal Council for Advancement of Aboriginals was founded in 1959.

Afro-Latin organization dates from a little later. In Brazil, the *Movimento Negro Unificado* was founded in 1978. In Colombia, small university-based groups laid the basis for a national organization, *Cimarrón* (1982). The international context of the US black social movement, African decolonization, and protest against South Africa's apartheid regime fed these movements. More generally, both indigenous and Afro-Latin movements were part of the worldwide trend of the so-called new social movements which moved away from classic left-wing-oriented political protest, based on concepts of the working class and class struggle, toward multiple sites of resistance around more specific issues and identities (sexuality, gender, ethnicity, environment, housing, land).

The Afro-Latin and indigenous movements are very heterogeneous. In Brazil and Colombia, the black movement includes organized groups such as the *Movimento Negro Unificado*, but can also encompass study groups in universities, carnival groups, rap and other music groups, Afro-Brazilian religious centers, theater and dance companies, groups of black artists and writers, local peasant associations, urban neighborhood groups, black politicians running for office, Church-based organizations such as the *Pastoral Negro* or *Afro-Americano*, and some professional associations that have a significant black presence. Indigenous movements encompass national and local organizations, peasant associations, village councils, groups of Church-trained indigenous catechists, research groups, associations of indigenous lawyers, indigenous politicians, and so on. At the risk of overgeneralization, it is commonly the better-educated and more urban-based who tend to drive these movements forward.

The agendas of these movements are equally varied. Rights to land and, more broadly, territory (i.e., expanses of land, which underwrite a cultural way of life, rather than subsistence plots) have been central, although more so to indigenous than Afro-Latin movements. Language is also important, with campaigns for bilingual education and indigenous teacher training. Demands for broader cultural rights and human rights include ending discrimination in the labor market and revaluing the image of Afro-Latin and indigenous identities as represented in the public sphere (e.g., the media, education). Political demands often center on getting Afro-Latin and indigenous representatives into elected government and other state entities and on obtaining greater autonomy for indigenous and Afro-Latin communities.

To give some idea of the variety of the black social movement, I will selectively outline some of its aspects in Colombia. The black movement started with small university-based groups (Wade 1995, 1999). One such was called Soweto – attesting to the transnational vision of its founders – and included Juan de Dios Mosquera, a black student from the Pacific coastal region of the country, a poor and underdeveloped area that has historically been 80–90 percent black. These students were as disillusioned by the inability of current left-wing discourses to address issues of racism and racial identity as they were inspired by the example of US and South African black resistance. Mosquera, who was reading Martin Luther King, Frantz Fanon, and Léopold Senghor (an African intellectual who, with the Martinican Aimé Césaire, founded the *négritude* movement in 1930s Paris), went on to found *Cimarrón* as a national black organization. Its name is the colonial term for the escaped slaves who founded renegade communities called palenques in remote areas of the countryside. This imagery – which is found in Brazil (where quilombo is the term for a renegade community) and throughout the Caribbean in the figure of the maroon – was important in defining a home-grown identity for blackness, different from the USA. Cimarrón is a small urban group, based in Bogotá, with chapters in provincial capitals. It has little impact on the mass of Afro-Colombians, is intellectual in orientation, and concerned with protesting about racism and raising black consciousness.

A different current of the Colombian black movement is represented by peasant associations in the Pacific coastal region, many of them sponsored by the Church in the 1980s, to help defend local people's position in the face of rapid change. Organizations such as *Asociación Campesina Integral del Atrato* (ACIA) entered into ad hoc partnerships with indigenous organizations, often better funded and with more church and international NGO (non-governmental organization), support, to create interethnic coalitions. ACIA, among others, became a significant player in the process of constitutional reform that took place in Colombia in the 1990s and which resulted in legislation that gave special rights to "black communities," especially rural ones in the Pacific coastal region (of which more below). This spurred the formation of many community-based peasant organizations, which primarily lobby the state to secure land rights, and more recently to defend themselves against paramilitary/guerrilla conflicts which are terrorizing and displacing the local population. Such community groups, however, also interact with national or regional organizations such as the *Proceso de Comunidades Negras*, which represents a larger agenda of black rights and cultural identity. Contrast with this the numerous urban *barrio* (neighborhood) black organizations that exist in cities such as Cali and Bogotá, which have substantial black populations, many of them migrants. These are often focused on local barrio issues (housing, employment, etc.), but may also be cultural groups which stage performances of rap and hip-hop, tap into NGO, church, and state funding streams for both ethnic diversity and youth culture and are conscious of wider issues of racism and black identity. In some cases, there are separate black women's organizations which address the intersection of race and gender that constructs specific images and positions for black women (servant, sexual object) and may also create divisions within the black movement when black women feel that black men are marginalizing gender issues. NGO funding, which targets gender as well as ethnic diversity, may also help create organizations (often income-generating projects) for black women.

A similar heterogeneity can be seen in Guatemala, where there are hundreds of Mayan organizations of different types. One element in the complex panorama are the indigenous Q'echi-speaking catechists of the north of the country, who have been particularly active since the 1990s, after more left-wing catechists were repressed by the military regime (Wilson 1995). The catechists are instrumental in a process of Maya resurgence – the emergence of an ethnic identity – that in this case is channeled mainly through religious practices. Symbols such as mountain spirits are reinflected from being seen as white landowners to being ancient Mayas. The Church is in nominal control of rural catechists, but often they are trained by urban catechists in workshops that use texts written by priests, creating a significant distance between priests and the Q'echi people who are addressed by rural catechists. The better-educated urban catechists are more influential in ethnic resurgence, but they have varied ideas about indigenousness. Some of them have little time for a version of indigenous identity in which rural symbols are important; others, affected by evangelical currents, reject rituals that involve alcohol (which tend to be more central for rural people).

This complex grass-roots scene exists alongside the more urban, intellectual pan-Mayanist movement studied by Warren (1998; see also Hale 2002). This involves activists who are national, urban figures (although perhaps of rural origins), who have publications to their name and columns in national newspapers, as well as school-teachers, extension workers in development projects and local, rural people, who are experts in local history and culture. The emphasis in this movement is on promoting indigenous languages and dress styles, campaigning for educational curricula that include Maya history and indigenous languages and cultures, recovering Maya history, and fostering *autodeterminación* (self-determination). The movement's activists, who vary greatly in their perspectives, engage in debates with ladino (non-indigenous) intellectuals and others who accuse some of them of not being authentically indigenous, of being too "radical" and of creating destructive ethnic divides ("racism in reverse"), and of opportunistically using Maya identity as a strategy to mobilize support. As in Colombia, gender is a cross-cutting issue: Mayan women have particular concerns, such as the effects of violent state repression in the 1980s (widowhood, rape), gender differences in use of Spanish, and reproductive health issues.

Context and Causes

Many factors have played a role in the rise of these ethnic movements. The apparent failure of "development" and of modernizationist ideals of progress, especially for the poorest, amongst whom Afro-Latins and indigenous peoples figure prominently, helped create a climate in which visions of modernization that went hand-in-glove with homogenization through mestizaje seemed less convincing than before (although they have by no means lost all their force). Neoliberal reform made poverty worse for many in the region, encouraged governments to exploit natural resources (often located in indigenous and Afro-Latin areas), and undermined collective landholding. Processes of democratization in many Latin American countries opened spaces for protest and the expression of diverse identities (Yashar 1998). The rise of the Brazilian black movement was undoubtedly fostered by the dismantling of the military regime in the late 1970s. A global climate in which the authority of the West was being challenged through decolonization, postcolonial critique, and postmodernist relativism has also been conducive to the proliferation of subaltern diversity. Currents of liberation theology, while mainly aimed at the poor, were also open to ethnic diversity. The Church was a ubiquitous sponsor of ethnic organizations, even if the processes it supported could not go beyond the limits it favored. International agencies began to produce global statements about indigenous rights: in 1989 the International Labour Organization of the UN produced its influential Convention 169 (concerning Indigenous and Tribal Peoples in Independent Countries); in 1985, the UN Working Group on Indigenous Populations began to write the Draft Universal Declaration of Rights of Indigenous Peoples (1994). In the 1990s, major development agencies began to take an interest in Afro-Latinos and indigenous communities: the Inter-American Development Bank (IDB), the World Bank, the UN, and the Inter-American Foundation all became involved in researching and funding such communities. Globalization meant that black and indigenous university students in provincial Latin American cities could increasingly gain access to information about ethnic movements elsewhere: the transnationalization of ethnic revitalization has been essential in giving Latin American ethnic minorities inspiration and material support from international sources. At the same time, Afro-Latin and indigenous people are themselves part of globalizing flows, migrating to the USA and, to a lesser extent, to Europe. Mexican indigenous migrant organizations in California have worked not only to defend their position in the USA, but to promote indigenous causes in Mexico (Kearney 2000).

These global processes of course include commodity flows as well as exchanges of political solidarity: images of Brazilian indigenous people as naturally Green circulate in global markets, just as reggae and rap music have become global commodities. Afro-Latin identity has fed as much or more on consumer culture as on intellectual and political stimulus. Sansone (2003) argues that in Bahia, Brazil, the new black ethnicity is "based on aestheticization of black culture and a conspicuous use of the black body." More than previously, it feeds on, but also itself feeds, youth culture, the leisure industry, and consumption. Indigenous culture can also sell, whether it is healing powers or primitivist images of being at one with nature. Indigenous people are as adept at selling or at least using these images as are commercial companies (Ramos 2003). In short, Afro-Latin and indigenous groups are agents of commodification as well as its objects.

Ethnic Movements, Legal Reform, and Social Policy

In considering how ethnic movements have managed to achieve their profile, it is vital to explore the reaction of Latin American states to these mobilizations. What stands out is a series of shifts, from about 1990, toward official multiculturalism, constitutional reforms recognizing ethnic minorities, and legislation according them special rights, in some cases (notably Brazil) including affirmative action programs that rival those made famous in the USA. Such legal and policy reforms are designed to address problems of social and political exclusion, which have been increasingly documented by research, not least that carried out by major funding agencies who are interested in promoting social inclusion and political participation in ethnically diverse countries.

These reforms have spurred ethnic movements, as new spaces are opened up for action and participation. The reforms were, of course, partly the result of political mobilization by ethnic movements, but this needs to be examined carefully, as other scholars argue that reforms actually also meet the needs of new neoliberal forms of governance and suit the interests of Latin American states, as long as the ethnic movements they address remain within certain limits of action. I will discuss this in more detail below, after examining the scope of the reforms, with particular reference to those aimed at Afro-Latins, as these are less often discussed.

The reforms vary substantially from one country to another, but include several of the following elements: recognition of the nation's multicultural character and the distinctive collective nature of indigenous peoples, recognition of indigenous customary law, recognition of collective property rights, official status for indigenous languages in indigenous communities, and provision of bilingual education (Assies et al. 2000; Van Cott 2000b; Sieder 2002).

Reforms that target Afro-Latin populations have been less numerous (Wade 1997; Htun 2004; Hooker 2005). In Nicaragua under the Sandinistas, laws were introduced in 1987 that gave some autonomy to the country's Atlantic coast region, recognizing at the same time a series of ethnic rights for the region's various indigenous groups and black and mulatto Creole population. In Honduras and Guatemala, groups claiming African descent (Garifuna- and English-speaking black groups) nominally have the same rights as indigenous peoples. In Ecuador, the 1998 constitutional reform that accords 15 collective rights to indigenous peoples in Ecuador also accords them to Afro-Ecuadorians "to the extent that they are applicable."

In Brazil, the 1988 constitution included transitory article 68, allowing land titles for so-called *remanescentes das comunidades dos quilombos* (communities derived from those originally formed by runaway slaves). Although there are said to be over 2,000 quilombos in Brazil, only 743 of these are officially recognized. By 2003, only about 70 of these had had their lands titled. In early 2003, Brazil also implemented a policy of affirmative action directed at getting more Afro-Brazilians into higher education, with some universities allocating quotas for black students. In 2005, Congress was debating the Statute of Racial Equality, originally drafted in 2000, which proposed 20 percent quotas for Afro-Brazilians in federal government, as well as the monitoring of black participation in television output and political parties.

Colombia also has detailed legislation directed at Afro-Colombian communities (Arocha 1998; Wade 2002). Law 70 of 1993 opened the way for rural black communities in Colombia's Pacific coastal region to gain collective title to land. By 2001, 80 collective titles had been allocated there. Meanwhile, the state has pushed forward *Plan Pacífico*, a major development plan with IDB funding directed at the modernization of the Pacific coastal region. In addition, between 1993 and 1997 two special seats were reserved for black delegates in the House of Representatives, while black representatives now participate in major state bodies. Recent legislation has promoted the creation of Afro-Colombian studies in the national curriculum and given black students special access to grants for university studies. Ethnic groups have been given special access to airtime on certain TV channels and government research bodies have funded research on Afro-Colombian themes. The basic idea of "positive differentiation" in favor of Afro-Colombians was legitimated by the Constitutional Court in 1996, which ruled that it was permissible to introduce a racial criterion into matters regarding educational policy, even though racial discrimination is in principle proscribed by the constitution.

There are a number of reasons why Latin American states have adopted these reforms. The most obvious might seem to be the desire of the state to combat social exclusion and create more democratic regimes. This would accord with the government rhetoric surrounding reform, but true intentions are of course difficult to measure, especially within a heterogeneous entity such as "the state." Van Cott reckons that the impetus for constitutional change was not a desire to include ethnic minorities, but rather "dissatisfaction with the state and the regime" on the part of political elites and common citizens, not to mention international experts, who saw states as overcentralized, inefficient, locked in internecine stalemate, and with weak and politically compromised judiciaries (Van Cott 2000b: 51). She also mentions the susceptibility of Latin American political elites to the pressures of an "international political culture" and discourse about human and minority rights. In this sense, a key motive might have been the desire to present a more democratic face on the international scene, respectful of human rights in ways that have become increasingly monitored by the major funding agencies, which, as noted above, in the 1990s took an increasing interest in the social inclusion of marginal groups in general and in Afro-Latin and indigenous populations in particular.

The interests of the neoliberalizing state are also adduced by a number of authors who argue that states now embrace difference as a new way to govern in an era in which "development" is in crisis, structural adjustment and neoliberalism have made savage impacts on welfare, and the colonization of frontiers continues apace. Neoliberal forms of governance seek to control indirectly through creating and/or co-opting indigenous organizations and encouraging them into a formal dialogue with the state. Hale expands on this, arguing that multiculturalism fits well with neoliberal forms of governance which seek to promote subjects, individual and collective, who are self-regulating and self-organizing. Such subjects can include ethnic subjects, whether they are located in remote areas or not. "Specifically, powerful political and economic actors use neoliberal multiculturalism to affirm cultural difference, while retaining the prerogative to discern between cultural rights consistent with the ideal of liberal, democratic pluralism, and cultural rights inimical to that ideal" (Hale 2002: 491). States thus encourage cultural difference within certain limits and discourage ethnic assertion that is deemed too radical and conflictive. These limits are partly about allowing recognition of cultural difference while not allowing economic and political empowerment and self-determination, but Hale argues this is too crude a distinction. Culture and politics are too intertwined to be separated out in this way and, anyway, a key concession by states has been precisely on the economic issue of land rights. Instead, limits are about constraining the space in which indigenous organizations can operate and defining the very language and modes of engagement. Hale argues that states will not allow indigenous rights to "violate the integrity of the productive regime" nor "call basic state prerogatives into question" (Hale 2004: 19) Further, "the concessions and prohibitions of neoliberal multiculturalism structure the spaces that cultural rights activists occupy: defining the language of contention; stating which rights are legitimate, and what forms of political action are appropriate for achieving them; and even weighing in on basic questions of what it means to be indigenous" (Hale 2002: 490).

Hale illustrates his ideas with ethnography from the department of Chimaltenango, in northern Guatemala. He traces how local ladinos now actively endorse multiculturalism, but at the same time hold out fears that Maya ethnic assertiveness that seems to them too radical will generate racism in reverse, ethnic polarization, and even conflict. The indigenous mayor of a local town, a member of the *Partido de Avanzada Nacional* which was actively seeking indigenous candidates, took a similar line: identifying himself strongly as Maya and with a good track record of indigenous activism in the 1970s (subsequently crushed by the government), by the 1990s he nevertheless stood against Maya ethnic organization and preferred to work for collective goals, eschewing radical indigenous politics.

Escobar (1997) adds a twist to the argument that links neoliberalism with multiculturalism. He points out that capitalism has adopted new forms of exploitation in which nature is no longer simply exploited as, apparently, an inexhaustible resource to be plundered at will. Instead, the idea of conserving nature as a potential resource for the future becomes practicable; hence an interest in, for example, biodiversity, which encompasses untapped wealth and unknown chemical and genetic materials. It is no accident that the Pacific coastal region of Colombia is one of the world's most biodiverse areas. The Colombian state is intent on developing the area, but at the same time there is an interest in conserving it, for who knows what valuable resources it might prove to contain? Black and indigenous communities are then charged with using the land to which they hold collective titles in a sustainable and "traditional" way. This is, perhaps, a valuable move, but it may also trap these communities into roles of stewardship over which they have little control. Meanwhile, they are surrounded by standard processes of development which may destroy the ecological balance of areas in their immediate vicinity, but which they do not control. There are clear tensions between conservation initiatives, which consolidate ethnic communities, and standard state-led development processes (roads, ports, canals), which tend to displace them – not to mention the paramilitary terrorism, linked by many to the state, which also displaces local people and, some say, clears the way for capitalist enterprises. But it would be simplistic to see the state as pursuing only one strategy in these situations. Both capitalism and governance can work through mixed strategies, co-opting land-titled black communities for the production and export of certain forest goods (e.g., palm hearts) and displacing them for other enterprises (e.g., shrimp farming).

A different argument about why Latin American states have adopted constitutional reforms highlights the power and agency of black and indigenous social movements, who wrested hard-won concessions from recalcitrant states. Van Cott thinks that, "in no case in Latin America was the demand for special rights and recognition the most important reason for the decision to reform the political constitution" (Van Cott 2000b: 51). She argues, however, that indigenous mobilization, with its international dimensions, was able to influence political elites in their attempts at reform. Black social movements were generally weaker in the region, but arguably had a similar trajectory. This view is a little different from that of, say, Arocha (1998) who presents the rights given to indigenous and particularly black populations in the 1991 Colombian constitution as concessions forced out of a reluctant or indifferent Constituent Assembly by black and indigenous protest and mobilization. Some of the difference between the views of Van Cott and Arocha is undoubtedly because the concession of *black* rights in Colombia was indeed only just won in the constitution, riding in part on the coattails of indigenous rights, and that various protests and demonstrations by black organizations certainly had an important role to play, as did black–indigenous coalitions.

In the Brazilian case, Arruti (1998) notes that "if the attribution of land rights to 'remnants of quilombo communities' had indeed been won by social movements in the Constituent Assembly of 1988, it was clear that this measure [Article 68] had only been taken because of the apparently insignificant number of these communities, estimated, at the time, to be about twenty in the whole of Brazil." It is also noticeable that concrete proposals for and debate around Article 68 did not emerge until seven years after the constitutional reform. For Nicaragua, the case is somewhat different, as the passing of the 1987 Law on Autonomous Regions of the Atlantic Coast, which gave a good deal of local autonomy to various ethnic groups in the coastal region and instituted bilingual and bicultural educational programs, was arguably a result of the armed resistance of Miskito and other indigenous groups to the Sandinistas, in the complex context of the US–Contra–Sandinista war. Again, it is notable that rights for black Creole groups in a sense rode on the coattails of rights for indigenous groups.

In sum, the role of ethnic mobilization in winning, and even more in *shaping*, constitutional rights is clearly important, even if Van Cott may be right that it was not the "most important." It is hard to see that constitution writers would have included such rights in the absence of such mobilization and the participation of indigenous and black activists, or their supporters, in constituent assemblies. And it is indubitable that black and indigenous organizations have in many cases been important in shaping subsequent legislation, albeit often in arenas of negotiation set up by the state, and in lobbying for legal accords to be put into practice. But this has to be set alongside the idea that recognizing ethnic rights also harmonized with a number of political interests in state circles which were, as I argued above, tied to strategic objectives of governance and development that would take precedence over these rights. Hence perhaps the most important role for ethnic organization is to make formal rights translate into meaningful rights in practice.

Achievements and Challenges

There is no doubt that the public profile of blackness and indigenousness has been raised and in some sense improved in Latin America. The notion that black and indigenous people constitute a marginalized sector of the population that has historically been excluded and still today suffers racial discrimination has become much more current and has achieved some official recognition. This public profile is in one sense purely symbolic but it has had a very important impact in countries where blackness was generally associated with inferiority and seen as a status to be avoided. Legislative reforms hard to envisage even a few decades ago have occurred and made a real difference to the lives of at least some black and indigenous people. However, many dilemmas and obstacles remain.

If one of the key objectives of ethnic movements was autodeterminación, what kind of autonomy has been won in the context of regional processes of democratization and continuing social inequality? The answer is that some autonomy has been won, but it tends to be constrained. In the Mexican state of Oaxaca, indigenous *municipios* (municipalities) were given greater political and legal autonomy in 1995 electoral reforms, but this has also fostered fragmentation: the ethnically diverse state of Oaxaca has 570 municipios. There are competing tendencies of social unity and political factionalism in which party politics continues to play an important role. In

Chiapas, the Mexican state has been intent on restricting the demands for autonomy of the *Ejército Zapatista de Liberación Nacional* (EZLN), some of which were recognized in the 1996 San Andrés peace accords, and bringing these into line with existing municipal-based autonomy. Sieder argues that, in Bolivia, decentralization and multiculturalism together "strengthened the spaces and opportunities for indigenous movements," but that they could also reinforce local power elites, increase fragmentation of indigenous authorities, and further the penetration of party politics. Such policies may in fact have "extended the territorial outreach of the state" (Sieder 2002: 8). In some countries, indigenous politicians are now part of the state – in Colombia, there are specially elected indigenous senators – but Hale cautions that "it would be a mistake to equate the increasing indigenous presence in the corridors of power with indigenous empowerment" in "the era of the '*indio permitido*,'" the "permissible Indian" who can go so far, but no further (Hale 2004: 18). Afro-Latin autonomy is even more constrained: in the Colombian Pacific coast region, community autonomy is about gaining collective land title and much less about political or legal control. Meanwhile, waves of violence and displacement in the region severely undermine any progress made.

Another key objective for ethnic movements is economic inclusion. Multicultural reforms have led to greater inclusion of ethnic minorities in development policy, and major funding agencies also pursue "ethno-development" initiatives that target ethnic communities. But it is difficult to make a case that things have improved in this respect at a time when, with neoliberalization, social inequality has been growing in the region as a whole and poverty has been increasing for many of the poor, including indigenous and black people. Afro-Colombian land rights are vitiated by violence. Progress on Afro-Latin land rights in Ecuador and Brazil has been slow and weak. Indigenous land rights have made most progress in the Amazon region, but there they confront state interests in promoting logging, mineral exploitation, and road building. Outside that region, with a common scenario of peasant agriculture based on small plots and strong patterns of seasonal and out-migration, things have been tougher still. In Guatemala in early 2003, eight years after the Accord on the Identity and Rights of the Indigenous Peoples, the Pro-Indigenous Accord Committee (COPAI) brought indigenous representatives from 100 municipalities to Guatemala City, demanding that Congress reactivate the Accord.

Other results of the reforms concern issues of identity. One clear outcome of multicultural policies has been the "indigenization" of blackness (Wade 1995; Hooker 2005). Many countries have piggy-backed Afro-Latin rights onto models of indigenous rights. *Negros* and *indígenas* have historically had – and still to a great extent have – very different locations in the "structures of alterity" of Latin American nations (Wade 1997: 35–7). Indigenous peoples have been seen as classic Others, often with a special legal position (albeit as minors); seen as a basically rural population, glorified as the ancestral roots of the nation, and made the object of academic study. Afro-Latins have generally been seen as second-class citizens, part of the general population, often rather urban in location (with the notable exception of the Pacific coastal populations of Colombia and Ecuador), not set apart, often ignored by academics, and less likely to be hailed as a symbol of national roots. These differences fed into differences in political mobilization, as indigenous peoples generally organized earlier and with greater backing from international NGOs and the Church. Governments were also more prepared to listen to indigenous demands. They were able to "hear" those subalterns speak, precisely because they were constituted as Other. When black demands were made, one typical response in Colombia was that they were not "an ethnic group."

With the reforms, black groups began to look more like indigenous ethnic groups. The image of blackness in Colombia and Ecuador becomes that of the Pacific coastal region: rural, regionally specific, "traditional," and indigenous-looking. Yet in Colombia the black population in the Pacific coast region is easily outweighed by the number living in the major cities. In Nicaragua, Honduras, and Guatemala, Afro-Latin rights are focused around Garifuna groups, who are seen as ethnic groups on a par with other indigenous ethnic groups. In Brazil, land rights were offered to "remnants" of quilombo communities, seen as isolated, rural, and ancestral; and there has been a process of "re-indigenization" in which communities that might easily have been considered Afro-descendant have resuscitated their indigenous histories partly in order to facilitate land claims (Warren 2001). But anyway the vast majority of Afro-Brazilians live in cities where such land rights are irrelevant. The affirmative action reforms that do affect black urban populations are more recent – and much more controversial.

The implications of this indigenization of blackness are not unidirectional. On the one hand, there is the danger that urban black populations and urban labor market discrimination are left out of the picture. To gain recognition, black people have to represent themselves as culturally different, which itself is not a strategy with clear outcomes: there are both pros and cons to identity politics. On the other hand, interesting alliances can form between indigenous and black groups. This has occurred to some extent in Ecuador, Colombia, and Nicaragua (with hints in Guatemala and Honduras too). Such cross-cutting alliances are important in the context of official multiculturalism which, while it might expect black ethnicity to "look like" indigenous ethnicity and be amenable to the same structures of governance, also tends to separate different "cultures" out into defined spaces and undermine horizontal connections between them.

Another set of dilemmas surrounds the tendency for ethnic movements to engage in essentialist representations of identity, although this seems to have been more of a concern for liberal scholars, wedded to anti-essentialist politics, than for activists themselves. It is perhaps not surprising, in a political and cultural climate that encourages indigenization, ethnicization, and the definition of group boundaries, that ethnic activists will produce images of their history and culture that appear essentialist and even naturalizing. Anti-essentialism may be a luxury of well-fed liberal intellectuals, intent on showing how ethnic cultures are social and historical constructs. Scholars have made recourse to the idea of "strategic essentialism" to legitimate activists' essentialist representations as a conscious tactic in a political struggle and this is undoubtedly partly true, although such an argument is more than a little patronizing in its implication that such tactics need such an intellectual green light. Warren (1998: 201–3) argues that Mayan activists use both essentialist and non-essentialist discourses about Mayanness. In my view, the key point is not so much the nature of the discourse being deployed, but what its practical political consequences are. Whom does it include and exclude? Whom does it empower and disempower? Anthropologists and historians may find themselves at odds with some cultural activists over these issues, but the likelihood is that there will be disagreement between different cultural activists too (not to mention different scholars). It is a red herring to phrase the problem in terms of an anti-essentialist academy versus essentialist activists. There can be dialogues (sometimes admittedly of the deaf) about the practice of politics which cross-cut this difference.

In sum, reforms have created a new public profile for indigenousness and blackness: they have laid the basis for conditional political autonomy; they have tended to "indigenize" blackness; they have helped to consolidate a basis of land titling for some communities, but this has been slow and is often ineffective in practice against forces of displacement and the worsening conditions that are evident in many Latin American countries as a result of neoliberalization and economic crisis. These conditions are shaped by political and economic forces that override the reforms. Reforms have also helped to create new networks and social capital by channeling resources, albeit in controlled ways, into ethnic organizations, whether around land claims, income generation, or issues of ethnic identity. However much multicultural reforms fit a neoliberal agenda, they also open up spaces for ethnic movements which may then have their own dynamic and are not necessarily always controlled by that agenda. Unforeseen coalitions and networks forming between black and indigenous organizations, indigenous groups emerging from what was previously seen to be a homogeneous, mestizo, peasant society (as in northeast Brazil), black rap groups using Church and state "youth culture" funding streams to promote a radical agenda of black consciousness, indigenous organizations allying with unions and other popular movements to oust a national president (as in Ecuador and Bolivia) – all these are hints of the ways ethnic politics can take on unexpected dimensions in the long struggle for social justice.

BIBLIOGRAPHY

Andrews, G. R. (1991) *Blacks and Whites in São Paulo, Brazil, 1888–1988*. University of Wisconsin Press, Madison.

Arocha, J. (1998) "Inclusion of Afro-Colombians: An Unreachable Goal," *Latin American Perspectives*, 25:3.

Arruti, J. M. A. (1998) "Subversions Classificatoires: Paysans, Indiens, Noirs. Chronique D'une Ethnogenèse," *Genèses. Sciences Sociales et Histoire*, 32.

Assies, W., Van der Haar, G., & Hoekema, A. (eds.) (2000) *The Challenge of Diversity: Indigenous Peoples and Reform of the State in Latin America*. Thela Thesis, Amsterdam.

Brysk, A. (1996) "Turning Weakness into Strength: The Internationalization of Indian Rights," *Latin American Perspectives*, 23:2.

De la Cadena, M. (2000) *Indigenous Mestizos: The Politics of Race and Culture in Cuzco, 1919–1991*. Duke University Press, Durham.

Escobar, A. (1997) "Cultural Politics and Biological Diversity: State, Capital and Social Movements in the Pacific Coast of Colombia." In R. G. Fox & O. Starn (eds.), *Between Resistance and Revolution: Cultural Politics and Social Protest*. Rutgers University Press, New Brunswick.

Field, L. W. (1994) "Who Are the Indians?: Reconceptualizing Indigenous Identity, Resistance and the Role of Social Science in Latin America," *Latin American Research Review*, 29:3.

Hale, C. R. (2002) "Does Multiculturalism Menace? Governance, Cultural Rights and the Politics of Identity in Guatemala," *Journal of Latin American Studies*, 34.

Hale, C. R. (2004) "Rethinking Indigenous Politics in the Era of the 'Indio Permitido'," *NACLA Report on the Americas*, 38:2.

Hanchard, M. (1994) *Orpheus and Power: The Movimento Negro of Rio de Janeiro and São Paulo, Brazil, 1945–1988*. Princeton University Press, Princeton.

Helg, A. (1995) *Our Rightful Share: The Afro-Cuban Struggle for Equality, 1886–1912*. University of North Carolina Press, Chapel Hill.

Hooker, J. (2005) "Indigenous Inclusion/Black Exclusion: Race, Ethnicity and Multicultural Citizenship in Contemporary Latin America," *Journal of Latin American Studies*, 37:2.

Htun, M. (2004) "From 'Racial Democracy' to Affirmative Action: Changing State Policy on Race in Brazil," *Latin American Research Review*, 39:1.

Kearney, M. (1996) "Introduction (to Special Issue on Indigenous Ethnicity and Mobilization in Latin America)," *Latin American Perspectives*, 23:2.

Kearney, M. (2000) "Transnational Oaxacan Indigenous Identity: The Case of Mixtecs and Zapotecs," *Identities – Global Studies in Culture and Power*, 7:2.

Pallares, A. (2002) *From Peasant Struggles to Indian Resistance: The Ecuadorian Andes in the Late Twentieth Century*. University of Oklahoma Press, Norman.

Porras, A. (2005) *Tiempo de indios: La construcción de la identidad política colectiva del movimiento indio ecuatoriano (las movilizaciones de 1990, 1992 y 1997)*. Abya Yala, Quito.

Ramos, A. (1998) *Indigenism: Ethnic Politics in Brazil*. University of Wisconsin Press, Madison.

Ramos, A. (2003) "Pulp Fictions of Indigenism." In D. S. Moore, J. Kosek, & A. Pandian (eds.), *Race, Nature and the Politics of Difference*. Duke University Press, Durham.

Sanders, J. (2003) "Belonging to the Great Granadan Family: Partisan Struggle and the Construction of Indigenous Identity and Politics in Southwestern Colombia, 1849–1890." In N. Appelbaum, A. S. Macpherson, & K. A. Rosemblatt (eds.), *Race and Nation in Modern Latin America*. University of North Carolina Press, Chapel Hill.

Sansone, L. (2003) *Blackness without Ethnicity: Constructing Race in Brazil*. Palgrave Macmillan, New York.

Sieder, R. (ed.) (2002) *Multiculturalism in Latin America: Indigenous Rights, Diversity and Democracy*. Macmillan, Basingstoke.

Van Cott, D. L. (2000a) *The Friendly Liquidation of the Past: The Politics of Diversity in Latin America*. University of Pittsburgh Press, Pittsburgh.

Van Cott, D. L. (2000b) "Latin America: Constitutional Reform and Ethnic Right," *Parliamentary Affairs*, 53:1.

Wade, P. (1995) "The Cultural Politics of Blackness in Colombia," *American Ethnologist*, 22:2.

Wade, P. (1997) *Race and Ethnicity in Latin America*. Pluto Press, London.

Wade, P. (1999) "Working Culture: Making Cultural Identities in Cali, Colombia," *Current Anthropology*, 40:4.

Wade, P. (2002) "The Colombian Pacific in Perspective," *Journal of Latin American Anthropology*, 7:2.

Warren, J. W. (2001) *Racial Revolutions: Antiracism and Indian Resurgence in Brazil*. Duke University Press, Durham.

Warren, K. B. (1998) *Indigenous Movements and Their Critics: Pan-Maya Activism in Guatemala*. Princeton University Press, Princeton.

Warren, K. B. & Jackson, J. E. (eds.) (2003) *Indigenous Movements, Self-Representation, and the State in Latin America*. University of Texas Press, Austin.

Wilson, R. (1995) *Maya Resurgence in Guatemala: Q'echi' Experiences*. University of Oklahoma Press, Norman.

Winant, H. (1994) *Racial Conditions: Politics, Theory, Comparisons*. University of Minnesota Press, Minneapolis.

Yashar, D. J. (1998) "Contesting Citizenship: Indigenous Movements and Democracy in Latin America," *Comparative Politics*, 31:1.

Chapter Twenty-Eight

SOCIAL AND ECONOMIC IMPACT OF NEOLIBERALISM

Duncan Green

The last 25 years in Latin America have seen a process of intense market reform. Since the onset of the debt crisis, triggered by the Mexican default of August 1982, a combination of influences has transformed the Latin American economy in a "silent revolution" that has affected every corner of the continent and its half billion citizens. This chapter explores the causes of the continent's abrupt change of economic direction and the economic, social, and political impact of economic reform and the region's integration into the global economy.

The forces driving market reforms were both domestic and external. Domestically the debt crisis was a symptom of the exhaustion of the previous model of import substitution, which, while it had led to the successful industrialization of the larger economies, bequeathed a legacy of underinvestment, inefficient industry reliant on high levels of state protection, and deep social and economic inequality. In the 1970s Latin American governments had postponed the inevitable adjustment by indulging in an unprecedented borrowing spree. When the influx of hard currency came to an end, the region was forced to opt for austerity at a time of global recession.

Within the political and business elite, the travails of the import substitution model prompted an increased questioning of its assumptions and policies, notably its heavy reliance on the state and state-owned enterprises in managing the economy, its emphasis on producing for the domestic market, and the relatively low priority given to exports. The first signs of the impending neoliberal triumph came in Chile, where, shortly after the coup of 1973 brought a military regime to power, led by General Augusto Pinochet, a team of economic technocrats known as the "Chicago Boys" (after their neoliberal *alma mater*, the University of Chicago) took over the reins of the economy and instituted one of the most violent market transformations of recent times.

Internationally, the start of the debt crisis came at the high point of the neoliberal assault on Keynesianism, marked by the elections of Margaret Thatcher in Great Britain in 1979 and Ronald Reagan in the USA 1980, and the collapse of the French Socialist government's attempt to reflate the economy following François Mitterrand's election in 1981. The neoliberals had the winds of history in their sails, and Latin America's crippling shortage of foreign exchange forced government after government to turn to the International Monetary Fund (IMF) for relief, placing unprecedented power in the Fund's hands, which it used to implement a rapid market reform program across the region.

The program broadly consisted of two stages. The first involved currency stabilization, since the neoliberals saw inflation as the greatest obstacle to growth. During this phase, economic policy consisted of little more than severe austerity, with public sector spending cuts and sharp increases in interest rates. These were designed both to reduce domestic demand, and therefore inflation, and to reduce demand for imports, enabling countries to build up a trade surplus with which to meet debt service obligations.

This was followed by a broader and more complex process of "structural adjustment" to implant a functioning market economy in the country by "getting the prices right," removing artificial distortions such as price controls or trade tariffs, and allowing the unregulated market to determine the most efficient allocation of resources.

Because of its role in distorting prices and generally interfering with the free operation of the market, the state was generally seen as the problem, not the solution; the economy had to be restructured to reduce the state's role and unleash the private sector. This meant the privatization of state firms and the broader deregulation of trade, finance, and investment. Deregulation also aimed to remove expensive "structural rigidities" in the labor market by making it easier to hire and fire employees, restricting trade union activities, and encouraging greater labor "flexibility" through short-term contracts and subcontracting.

Like stabilization, structural adjustment involved eliminating government spending deficits, which were seen as inflationary; however, adjustment differed in that it more frequently involved closing the deficit by enhancing revenue as well as cutting spending. This was usually achieved by a mixture of income from privatization and raising sales taxes such as Value Added Tax. Following severe cuts in social service spending in the 1980s, the later stages of adjustment saw a sharp increase in health and education budgets, as governments sought to repair the damage and create a healthy, educated workforce.

The ultimate aim of structural adjustment was to enable countries to pursue export-led growth. Under these policies governments should give priority to exports, encouraging the private sector to diversify and find new markets for its products. This sometimes involved suppressing domestic demand (which diverts goods away from exports to local consumption). Removing all trade barriers on both imports and exports along with capital controls would, argued the neoliberals, ensure that resources were allocated efficiently, and that exports were made more competitive. Producers would be able to cut costs by importing the cheapest inputs available, whether fertilizers and pesticides for agro-exports or manufactured inputs for industry. The search for export-led growth generally meant encouraging foreign investors to bring in new technology and capital, requiring further deregulation in these areas.

Reality has, needless to say, been rather more messy than such neat generalizations. The phases often overlapped, with differences over the sequencing of different reforms provoking lively debates among economists. No one country implemented the full neoliberal recipe; for example, several supposedly exemplary neoliberal regimes clung on to lucrative and strategically important state enterprises in copper (Chile) and oil (Mexico). Several of the most successful countries mixed orthodox neoliberal adjustment with heterodox government controls; Mexico set wages and prices in its successful adjustment program in the late 1980s, while Brazil, Mexico, and Argentina all deliberately kept the exchange rate overvalued at different points in the 1990s in order to bring down inflation, flouting the IMF's emphasis on "getting the prices right."

Moreover, the neoliberal recipe has evolved over time, as proponents of reform such as the World Bank have tried to learn from their failures. Compared to the "savage capitalism" of the 1980s, they now give more weight to institutional issues, to the importance of an effective state regulation of markets; and they focus more on poverty and inequality. However, the change in stated purpose has not been matched by a change in the underlying ideology, which continues to place an enormous degree of faith in the efficiency of markets.

This shift also reflected political developments in the region, where, in part due to public unhappiness with the results of neoliberal reforms, most of South America elected centre-left governments after the turn of the century. Governments in Brazil, Argentina, and Venezuela had little in common with the blood-and-thunder free marketeers of the 1980s, but opted for different degrees of dissent from neoliberal orthodoxy.

By 2006, the pure neoliberalism of the early years had become fragmented and confused. In other circumstances, Latin America's economic orthodoxy might have seemed ripe for a paradigm shift, but a number of obstacles stood in the way of the kind of transformation that swept away the import substitution model: the lack of a clear alternative vision; the power of capital markets; and the region's continued dependence on foreign investment and technology.

Economic Impact: The 1980s

The initial impact of stabilization programs in the early 1980s was the region's most severe recession since World War II, as the region slashed imports and used the resulting trade surplus to repay its debt service obligations. By the time the trade balance swung back into the red again in 1992, Latin America had generated a total trade surplus of $242.9 billion. Almost all of this promptly left the region in debt service payments. The transfer of wealth from the poor countries of Latin America to the institutions of the First World went on until 1991, a net flow of $218.6 billion, or $534 for every man, woman, and child in the continent. Even debt service payments on this scale failed to keep up with the interest falling due, and the region's total external debt rose steadily throughout the decade from $220 billion in 1980 to $447 billion in 1990 (CEPAL various years b).

This extraction of wealth from the region left a large hole in the economy, in the form of an investment collapse. Governments forced to adopt austerity measures found it less politically costly to cut public investment than to dismiss employees in the middle of a recession (although many did that as well), while the private sector was deterred from investing both by the impossibility of borrowing abroad, and the recession and high interest rates at home, as governments raised interest rates to fight inflation. Foreign investors also took fright. Bank loans dried up and annual foreign direct investment fell from $8 billion in 1981 to $3 billion in 1983. Across the region, gross domestic investment (which includes both local and foreign investment) collapsed from $213 billion in 1980 to just $136 billion in 1983 (IDB various years, 1990: 297).

Throughout the mid-1980s, investment continued to languish well below its 1980 figure, becoming, in the words of the Inter-American Development Bank (IDB), "the great casualty of the debt crisis" (IDB various years, 1988: 29). In practice, the investment slump created a backlog of what became known as the "social debt" – a disintegrating education and health service, and an economy dogged by crumbling infrastructure: potholed roads, intermittent electricity supplies, and millions of families without access to drinking water or sewer systems.

The mid-1980s saw a number of so-called "heterodox" stabilization programs in countries such as Mexico, Argentina, and Brazil, as governments sought less damaging alternatives to the standard IMF stabilization packages. These used temporary government freezes on wages, prices, and exchange rates and introduced a series of new currencies to symbolize a new start and to break "inflationary expectations," whereby producers and employers constantly raise prices and wages in a self-fulfilling inflationary spiral. Heterodox programs are designed to give the economy a cooling-off period while the government takes steps to remedy the underlying causes of inflation, such as the orthodox measure of cutting the fiscal deficit (hence the "heterodox" nature of the formula).

Such programs showed mixed results in achieving stabilization, registering a significant success in Mexico in 1988. But in the best-known cases – the *Austral* plan in Argentina (June 1985), the *Cruzado* plan in Brazil (February 1986), and the *Inti* plan in Peru (July 1985) – the governments failed to deal with their spending deficits and merely succeeded in temporarily suppressing inflation through price controls. When the controls were finally removed, the underlying imbalances drove inflation even higher than before the programs were introduced.

The failure of the heterodox plans left the neoliberal program in a dominant position – governments and political parties of all persuasions accepted the need for a market-led approach to policy formation, and more active engagement with the global economy and foreign investment. The collapse of Eastern European statist systems in the late 1980s and early 1990s merely served to strengthen such beliefs. By the turn of the decade, neoliberalism was the only game in town.

The Economy from 1991 to 1997

After the lost decade of the 1980s, the economy picked up somewhat in the following decade, leading to premature claims that Latin America had turned the corner and was headed for an East Asian-style miracle. The silent revolution's most convincing success was inflation. Although the initial impact of stabilization programs was to increase prices, by 1997 regional inflation had fallen to single figures and has remained close to 10 percent ever since (ECLAC 2005a: Table A-1). The most startling success story of the decade was Brazil, where Finance Minister (and later President) Fernando Henrique Cardoso's *Real* plan cut inflation in Latin America's largest economy from 2,500 percent in 1993 to 4 percent in 1997. The region's performance on growth was less impressive. After a deep recession in the early 1980s, and stagnation in the latter part of the decade, the region returned to moderate growth in the 1990s, averaging 3.5 percent from 1991 to 1997 (CEPAL various years b, 1997: 49, 51). However, this was only 1.8 percent once population growth was taken into account, well short of the region's performance in previous decades.

Investor confidence in the region returned, encouraged by the announcement in March 1989 of the "Brady Plan," proposed by US Treasury Secretary Nicholas Brady, which consisted of a series of debt reduction measures. A Brady Plan deal came to be seen, like an IMF Stand-by Arrangement, as a bill of good economic health, opening the door to foreign investment. After squeezing nearly $220 billion out of Latin America from 1982 to 1990, the international capital markets suddenly began pouring money into the region, and by 1991 the capital tide had turned. Although Latin America's debt has continued to rise, reaching $753 billion in 2004 (ECLAC 2005a: Table A-18), booming exports have meant that, for all but the most vulnerable countries (such as Honduras, Nicaragua, and Bolivia), debt now exerts a smaller burden on the economy.

Incoming capital was a mixture of portfolio investment in equities and bonds, and foreign direct investment (FDI). FDI expanded steadily from $6.7 billion in 1990 to reach $44 billion in 1997 (CEPAL various years b, 1997: 58). In the initial stages, much of this investment was the result of the region's privatization program, inaugurated in the late 1980s, and was confined to the larger economies. Such FDI initially brought fewer social benefits as it only represented a transfer of ownership, rather than new investment, and was often accompanied by job losses as privatized companies shed labor either in the run-up to, or immediately after, the sell-off. However, according to CEPAL, the UN Economic Commission for Latin America and the Caribbean, the mid-1990s saw a greater range of countries benefiting from foreign investment, and, by then, privatization accounted for only 30 percent of the total influx, suggesting the FDI was starting to play a more productive role in terms of jobs (CEPAL 1996–7: 134).

The influx of foreign investment did little to solve Latin America's long-term economic Achilles heel – low savings and investment rates. Gross domestic investment in 2004 came to just 20.8 percent of GDP, unaltered for most of the previous 20 years. This figure compares to 27.6 percent in 1980, the year before the start of the debt crisis, and is well short of the investment rates in the successful economies of East and Southeast Asia. Furthermore, in foreign investment more than in most other subjects, there is no such thing as a free lunch. From 1991 to 2004, profit repayments rose from 4.1 percent of GDP to 6.5 percent (ECLAC 2005a: Tables A-5, A-15).

Privatization of government assets became a crucial, if unsustainable, source of revenue in the 1990s. The growing fiscal crisis of the state sector, provoked by both foreign and domestic debt payments, has forced governments to increase revenue or cut expenditure; privatization achieves both, shedding loss-making companies while raising substantial amounts of cash. In Argentina, President Carlos Menem's privatization program raised $9.8 billion in cash; it enabled the government to cut a further $15.6 billion off its foreign debt between 1989 and 1993, as transnational corporations bought up debt paper and swapped it for a stake in the newly privatized companies (West Merchant Bank 1994). In Mexico, privatization raised a total of $13.7 billion in 1990–1, providing just under a tenth of government revenues (Devlin 1993: 159).

From 1990 to 1996, the total value of Latin American privatizations came to $73 billion. By the mid-1990s, Mexico and Argentina had little left to sell, while Brazil was just beginning its program. In recent years the main privatizations have been in electricity generation, telecommunications, and oil and gas. Government concessions to the private sector to build infrastructure such as airports and seaports is also becoming an increasingly important source of revenue (CEPAL 1996–7: 50). For some countries, the renewed capital influx also helped to ease the pain (and political costs) of economic stabilization. In the early 1980s, stabilizing countries had both to reduce inflation and generate a massive trade surplus with which to keep up their debt service. The only means to achieve this double objective was to inflict a huge recession at home.

From the late 1980s, there was another option, as foreign capital came to provide a cushion against the worst effects of adjustment. Latecomers to stabilization, such as Argentina's Carlos Menem and Brazil's Fernando Henrique Cardoso, found themselves able to get inflation under control without the same degree of austerity, by using capital inflows to keep up debt repayments. Large capital inflows also led to overvalued currencies, which helped suppress inflation by holding down import prices. The effects were spectacular: Argentina's inflation fell from 4,923 percent in 1989 to 18 percent three years later (CEPAL various years b, 1993: 35), and within months of the adjustment package, the economy moved smoothly into four years of record-breaking growth – over 6 percent in every year from 1991 to 1994 (CEPAL various years c, 1994: 18).

The cost of this strategy was a loss of export competitiveness and ensuing trade deficit, which could only be covered as long as capital inflows lasted. The Mexican crash of early 1995 graphically demonstrated what happens when dollar inflows stop. On December 20, 1994, the Mexican government finally responded to a year of disastrous political and economic news that had alarmed investors already concerned about the country's overvalued currency and escalating trade deficit. Mexico's reserves had fallen from $30 billion in February to just $5 billion, and Mexico was in danger of defaulting on debt repayments in a repeat of the 1982 crash that precipitated the region's debt crisis.

In the end, an unprecedented $50 billion bail-out coordinated by Washington prevented collapse, but in return Mexico was forced to abandon the end of this "easy option" of foreign investment-driven stabilization, announcing an austerity package on March 9 which raised taxes, cut public spending, floated the interest rate, and relied on rocketing interest rates to get inflation under control. The results were predictably catastrophic as growth ground to a halt, a wave of bankruptcies ensued, and an estimated 1.2 million jobs were lost by the end of May 1995 (*Latin America Monitor* 1995: 3).

Latin America since 1997

The speed with which Latin America has become integrated with the global economy over the course of the silent revolution has been truly remarkable. Latin America's courtship of global capital markets has been a whirlwind affair. The spread of regional stock markets, privatization programs, bank deregulation, bond issues, and the growing number of Latin American companies whose shares trade on the stock exchanges of New York and London have greatly increased the region's openness to international capital flows.

As Latin Americans have learned to their cost, these different sources of capital behave in radically different ways, in terms of their potential social benefits and their degree of unreliability. Capital flows can come in the form of "hot money," which can disappear overnight, or enter in less volatile "stickier" varieties, such as foreign direct investment, which is both more stable and produces more benefits in the form of jobs and improved infrastructure. While other forms of foreign investment were varying wildly, net FDI remained above $30 billion per year through 1997–2004 (ECLAC various years a 2005: Table A-16). Although capital market integration has provided the region with much-needed capital, it has made the region vulnerable to external shocks by increasing the impact of any sudden withdrawal of foreign capital.

Mexico proved to be the harbinger of the end of the 1990s boom. The *coup de grâce* was administered in 1997, when the global financial turmoil precipitated by a number of crises in East Asia rapidly spread to Latin America. Capital flows dried up, and governments that had relied on fixed and overvalued exchange rates to stabilize inflation saw their currencies come under concerted attack on international markets. The Brazilian currency crashed in 1998, but Argentina undoubtedly suffered the greatest trauma, as a run on the currency led to government spending cuts and a decision to freeze dollar-denominated bank accounts. The actions sparked protests in which 27 people died, and five governments fell in the space of two weeks. The political chaos triggered one of the worst peacetime economic and social collapses in Latin American history, as GDP fell by 11 percent in 2002 (ECLAC various years b 2005, Table A-2).

The reversal of capital flows triggered a "lost half decade" from 1997 to 2003, after which the economic rollercoaster zoomed upward once more, driven by high commodity prices. The motor for much of this latest boom was rising demand in the USA and China, whose voracity for metals and foodstuffs gave another twist to the wider impact of the silent revolution in pushing the region back toward dependence on the export of raw materials.

Events such as the Argentina crisis drew new attention to the impact of capital market integration, which had previously received far less attention than trade liberalization. According to Harvard's Dani Rodrik (1999: 18):

> For the 1990s, the evidence suggests that the instability in private capital flows has been perhaps the most important single determinant of macroeconomic volatility . . . some of the smaller countries of the region with little access to private capital flows (Bolivia and Guatemala) have experienced the lowest levels of macroeconomic volatility. Argentina and Venezuela are at the other extreme, with very high levels of exposure to volatility in private capital flows and correspondingly high levels of macro-volatility. Countries like Brazil, Chile, and Colombia, which have managed private capital flows, are somewhere in between.

The successive crises have also prompted much debate on exchange rate regimes. While pegging exchange rates to the dollar produced enormous benefits in curbing inflation, the difficulty appeared to lie in designing a stabilization program with a clear exit strategy, enabling governments to come off a pegged exchange rate once stabilization had been accomplished. No governments did so willingly, but in retrospect Brazil's exit from a less rigid pegged currency arrangement in 1999 was more successful than that of Argentina, which clung on to its more draconian currency board system until the very last minute, thereby greatly increasing the economic and social costs of devaluation.

But beyond the technical aspects of the debate, the main lesson is that capital account liberalization is not the answer to Latin America's historical inability to save and invest in sufficient quantities to generate growth and jobs. Moreover, continued dependence on capital inflows will remain costly. In April 1999, Javed Burki, World Bank Vice President for Latin America and the Caribbean, told reporters: "My belief is that we should stop talking about crises and start talking about extreme volatility. Essentially, I think we should be preparing ourselves for a perpetual state of volatility rather than a recurring crisis" (World Bank 1999).

Observers such as CEPAL continue to stress the need for Latin America to increase its savings rate, thereby reducing its dependence on foreign capital flows. They also point to the dangers of excessive deregulation, which has led to a rash of banking crises in countries such as Mexico and Venezuela, as poorly supervised banks have been allowed to pile up bad debts. Bailing out such crashes is a costly business: the Venezuelan crisis of 1994 cost the government 13 percent of GDP, while in Mexico in 1995, the bill came to 8.5 percent of GDP (CEPAL 1996–7: 57).

Trade

By 2003, Latin America was starting to turn the corner. The regional GDP rose to 6 percent the following year, and the reason behind this latest boom was trade. Like capital account liberalization, booming trade has bound the region ever more tightly to the world economy. Since the mid-1980s exports have risen much faster than the economy as a whole, more than quintupling in value between 1988 and 2004 to reach $460 billion (CEPAL various years b 2004: 2). New primary products, such as soybeans, fresh fruit and vegetables, mining, and manufactured goods produced in cheap labor assembly plants, or *maquiladoras*, have led the growth in exports.

Imports have risen at a similar pace, as Latin America has become increasingly oriented toward trade with the rest of the world, leaving behind import substitution's emphasis on production for the domestic market.

From the late 1980s, under pressure from the international financial institutions, Latin America began to liberalize imports at a breakneck rate, despite the lack of any reciprocal opening from US or European governments. Neoliberals argue that liberalizing imports improves economic efficiency and benefits everyone. Local factories can import the best available machinery and other inputs to improve their productivity, while consumers can shop around, rather than be forced to buy shoddy home-produced goods. Competition from abroad will force local factories either to close, or to improve their products until they become competitive with other countries' goods, paving the way for increased manufactured exports.

Two respected Latin American economists, Ricardo Ffrench-Davis and Manuel Agosín (1994), have laid out some clear conditions for a successful trade reform: the value created by new activities must exceed that lost due to the number of factories destroyed by competition from cheap imports; export industries must be sufficiently linked to the rest of the national economy to spread the benefits of improved exports throughout the country; and increased competitiveness must be achieved by continuous gains in productivity rather than through low wages or ever-greater subsidies or tax breaks. The authors do not believe these conditions have been met in the recent Latin American trade reforms and point out numerous serious failings:

- Countries have unilaterally opened up their economies in a protectionist and stagnant world economy, allowing other regions to increase their imports to Latin America without having to reciprocate by buying the region's exports.
- Countries have liberalized far too rapidly, not allowing local firms sufficient time to make the necessary changes and investments to adapt to the new rules and improve their productivity before the import floodgates open. This has wiped out numerous potentially competitive companies in a wholly avoidable manner.
- Latin America has fallen back into relying on its static comparative advantage, which has led it to concentrate its efforts in the least dynamic areas of the world economy, such as commodity exports.

Regional Integration

An important aspect of the new emphasis on trade has been the burgeoning number of free trade agreements (FTAs) between Latin American countries and between Latin America and other regions. Best known is NAFTA, the North American Free Trade Agreement between Mexico, Canada, and the United States, which came into force in 1994.

Different kinds of free trade agreement have had contradictory effects on the Latin American economies. FTAs such as NAFTA with more industrialized, advanced nations have served to increase Latin America's reliance on its traditional "comparative advantage" in raw materials, commodities, and goods produced with cheap labor. Intra-regional trade, on the other hand, tends to include a higher proportion of manufactured goods, and so can have a more positive effect in developing local industry. By 2004, intraregional trade accounted for just 17 percent of the total, considerably less than in Asia or Europe (ECLAC 2005b: 13). The main subregion has been the Mercosur FTA, comprising Argentina, Brazil, Uruguay, and Paraguay.

In 1994, the North American and Latin American leaders announced their intention to negotiate a "Free Trade Area of the Americas" covering the whole hemisphere, by the year 2006. However, long before then, talks had become bogged down because the USA demanded access to Latin American markets while offering little in return, for example in curbing its agricultural subsidies. (High levels of subsidies to US agribusiness leads to overproduction and dumping on world markets, which in turn harms Latin American exporters.) Instead, Latin American governments, especially those of Mercosur, continued to make the running on regional integration, notably by incorporating Bolivia and Chile into Mercosur's free trade area. Mercosur has also completed a Free Trade Agreement with the Andean Community.

Social Impact

Shrinking wages, rising prices for food and other essentials, increased unemployment or "underemployment," and collapsing government services – the human cost has mounted inexorably throughout the silent revolution, exacting a toll of hunger, disease, and despair. Throughout the region, after decades in which the percentage of Latin Americans living in poverty had been falling (though not their actual number), poverty is once again on the rise. The pattern of poverty over the two decades of the silent revolution was one of an explosion in the 1980s, followed by a slow increase in the absolute numbers of the poor in the 1990s. Due to growing population this meant that the proportion of poor people fell back from a high of 48 percent in 1990 to 44 percent in 2002 (ECLAC various years a, 2004: 6). Latin America ended the two decades of turmoil reform with a greater proportion of poor people than in 1980. One in five Latin Americans did not earn enough to feed themselves properly.

Traditionally in Latin America, the poor are concentrated in rural areas, but the impact of neoliberalism shifted poverty to the cities, more than doubling the number of poor people in urban areas. From 1980 to 1999 the number of poor Latin Americans in rural areas increased from 73 million to 77 million, but was overtaken for the first time by the battalions of the urban poor, which jumped from 63 million people to 134 million (ECLAC various years a). Indigence, sometimes known as absolute or extreme poverty, remains mainly a rural blight.

While Latin America is not as poor overall as Africa or parts of Asia, it leads the world in inequality and, since 1982, inequality has got worse. Total GDP grew by 52 percent between 1980 and 2000 (CEPAL various years a, 2003: 196), so why has poverty increased, both in absolute and percentage terms? The answer lies both in population growth of 44 percent, and in inequality, which ensured that even the paltry 8 percent improvement in per capita GDP failed to reach the poor. The World Bank concluded that in the 1980s, "the wealthy were better able to protect themselves from the impact of the recession than were the poor" (Psacharopoulos et al. 1995: ix). *The Economist* (1993) put it more bluntly, commenting that "stabilization and structural adjustment have brought magnificent returns to the rich."

The link between inequality and poverty reduction is best illustrated by comparing Chile, one of the region's most unequal countries, with Uruguay, one of its most equitable. In Chile, the 52 percent increase in per capita GDP between 1990 and 1998 translated into a 46 percent decline in poverty. In Uruguay, a much smaller increase in per capita output (26 percent) gave rise in a similar period to a somewhat larger relative fall in poverty than in Chile. Because the cake was shared out more fairly, in Uruguay more people benefited from less growth (ECLAC various years a, 2001: 30).

Latin American inequality is on such a scale that a comparatively minor move toward a fairer distribution of income could eradicate poverty overnight, according to the World Bank: "Raising all the poor in the continent to just above the poverty line would cost only 0.7 percent of regional GDP – the approximate equivalent of a 2 percent income tax on the wealthiest fifth of the population" (*Financial Times* 1993).

There has been a vigorous debate over the relationship between structural adjustment and rising poverty – is it the cure or the cause? In the early years, the World Bank believed that "without adjustment, the condition of the poor would undoubtedly have been worse" (Psacharopoulos et al. 1995, preface). In more recent years, doubts have surfaced even in this dogged advocate of liberalization. Its flagship *World Development Report* (2006: 16) on equity admitted:

> In many countries, opening to trade (often coinciding with opening to foreign direct investment) has been associated with rising inequality in earnings in the past two decades. This is especially so for middle-income countries, notably in Latin America. Opening to trade often boosts the premium on skills as firms modernize their production processes (skill-biased technical change, in the jargon of economists). This is bad for equity if the institutional context restricts the capacity of workers to shift into new work – or limits future cohorts' access to education.

Back in real life, the link between neoliberalism and Latin America's increased poverty and inequality can be all too obvious. In Bolivia the redundancy notices issued to thousands of factory workers when the government began its structural adjustment with the infamous "Decree 21060" made their neoliberal origins brutally clear: "The Company has found it necessary to rationalize the workforce," went the notice to Richard Ardaya, a trade union activist, from his employers at the La Modelo textile plant, "therefore with recourse to Article 55 of Decree 21060 of 1985, I regret to inform you that your services are no longer required." The headed notepaper is bordered with the logos of La Modelo's fashionable customers: Pierre Cardin, Playboy, and Van Heusen (Green 2003: 94).

In other cases, however, the connection is less direct and harder to prove or disentangle from all the other influences on Latin America's economy: international commodity prices, the end of commercial bank lending to the region after 1982, world recession, international interest rates, and domestic influences such as political instability and the effectiveness (or otherwise) of government. The suffering in Bolivia's tin mines is a good example; critics blame it on structural adjustment, yet the government's supporters point out, with considerable justification, that it would be unfair to blame adjustment for the collapse in world tin prices that occurred just two months after Decree 21060 was issued.

There are many ways that economic changes can affect people's quality of life: incomes, taxes, working conditions, prices, state services, the impact on home life and the family. Adjustment and stabilization measures have a profound influence on all of them.

A Living Wage

The rural poor sometimes have a plot of land on which to grow food, but the urban poor have few assets beyond their labor, so their well-being depends to a large extent on what they can earn. According to the UN ECLAC (1994: 16), the main causes of increasing poverty and inequality during the 1980s were the "massive decline in real wages, . . . the rise in unemployment and . . . the number of people employed in very low-productivity jobs."

After the "lost decade" of the 1980s, average real wages recovered in most countries, although they suffered setbacks following financial crises in Mexico (1995), Brazil (1998), and Argentina (2001). Only in Argentina, Brazil, Uruguay, and Venezuela were wages in 2004 lower than in 1990 (ECLAC 2005a: Table A-24).

But even as real wages recovered, unemployment rose to reach 10 percent in 2004. Worst hit were Colombia, the Dominican Republic, and Venezuela, all of which had rates over 15 percent. Even this grossly underestimates the problem, as it does not include the army of informal-sector workers and "underemployed" – in Latin America, regular waged work was rapidly becoming a luxury denied the majority of the population. One *Economist* headline (March 21, 1998) summed up the puzzlement of the neoliberals: "Great reforms, nice growth, but where are the jobs?" Government cutbacks have led to numerous redundancies, but their main impact has been a sharp fall in wages among remaining public employees, the sector worst hit by adjustment. Many of those worst affected are middle-class, thousands of whom end up joining the ranks of the "new poor" created by adjustment policies.

Adjustment policies have sought to "flexibilize" labor. In practice, this has meant cracking down on trade unions and making it easier for managers to hire and fire employees, shift to part-time work, and to cut costs by subcontracting work to smaller companies, often little more than sweatshops. The proportion of the workforce employed by large companies fell from 44 percent to 32 percent between 1980 and 1990 (Van der Hoeven & Stewart 1994: 5), the slack being taken up by a boom in small companies and the informal sector, where wages are generally lower. In Chile, the neoliberal tiger, a labor force once accustomed to secure, unionized jobs has been turned into a nation of anxious individualists. According to a World Health Organization survey, over half of all visits to Chile's public health system involve psychological ailments, mainly depression (*Mercurio*, 1993). In Argentina such changes meant that having a job was no longer enough to stave off hunger. By the early 1990s, 23 percent of wage-earners in the manufacturing sector were living below the poverty line, whereas before the debt crisis a job in a factory virtually guaranteed a pay packet big enough to keep a family out of poverty (CEPAL, various years c, 1993: 8).

During the recession of the 1980s and the adjustment of the 1990s, the informal sector acted as a gigantic sponge, soaking up those who had been sacked, or who were entering the work force for the first time. As Latin America's streets became clogged with vendors desperately seeking customers for their petty wares, incomes fell. In La Paz, where 60 percent of the workforce is now in the informal sector, there was one street trader for every three families; there were just not enough buyers to go round (Green 2006: 69). By 1989 the income of the average Latin American working in the informal sector had shrunk to just 58 percent of its 1980 figure, harder hit than even the public sector (Van der Hoeven & Stewart 1994: 14).

In Latin America as a whole, the percentage of informal employment in urban areas has climbed by over five percentage points (nearly 20 million individuals) since 1990. What is more, the percentage of new jobs that were in the informal sector rose from 67.3 percent in 1990–4 to 70.7 percent in 1997–9 (ECLAC, various years a, 2002: 10). Of every 10 jobs now being created, seven are in the low-tech, low-wage economy with only the most tenuous connection with the modern world and international markets. Globalization, Latin America-style, is excluding nearly three-quarters of its citizens.

Incomes for non-wage-earners have also taken a battering at the hands of adjustment. Government cutbacks have whittled away at Latin America's already paltry welfare system, as the elderly in particular have seen state pensions dwindle in value.

Overall, ECLAC sees a pattern in which economic shocks exacerbate poverty, but subsequent upturns fail to repair the damage. It concludes (various years a, 1999: 25): "The experience of several countries has shown that even after the economy picks up again, it takes longer to bring poverty levels down to where they were previously and much longer still before any new reduction can be achieved." A prime example is Brazil, where wages slumped after the 1998 financial crisis and had not recovered by 2004.

Taxes

The tax system is important in determining what portion of income actually reaches the home as well as how much the government has to spend on social services. Since the late 1980s, tax reform has also gained increasing importance as a means of balancing government budgets and curbing inflation. However, some of the resulting changes in the tax regime have penalized the poor.

On the positive side, as part of their adjustment program, several countries have improved their level of income tax collection either by closing loopholes (Mexico, Argentina) or, in some instances (Chile, Colombia), by increasing taxation rates (Cardoso & Helwege 1992: 178). Most countries, however, have switched away from income taxes (already among the lowest in the world, since the Latin American elite has always been violently averse to parting with its wealth) toward greater emphasis on sales taxes. Governments argue that this is easier to collect, especially where in some cases over half the workforce are in the informal sector and therefore are not registered to pay income taxes. However, sales taxes are usually regressive, costing the poor proportionally more of their income than the rich, since the poor spend a larger share of their income on buying goods and services. Tax reform thus helped fuel rising social inequality.

Credit

Since the neoliberal understanding of the economy is essentially monetarist, it believes that cutting the amount of money circulating in the economy is the best means of curbing inflation. Removing money from the economy means reducing credit, which has largely been achieved by imposing high interest rates to make borrowing more expensive. The result has been a collapse in demand for credit and a deep recession in many countries, as local industry has suddenly found it impossibly expensive to take out loans for investment.

When many economies returned to growth in the late 1980s, they often relied for their success on continued inflows of foreign capital, which had to be lured in by offering appetizingly high interest rates. The squeeze on borrowers has continued, as only the largest firms have been able to borrow abroad at lower interest rates. Since the late 1980s, privatization has also done away with numerous state banks, some of which targeted at least some of their credit to small and medium-sized farmers and small businesses in the towns. Experience shows that, left to their own instincts, private banks, especially those in foreign hands, prefer to lend to big business. Just as millions of people have been joining the informal sector, they have seen their attempt at self-help crippled by the scarcity of credit.

Prices

Inflation has been aptly described as "a tax on the poor." In a high-inflation economy, the better off usually find ways to defend their incomes from its erosive effects by investing their money in index-linked bank accounts or turning it into dollars. The poor have no such options, and for them, the sustained fall in inflation since the mid-1990s was neoliberalism's single greatest achievement.

But different facets of adjustment have different winners and losers. Often the winners from one measure lose from another, creating a complex pattern of costs and benefits. The end of government subsidies and price controls on many basic foods and fuel has hit the urban poor hard. The sudden removal of fuel subsidies, and the subsequent increase in public transport fares, has been one of the commonest causes of anti-IMF rioting in the region, notably in Venezuela in 1989.

Most governments have replaced general subsidies with attempts to "target" subsidies at the poorest. Although the neoliberal argument (that general subsidies are a waste of money and often end up subsidizing the wealthy middle-class consumer) is at first sight convincing, talk of targeting is in practice often little more than a smoke-screen for government cuts, while the logistical difficulties of identifying the poor and getting subsidies to them often mean that many slip through the extremely tattered safety net. When Jamaica replaced a general subsidy with a targeted subsidy, it managed to reach only 49 percent of those identified as the target group. Those it reached were better off than under the general subsidy, but the remainder were faced with a jump in food prices and no help from the state (Van der Hoeven & Stewart 1994: 24).

Trade liberalization can benefit the urban poor, bringing cheaper food imports. Removing protective tariffs on imports often means lower prices and higher quality for the consumer. Frequently, however, such gains are captured by the food-processing companies (often themselves multinationals) that import the food. Moreover, simultaneous adjustment measures such as the removal of food subsidies often undo any potential benefits to the poor. In reality, the main beneficiaries of this kind of economic integration are often the middle class, from buyers of computers to those in need of a Big Mac.

In the countryside, the effects have been different. An end to controlled prices has in some cases allowed farmers to sell their crops at a better price, but trade liberalization has swamped markets with cheap imported food, which has had the opposite effect.

State Services

Despite the pressures on public spending in the wake of the debt crisis, over the region as a whole, health indicators such as infant mortality continued to improve.

Infant mortality fell from 38 per 1,000 in 1990 to 27 per 1,000 in 2003 (in 1970 it was 86 per 1,000) (UNDP various years, 2005: 253). Access to drinking water improved greatly; those without access fell from 31 percent to 11 percent (ECLAC various years b, 2004: 111). Improvements in health stemmed from the spread of low-cost, effective technology such as vaccinations, which helped counteract the health impact of rising poverty under adjustment.

Average spending on primary education fell from US$164 per child in the early 1980s to US$118 by the end of the decade (Watkins 1995: 79). An extreme example occurred in Peru, where in August 1990 the newly elected President Alberto Fujimori unleashed a particularly radical adjustment program that became known as "Fujishock." Educational spending, which in 1980 had averaged $62.50 per student fell to just $19.80, according to Ministry of Education figures. Teachers' wages fell to a quarter of their former value, leading to a mass exodus from the profession (*Latinamerica Press* 1992: 5), while 30 percent of registered students dropped out, as children left school to supplement dwindling family incomes (Poole & Rénique 1992: 152).

Since 1990, pressure from the World Bank, coupled with the growing realization that cutting social spending undermines the region's prospects for growth, has reversed the trend. The greater effort resulted in a sizeable increase (around 50 percent) in per capita social spending. From an average of US$360 per capita at the start of the decade, social expenditure climbed to US$540 per capita by its end.

The rise was prompted both by a reactivation of economic growth and a decision to give greater priority to social spending, which climbed from nearly 42 percent to almost 48 percent of total public expenditure during the decade. Evidence suggests that governments have also become more determined to protect social spending when crises hit: in six countries in which GDP contracted in 1999 (Argentina, Chile, Colombia, Honduras, Uruguay, and Venezuela), governments shielded social services from the effects of the downturn (ECLAC various years a, 2000–1: 13). The World Bank's conversion to the cause of increased social spending looks like a remarkable U-turn. Figures for the share of government spending devoted to education and health between 1981 and 1989 show that all those countries defined by the World Bank as "intensively adjusting" cut health expenditure, and only one failed to cut spending on education.

Total spending is only part of the story. In many Latin American countries, government welfare spending is actually quite high compared to other developing countries at a similar stage of development, but the way the money is spent increases inequality by giving priority to the needs of the better off (Lloyd-Sherlock, undated). Compared to its per capita GDP, Brazil's education budget is one of the highest in the world, but too much of it goes to fund public universities that in practice cater to the children of the middle classes (*Economist*, February 22, 2003). Primary education is far more effective in improving the prospects of the poor than spending on universities that they are unlikely to attend. Similarly, preventive medicine and local clinics are more effective than expensive operating theatres in hospitals. Yet historically, Latin American governments have put hospitals and universities first. The evidence here is that the poor have benefited from changes in education spending over the last 20 years, which have placed more priority on primary education, but that there has been a deterioration in their slice of health sector expenditure in all the intensively adjusting countries (Van der Hoeven & Stewart 1994: 20). Cuts in health spending are all the more painful since the social impact of adjustment has simultaneously undermined people's health. In Lima, the 1990 Fujishock program led to a 30 percent fall in the average protein intake between July and November (International Save the Children Alliance 1992: 45).

Home and Family

At the eye of the social and economic storm unleashed by the silent revolution lay the family. The central figure in the Latin American family is the mother. Traditionally, her main role may have been childbearing, childrearing, and housework, but economic and social change added new tasks to her workload. Women formed an increasing percentage of the workforce, rising from 22 percent in 1980 to 45 percent by the mid-1990s. Among the 25–49 age range, there was little difference between the proportions of women and men in work (ECLAC various years a, 1996: 64).

Many of the new, low-waged or part-time jobs generated by adjustment went to women, while many men lost their role as family breadwinner as full-time waged jobs disappeared, or wages fell so far that a single income was no longer enough to feed a family.

A study by Caroline Moser (1993) offers a unique glimpse of how adjustment and the debt crisis affected the women of one poor community in Guayaquil, Ecuador's largest city. From 1978 to 1988, Moser regularly visited and studied the community of Indio Guayas, an area of swampland shantytown which in 1978 had about 3,000 residents. She was therefore able to take a series of socioeconomic snapshots of the community as the Ecuadorean government adopted eight different stabilization/adjustment packages between 1982 and 1988. Moser found that women reacted in three different ways to the impact of adjustment on their lives. About 30 percent of the women were coping, juggling the competing demands of their three roles in the workplace, home, and community. They were more likely to be in stable relationships with partners who had steady jobs. Another group, about 15 percent of the women, were simply "burnt out," no longer able to be superwomen 24 hours a day. They were most likely to be single mothers or the main breadwinners and were often older women, physically and mentally exhausted after the effort of bringing up a family against such heavy odds. They tried to hand over all household responsibilities to their oldest daughter, while their younger children frequently dropped out of school and roamed the streets. The remaining group, about 55 percent, Moser described as simply "hanging on", sacrificing their families by sending sons out to work or keeping daughters home from school to help with the housework.

Conclusion

Ever since independence, Latin American governments and planners have veered between state and market in search of the elusive path to long-term development. The transformation of the world economy in the last 30 years may have destroyed full-blown central planning as a viable economic model, but the crude recipes of the free marketeers have failed to create the foundations for long-term success in the new world order. Rather, neoliberalism is in danger of locking Latin America into a model of export-led growth based on raw materials and cheap labor, leading to growing impoverishment and irrelevance within the global economy.

If neoliberalism has failed the majority of Latin America's people, what realistic alternatives are there? Although supporters of the silent revolution routinely dismiss their critics as economic dinosaurs bereft of alternative ideas, there is already a rich debate over the ingredients for building a better economic model for the region. Such a model would need to move away from the silent revolution's overreliance on exports as panacea, and focus on the domestic economy, building linkages between sectors, upgrading skills and technology, and building on Latin America's rich web of associative structures such as cooperatives to ensure that growth benefits the poor. A new model should also recognize that Latin America's traditional preference for "slash and burn" shifts in policy making may not be the best approach. As Dani Rodrik (2000) argues, partial and gradual reforms have often worked better because they are sensitive to the institutional and political peculiarities of particular countries.

There seems little doubt that if the region is to achieve long-term development, it must find a way of combining economic growth with a far higher degree of social and economic equality. This combination of "growth with equity" has always eluded Latin America but other countries have shown not only that it is possible, but that the two are mutually reinforcing: equal societies tend to grow faster than unequal ones (Hanmer et al. 1999: 547–63). Growth with inequality leads to political instability, social breakdown, and a substandard workforce, while seeking equity without ensuring growth is a recipe for political conflict and eventual collapse.

The Achilles heel of all attempts to transform the neoliberal model into one that works for growth with equity is the difficulty of building a sufficiently powerful political coalition behind the movement for change. The recent shift to centre-left governments in countries such as Brazil and Argentina has not been matched by a concomitant shift in economic policy, except in those countries, such as Venezuela and Bolivia, where a boom in oil and gas prices has enabled governments to pursue a free-spending "petro-populist" agenda that is unlikely to survive a subsequent collapse in energy prices.

Latin America's silent revolution required the catastrophe of the debt crisis and the unceasing arm-twisting of the international financial institutions to bring it about, and history suggests that another such trauma will be required to achieve the degree of change in economic and political thinking which is of life-and-death importance to the poor of Latin America. For them, the trauma is already happening, but they may have to wait until it touches the elites within the region and powerful interests abroad, before a definitive shift can take place.

BIBLIOGRAPHY

Cardoso, E. & Helwege, A. (1992) *Latin America's Economy: Diversity, Trends and Conflicts.* Cambridge, MA.
CEPAL (various years a) *Anuario estadístico de América Latina y el Caribe.* Santiago, Chile.
CEPAL (various years b) *Balance preliminar de la economía de América Latina y el Caribe.* Santiago, Chile.

CEPAL (various years c) *Panorama económico de América Latina*. Santiago, Chile.

CEPAL (1996–7) *Estudio económico de América Latina y El Caribe*. Santiago, Chile.

Devlin, R. (1993) "Privatisations and Social Welfare," *Cepal Review*, No. 49, Santiago, Chile, p. 159.

ECLAC (1994) *The Social Summit: A View from Latin America and the Caribbean*. Santiago, Chile.

ECLAC (2005a) *Economic Survey of Latin America and the Caribbean*. Santiago, Chile.

ECLAC (2005b) *Latin America and the Caribbean in the World Economy*. Santiago, Chile.

ECLAC (various issues) *ECLAC Notes*. Santiago, Chile.

ECLAC (various years a) *Social Panorama of Latin America*. Santiago, Chile.

ECLAC (various years b) *Statistical Yearbook*. Santiago, Chile.

Economist (1993) "A Survey of Latin America." November 13.

Ffrench-Davis, R. & Agosín, M. (1994) "Liberalización comercial y desarrollo en América Latina," *Nueva Sociedad*, Caracas, September/October.

Financial Times (1993) London, March 26.

Green, D. (2003) *Silent Revolution: The Rise and Crisis of Market Economics in Latin America*. Monthly Review Press, New York.

Green, D. (2006) *Faces of Latin America*, 3rd ed. London.

Hanmer, L., De Jong, N., Kurian, R., & Mooij, J. (1999) "Are the DAC targets Achievable? Poverty and Human Development in the Year 2015," *Journal of International Development*, 11:4, pp. 547–63.

IDB (various years) *Economic and Social Progress in Latin America*. Interamerican Development Bank, Washington.

International Save the Children Alliance (1992) *El impacto de la crisis económica, el ajuste y la deuda externa sobre la niñez en América Latina*. Lima.

Latin America Monitor (1995) Mexico City, Mexico, August.

Latinamerica Press (1992) Lima, June 18.

Lloyd-Sherlock, P. F. (undated) "The Needy: Public Social Spending In Latin America." Mimeo.

Mercurio (1993) Santiago, Chile, September 30.

Moser, C. (1993) "Adjustment from Below: Low-income Women, Time and the Triple Role in Guayaquil, Ecuador." In S. Radcliffe & S. Westwood (eds.), *Viva: Women and Popular Protest in Latin America*. London.

Oxfam (1995) *The Oxfam Poverty Report*. Oxford.

Poole, D. & Rénique, G. (1992) *Peru: Time of Fear*. London.

Psacharopoulos, G. et al. (1995) *Poverty and Income Distribution in Latin America*. World Bank, Washington DC.

Rodrik, D. (1999) *Why Is There So Much Economic Insecurity in Latin America?* Harvard University Press, Cambridge, MA.

Rodrik, D. (2000) *Development Strategies for the Next Century*. Harvard University Press, Cambridge, MA.

UNDP (various years) *Human Development Report*. United Nations, New York.

Van der Hoeven, R. & Stewart, F. (1994) *Social Development during Periods of Structural Adjustment in Latin America*, ILO, Geneva.

Watkins, K. (1995) *The Oxfam Poverty Report*. Oxfam, London.

West Merchant Bank (1994) *Investment Review*. London.

World Bank (1999) *Press Briefing: Responding to the Crisis*. Washington, DC, April 25.

World Bank (various years) *World Development Report*. Washington, DC.

Index